BLACK NAMES IN AMERICA: ORIGINS AND USAGE

Collected by
NEWBELL NILES PUCKETT

Edited by
MURRAY HELLER

G. K. HALL & CO. 70 LINCOLN STREET, BOSTON, MASS.

Library of Congress Cataloging in Publication Data

Puckett, Newbell Niles.
    Black names in America.

    At head of title: Newbell Niles Puckett memorial
gift, John G. White Department, Cleveland Public Library.
    1. Negroes--Names. 2. Names, Personal--United
States. I. Heller, Murray, ed. II. Cleveland. Public
Library. John G. White Dept. III. Title.
E185.89.N3P82   929.4'0973   74-13553
ISBN 0-8161-1140-5

This publication is printed on permanent/durable acid-free paper.

This book is dedicated to the memory of
Professor Newbell Niles Puckett,
Western Reserve University, Cleveland, Ohio.
Whatever value resides in these pages is due to his efforts;
whatever deficiencies the reader finds should be laid at my door.

Foreword

Dr. Newbell N. Puckett has made a valuable contribution to understanding the history of our nation and the "black experience" in America. Born and raised in Mississippi, Dr. Puckett's work in sociology and folklore at Western Reserve University in Cleveland, Ohio, presents us with a deep appreciation of our past culture. His publications relating to folklore and humor include Folk-Beliefs of the Southern Negro, Ohio Folk-Beliefs and The Religious Life of the Southern Negro.

Black Names in America is based on Dr. Puckett's research in the genesis, use and metamorphosis of the names of black Americans. The first stage of this study, "Names of American Negro Slaves," appeared in G. P. Murdoch's Studies in the Science of Society, published by the Yale University Press in 1937. The evolution of the naming process is a little-known aspect of the American socio-cultural heritage, yet those who have been part of the black experience know well and feel keenly the importance of a name and its impact on the individual. The material amassed for this work reveals how individual aspirations and the pressures of the larger society affected the naming practices of an entire race.

Names have been used not only to identify a human being but also to villify, depersonalize and dehumanize. Sam and Sambo, which Dr. Puckett identifies as common slave names of the seventeenth century, became racist slurs in the twentieth century when black men were commonly summoned by these names. The social significance of names is also manifested in summoning forms such as "boy" or "nigger" which supplanted the use of a name. The psychic impact was to reduce one to the level of a stereotype or non-person.

Students of sociology, anthropology and history will find this book a valuable resource for developing an understanding of social values related to naming. One recognizes the emergence of blacks from degradation to dignity through their rejection of "bestowed" names and their adoption of names suggesting self-esteem. Consider the nameless slave boy whose purchase price was a horse and who as a free man bore the name George Washington Carver. Black Names in America gives meaning to the name change of a great American from Thoroughly Good Marshall to Thurgood Marshall.

Dr. Puckett has investigated an area of historical importance. The once subtle black protest and the process of seeking status, recognition and a sense of humanity take on added significance in this work. Black Names in

FOREWORD

<u>America</u> provides the raw material for future study of the sociological effects of naming and the reflection, through names, of the self-image of a people.

George J. Livingston
Assistant Professor
School of Applied Social Sciences
Case Western University

Member, Board of Trustees,
Cleveland Public Library

Secretary Treasurer, Board of
John G. White Estate

Preface

In the spring of 1968 I had the opportunity, through the good offices of Professor Francis L. Utley, of The Ohio State University, and Mrs. Newbell Niles Puckett, to examine a large collection of names of Black Americans. These names formed part of a larger collection of material gathered over many years by Professor Puckett, of Western Reserve University. His untimely death precluded his witnessing the fruits of many of his scholarly labors, but it has been the wish of Mrs. Puckett, as well as that of his colleagues, that Professor Puckett's work not be confined to the dusty but populated world of unfinished research--especially since his research is both of great interest in its own right and, in fact, one more important tool for understanding the American experience.

With this in mind, I have completed the task of organizing the material which is housed in the John G. White Department of the Cleveland Public Library. There are in this collection approximately 500,000 names listed: 340,000 Black and 160,000 White. The former is the largest collection of Black names in America, and it dates from 1619 to the mid-1940's.

Professor Puckett's involvement in the culture and history of Black Americans began long before Black Studies programs became popular on college campuses. In 1926 his researches at Columbia University led to the publication of his Folk Beliefs of The Southern Negro (Chapel Hill, University of North Carolina Press), and in 1937 he published the initial findings of what he hoped to be this present study, "Names of American Negro Slaves," in Studies in The Science of Society, edited by George Murdock (New Haven, Yale University Press).

Professor Puckett's contributions have been acknowledged and appreciated by his colleagues within the academic world. In addition, students of American culture and language not associated with universities have also benefited from his research. The following note was among Dr. Puckett's papers; the correspondent is one we all know:

June 7, 1937

Dear Dr. Puckett:

It goes without saying that I was greatly interested in your paper on slave names in the Keller Festschrift. In it you say that you have under way a similar study of the names of present-day

negroes. May I bother you to let me hear of it whenever you publish
it? I'd certainly like to have it in my files, and to refer both to
it and to the paper on slave names in the next edition of my book,
"The American Language."

Your "Folk Beliefs of the Southern Negro," published in 1926, is
still on my shelf--a capital book!

Sincerely yours,

H. L. Mencken
1524 Hollins St.
Baltimore

Some of the interpretations offered in the 1937 article have been slightly
revised, since material collected after that publication offers access to a
greater number of names. For example, 703 Black slave names were listed for
the eighteenth century; the collection now totals 1,713 Black slave names,
more than double the original number, and 1,170 free Black names, a group not
the concern of the original article. Additional material has also indicated a
need to reevaluate the shift to unusual names in the nineteenth century. However, much of the discussion presented in Professor Puckett's article is as
valid now as then, and with the intent of offering the present reader a taste
of the lucidity of style and wit and the clarity of expression characteristic
of Professor Puckett, I have taken the liberty of referring to the article in
the early sections of this book.

With the great interest in Black history and the enormous amount of literature being published today to satisfy this interest, another general discussion of West African history, the slave trade and the effects of slavery upon
Blacks in America appears to me to be presumptuous as well as redundant. Instead, a short description of the development of names and naming practices
precedes the main concern of the book. The discussion itself is along prin-
ciples well known to students of names, but it may also be of interest to the
general reader. In addition, this discussion provides a basis for establish-
ing many of the categories of Black names in America.

The material is divided chronologically. The first chapter deals with
two centuries, the seventeenth and the eighteenth. I would suggest here, as
I do again later, that the reader treat with caution the temptation to read
trends into these naming practices; the number of names constitutes too small
a sample. Chapter Two deals with the period 1800-1864, and here we are on
safer ground since the number of Black and White names collected is sizeable.
Still, generalizations should be tentative. Chapter Three covers the period
following the Civil War, to the mid-1930's, when almost all of Professor
Puckett's collecting was terminated. Chapter Four deals with one aspect of
this period, the names of college students. The last chapter lists Black and
White names of African origin and their meanings.

Throughout the collection, distinctions are made among names that are
"usual," "unusual" and "old-fashioned." For these distinctions I have

maintained the criteria developed by Professor Puckett. The following comes
from the 1937 article:

> ...names which would be considered unusual according to present-day
> white standards in the South; ...names, like Abigail...and Saph-
> ronia,...would today be regarded merely as old-fashioned....
> p. 482

Thus, 1937 White standards of name usage were Professor Puckett's test for determining whether a name was "usual" or not. He notes the difficulty in pro-
jecting one's self backward into an earlier period and determining just what
would or would not have been considered normal then. It is a difficulty worth
accepting since, despite a certain amount of subjectivity, some rich insights
reward the reader in noting shifts in name usage using this test.

The task confronting an editor of such a large and significant body of
material is almost overwhelming. The lists of names offered are the product
of an exhaustive examination and sifting of innumerable lists collected over
the years. It seems to me that my primary responsibility, and therefore, the
primary purpose of this book, is to make available to the reader a coherent
and intelligible panoramic view of all the names. Thus, there is no attempt
to investigate individual names or to discuss the significance of names in any
but the most cursory way. Rather, the purpose is to present the wealth of
names in such a way that the general reader will acquire a grasp of the movement and character of Black name usage over the years, and the scholar will
have access to a body of name material never available before. The finest
compliment possible would be a more penetrating study based upon the material
in this book.

I am indebted to the Puckett Memorial Committee and especially to Mrs.
Puckett for the opportunity to edit Professor Puckett's material. In addition,
Mrs. Alice N. Loranth, Head of the John G. White Department, Cleveland Public
Library, has been vitally concerned with the success of this book. Her aid
in arranging and processing material has been invaluable. I wish to acknowl-
edge my gratitude for the support and advice offered me by a number of
scholars at The Ohio State University, especially Dr. Alan Brown, whose read-
ing of the final draft was of great help to me.

To Dr. Utley, for his faith in me over the years as well as for the acuity
and scholarly skills he brought to the manuscript, I owe a debt so great only
he and I knew its magnitude. His death last year is a great loss to the academic world and a personal loss to a great many people. He had become for me
much more than a teacher--or rather, he had become for me, finally, a teacher.

Most importantly, I would like to thank my wife, Madge, for the patience
with which she read my notes, the sympathy and devotion she has felt toward
me and my efforts, and the innumerable cups of coffee made on my behalf.

Contents

Guide to Source Lists

Chapter I

Chapter IV

Acknowledgments

Amongst many who aided in this collection, the following individuals and organizations seem to have warranted Dr. Puckett's special thanks:

Adomeit, Ruth, Cleveland, Ohio
Barrow, Miss S. F., Cleveland, Ohio
Brannon, Peter A., Montgomery, Alabama
Cheves, Miss Parmalee, Charleston, South Carolina
Cutler, Mrs. J. E., Cleveland, Ohio
Davis, Professor R. H., Canard Jr. High School, Cleveland, Ohio
Dickson, Harris, Vicksburg, Mississippi
Dockery, Joe R., Dockery, Mississippi
Evans, Dr. Gus, Aberdeen, Mississippi
Evans, Miss Moina, Columbus, Mississippi
Fairchilds, Mrs. V. A., Cleveland, Ohio
Hellerstein, Rebecca, Cleveland, Ohio
House, Dorothy E., Maternity Hospital, Cleveland, Ohio
Hudson, Dr. Arthur P., Chapel Hill, North Carolina
Hudson, Sadie, Columbus, Mississippi
Johnson, Dr. Charles S., Fisk University, Nashville, Tennessee
Jordan, Harvie, Atlanta, Georgia
Kennedy, R. Emmet, Gretna, Louisiana
Leiding, Mrs. Harriet K., Charleston, South Carolina
Lyons, Miss A., Cleveland, Ohio
Lyles, Mrs. Anna, Cleveland, Ohio
McCray, Miss H. H., Friendly Inn, Cleveland, Ohio
Peterkin, Mrs. Julia M., Fort Motte, South Carolina
Randolph, Vance, Pittsburg, Kansas
Ripley, Mrs. Katharine Ball, Charleston, South Carolina
Ross, Harold H., Cleveland, Ohio
Saxon, Lyle, Melrose, Louisiana
Sibley, Mrs. C. L., Birmingham Baptist Hospital, Birmington, Alabama
Thompson, George, Assoc. for Colored Community Work, Akron, Ohio
Toth, Father Joseph, Cleveland, Ohio (Names mostly from the files of the
    Cleveland City Hospital)
Watts, Mrs. C. A., Miami, Florida

The following informants were furnished by Professor A. P. Hudson, Chapel Hill, North Carolina:

Bowen, Ellen M., Greenville, North Carolina
Comer, Mrs. Harry, Chapel Hill, North Carolina

Acknowledgments

Deans, Clyde, Chapel Hill, North Carolina
Ewing, J. M., Chapel Hill, North Carolina
Graves, Mrs. J. C., Wilmington, North Carolina
Grubb, Rev. G. G., Chapel Hill, North Carolina
Hawthorne, Phyllis, Scarsdale, New York
Henry, Mrs. G. K. S., Chapel Hill, North Carolina
Horrell, Joe, Chapel Hill, North Carolina
Hulme, Francis, Buncombe County, North Carolina
McKee, Jane, Chapel Hill, North Carolina
McLean, James K., Maxton, North Carolina
McNeir, W. F., Chapel Hill, North Carolina
Mitchell, Allie C., Chapel Hill, North Carolina
Miller, E. S., Chapel Hill, North Carolina
Pebbles, Julia, Jackson, North Carolina
Sams, H. W., Chapel Hill, North Carolina
Sharpe, Mrs. H. B., Chapel Hill, North Carolina
Smithy, Len B., Bath, North Carolina
Wallace, Mrs. L. De L., Chapel Hill, North Carolina
Wallace, M., Athens, Alabama

AGENCIES AND ORGANIZATIONS

Anne Arundel County Welfare Board, Annapolis, Maryland
Associated Charities, Cincinnati, Ohio
Baltimore County Welfare Board, Towson, Maryland
Brooklyn Association for Improving the Condition of the Poor, Brooklyn,
    New York
Bureau of Vital Statistics (Mr. Butler Toombs), Atlanta, Georgia
Cook County Bureau of Public Welfare, Chicago, Illinois
Department of Public Welfare (Mr. F. G. Flowers), Baltimore, Maryland
Department of Public Welfare, Hartford, Connecticut
Department of Public Welfare, Macon, Georgia
Department of Public Welfare, New Orleans, Louisiana
Division of Social Service (Miss Aberdeen Johnson), St. Petersburg, Florida
Duval County Family Welfare Society, Jacksonville, Florida
Emergency Relief Bureau, Buffalo, New York
Family Bureau of Franklin County, Columbus, Ohio
Family Service Association, Jersey City, New Jersey
Family Service Organization, Louisville, Kentucky
Family Service Society, Canton, Ohio
Family Service Society (Miss Eva Smill), New Orleans, Louisiana
Family Service Society of Richmond (Mrs. Marian Yingling Frost), Richmond,
    Virginia
Family Society of Allegheny County, Pittsburgh, Pennsylvania
Family Society of New Haven, New Haven, Connecticut
Family Welfare Agency, Memphis, Tennessee
Family Welfare Association (Miss Dorothy Pope and Miss Isabel L. Bride-
    good), Baltimore, Maryland
Family Welfare Association, Minneapolis, Minnesota
Family Welfare Assocation, Springfield, Illinois
Family Welfare Association, Springfield, Massachusetts

ACKNOWLEDGMENTS

Family Welfare Association, Wichita, Kansas
Family Welfare Society, Columbia, South Carolina
Family Welfare Society, Indianapolis, Indiana
Family Welfare Society, Providence, Rhode Island
Family Welfare Society of Queens, Inc., Jamaica, New York
Family Welfare Society, Roxbury, Massachusetts
Genese County Welfare Relief Commission, Flint, Michigan
Guilford County Board of Public Welfare, Greensboro, North Carolina
Houston County Department of Public Welfare, Dothan, Alabama
Houston Social Service Bureau, Houston, Texas
Jefferson County Department of Public Welfare, Birmingham, Alabama
Kansas City Provident Association, Kansas City, Missouri
Lincoln House Association, Waterbury, Connecticut
Macon County Department of Public Welfare, Tuskegee, Alabama
Mobile County Department of Public Welfare, Mobile, Alabama
Pickens County Department of Public Welfare, Carrollton, Alabama
Polk County Emergency Relief Commission, Des Moines, Iowa
Provident Association, St. Louis, Missouri
Public Assistance Division, Board of Public Welfare, Washington, D. C.
Public Health Nursing Association (Miss Elizabeth H. Rath), Pittsburgh,
    Pennsylvania
Pulaski County Public Welfare Commission, Little Rock, Arkansas
Richmond County Department of Public Welfare, Augusta, Georgia
St. Louis County Welfare Association, Clayton, Missouri
Social Service Bureau, Newark, New Jersey
Social Service Bureau, Petersburg, Virginia
State School for Girls (Miss Eva E. Veirs and Miss Florence Monohan),
    Geneva, Illinois
Temporary State Department of Public Welfare (Miss Dorothy F. Churchill),
    Charleston, South Carolina
United Charities, Dallas, Texas
United Provident Association, Oklahoma City, Oklahoma
Winston-Salem Associated Charities (Miss Mary E. Judy and Miss Florence H.
    Gray), Winston-Salem, North Carolina

CHAPTER I

In the Beginning: 1619-1799

Along with taxes and death there appears in every human society a third
phenomenon whose universality is as personal and at the same time as collec-
tive: the bestowal upon every member in the community of a personal name.
Unlike the first two, which point to the commonality of all men, types of
personal names reflect distinctions not only between members of a community,
but also between communities of men. And although forms of taxation differ -
from tributes of salt to graduated income taxes - the practice is indigenous
to human society. Similarly although names and naming customs differ, the
practice of conferring a name upon every member in a group is universal.

Furthermore, despite differences in languages and cultures, very marked
similarities exist both in personal naming beliefs and in naming practices and
types of names given. It is most striking, for example, that in both ancient
Hebrew and Babylonian thought, nothing existed unless it had a name. To
eliminate the name was tantamount to eliminating the thing.[1] Similarly, the
ancient Egyptians, for whom a man was divided into eight parts, one of the
most important being his name, believed that if the name were blotted out, the
man and all his afterlife would be destroyed.[2]

Navaho Indians believed that there was a certain amount of power in a
name which would ultimately be used up. When this happened, the name was ex-
hausted. In Australia each aboriginal has at least two given names. Of these,
the second is the secret or sacred name, used only in a whisper after the most
elaborate precautions have been made.

Some American Indians and peoples in Tibet believed that sickness was
caused by names that "did not fit" and that a cure would be effected only by

_____

[1]Elsdon C. Smith, _Treasury of Name Lore_ (New York: Harper and Row,
1967), p. 218. I am greatly indebted to this excellent little book, as well
as Lambert and Pei's _Our Names_ (New York: Lothrop, 1969) for the discussion
in the following pages.

[2]S. & K. Waddell, "Buddhism of Tibet," _Science of Sociology_, II, Vol. I,
p. 498: On the other side of the world this belief is to be found. "Tibetan
ghosts are always malicious and their names have to be burned: ultimately a
piece of paper is thrown into the flames, on which is written the name of the
deceased person - always a relative - whose ghost is to be suppressed. When
this paper is burned the particular ghost has received its quitus, and never
can give trouble again."

In the Beginning: 1619-1799

acquiring a new name that would "fit." And although medication proved a more reliable way of regaining health, ancient times saw Chinese doctors writing a patient's name on paper, which they subsequently burned, and mixing the ashes with medicine to insure the identification of the medicine with the sick man.

Amongst German Gypsies "the child is given a name..., but which is immediately changed if its owner has succeeded in surviving a serious illness. The precaution is taken to prevent the Sickness Spirit from recognizing the child."[3] And finally, it is the custom among the peasants of Bulgaria to name children born after the death of a first child Zhivko (life) if a boy, and Zhivka, if a girl, to insure the life of the second child.[4]

This close connection between a name and its owner's life and health appears as one application of Lévy-Bruhl's Law of Participation; that is, a connection is believed to exist between two things which are regarded as partially identical or as having a direct influence on one another although there is no spatial contact nor intelligible causal relation between them. Lévy-Bruhl is wise enough not to confine this law to the primitive mind. On the contrary, he suggests that this, as well as other characteristics, may also be elements in civilized communities. And when Piaget notes both that the children he was dealing with began by confusing words with things, and that names were intimately bound up with the objects they denoted so that they shared in the nature of things, we can readily understand that modern man can attribute to names some of the qualities felt by ancients and primitives.[5]

A very common custom among many primitives is for boys and girls to take a new name at puberty in the belief that in doing so they acquire a new identity, become entirely different people. And in modern times initiates into religious orders such as those of the Catholic Church do the same. Thus, it is not very strange that Quamina, newly christened Timothy, refused to pay a debt. "He said that the old man lent the doubloon to Quamina but he was not Quamina now; he was a new man, born again and called Timothy, and was not bound to pay the debt of the dead man."[6]

Modern American Jews often retain the ancient Ashkenazic custom of refusing to name a child after an older living person in order to insure that the Angel of Death will not take the young child by mistake. Similar to this is the custom of changing the name of a sick person in order to save his life by hoodwinking the Angel of Death. This Jewish custom parallels that of some

[3]Martin Block, Gypsies, Their Life and Their Customs (London and New York: D. Appleton, 1939), p. 182.

[4]Frederick, W. H. Megeod, "Personal Names Amongst Some West African Tribes," Journal of African Society, XVII (1917), p. 43: "Another Vai known to Koelle bore the name Momoru Doaru Wonye, Wonye meaning a large kind of ant, possibly the great stink ant. He himself told Koelle the origin of the name. His mother had several children before him, all of whom died. When he was born, people said to his mother, 'You must give a bad name to this one, else he will die also!' Hence she called him Wonye, and he lived."

[5]James Dougall, "Characteristics of African Thought," International Institute of African Language and Culture Memorandum X (London: Oxford University Press, 1932), pp. 8-11.

[6]Cynric R. Williams, A Tour Through the Island of Jamaica in 1838, p. 19.

In the Beginning: 1619-1799

North American Indians and seems somewhat related to the practices of German Gypsies and Bulgarian peasants.

Parents everywhere usually attempt to give a child a "good" name, one that will benefit him in infancy and in later life. Thus, aside from causing some eyebrow raising, naming a child Dirt or Filth, when translated into English, in order to convince the evil spirits that it is not worth their trouble to injure it, has very much the same spirit, albeit negatively expressed, as that which motivated Mr. and Mrs. Frederick Lindloff of Clinton County, Iowa, to name their child, in 1880, Through-Much-Trial-and-Tribulation-We-Enter-the-Kingdom-of-Heaven.

Names, then, can be viewed in terms of the anthropologist's Law of Participation and the psychologist's analysis of the child's vision of the world. It is enough for our concerns at the present to say that certain attitudes toward personal naming practices, such as the investment of the name with magical, healing and prestigious powers seem very similar, as do the naming practices themselves, the world over.

The Latins bestowed names indicative of the order in which the holder of the name was born. Examples include the Latin Una ("One"), Quintus ("Fifth"), Octavius or Octavian ("Eight") or a Spanish name like Primo (today the word, which originally meant "First," means "cousin" or "first cousin "). A similar practice on the other side of the globe appears in Japan, where children are often numbered instead of named; Ichiko, for example, means "number one child" or "first born." An Armenian gentleman of my acquaintance has the name Antranig or "little first born."[7] And there was a family in Detroit, Michigan where the sons were called One, Two, Three Stickney, and the daughters First, Second, Third Stickney.[8]

Something similar is done by the Ashanti tribes of Ghana, West Africa, who occasionally name their children, from the second on, in the order in which they are born: Manu, Mensah, Avan ("Second," "Third," "Fourth," etc.), up to Badu, "Tenth." But the Ashanti have an additional custom; they name their children according to the day of the week on which they were born. This practice persisted in Jamaica, and a number of these traditionally Jamaican[9]

---

[7]Compliments of Mrs. Gloria Avazyian, South Orange, New Jersey.

[8]National Magazine, 10, 1857, p. 183.

[9]M. W. Beckwith, Black Roadways (Chapel Hill, 1929), p. 59; F. W. Pitman, "Slavery on British West India Plantation in the Eighteenth Century," Journal of Negro History XI (1926), p. 641; see also E. Clodd, Magic in Names and Other Things (London, 1920), p. 66; F. S. and M. J. Herskovits, Rebel Destiny (New York and London, 1934), pp. 222-223, for similar usages among the Saramacca Negroes of Suriname.

In the Beginning: 1619-1799

names are found in the United States, e.g., <u>Quashe</u>, <u>Cudjo</u>, <u>Quaco</u> and <u>Cuffee</u> among male slaves and <u>Juba</u>, <u>Beneba</u>, <u>Cooba</u> (spelled Cubah or Cubbah) and <u>Abba</u> (spelled Abah) among female slaves.[10] We might note in passing that when twins were born to a couple in England one midnight, the eldest was named <u>Tuesday</u> and the youngest <u>Wednesday</u>.

Just as attitudes and personal naming practices seem universally similar, types of names employed seem also to reflect the commonality of the human animal. Many in ancient Egypt were known to each other by such nicknames as <u>Mouse</u>, <u>Ape</u>, <u>Cat</u>, <u>Big Head</u>, <u>Baldy</u> and <u>Lazy</u>. The name of the Italian painter Cimabue translates into "Oxtop"; Emperor Frederick Barbarossa was really known as "Red Beard." Many nicknames have evolved into family names. Unfortunately some original descriptive meanings have been lost; fortunately others have not. Cameron meant "Crooked nose," and Cruickshanks was one with bow legs. Foljambe referred to an awkward legged man, and Kennedy to a man with a big head.

In the Middle Ages almost every man was known among his neighbors by a nickname more or less harsh. In the London records of the twelfth and thirteenth centuries such nicknames as <u>Forfot</u> (pig feet), <u>Holebuc</u> (hollow belly), <u>Hore</u> (dirt and filth), <u>Stunch</u> (smell) and <u>Wigga</u> (beetle) attest to the descriptive powers of our English forefathers. A look through his auto-biography culls such names from Malcolm X's days on the streets of Harlem as <u>Brown Sugar</u> and <u>Creole Bill</u>, <u>Black Sammy</u>, <u>King Padmore</u>, <u>Cadillac Drake</u>, <u>Alabama Peach</u>, <u>Dollarbill</u>, <u>Fewclothes</u> and <u>Jumpsteady</u>.[11] The author himself was known at various stages of his life as <u>Malcolm Little</u>, <u>Homeboy</u>, <u>Detroit Red</u>, <u>Big Red</u>, <u>Satan</u>, <u>Malcolm X</u> and <u>El-Hajj Malik El-Shabozz</u>.[12]

What emerges from this cursory description is the fact that personal name practices and beliefs show remarkable similarities throughout the world and through the ages.

Also, there are some general categories of given and surnames which appear the world over. Of the surnames there is a general agreement upon at least these four types: Descriptive, Location, Occupation and Relationship. Descriptive surnames, e.g., Young, Whitehead, Small, Brown, Lightfoot, denote characteristics such as age, color, size and physical appearance. Location names, such as Hill, Poole, Blackwood, Radcliff, may refer to village, town and other place names. Occupation names like Cook, Taylor, Smith, Goldsmith and Miller refer to the variety of human endeavors. But difficulties arise in interpreting meanings of names without knowledge of the cultural and linguistic characteristics of the period. For example, how does one differentiate between occupation and class distinctions when confronted with the

---

[10]Newbell N. Puckett, "Names of American Negro Slaves," p. 474. Preface.

[11]Malcolm X, The Autobiography of Malcolm X (New York: Grove Press, 1964), pp. 88-97.

[12]Ibid., p. 451.

In the Beginning: 1619-1799

name <u>Knight</u>? Again, is a <u>Miller</u> one who owned the mill, <u>i.e.</u>, is it an occupation name, or is Miller one who lived near the mill, <u>i.e.</u>, is it a location
name?[13] Relationship names such as Robertson and Wilson (the sons of Robert
and Will) sometimes reflect other than parental relationships. At times the
name of the lord of the manor, or that of the owner of the field or of the
slave master might be the origin of the surname.

Given names show even greater variety. They were the first names people
had,[14] of course, and their origins lie in description, Biblical references,
titles, animal life, flora, fauna, jewels, calendar, episodes, places, occupations and individual fancy. Another source of infinite variety lies in pet
or hypocoristic names. From the variety of given names Elsdon Smith notes
ten principal types of girl's names ranging from common Biblical names to
artificial or invented ones such as <u>Jiola</u> and <u>Uana</u>; and seven principal types
of boy's names from common Biblical names to titles such as <u>Colonel</u>, <u>Duke</u> and
<u>General</u>. The more common pet or hypocoristic types of names express the idea
of smallness, incompetency or contempt or endearment.

Although the trait of combining given names into new forms is not unique
in America (French <u>Marianne</u> is a combination of <u>Marie</u> plus <u>Anne</u>), we are ad-
dicted to this custom to a greater degree than most other people. <u>Georgianna</u>,
<u>Joanna</u>, <u>Charlene</u>, are some obvious examples.[15]

Personal names, both given and familial, change, often inadvertently, but
just as often by choice. Thus the number and variety of surnames in use have
been and, to a lesser extent still, are being increased in numerous ways,
ranging from corruption by scribes' use of Latin to shifts of local pronunciation. The principal reasons for conscious name changing in America range
from difficulties in spelling and punctuation to a desire to break with the
past. Not all of these intentional changes produce new names, of course, but
many of them do.

Given the infinite possibilities of variety in the bestowal of names and
a situation wherein large numbers of Blacks were hauled out of their cultural
and linguistic contexts,[16] a study of the personal names of Black Americans
can serve a number of purposes. It can, for one, serve as a recording of the
names used by Blacks, both slave and free, in this country; secondly, it can

---

[13]C. N. Matthews, <u>English Surnames</u> (New York: Charles Scribner's Sons,
1966), pp. 69 and following.

[14]The need for a second or surname becomes felt when the group becomes
so large that another name is needed to distinguish one individual from another; cf. Megeod, <u>Languages of West Africa</u> (London: K. Paul, French, T.
Truber and Co., 1911-1913), II, 339.: "Usually there is only a single personal name. Certainly it is so in the smaller tribes. In larger tribes a
second name--totemic, family, local, or descriptive--may be added; and these,
like the surnames in Europe, may be of quite recent invention."

[15]See the list offered by Lambert and Pei, pp. 59-60.

[16]A rough estimate indicates that less than 17,000 Blacks lived in the
Colonies prior to 1700. See J. Hope Franklin, <u>From Slavery to Freedom</u>, 3rd
Edition (New York: Alfred A. Knopf, 1967), pp. 73-104. Another estimate
suggests about 30,000. See Farley Reynolds, <u>Growth of the Black Population</u>
(Chicago, Ill.: Markham Publishing Co., 1970), p. 20.

In the Beginning: 1619-1799

enable us to determine the extent to which universal naming practices reflect themselves amongst Black Americans; thirdly, it can serve to indicate to us the nature of the relationships existing between Whites and Blacks in America from the days of the earliest slave trading to the mid-twentieth century, a period of some three hundred years. And even further, as Dr. Puckett put it, it can serve as a study of the social role of names in general.

"This collection includes only sixty-five names of slaves prior to 1700-- thirty-six from Virginia, twenty-seven from New York and two from Maryland. In the hands of the earlier slave traders slaves seem to have been simply merchandise en masse, not distinguished by individual names until they had entered into the occupational life of their subsequent owners."[17] The slave ship James' Journal (1675) mentions on April 17 that "a stout man slave leaped overboard and drowned himself." Again on September 6 the Journal notes that "a neaggerman dep'ted this life whoe died suddenly."[18]

Some names, of course, were foisted upon Black captives in transit to the New World. But the transitional nature of the situation produced names highly fanciful and short-lived. Edward Manning of the slaver Thomas Watson in 1860 writes:

> I suppose they...all had names in their own dialect, but the effort required to pronounce them was too much for us, so we picked out our favorites and dubbed them 'main-stay,' 'cats head,' 'Bull's eye,' 'Rope-yarn,' and various other sea phrases.[19]

That only those Blacks who became "favorites" received names, however eccentric, underscores the significance of the bestowal of a name. That is, to name a person is to recognize his existence.

Most Blacks were not named on ship or even after landing until they were purchased and transported to their owners. A New England slave notice announced even into the eighteenth century, "a very likely negro man" for sale.[20] These Blacks, then, had no real identity to Whites as human beings for they had no names. Only when the slave acquired a name did he assume some degree of dignity in the White owner's eyes, and it would seem that the type of names used would reflect the relationship.

Of the sixty-five slave names prior to 1700, twenty are English with a total incidence of thirty-five; eighteen are Spanish with a frequency of twenty-six; the diminutive Tony could be either English, as in Anthony, or Spanish, as in Anthonio; and three are African.

---

[17]Puckett, op. cit., pp. 472-473.

[18]E. Donnan, Documents Illustrative of the History of the Slave Trade to America, 4 vols. (Washington, D. C., 1930-35), Vol. I, 199.

[19]George F. Dow, Slave Ships and Slaving (Salem, Mass., 1927), p. 295.

[20]To be more precise, 1712-1714 sales notices.

In the Beginning: 1619-1799

The sixty-five names are listed below; the number
after a name indicates the frequency with which the name
was used, and no number indicates the name was used that
one time.[21]

Andrew	Eliz	Mary 3
Angelo	Emanuel	Madelina
Angeli	Fernando	Manuel
Anthonio 4	Figa	Margaret
Anthony 3	Frances	Mitchaell
Antonio	Francisco 2	Mookinga
Balthazar	Gasinte	Palassa
Barbara	Isabella	Phillip
Bastiaen	Jacob	Paulo
Brase	John 10	Samba
Christopher	Julianna	Susanna
Couchazello	Joseph	Tony
Diego	Lucia 2	Will
Edward 2	Maria 4	William 2

If we were to ignore John for the moment, since it may have been Juan, the
figures would indicate an approximately equal distribution between English and
Spanish names and frequencies (English: nineteen names with a frequency of
twenty-five; Spanish: eighteen names with a frequency of twenty-six. Further-
more, in the group of Black slaves originally brought into Virginia in 1619
there seem to have been three Anthony's, two John's and an Angelo, Isabella,
William, Frances, Edward and Margaret. Angelo is a very uncommon name in
England, and the rest may represent Anglicizations of original Spanish names.[22]
Thus, Anthony might be a metamorphized Anthonio, John may have emerged from
Juan, William from Guillaume, Frances from Francisca, Edward from Eduardo, and
Margaret from Margarita. In addition, two children born in Virginia received
the English names Mary and Elizabeth. There is a strong possibility that the
majority of slaves brought to the Colonies before 1700 had Spanish names.

A few surnames appear among slaves even prior to 1700. Andrew Moore and
Philip Gowen, who probably took their masters' surnames, show rather complete
Anglicization. John Pedro (Virginia, 1623) may have received an earlier
Spanish baptism; his name is only partially Anglicized,[23] and represents a
juxtaposition of two given names, one English and the other Spanish. Edward
Mozingo (Virginia, 1672) may well have had the English Edward added to an
original African name.

Only three given names are of African derivation: Mookinga, Samba and
Palassa; these names, two male and one female, in that order, comprise 04.6

---

[21]This will be the case throughout this work. In addition, a number
after a name usually indicates the frequency with which that name was used in
the period under discussion.

[22]H. T. Caterall, Judicial Cases Concerning American Slavery and the
Negro, 3 vols. (Washington, D. C., 1926-32), Vol. I, pp. 55-56.

[23]Puckett, op. cit., p. 473.

In the Beginning: 1619-1799

per cent of the total sixty-five names on this list. Initially, then, it seems that the earliest of slave traders to the Colonies, when indeed they deigned to use names at all, and slave owners in the New World, foisted upon Blacks names foreign to their origins.

Of the English names represented in this early collection John (10), the most frequently used name, heads the list of Biblical names, followed by Mary (3), Balthazar, Emanuel, Jacob and Joseph: a total of six names with a frequency of eighteen. Spanish names clearly derived from the Bible include Maria (4) and Paulo, two names with a frequency of five. English and Spanish names with obvious Biblical derivation thus account for at least twenty-three, or 35.3 per cent, of the sixty-five names. The percentage would be considerably higher were we to include names which might easily have Biblical origin such as Manuel, not to mention the Saints Andrew, Anthonio (4), Anthony, Antonio, Christopher, Frances, Francisco (2), Lucia (2), Madelina and Phillip.

It appears then that whether or not baptism was involved, Whites tended to supply their Black slaves, to a great extent, with Biblical and Christian names. The desire to propagate the Faith was undoubtedly an important motivating factor, especially amongst Spanish Catholics; however, an element of fancy may have entered in. James Arnold, the surgeon on the English slaver, The Ruby, wrote in 1787: "The first slave that was traded for, after the brig anchored at the Island of Bimbe (small island south of Old Calabar, 1787), was a girl of about fifteen who was promptly named Eve, for it was usual on slave ships to give the names of Adam and Eve, to the first man and woman brought aboard."[24]

For the period between 1700 and 1800 the names of 2,883 Blacks were available, including 143 from Louisiana almost all of whom are of French or Spanish origin. Collected were 1,713 Black slave names, 962 male and 608 female, excluding the Louisiana slaves with French or Spanish names (see Source List D), and 1,170 names of free Blacks, 763 male and 407 female, within the bounds of the Continental United States (see Source Lists A, B, C).

The thirty-eight most frequently used names of Black male slaves, using five as a cut off point, are in order of frequency[25] (see Source List A):

Jack 57	Peter 20	Ben 12
Tom 47	John 18	George 12
Harry 34	Robin 18	Tam 12
Sam 30	Frank 16	James 11
Will 23	Charles 15	Piet 9
Caesar 21	Joe 14	Cato 8
Dick 20	Prince 14	Daniel 8

---

[24]Dow, op. cit., p. 172.

[25]Unless otherwise stated, all lists have as a cut off point a frequency of 5.

In the Beginning: 1619-1799

Simon 8	Thom 7	Pompey 6
Abram 7	Andrew 6	Isaac 5
Jacob 7	Bob 6	Jupiter 5
Lew 7	Cof 6	Ned 5
Sambo 7	Francis 6	York 5
Stephen 7	Joseph 6	

The twenty-six most frequently used female Black slave names are, in order of frequency:

Bet 38	Sary 12	Ginny 7
Mary 22	Gin 10	Grace 7
Jane 18	Gen 9	Jenny 7
Hannah 16	Dien 8	Maria 6
Betty 15	Dinah 8	Nancy 6
Sarah 15	Isabel 8	Rose 6
Phillis 14	Judy 8	Amy 5
Nan 13	Lucy 8	Dine 5
Peg 12	Susan 8	

The thirty-one most frequently used Southern Free Black male names are, in order of frequency (see Source List B):

John 28	Ben 15	Richard 9
James 25	Harry 13	Caesar 8
George 24	Samuel 13	Robert 8
Sam 24	Thomas 13	Daniel 7
William 23	Will 13	Frank 7
Peter 22	Charles 12	Henry 7
Dick 19	Joseph 11	Abraham 6
Jacob 18	Bob 10	Ned 6
Jack 17	Davey 9	David 5
Tom 17	Joe 9	Mingo 5
		Toby 5

The nineteen most frequently used Southern Free Black female names are, in order of frequency:

Sarah 24	Jane 10	Grace 7
Hannah 19	Ann 8	Nan 7
Rachael 19	Elizabeth 8	Lucy 6
Bet(t) 12	Nancy 8	Nanny 6
Mary 12	Pegg 8	Patience 6
Phillis 12	Dinah 7	Rose 6
		Betty 5

From a list of 118 Northern Black Soldiers, Colonial Patriots, the ten most common given names, in order of frequency, using three as a cut off point are (see Source List C):

BLACK NAMES IN AMERICA

In the Beginning: 1619-1799

John 9	Cato 6	Thomas 4
Prince 8	Caesar 4	Cuff 3
Peter 7	Richard 4	Joseph 3
		Pomp 3

These ten names account for fifty-one, or 43.2 per cent, of all the names in the list. The thirteen most common surnames of the Black Patriots, in order of frequency, using two as a cut off point are:

Freeman 7	Rogers 3	Liberty 2
Johnson 4	Ball 2	Phillips 2
Brown 3	Caesar 2	Rhodes 2
Greene 3	Jackson 2	Vassall 2
		Williams 2

The popularity of Freeman (7), along with the use of Liberty (2), suggests a unique social position for these Blacks in America. Here we can surely hypothesize that the surname represents not only aspirations, but also achievement. Freeman and Liberty represent 7.6 per cent of all the surnames used by the members of this Black Patriot Company.[26]

Jack, Tom and Harry, the first three names on the slave list, in that order, account for 138 names in all, or 14.3 per cent of all slave males; yet amongst free Black males Jack and Tom appear ninth and tenth with seventeen occurrences each and Harry appears twelfth with thirteen occurrences, a total of forty-seven, or 7.2 per cent. This suggests that free Blacks eschewed the most frequently used names of their slave brothers.

Sam (30), the fourth most popular slave name, is also fourth amongst free Blacks (24). Will occurs twenty-three times amongst Black slaves, appearing fifth on the list; William appears fifth on the list of free Blacks, occurring twenty-three times, whereas Will occurs thirteen times amongst free Blacks, coming in fifteenth.

William (23), Samuel (13), Thomas (13), Davey (9), Richard (9), Robert (8), Henry (7), Abraham (6), David (5), Mingo (5) and Toby (5) appear amongst free Blacks but do not appear on the list of most commonly used slave names. Conversely, Robin (18), Prince (14), Tam (12), Piet (9), Cato (8), Simon (8), Abram (7), Lew (7), Sambo (7), Stephen (7), Thomas (7), Andrew (6), Cof (6), Francis (6), Pompey (6), Isaac (5), Jupiter (5) and York (5) are common slave names which do not appear as common free Black names in the South.

The attitude of the master toward the slave was less that of a parent toward his child than that of an owner toward his property. Probate records

---

[26]"Negro Names," Opportunity, V, p. 37. "Woodson's Mind of the Negro relates the story of a fugitive who decided that on becoming a man he would adopt as his name Be-man. There are now many Negro families of Beman. In New York, in the listings of Free Negro Heads of Negro Families, there were six families of Jubilees, and other families of Liberty's, Freebob's, Freeman's and names that carry on through generations...."

In the Beginning: 1619-1799

reveal a tendency to personalize and identify accurately by name all live-
stock, human or otherwise; mules and cows are often listed by name, and are
distinguished from slaves mainly in terms of appraised value. To furnish an
interesting comparison, 235 names of mules were abstracted from Lowndes County,
Mississippi, Probate Records for 1858. Of this number, 197, or 84 per cent,
occur also as slave names, including not only such common names as Bet, Eliza,
Jinny and Tobe, but also such classical names as Cato, Dianna, Hector and
Pompey.

The ten most common mule names were, in order of frequency:

Jack	John	Tom
Kitt	Mike	Bill
Beck	Ned	Jim
		Dolly

Most of these also occur among the most common slave names. Certain names,
on the other hand, seem to have been distinctive to mules, e.g., Blaze,
Dragon, Five Cents, Fly 3, Lightfoot, Pick, Rock, Shot, Telegraph, Value and
Yanky. In general, however, mule names resemble many of the slave diminutives
in being short and terse, designed rather for property than personal distinction.

Jack, Tom and Harry reflect a level of impersonality best described by
its echo of any "Tom, Dick and Harry." The three most popular free Black
names, on the other hand, reflect not impersonality, but rather, an assimilation represented in the standard English names of John, James and George. In
addition, it appears that slave names tended to take shortened or contracted
forms; for example, Sam, Will, Dick, Abram, Thom and Bob. Although free
Blacks used these forms also, there is a tendency for them to employ Richard,
Abraham, Thomas and Robert.

These two impressions tend to suggest that the free Southern Black employed his freedom in adopting a name that offered him more dignity and individuality while, at the same time, reflecting an English tradition.

The free Black names in the North, represented by the members of the 2nd
Co. Revolutionary soldiers(Source List C), offer interesting speculation. As
among their free brothers in the South, John is the most popular name. Yet
the next most frequently used name, Prince (8), is not found at all in the
list of commonly used names of Southern free Blacks; however, it is found
fourteen times amongst slaves. Cato and Cuff (Cof in the slave list) share
this peculiarity with Prince. And Richard and Thomas, used by the Black
soldiers and free Blacks, are not found on the Black slave list.

One might conjecture that along with the desire for dignified names such
as Richard and Thomas, instead of Dick and Thom, the free Northern Blacks
found attractive such titular and classic names as Prince and Cato, as well
as the derivation from the African, Cuff. This predilection for more elegant

In the Beginning: 1619-1799

names is supported by noting that 8.4 per cent of the Black Revolutionary soldiers took as surnames Freeman, Freedman and Liberty.

Of the female slave names Peg (12), Sary (12), Gin (10), Gen (9), Dien (8), Isabel (8), Judy (8), Susan (8), Ginny (7), Jenny (7), Maria (6), Amy (5) and Dine (5) are not used by free Black women. They employ instead: Rachael (19), Ann (8), Elizabeth (8), Nanny (6) and Patience (6).

There seems to be a tendency amongst the free Black women to avoid the shortened and patronizing Sary, Gin, Gen, Amy and Dine forms and employ instead the more dignified as well as Biblical Sarah, Hannah, Rachael and Mary. Indeed, these four alone total 74, or 18.1 per cent, of all the free Black female names. Contracted or non-English names on the slave list such as Isabel (8) and Maria (6) are either replaced with Elizabeth (8) or transformed into Mary (12) by free Black women. We find also the influence of Puritan nomenclature in these Black women with the appearance of Grace and Patience.

Of the male slaves, 13.09 per cent employed Biblical or Puritanic names; 14.48 per cent of the female slaves also used these types. This would suggest a slightly greater influence of Christianity upon female slaves. Amongst free Black males in the South 29.45 per cent used Biblical or Puritanic nomenclature, a significant jump. And similarly, free Black women employed this type of name at a very high rate of 26.28 per cent. It would seem, then, that amongst male and female Blacks freedom allowed them to use a type of nomenclature they found attractive and perhaps more dignified. This is reflected as well amongst Black Colonial soldiers who employed Biblical names at a rate of 33.05 per cent--almost a third of all the names used in the entire Company.

The most popular of Biblical names amongst male slaves were Peter (20), John (18), James (11), Daniel (8), Simon (8), Abram (7) and Jacob (7). Male slaves employed Old Testament names fourteen times with a total number of 44; they used New Testament names thirteen times with a frequency of 79. Amongst male slaves Puritanic names were not used at all.

Female slaves employed Mary (22) most often, followed by Hannah (16) and Sarah (15). As with the males, slave women used both New and Old Testament names, and the contrast is even more evident here. Only three New Testament names are employed, Mary, Dorcas and Tabitha.[27] Thirteen Old Testament names are used with a total frequency of 54. We see here the emergence of Puritan influences reflected in female names with the use of Grace (7), Mercy, Patience and Temperance.

Free Black males in the South found John (28) the most attractive, followed by James (25) and Peter (22). They then turned Abram into Abraham (6), retained Daniel (7) and dropped Simon. Samuel (13), Thomas (13) and Joseph (11) were also attractive.

---

[27]"Dorcas, interchangeable with Tabitha: A woman of good deeds. Made coats and garments for the poor; hence, a Dorcas Society of Women of the Church who supply garments to the needy." New Century Cyclopedia of Names, 3 vols., ed. Clarence L. Barnhart (New York: Appleton-Century-Crofts, 1954), p. 1313.

BLACK NAMES IN AMERICA

In the Beginning: 1619-1799

Free Black men tended to employ more Old Testament names than did the slaves. Nineteen Old Testament names with a frequency of 77 were employed, whereas only thirteen New Testament names with a frequency of 113 were used. The pattern remains the same for free and slave males: more Old Testament names but a greater frequency of New Testament names.

Free Blacks in the North found John (9), Peter (7) and Thomas (4) the most attractive Biblical names. Yet eleven Old Testament names were used with a frequency of twelve, and although New Testament names were employed with a frequency of twenty-seven, only seven New Testament names were actually used. As in other male groups, no Puritanic names are found amongst these Black soldiers.

Free Black women in the South continue the marked distinction in the use of Old and New Testament names. Mary (12) is replaced as the most frequently used name by Sarah (24), and only two other New Testament names, Christian and Jude, are employed. Hannah (19), along with Sarah, continues to be highly regarded by these free Black women, as they were by slave women. Eleven Old Testament names with a frequency of 78 appear, whereas only three New Testament names with a frequency of fourteen are found in this list. And again Puritanic names such as Charity, Grace (7), Patience (6) and Prudence find greater favor with free Black women and have a frequency of 14.01 per cent of the total names in this category, a 2.63 per cent increase over Puritanic names used by the female slave group.

6.13 per cent of slave male names were Classical or Literary; yet only 1.49 per cent of female slave names fall into this category. It would seem that male slave owners, choosing names for their slaves, had a greater propensity and infatuation for classical and literary names than their wives, who presumably would have a greater amount of control in naming female slaves.

Amongst free Black males in the South 4.03 per cent continued using classical or literary names, a slight drop, but free Black women evidently found this type of name attractive as is reflected in a rise from 1.49 per cent to 2.69 per cent. Colonial Black soldiers also found classical and literary names to their liking; 16.10 per cent of their given names and 2.54 per cent of their surnames belong in this category.

Caesar (21) is by far the most frequently used Black slave male classical name, followed by Cato (8), Pompey (6) and Jupiter (5). Rome seems to have had a greater influence in these classical names than Athens. This is also true amongst slave women, with Dianna (2), Dido (2), Phoebe (2) and Venus (2).[28] Southern free Black classical and literary names also center around ancient Rome as Caesar (8) remains the favorite, followed by Pompey (4) and Sipio (3) and its variant Sipeo. Hellenic influences are reflected in Poladore (2), Alexander, Hector, Hercules and Troyles.

---

[28]Greek but synonymous with the Latin Diana, goddess of the name Dice is also Greek, daughter of Zeus, the personification of justice. New Century Cyclopedia of Names, ibid., Vol. I, p. 1271 and Vol. III, p. 3171.

In the Beginning: 1619-1799

Amongst free Black soldiers Cato (6) replaces Caesar (4) in popularity as a given name, followed by Philo (2) and Scipio (2). However, Caesar appears two more times as a surname. Again Latin is more frequently the source of these classical names than Greek. Of the latter, Hector is again present, but Hercules is ignored by these Black soldiers and Plato is picked up--a remarkable shift for soldiers. Literary names occur with the use of Hamlet and Ichabod which is also Biblical.

Free Black women also employ more Latin names than Greek. Venus is often used, as are Dianna and Dido. Free women employ the Greek Pheba as well as Pheby; to this they add Chloe (2) for the first time, and we also see the use of Penelope and Cassandra. One literary name emerges, that of Priscilla.

Geographical location names account for 2.48 per cent of all the male slave names. There are no location names for female slaves. This would suggest that male identification relied more heavily upon making some kind of connection between an individual and some place of residence or birth. Perhaps it suggests that male slaves were more migratory than female slaves.

Free males in the South show a very slight decline in the number of geographical names used, from the slave 2.48 per cent to 2.17 per cent. But although free females reflect a greater attraction for this type of name, going from 0 to .24 per cent, the change is too insignificant to mean anything. Free Black soldiers reflect a greater interest in geographical names; they employ 2.54 per cent as given names and 5 per cent as surnames. It is possible that this relatively higher percentage of location names employed by Black soldiers is due to the Whites who registered them for duty in the Colonial Army.

York (5) is the most frequently used location name among Black male slaves; this is followed by London (3). Other British place names, comprising the large majority listed are: Bristoll, Cambridge, Essex, Lancaster, Limehouse,[29] Malborough, Newport, Oxford, Portsmouth, Salisbury, Willoughby and Warwick. The only definite case of a male slave being given a feminine name is Carolina (South Carolina, 1799); this may have referred to the state from which he came, and was possibly followed by Tom or some other name not included in the listing.

Free Southern Black males retain the British York (3) and London (2). They also use Bristol and Oxford but drop many others in favor of Sussex, Yarmouth and Isle of Wight. Unlike the male slaves, the females dropped the name Carolina. Place names of non-British origin such as Portroyal and Prussia appear reflecting perhaps a sense of freedom and mobility. Black patriot soldiers use Boston, Glosaster and York as given names, which seem to parallel slave names; however, the surnames employed by these soldiers reflect other areas. Holland, Holsted and Northup are not found elsewhere, and

---

[29] N. E. London, on the North bank of the Thames. It contains London's "Chinatown" and has long been noted as a rendezvous of British and foreign sailors. New Century Cyclopedia of Names, ibid., Vol. II, p. 2466.

In the Beginning: 1619-1799

Middletown, although listed amongst slave names, is too common to demand an exact placement.

Finally, of the free Black females only one name, Carolina, appears. This is identical with the incidence among slave males.

Descriptive or occupational or episodic male slave names occur 6.54 per cent; female slave names of this type occur 3.12 per cent. It would appear that the same motivation develops here as it does amongst location names; that is, identification between individual and name depends to a greater extent among male slaves upon external incidents more than upon familial patterns.

Among free Southern Black males only 2.36 per cent of their names depend upon these external incidents. Similarly, female names of this type drop to 2.72 per cent. Again, as with location names, the change in female percentages seems statistically insignificant, but the change in male frequencies seems noteworthy. Quite by contrast, Black soldiers show 4.23 per cent given names of this type and a dramatic 27.96 per cent surnames of this type. This also may reflect the need to coin some identifying surname for recruitment purposes, if indeed the Black recruit had no surname.

Of the descriptive or occupational or episodic names used by Black male slaves Robin (18) has the greatest frequency. Tie (3) comes next in number. The descriptive names are: Boomy, Jade, Lemon, Mink, Narow, Notice, Obey, Orange, Oxfoot, Pomp (2), Prime, Punch, Robin (18), Same, Scrub, Slam, Sharp, Sherry, Smart (2), Strap, Such, Tie (3), Tight (2), Tite, Tomboy, Ton (2), Ventured, Willing, Yallah, Yeary and Young. The occupational names are Boatswain and Ploughman, and the episodic names are June, Seas and Quarto. For the females the descriptive names are: Chat, Cherry, Darkis, Fill, Floor (4), Lies, Loos, Present and Violet (2). There are no occupational names at all amongst female slaves. Episodic names are Easter (3), Feb, June and Paddle.

Of Free Southern Black male descriptive names, only Lemon, Pomp and Sharp reflect any connection with slaves. Instead Darky (Browne), Fortune, Freeman, Greenage, Lamb, Liberty, Mosses, Mountain, Palm and Turkey (Smith) are used. This, of course, reflects the sense of freedom and liberty which must have been felt by these Southern Blacks. Occupational names are Boatswain, Tooler and Topmain, and the one episodic name, Holiday.

The free Black soldiers employ two descriptive given names, Pomp (3) and Sharp (2). These coincide with free and slave Blacks. Surnames of this type are more profuse among the Black soldiers. They use these descriptive surnames: Brown (3), Freedom, Freeman (7), Green, Greene (3), Hazard, Liberty (2), Lion, Little, Low, Mix, Power, Strong, Vassall (2) and Violet. Occupational names are: Baker, Dyer, Gardner, Miller and Sowers. The one episodic name is Fayerweather. What is suggested by the names used is that along with the sense of freedom felt by these Black males in the North and South is a feeling of partial integration into the larger community. This is also reflected in the growing number of occupational names (Slaves: 2; Southern free: 3; and Northern free: 5)

15

BLACK NAMES IN AMERICA

In the Beginning: 1619-1799

The free females employ only one descriptive name used by their slave sisters, <u>Violet</u>. To these are added <u>Comfort</u>, <u>Flowrah</u>, <u>Memory</u> (2), <u>Obedience</u>, <u>Pink</u> (3) and <u>Pinky</u>. Perhaps a lightening of color was esteemed and reflected in these names. There are no occupational names used and only one episodic name, <u>Friday</u>. It is interesting to note that females, both slave and free, employ <u>Violet</u> whereas males do not. But one Black Colonial soldier did use <u>Violet</u> as a surname.

Titular names were employed by male slaves at a rate of 1.76 per cent and by female slaves at a rate of .65 per cent. This very low rate of use continues amongst Free Southern Blacks, male and female. Indeed free Black males in the South employ titular names at a rate of only .306 per cent. And although free women increase the rate to 1.71 per cent these frequencies are still exceedingly low. Only among Free Black Patriot Soldiers is there a significant rate of usage of titular names. These Blacks employed title names at a rate of 6.77 per cent for given names and .84 per cent for surnames. Of the titular names employed by slave males, <u>Prince</u> (14) is most popular, followed by <u>Duke</u> and <u>Esquire</u>. Slave females were restricted to titular names reflecting familial roles with <u>Nanny</u> (3) and its variant, <u>Nanne</u>.

Free males in the South dropped all but two instances of titular names, <u>Duke</u> and <u>Prince</u>. These two constitute the extent of titular names used by free Black males. In the North, Free Black males tended to find greater attraction in these names. Of the given name, <u>Prince</u> (8) is the only titular name used, but its frequency seems quite high. Among the surnames of Black soldiers, <u>Earl</u> appears for the first time. Interestingly enough, one free woman found the titular name <u>Prince</u> attractive and employed it as <u>Princess</u>, but for the most part the familial <u>Nanny</u> (6) reappears with increased frequency. All in all it seems that Blacks did not find titular names especially to their liking, but chose other names to reflect a sense of dignity, pride and individuality.

Famous names, like titular ones, are rare amongst Blacks. The only incidence occurs in the slave male list. One slave owner, moved by some historical or fanciful inclination, called one of his slaves <u>Cromwell</u>, But amongst slave women and free Blacks, North and South, names of this sort do not appear.

Amongst Black male slaves, names of African origin appear in small number; 9.25 per cent of all male slaves employ African or African derived names. Slave females employ an even smaller, 6.57 percent, of African names. It would appear that very few slaves were allowed to retain those names with which they were familiar before disembarking in America. And among free male Blacks in the South, the rate of African names drops even lower to 3.01 per cent and among free women to 4.66 per cent. The African background recedes in memory and these names reflect only lingering vestiges. Free soldiers of the North, on the other hand, exhibit a continued, if infrequent, use of African names; 9.40 per cent of their surnames are derived from their former homeland.

BLACK NAMES IN AMERICA

In the Beginning: 1619-1799

The most popular African name amongst slave males is Cof (6) and its
variants: Coffee (2), Coffie, Cuff, Cuffo (2), Cuffee, Cuffy (4) and Kof (3).
Sambo (7) and variant, Samba, follow. Quashey (3), Qua (2), Quack (2), Quaco
(2), Quam, Quamana, Quamina, Quamno, Quas, Quashoo and Quay represent a significant number of names initially characterized by the Qu sound. Mingo (4)
is another name with a relatively high frequency of usage. For a complete
dictionary of African origins of names, see Chapter V.

Coffee, Quashey and Quashoo are mentioned among the slaves of the Royal
African Company in Africa about 1680.[30] Phillips attributes the continuation
of some few African names to the persistence of the maritime slave trade,
bringing new slaves of the same name from Africa.[31] But Cobb, in mentioning
four native Africans, named Capity, Saminy, Quominy and Quor, who were slaves
in Georgia, states that they had facial tatooing and "were treated with
marked respect by all the other Negroes for miles and miles around."[32] This
suggests that the cultural value of American names may not have been the same
with the slave as with the modern immigrant. African captions may even have
conferred a certain amount of distinction among the slaves, and thus have
continued where the master allowed it.[33] However, E. Franklin Frazier con-
tends that the preservation of African institutions in the Americas, if viable
in Brazil, is not characteristic of the United States. "As Frazier says, the
array of isolated instances of African survivals only indicates how thoroughly
American slavery wiped out African social organization, habits, and ways of
thought."[34] This position seems to be supported by the very small percentage
of African names used by Blacks during this period.

For slave women, Beck (4), Bat (2) and Mally (2) are the only names occurring more than once. There seems to be little resemblance between male
and female names except in the cases of Abah (male: Abra), Kouba, Comba and
Cumba (male: Cubah (2), Cubbah, Cudah and Sumba) and Simbo (male: Sambo (7)
and Samba).

Of the free Southern Black males, Cuff (3) and its variants Caffee,
Coffee, Cuffee and Cuffy make up the majority of African names. Mingo (5)
seems even more popular than it did amongst slaves, and Quash and Samboe also
find a place amongst free Black males in the South. One name not amongst
male slaves appears: Congo.

Free Northern Black soldiers use as given names Cuff (3), Congo and Mingo,
as do their free Southern brothers. Cuff remains the most popular. But interestingly enough these Black soldiers use as often as Cuff a name found

---

[30]C. G. Woodson, "Extracts from the Records of the African Companies,"
Journal of Negro History, XIII (1928), 290 ff.

[31]U. B. Phillips, Life and Labor in the Old South (Boston, 1935),
p. 195.

[32]J. B. Cobb, Mississippi Scenes (Philadelphia, 1851), p. 173.

[33]Puckett, op. cit., pp. 474-475.

[34]Eugene D. Genovese, The Political Economy of Slavery (New York:
Random House, 1967), p. 73. See E. Franklin Frazier, The Negro in the U. S.
(New York, 1949), pp. 6-11.

In the Beginning: 1619-1799

before and among slave women, <u>Juba</u> (3). Either the meaning or the traditional
gender of this name had been forgotten by this time.

All free Blacks employ 4.11 per cent African names; all slave Blacks use
7.53 per cent African names. Free Blacks in the eighteenth century dropped
almost half of even that small number of African names left to Black slaves.

Biblical names constituted the largest percentage of names of all the
above categories for Black male slaves during the eighteenth century. African
names appear next in frequency followed by descriptive or occupational or
episodic names, classical or literary, geographical, titular and famous, in
that order. Female slaves also show a greater use of Biblical and Puritanical
names (14.48 per cent) followed then by African names (6.57 per cent). Descriptive, occupational or episodic, classical or literary, titular, geographical and famous follow in that order. It would appear that the greatest
number of names employed by slaves, male and female, were Biblical and African
in that order.

Free male Blacks of this period tend to forego African names for Biblical
ones to a great extent (Biblical 20.31 per cent in the South; 26.27 per cent
Northern Black Soldiers contrasted with 13.09 per cent Biblical slave names,
and 3.01 per cent African names of free males, in the South; 9.40 per cent
African of Northern Black soldiers contrasted with 9.25 per cent African slave
names). The use of classical and literary, geographical, descriptive, occupational or episodic, titular and famous names becomes less frequent among free
Black males in the South than among their slave brothers.

Free Black soldiers tend to rely primarily upon Biblical and classical or
literary names: these make up 43.2 per cent of all given names. African and
titular names, 9.40 and 6.77 per cent, respectively, are followed by descriptive, occupational or episodic (4.23 per cent) and geographical (2.54 per
cent). There are no famous names as such among Black soldiers. Interestingly
enough 27.96 per cent of all Black soldiers' surnames are descriptive, occupational or episodic, a very large percentage.

Like males, free women found Biblical and Puritanic names to their liking,
employing 26.28 per cent contrasted with 14.47 per cent used by slave women.
They rejected, as their men, the use of African names, dropping from 6.57 per
cent as slaves to 4.66 per cent as free women. Classical and literary names
showed an increase to 2.69 per cent from 1.49 per cent; titular names also
rose from .65 per cent to 1.71 per cent as did geographical names from none to
.24 per cent. Descriptive, occupational and episodic names fell from 3.12
per cent as slaves to 2.94 per cent for free women, and famous names were not
found among slave or free women.

There is one further classification to be made, that between names which
would be considered unusual and/or old-fashioned, and those which we would
consider common. These distinctions reflect the sense of assimilation or
alienation, either real or perceived, by the members of an ethnic or racial
group in relation to the predominant group in a community. Male Black slaves,

In the Beginning: 1619-1799

using such names as Anbe, Argile, Demmy, Go, Libb, Pawby, Savl and the like, employ 40.12 per cent unusual names. If we deduct names merely old-fashioned and not inherently unusual such as Caesar and Josey, a total of 142 names, we see that Black male slaves used unusual names at a rate of 25.36 per cent.

Female slaves using such names as Abb, Essee, Janna, Post, Sena and Zibia have an unusual rate of 42.59 per cent. When we deduct old-fashioned names such as Abigail, Clarissa, Patience and Sary, we are left with an unusual rate of 18.09 per cent.

When we turn to free Black males in the South, we see that such names as Brazilde, Judsom, Loudos, Palm and Tepio contribute to a rate of unusualness of 21.08 per cent. By eliminating old-fashioned names we see a rate of unusualness of 13.64 per cent. Of the free females there is an unusual rate of 40.78 per cent and the deduction of the old-fashioned names creates a rate of unusualness of 15.23 per cent.

The free Black females in the South, unlike their slave sisters, employed approximately twice as many unusual names as their counterpart males, but after old-fashioned names are deducted it appears that unusual names are employed with relatively the same rate among free males and females. It would seem, then, that free females chose a great many more old-fashioned names than did free males. This seems to reflect a pattern similar to that seen amongst slaves.

Black slaves, male and female, show a rate of 39.29 per cent unusualness, with 22.47 per cent being bona fide unusual and 16.82 per cent old-fashioned. Free Black names in the South are characterized by a rate of only 28.61 per cent unusual, 14.25 per cent unusual and 14.35 per cent old-fashioned. We may conjecture that on the basis of these figures slaves were more prone to be the recipients of names more unusual than those of free Blacks.

Louisiana, with its transition from Latin to American ownership, offers an interesting illustration of how slave names are altered in response to changes in cultural surroundings. Of 143 slaves listed there prior to 1800,[35] (Source List D), 100, or 69 per cent, had names of French or Spanish provenance. However, in the case of 339 Louisiana slaves listed after 1800 only 47, or 14 per cent, had names so derived.[36]

Taken as a whole the group of Black names, slave and free, shows a transition from a foreign to an English setting. However, the total number of names

---

[35]Tabulated from Caterall, op. cit., Vol. III. Doubtful names such as Louis, Maria, and Marie, which might possibly be of English derivation as well as French or Spanish, are omitted altogether in this analysis. See Source List D for complete list.

[36]It is interesting that the free Blacks seem more conservative than the slave in the matter of name changes, from French to English as in the case of the change from African to English. Of some 2,360 Louisiana free Blacks listed by Woodson in 1830, 1,647, or approximately 70 per cent, possessed names of French or Spanish origins. This suggests that many name changes were forced upon slaves by their masters. See Source Lists E, F, G and H for slave names of Dutch, French and Spanish origin.

In the Beginning: 1619-1799

available--2,883--is too small to be regarded as entirely typical of the
period. A more adequate sampling exists for the period of 1800 to 1860.

Source List A: SLAVE BLACK NAMES, 1700-1800

The names of free Blacks were collected from the first census in the
South in 1790, Patriots of the American Revolution and Free Negro Family.
Black slave names were collected through Mississippi probate records, will
books and deed registers in Monroe, Lowndes and Hinds counties, and from
plantation records, old church minute books, the files of the Mississippi
State Department of Archives and History, and the files of the Vicksburg Re-
publican and Eagle. Available published sources include H. T. Caterall,
Judicial Cases Concerning American Slavery and the Negro (3 vols., Washington,
1926-32); the most important source; E. Donnan, Documents Illustrative of the
History of the Slave Trade to America (4 vols., Washington, 1930-35); various
articles on the subject in Journal of Negro History; H. L. Mencken, The Ameri-
can Language (4th ed., New York, 1936), p. 524; U. B. Phillips, A Documentary
History of American Industrial Society (Cleveland, 1909), Vols. I & II; T. S.
Weld, American Slavery as It Is (New York, 1839); and Census of Slaves, from
E. B. O'Callaghan, The Documentary History of the State of New York (4 vols.,
Albany, New York, 1850), Vol. III, Chap. XI, pp. 503-521. This is a very
small percentage of the total Black population. Franklin (p. 184) numbers
the slave population in 1790 at something less than 700,000. Therefore, what-
ever trends are indicated should be viewed most cautiously.

Of the slave names, 972 are male and 603 are female. These figures ex-
clude the 143 slave names from Louisiana. The number of slave names from
each state are as follows:

New Jersey 5	Maryland 42
Rhode Island 5	Kentucky 46
Georgia 15	North Carolina 66
Pennsylvania 24	South Carolina 81
Louisiana 26	Virginia 105
(exclusive of the list of	Massachusetts 120
Louisiana slave names of	New York 986
French or Spanish origin)	Unknown 54

This is not to suggest that New York and Massachusetts were greater slave
holding states than those of the Southern edge of the country, but that the
census of slaves taken in New York in 1755 made available a relatively large
list. It does underscore the fact, however, that tobacco and cotton were not
the only motivating forces behind the acquisition of slaves in America.

Following is a listing of Black slave names, male and female, in the United
States in the eighteenth century. The first number after the name indicates
the frequency with which the name was used; the second number indicates the
rate of usage per 100,000 Black slaves. No number after a name indicates that
only one Black slave used that name.

20

In the Beginning: 1619-1799 -- A. SLAVE BLACK NAMES, 1700-1800

MALE
    Alphabetical (Sample: 972)
    Untabulated names have rate of 104 per 100,000.

Abel	Bowzar	Cuffy 4 416
Abelard	Boyyas	Dan
Aberdeen	Braboo	Daniel 8 832
Abra	Bris	Dave
Abraham 2 208	Bristo 4 416	David 3 312
Abram 7 728	Bristoll	Davis
Acavan	Bromley	Demmy
Adam 4 416	Bumbo	Dennis
Alston	Bungoh	Devon
Alyema	Burrah	Dick 20 2079
America	Caesar 21 2183	Dickinson
Anbe	Cambridge	Dirck
Ando	Carey	Doll
Andrew 6 624	Carolina	Ducko
Andries	Caser	Duke 2 208
Ankque	Cato 8 832	Ebo Roben
Anthony 3 312	Chalsey	Eliah
Argile	Chaney	Ephraim
Arron	Charis	Esop 2 208
Arthur	Charles 15 1559	Esquire
Austin 2 208	Chuffee	Essex
Awaan	Ciah 2 208	Fait
Bacches	Cicero	Fantee
Bal	Cilkenney	Fell
Ball	Cipio	Flink
Bamba	Claes 2 208	Flip
Banma	Class	Fort 2 208
Bass 2 208	Claus	Forten
Bastian	Clem	Fortune 2 208
Batt	Clement	France
Been	Clos	Francis 6 624
Bel	Cof 6 624	Frank 16 1663
Ben 12 1247	Coffee 2 208	Frans
Bendo	Coffie	Frederick 3 312
Benjamin	Combwood	Fuller
Bern	Commenie	Gato
Beverly	Cornelias	Geffrey
Bill 3 314	Cornelis	Gem
Billy Bink	Corso	George 12 1247
Boatswain	Cromwell	Gif
Bob 6 624	Cubah 2 208	Go
Bohaneo	Cubbah	Graham
Bongeos	Cubit	Gumba
Bonner	Cudah	Guy 2 208
Boohum	Cudjo 2 208	Gye
Boomy	Cuff	Hammel
Bos	Cuffe 2 208	Harry 34 3534
Boston	Cuffee	Henck

21

In the Beginning: 1619-1799 -- A. SLAVE BLACK NAMES, 1700-1800

Hendrick	Lando	Nienus
Henry 2 208	Lango	Norton Minors
Herculus	Lans	Notice
Hithro	Lazer	Obey
Honnyball	Leendert	Ocra
Imdus	Lemon	Ocrague
Isaac 5 520	Lett	Ocrasan
Ishamel	Lew 7 728	Ocreka
Ishener	Lewis 3 312	Ocumah
Jack 57 5925	Libb	Oliver
Jackes	Limehouse	Orange
Jacob 7 728	London 3 312	Ossan
Jade	Lonnon	Oxfoot
Jaek	Lou 2 208	Oxford
Jafta 3 312	Louis 4 416	Pamo
James 11 1143	Lue	Pamp
Jamie	Luke 2 208	Papav
Jan 2 208	Maan	Parker
Japhory	Maatt	Parris
Jasper	Maison	Partrick
Jeams	Malborough	Pater
Jeck	Mamillus	Patrick
Jeffery 2 208	Manuel	Pattoe
Jeffre	March	Paul
Jefroy	Mars	Pawby
Jem	Matthew	Peet
Jemmy	Michael	Penney
Jeremiah	Middletown	Pero 2 208
Jerre	Miley	Peter 20 2079 [37]
Jesserve	Minas	Peyton
Jim 4 416	Minck 3 312	Philander
Job	Mingo 4 416	Phillip 3 312
Jobah 2 208	Mink	Phillips
Joe 14 1455	Monk	Piet 9 936
John 18 1871	Moses	Pieter 2 208
Joo	Mowoori(a)e	Pinna
Joseph 6 624	Munen	Ploughman
Josey	Nance	Pomp 2 208
Julus	Napten	Pompey 6 624
June	Narow	Portsmouth
Jupiter 5 520	Nat	Praemis [37]
Kandol	Nease	Primax [37]
Kellis	Ned 5 520	Prime
Kidder	Nenes	Primes
Kinck	Nero 2 208	Primus
Kof 3 312	Newport	Prince 14 1455
Lancaster	Nicholas 2 208	Punch

---

[37]The New Century Cyclopedia of Names, ed. Clarence L. Barnhart.
(New York: Appleton-Century-Crofts, 1954), Vol. 2, p. 1786. Peter, Praemis,
Primax and Quod merely smack of classical Latin and Titus can be Biblical -
The Good Thief.

In the Beginning: 1619-1799 -- A. SLAVE BLACK NAMES, 1700-1800

Qua 2 208	Seas	Tobe 3 312
Quack 2 208	Sem	Tobias
Quaco 2 208	Sham	Toby 4 416
Quam	Shante	Tom 47 4886
Quamana	Sharp	Tomboy
Quamina	Sherper	Tomma
Quamno	Sherry	Ton 2 208
Quarto	Sidney	Tone
Quas	Simbo	Toney 3 312
Quash 3 312	Simon 8 832	Tonney
Quashey 3 312	Sive	Toon 4 416
Quashoo	Smart 2 208	Tower
Quay 37	Sopus	Trump 2 208
Quod	Spencer	Ulysses
Quoney	Stephen 7 728	Ventured
Ralph	Strap	Wann
Reuben 2 208	Such	Warrah
Rhodick	Sym	Waterford
Richard 3 312	Taliver	Warwick
Robin 18 1871	Tam 12 1247	Will 23 2391
Roger 2 208	Tamma	William 3 312
Roos	Tance	Willing
Sackoe	Tanoe	Willis
Salisbury	Taynay	Willoughby
Sam 30 3119	Temba	Yaff
Samba	Thom 7 728	Yallah
Sambo 7 728	Thomas	Yamboo
Same	Tie 3 312	Yaumah
Sampson 4 416	Tight 2 208	Yearie
Savl 2 208	Tim 2 208	Yonaha
Sawney	Tiss	Yono Cish
Scipio 3 312	Tite	York 5 520
Scrub	Titus 3 312 37	Young

Biblical and Puritanical

Peter 20	Adam 4	Eliah
John 18	Anthony 3	Ephraim
James 11	David 3	Jeremiah
Daniel 8	Titus 3	Job
Simon 8	Abraham 2	Matthew
Abram 7	Luke 2	Michael
Jacob 7	Reuben 2	Moses
Andrew 6	Thomas 1	Paul
Joseph 6	Abel	Tobias
Isaac 5		

Classical and Literary

Caesar 21	Jupiter 5	Nero 2
Cato 8	Scipio 3	Abelard
Pompey 6	Esop 2	Bacches

23

In the Beginning: 1619-1799 -- A. SLAVE BLACK NAMES, 1700-1800

Cicero	Pater	Primax
Cipio	Philander	Quod
Herculus	Praemis	Ulysses
Mars		

Geographic Location

York 5	Esses	Oxford
London 3	Lancaster	Portsmouth
Aberdeen	Limehouse	Salisbury
America	Malborough	Waterford
Bristoll	Middletown	Willoughby
Cambridge	Newport	Warwick

Descriptive, Episodic, Occupational

Robin 18	Narow	Sham
Tie 3	Notice	Sharp
Pomp 2	Obey	Sherry
Smart 2	Orange	Strap
Tight 2	Oxfoot	Such
Ton 2	Ploughman	Tite
Trump 2	Prime	Tomboy
Boatswain	Punch	Tone
Jade	Quarto	Ventured
June	Same	Willing
Lemon	Scrub	Yallah
Mink	Seas	Young

Titular

Prince 14	Duke 2	Esquire

Famous

Cromwell

African

Sambo 7	Quack 2	Cubbah
Cof 6	Quaco 2	Cudah
Cuffy 4	Ankque	Cuff
Mingo 4	Bamba	Cuffee
Kof 3	Batt	Demmy
Quashey 3	Bendo	Ducko
Ciah 2	Boomy	Ebo Roben
Coffee 2	Boyyas	Fait
Cubah 2	Bumbo	Gato
Cudjo 2	Bungoh	Gumba
Cuffe 2	Burrah	Joo
Jobah 2	Coffie	Kinck
Qua 2	Commenie	Lando

In the Beginning: 1619-1799 -- A. SLAVE BLACK NAMES, 1700-1800

Lango	Quashoo	Taynay
Nease	Quay	Temba
Pinna	Sackoe	Tomma
Roos	Samba	Wann
Quam	Sawney	Warrah
Quamana	Sem	Yamboo
Quamina	Simbo	Yaumah
Quamno	Sive	Yearie
Quas	Tanoe	

FEMALE

Alphabetical (Sample: 603)
Untabulated names have rate of 164 per 100,000.

Abah	Carie	Dyne 2 329
Abanna	Cate 2 329	Easter 3 493
Abb	Catharien	Edy
Abigail	Charlotte 2 329	Elecate
Abigal	Chat	Elena
Abigall	Cherry	Elizabeth 3 493
Abnabea	Clarissa	Elly
Addy	Comba	Emme
Adalaide 2 329	Cumba	Essee
Aggy	Curiarah	Esther
Agnes	Darkis	Eva 2 329
Agonna	Defne	Eve
Ailce	Dean 2 329	Fan
Aloy	Deana	Fanny
Ambo	Deddie	Farih
Amy 5 822	Deen 4 658	Farry
Anna 2 329	Demeca	Fassiah
Anne 2 329	Derinda	Feb
Annika	Diana 2 329	Fill
Armenda	Diane	Floar
Barbara 2 329	Diannah 2 329	Floor 4 658
Bass	Dibb	Flora 4 658
Bat 2 329	Dice	Flore 2 329
Battah	Dido 2 329	Frances
Bayna	Diean	Geany
Beck 4 658	Dien 8 1316	Gen 9 1480
Bek	Dijaen 3 493	Gilly
Bekinda	Dill	Gin 10 1645
Belis	Dinah 8 1316	Ginny 7 1151
Belle	Dine 5 822	Grace 7 1151
Benabah	Doll	Greech
Bess 3 493	Dorcas	Habella
Bet 38 6250	Dorrity	Hagar 3 493
Betsy	Dosh	Hage
Betty 15 2467	Durah	Hager 2 328
Biblor	Dyaen 2 329	Hagor
Bilah	Dyan 3 493	Hanch 2 328
Binah	Dyane 2 329	Hannah 16 2632

In the Beginning: 1619-1799 -- A. SLAVE BLACK NAMES, 1700-1800

Hes	Maria 6 987	Rhoda
Hester 3 493	Marie	Riet
Ida 2 329	Marion	Roos
Isabel 8 1316	Marrian	Rosa
Isabelle	Martha	Rose 6 987
Jan	Mary 22 3618	Ruth
Jane 18 2960	Mat	Sal
Janna	Matilda	Sale
Jean 3 493	Mercy	Sally 4 658
Jemima	Mereum	San
Jenny 7 1151	Mila	Sar
Joan 2 329	Milly 2 329	Sarah 15 2467
Juba	Mima	Sary 12 1974
Jud 2 329	Minda	Sena
Judith	Moll 3 493	Sib
Judy 8 1316	Molly 2 329	Silpa Fortune
June	Monimea	Silva
Kate 2 329	Morandah	Simboh
Kauchee	Moryn	Sivil
Kea	Nab	Sobett
Keet	Nan 13 2138	Sooh
Kin	Nancy 6 987	Suckey 3 493
Kitty	Nann	Sue 2 329
Kouba	Nanne	Susan 8 1316
Lade	Nanny 3 493	Susanah 2 329
Lander	Nanot	Susanna 2 329
Lane 2 329	Nans	Susannah 3 493
Leane	Nell	Susie
Libe	Nen 3 493	Syne 4 658
Lies	Oessah	Tabitha
Lil	Paddle	Tammes
Lill	Pagg	Teen
Lille 2 329	Pat	Temperance
Loos	Patience	Terressa
Lucy 8 1316	Peg 12 1974	Theribah
Lue 2 329	Peggy 3 493	Tiller
Lybe	Pen	Tittie
Lydia	Pendor	Tobby
Lysett	Phillis 14 2303	Tracey
Mally 2 329	Phoebe 2 329	Tryn
Mander	Polly	Venus 2 329
Mar	Post	Violet 2 329
Marcy	Present	Winney
Mare	Qussuba	Wyne
Marget	Rachael 4 658	Wyntje
Margett	Regein 2 329	Yud 2 329
		Zibia

Biblical

Mary 22	Sarah 15	Grace 7

Black Names in America

In the Beginning: 1619-1799 -- A. SLAVE BLACK NAMES, 1700-1800

Hannah 16	Dinah 8 [38]	Rachael 4
Hagar 3	Esther	Mereum
Abigail	Eve	Patience
Abigal	Judith	Ruth
Abigall	Mercy	Tabitha
		Temperance

Classical and Literary

Diana 2	Phoebe 2	Dice
Dido 2	Venus 2	

Geographic Location

(None)

Descriptive, Episodic, Occupational

Floor 4	Cherry	June
Easter 3	Darkis	Lies
Violet 2	Feb	Loos
Chat	Fill	Paddle
		Present

Titular

Nanny 3	Nanne

Famous

(None)

African

Beck 4	Bilah	Kauchee
Bat 2	Binah	Kea
Mally 2	Comba	Kouba
Abah	Cumba	Libe
Abanna	Demeca	Loos
Abb	Dibb	Mila
Alyema	Durah	Mima
Ambo	Farih	Minda
Annika	Farry	Roos
Battah	Fassiah	Sena
Bayna	Janna	Simboh
Bek	Juba	Sooh
		Tiller

---

[38]Also Dina: Daughter of Jacob by Leah, The New Century Cyclopedia of
Names, ed. Clarence L. Barnhart, 3 vols., p. 1283, Vol. I.: also Bardsley,
C. W., Curiosities of Puritan Name Clatins (London, 1880), p. 72, "became
great favorite in England during the Elizabethan Age."

In the Beginning: 1619-1799

Source List B: FREE BLACK NAMES, SOUTH, 1700-1800[39]

Of the 1170 free Black names, 763, including 118 Black soldiers, are male and 407 are female. The states contributing to this list are as follows-- the number following the state indicates the number of Black free names from that state:

North Carolina 26   Virginia 294
Connecticut 118   Maryland 549
    (See Source List C)   Unknown 27
South Carolina 156

MALE
    Alphabetical (Sample: 645)
    Untabulated names have rate of 155 per 100,000.

Aaron 4 620	Chester	Frederick 2 310
Abednego	Cirus	Freeman
Aberdeen	Clem	George 24 3721
Abraham 6 930	Cock	Godfrey
Abram	Coffee	Goffe
Adam 3 465	Colemus	Greenage
Alexander	Con	Hamutt
Ambrose	Congo	Hannibal
Andrew 3 465	Cornelius	Harry 13 2016
Anthoney 2 310	Cornish	Hector
Anthony 3 465	Courtney	Hendley
Archibald	Cuff 3 365	Henly
Barjona	Cuffee	Henney
Barton 3 465	Cuffy	Henry 7 1085
Battis	Cupid	Hercules
Ben 15 2326	Cyrus	Holiday
Benjamin	Dampier	Humphrey
Billy 2 310	Daniel 7 1085	Ignatius
Boatswain	Darby	Isaac 4 620
Bob 10 1550	Darky (Brownie)	Isham
Booker	Davey 9 1395	Isle of Wight
Boston	David 5 775	Israel
Brazilde	Dennis	Jack 17 2636
Bristol	Dick 19 2946	Jacob 18 2791
Caesar 8 1240	Donpedro	James 25 3876
Caffee	Draper	Jeffrey 3 465
Cain	Duke	Jem 3 465
Caleb	Dundy	Jere
Cato 3 465	Edward	Jeremiah
Charles 12 1860	Finton	Jesse
	Fortune	Jethro 2 310
	Frank 7 1085	Jim 3 465

[39]See references in Source List A, particularly First Census, 1790.

BLACK NAMES IN AMERICA

Joe 9 1395
John 28 4341
Johnson
Jonas
Jordan
Joseph 11 1705
Joshua 2 310
Josias
Judea 2 310
Judsom
Kane
Kitt
Lamb
Lambold
Lander
Lemon
Leonard
Lewis 2 310
Liberty
Limas
Limus 2 310
London 2 310
Lonnon
Loudos
Lougo
Manuel
Manus
Marlow
Martin
Matthew 3 465
Mial 3 465
Michael
Mingo 5 775
Mitchell
Mole
Moore

Mose
Moses 3 465
Mosses
Mountain
Nace
Nance
Nate
Ned 6 930
Nero
Noah
Orson
Oxford
Pace
Paddy
Palm
Paraway
Pat
Patt
Paul 2 310
Pearce
Peter 22 3411
Phil (1) 3 465
Phillip 2 310
Poladore 2 310
Pomp
Pompey 4 620
Portroyal
Prince
Prusia
Quash
Rawley
Razin
Reddin
Rice
Richard 9 1395
Robert 8 1240

Robin 3 465
Sam 24 3721
Samboe
Sampson 2 310
Samuel 13 2016
Santo
Saul 2 310
Scipio
Scott
Sharp
Sindey 2 310
Simon 4 620
Sipeo
Sipio 3 465
Stephen 3 465
Sussex
Sylvanus
Tepio
Thomas 13 2016
Tim 2 310
Toby 5 775
Tom 17 2636
Tooler
Topmain
Tower 4 620
Townly
Troyles
Turkey (Smith)
Valantine
Webster
Will 13 2016
William 23 3566
Wilson
Yarmouth
York 3 465
Zachariah 2 310

Biblical and Puritanical

John 28
James 25
Peter 22
Jacob 18
Samuel 13
Thomas 13
Joseph 11
Daniel 7
Abraham 6
David 5
Aaron 4

Isaac 4
Adam 3
Andrew 3
Anthony 3
Ignatius Saint 3
Matthew 3
Joshua 2
Judea 2
Paul 2
Sampson 2
Saul 2

Zachariah 2
Abednego
Abram
Abrose
Benjamin
Cain
Israel
Jeremiah
Michael
Noah

In the Beginning: 1619-1799 -- B. FREE BLACK NAMES, SOUTH, 1700-1800

Classical and Literary

Caesar 8	Alexander	Hercules
Pompey 4	Cupid	Sipeo
Sipio 3	Hannibal	Sylvanus
Poladore 2	Hector	Troyles
		Valantine

Geographic Location

York 3	Bristol	Prusia
London 2	Isle of Wight	Sussex
Aberdeen	Oxford	Yarmouth
Boston	Portroyal	

Descriptive, Episodic, Occupational

Boatswain	Lamb	Pomp
Darky (Brownie)	Lemon	Sharp
Fortune	Liberty	Tooler
Freeman	Mosses	Topmain
Greenage	Mountain	Turkey (Smith)
Holiday	Palm	

Titular

Duke	Prince

Famous

(None)

African

Mingo 5	Congo	Kitt
Cuff 3	Cuffee	Mial
Caffee	Cuffy	Nace
Cock	Goffe	Quash
Coffee	Hamutt	Razin
		Samboe

FEMALE
Alphabetical (Sample: 406)
Untabulated names have rate of 246 per 100,000.

Abigal	Anne	Bet(t) 12 2948
Abigail	Annie 2 491	Betty 5 1229
Affee	Becae	Binah 3 737
Aggy 3 737	Beck 2 491	Bridget
Alice	Bek	Carolina
Amy 2 491	Beno	Caroline
Ann 8 1966	Bess 3 737	Cassandra

In the Beginning: 1619-1799 -- B. FREE BLACK NAMES, SOUTH, 1700-1800

Cate 2 491	Jude	Pheba
Catherina	Judy 3 737	Pheby
Catherine 2 491	Judit	Philler
Cecily	Julet	Phillis 12 2948
Charity	Kate 3 737	Pink 3 737
Charlotte	Keziah	Pinky
Chloe 2 491	Kitty 2 491	Ply
Christian	Leria	Polly
Clarissa 2 491	Lett	Princess
Clementine	Letty	Priscilla
Comfort	Lin	Priss 2 491
Conney	Linder	Prudence
Conny	Lucy 6 1474	Rachael 19 4668
Crecy	Lydia 3 737	Rebecca
Daphna	Mable	Rhode
Daphny	Maggy	Rhody
Deborah	Manzey	Rose 6 1474
Dianna	Margaret 4 983	Ruth 2 491
Dice	Margarite 2 491	Sal
Dide	Margrete	Sall 3 737
Dido	Maria(h) 4 983	Sally
Dinah 7 1720	Marian 2 491	Sarah 24 5897
Dolly	Martha	Sary
Edy 2 491	Mary 12 2948	Serah
Ege	Memory 2 491	Sibb
Eleanor 3 737	Mercer	Siller 2 491
Elizabeth 8 1966	Meriah	Silvia
Eve	Mill	Sindy
Fanny 2 491	Milly 4 983	Sue
Feeby	Minta	Suck
Flora	Moll 3 737	Su(c)key 3 737
Flowrah	Molly 4 983	Susan
Frances 4 983	Murriah	Susanna 2 491
Friday	Nan 7 1720	Susannah
Grace 7 1720	Nancy 8 1966	Tamer 2 491
Hagar 2 491	Nann 2 491	Tene
Hager	Nanny 6 1474	Tilly
Hannah 19 4668	Nell 2 491	Tinah
Heany	Nelly 3 737	Treasie
Henrietta	Ninian	Venus
Hester	Obedience	Vin
Ibby	Patience 6 1474	Viney
Jane 10 2457	Patt 2 491	Vinney
Jean	Patty 2 491	Violet
Jennett 2 491	Peg 3 737	Winna
Jennie	Pegg 8 1966	Winney
Jenny 2 491	Peggy 2 491	Zenith
Jinny	Penelope	Zilphy
Judah	Penny	

31

In the Beginning: 1619-1799 -- B. FREE BLACK NAMES, SOUTH, 1700-1800

Biblical and Puritanical

Sarah 24	Patience 6	Christian
Hannah 19	Hagar 2	Deborah
Rachael 19	Ruth 2	Judah
Mary 12	Abigal	Jude
Dinah 7	Abigail	Prudence
Grace 7	Charity	Rebecca

Classical and Literary

Chloe 2	Dice	Pheba
Cassandra	Dido	Pheby
Dianna	Penelope	Priscilla
		Venus

Geographic Location

Carolina

Descriptive, Episodic, Occupational

Pink 3	Flowrah	Pinky
Memory 2	Friday	Violet
Comfort	Obedience	

Titular

Nanny 6	Princess

Famous

(None)

African

Binah 3	Bek	Manzey
Beck 2	Conney	Murriah
Siller 2	Conny	Sibb
Affee	Ege	Tene
Becae	Ibby	Tinah

In the Beginning: 1619-1799

Source List C: FREE BLACK PATRIOTS, NORTH, 1700-1800[40]

MALE
Alphabetical (117 names)
Payroll 2nd Co. 4th Reg. Connecticut.

Alex Judd
Andrew Jack
Anthony Bettis
Arthur Davis
Bill Sowers
Boston Ballard
Brister Baker
Caesar Bagdon
Caesar Chapman
Caesar Fayerweather
Caesar Power
Cato Gardner
Cato Greene
Cato Morey
Cato Rawson
Cato Robinson
Cato Wilbrow
Congo Zado
Cuff Freeman
Cuff Greene
Cuff Liberty
Cyrus Vassall
Daniel Bradley
David Humphreys,
    Captain of the Co.
Derby Miller
Derby Vassall
Dick Freedom
Dick Violet
Ezekiel Tupham
Gamaliel Terry
George Jackson
George Middleton
Glosaster Haskins
Guy Watson
Hamlet Earl
Hannibal Allen
Harry Williams
Hector Williams
Heman Rogers

Henry Tabor
Ichabod Northup
Isaac Higgins
Isaac Johnson
Jack Arabus
Jack Little
James Dinah
James Hawkins
Jeremiah Green
Jesse Vose
Jo Otis
John Ball
John Clark
John Cleveland
John Decruse
John Harrison
John Johnson
John McLean
John Phillips
John Rogers
Job Caesar
Joseph Ball
Joseph Low
Joseph Ocruman
Juba Freeman
Juber Holland
Lent Munson
Lewis Jones
Lewis Martin
Mingo Freeman
Ned Fields
Ned Freeman
Peter Bailey
Peter Branch
Peter Freeman
Peter Gibbs
Peter Lion
Peter Mix
Peter Morando

Philo Freeman
Philo Phillips
Phineas Strong
Plato Alderson
Pomp Cyrus
Pomp Liberty
Pomp McCuff
Prince Brown
Prince Crosbee
Prince George
Prince Greene
Prince M. Harris
Prince Lenks
Prince Johnson
Prince Vaughn
Primus Rhodes
Reuben Roberts
Richard Holsted
Richard Marshall
Richard Rhodes
Richard Stanley
Rufus Callehorn
Sampson Cuff
Samson Hazzard
Scipio Brown
Scipio Dalton
Sear Kimball
Serico Collens
Sharp Camp
Sharp Rogers
Shubael Johnson
Solomon Sowtice
Thomas Brown
Thomas Burdine
Thomas Jackson
Thomas Lewis
Tom Freeman
Tim Caesar
York Champlin

---

[40]From William C. Nell, "Colored Patriots of the American Revolution,"
American Negro: His History and Literature (Ser. No. 1, 1968). Reproduction
of 1855 edition (Arno).

In the Beginning: 1619-1799 -- C. FREE BLACK PATRIOTS, NORTH, 1700-1800

Given Names

Biblical and Puritanical

John 9	Andrew	Job
Peter 7	Daniel	Lent
Thomas 4	David	Reuben
Joseph 3	Ezekiel	Sampson
Isaac 2	Ichabod	Samson
James 2	Jeremiah	Solomon

Classical and Literary

Cato 6	Scipio 2	Hector
Caesar 4	Hamlet	Ichabod [41]
Philo 2	Hannibal	Phineas
		Plato

Geographic Location

Boston	Glosaster	York

Descriptive, Episodic, Occupational

Pomp 3	Sharp 2

Titular

Prince 8

Famous

(None)

African

Cuff 3	Juba 1	Congo
	Juber	Mingo

Surnames

Biblical and Puritanical

(None)

Classical and Literary

Caesar 2	Arabus

---

[41]Biblical poem by J. G. Whittier. (Named "Inglorious" by mother who died giving him birth.) The New Century Cyclopedia of Names, ed. Clarence L. Barnhart, 3 vols., p. 2101, Vol. 2.

In the Beginning: 1619-1799 -- C. FREE BLACK PATRIOTS, NORTH, 1700-1800

Geographic Location

Champlin	Holland	Middletown
Cleveland	Holsted	Northup

Descriptive, Episodic, Occupational

Freeman 7	Fayerweather	Low
Brown 3	Freedom	Miller
Greene 3	Gardner	Mix
Liberty 2	Green	Power
Vassall 2	Hazzard	Sowers
Baker	Lion	Strong
Dyer	Little	Violet

Titular

Earl

Famous

(None)

African

Cuff
McCuff
Zado

In the Beginning: 1619-1799

Source List D: LOUISIANA SLAVES - FRENCH OR SPANISH NAMES PRIOR TO 1800[42]

Aimee 2	Felicite	Marguerita
Alexandro	Florestine Cecile	Maria 3
Alphonse	Francaise Gabrielle	Mariana 2
Anaise	Lorio	Maire Aram
Andres	Franchon	Marie Jeanne
Angelica	Franchonet	Marie Louise 2
Angelique	Francisco 6	Mariquina
Antonio 2	Francois 5	Maturina
Arsene 2	Frosina	Maturine
Augustine	Gil La Rose	Melite
Bambara	Gonzalo	Meme
Bernardine	Guaissecamant	Miguel La Rose
Bernardo	Guela	Modeste
Biron	Helene	Morieux
Boucaud (John)	Hibou	Mulet
Brunet	Honorato	Myrthee
Calais	Isabella 2	Naneta 3
Carlos	Jacques	Narcisse
Carmelite	Janot	Nicholas 2
Catalina	Jasmin	Paya
Catarina	Jean 5	Pedro 3
Catin	Jeanneton	Petit
Celesie	Jeannot	Petit Jean
Celeste	Juan Luis	Pierre 3
Celestine	Juana 2	Pierrot
Cesard	Junon 2	Pistolet
Changereau	Langulo	Raphael
Charles	Leon 2	Reynaldo
Charlot 2	Lizeta	Robinette
Choucoura	Louison	Rosine
Colas	Lubin	Rosette 2
Crusquet	Luis	Sans Quartier
Cupidon	Magdalena 2	Sebany
Delphine 2	Maillon	Songot
Doninic	Manon 4	Therese
Eugenie	Maranthe	

[42]From H. T. Caterall, "Judicial Cases Concerning American Slavery and the Negro," 3 vols. (Washington, D. C., 1926-1932).

In the Beginning: 1619-1799

Source List E: BLACK SLAVES WITH UNAMERICANIZED DUTCH NAMES (N. Y., 1755)[43]

Andries	Maan	Deen 4
Awaan (Aaron)	Maatt	Diean
Claes 2	Minck 3	Dien 8
Clos	Peet	Dijeen 3
Dirck	Piet 9	Dijean
Frans	Pieter 2	Dyaen 2
Henck	Roos	Keet
Jaek	Tam 12	Pagg
Jan 2	Tamma	Regein 2
Jeams	Toon 4	Riet
Jeck	Catharien	Roos
Jessewe	Dean 2	Wyntje
Leendert	Deana	Yud 2

---

[43]See references for Source List A, particularly O'Callaghan, E. B., "The Documentary History of the State of New York."

In the Beginning: 1619-1799

Source List F: SLAVES, VIRGIN ISLANDS[44]

Abel	Johanna	Pody
Abraham	John 2	Pompey
Andrias	Johns	Prince Qvakoe
Belli	John Saby	Quamina
Cesar	Jonathan	Qvakoe
Coffee	Josse	Qvaso Withe
Coffe Mulaet	Jupiter 2	Roe Jah
Colla	Laurentia	Sam 2
Cudio	Lena	Sam Hector
Cudjo	London	Samson
Cupido	Lorgent	Sara
Decbr	Maria	Schous
Doblin	Marianna	Seiman
Dorinda	Marina	Simon
Franch	Merckel	Sue
Frantz	Michel	Sylvester 2
Gall	Neptune	Sylvia
George 2	Nicol	Tham 2
George Foot	Paris	Tony
Gomas	Pedro	Turlun
Hans	Pelot	Wano
Harry 2	Peru	Wenus
Jach 4	Perupey	Will 3
Jasper	Phoenix	William 2
Joh	Pieter	

---

[44]W. Westergaard, "Account of the Negro Rebellion in St. Croix, Danish West Indies," J. N. Hist., XI (1926), 50-61 (1759).

In the Beginning: 1619-1799

Source List G: JAMAICA SLAVES - 1803[45]

Abraham	Flora	Moses
Adam	Franky	Nancy
Bacchus	George	Ned
Betsey	Gerard Cohen	Patrick
Clarissa	Jack	Patty
Cork	James	Peter
Countess	James Richards	Providence
Cupid	Jemmy	Richard
Cyrus	Joe 3	Richard Payne
Davey	John 4	Robert 3
Dick	John Davis	Tom
Dominick	John Williams	Trust
Douglas	Juliet	Wheedle
Dragon	Lewis Vincent	Will
Fanny	March	William 2

---

[45]F. W. Pitman, "Slavery on British West India Plantations in the Eighteenth Century," J. N. Hist., XI (1926), 584-668.

In the Beginning: 1619-1799

Source List H: FRENCH-CANADIAN BLACK SLAVES[46]

Note: Numbers following the name refer to years.

Andre 1762	Kitts 1792	Pierre 1793
Caesar 1784	Louise Lepage 1744	Prince 1795
Flora 1784	Louison 1749	Robert 1748
Isabella or Bell 1778	Manuel 1797	Rose 1796
Jack 1790	Neptune 1747	Rubin 1795
Jean Mousange 1751	Nicholas 1757	Sarah 1784
Joequo 1796	Patrick 1781	Tanus 1793
Joseph 1785	Pierre 1757	Tobi 1785

---

[46]William P. Riddell, "Notes on the Slave of Nouvelle-France," J. N. Hist., 8 (1923), 316-330.

CHAPTER II

Names, Slave and Free: 1800-1864

For the period 1800-1860 the names of 14,177 Black slaves from the Southern states were available, 7,705 males and 6,472 females (see Source List I).[1]
Of the free Blacks in the South from 1800 to 1860 the names of 13,356 were
collected. Of this number, 8,668 were male and 4,688 female (see Source
List J).

In these slave lists it has seemed best to record each name as listed on
the individual document, even though owners and overseers obviously twisted
identical names into many curious forms. The orthographic situation with the
slaves resembles that in early England, when spelling was roughly phonetic.
Even up to the Elementary Education Act of 1870 a considerable proportion of
the English people did not spell their own names but trusted to the parson
and the clerk, who wrought strange and wonderful creations from unfamiliar
names.[2] Similarly, among our slave names we find Liz (2), Liza (6), Lizar,
Lize, Lizee, Lizy, Lizza, Lizzie (5) and Lizzy (9), making it sometimes difficult to say just where Eliza ends and Lizzie begins. Rachel (60) blossoms
forth into Rachael (20), Raechel, Rachell and Rachiel, while Cina (2), Cind,
Cinda (3), Cindy (3), Sina (2), Sinah, Sinda and Sindy (5) leave one wondering
whether to blame Cindarella or Lucinda for such cryptographic confusion.
Lucy (117) appears also as Lussee and Luce; Sarah (116), as Sara, Saraugh and
Sary; Charlotte (47), as Chalath, Charlette, Charlott (12), Scharlotte, Shar-
lot, Sharlott and Sharlotte (5); Sukey (13), as Soockey, Sookey (4), Suck (2),
Sucky (8) and Sucy; and Violet (16), as Vilet (3), Vilett (4) and Violette.
Lucretia (6) is not only the mother of Lucresha but also the stepmother of
Creacy, Creasey, Creasy (2), Creecy (2), Cresa, Crese, Cresy (2), Cricy,
Cressy and perhaps even Cretia (2) and Critty. The names of male slaves seem
to run into fewer vagaries of spelling, although we do find Peter (109) ap-
pearing as Peater, and Caesar (23) as Caezar, Cesar (4) and Seasar (2).

The slave himself may well have enjoyed playing around with the spoken
word. Slave boy Malachi, for instance, "was baptized seven times, under different names, and with different sponsors, the good rector, to whom all young
Negroes looked alike, not recognizing him,"[3] although in this case the

---

[1]This is a more adequate, however, again a smaller sample. Franklin
estimates 2,000,000 slaves by 1830, and 3,953,760 by the time of the Civil War. (p. 186)

[2]E. Weekley, The Romance of Names (London, 1922), pp. 27-28.

[3]F. Clayton, "A Sketch in Black and White," Atlantic Monthly, XCVII (1906), p. 605.

Names, Slave and Free: 1800-1864

enticement may have been the ceremony rather than a delusion of nomenclatural grandeur expressing itself in terms of quantity rather than quality. Quite possibly many slave names were developed by Blacks themselves and used to express social distinctions current in slave society. Just as younger slaves were required to show respect to older ones by addressing them as "Uncle,"[4] so other factors, such as differences in occupation, led to social distinctions. House servants, drivers (foremen), carpenters, carriage drivers, fiddlers, cartwrights and shoemakers were high in the slave aristocracy, color entering in indirectly through the fact that mulattoes were more often chosen to be domestics and artisans. Moreover, slaves of "quality folk" held themselves above those owned by "trash."[5] Something of this element of social distinctions among slaves is expressed in a Mississippi Negro folk-rhyme formerly used in connection with cake walks. The latter, being "pay parties," required a doorkeeper possessing a sense of both financial and social discrimination. The rhyme runs as follows:

> "Is dat you, Sambo?" "No, dis am Cin."
> "Your'se potty good looking, but you can't come in."[6]

In order to use the name as a mark of social distinction among his fellows, the slave had to have freedom of choice. When this was allowed, as happened in at least some cases, it resulted, sometimes, in the selection of a master's given name, perhaps in the hope of receiving a special gift;[7] sometimes, in such descriptive names as Monday ("He oughter been name' Sunday, de day o' rest! He been sittin' down all his life."); and sometimes in such combinations as Willis Silblumus Quintellius Cerlarius Thomas William, called "literally 'fo' short', Willis."[8] Such slave names as April, August (3), Friday (7), January (3), July (5), June, March (7), Monday, Morning, Winter (2), and, for women, Easter (7), Easther, July and Morning, may refer to events associated with birth,[9] as was true in England at the eve of the Reformation, where Easter was the name longest to survive.[10]

Certain slave names on our list refer to localities: Aberdeen (3), Alabama, Baltimore, Boston (2), Dallas, Dublin (2), Erie, French (2), Galilee,

---

[4]E. F. Frazier, "The Negro Slave Family," Journal of Negro History, XV (1930), p. 213.

[5]Ibid., p. 209; See also Harper's Monthly Magazine, XVII (1858), p. 422; R. Q. Mallard, Plantation Life before Emancipation (Richmond, Va., 1892), p. 46.

[6]Informant: Colonel W. A. Love, Columbus, Mississippi.

[7]"Gift-names" are still found among Virginia Negroes. One colored woman named her daughter Annie Virginia Cordelia Idella Pigram, received a gift from each white person included in this list, and then called the child Tumps "for short." (Informant: Miss S. F. Barrow, Cleveland, Ohio.)

[8]O. K. Armstrong, Old Massa's People (Indianapolis, Ind., 1931), p. 59.

[9]Unquestionably, Sunday May the Ninth, a name bestowed upon a slave in the 1850's, was meant to guarantee the bearer's remembrance of his birthday. Informant: G. G. Grubb, Chapel Hill, North Carolina.

[10]C. W. Bardsley, Curiosities of Puritan Nomenclature (London, 1880), pp. 36, 96.

Names, Slave and Free: 1800-1864

Glascow, Holland (5), Jersey, London (5), Newport, Paris, Richmond (8), Scot-
land (4), Carolina (4), Dallas, Georgia (2), India (2), Indiana (2), Louisiana,
Louisianna, Misourie, Missouria, Savannah (2), Tennessee, Venice (2), Virginia
(9) and Virginie. Some may have been chosen by slave parents in reference to
place of birth; some, by masters to indicate place of purchase. Others refer
to localities known by name rather than through contact. In the rice plantation section, there was much coming and going of ships from England, and
slave mothers sometimes named their children York, London, or the like, according to the port of sail or destination of various vessels.[11] Holland was
a fairly common name among whites in England[12] and in colonial Massachusetts,
where London, Boston, America, and many similar names were also found.[13]

Nicknames might come either from a slave source or from the masters. They
are, of course, common all over the world, being used frequently by uncivil-
ized folk for the purpose of concealing their true names from the machinations
of sorcerers. Ordinarily they were too informal to be entered in official
records, although in the Esher Parish Register we do find "Bacchus alias Hog-
tub alias Fat Jack alias John from Ld. Clive at Claremont, buried 1772."[14]
Relatively few traces survive of the nicknames used among plantation Blacks
in addressing other slaves. Carmer,[15] cites the following from Thorn Hill
Plantation in Alabama: Pie Ya, Puddin'-tame, Frog, Tennie C., Monkey, Mush,
Cooter, John De Baptist, Fat-man, Preacher, Jack Rabbit, Sixty, Pop Corn, Old
Gold, Dootes, Tangle-eye, Bad-Luck, Fly-up-de-Creek, Cracker, Jabbo, Cat-fish,
Bear, Tip, Odessa, Pig-Lasses, Rattler, Pearly, Luck, Buffalo, Old Blue, Red
Fox, Coon and Jewsharp. Several of these suggest personal traits or episodes
in the life of the individual, and hence approach closely the character of
certain types of primitive names. Some nicknames occurring in our own list
are: Bap, Bebb, Bingo, Binkey (2), Biby, Bus, Fell, Fodder, Fute, Gallon,
Jacko, Luck, Money, Moon, Nig, Pillow, Pool, Quince (2), Ratler, Rep, Roller,
Sandy (10), Tabs, Tell, Tink, Tip, Top, Town, Toy, Bis, Icy, Mopsy, Munny,
Pussy (2), Spice and Spicy.

Such titular nicknames among men as Dock (6), Doctor (5), Esquire, General, Govenor, Judge (5), King (6), Major (8), Parson and Squire (8) seem to
indicate a recognition of slave social distinctions, although both Squire and
Major were common among ordinary folk in England before the death of Queen
Elizabeth.[16] Possible slave derivation is also indicated in those names that
seem to be based on personal pecularities,[17] of which the following occur in

---

[11]Armstrong, op. cit., p. 62.

[12]Weekley, op. cit., p. 98.

[13]N. I. Bowditch, Suffolk Surnames (Boston, Mass., 1858), pp. 16-18.

[14]C. L. Ewen, A History of Surnames of the British Isles (London, 1931),
pp. 203, 330, 328.

[15]C. Carmer, Stars Fell on Alabama (New York, 1934), p. 96.

[16]Bardsley, op. cit., pp. 196-197.

[17]W. F. Allen (Slave Songs of the United States (New York, 1867),
p. xxxiii) mentions a slave named After-dark, "so called because he was so
black that 'you can't sh'um 'fo' day-cleam'."

Names, Slave and Free: 1800-1864

our list: <u>Baldy</u> (2), <u>Bellow</u>, <u>Bold</u>, <u>Boney</u>, <u>Brag</u>, <u>Brave Boy</u>, <u>Crip</u>, <u>Grizzy</u>, <u>Hardtimes</u>, <u>Junior</u>, <u>Live</u>, <u>Lively</u>, <u>Mangy</u>, <u>Muss</u>, <u>Polite</u>, <u>Racket</u>, <u>Senior</u>, <u>Short</u>, <u>Smart</u> (6), <u>Tartar</u>, <u>Babe</u>, <u>Bitsey</u> (2), <u>Bonny</u>, <u>Grief</u>, <u>Happy</u> (2), <u>Mourning</u>, <u>Peachy</u>, <u>Queen</u> and <u>Sis</u>.[18]

Of the 247 most frequently used names of Black male slaves, <u>John</u> (295) is the most popular, followed by <u>Henry</u> (260), <u>George</u> (221), <u>Sam</u> (162), <u>Tom</u> (156), <u>Charles</u> (155), <u>Jim</u> (150), <u>Jack</u> (140), <u>Peter</u> (135) and <u>William</u> (126). These ten names comprise 23.36 per cent of all male slave names, almost a quarter. Of the most frequently used free Black names, on the other hand, the names most often used total 36.25 per cent of that list.

This pattern continues for the complete lists of most frequently used names. Black slaves employ 247 names with a total incidence of 6,130, or 79.55 per cent, of all Black male slave names. Free Blacks use 103 names with a total incidence of 6,132, almost exactly the same incidence as slaves, but with 70.74 per cent rate. This difference can perhaps be attributed to the ability of free Blacks to acquire surnames. This would allow them to use the surnames in an identifying way and enable them to choose given names without the pressure of having them function as the sole identification. Slaves, on the other hand, generally lacking a surname, used a greater number of given names for identification.

<u>James</u>, <u>Thomas</u>, <u>Samuel</u> and <u>David</u> appear amongst the first ten free Black names and not amongst the first ten slaves. They replace <u>Sam</u>, <u>Tom</u>, <u>Jim</u> and <u>Jack</u>. It would seem that <u>Samuel</u> and <u>Thomas</u>, preferred by free Blacks over the familiarized shortened <u>Sam</u> and <u>Tom</u>, reflect yearnings for greater dignity. The popularity of <u>James</u> and <u>David</u> rather than <u>Jim</u> and <u>Jack</u> tends to support this possibility.

The following is intended to help indicate some of the shifts from slave to free Black in the popularity of names. Below is a list of the fifty most frequently used free Black names; the number after the name indicates the position of that name in the slave list (Source Lists I, J):

John 1	Daniel 24	Anthony 34
William 10	Richard 66	Harry 19
James 18	Robert 37	Frank 22
Thomas 52	Benjamin 116	Solomon 62
George 3	Jesse 35	Allen 39
Henry 2	Jacob 21	Sam 4
Samuel 78	Moses 14	Reuben 48
David 33	Stephen 25	Philip 90
Charles 6	Lewis 20	(spelled Phillip)
Peter 9	Edward 61	Elijah 80
Joseph 67	Billy 29	Joshua 88
Isaac 15	Jack 8	Ned 23

---

[18]Puckett, <u>op. cit</u>., pp. 483-487.

Names, Slave and Free: 1800-1864

Abraham 46	Tom 5	Abram 26
Alexander 65	Nathan 55	Aaron 45
Edmond 40	Jerry 27	Elisha 133
Isham 81	Simon 31	Jeremiah
Willis 38	Matthew	(not listed)
Andrew 32	(not listed)	

Adam, Albert, Alfred, Bill, Ben, Bob, Caesar, Dave, Dick, Ellick, Jim, Joe, Nelson, Phil, Washington and Will, sixteen names in all, lost popularity with free Blacks and are not found amongst the fifty most commonly used names. They are replaced by Alexander, Benjamin, Edward, Elisha, Elijah, Isham, Jeremiah, Joseph, Joshua, Matthew, Nathan, Philip, Richard, Samuel, Solomon and Thomas.

This shift gives rise to interesting conjectures. The sixteen slave names which lost popularity are characterized by nine shortened forms, two Biblical names, one classical, one famous and three common names; the free names which replace these are characterized by twelve Biblical names, one classical, three common and no shortened forms at all. In addition, the slave names are composed of nine names with one syllable, the shortened forms, six names of two syllables, and one trisyllabic name. The free Blacks replace these with ten names of two syllables, four trisyllabic names and two names with four syllables each. Thus the free Blacks tend to employ names with sound patterns less stacatto and names more dignified and elevated than those employed by, or foisted upon, their slave contemporaries.

The most commonly used slave names in the nineteenth century show changes from those on the eighteenth century list. Perhaps the most significant shift is that which sees John move from ninth position in the eighteenth century to first in the nineteenth. This reflects the general movement to Western nomenclature even amongst slaves, upon whom less than dignified names were generally foisted. The shift from such names as Caesar, Dick, Harry, Robin and Will to Charles, George, Henry, Jim and William from the eighteenth to the nineteenth centuries on the ten most frequently used slave names lists tend to support this possibility. The shift can be seen not only in terms of slave names from one century to another, but also in terms of names chosen by free Blacks from the eighteenth to the nineteenth century. Free Blacks in the later period shun the monosyllabic Sam, Dick, Jack and Tom for Samuel, Charles, Henry and Thomas. This tendency to a more elevated nomenclature can be illustrated by comparing the ten most frequently used names by Blacks in the eighteenth and nineteenth centuries.

The following lists reflect slave and free Black names
in the eighteenth and nineteenth centuries (Source Lists
A, B, I, J):

BLACK NAMES IN AMERICA

Names, Slave and Free: 1800-1864

Eighteenth Century		Nineteenth Century	
Slave	Free	Slave	Free
Jack	John	John	John
Tom	James	Henry	William
Harry	George	George	James
Sam	Sam	Sam	Thomas
Will	William	Tom	George
Caesar	Peter	Charles	Henry
Dick	Dick	Jim	Samuel
Peter	Jacob	Jack	David
John	Jack	Peter	Charles
Robin	Tom	William	Peter

Turning to the nineteenth century females, we find that amongst Black slave women Mary (321) is the most popular name, followed by Maria(h) (178), Nancy (157), Sarah (150), Lucy (139), Harriet (129), Elisa (122), Jane (119), Hannah (115) and Martha (108). These ten names comprise 23.76 per cent of all female slave names, almost a quarter. Of the most frequently used free Black female names, the ten most commonly used names total 35.36 per cent. This pattern continues for the complete lists of most frequently used names, although to a lesser degree than with males. Black female slaves employ 172 names with a total incidence of 5,003, or 77.30 per cent, of all Black female slave names. Free Black females use 87 names with a total incidence of 3,552, or 75.76 per cent, of all free Black female names.

The percentage of the first ten names appears almost identical with that of the male names; with the entire listing of most frequently used names the difference in concentration of names amongst slave and free Black women lessens. However the pattern seems to be the same with both sexes; slave given names appear less concentrated than those of free Blacks, and the probability suggests itself that free Blacks chose popular given names which clustered around fewer choices, trusting to their surnames to provide identification. Slaves, on the other hand, rarely having surnames, found the given name functioning as the sole identification symbol and tended to employ a greater variety of names.

This tendency is reflected another way. In the eighteenth century male slaves employed 38 names most frequently out of a total of 384 names, or 9.89 per cent. At the same time free males chose 31 names out of 202 most often, a 15.35 per cent. Thus, free Black males in the eighteenth century show a markedly greater tendency to concentrate their names than did their slave counterparts.

Females, on the other hand, show a greater stability in this area. Slaves used 26 out of 254 names most often, a 10.23 per cent, and free women chose 19 out of 169 names most often, a 11.24 per cent. It is possible that the male, in greater contact with the larger White population, employed the surname more frequently than the female and tended to restrict his choice of given names since he could rely upon his surname for identification.

Names, Slave and Free: 1800-1864

Betsy, Elizabeth, Polly and Sally appear amongst the first ten free female names and not amongst the first ten slave names. They replace Elisa, Harriet, Maria(h) and Martha. Like their male counterparts, free females avoid the familiar form of a name, preferring instead its more formal and dignified form. Thus, Elisa loses favor and is replaced by Elizabeth. Nevertheless, free women favor Betsy, Polly and Sally. There seems to be a tendency to drop the Spanish Maria(h) for the English Mary, although unlike in the dominant White group, it is second in popularity to Nancy.

Following is a list of the fifty most frequently used free Black female names. The number following the name indicates the order of that name in the slave list (Source Lists I, J).

Nancy 3	Ann 13	Phillis 26
Mary 1	Susan 24	Katy (not listed)
Sally 14	Maria 2	Caty 55
Betsy 16	Rebecca 61	Kate 58
Polly 32	Charlotte 25	Matilda 20
Lucy 5	Martha 10	Agnes 90
Elizabeth 38	Margaret 22	Louisa 19
Jane 8	Catharine 42	Dolly 68
Sarah 4	Judy 29	Edy 77
Hannah 9	Lydia 48	Grace 47
Fanny 18	Betty 28	Kitty 33
Milly 17	Nelly 36	Rhoda 72
Rachael 11	Esther 46	Leah 89
Patsy 51	Su(c)key 63	Aggy 59
Peggy 27	Winn(e)y 45	Anna 75
Eliza (not listed)	Rose 23	Charity 34
Liza 132	Harriet 6	Phoebe 52
Elisa 7	Priscilla 80	Caroline 12

Adeline, Amanda, Amy, Becky, Celia, Clarissa, Dinah, Elisa, Ellen, Emily, Frances, Julia, Lucinda and Malinda, fourteen names in all, lost popularity with free Black women and are not found amongst the fifty most commonly used names. They are replaced by Aggy, Agnes, Anna, Dolly, Edy, Eliza, Katy, Leah, Patsy, Phoebe, Priscilla, Rebecca, Rhoda and Su(c)key.

Unlike their male counterparts, free Black women tended to replace tri-syllabic names with those of two syllables. The fourteen names dropped from those most commonly used contained seven with two syllables and seven with three; the fourteen names replacing them contain eleven with two syllables and only three with three syllables. Again unlike their male counterparts, women, both slave and free, show no names of either one or four syllables. The shift in the types of names themselves seems to reject any pattern.

Bet and Betty, first and fifth amongst eighteenth century female slaves, are eschewed by nineteenth century females. This is also true for Phillis, Nan, Peg and Sary. They are replaced by Maria(h), Nancy, Lucy, Harriet and

Names, Slave and Free: 1800-1864

Elisa. The short, stacatto, one-syllable names, Bet, Nan and Peg - all
shortened forms - give way to names which perhaps reflect a greater awareness
of human qualities belonging to the holder of those names.

> This tendency can perhaps be illustrated by a compari-
> son of the ten most popular names amongst slave and free
> women during the two periods 1700-1800 and 1800-1860 (see
> Source Lists A, B, I, J).

Eighteenth Century		Nineteenth Century	
Slave	Free	Slave	Free
Bet	Sarah	Mary	Nancy
Mary	Hannah	Maria	Mary
Hannah	Bet(t)	Sarah	Betsy
Jane	Rachael	Nancy	Sally
Betty	Mary	Lucy	Polly
Sarah	Phillis	Harriet	Lucy
Phillis	Jane	Elisa	Elizabeth
Nan	Ann	Jane	Jane
Peg	Elizabeth	Hannah	Sarah
Sary	Nancy	Martha	Hannah

It seems probable that the Biblical names of Blacks came more from the
masters than from the slaves themselves. However, it is very possible that a
Biblical name represented social as well as inspirational possibilities.
There existed a long tradition in Africa of bestowing sacred names so that
the recipient became familiar with the qualities and history of his name.
This oral tradition clearly functions in an educational way. Perhaps this
holds true in America; religious Blacks may have used Biblical names so that
their children would be familiar with the teachings of Christianity. Secondly, as Franklin points out, in the latter half of the eighteenth century the
Church represented the lone hope for freedom - in this world as well as the
other. It was only later - well into the nineteenth century - that America's
churches in the South supported the institution of slavery.[19] Most of these
Biblical and Puritan names were found with the early Whites of Columbus,
Missippi, listed in various Probate Records; though such nomenclature is less
frequent in the South than it was in early New England.[20] They were at one
time exceedingly common among the English,[21] and appear frequently in Colonial
New England,[22] in the roll of the United States Congress and in Who's Who in
America[23] as well as among contemporary Southern Mountaineers.[24]

---

[19]Franklin, op. cit., pp. 161-163 and 227-228.

[20]W. D. Bowman, The Story of Surnames (London, 1931), p. 92.

[21]Ibid., 89-90 and 250 ff. Bardsley, op. cit., 38-116. Weekley, op. cit., 85-89.

[22]Bowditch, op. cit., pp. 12-20.

[23]Mencken, see p. iii.

[24]J. C. Campbell, The Southern Highlander and His Homeland (New York, 1921), p. 2.

Black Names in America

Names, Slave and Free: 1800-1864

Black male slaves in the nineteenth century used 104 names of Biblical origin and one name, <u>Providence</u>, which can be classified as Puritanical. <u>John</u> (295) and <u>Peter</u> (135) were the most popular, followed by <u>Moses</u> (96) and <u>Isaac</u> (94). There were a total of 1,820 incidences from the 7,705 slave names collected, or 23.62 per cent. That is, almost a quarter of all male slave names in the nineteenth century were Biblical in origin. Of these names, 72, or 69 per cent, were Old Testament and 32, or 31 per cent, were from the New Testament.

Although Old Testament names were employed more than twice as often as those from the New Testament, the overwhelming popularity of <u>John</u> and <u>Peter</u> made the incidence of New Testament names 872, or 48 per cent. Old Testament names, on the other hand, accounted for 947 incidences, or 52 per cent.

Slaves in the eighteenth century employed Biblical names to an extent of 13.09 per cent; slaves in the nineteenth century almost double that figure to 23.62 per cent. In the eighteenth century, 35 per cent of male slave names were of Old Testament origin and 65 per cent originated in the New Testament. It would seem that Old Testament names found great favor amongst slaves and their owners in the nineteenth century.

Below is a list of the ten most frequently used Biblical
names amongst eighteenth and nineteenth century Blacks,
slave and free (<u>see</u> Source Lists A, B, I, J).

Eighteenth Century		Nineteenth Century	
Slave	Free	Slave	Free
Peter	John	John	John
John	James	Peter	James
James	Peter	Moses	Thomas
Daniel	Jacob	Isaac	Samuel
Simon	Joseph	James	David
Abram	Daniel	Jacob	Peter
Jacob	Abraham	Daniel	Joseph
Andrew	David	Stephen	Isaac
Joseph	Aaron	Abram	Daniel
Isaac	Isaac	Simon	Benjamin

Slave women in the nineteenth century employed forty-five Biblical and seven Puritanical names. <u>Mary</u> (321) and <u>Maria</u>(h) (178) head the list, followed by <u>Sarah</u> (150), <u>Hannah</u> (115) and <u>Rach(a)el</u> (98). There were a total of 1,183 incidences from the 6,472 female slave names collected, or 18.27 per cent. Of these names, 33, or 63.5 per cent, were Old Testament, 12, or 23 per cent, were New Testament and 7, or 13.5 per cent, were Puritanical.

The pattern established by females was similar to that established by males. Old Testament names were employed more than twice as frequently as those emanating from the New Testament, and, consistent with that pattern, was the great popularity of one name, <u>Mary</u> or <u>Maria</u>(h), which made the incidence

Names, Slave and Free: 1800-1864

of New Testament names total 542, or 46 per cent. Old Testament names, notwithstanding their markedly greater employment, account for only two more incidences than those from the New Testament, a total of 544 incidences, or 46 per cent. The seven Puritanical names total 97 incidences, or 8 per cent.

Female slaves in the eighteenth century employed Biblical and Puritanical names to an extent of 14.48 per cent; female slaves in the nineteenth century show a slight rise to 18.27 per cent. The use of this type of name appears to have found more favor amongst males than females in the nineteenth century. Of the names used in the eighteenth century, females looked to the Old Testament for 61.4 per cent. From the New Testament came 27.2 per cent and Puritanical names accounted for 11.4 per cent.

Puritanical names show a slight decrease of approximately 3 per cent in the nineteenth century. Old Testament names decrease markedly, approximately 15 per cent. New Testament names increase in popularity from the eighteenth to the nineteenth century by approximately 18 per cent. Unlike their male counterparts, female slaves in the nineteenth century employ a greater number of New Testament names than their sisters in the previous century.

Below is a list of the seven most frequently used Biblical names amongst eighteenth-and nineteenth-century women, slave and free. This number is used rather than ten since in the eighteenth- century slave list all names after the seventh have a frequency of one (see Source Lists A, B, I, J).

Eighteenth Century		Nineteenth Century	
Slave	Free	Slave	Free
Mary	Sarah	Mary	Mary
Hannah	Hannah	Maria(h)	Sarah
Sarah	Rachael	Sarah	Hannah
Dinah	Mary	Hannah	Rachael
Grace	Dinah	Rach(a)el	Maria
Rachael	Grace	Charity	Rebecca
Hagar	Patience	Dinah	Esther

Turning to the category of classical and literary names, we find that 2.92 per cent of all Black male slaves in the nineteenth century employed this type of name. The ten most frequently used were Caesar, Cato, Pompey, Cyrus, Julius, Scipio, Hector, Horace, Nero and Hannibal. Latin or Roman names appear more popular than Greek or literary names. Male slaves in the eighteenth century employed classical and literary names to the extent of 6.13 per cent, a little less than twice as often as nineteenth-century slaves. Males in both periods found Latin more appealing than Greek names.

Following is a list of eighteenth- and nineteenth-century classical and literary names found amongst slaves.

BLACK NAMES IN AMERICA

Names, Slave and Free: 1800-1864

The first seven are given since all names after that
amongst eighteenth-century males have a frequency of one
(<u>see</u> Source Lists A, I).

Slave Names: Eighteenth Century	Slave Names: Nineteenth Century
Caesar	Caesar
Cato	Cato
Pompey	Pompey
Jupiter	Cyrus
Scipio	Julius
Esop	Scipio
Nero	Hector

From the list of most frequently used names of free male Blacks in the
nineteenth century appear the classical ones <u>Alexander</u>, <u>Caesar</u>, <u>Cato</u> and
<u>Pompey</u>; free Blacks in the eighteenth century employed <u>Caesar</u> most frequently,
followed by <u>Pompey</u>, <u>Sipio</u> and <u>Poladore</u>. The remaining eight names have a frequency of one. <u>Caesar</u> seems the most popular of classical names with all
groups other than free Blacks in the nineteenth century. With this group,
<u>Alexander</u> appears most often, although it had not shown to be especially popu-
lar before. <u>Cato</u> and <u>Pompey</u> remain popular, along with <u>Caesar</u>, from one
century to another with both slaves and free Blacks.

Nineteenth-century slave females employ literary and classical names to
an extent of 5.19 per cent. Literary names such as <u>Clarissa</u> and <u>Celia</u> head
the list, followed by classical <u>Phoebe</u>, <u>Venus</u> and <u>Chloe</u>. Eighteenth-century
slave women used an exceedingly low 1.49 per cent of classical names, limiting
themselves to <u>Diana</u>, <u>Dice</u>, <u>Dido</u>, <u>Phoebe</u> and <u>Venus</u>. Nineteenth-century slave
women employ these five names and add to them names such as <u>Minerva</u>, <u>Cynthia</u>
and <u>Juno</u>, but a glance at the nineteenth-century list (Source List I) would
suggest that a good part of the increase is due to the use of literary names,
especially <u>Clarissa</u> and <u>Celia</u>. Southern mistresses seem to have had a great
affection for British novels.

Nineteenth century free women employ such classical and literary names as
<u>Phoebe</u>, <u>Dicy</u>, <u>Celia</u>, <u>Lavinia</u>, <u>Chloe</u>, <u>Clarissa</u>, <u>Lucretia</u>, <u>Penelope</u> and <u>Minerva</u>;
eighteenth century free females used <u>Chloe</u>, <u>Cassandra</u>, <u>Dianna</u>, <u>Dice</u>, <u>Dido</u>,
<u>Penelope</u>, <u>Pheba</u>, <u>Priscilla</u> and <u>Venus</u>.

In the nineteenth century 1.59 per cent of all Black male slave names indicate some geographical location, primarily place names, a decrease of almost
1 per cent over slave usage in the eighteenth century. Of the thirty-six
names only <u>Charleston</u>, <u>Alabama</u>, <u>America</u>, <u>Antrim</u>, <u>Baltimore</u>, <u>Jersey</u>, <u>Montgomery</u>
and <u>Somerville</u>, 8 in all, seem American; the remaining twenty-eight are
foreign, mostly British. <u>York</u> and <u>Essex</u> head the list followed by <u>Richmond</u>,
<u>London</u>, <u>Aberdeen</u>, <u>Holland</u>, <u>Glasgow</u>, <u>Scotland</u>, <u>Boston</u> and <u>Dublin</u>.

BLACK NAMES IN AMERICA

Names, Slave and Free: 1800-1864

Free Blacks in the nineteenth century used only two geographical names, London and York; free Blacks in the earlier century employed York, London and nine others with an incidence of one each. York and London show the greatest popularity amongst free and slave Blacks in both centuries.

Slave women in the nineteenth century employed 3.24 per cent geographic names. Charlotte leads the list, followed by one African place name, Malinda. Virginia, America, and another African place name, Mahala, follow. Female slave geographic names total slightly more than twice the percentage used by their male counterparts. This is striking, for in the eighteenth century female slaves used no geographic names at all. This may suggest a greater mobility on the part of women, and a need to identify female slaves in this manner.

Free Black females in the nineteenth century employ Charlotte and Mahala as their only geographical names. It is perhaps that free Black women once more were identified in other ways than those dealing with geographical or place names. Free Black women's names in the eighteenth century reflect only one incidence of a location name, Carolina. It seems significant that amongst Black women the only group to show any great use of location names is the slave group in the period 1800-1864.

Descriptive, episodic and occupational names amongst Black slaves in the nineteenth century total 4.20 per cent of the complete list of 7,705 names. Green heads the list, followed by Primus, Pleasant, Hardy, Robin, Sandy, Friday, March and Orange. In the eighteenth century, this type of name, headed by Robin, totaled 6.54 per cent, an insignificantly higher figure.

Free males in the nineteenth century used Pleasant, Robin, Green and Sandy. These, of course, were quite popular with slaves in this period. Free males in the eighteenth century employ 2.36 per cent descriptive, episodic or occupational names, and this list is characterized by the non-use of Robin, a name popular with slaves in that period, as well as with both groups in the later century. Pleasant, incidentally, is found amongst female slaves as well as amongst males.

Slave women in the nineteenth century employ descriptive, episodic or occupational names to an extent of 2.34 per cent. Flora, Violet, June and May head the list, followed by Marina, Nicy, Prissy, Die, Mealy and Tiller. In the eighteenth century 3.12 per cent of female slave names were of this type. Eighteenth-century females used Floor, Easter and Violet along with nine other names with incidences of one.

Free females in the nineteenth century employ Mourning, Comfort, Cherry, Flora and Grief as descriptive names. In the eighteenth century 2.36 per cent of the free Black women chose Pink, Memory, Comfort, Flowrah, Friday, Obedience or Violet. It appears that amongst all females, free or slave in both centuries, Violet and Flora or Flower are perennials.

BLACK NAMES IN AMERICA

Names, Slave and Free: 1800-1864

Male slaves in the nineteenth century used 1.15 per cent titular names headed by Prince and Major. These are followed by Squire, King, Dock, Doctor and Judge. Slaves in the eighteenth century employed 1.76 per cent titular names: Prince, Duke and Esquire. Prince was clearly the most popular titular name for slaves in both centuries. Nineteenth-century free Black males employ the names Major, Squire and Prince, whereas free Black males in the eighteenth century use only Prince and Duke, with a very low .306 per cent.

Slave women in the nineteenth century use titular names at a rate of .37 per cent. Nanny is the most popular, followed by Queen, Granny, Senior and Madame. In the eighteenth century slave women used only Nanny, with a rate of .65 per cent. Free Black women in the nineteenth century employ Nanny, and free women in the eighteenth century employ Nanny and Princess, for a total of 1.71 per cent. Nanny seems the one favorite female titular name for both slave and free women in both centuries, as Prince is among males. Titular names, then, are generally avoided by Blacks, notwithstanding popular misconceptions concerning Black naming practices.

Male slaves in the nineteenth century used famous names at a 1.15 per cent rate. Washington was the most popular name, followed by Madison, Jefferson, Napoleon, Lafayette, Columbus, Van Buren, Middleton and Winston. All but Napoleon played a direct role in American history, and all were internationally known except Middleton and Winston, two men famous in the South in the first half of the century. Eighteenth-century slaves used only one famous name, Cromwell, for a rate of .10 per cent. In the nineteenth century free Blacks used Washington and Jefferson; eighteenth-century free Blacks used no famous names.

In the nineteenth-century female slaves show a .13 per cent use of famous names with Victoria, Airy and Zenobia. Their eighteenth century counterparts use no famous names. Nineteenth-century free females employ no famous names as such, nor do their eighteenth-century sisters.

Washington and Jefferson, used by Black males both free and slave in the nineteenth century, seem to be the only famous names used with any degree of consistency and frequency as given names. Like titular ones, famous names did not find an especially strong acceptance amongst Blacks.

In the nineteenth century male slaves used African names to an extent of 1.73 per cent. Mingo, Quash, Sambo, Cuffee, Juba, Quam and Sango head the list. In the eighteenth century Sambo, Cuf, Cuffy, Mingo, Kof and Quash head a list which has a rate of 9.25 per cent. It appears that male slaves in the nineteenth century used appreciably fewer African names than those in the preceding period. Free eighteenth-century Black males used 3.01 per cent African names headed by Mingo and Cuff. Thus, although a few names appear amongst free and slave males in both centuries, the percentage of names which derive from Africa is a small 7.53 per cent amongst slaves in the eighteenth century and dwindles amongst eighteenth-century free Blacks and nineteenth-century free and slave Blacks.

Names, Slave and Free: 1800-1864

Female slaves in the nineteenth century use African names at a rate of
3.02 per cent. Juba, Anaca, Cuffee, Sara, Cotta, Gabi, Anecky and Cusha head
the list. In the eighteenth century Beck heads the list of African names
which includes Cumba and Juba, for a rate of 4.57 per cent. The pattern established by male slaves holds good for the females; i.e., eighteenth-century
female slaves use African names with more frequency than those in the nineteenth century. Again, like their men, free females eschew African names.

A very large class of slave names, such as Eugene, Nathaniel, Ella and so
on, which were clearly identical with White nomenclature of the period, show
the direct or indirect influence of the owner in the naming of the slave
child, and the same thing is indicated even more strongly by another large
group of slave given names which include Addison, Campbell or Robinson, apparently derived from the surnames of the Whites. Still another large group includes the various diminutives, such as Dan, Pete, Ebby, Litt, Nell, Tabby and
so on, which follow closely American White patterns. These three groups, together with the 100 most common slave names, constitute the bulk of slave
nomenclature and indicate his growing alliance with American usage in this
respect. In fact, the actual naming of the slave child was often (probably
most often) done by the master or mistress, resulting not only in names of
the master's family being given to slaves,[25] but also in such names as Fed[26]
or Last Night (the master being roused from his morning sleep by the news
that Clementine "had a little boy last night").[27]

Male slaves in the nineteenth century used 1,663 unusual names; of these
928 would be considered old-fashioned. Thus the incidence of unusual names
totals 735 out of 7,705, or 9.52 per cent. Eighteenth-century male slaves employed unusual names at a rate of 25.36 per cent. Female slaves in the nineteenth century used 2,041 unusual names; those old-fashioned total 1,406,
leaving 635 unusual names, or 9.79 per cent. In the eighteenth century female
slaves used unusual names at a rate of 18.09 per cent.

With both male and female slaves, then, 1800-1860 saw a diminished percentage of unusual names, approximately 14 per cent less among male and a
little less than 9 per cent for female slaves. The amount of decrease creates
a situation in which both sexes in the nineteenth century use almost the same
amount of unusual names.

Free Black males in the nineteenth century use 1,396, or 16.10 per cent,
unusual names (see Source List J). Free Black males in the preceding century

---

[25]Armstrong, loc. cit.

[26]Frazier, op. cit., p. 229. "When in slavery I was called Fred. Why
I was so named, I cannot tell. I never knew myself to have any other name,...
for it is common for slaves to assume any name as it suits the humor of the
master."

[27]"Negro Minstrelsy, Ancient and Modern," Maga Social Papers (New York,
1867), p. 286.

Names, Slave and Free: 1800-1864

use unusual names at a rate of 13.64 per cent. Free females in the nineteenth century employ 1,046 unusual names, or 22.31 per cent of the names collected; for free females in the earlier century the figure was 15.23 per cent.

It appears that one trend started in the eighteenth century is reversed in the nineteenth; in the former period slaves used a higher percentage of unusual names than did free Blacks. In the later period, on the other hand, slaves used a lower percentage of unusual names than did free Blacks. Secondly, free males in the nineteenth century show a greater use of unusual names than females; this also reverses a pattern established in the eighteenth century. Finally, in the eighteenth century male slaves reflected a greater percentage of unusual names than did females, but in the nineteenth century the percentage of unusual names appears about equal amongst both sexes.

The following table represents the percentage of names in each of the categories for males and females, slave and free, in the eighteenth century, excluding Northern free Blacks, and slave males and females in the nineteenth century. We can also include the rate of unusualness for free Blacks in the nineteenth century (see Source Lists A, B, I, J).

Century	Male %	Female %	Total %
Biblical/Puritanical			
Slave--18th	13.09	14.48	13.63
Slave--19th	23.62	18.27	21.18
Free--18th	29.45	26.28	28.23
Classical/Literary			
Slave--18th	6.13	1.49	4.33
Slave--19th	2.92	5.19	3.95
Free--18th	4.03	2.69	3.51
Geographic			
Slave--18th	2.48	0	1.52
Slave--19th	1.59	3.24	2.23
Free--18th	2.17	.24	1.42
Descriptive/Episodic/Occupational			
Slave--18th	6.54	3.12	5.22
Slave--19th	4.20	2.34	3.35
Free--18th	2.36	2.72	2.66
Titular			
Slave--18th	1.76	.65	1.33
Slave--19th	1.15	.37	.79
Free--18th	.306	1.71	.85

BLACK NAMES IN AMERICA

Names, Slave and Free: 1800-1864

Century	Male %	Female %	Total %
Famous			
Slave--18th	.10	0	.06
Slave--19th	1.15	.13	.88
Free--18th	0	0	0
African			
Slave--18th	9.25	4.57	7.53
Slave--19th	1.73	3.02	2.32
Free--18th	3.01	4.66	4.11
Unusual			
Slave--18th	25.36	18.09	22.47
Slave--19th	9.52	9.79	9.66
Free--18th	13.64	15.23	14.25
Free--19th	16.10	22.31	18.28

In the nineteenth century the greatest percentage of slave names were of Biblical and Puritanical origin, 21.18 per cent; descriptive, episodic and/or occupational names follow classical and/or literary names which are second in frequency. Then come names of geographic location, African origin, famous and titular. Finally, unusual names account for 9.66 per cent, or almost one-tenth of all slave names in the period 1800-1860.

By contrast slaves in the eighteenth century used names in this order of popularity: Biblical, Puritanical, African, descriptive, episodic and/or occupational, literary-classical, geographical, titular and famous. Their rate of unusualness was a very high 22.47 per cent: almost one-quarter of all names used. It appears that amongst slaves in the nineteenth century Biblical names became exceedingly popular at the expense of African and unusual names.

Eighteenth-century free Blacks employ a substantial number of Biblical names, 28.23 per cent; literary-classical names follow with 3.51 per cent. Next in frequency are descriptive, episodic and/or occupational names, African, geographical and titular.There are no famous names as such amongst free Southern Blacks, male and female, and the rate of unusualness is 14.25 per cent, much lower than amongst slaves in the eighteenth century but higher than amongst slaves in the nineteenth century. The trend is obviously toward fewer and fewer unusual names.

The following list is highly reflective of the high degree of assimilation, at least in terms of nomenclature, of free Black men into the main pattern of White naming practices in the period preceding the Civil War. It consists of the first twenty-five most frequently used White male given names in order of popularity from Blair's Listing of Early Tax Digests of Georgia, 1790-1818 (see Source List K); next to the name is a number which indicates that name's position amongst free Black males (see Source List J).

Names, Slave and Free: 1800-1864

John 1	George 5	Isaac 12
William 2	David 8	Lewis 21
James 3	Jesse 17	Edward 22
Thomas 4	Richard 14	Joshua 34
Joseph 11	Jacob 18	Moses 19
Robert 15	Daniel 13	Stephen 20
Henry 6	Charles 9	Nathaniel 59
Samuel 7	Peter 10	Abraham 36
Benjamin 16		

Of the first twenty-five most popular names amongst White males all but Joshua, Nathaniel and Abraham belong to the first twenty-five most popular names amongst the free Black male population. In other words, twenty-two out of the first twenty-five most frequently used White names are to be found amongst the first twenty-five most popular free Black male names. The three names not on the list amongst free Blacks are replaced by Billy, Jack and Anthony, which appear twenty-third, twenty-fourth and twenty-fifth among them. This means, then, that the first twenty-two names amongst White males correspond to the first twenty-two names amongst free Black males. And, the first four names are exactly the same on both lists. John, William, James and Thomas, then, are the most popular names for both White and free Black males.

Of these twenty-five White names only thirteen appear among the first twenty-five male slave names in the nineteenth century. It becomes evident, then, that, certainly in terms of naming practices in the nineteenth century, free Blacks were considerably more prone to choose names identical with White practices than were their slave brothers.

In the eighteenth century the first twenty-five free Black male names include, as did the slaves in the nineteenth century, thirteen names which correspond to the most popular White male given names. And slaves in the eighteenth century used only eight names which correspond to those on the White list in the nineteenth century. The pattern among men is quite interesting. Of the most frequently used twenty-five names amongst Whites, male slaves in the eighteenth century used eight, free Blacks in the same century used thirteen, slaves in the nineteenth century used thirteen and free Blacks in the nineteenth century used twenty-two out of twenty-five.

The twenty-one most frequently used White female given names are listed below with a figure next to each name which represents that name's position amongst free Black women in the nineteenth century (see Source Lists J, K). Using a cut-off of five, there appear only twenty-one White female given names in the nineteenth century from our collected list which hold that minimum of popularity.

Mary 2	Nancy 1	Sally 3
Elizabeth 7	Eliza 16	Asia*
Sarah 9	Priscilla 34	Hannah 10
Ann 17	Rach(a)el 13	Martha 22

---

*Not among 106 names with a frequency of 5 or more.

Names, Slave and Free: 1800-1864

Jane 8	Rebecca 20	Betsy 4
C(k)atherine 24	Frances*	Esther 29
Margaret 23	Lydia 26	Ruth*

Of the first twenty-one most popular names amongst White females, twelve
are to be found amongst the twenty-one most frequently chosen nineteenth-
century free Black female names, a decidedly lower correspondence than that
found amongst males. It would seem that free Black females found it less
necessary to emulate White naming practices.

Slave females in the nineteenth century either chose or were given nine
names which correspond with those on the list of twenty-one most popular White
female names. Slave females like their free sisters manifest a lesser degree
of assimilation in terms of name usage than males. It should be noted, however, that <u>Mary</u> finds greatest favor with slave females, as indeed it does
with White women, whereas <u>Nancy</u> is elevated to first position and <u>Mary</u> rele-
gated to second position by free Black women.

In the eighteenth century the first twenty-one free Black female names
include eight which are found on the White female list, one less than those
on slave female lists in the nineteenth century. Slave females in the
eighteenth century were given, or chose, only four names which correspond to
those most frequently used by White women.

The pattern established by Black males appears to hold true for their
women. Of the most frequently used twenty-one names amongst White females,
Black female slaves in the eighteenth century use four, free Black females
in the same period use eight, female slaves in the nineteenth century use
nine and free Black women in the same period use twelve out of twenty-one.
So it appears true for females, although more so for males, that the passage
of time sees Blacks acquiring nomenclature more similar to that of Whites
and that free Blacks move in this direction faster than slaves.

As long as a farmer had but five or six mules, <u>Betty</u>, <u>Fanny</u>, <u>Matilda</u> or
<u>Henry</u> would serve fairly well as titles, but on plantations with more abundant
mule-power, we find appearing on the records such secondary descriptions as
<u>Young Beck</u>, <u>Old Dick</u>, <u>Little John</u>, <u>Big Kitt</u>, <u>Yellow Jim</u>, <u>Leader Kit</u> and even
such regular surnames in muledom as <u>Jane Henkel</u>, <u>Sam Nelson</u> and <u>Pol Jones</u>,
which may or may not have been patterned after the surname of the owner.
Similar secondary descriptions appeared in the lists of slave names.

A glance at the development of secondary distinctions in English history
will shed light on this tendency. In the eleventh century the majority of
people in England had but a single name, but with the rise of large towns and
a growing country population, it became increasingly difficult to identify an
individual with only one name.[28] Hence, by the end of the twelfth century it

---

*Not among 106 names with a frequency of 5 or more.

[28]Bowman, <u>op. cit.</u>, p. 5.

Names, Slave and Free: 1800-1864

had become exceptional for a person to lack an official description or surname.[29] These were at first of secondary importance, being placed after the
fontname. They were derived mainly from such various sources as the individual's personal appearance, his place of residence, parentage and occupation,
and it was not uncommon for a person to have several such additions. Secondary
appellatives, first noticed as hereditary in 1267, gradually became recognized
as family names, and eventually became more important than the forename.[30]

A very similar situation existed among American Black slaves. The development of names among slaves followed essentially the same pattern as that
of surnames in early England if we include another category, that of ownership, the freed slave taking in many cases the surname of his former owner.
"For example, in 1831 Sophia, the property of Eli Fenn, was freed and given
the name of Sophia Fenn...."[31] Just as one might suspect, very often Blacks,
when freed not by their master, took surnames which did not reflect their
former relationship. Of the list of surnames taken after the Civil War by
Blacks from the same plantation, only one chose the name of his former owner
(Jones). The surnames were apparently added to the given name in the plantation records at a later date. Evidence to support this lies in the fact that
the ink used for recording these was of a different kind. It is interesting
to note the wide variety of surnames used by Blacks coming from the same
plantation.[32]

Niger Brown	Eli Verdier
Spencer Jackson	Anthony Golphine
Jackson Quinton	Cato Ash
Richard Nellicliff	Robert Yeomans
Joe Thompson	Winter Baker
Ben Wallace	Primus Goodwin
O. Simon Marshall	Ancil Pinckney
Charles Howard	O. Sam Jones

In Johnson Vs. Field (La., 1827) it was ruled, "Slaves being men, are to
be identified by their proper names...and when there are two or more of the
same name, by some other, which distinguishes them in relation to physical,
or, perhaps, moral qualities."[33] But one suspects here, as in many another
situation, that the law reflects rather than directs human activity. It seems
likely that the great influx of slave labor forced white owners to distinguish
more fully between one slave and another. "As slaves, each had as a rule but
a single name (Andrew, Barrack, Brave Boy, Caesar, England, Esau, Isham, Isha-
mel, Polydore, Profit); but when there were two or more of the same name, distinction was made by adding a parent's name (Nancy Isham, Nancy Flora), or a

---

[29]Ewen, op. cit., p. 218.

[30]Ibid., pp. 47, 90-92, 218-219.

[31]Ralph B. Flanders, Plantation Slavery in Georgia (Chapel Hill, N. C.,
1933), p. 250. From Acts of the General Assembly, 1831, pp. 225-226.

[32]Phillips and Glunt, Florida Plantation Records, G. N. Jones Plantation, 1834-35, p. 33.

[33]Caterall, op. cit., III, p. 482.

Names, Slave and Free: 1800-1864

surname which was sometimes that of a preceding owner (Prince Habersham, Ben Jackson, John Sails, Mary Cain, Nancy Harris), or by prefixing an adjective (Big Ben, Short-foot Billy, Old Joe, Black Maria, Little Marie, Young Polly)."[34]

But in 1831, in Louisiana, we find that "the slaves had so many sobriquets, and were known by so many names that...embarrassment remains, from the designation in the deeds, not corresponding."[35] Into the property records crept a great many aliases in an effort to identify slaves more exactly. Some were simply diminutives, as Alexander or Aleck, Alice or Else, Appling or App, Charlotte or Lotty, Doritha or Doll, Francis or Franky, Simon or Si, Sucky or Susan. Others possibly represent differences due to transfer of ownership and change of name, as Clara or Hager, Henrietta or Mary, John or Jupiter, Juba or Jupiter. Still others represent nicknames, as Anthony or Nig, and Old Nat, commonly called Capt. Nat.

Secondary names became almost a necessity on the larger plantations.[36] In the will of Nathanel H. Hooe (Louisiana, 1844), three slaves named Bill were distinguished as Blacksmith Bill, Billy Monroe and Bill Beverly.[37] Age was often made a basis for such distinctions, and in the slave lists we find such descriptions as Old Isaac, Young Ned, Old Man Peter, Granny Sarah, James the Babe, Andrew (7 yrs.), Paul (born March, 1839) and Benty (purchased Feb'y, 1837). The terms "big" and "little," which were used very frequently, usually referred to age rather than to physical size, and sometimes led to such curiosities as Big Patience and Little Patience (Mississippi, 1838). In England, even as late as 1545, the will of John de Gyton refers to his two sons as "Olde John" and "Young John," and "John the Bigg" is used in other instances.[38] In France, such names as Grandjacques and Petitjean were fairly common.[39] Personal traits other than age also served to distinguish between slaves, as in the cases of Jack (short), Jenny (blind), Miley (prime), Long, Poll and possibly Blush, Billy. Reference is made to Mulatto, Will or Will, Brown, and to Yellow, Jane, and color may even have given rise to an actual surname in the case of John, Mulatto or Joe, Creole. Location figures in such names as Guinea, Jack, Kentucky, Tom, Prairie, Jim (possibly from the prairie section of Mississippi), Columbia, Bitsey (from Columbia, Mississippi?), and perhaps, John, Kentuck. On the plantation of John Palfred in Louisiana, in 1807, American, Hercules "was so styled to distinguish him from an African of the same name."[40] America, a name in use in England four centuries ago,[41]

---

[34]Phillips and Glunt, op. cit., p. 33.

[35]Caterall, op. cit., III, pp. 493-494.

[36]See Chapter I, footnote 14.

[37]Caterall, op. cit., III, p. 315.

[38]Bardsley, op. cit., p. 4.

[39]Weekley, op. cit., p. 59.

[40]Phillips, Life and Labor in the Old South, p. 293.

[41]Bardsley, op. cit., p. 212.

was a fairly common name among female slaves and also occurs with modern Blacks.

Occupation and working ability served as a basis for many secondary distinctions among slaves, as in the cases of Tinker, Jack, Isaac, the Potter, Preaching, Dick, Captain (Chimney Sweep), George (carpenter), Fortune (Head Bird Minder with Gun), Stephney (best ploughman), John (Driver), Clary (Plantation Cook), Dolly (in house), and Miller, Joshua (at mill). Ben, Shipman and Isaac, Butcher may conceivably have derived their surnames from occupations as truly as did the early English Cooks, Fishers or Smiths. Genealogical relationships were sometimes noted, e.g., Rose's, Giney, Ann (Mingoe's mother), Pompey (Phillis's son), Katrina's, York, Jenny's, Dolly, and in some instances these maternal[42] descriptives may have laid the basis for a true surname, such as Julianna, Eliza or Lindsey, Walton (son of Lindsey). With an increase in numbers came a need for still further differentiation, and we find a few cases of double distinctions, e.g., Black, Fat, Eliza's, Rattra (child), Old, Penny, Boon and Old, Penny at Mill, Old, Cook, Woman, Jinny. The case of "Old Woman named Little Mary" shows that the childhood distinction of "Little" was sometimes difficult to shake off in later life. These double distinctions, all from Mississippi after 1840, give some indication of the need for actual surnames.

"Even during slave days the surname of the master was used for identification purposes among servants...'Who dat?' you say. 'Dat William Dunbar.' 'An' you know he b'long to di Dunbars.'"[43] Thus Matilda, Davis was the slave of Thomas Davis (Kentucky, 1855), William Isaac Rawlings (Tennessee, 1837), was the son of his master Isaac Rawlings by a slave mother, and Isaac of Cowling (Virginia, 1800) belonged to Thomas Cowling. In the cases of Jane Harper, owned by a Mr. Wallis, and of Mary Harry, owned by the McCants, the surname was probably that of a former owner. In some instances, a double name may have been amalgamated into a single one by an owner or overseer. Thus Jimboon (Mississippi, 1840) might originally have been Jim Boone.

With freedom, these simple distinctions of slavery days were naturally expanded. Romeo Jones now signed his name Romey O. Jones, and Pericles Smith becomes Perry Clees Smith. A boy who had always been known as Polly's Jim, having learned to read the New Testament, became Mr. Apollo's James.[44] Slave Sam of Mississippi became Sam Buck when his master acquired another Sam, but under the exhilaration of freedom he expanded into Sam Buck Jeemes Ribber Highoo.[45] Corinthia Marigold Wilkinson Ball Wemyss Alexander Jones Mitchell owed her collection of names to the fact that she had been owned successively by half a dozen families and after Emancipation took the names of them all.[46]

[42]The slave child in many cases had little or no contact with his father, who might be unknown to him or be living on some other plantation. For illustrations, see Frazier, op. cit., p. 228.

[43]Armstrong, op. cit., p. 60.

[44]J. B. Harrison, "Studies in the South," Atlantic Monthly, L (1882), p. 447.

[45]Informant: Colonel W. A. Love, Columbus, Mississippi.

[46]D. Macrae, The Americans at Home, 2 vols. (Edinburgh, 1870), II, p. 332.

BLACK NAMES IN AMERICA

Names, Slave and Free: 1800-1864

Of the free Blacks in the South the surnames of 13,129 Blacks were collected (see Source List L). And in spite of the vagaries described above, the following list suggests the direction taken by most Blacks during the period in the South before the Civil War.

Following is a list of the fifty most popular White surnames in order of frequency. The number after the name represents the position of that name amongst the most popular free Black surnames (see Source List L).

Jones 1	Simmons 98	Parker 62
Smith 4	Mitchell 12	Harrison 61
Williams 10	Evans 11	Miller 52
Davis 24	Gray 51	Phillips 86
Moore 18	Griffin 40	Cox 105
Hill 14	White 15	Green 21
Brown 5	Wilson 8	Kelly 53
Wright 43	Clark 59	Wood 74
Johnson 3	Jackson 6	Adams 80
Carter 9	Hall 56	Cooper 33
Harris 7	Allen 28	Robertson 67
Johnston 31	Powell 71	Willis 120
Walker 45	Roberts 30	Young 54
Taylor 39	Rogers 131	Ward 132
Edwards 72	Brooks 104	Hart
Martin 25	Lewis 20	(not on Black list)
Baker 44	Turner 26	King 35

Of the first ten most popular surnames among Whites it appears that six are identical with the list of most popular free Black surnames; of the first twenty-five names on the White list, twelve are repeated on the list of most frequently used twenty-five Black names, and of the first fifty surnames among Whites, twenty-nine appear on the list of most popular fifty Black surnames. It seems clear that Black surname practice was at that point in time very similar to White surname usage. This is true as well, as we have seen, for given name usage.

The following list, drawn from Woodson,[47] reflects the 100 most common free Black surnames for the entire country, including the 13,129 Southern free Black surnames. It is derived from an examination of 37,519 names in all. Following is an alphabetical listing showing frequency of usage and rates per 100,000; a second list offers the frequency of usage and a second number in parentheses which reflects

---

[47] Carter G. Woodson, Free Negro Heads of Families in the United States in 1830 (Washington, D. C., 1925).

Names, Slave and Free: 1800-1864

that name's frequency position amongst the first 152
Southern free Black names. NSL means that the name was
not on the Southern list.

Alphabetical Listing

Adams	114	304	James	136	362
Alexander	51	136	Jenkins	84	224
Allen	145	386	Johnson	830	2212
Anderson	279	744	Jones	601	1602
Bailey	74	197	Jordon	47	125
Baker	73	195	King	98	261
Banks	72	192	Lee	128	341
Barnes	40	107	Lewis	98	261
Bell	104	277	Lucas	70	187
Brooks	86	229	Martin	121	322
Brown	753	2007	Mason	83	221
Butcher	38	101	Miller	241	642
Butler	215	573	Mitchell	101	269
Campbell	54	144	Moore	201	536
Carter	147	392	Murray	46	123
Clark	124	330	Myers	41	109
Coleman	51	136	Parker	121	322
Collins	143	381	Patterson	66	176
Cooper	149	397	Perry	38	101
Cox	49	131	Phillips	58	155
Davis	289	770	Pierce	60	160
Dixon	43	115	Porter	51	136
Edwards	62	165	Price	77	205
Fisher	74	197	Reed	85	227
Franklin	42	112	Richardson	112	298
Freeman	316	842	Roberts	166	442
Gardner	61	163	Robinson	149	397
Gibson	73	195	Rogers	54	144
Gordon	30	80	Ross	56	149
Grant	34	91	Russell	46	123
Gray	101	269	Saunders	39	104
Green	255	680	Scott	341	909
Griffin	77	205	Simmons	63	168
Hall	162	432	Smith	718	1913
Hamilton	42	112	Stevens	39	104
Harris	298	794	Stewart	146	389
Hawkins	83	221	Taylor	151	402
Henderson	42	112	Thomas	313	834
Henry	106	282	Thompson	349	930
Hill	192	512	Tucker	34	91
Holland	48	128	Turner	141	376
Holmes	47	125	Walker	89	237
Hopkins	54	144	Ward	64	171
Howard	103	274	Washington	52	139
Hunter	40	107	Watkins	43	115
Jackson	697	1858	Watson	63	168

Names, Slave and Free: 1800-1864

West 72 192
White 201 536
Williams 666 1775
Willis 30 80

Wilson 296 789
Wood 69 184
Wright 137 365
Young 122 325

Frequency Listing

Johnson 830 (3)
Brown 753 (5)
Smith 718 (4)
Jackson 697 (6)
Williams 666 (10)
Jones 601 (1)
Thompson 349 NSL
Scott 341 (2)
Freeman 316 (13)
Thomas 313 NSL
Harris 298 (7)
Wilson 296 (8)
Davis 289 (24)
Anderson 279 (17)
Green 255
Miller 241 (52)
Butler 215 (32)
Moore 201 (18)
White 201 (15)
Hill 192 (14)
Roberts 166 (30)
Hall 162 (58)
Taylor 151 (39)
Cooper 149 (33)
Robinson 149 (57)
Carter 147 (9)
Stewart 146 (23)
Allen 145 (28)
Collins 143 (16)
Turner 141 (26)
Wright 137 (43)
James 136 (22)
Lee 128 (70)
Clark 124 (59)
Young 122 (54)
Martin 121 (25)
Parker 121 (62)
Adams 114 (80)
Richardson 112 (27)
Henry 106 (74)
Bell 104 (38)
Howard 103 (69)
Gray 101 (51)
Mitchell 101 (12)
King 98 (35)

Lewis 98 (20)
Walker 89 (45)
Brooks 86 (104)
Reed 85 (42)
Jenkins 84 (47)
Hawkins 83 (55)
Mason 83 (56)
Griffin 77 (40)
Price 77 (64)
Bailey 74 (34)
Fisher 74 NSL
Baker 73 (44)
Gibson 73 (73)
Banks 73 (37)
West 72 (46)
Lucas 70 (29)
Wood 69 (76)
Patterson 66 (66)
Ward 64 (132)
Simmons 63 (98)
Watson 63 (133)
Edwards 62 (72)
Gardner 61 (147)
Pierce 60 (78)
Phillips 58 (86)
Rose 56 NSL
Campbell 54 (63)
Hopkins 54 (130)
Rogers 54 (131)
Washington 52 (110)
Alexander 51 (99)
Coleman 51 (49)
Porter 51 (84)
Cox 49 (105)
Holland 48 (116)
Holmes 47 (68)
Jordon 47 (41)
Murray 46 (141)
Russell 46 (75)
Dixon 43 (65)
Watkins 43 (79)
Franklin 42 (113)
Hamilton 42 (114)
Henderson 42 (102)
Myers 41 NSL

Names, Slave and Free: 1800-1864

Barnes 40 NSL	Perry 38 NSL
Hunter 40 (122)	Grant 34 (121)
Saunders 39 (108)	Tucker 34 (109)
Stevens 39 (103)	Gordon 30 (81)
Butcher 38 (77)	Willis 30 (120)

Of the first ten surnames, seven used by Southern free Blacks are incorporated into the nationwide list. Thompson and Thomas, seventh and tenth on the main list, are not found amongst Southern free Blacks at all, nor does Freeman, a most exhilarating surname, appear in the first ten of Southern free Blacks, coming thirteenth.

Another dramatic shift seems to involve the elevation of Johnson and Brown by Northern free Blacks at the expense of Jones and Scott. And amongst the first twenty names throughout the country Miller and Butler, sixteenth and seventeenth, find great favor with free Northern Blacks, having been fifty-second and thirty-second, respectively, amongst Southern free Blacks.

From the 38th Congress, 1st session (1863-64), House Executive Document No. 42, Vol. IX, pp. 17-74, come the surnames of 2,758 freed slaves in Washington, D. C., in 1864 (see Source List M).

The following list reflects the popularity of the fifty-three most frequently used surnames by these Blacks freed in 1864 in Washington, D. C. in terms of Southern free Blacks, Southern Whites and all free Blacks in the United States between 1800 and 1860. The number after each name indicates that name's popularity amongst these groups. NL means that the name was not on the list (see Source Lists L, M).

Blacks Freed in 1864	Southern Free Blacks	Southern Whites	All Free Blacks
Brown	5	7	2
Johnson	3	9	1
Lee	NL	NL	33
Smith	4	2	3
Thomas	NL	NL	10
Clarke	NL	NL	NL
Butler	32	NL	17
Jackson	6	15	4
Jones	1	1	6
Carter	9	10	26
Simms	NL	NL	NL
Steward	NL	NL	NL
Williams	10	3	5
Shorter	NL	NL	NL
Hawkins	NL	NL	51
Dorsey	NL	NL	NL

Names, Slave and Free: 1800-1864

Blacks Freed in 1864	Southern Free Blacks	Southern Whites	All Free Blacks
Taylor	39	14	23
West	46	NL	NL
Bell	38	NL	41
Carrol	NL	NL	NL
Green	21	40	15
Bowie	NL	NL	NL
Brooke	NL	NL	NL
Forrest	NL	NL	NL
Davis	24	4	13
Fletcher	NL	NL	NL
Gray	51	35	43
Ross	NL	NL	NL
Young	NL	47	35
Tyler	NL	NL	NL
Hall	NL	16	22
Washington	NL	NL	NL
Waters	NL	NL	NL
Allen	28	17	28
Bruce	NL	NL	NL
Hutchinson	NL	NL	NL
Snowden	NL	NL	NL
Wallace	48	NL	NL
Coleman	49	NL	NL
Curtis	NL	NL	NL
King	35	50	45
Lancaster	NL	NL	NL
Lewis	20	22	46
Mathews	NL	NL	NL
Bealle	NL	NL	NL
Diggs	NL	NL	NL
Dodson	NL	NL	NL
Mason	NL	NL	52
Brisco	NL	NL	NL
Cole	NL	NL	NL
Holmes	NL	NL	NL
Meredith	NL	NL	NL
Smallwood	NL	NL	NL

Clarke, sixth in popularity amongst freed Blacks in Washington, D. C., does not appear on the other lists, but Clark finds favor with Southern Whites and appears on that list in thirty-ninth place, and Blacks throughout the nation employ Clark frequently, as it appears in thirty-fourth place on that list. Steward, twelfth on the list of freed Washington, D. C. Blacks, does not appear on the other lists, but Stewart does, appearing twenty-third amongst free Southern Blacks and twenty-seventh amongst all Blacks; it does not find favor with Southern Whites. In addition, Brooke, twenty-third, amongst Washington, D. C. freed Blacks, but not listed with other groups, appears as Brooks among Southern Whites and all free Blacks, coming twenty-first and

Names, Slave and Free: 1800-1864

forty-eighth, respectively, although not employed by Southern free Blacks. Variations in spelling seem to account for the difference in usage of the surnames Clark and Stewart, and perhaps this along with variations in pronunciation holds true for Brooks as well.

Of the ten most popular surnames employed by these freed Blacks in 1864, six are found amongst the ten most popular surnames of free Blacks from 1800-1860 throughout the country. Brown and Johnson, first and second amongst the Washington group, appear on the nationwide list with Johnson first and Brown second. It seems that although the Washington group has reversed the order of popularity of these two names, the frequency figures tend to support the belief that the Washington group reflected accurately the enormous popularity of these two surnames amongst Blacks in every part of the country.

Of these ten most popular Washington, D. C. surnames, six also appear amongst Southern free Blacks, and five appear amongst Southern Whites. The following are lists of the ten most popular surnames found amongst these four groups (see Lists L, M).

Blacks Freed in 1864	Southern Free Blacks	Southern Whites	All Free Blacks
Brown	Jones	Jones	Johnson
Johnson	Scott	Smith	Brown
Lee	Johnson	Williams	Smith
Smith	Smith	Davis	Jackson
Thomas	Brown	Moore	Williams
Clarke	Jackson	Hill	Jones
Butler	Harris	Brown	Thompson
Jackson	Wilson	Wright	Scott
Jones	Carter	Johnson	Freeman
Carter	Williams	Carter	Thomas

Lee and Butler stand out as surnames found only, with any great degree of popularity, amongst Blacks in the Washington, D. C. area. Perhaps the fame of Confederate generals impressed itself upon Blacks who received freedom from the enemy of those Confederate heroes.

Of the unusual names from the list of 3,224 freed Washington, D. C. Blacks in 1864, 1,324 are males and 1,900 are females (see Source List M). There are 142 unusual male names in all, or 10.7 per cent. Excluding such names as Ananias, Cato, Judah and Tobias, which can be considered old-fashioned rather than unusual, a total of 57, there are left 85 names intrinsically unusual, or 6.4 per cent. For females, out of 1,900 persons there are 307 unusual names with 220 considered old-fashioned. This leaves a total of 87 unusual names, or 4.6 per cent. Males and females together employed 172 unusual names, or 4.6 per cent.

Male slaves in the eighteenth century show a rate of unusualness of 25.36 per cent; in the nineteenth century, i.e., 1800-1860, the rate drops to 9.52 per cent, and amongst the freed Washington, D. C. Blacks the rate drops even

Names, Slave and Free: 1800-1864

lower to 6.4 per cent. However, free Blacks in the eighteenth century employ
unusual names at a rate of 13.64 per cent, and in the nineteenth century the
rate increases to 16.10 per cent. It appears that males in the Washington,
D. C. area were less prone to adopt unusual names than Blacks who were freed
prior to 1860. Female slaves in the eighteenth century used unusual names at
a rate of 18.09 per cent; in the nineteenth century the rate drops to 9.79
per cent, and amongst the freed Washington, D. C. females the rate drops to a
very low 4.6 per cent. Free females in the eighteenth century employed unusual names at a rate of 15.23 per cent; in the nineteenth century the rate
increases to 22.31 per cent. Like males, then, the freed Black females in the
Washington, D. C. area were less prone to use unusual names than their freed
sisters of the earlier period.

The pattern established in the nineteenth century amongst free Blacks apparently changes in Washington; free Black males employ a lesser percentage
of unusual names than do females. However, males and females combined show
the lowest rate of unusual names in Washington, D. C. than at any previous
time.

Most of the unusual names employed by freed Blacks in the Washington area
can be easily traced back to previous groups. Cagy, for example, can be found
amongst the random sample of unusual names of free Blacks throughout the
country in 1830 (see Source List J), and German is an unusual name found
amongst New England free Blacks. For the females, Binah is found amongst
slaves in the nineteenth century, and Zilphia is found amongst free Black females in New England in the first half of the nineteenth century.

It is interesting to note that Ignatius and Noble are found only amongst
White males in Georgia, 1790-1818 (see Source List K); they are not found with
any other Black group save the Washington, D. C. males. The females' unusual
name Acquilla is found only with White females in Georgia, 1790-1818; Avonia
is found amongst White unusual names in Colonial Massachusetts, as is Sophronia (spelled Saphronia). These three unusual names found amongst free Black
females in Washington, D. C. do not appear with any other Black group; they
appear only in White name lists.

The following is a listing of those male and female
unusual names in the Washington, D. C. area which seem to
have no precedents in earlier groups, Black or White (see
Source List M).

Male, Unusual, Washington, D. C.

Aloysius	Lamertine
Boker	Loretto
Bosquet H'Y Shorter	Marshack
Feudal	Otho
Floreed	Protus
Kaliski	Reverdy
	Steptoe

Names, Slave and Free: 1800-1864

Female, Unusual, Washington, D. C.

Aldezena
Ariana
Arilla
Bohemia
Chia
Chissa
Delozier
Fatina

Genora
Henny
Hortensi
Landonina
Lishy
Mazella
Valinda
Verlinda
Zora

Finally, we might note some unusual features of the use of Junior amongst Black females granted freedom in Washington, D. C. There are four incidences of the use of Junior among females: Kitty Taylor, Jr.; Mary Carroll, Jr.; Mary Butler, Jr.; and Ellen Covington, Jr. We might also note these two odd combinations: Nellie Jennie and William Williams.

There are listed (see Source List M) 2,758 surnames and 3,224 given names; the discrepancy exists because surnames were not always included in the Congressional listing. The choice of surnames is quite interesting; out of 1,005 petitions for freedom in which the surname of the slave's owner was mentioned, only sixteen Blacks chose the same surname as their former owners. And of these sixteen, five Blacks had been owned by other Blacks. The remainder of the 1,005 petitioners, 989, whose owners' surnames were mentioned in their petitions for freedom chose surnames other than those of their former owners.

Names, Slave and Free: 1800-1864

Source List I: SLAVE BLACK NAMES, 1800-1860[48]

The states which contributed to the list are as follows--the number after the state indicates the number of slave names from that state:

Arkansas 4	Florida 532
District of Columbia 4	Kentucky 589
Missouri 6	Virginia 619
Maryland 57	North Carolina 745
Texas 123	Georgia 821
Alabama 355	Louisiana 1,656
South Carolina 475	Mississippi 7,505
Tennessee 487	Unknown 164

Following is a listing of Black slaves, male and female, in the United States, for the period 1800-1860. The first number after the name indicates the frequency with which the name was used; the second number indicates the rate of usage per 100,000 Black slaves. No number after a name indicates that only one Black slave used that name.

MALE
　Alphabetical (Sample: 7,700)
　Untabulated names have a rate of 12.978 per 100,000.

Aaron 30　389	Alexander 20　260	Amoritt
Abe 12　156	Alfonso 2　26	Amos 22　285
Abel 7　91	Alford 3　39	Ancil
Aberdeen 6　78	Alfred 53　688	Anderson 25　324
Abduhl	Alick 6　78	Andrew 50　649
Abner	Alin	Andy 17　221
Abraham 30　389	Allen 36　467	Angus
Abram 57　740	Aller	Annaky
Absolom 6　78	Allick	Annanias 2　26
Achilles	Allison	Ansel 3　39
Ackerly	Allsip	Anthony 44　571
Adam 34　441	Alonzo 3　39	Antoney 3　39
Addison 7　91	Alphaid	Antonio
Adolphe	Altamont	Antram
Adolphus	Alvest	Antrem
Africa 2　26	Alvin 2　26	Antrim
Ager	Alvis	Apollo
Aham	Amand	Appling
Airdens	Ambrose 10　130	April
Alabama	Amburke	Ara
Albert 30　389	Amces	Arch 4　52
Albinus	America	Archer 4　52
Alec	American Hercules	Archie 2　26
Aleck 8　104	Amis	Archy 6　78
Alex 4　52	Amisteid 2　26	Armisted

---

[48]See References for Source List A.

Names, Slave and Free: 1800-1864 -- SLAVE BLACK NAMES, 1800-1860

Armstead 4 52	Benona	Brit 3 39
Armstid	Benson	Brittum
Armstrong	Benty	Brooks 3 39
Aron 3 39	Beny	Brown 4 52
Arthur 15 195	Berry 11 143	Brutus 6 78
Asa 2 26	Bertrand	Buck 9 117
Asbury 4 52	Beverly 2 26	Bulger
Ashing	Bill 97 1259	Buncum
August 3 39	Billy 54 701	Bunkey
Augustus 5 65	Binga	Buny
Austin 13 169	Bingo	Burgess
Avis	Binkey	Burke
Aylup	Bipy	Burkey
Baal	Bird	Burr
Babert	Birkey	Burrel 2 26
Babtiste	Bishop 2 26	Burrell 5 65
Bacchus	Black Fat	Burt
Bachus	Black Hawk	Burwell 4 52
Bailey	Blair	Bus
Bailley	Blango	Bush
Baldy 2 26	Blender	Butler
Baltimore	Blunt	Butter
Baltissum	Bob 105 1379	Bvely
Bann	Bold	Byas
Bap	Boling	Byron
Baraber	Bond	Cader
Barac	Boney	Caesar 29 376
Barney 2 26	Bonta	Caezar
Barrack	Bonum	Cage
Barry	Booker 2 26	Cager 2 26
Bart 2 26	Boordem	Cain 5 65
Barte	Boreden	Caleb 12 156
Bartee	Boson	Calvin 14 182
Bartlett 4 52	Boston 3 39	Calypso
Bartley	Bosum	Campbell
Basil 2 26	Bowling	Canada
Bass	Boxo	Capity
Battiste	Braboy	Caplain
Battle	Brack	Captain 3 39
Bayley	Bradley	Carney
Bazie	Bradly 2 26	Caro
Bazil	Brag	Carpenter
Bebb	Brandon	Carrell
Bell	Braters	Carroll
Belleford	Brave Boy 2 26	Carter 10 130
Bellommond	Braxton	Case
Bellow	Brent	Cassius
Ben 91 1181	Bresten	Caswell
Benbow	Brigut	Cato 17 221
Bency	Bris	Cavannah
Bendy	Brister	Celim 2 26
Benjamin 11 143	Bristoe	Cesar 4 52

Names, Slave and Free: 1800-1864 -- SLAVE BLACK NAMES, 1800-1860

Chain	Coon	Demarins
Chamb	Cooper 7 91	Demps 2 26
Chance	Corey 2 26	Dempsey 5 65
Chancey	Cornelius 5 65	Dennis 27 350
Chane	Correll	Denny 4 52
Chaney 11 143	Cotteen	Deny
Chang	Coty	Dick 87 1129
Chantis	Courtney	Dicky
Chanty	Cow	Dilas
Charles 155 2011	Crakii	Dock 6 78
Charleston 2 26	Crawford	Doctor 6 78
Charley	Creed	Dodson
Charlton	Crip	Doe
Chary	Crockett	Dolphin
Chat	Crumbo	Donas
Chesley	Crummel	Donelson
Cheslie	Cubet	Dorsey 4 52
Chitt	Cudge 2 26	Dosh
Christian 2 26	Cudgo	Dosly
Christopher 2 26	Cudjo 2 26	Douglas 2 26
Christy	Cudjoe 2 26	Dow 2 26
Cicero 3 39	Cuff	Dowd
Cimon	Cuffee 4 52	Drara
Cinton	Cuffey 3 39	Drew 3 39
Claban	Cuffy 2 26	Dublin 3 39
Claborn	Cummings 2 26	Dudley 6 78
Clabourne	Cupid 4 52	Duke 4 52
Claiborn 2 26	Curtis	Dumas
Claiborne 8 104	Cy	Dunah
Claibourn	Cyrus 14 182	Duncan
Claiburn	Cyfax	Dunney
Clander	Dago	Eaton
Clarence	Dale	Eben
Clark 5 65	Dallas	Edd
Clarke 2 26	Dan 11 143	Eddy 4 52
Claniho	Daniel 68 882	Eden
Clay 8 104	Dann	Edmond 35 454
Clem 4 52	Danny	Edmondson
Clenen	Danrille	Edmun
Clement	Darret	Edmund 6 78
Clinton 3 39	Dave 33 428	Edney
Coateen	Davy 29 376	Edom
Coatney	David 48 623	Edward 22 285
Colbert	Davidson	Edwin 5 65
Coleman 11 143	Davis 2 26	Edwood
Columbus 3 39	Dawson	Egbert 4 52
Comas	Day	Egerton
Conder	Dealy	Eincline
Congo 2 26	Dean	Elbert 4 52
Conky	Dedon	Eldridge
Contee	Dee	Elaxander
Conrad	Delany	Eli 14 182

Names, Slave and Free: 1800-1864 --   SLAVE BLACK NAMES, 1800-1860

Elias 16 208	Fielding 3 39	Gerral
Elijah 16 208	Fiscal Philly	Gib 3 39
Elis	Fisher 2 26	Gifford
Elish	Flanders 5 65	Gilbert 18 234
Elisha 10 130	Flemming	Giles 12 234
Elizah	Florence	Gill 2 26
Elizus	Floyd 2 26	Gilly
Ellic 4 52	Foard	Gilmer
Ellick 35 454	Fodder	Gim
Ellis	Fortune 6 78	Gingo
Elup	Foster	Giverson
Elusher	Fountain 3 39	Glasgow 4 52
Elvoid	Francesco	Gloster
Ely	Francis 6 78	Godfrey 2 26
Emanuel 11 143	Frank 74 960	Godson
Ember	Franklin 3 39	Golding
Emmerson	Fravas	Goodson
Emory	Frazur	Gorr
England	Fred 6 78	Goservar
Enoch 6 78	Freden	Gosh
Enox	Ferdinand 12 156	Gosport
Ephriam 26 337	Freeman 4 52	Governor
Ephrim	Freling	Graham
Erasmus	Frelingheizsen	Grandison 5 65
Erie	Fremon	Grant
Ernest	French 3 39	Granville
Erwin	Freno	Green 25 324
Esau 2 26	Frenoli	Greenburg
Esaw	Friby	Grey
Esop	Friday 8 104	Griffin 6 78
Esquire	Fute	Grizzy
Essex 11 143	Gabe 7 91	Grunderson
Eugene 2 26	Gabriel 14 39	Grundy
Evan	Gadson 3 39	Gruss
Evans 3 39	Gage	Guilford 3 39
Everett	Galilee	Gulliah 2 26
Exom	Gallon	Gus 2 26
Ezekiel 5 65	Gambo	Gustus 2 26
Fab	Ganibo	Guy
Fabby	Ganza	Hacaliah
Faro	Ganzo	Haiden
Fayette 4 65	Garisan	Hal 3 39
Feb	Garland	Hall
Febber	Garnett	Hallary
Fed 6 78	Garrard	Ham 2 26
Felix 8 104	Garrat	Hambleton 3 39
Fell	Garrison 2 26	Hamet
Fenton	Garry	Hamlet
Ferdinand	General 4 52	Hamp
Fering	General Washington	Hampton 5 65
Ferreby	Genus	Han
Fielden	George 221 2868	Handen

73

Names, Slave and Free: 1800-1864 -- SLAVE BLACK NAMES, 1800-1860

Handy 2 26	Howard 9 117	Jent
Hannibal 7 91	Hubbard 2 26	Jenz
Hansel	Huger	Jepe
Hansen	Hugh	Jepey
Happy 2 26	Hughey	Jeremiah 2 26
Herbert	Humphrey 3 39	Jerome 3 39
Harculos	Hunt	Jerrimy
Hardtimes	Hunter	Jerry 57 740
Hardy 17 221	Ian	Jersey
Harise	Ihurad	Jerusha
Harman 2 26	Ike	Jess 5 65
Harper 3 39	Ira	Jesse 43 558
Harris	Irvey	Jethro
Harrison 15 195	Irvin 2 26	Jiles 2 26
Harry 80 1038	Isaac 94 1220	Jilson
Harty	Isaiah 5 65	Jiltson
Harvey 6 78	Isam 3 39	Jim 150 1946
Hasty 2 26	Isare	Jimboon
Hatten	Isham 16 208	Jimboy
Hayden 2 26	Ishmael 5 65	Jimmey 2 26
Hayes	Ishmel 2 26	Jimmy 8 104
Hayward 2 26	Ishum	Jo 2 26
Healen	Isiah 2 26	Job 6 79
Heary	Isom 2 26	Joe 122 1583
Hector 10 130	Israel 4 52	Johann
Hemutal	Isum 3 39	John 295 3828
Henderman	Ive	Johnny 5 65
Henderson 18 234	Iverson 3 39	Johnson
Henly	Jack 140 1817	Johnston 2 26
Henny	Jackey	Jonas 10 130
Henson	Jacko	Jonathan
Henry 260 3374	Jackson 21 272	Jordan 21 272
Herbert	Jacksoney	Joseph 19 247
Hercules 5 65	Jacob 77 999	Josh 5 65
Hermon	Jacosin	Joshua 15 195
Hernie	Jake 17 221	Josiah 7 91
Herter	James 86 1116	Jub
Heyward	January 4 52	Juba 4 52
Hezekiah 2 26	Jarrett	Jube 2 26
High	Jarrott 2 26	Juber
Hill	Jasby	Jubice
Hillard	Jason 2 26	Jubis
Hinson	Jasper 6 78	Jubiter
Hinton 2 26	Jayly	Juble
Hiram 3 39	Jeff 25 324	Juby
Holland 6 78	Jeffers	Judah 4 52
Hollon	Jefferson 14 182	Judge 5 65
Honey	Jeffoy	Judin
Horace 9 117	Jeffrey	Judson
Horation 4 52	Jeffro	Julian
Hosea	Jemmy 2 26	Julius 13 169
Hover	Jennings	July 6 78

Names, Slave and Free: 1800-1864 -- SLAVE BLACK NAMES, 1800-1860

Junior	Leonard 2 26	Mangy
Junius 2 26	Levi 7 91	Manuel 11 143
Jupiter 6 78	Levin 4 52	March 7 91
Justine 2 26	Levy 2 26	Marcus
Kadjer	Lew	Marine
Kanko	Lewis 78 1012	Mark 13 169
Keas	Lias	Marke
Kelly	Limbeck	Marlowe
Kennedy	Lige 5 65	Marmaduke
Kertus	Lijah 2 26	Mars 2 26
Ket	Limerick	Marsh 2 26
Kiah	Lindor	Marshall 7 91
Kider	Lindsay	Marson
Kinder	Lindsey 2 26	Martain
Kindy	Littleton 4 52	Martesia
King 8 104	Live	Martin 15 195
Kit 3 39	Lively	Mason 5 65
Kitt 4 52	Liverpool	Mat 5 65
Klar	Lize	Mathias
Knap	Lloyd 2 26	Mathison
Knowledge	London 8 104	Matt 5 65
Kumba	Lonize	Matterson
Lafayette 4 52	Lorenzo	Matthew 3 39
Lake	Lot	Mattimore
Laman 2 26	Louis 7 91	May
Lambert	Lovelace	Mayfield
Lanius	Lowey	McHenry
Lank	Lucas	McTreymone
Lany 2 26	Luck 2 26	Meaken
Lappo	Lucky	Means
Larkin 2 26	Luis	Medoza 2 26
Larry 2 26	Luke 7 91	Megee
Lary	Lum	Merney
Lash	Lurse	Merrick
Last Night	Luturn	Merrill
Laverty	Lymas	Merryman
Lawrence 6 78	Lymon	Meshac
Lawson 2 26	Lymous	Micajah 2 26
Lawyer	Macia Joe	Mice
Lean	Mack 10 130	Michael
Lear	Macon 3 39	Michel
Leathy	Macy	Middleton
Leba	Madison 17 221	Mike 6 78
Lebo	Mado	Milburn
Lee 14 182	Mahalz	Miless 13 169
Lem 16 208	Maitland	Mill
Lemuel 3 39	Major 10 130	Millary
Lemon	Malery	Miller 5 65
Len	Mallica	Milton 4 52
Lenias	Man	Milus 2 26
Lenn 2 26	Mance	Mingo 13 169
Leo	Manga 2 26	Minor

Names, Slave and Free: 1800-1864 -- SLAVE BLACK NAMES, 1800-1860

Minter	Nicholson	Patrick 12 156
Mintz	Nick 10 130	Patt
Missing	Nicker 2 26	Paul 11 143
Missouri	Nicodemus	Payne
Mitchell 5 65	Nicolis	Payton
Monday 6 78	Nig	Peater
Money	Niger	Peck
Monroe 3 39	Nimrod 5 65	Peeter
Montgomery	Noah 6 78	Pelson
Moody	Nolly	Pemberton
Moon	Nonen	Pembroke
Moonrey	Nong	Pender
Moore	Norman 2 26	Penn
Morcel	Norris	Pereson
Morning	Norton	Perine
Morris 9 117	Obadiah	Perry 11 143
Mose 11 143	Obed	Pete 2 26
Mosely	Octo	Peter 135 1752
Moses 96 1246	Oliver 10 130	Peyton 3 39
Munday	Olney	Pharo
Munford 2 26	Onash	Pharoah
Munroe	Oney	Phell
Munrow	Orange 7 91	Phil 34 441
Muss	Organ	Philan
Myal	Orville	Philander 2 26
Myer	Osborn 8 104	Phillip 15 195
Nace 5 65	Osborne	Phinzy
Nael	Osbourn	Phylander
Naise	Osburn	Pickens
Nance 4 52	Oscar 5 65	Pickett
Napoleon 5 65	Osmgon	Pillow
Nat 16 208	Osmon	Pinckney 3 39
Nathan 26 337	Osmond	Plato 3 39
Nathaniel	Osten	Pleas
Natt	Oswego	Pleasant 18 234
Nausea	Ottoway	Pliny
Nazareth	Ottowny	Plummer
Neal	Ovid	Poldo
Neale	Owen 2 26	Pole
Ned 69 895	Packer	Polite
Neece	Page	Polk 3 39
Neel	Pagy	Polute
Neger	Pall 2 26	Pomp
Nehemiah 2 26	Paris 3 39	Pompey 16 208
Nelson 42 545	Park	Pompy
Nero 8 104	Parker 3 39	Pool 2 26
Neuben	Parrot	Porter
Newman	Parry	Potiphar
Newport	Parson	Powell
Newsom 2 26	Parsons	Powhatan
Newton	Pat 6 78	Pressley
Nicholas 6 78	Pateloe	Preston 6 78

Names, Slave and Free: 1800-1864 -- SLAVE BLACK NAMES, 1800-1860

Prickson	Ricker	Saunderville
Primus 19 247	Rickey	Sawney 5 65
Prince 26 337	Rigdon	Scearse
Profit	Riley 5 65	Sceyar
Prophet	Rippin	Scipio 13 169
Providence	Ritter 2 26	Scotland 4 52
Purnell	Rob	Scott 12 156
Quack	Robbin	Seaborn 4 52
Quacko Minisee	Robert 40 519	Seabourn
Quah	Robertson	Seac
Quam 3 39	Robin 15 195	Seanby
Quaminah	Robinson 3 39	Seantry
Quaminy	Rodney 2 26	Seasar 2 26
Quarco	Roland	Semon
Quash 11 143	Rolla 2 26	Seneca
Quay	Roller	Senior
Quico (Quaccoo)	Ronemo	Serard
Quince 2 26	Rooey	Sessee
Quinny	Ross 2 26	Seth
Quintos	Row	Severin
Quomana	Rowden	Seymour
Quominy	Rube	Sezar
Quor	Rubin	Shad 2 26
Racket	Rucker 3 39	Shaderick
Rafe	Rue	Shadrack 8 104
Ralph 10 130	Ruffin 3 39	Sharper
Randall 11 143	Rufus 3 39	Shas
Randel 2 26	Russell 3 39	Shedrick 2 26
Randle 6 78	Rusus	Sheedrick
Randolph 2 26	Saba Quaico	Sheldon
Rane	Sac	Shelton
Ransom 4 52	St. George	Shepherd
Rastin	Salisbury	Sheppard
Ratler	Salsbury 2 26	Sherrod
Rattra	Sam 162 2103	Shields
Ray	Saman	Short
Raymond	Sambo 6 78	Shorum
Reason	Saminy	Sibley
Reddick	Sammy 4 52	Sibyo
Reed	Sampson 18 234	Sicum
Rentor	Samson	Sid
Rep	Samuel 17 221	Sidney 13 169
Resen	Sancho	Silas 7 91
Resin	Sanco	Siles
Reuben 30 389	Sanders	Silgress
Rezin	Sandy 11 143	Sim 3 39
Rial	Sanford 3 39	Simeon 2 26
Rich 2 26	Sango 3 39	Simon 53 688
Richard 20 260	Sanney	Simond
Richardson 3 39	Sanny	Simpson
Richman	Santon	Simson
Richmond 10 130	Saul 2 26	Sinclair

Names, Slave and Free: 1800-1864 -- SLAVE BLACK NAMES, 1800-1860

Sip 3 39	Tartar	Trussvan
Sipio	Taylor 5 65	Tucker
Sipp	Tayton	Tui
Sirar	Teacy	Tull
Skinner	Teams	Tumer
Slivey	Ted 2 26	Tumps
Smart 6 78	Teener	Turner 9 117
Smith 5 65	Tell	Umphrey
Sol 3 39	Telmachus	Umstead
Solimon	Temple 2 26	Uriah 2 26
Solomon 22 285	Terrill	Usly
Somerville	Terry	Valentine
Spence	Thaddeus	Van Buren 2 26
Spencer 15 195	Thadius	Vaughan
Spotswood	Thamil	Vickers
Squash	Theophilus	Vincent 6 78
Squire 9 117	Thereby	Vind
Stacy	Therry	Visa
Stander	Thom	Walker 5 65
Staney	Thomas 28 363	Wallace 4 52
Stanley	Thompson 2 26	Wallice
Stanton	Thornton 6 78	Wallock
Starkey	Thorton 5 65	Wally 2 26
Starling 2 26	Tiller	Walter 6 78
Staten	Tillman	Walton
Station	Tim 2 26	Warley
Staywood	Timothy 4 52	Warner 5 65
Stephen 63 817	Tingo	Warren 12 156
Stephney 2 26	Tink	Warriner
Sterling 3 39	Tinker	Wash 14 182
Steve	Tinsley	Washington 55 714
Steven	Tip	Wasset
Stewart 2 26	Tippo	Watson 2 26
Stokes 3 39	Titus 3 39	Watt 7 91
Stovall	Toby 5 65	Watty 2 26
Strato	Toland	Websha
Strawder	Tolbert	Wellsby
Stroden	Tom 156 2024	Wesley
Stuart	Tommy 5 65	Wesly 15 195
Sucurda	Toney 4 52	West 2 26
Sully 2 26	Tonim	Westley 12 156
Summerset	Tony 11 143	Whatley
Sunna	Toosh	Whit
Surry 2 26	Top	Wilcher
Syke	Town	Wiley 3 39
Sylvester 2 26	Townsend	Wilkinson 2 26
Syphax	Toy	Will 30 389
Syrus 4 52	Tracy	William 126 1635
Syvill	Travis 2 26	Willie 2 26
Tabs	Trim	Willis 38 493
Taffy	Trover	Willoby
Tarlton	Troy 2 26	Willy

Names, Slave and Free: 1800-1864 -- SLAVE BLACK NAMES, 1800-1860

Wilson 8 104	Wyatt 9 117	Zadock
Winchester	Yaff	Zadork
Windsor	Yapt Crud	Zanga
Winfield	Yenix	Zango 2 26
Winston	Yorick	Zank
Winter 3 39	York 16 208	Zanza
Wisdom	Yot	Zediah
Wittum	Young	Zeke
Woodley	Zachariah 2 26	Zephyr
Woodson	Zack 6 78	Zimri
Woodward	Zacko	Zingo
Wright 3 39	Zadoc	Zoomm

Frequency Listing (using 5 as a cut-off point)

John 295	Robert 40	Andy 17
Henry 260	Willis 38	Cato 17
George 221	Allen 36	Hardy 17
Sam 162	Edmond 35	Jake 17
Tom 156	Ellick 35	Madison 17
Charles 155	Adam 34	Samuel 17
Jim 150	Phil 34	Elias 16
Jack 140	Dave 33	Elijah 16
Peter 135	Aaron 30	Isham 16
William 126	Abraham 30	Lem 16
Joe 122	Albert 30	Nat 16
Bob 105	Reuben 30	Pompey 16
Bill 97	Will 30	York 16
Moses 96	Caesar 29	Arthur 15
Isaac 94	Davy 29	Harrison 15
Ben 91	Thomas 28	Joshua 15
Dick 87	Dennis 27	Martin 15
James 86	Ephriam 26	Phillip 15
Harry 80	Nathan 26	Robin 15
Lewis 78	Prince 26	Spencer 15
Jacob 77	Anderson 25	Wesly 15
Frank 74	Green 25	Calvin 14
Ned 69	Jeff 25	Cyrus 14
Daniel 68	Amos 22	Eli 14
Stephen 63	Edward 22	Gabriel 14
Abram 57	Solomon 22	Jefferson 14
Jerry 57	Jackson 21	Lee 14
Washington 55	Jordan 21	Wash 14
Billy 54	Alexander 20	Austin 13
Alfred 53	Richard 20	Julius 13
Simon 53	Joseph 19	Mark 13
Andrew 50	Primus 19	Miles 13
David 48	Gilbert 18	Mingo 13
Anthony 44	Henderson 18	Scipio 13
Jesse 43	Pleasant 18	Sidney 13
Nelson 42	Sampson 18	Abe 12

Names, Slave and Free: 1800-1864 -- SLAVE BLACK NAMES, 1800-1860

Caleb 12	King 8	Pat 6
Ferdinand 12	London 8	Preston 6
Giles 12	Nero 8	Randle 6
Patrick 12	Osborn 8	Sambo 6
Scott 12	Shadrack 8	Smart 6
Warren 12	Wilson 8	Thornton 6
Westley 12	Abel 7	Vincent 6
Benjamin 11	Addison 7	Wakter 6
Berry 11	Cooper 7	Zack 6
Coleman 11	Gabe 7	Augustus 5
Emanuel 11	Hannibal 7	Burrell 5
Essex 11	Josiah 7	Cain 5
Manuel 11	Levi 7	Clark 5
Mose 11	Louis 7	Cornelius 5
Paul 11	Luke 7	Dempsey 5
Perry 11	March 7	Edwin 5
Quash 11	Marshall 7	Ezekiel 5
Randal 11	Orange 7	Flanders 5
Sandy 11	Silas 7	Grandison 5
Tony 11	Watt 7	Hampton 5
Ambrose 10	Aberdeen 6	Hercules 5
Carter 10	Absolom 6	Isaiah 5
Chaney 10	Alick 6	Ishmael 5
Dan 10	Archy 6	Jess 5
Elisha 10	Brutus 6	Johnny 5
Hector 10	Dock 6	Josh 5
Jonas 10	Doctor 6	Judge 5
Mack 10	Dudley 6	Lige 5
Major 10	Edmund 6	Mason 5
Nick 10	Enoch 6	Mat 5
Oliver 10	Fed 6	Matt 5
Ralph 10	Fortune 6	Miller 5
Richmond 10	Francis 6	Mitchell 5
Buck 9	Fred 6	Nace 5
Horace 9	Griffin 6	Napoleon 5
Howard 9	Harvey 6	Nimrod 5
Morris 9	Holland 6	Oscar 5
Randall 9	Jasper 6	Riley 5
Squire 9	Job 6	Sawney 5
Turner 9	July 6	Smith 5
Wyatt 9	Jupiter 6	Taylor 5
Aleck 8	Lawrence 6	Thornton 5
Claiborne 8	Mike 6	Toby 5
Clay 8	Monday 6	Tommy 5
Felix 8	Nicholas 6	Walter 5
Friday 8	Noah 6	Warner 5
Jimmy 8		

Biblical and Puritanical

John 295	Peeter	Isaac 94
Peter 135	Moses 96	James 86

BLACK NAMES IN AMERICA

Names, Slave and Free: 1800-1864 -- SLAVE BLACK NAMES, 1800-1860

Jacob 77
Daniel 68
Stephen 63
Abram 57
Simon 53
Andrew 50
David 48
Anthony 44
Adam 34
Aaron 30
Abraham 30
Reuben 30
Thomas 28
Ephraim 26
Nathan 26
Amos 22
Solomon 22
Solimon
Joseph 19
Sampson 18
Samson
Samuel 17
Elias 16
Elijah 16
Lijah 2
Joshua 15
Josiah 7
Eli 14
Ely
Gabriel 14
Mark 13
Caleb 12
Benjamin 11

Emanuel 11
Manuel 11
Paul 11
Ambrose 10
Elisha 10
Jonas 10
Shadrack 8
Abel 7
Levi 7
Luke 7
Silas 7
Absolom 6
Enoch 6
Job 6
Noah 6
Vincent 6
Cain 5
Ezekiel 5
Isaiah 5
Isiah 2
Ishmael 5
Ishmel 2
Israel 4
Judah 4
Timothy 4
Jerome 3
Lemuel 3
Matthew 3
Titus 3
Thadius 3
Thaddeus
Annanias 2
Asa 2

Christian 2
Esau 2
Esaw
Gulliah 2
Ham 2
Hezekiah 2
Jeremiah 2
Nehemiah 2
Saul 2
Uriah 2
Zachariah 2
Abner
Eden
Galilee
Hosea
Jethro
Jonathan
Jordan
Lot
Meshac
Michael
Nathaniel
Nazareth
Nicodemus
Obadiah
Pharo
Pharoah
Potiphar
Prophet
Rubin
St. George
Steven
Providence
   (Puritanic)

Classical and Literary

Caesar 29
Caezar
Cesar 4
Seasar 2
Sezar
Cato 17
Pompey 16
Cyrus 14
Syrus 4
Julius 13
Julian
Scipio 13
Sipio
Sipp
Sip 3

Hector 10
Horace 9
Nero 8
Hannibal 7
Brutus 6
Jupiter 6
Jubiter
Augustus 5
Hercules 5
Harculos
American Hercules
Cupid 4
Horatio 4
Cicero 3
Plato 3

Mars 2
Ovid 2
Philander 2
Phylander
Achilles
Adolphe
Alexander
Elexander
Baal
Bacchus
Bachus
Byron
Cassius
Dumas
Erasmus

81

Names, Slave and Free: 1800-1864 -- SLAVE BLACK NAMES, 1800-1860

Esop	Marcus	Syphax
Hamlet	Pliny	Telmachus
Hansel	Seneca	Valentine
Justine	Strato	Yorick
Malery	Syke	

Geographic Location

York 16	Pool 2	Gloster
Essex 11	Salisbury	Jersey
Richmond 10	Salsbury 2	Liverpool
London 8	Surry 2	Montgomery
Aberdeen 6	Troy 2	Hill
Holland 6	Alabama	Somerville
Glasgow 4	America	Station
Scotland	Antrim	Summerset
Boston 3	Baltimore	Syvill
Dublin 3	Bristoe	Willoby
Paris 3	Canada	Winchester
Africa 2	England	Windsor
Charleston 2	Erie	

Descriptive, Episodic, Occupational

Green 25	Winter 3	Chance
Primus 19	Brave Boy 2	Chancy
Pleasant 18	Cager 2	Chanty
Hardy 17	Cage	Chat
Robin 15	Handy 2	Coon
Robbin	Happy 2	Cow
Sandy 11	Hasty 2	Creed
Friday 8	Luck 2	Day
March 7	Lucky	Ember
Orange 7	Rich 2	Emory
Fortune 6	Rolla 2	Fiscal Philly
Monday 6	Roller	Foard
Munday	Starling 2	Fodder
Smart 6	April	Genus
Grandison 5	Bird	Grey
Miller 5	Black Fat	Hardtimes
Smith 5	Black Hawk	Healen
Taylor 5	Blunt	High
Brown 4	Bold	Honey
Freeman 4	Boney	Hunter
January 4	Boordem	Jimboy
Ransom 4	Boson	Knowledge
Seaborn 4	Bosum	Lank
Seabourn	Brag	Lash
August 3	Calypso	Last Night
French 3	Capity	Limerick
Pinckney 3	Carpenter	Live
Sterling 3	Chain	Lively
	Chane	

Names, Slave and Free: 1800-1864 -- SLAVE BLACK NAMES, 1800-1860

Man	Pleas	Shepherd
Marsh	Pole	Sheppard
May	Polite	Short
Means	Polute	Shorum
Mill	Pomp	Sicum
Missing	Pompy	Skinner
Money	Porter	Squash
Moody	Ratler	Taffy
Moon	Reason	Tell
Morcel	Resen	Tiller
Morning	Resin	Tillman
Muss	Rezin	Tinker
Niger	Rippin	Tip
Nausea	Row	Top
Octo	Rue	Town
Packer	Sac	Toy
Parrot	Scearse	Trim
Pillow	Sharper	Wisdom
		Young

Titular

Prince 26	Judge 5	Governor
Major 10	Duke 4	Junior
Squire 9	General 4	Lawyer
King 8	Captain 3	Page
Dock 6	Bishop 2	Senior
Doctor 6	Esquire	

Famous

Washington 55	Jefferson 14	Van Buren 2
Wash 14	Napoleon 5	Middleton
George Washington	Lafayette 4	Winston
Madison 17	Columbus 3	

African

Mingo 13	Jubice	Annaky
Quash 11	Jubis	Ara
Sambo 6	Juby	Bann
Nace 5	Kitt 4	Bap
Naise	Kit 3	Barte
Sawney 5	Quam 3	Bartee
Cuffee 4	Sango 3	Bebb
Cuffey 3	Congo 2	Binga
Cuffy 2	Laman 2	Bingo
Cuff	Gill 2	Cavannah
Juba 4	Gulliah 2	Comas
Jube 2	Manga 2	Dago
Jub	Rolla 2	Dunah
Juber	Zango 2	Faro

Names, Slave and Free: 1800-1864 -- SLAVE BLACK NAMES, 1800-1860

Fute	Nong	Sessee
Gambo	Pateloe	Sim
Ganibo	Quaccoo	Sirar
Ganza	Quack	Sunna
Gilly	Quacko Minisee	Tingo
Hamet	Quah	Tippo
Kanko	Quarco	Toosh
Keas	Quay	Visa
Ket	Quico	Zacko
Kiah	(Quaccoo)	Zanga
Kumba	Saba Quaico	Zank
Labo	Saminy	Zanza
Leba	Sanco	Zingo
Mado	Sanney	Zoomm
Mallica	Sanny	

FEMALE
Alphabetical (Sample: 6,442)
Untabulated names have a rate of 15 per 100,000.

Abache			Airey			Angelina	3 44
Abb			Airy			Angeline	5 74
Abba			Alamy			Anika	
Abbe			Alcy	3	40	Anikee	
Abergall	2	30	Aleathea			Anilesa	
Abby	5	74	Alesia			Anky	
Abial			Aley			Ann	95 1409
Abigail			Algo			Anna	16 237
Accoo			Alice	14	208	Annaka	
Ada	3	44	Alley	4	59	Anne	3 44
Adah			Alli			Annetta	
Adalicia			Alline			Annette	
Adaline	41	608	Ally			Annie	3 44
Addela			Almyra	3	44	Anny	5 74
Addie			Alsey	5	74	Anonicat	
Adelaide	2	30	Alvira			Antoinette	4 59
Adele			Alzeria			Antona	
Adella			Ama			Antonia	
Adelle			Amanda	38	564	Aphnah	
Adline			Amelia	12	178	Appa	
Affa			America	9	133	Arabella	6 89
Affey			Amity			Aralanta	
Affiah			Amy	89	1320	Arena	
Agg			Ana	2	30	Arie	
Agga			Anaca	4	59	Armitta	
Aggaby			Anada			Arteta	
Aggy	22	326	Anaka	2	30	Artimesia	2 30
Agnes			Andrinette			Ary	8 119
Agusta			Aneca			Arzilla	
Agy			Aneky			Ascena	
Ails	2	30	Angela			Asy	
Ailsey	3	44	Angelia			Atsey	

Names, Slave and Free: 1800-1864 -- SLAVE BLACK NAMES, 1800-1860

Augusta	Binkey	Cessa
Aunice	Bis	Cessy
Avaline	Bitsey 2 30	Chalath
Avarilla 2 30	Blinda	Chaney
Averline	Bonny	Charity 42 623
Avis	Bridget 3 44	Charlette
Aylsey	Britcha	Charlot
Azilla	Cady 2 30	Charlott 12 178
Azuba	Caledonia 4 59	Charlotte 62 920
Azzy	Callie	Chatt
Babb	Camelia	Chena
Babe	Camilla	Cherry 8 119
Baket	Camille	Cherrylane
Barba	Candes 2 30	Chima
Barbara 2 30	Candis 7 104	Chitta
Barbary 4 59	Candy	Chloe 24 356
Barsilla	Canna	Chris
Barthena	Cardine	Christian
Barzella	Carline 5 74	Christiana
Batsey	Carolina 4 59	Chritianah
Bazilla	Caroline 97 1439	Cicely 2 30
Becca 4 59	Cary	Cicilia
Beccy	Cassey	Cilia
Beck 9 133	Cassie	Cilla 4 59
Becker	Cassilly	Ciller
Becky 25 371	Casy	Cina 2 30
Bela	Cate 9 133	Cind
Belinda	Catey	Cinda 5 74
Bell	Catharina	Cintha
Bella(h) 11 163	Catharine 33 489	Cinthia
Beller	Cathleane	Cit
Bellesames	Cathelln	Claire
Bena	Catie	Clara 13 193
Benadd	Catrane	Clarasy
Benah	Catura	Clarentine
Benetta	Caty 24 356	Clarinda 6 89
Berkey	Ceala	Clarissa 33 489
Bess 9 133	Cealey	Clairssey 4 59
Bessie 3 44	Cealy 2 30	Clary 11 163
Bet 4 59	Cebille	Clemensa
Betsia	Cecilia	Clementina
Betsy 87 1290	Cecillia	Clementine 4 59
Bett	Cela 3 44	Cleonder
Betta 2 30	Celesta	Cloah
Bettie 4 59	Celestia	Coelia
Betty 57 845	Celey	Coffie
Bicky	Celia 25 371	Collia
Biddy 10 148	Cellar	Columbia Bitsy 2 30
Bijah	Cely 5 74	Comelia
Bina 3 44	Cemente	Comfort 2 30
Binah 4 59	Centilla	Coose
Biner 4 59	Ceries	Cora 4 59

Names, Slave and Free: 1800-1864 -- SLAVE BLACK NAMES, 1800-1860

Cordelia	Dianna 4 59	Elenora
Cornelia 3 44	Dibby	Elisa 122 1810
Corrina	Dice 2 30	Elise 2 30
Coteler 2 30	Dicey 8 119	Eliza 2 30
Cotta	Dicy 3 44	Elizabeth 40 593
Creasey	Dido 2 30	Elizas
Creasy 2 30	Die 3 44	Elizer
Creecy 2 30	Dilce	Ella 2 30
Creesy	Dilcy 2 30	Ellen 53 786
Cresa	Diley	Ellender 2 30
Crese	Dilla	Ellie 2 30
Cresy 4 59	Dilly 3 44	Ellinor
Cretia 3 44	Dils	Elmira 4 59
Cricy	Dilsey 3 44	Elsa
Crissy	Dina 6 89	Elsey 13 193
Critty	Dinah 32 475	Elsy 2 30
Cuddy	Dine	Elve
Cuff 2 30	Diner 2 30	Elvia
Cuffee 4 59	Dinne	Elvina 2 30
Cuffey	Docia 2 30	Elvine
Cuffy 2 30	Doll 9 133	Elvira 17 252
Cusha 2 30	Dolley	Emaline 3 44
Cynthia 12 178	Dolly 18 267	Emeline 2 30
Cynthy	Dolphin	Emely 2 30
Daisy	Dorcas 16 237	Emiline 21 311
Dallas	Dorcia 2 30	Emily 70 1038
Daphe	Dorcus 4 59	Emma 19 282
Daphna 2 30	Doritha	Emmeline 2 30
Daphne 5 74	Doshia	Emmellia
Daphney 3 44	Dosia	Emmy
Daphny 3 44	Dru	Ersey
Dasy	Drucilla 2 30	Ester 10 148
Dausey	Dulcinea	Esther 28 415
Davidella	Dyche	Eoy Ann
Deb	Dye	Eugenia
Debby 2 30	Eady 2 30	Eulalie 2 30
Deborah 2 30	Eane	Euphemie
Dehlia	Easter 9 133	Eve 11 163
Delia 20 297	Easther	Eveline 11 163
Delila 5 74	Eba	Evy
Delilah	Ebby 2 30	Fan 5 74
Delitha	Eda 2 30	Fannie 3 44
Delpha	Edith 2 30	Fanny 80 1187
Delphine	Edmonia	Farilda
Delphy 2 30	Edy 16 237	Farina
Delsey 4 59	Effy 2 30	Fay
Dely	Elcy 3 44	Fee
Denara	Eleanor 5 74	Feeby
Desdamona	Eleanora	Fender
Desibri	Elen	Feriby
Di	Elena	Ferina
Diana 7 104	Elenor 2 30	Fernaster

Names, Slave and Free: 1800-1864 -- SLAVE BLACK NAMES, 1800-1860

Ferreby	Harriet 129 1913	Jincey
Fety Ann	Hedy	Jinne
Fibbe	Helen 2 30	Jinnie
Fibby	Henrietta 15 222	Jinn(e)y 17 252
Fil 2 30	Hepsey 2 30	Jinnet
Filis	Hester 22 326	Jinsey
Fill	Hestor 2 30	Jissie
Fillis 3 44	Hesty	Jo 3 44
Fiscal Fanny	Hetty 10 148	Joan Senior
Flarah	Hilly	Joana
Flerah	Holdy	Joaney 3 44
Flora 24 356	Hulda 5 74	Joanna 2 30
Florence 2 30	Huldy	Johanna
Florer	Ibby 2 30	Joice 2 30
Florida 2 30	Icy	Joicy
Florinda 2 30	Ida 2 30	Josephine 10 148
Frances 42 623	Idella	Josey
Francina	Inda 2 30	Juba 5 74
Francis 2 30	India 2 30	Jube 2 30
Frankey 2 30	Indiana 2 30	Juby
Frankie	Indy	Juda 5 74
Franky 4 59	Irena	Jude 8 119
Frinah	Irene	Judea 3 44
Gabby	Iris 2 30	Judith 3 44
Gabi 3 44	Isabel 4 59	Judy 55 816
Genette	Isabella 17 252	Julia 39 578
Genevieve	Isva	Juliana Johnson
Genie	Itse	Julianna Eliza 3 44
George Ann	Izetta	Julie
Georgeanna	Jane 119 1765	Juliet
Georgia 2 30	Janett 3 44	Juliett
Georgiana 3 44	Janey	July 2 30
Georgietta	January	Juna 2 30
Gertrude 2 30	Jany	June 9 119
Gilly	Jeanett	Juner
Gin	Jeanette	Juno 9 119
Gincy 2 30	Jeannet	Kanice
Giney	Jeanny	Kanzada
Ginney 2 30	Jeine	Kasina
Ginny 9 133	Jelia	Kate 24 356
Grace 26 386	Jemima	Katrina 2 30
Gracey 2 30	Jenne	Keria
Gracieuse	Jennett 2 30	Kesiah 2 30
Granny Mack	Jennetta 2 30	Kessiah
Grasey	Jennette	Kettera
Grieg 2 30	Jennie 4 59	Keyah
Gwyn	Jenny 8 119	Keziah 2 30
Hagar 7 104	Jes	Kiah
Hagur	Jessey	Kinah
Halda	Jessy 2 30	Kissee
Hanna 4 59	Jill	Kissiah
Hannah 115 1706	Jin	Kit

Names, Slave and Free: 1800-1864 -- SLAVE BLACK NAMES, 1800-1860

Kitty 43 638	Lindy 3 44	Magdaleen
Kity 2 30	Linn	Magdeline
Kiziah	Linney	Mage
Kizziah	Lisa	Magg
Kizzy 2 30	Liss	Mahala
Klima	Litt	Mahaley
Kora	Litty	Mahaly
Laenia	Livinia	Mahola
Larinda	Liz 2 30	Mahuldy
Laticia	Liza 7 104	Maina
Latitia	Lizar	Maisa
Latria	Lize 3 44	Malinda 34 504
Laura 14 208	Lizee	Malindy
Laurina	Lizy	Malisa
Lavina	Lizza	Malsa
Lavinera	Lizzie 5 74	Malvina 6 89
Lavinia 11 163	Lizzy 9 133	Manah
Leah 13 193	Loosa	Manda 5 74
Leaner	Loosy	Mandana
Leanora	Loretta	Mandy 3 44
Leanna 2 30	Loticia	Manerva
Lear	Lottie	Manna
Leathy	Lotty	Manzy
Leila	Lou	March
Lenah	Louellynn	Marena
Leonora 2 30	Louisa 78 1127	Margaret 66 979
Lerona	Louisiana 2 30	Margaretta
Lesa	Louisianna	Margarette 2 30
Let	Louiza 2 30	Margarita
Letha	Luce	Margery 2 30
Letitia 2 30	Lucinda 54 801	Margrath
Letta 2 30	Lucinyd	Margueritte
Lettia 3 44	Luckey	Maria(h) 178 2640
Lettie 3 44	Lucky 2 30	Mariana 4 59
Lettitia	Lucresha	Mariann
Letty 15 222	Lucretia 8 119	Marie 4 59
Leveny	Lucy 139 2062	Marier
Levinia 2 30	Lueaser	Marietta
Lid	Luida 2 30	Marina 6 89
Liddy 2 30	Luly	Mariner
Lidia	Lundy	Marteria 2 30
Lidy	Luri	Martha 108 1602
Liggina	Lussee	Marthy 2 30
Lila 3 44	Luvenia	Martille
Liley 2 30	Lydia 26 386	Marvel
Lilla 3 44	Lyla	Mary 321 4761
Lillie	Lylla	Marz
Lilly 6 89	Lysa	Matilda 76 1127
Lina	Lytha	Matiler
Lind	Madame	Matta
Linda 9 133	Madeleine	Mattie
Linder 2 30	Madora	Matty 3 44

Names, Slave and Free: 1800-1864 -- SLAVE BLACK NAMES, 1800-1860

Mauria	Moriah	Patient
May 9 133	Morina	Patsy 25 371
Mealey	Morning	Patt 2 30
Mealy 3 44	Motta	Pattie
Melia 81 1201	Mourning	Patty 9 133
Melly	Munny	Pauladore
Melvina 2 30	Muttpuin	Paulina 2 30
Mema	Myra 6 89	Pauline 3 44
Menia	Nan 3 44	Peachy
Merica	Nance 3 44	Peg 5 74
Merilla	Nancy 157 2329	Pegg 2 30
Mernervey	Nanie	Peggy 59 875
Meroh	Nanky	Penelope
Messeniah	Nann	Pennine
Mila	Nannie	Penny 20 297
Milcha	Nanny 17 252	Pheby 6 89
Mildred	Narcissa 3 44	Pheraby
Miley 2 30	Natty 2 30	Pherady
Milla 2 30	Necy 2 30	Phereby
Milley 4 59	Nel	Phibby
Millie	Nell 3 44	Philis 3 44
Mima 14 208	Nelle	Phillis 60 890
Mimey Mann	Nelly 42 623	Phillissia
Mimy 2 30	Netta	Phillisy
Mina	Netty	Philomonia
Minda 4 59	Nicey 3 44	Ph(o)ebe 25 371
Minerva 16 237	Nicy 4 59	Piety
Minervi	Nilla	Pillis
Miney	Nina	Pink
Minna	Nine	Pinna
Minney 2 30	Nona	Pleasant 2 30
Minnie 2 30	Nora(h) 7 104	Plina
Minny 3 44	Notice	Pol
Minty 2 30	Numa	Poll 6 89
Mira 3 44	Nutta	Polly 49 727
Mirah 2 30	Nutty	Polydore
Miranda	Octavia 3 44	Posha
Mirnia	Olivia 3 44	Pounds
Misha	Oll	Preepey
Misourie	Olly	Priscilla 16 237
Miss Martineau	Oney 2 30	Prichanna
Missoney	Opheeler	Prissy 4 59
Missouria	Orasha	Prosper
Mitty 2 30	Orsta	Prudence 7 104
Moll	Palsey	Prudy 4 59
Molly 16 237	Pamela	Prue
Monachee	Pamelia 3 44	Pussy 3 44
Monah	Paralee	Queen 2 30
Monda	Parthena 2 30	Quinn
Mooning	Parthenia 2 30	Rach(a)el 98 1454
Mopsy	Patcey	Rachee
Morgan	Patience 18 267	Rachell

Names, Slave and Free: 1800-1864 -- SLAVE BLACK NAMES, 1800-1860

Rachiel	Salina	Siby
Raechel 2 30	Sall 5 74	Silla 8 119
Ramaiah	Sallie	Siller 6 89
Reanna	Sally 93 1397	Sillva
Rebecca 22 326	Saly	Silva 7 104
Recy	Samantha	Silvey 25 371
Reno	Sambo	Silvia 6 89
Renta	Samy	Sina 3 44
Reny	Sanina	Sinah
Retta	Saphroney	Sinda
Reuta	Saphronia	Sinder
Rhina	Sappo	Sindy 5 74
Rhinor	Sara 3 44	Sinethas
Rhoda 8 119	Sarah 150 2225	Sintha
Rhody 2 30	Saraugh	Sis
Rihna	Sarena	Smiley
Rina 2 30	Sarenah	Sobuty
Rinah	Sariah	Sofa 3 44
Rindy	Sary 15 222	Sofia
Riner	Satera	Sofiah
Riney 2 30	Satere	Soockey
Rintha	Satirah 3 44	Sookey 4 59
Ritta 2 30	Satty	Sooky
Roda 3 44	Savannah 2 30	Sopha 2 30
Rollie	Savinia	Sophia 12 178
Rosa	Savory	Sophie 2 30
Rosalinda	Scamby	Sophy 10 148
Rosaline	Scharlotte	Spice
Rosanna	Scylla	Spicy
Rosannah	Sealey	Spinar
Rose 63 934	Sealy 4 59	Suck 2 30
Roseanna	Seeley	Sucky 8 119
Rosella	Selah	Sucy
Rosetta 6 89	Seley	Sue 6 89
Rosette	Selina	Sukey 21 311
Rosetty	Seller	Sully 2 30
Routh	Selma	Susan 63 934
Rozana	Seloy	Susana
Rozetta 6 89	Selvia	Susanna 2 30
Ruhamah	Sena	Susannah
Ruth 8 119	Senna	Susany
Rutha	Serena 3 44	Susey
Ruthy 2 30	Sethy	Suzan
Sabarah	Sevenia	Sylla 3 44
Sabra 4 59	Sevilla	Sylva 3 44
Sabry	Shamber	Sylvania
Saby	Sharlit	Sylvia 17 252
Sadie	Sharlot	Syrena
Safrona	Sharlott	Szela
Sal	Sharlotte 5 74	Tabb 2 30
Salena 3 44	Sheba	Tabby 2 30
Saley	Sib	Tabitha

Names, Slave and Free: 1800-1864 -- SLAVE BLACK NAMES, 1800-1860

Tamar 5 74	Tona	Vina
Tamer 3 44	Treasy	Viney 4 59
Tandy	Trice	Viny 2 30
Taner	Trusty	Violet 21 311
Tay	Tyra 3 44	Violetta
Tempe 2 30	Tyrah 2 30	Violette
Tempie 2 30	Tyre	Virgin
Tempy 2 30	Unis	Virginia 11 163
Tena	Ursey	Virginie
Tenah 4 59	Ursilla	Viva 2 30
Tenar	Ursley	Viza
Tener 2 30	Venice 2 30	Wenny
Teney 3 44	Vennah	Winn(e)y 31 460
Tennessee	Venus 25 371	Winnia
Tenny	Venie	Winnie 4 59
Tenor 2 30	Verg	Woody
Terese	Veria	Writ
Thamer	Vertie	Wyn
Thena	Vesta	Yanaky
Theodocia	Vevis	Zada
Tibby 2 30	Vic	Zellah
Tildy 2 30	Vicey	Zenobia
Tilla 3 44	Victoria 7 104	Zera
Tiller 3 44	Victory	Zie
Tilly 2 30	Vicy	Zila
Tina 2 30	Vilet 3 44	Zilphy
Tinia	Vilete	Zinda
Tinney	Vilett 4 59	Zinny
Tisha	Villy	Ziphy
		Zody

Frequency Listing (using 5 as a cut-off point)

Mary 321	Matilda 76	Julia 39
Maria(h) 178	Emily 70	Amanda 38
Nancy 157	Margaret 66	Malinda 34
Sarah 150	Rose 63	Catharine 33
Lucy 139	Susan 63	Clarissa 33
Harriet 129	Charlotte 62	Dinah 32
Elisa 122	Phillis 60	Winn(e)y 31
Jane 119	Peggy 59	Esther 28
Hannah 115	Betty 57	Grace 26
Martha 108	Judy 55	Lydia 26
Rach(a)el 98	Lucinda 54	Becky 25
Caroline 97	Ellen 53	Celia 25
Ann 95	Polly 49	Patsy 25
Sally 93	Kitty 43	Ph(o)ebe 25
Amy 89	Charity 42	Silvey 25
Betsy 87	Frances 42	Venus 25
Milly 81	Nelly 42	Caty 24
Fanny 80	Adeline 41	Chloe 24
Louisa 76	Elizabeth 40	Flora 24

91

Names, Slave and Free: 1800-1864 -- SLAVE BLACK NAMES, 1800-1860

Kate 24	Clary 11	Nora(h) 7
Aggy 22	Eve 11	Prudence 7
Hester 22	Eveline 11	Silva 7
Rebecca 22	Lavinia 11	Victoria 7
Emiline 21	Virginia 11	Arabella 6
Sukey 21	Biddy 10	Clarinda 6
Violet 21	Ester 10	Dina 6
Delia 20	Hetty 10	Lilly 6
Penny 20	Josephine 10	Malvina 6
Emma 19	Sophy 10	Marina 6
Dolly 18	America 9	Melinda 6
Patience 18	Beck 9	Myra 6
Elvira 17	Bess 9	Pheby 6
Isabella 17	Cate 9	Poll 6
Jinn(e)y 17	Doll 9	Rosetta 6
Nanny 17	Easter 9	Siller 6
Sylvia 17	Ginny 9	Silvia 6
Anna 16	June 9	Sue 6
Dorcas 16	Juno 9	Abby 5
Edy 16	Linda 9	Alsey 5
Minerva 16	Lizzy 9	Angeline 5
Molly 16	May 9	Anny 5
Priscilla 16	Patty 9	Carline 5
Henrietta 15	Ary 8	Cely 5
Letty 15	Cherry 8	Cinda 5
Sary 15	Dicey 8	Daphne 5
Alice 14	Jenny 8	Delila 5
Laura 14	Jude 8	Eleanor 5
Mima 14	Lucretia 8	Fan 5
Clara 13	Rhoda 8	Hulda 5
Elsey 13	Ruth 8	Juba 5
Leah 13	Silla 8	Juda 5
Agnes 12	Sucky 8	Lizzie 5
Amelia 12	Candis 7	Manda 5
Charlott 12	Diana 7	Pag 5
Cynthia 12	Hagar 7	Sall 5
Sophia 12	Liza 7	Sharlotte 5
Bella(h) 11	Mahala 7	Sindy 5
		Tamar 5

Biblical and Puritanical

Mary 321	Raechel 2	Grace 26
Maria(h) 178	Rachiel	Rebecca 22
Sarah 150	Charity 42	Patience 18
Sara 3	Dinah 32	Dorcas 16
Hannah 115	Dina 6	Darcus 4
Hanna 4	Esther 28	Leah 13
Rach(a)el 98	Ester 10	Eve 11

Names, Slave and Free: 1800-1864 -- SLAVE BLACK NAMES, 1800-1860

Easter 9	Adah	Amity
Jude 8	Judes 3	Christian
Ruth 8	Judith 3	Christiana
Hagar 7	Comfort 2	Christianah
Prudence 7	Deborah 2	Magdaleen
Delila 5	Susanna 2	Magdeline
Delilah	Susannah	Moriah
Juda 5	Susana	Piety
Judah 2	Susany	Sheba
Ada 3	Abigail	Tabitha

Classical and Literary

Clarissa 33	Juno 8	Camilla
Clarissey 4	Lucretia 8	Camille
Celia 25	Lucresha	Clementina
Ph(o)ebe 25	Cretia 3	Corrina
Phoeby 4	Diana 7	Delph
Pheby 6	Dianna 4	Delpha
Venus 25	Myra 6	Delphia
Chloe 24	Mira 3	Delphine
Delia 20	Mirah 2	Delphy 2
Minerva 16	Daphne 5	Desdamona
Minervi	Daphney 3	Dido
Cynthis 12	Daphny 3	Euphemie
Cintha	Daphna 2	Lear
Cinthia	Narcissa 3	Letha
Cynthy	Octavia 3	Marz
Sinethas	Artimesia 2	Polydore
Sintha	Dice 2	Pauladore
Manerva	Dicey 8	Penelope
Mernervey	Dicy 3	Scylla
Lavinia 11	Iris 2	Sylla 3
Levinia 2	Parthenia 2	Silla 8
Livinia	Augusta	Siller 6
Luvinia		Theodocia

Geographic Location

Charlotte 62	America 9	India 2
Charlott 12	Mercia	Indiana 2
Charlot	Mahala 7	Louisiana 2
Charlette	Mahaley	Louisianna
Scharlotte	Mahaly 4	Savannah 2
Sharlit	Clarinda 6	Venice 2
Sharlot	Tamar 5	Dallas
Sharlotte 5	Caledonia 4	Marietta
Malinda 34	Carolina 4	Misourie
Malindy	Elmira 4	Missouria
Melinda 6	Columbia Bitsy 2	Selma
Virginia 11	Ellender 2	Seville
Virginie	Florida 2	Sylvania
	Georgia 2	Tennessee

Names, Slave and Free: 1800-1864 -- SLAVE BLACK NAMES, 1800-1860

Descriptive, Episodic, Occupational

Flora 24	Airey	Morning
Florer	Alley	Mourning
Florah	Arena	Munny
Violet 21	Babe	Nine
Violetta	Cellar	Notice
Violette	Chatt	Nutty
June 9	Cherry	Palsey
Juner	Cherrylane	Patient
May 9	Dye	Peachy
Marina 6	Fiscal Fanny	Pink
Nicy 4	Gabby	Pounds
Nicey 3	Gracieuse	Prosper
Prissy 4	Grasey	Savory
Die 3	Hilly	Sis
Mealy 3	Icy	Smiley
Mealey	Itse	Spice
Tiller 3	January	Spicy
Ails 2	March	Taner
July 2	Mariner	Trusty
Lucky 2	Marvel	Victory
Luckey	Mimey Mann	Virgin
Pleasant 2	Mooning	Woody
Tenor 2	Mopsy	Writ

Titular

Nanny 17	Queen 2	Joan Senior
Nann	Granny Mack	Madame
Nanie		

Famous

Victoria 7	Airy	Zenobia

African

Abb	Anada	Bijah
Abba	Anaka 2	Bina 3
Accoo	Aneca	Binah 4
Ada 3	Aneka	Bis
Adah	Anika	Canna
Affa	Anikee	Catura
Affey	Annaka	Chima
Affiah	Aphnah	Chitt
Agga	Azuba	Chitta
Aley	Azzy	Coffie
Alli	Becca 4	Collia
Ally	Bena	Coose
Ama	Benah	Cotta
Anaca 4	Betta 2	Cuddy

Names, Slave and Free: 1800-1864 -- SLAVE BLACK NAMES, 1800-1860

Cuff 2	Kora	Pinna
Cuffee 4	Loosa	Retta
Cuffey	Mahaly	Rhina
Cuffy 2	Maina	Rihna
Cusha 2	Maisa	Sabarah
Dibby	Malsa	Saby
Eba	Manah	Sambo
Ebby 2	Manda 5	Sanina
Eda 2	Mandana	Sariah
Gabi 3	Manna	Satera
Gilly	Manzy	Selah
Hagur	Matta	Sena
Juba 5	Mema	Senna
Jube 2	Menia	Sib
Juby	Milla 2	Siby
Kanuce	Mina 14	Sina 3
Kesiah 2	Minda 4	Sinah
Kessiah	Minna	Tamar 5
Kettera	Mira 3	Tena
Keyah	Mirah 2	Tenah 4
Kiah	Misha	Vennah
Kinah	Monah	Yanaky
Kissee	Motta	Zada
Kissiah	Nilla	Zellah
Kit	Numa	Zie
Kiziah	Nutta	Zinda
Kizziah	Olly	Zody
Kizzy 2		

Names, Slave and Free: 1800-1864

Source List J: FREE BLACK NAMES, 1800-1860

Most Common Given Names, South

Following is a listing of the most common given names. For convenience an alphabetical listing with the frequency of occurrence and rate of 11.536 per 100,000 will be followed by a frequency listing with the frequency number.

Male, Alphabetical (141 names)

Aaron 30 346	Enoch 9 104	Kenneth 1
Abram 31 358	Ephraim 24 277	Lamb 5 58
Abraham 40 461	Ezekiel 13 150	Lawrence 7 81
Absolom 16 185	Frank 54 623	Leonard 4 46
Adam 18 208	Fred 5 58	Leroy 4 46
Albert 9 104	Frederick 27 311	Levi 25 288
Alexander 40 461	Gabriel 11 127	Lewis 76 865
Alfred 19 219	George 232 2766	London 6 69
Allen 47 542	Gilbert 10 115	Louis 3 35
Amos 11 127	Green 6 69	Major 13 150
Andrew 36 415	Harrison 12 138	Martin 21 242
Anthony 55 634	Harry 55 634	Matthew 32 369
Arthur 27 311	Harvey 8 92	Micajah 10 115
Ben 23 265	Henderson 6 69	Miles 17 196
Benjamin 117 1350	Henry 214 2469	Mingo 11 127
Berry 7 81	Herbert 7 81	Moses 103 1188
Bill 15 173	Hezekiah 11 127	Nat 11 127
Billy 73 842	Howard 1	Nathan 35 404
Bob 16 185	Isaac 132 1613	Nathaniel 23 265
Buck 5 58	Isham 39 450	Ned 41 473
Caesar 244 277	Ishmael 9 104	Nelson 9 104
Caleb 13 150	Isiah 5 58	Noah 14 162
Cato 11 127	Israel 10 115	Oliver 6 69
Charles 160 1846	Jack 73 842	Peter 149 1719
Charlie 1	Jackson 1	Phil 11 127
Curtis 1	Jacob 105 1211	Philip 43 496
Daniel 130 1590	Jake 1	Pleasant 17 196
Dave 2 23	James 499 5756	Pompey 8 92
David 166 1915	Jasper 1	Primus 3 35
Davy 8 92	Jeff 4 46	Prince 6 69
Dennis 13 150	Jefferson 7 81	Ralph 8 92
Dick 22 254	Jeremiah 29 335	Reuben 46 531
Edmond 40 461	Jerry 34 392	Richard 123 1419
Edward 75 854	Jesse 106 1223	Robert 123 1419
Edwin 1	Jim 26 300	Robin 15 173
Eli 16 185	Joe 29 335	Sam 47 542
Elias 14 162	John 681 7856	Sampson 15 173
Elijah 42 485	Jordon 22 254	Samuel 196 2261
Elisha 29 335	Joseph 148 1707	Sandy 5 58
Ellick 5 58	Joshua 41 473	Shadrack 11 127
Emanuel 14 162	Julius 4 46	Sidney 5 58

Names, Slave and Free: 1800-1864 -- FREE BLACK NAMES, 1800-1860

Simon 33 381	Tom 36 415	William 562 6483
Solomon 49 565	Wallace 1	Willie 16 185
Stephen 86 992	Walter 7 81	Willis 38 438
Squire 8 92	Washington 11 127	York 6 69
Thomas 334 2789	Wesley 1	Zachariah 18 208
Toby 6 69	Will 16 185	

Male, Frequency (142 names)

John 681	Jerry 34	Hezekiah 11
William 562	Simon 33	Mingo 11
James 449	Matthew 32	Nat 11
Thomas 334	Abram 31	Phil 11
George 232	Aaron 30	Shadrack 11
Henry 214	Elisha 29	Washington 11
Samuel 196	Jeremiah 29	Gilbert 10
David 166	Joe 29	Israel 10
Charles 160	Arthur 27	Micajah 10
Peter 149	Frederick 27	Albert 9
Joseph 148	Jim 26	Enoch 9
Isaac 132	Levi 25	Ishmael 9
Daniel 130	Caesar 24	Nelson 9
Richard 123	Ephraim 24	Shadrick 9
Robert 123	Ben 23	Davy 8
Benjamin 117	Nathaniel 23	Harvey 8
Jesse 106	Jordon 22	Pompey 8
Jacob 105	Dick 22	Ralph 8
Moses 103	Martin 21	Squire 8
Stephen 86	Alfred 19	Berry 7
Lewis 76	Adam 18	Herbert 7
Edward 75	Zachariah 18	Jefferson 7
Billy 73	Miles 17	Lawrence 7
Jack 73	Pleasant 17	Walter 7
Anthony 55	Absolom 16	Green 6
Harry 55	Bob 16	Henderson 6
Frank 54	Eli 16	London 6
Solomon 49	Will 16	Oliver 6
Allen 47	Willie 16	Prince 6
Sam 47	Bill 15	Toby 6
Reuben 46	Robin 15	York 6
Philip 43	Sampson 15	Buck 5
Elijah 42	Elias 14	Ellick 5
Joshua 41	Emanuel 14	Isiah 5
Ned 41	Noah 14	Fred 5
Abraham 40	Caleb 13	Lamb 5
Alexander 40	Ezekiel 13	Sandy 5
Edmond 40	Dennis 13	Sidney 5
Isham 39	Major 13	Jeff 4
Willis 38	Harrison 12	Julius 4
Andrew 36	Amos 11	Leonard 4
Tome 36	Cato 11	Leroy 4
Nathan 35	Gabriel 11	Louis 3

Names, Slave and Free: 1800-1864 -- FREE BLACK NAMES, 1800-1860

Primus 3	Edwin 1	Jasper 1
Dave 2	Howard 1	Kenneth 1
Charlie 1	Jackson 1	Louis 1
Curtis 1	Jake 1	Wallace 1
		Wesley 1

Female, Alphabetical (133 names)

Abigail 5 107	Emily 5 107	Marion 1
Adaline 2 43	Esther 30 640	Martha 44 939
Aggy 18 384	Eve 5 107	Mary 271 5781
Agnes 22 469	Eveline 3 64	Matilda 23 491
Alice 14 299	Fanny 87 1856	Mattie 1
Amanda 1	Flora 7 149	May 2 43
Amelia 10 213	Frankie 8 171	Mildred 7 149
Amy 11 235	Ginny 3 64	Milly 84 1792
Ann 71 1515	Grace 20 427	Mima 6 128
Anna 18 384	Grief 5 107	Minerva 5 107
Annie 3 64	Hannah 89 1898	Minnie 2 43
Becky 13 277	Harriet 27 576	Molly 16 341
Bellah 3 64	Helen 485	Mourning 13 277
Betsy 177 3776	Henrietta 2 43	Nancy 285 6079
Betty 37 789	Hester 7 149	Nanny 7 149
Biddy 5 107	Hagar 6 128	Nelly 36 768
Candis 6 128	Hetty 10 213	Patience 17 363
Caroline 17 363	Isabella 6 128	Patsy 75 1600
Catharine 41 875	Jane 108 2304	Peggy 75 1600
Celia 12 256	Jemima 5 107	Penelope 6 128
Charity 18 384	Jinny 11 235	Phillis 24 512
Charlotte 50 1067	Josephine 2 43	Phoebe 18 384
Cherry 5 105	Judah 6 128	Penney 5 107
Chloe 8 171	Judy 41 875	Polly 149 3178
Clara 5 107	Julia 12 256	Priscilla 26 555
Clarissa 8 171	Katy 23 491	Rachael 83 1770
Clary 1	Keziah 16 341	Rebecca 51 1088
Comfort 8 171	Kitty 20 427	Rhoda 20 427
Delia 5 107	Laura 2 43	Rhody 7 149
Dicy 14 299	Lavinia 10 213	Rosa 1
Dina(h) 15 320	Leah 19 405	Rose 28 597
Dolly 20 427	Letty 14 299	Ruth 4 85
Dorcas 10 213	Lillie 2 43	Sally 213 4544
Dorothy 1	Louisa 22 469	Sarah 107 2282
Edith 11 235	Lucinda 9 192	Silvey 6 128
Edy 20 427	Lucy 136 2901	Sophia 12 256
Effie 1	Lucretia 7 149	Su(c)key 30 640
Eleanor 13 277	Lydia 38 811	Susan 65 1387
Ellen 7 149	Mabel 1	Susie 3 64
Eliza 73 1557	Maggie 2 43	Tabitha 7 149
Elizabeth 123 2624	Malinda 2 43	Tamer 12 256
Elsie 8 171	Mahala 6 128	Venus 3 64
Elvira 5 107	Margaret 43 917	Violet 12 256
Emiline 1	Maria(h) 64 1365	Willie 1
		Winn(e)y 29 619

Names, Slave and Free: 1800-1864 -- FREE BLACK NAMES, 1800-1860

Female, Frequency (133 names)

Nancy 285	Leah 19	Isabella 6
Mary 271	Aggy 18	Judah 6
Sally 213	Anna 18	Mahala 6
Betsy 177	Charity 18	Penelope 6
Polly 149	Phoebe 18	Mima 6
Lucy 136	Caroline 17	Silvey 6
Elizabeth 123	Patience 17	Abigail 5
Jane 108	Molly 16	Biddy 5
Sarah 107	Keziah 16	Cherry 5
Hannah 89	Dina(h) 15	Clara 5
Fanny 87	Alice 14	Delia 5
Milly 84	Dicy 14	Elvira 5
Rachael 83	Letty 14	Emily 5
Patsy 75	Becky 13	Eve 5
Peggy 75	Eleanor 13	Grief 5
Eliza 73	Mourning 13	Jemima 5
Ann 71	Celia 12	Minerva 5
Susan 65	Julia 12	Penney 5
Maria 64	Sophia 12	Helen 4
Rebecca 51	Tamer 12	Ruth 4
Charlotte 50	Violet 12	Annie 3
Martha 44	Amy 11	Bellah 3
Margaret 43	Edith 11	Eveline 3
Catharine 41	Jinny 11	Ginny 3
Judy 41	Amelia 10	Susie 3
Lydia 38	Dorcas 10	Venus 3
Betty 37	Hetty 10	Adaline 2
Nelly 36	Lavinia 10	Henrietta 2
Esther 30	Lucinda 9	Josephine 2
Su(c)key 30	Chloe 8	Laura 2
Winn(e)y 29	Clarissa 8	Lillie 2
Rose 28	Comfort 8	Maggie 2
Harriet 27	Elsie 8	Malinda 2
Priscilla 26	Frankie 8	May 2
Phillis 24	Ellen 7	Amanda 1
Katy 23	Flora 7	Clary 1
Matilda 23	Hester 7	Dorothy 1
Agnes 22	Lucretia 7	Effie 1
Louisa 22	Mildred 7	Emiline 1
Dolly 20	Nanny 7	Mabel 1
Edy 20	Rhody 7	Marion 1
Grace 20	Tabitha 7	Mattie 1
Kitty 20	Candis 6	Rosa 1
Rhoda 20	Hagar 6	Willie 1

Names, Slave and Free: 1800-1864 -- FREE BLACK NAMES, 1800-1860

<u>Unusual Names, South</u>

<u>Male</u>

Able	Boston	Darling
Abraham	Bray	Derry
Abram	Brister	Dilson
Absolam	Bristo	Doctor
Absolem	Brittain	Dolphin
Absolom	Brutus	Dominick
Admiral	Buck	Donum
Africa	Bud	Dory
Agrippa	Bug	Dorry
Ahab	Burgoine	Dread
Ajar	Bushrod	Drue
Alamy	Byer	Dublin
Alesey	Cader	Duke
Alief	Caesar	Dunah
Amariah	Cain	Ebenezer
America	Caleb	Ecer
Ampy	Capio	Eden
Amsey	Captain	Egypt
Ananias	Carlos	Elam
Andrew Jackson	Castille	Eli
Annaky	Catice	Elias
Annias	Cato	Elijah
Appy	Cavano	Elisha
Aquil	Chavus	Ellet
Aquilla	Chedle	Elvy
Argal	Chertly	Elzey
Argy	Church	Emanuel
Atia	Cidea	Enoch
Atty	Cipio	Enus
Axom	Clack	Ephraim
Bacchus	Cleon	Erasmus
Balaam	Cold	Esau
Barach	Comfort	Esaw
Barnabas	Cordy	Esom
Baron	Craven	Etheldred
Bash	Crecy	Euphrozein
Battaille	Cudjoe	Exum
Batts	Cue	Ezekiel
Bazeel	Cuff	Ezeriah
Bazzle	Cuffee	Fabias
Bias	Cuffey	Fed
Bing	Cuffy	Findcastle
Bird	Cupid	Flanders
Bland	Cupit	Fortunalus
Bond	Custes	Fountain
Bonnet	Cyles	Fran
Bonny	Cyphax	Frankey
Booker	Dancy	French

Names, Slave and Free: 1800-1864 -- FREE BLACK NAMES, 1800-1860

Gabe	Juan Pedre Laverence	Minnis
Gabi	Juba	Minus
Gabriel	Jubice	Monday
Games	Jubiter	Mordica
Gamon	Judah	Moses
Ganibo	Julius Caesar	Nace
General	Jupiter	Naseal
George Washington	Justice	Nazareth
Gideon	Kadjer	Nazeriah
Gilliam	Kedar	Nead
Gingo	Kesia	Nealy
Glascow	Ket	Nehemiah
Glasgo	Keziah	Nero
Glasgow	King	Nimrod
Glasscoe	Kitter	Nisom
Gulliah	Kiver	Noah
Guy	Klar	Noel
Hago	Laban	Nunnelly
Ham	Lacky	Obadiah
Hannibal	Lamb	Obediah
Happy	Lazarus	Olphin
Harklas	Lenn	Oxey
Heart	Levi	Oxford
Hercules	Lewillin	Palladore
Herod	Lisha	Paschal
Hezekiah	Lishe	Perio
Holland	Littleberry	Pleasant
Hope	Lockey	Polidore
Hopeful	London	Pompey
Horsey	Lorenzo	Port
Ichabod	Lorid	Primus
Immanuel	Lot	Prince
Isaac	Luby	Quam
Isah	Lucky	Quaminy
Isariah	Lud	Quawk
Isham	Lury	Quiller
Ishmael	Lyeus	Quilly
Isiah	Madam	Rafe
Ison	Major	Ragis
Israel	Malachi	Reason
Izerish	Mallica	Rial
Jabex	Man	Riler
Jeremiah	Martes	Roll
Joanner	Masor	Rozarro
Job	Mastin	Ryal
Johia	Mesech	Sampson
Jolly	Meshac	Sanco
Jonas	Meshack	Sandy
Jose	Meshak	Sango
Josiah	Methias	Saul
Joshiah	Micajah	Schisms
Joshua	Mingo	Scipio

Names, Slave and Free: 1800-1864 -- FREE BLACK NAMES, 1800-1860

Scotland	Sy	Ursan
Sess	Syphax	Valentine
Sessee	Syphe	Venus
Shade	Taliaferro	Waggoner
Shadrac	Taliferro	Wat
Shadrach	Tascon	Whet
Shadrack	Tenny	Whitty
Shadrick	Theoderick	Witcher
Sigh	Theophilus	World
Sign	Theopilas	Zachariah
Simus	Theopulus	Zadek
Sinai	Thomas Jefferson	Zadork
Sion	Thoneas	Zanga
Solomon	Titus	Zebulon
Spanish	Tobias	Zed
Squire	Tobit	Zedakiah
Stilh	Toby	Zeddock
Strato	Topsail	Zedekiah
Sucurda	Trim	Zedick
Sivail	Tumer	Zephemiah
Swan	Uriah	Zilphy

Female

Abb	Arena	Celinda
Abba	Arrena	Cenry
Abby	Arrenia	Chaney
Abiah	Arrinah	Chanty
Abigail	Asphasia	Chany
Adelphi	Atha	Charity
Affey	Basheba	Chelsea
Affiah	Bazzila	Cherry
Affy	Becky	China
Agga	Belinda	Chiss
Aggy	Bellow	Chloe
Aicy	Bena	Chocolate
Ailey	Bershaba	Christian
Alotsa	Bijah	Claricy
Ama	Biner	Clarinda
Amanda	Bitty	Clarissa
Amelia	Brazillia	Clelista
Amia	Britcha	Cloey
Amaretta	Camilla	Clory
Anaka	Candass	Comfort
Aneca	Candis	Creasy
Anilesa	Capay	Crece
Anky	Carina	Crecia
Annalsa	Caron	Crecy
Annaritta	Casina	Cressa
Annica	Cassil	Cresy
Annis	Cassy	Cressy
Ansely	Celah	Cricey

Names, Slave and Free: 1800-1864 -- FREE BLACK NAMES, 1800-1860

Crissa	Frankie	Lannah
Crissey	Furlisy	Lavinia
Critty	Fury	Leanty
Croescy	Gatsey	Leavy
Cuffee	Gatty	Leddy
Cuffey	Gilly	Lehannah
Daphne	Gina	Lethe
Darkie	Ginny	Lethy
Darkis	Glathe	Letitia
Deborah	Grief	Lettuce
Deborough	Hagar	Levicy
Delilah	Hager	Levina
Delitha	Hannah	Levisa
Delpha	Hearty	Levita
Deluda	Hepsey	Liley
Desebri	Hetha	Linda
Dici	Heziah	Linder
Dicy	Honoria	Litha
Dido	Hulda	Liz
Dilcy	Huldy	Lizza
Diley	Ibby	Lovey
Dilly	Isley	Lot
Dilsey	Ivory	Lucena
Dinah	Ivy	Lucinda
Disa	Jamima	Lucrecy
Disey	Jamimah	Lucretia
Docia	Jemima	Madam
Doctor	Jerrydine	Madamoiselle
Dorcas	Jerusha	Mahala
Dula	Jimima	Main
Easter	Jincey	Malinda
Eba	Jinsy	Manna
Edme	Joama	Marenda
Elander	Joicy	Mariah
Elishea	Juba	Marinda
Elissa	Juda	Marsha
Elvey	Judah	Marshy
Encey	Judea	Massa
Endy	Judicke	Massey
Eppy	Juduh	Massy
Erlina	July	Matilda
Euphemia	Kata	Mealy
Eve	Kesiah	Meeky
Faith	Keziah	Mehala
Faitha	Kiddy	Melia
Faithy	Kinner	Meranda
Febe	Kipiah	Merit
Ferebe	Kissey	Milia
Ferebee	Kizzy	Milla
Ferebey	Laetitia	Mimy
Ferriba	Lana	Minty
Fortune	Laney	Miranda

Names, Slave and Free: 1800-1864 -- FREE BLACK NAMES, 1800-1860

Moaning	Quiviene	Tabby
Molsey	Raner	Tally
Molsy	Raney	Tamer
Morning	Reason	Tamzy
Mourning	Rebee	Tapley
Nabby	Reietta	Tareazer
Nanna	Rena	Tempe
Neely	Reny	Temperance
Nicey	Rhiney	Temperence
Obedience	Rhoda	Tempey
Oliph	Rhody	Temporence
Ollian	Rinah	Tempy
Orpha	Ritter	Tena
Pagey	Rodam	Tenah
Pamela	Rosina	Teresey
Pamelia	Rozetta	Teresy
Pamilia	Rusha	Thamar
Pankey	Ruthy	Thamer
Parma	Sabra	Theney
Parthenia	Sabry	Thummer
Patience	Salenia	Tiller
Pearth	Sample	Tincy
Penelope	Savory	Tinny
Penny	Scylla	Tissey
Penninah	Sealy	Trecy
Penney	Selah	Unis
Petsey	Sephas	Ursula
Phebey	Shady	Usley
Philette	Sicily	Usly
Phillis	Siller	Venous
Phoebe	Sina	Venus
Piety	Siney	Vicy
Pink	Sipha	Vina
Pleasant	Sisly	Viney
Poline	Smithey	Wafey
Pomona	Smithy	Willy Ricks
Portia	Sophia	Wincey
Portion	Sophy	Winney
Posha	Spicer	Zany
Presby	Starky	Zealous
Pricy	Suckey	Zelph
Priscilla	Sylvannah	Zena
Prudence	Tabatha	Zenia
Prudy	Tabitha	Zilea
		Zipha

Unusual Names, North[49]

The following is a list of unusual given names employed by free Blacks in New England, 1830.

_____

[49]Taken from Bowditch, N. I., "Suffok Surnames" (Boston, 1858).

Names, Slave and Free: 1800-1864 -- FREE BLACK NAMES, 1800-1860

<u>Male</u> (150 names)

Abiezer	Elikaim	Onando
Ackmit	Emer	Othello
Adolphin	Epaphroditus	Ozins
Agrippa	Eri	Pardon
Aliby	Esek	Parson
Alpheus	Esop	Patuner
Amor	Exeter	Pedro
Antoine	Farry	Peleg
Antonio	Fortunatus	Pender
Apollos	Gad	Peres
Araam	Gadock	Pero
Archilus	Gamby	Peteri
Ariel	German	Pharoah
Aron	Gurden	Pieros
Asabel	Hacaliah	Plato
Asahel	Hamlet	Polydore
Ashael	Handsaw	Prime
Bazil	Harlo	Primeth
Benajer	Hector	Prosper
Biather	Ishial	Quack
Bosem	Jabez	Quam
Boston	Japhet	Quarco
Brazillai	Jedidah	Rans
Brem	Jeduthan	Road
Byan	Jehu	Roman
Call	Joab	Royal
Cameralsmer	Jub	Ruel
Christmas	Juba	Saba
Coffin	Jube	Sabra
Colly	Lat	Sambo
Cornwallis	Leamer	Sango
Cozy	Leathurin	Sharper
Cubit	Leba	Shim
Cudjo	Limous	Shubel
Cuff	Lisnon	Sony
Cull	Lorezo	Soudon
Curon	Lot	Sunna
Curow	Lude	Suthy
Cury	Luzern	Thales
Czar	Mafus	Tibe
Darius	Mattrass	Tower
Deavius	Mehitable	Uriel
Dimon	Milo	Vemer
Dirius	Mineas	Whippy
Domp	Neptune	Yarmouth
Donas	Newport	Zackenas
Ebene	Nichabod	Zebiah
Eber	Obed	Zebulen
Electa	Obid	Zemilaino
Eliakim	Obier	Zimri

Names, Slave and Free: 1800-1864 -- FREE BLACK NAMES, 1800-1860

Female (58 names)

Acubeth	Gift	Pilea
Amarillis	Gisfey	Pink
Ami	Gist	Pinna
Apphia	Hope	Remembrance
Azuba	Ivan	Ritty
Bathsheba	Jedidiah	Roby
Berthana	Juda	Roker
Bethana	Losana	Rozinah
Birthena	Lovisa	Ruhamah
Bon	Lucitia	Sanina
Calez	Luna	Shewbel
Dana	Mahitable	Sibbel
Delight	Manna	Thankful
Diadama	Mercy	Time
Eliza	Meribah	True
Ezpearance	Nenus	Tuseance
Fidelia	Orange	Waity
Flow	Parcilla	Zelpha
Freelove	Pender	Zilpah
		Zilphia

(139) White Names, Colonial Massachusetts

Achsah	Cephorine	Hilus
Almeron	Chranston	Hirieli
Aloys	Comfort	Hope
Ambroscine	Consider	Increase
Amity	Corydon	Jehu
Ammial	Cotton	Jireh
Amphion	Cuff	Josehebeth
Anastasia	Dedrum	Justus
And	Delicia	Lately
Annaple	Delos	Latter
Ari	Demas	Leader
Ariel	Deodat	Loa
Aristides	Despire	Lobena
Armeda	Dipluma	Lodema
Arsmus	Dodavah	Lucitanus
Artaxerxes	Dwelley	Lunana
Avonia	Edee	Lusher
Bant	Egidus	Mama
Belitho	Elishaway	Maneer
Bellona	Elven	Maudit
Bethuel	Erdix	Merari
Biles	Euphrosyne	Mercy
Bonum	Experience	Milo
Bozoun	Galusha	Mungo
Briceno	Galutia	Nabby
Bunker	Given	Nion
Byby	Hadassah	Nymphas

Names, Slave and Free: 1800-1864 -- FREE BLACK NAMES, 1800-1860

Obid	Sabin	Tamyene
Odeardo	Salathiel	Tead
Oel	Salma	Temperance
Orison	Saloam	Urania
Orleas	Sarkis	Urbain
Orpha	Sarson	Usual
Orra	Sealum	Valorous
Ozia	Selah	Vistus
Pardon	Selthia	Welcome
Paschal	Semira	Winter
Patience	Sephamore	Zabdiel
Person	Seranus	Zarlock
Philura	Seraph	Zattu
Pilgrim	Shippie	Zeda
Pincus	Sparach	Ziba
Pruda	Suviah	Zibeon
Prudence	Sweet	Zina
Rahuman	Tade	Zion
Rezin	Talmuna	Zoa
		Zoeth

(33) White Names, Colonial Massachusetts, Easily Labelled Black

Almond	Iola	Orlando
Alpha	Ivory	Pamela
Alvira	Kosmos	Rozella
Amanda	Lazarus	Saphronia
America	Lemon	Sebeus
Ananias	Lorenda	Serena
Belinda	Lueva	Tamer
Cain	Luria	Thannie
Clem	Melinda	Vashti
Eldesta	Oral	Velzora
Hulda	Orange	

Unusual Names, North and South[50]

This next list of Unusual Names represents a random culling from all free Black names collected, North and South. If we keep in mind that the rate of unusualness amongst free Blacks is less than 20% of all the names collected, it will help keep this sometimes amusing example of extravagance in its proper perspective.

Male (290 names)

Abednago	Africa Griffin	Ananias
Able	Agrippa	Appy
Abiezer	Ahab	Archelaus
Ackro	Ally African	Asral
Adonis	Alpheus	Bachelor

---

[50]See Source List A for references.

Names, Slave and Free: 1800-1864 -- FREE BLACK NAMES, 1800-1860

Balaam	Debzil	Hop
Balthazar	Dibe	Hopeful
Baptist	Dives	Iber
Bash	Doctor Tucker	Ichabod
Battus	Donations	Indian Bill
Bazeel	Drara	Isah
Bazzle	Dread Smith	Ivory Hill
Benona	Dube Coal	Izerish
Black	Duincee	Jabez
Boaz	Duke	Jedidiah
Bony	Dunah	Jeduthan Mero
Booker Lawson	Edinburg	Jep
Bos	Egypt	Jeppo
Boxo	Electa	Job
Brave Brown	Eliakim	Johia
Brazillai	Eliphalit	Jolly Revils
Buck	Ellet	Joy
Buck Ben	Elymus	Juba
Bushrod	Emanuel	Jube
Cagy	Epaphroditus	Juber
Calemnius	Erasmus	Jubiter
Cano	Eri	Julius Caesar
Castille	Esop	Justice
Chesty Young	Esquire	Ket
Christmas	Etnah	Kettle
Christmas Johnson	Even	Kiar
Church	Expearance	King
Cidea	Exum	Lad
Clum	Flanders	Leba
Cobus	Flour Monk	Lebo
Cold Chain	Flow Cam	Led
Comb Bug	Fortunalus	Leu Leboo
Congo	Fortunatus	Leno
Conky	Fountain	Leven
Connecticut	Freborn	Looke
Constan Brown	Free Bob	Louder
Contee	Free Four	Lovey Griffin
Corns Jackson	Gabi	Lud
Cornwallis Lee	Gambo	Mado
Crumbo	Ganibo	Man Valentine
Cubit	George Washington	Mesbeck
Cudge	Ginger	Mink
Cudgo	Gingo	Moab
Cue	Gullaih	Monday
Cuff (old)	Gruff	Nace
Cupid	Custy	Nacht
Cupit	Hacaliah	Nazareth
Cyphax	Half	Neamy
Czar	Ham Folio	Nehemiah
Darby	Hannibal	Neptune
Darky Baily	Happy	Nice Johnson
Darling Bass	Herckiah	Noah

Names, Slave and Free: 1800-1864 -- FREE BLACK NAMES, 1800-1860

Nutter Nutter	Roll	Tibe
Obed	Ronemo	Tingo Stout
Oliver Cromwell	Rozarro	Tobit
Othello	Saba Quaico	Tone
Palladore	Saint Luke	Tower
Pardon	Sambo Hazzard	Tower Hill
Part Bartly	Sambo Holland	Trusty Maxwell
Pateloe	Sanco	Tui
Patrick Henry	Sandy Hill	Tunis
Peleg	Sango	Tusbey
Peregrine	Sanon	Valentine
Pero	Santy	Waggoner Labon
Pharoah	Sapiea	Wittum
Phelix	Sceyar	Yacht
Pieros	Schisms	Yaff
Plato	Seneca	Yapt Crud
Pleasant Fair	Shadrack	Yenix
Polidore	Sharper	Yon
Polydore	Shim Camp	Yot
Poplar	Sias	Zackenas
Priam	Sibby	Zacko
Priear	Sibyo	Zadoc
Prime Flowers	Sicum	Zadock
Prine	Sigh	Zadork
Punch	Sign	Zango
Quack	Sinai	Zanza
Quacko Minesee	Sindred	Zebiah
Quality	Sion	Zebulon
Quam	Sip	Zeddock
Quaminy	Sony	Zedick
Quawk Moore	Soudon	Zekia
Quiller	Sovereign	Zemiliano
Quilly	Spanish John	Zeno
Quintos Plato	Squash	Zenus
Reason	Squire	Zephaniah
Red Ben	Sucurda	Zepheniah
Resin	Sunna	Zingo
Return	Swan	Zilphy
Right	Tab Still Cold	Zimri
		Zip

Female (185 names)

Abagill	Annaka	Azuba
Adelphi	Annaritta	Balinda
Affy	Anty	Barbary Allen
Aicy Day	Apphia	Bazzilla
Algo	Ariminta	Britcha
Alotsa	Arrenia	Casandra
Amaziah	Arrinah	Casiah
Anilesa	Asphasia	Casina
Anky	Assent	Cassa

109

BLACK NAMES IN AMERICA

Names, Slave and Free: 1800-1864 -- FREE BLACK NAMES, 1800-1860

Celinda	Judy	Rebee
Cherry	Kata	Reietta
Chilla	Kesiah	Resin
China	Kettera	Roby
Chocolate Brown	Kiddy	Roker
Cloa	Lady	Rosealle
Coffie	Lallate	Rosetta
Comfort	Lazarus	Rosinda
Coose	Lethe	Rosina
Cressa	Lettuce	Rozinah
Critty	Lira	Rutha Lee
Darkie	Looky	Ruhamah
Deluda	Lorinda	Sabina
Dice	Love	Sabra
Dido	Lovey	Sabrina
Dinah	Lovisa	Sack
Eady	Lucky	Sambo
Easau	Luna	Sanina
Ersa	Mahitable	Satana
Esther Queen	Main Boon	Selah
Eulalie	Manna	Serena
Euphrozein	Marcy	Servilla
Eve	Mariah	Shady
Faitha	Massy	Sicily
Felicity	Meeky	Simp
Floro	Memory	Sooly
Fonda	Memory Devine	Starky
Fox Hill Sarah	Meribah	Sukey
Franky	Milky	Tabatha
Freelove Updike	Minis	Tamzy
Fury	Minty	Teanna
Gatty	Morning Locus	Temperance
Gift	Mourning	Temperence
Gift Johnson	Nanky	Tersha
Gitty	Naseal	Time
Grease	Naseyle	Tiny
Grief	Negro Milly	Tissey
Hearty	Nene	True
Herculous	Nicy	Trump
Hessy	Obedience	Trusilla
Holly	Orange	Unicy
Honour	Orasha	Unis
Hope	Parma	Unity
Ibby	Perica	Vicy
Indianna	Phippy	Wealy
Jasma	Piety	Widow Cowplane
Jemima	Pilea	Winny
Jerrydine	Pink	Winxy
Joam	Pinna	Zealous
Juby	Pomona	Zeicle
Juda	Posha	Zelph
Judicke	Quiviene	Zenia
		Zilpla

Names, Slave and Free: 1800-1864 -- FREE BLACK NAMES, 1800-1860

Most Common Given Names, North

These 238 names appeared in the <u>Massachusetts</u> <u>Mercury</u>, Boston, September 16, 1800. They refer to Blacks and Mulattoes, and the intent is to warn these people to leave the Commonwealth. The stated purpose is to reduce pauperism although one suspects racism is involved. It is interesting to note that even if these people were, indeed, paupers, their names reflect nomenclature well within the established white pattern. The number after the given name represents the frequency usage; no number indicates one time.

Male (136 names)

John 17	Lewis 2	Jacob
Thomas 14	Robert 2	Janus
Peter 12	Amos	Jeremiah
James 7	Boston	Julius
William 6	Bristol	Leville
Samuel 6	Britton	Moses
Joseph 5	Butterfield	Newell
Charles 4	Calo	Oliver
Prince 4	Casme	Paul
Richard 4	Cato	Plato
Cuffy 3	Douglas	Primus
David 3	Edward	Raney
George 3	Fortune	Scipio
Henry 3	Francis	Simon
Abraham 2	Frank	Stephen
Anthony 2	Hamet	Timothy
Caesar 2	Hamlet	Waley
Jack 2	Isaac	

Female (102 names)

Mary 10	Phoebe 2	Freelove
Hannah 8	Susannah 2	Hagar
Nancy 8	Abijah	Jane
Polly 7	Abijah, Jr.	Jenny
Sally 7	Amey	Judith
Rebecca 4	Anna	Katy
Sylvia 4	Anne	Kelurah
Betsy 3	Catherine	Lucinda
Elizabeth 3	Clarissa	Lydia
Lucy 3	Diana	Nelly
Margaret 3	Dinah	Rachel
Philis 3	Dolly	Rhode
Charlotte 2	Elone	Rosanna
Eliza 2	Esther	Sophia
Peggy 2	Flora	Stepney
		Violet

Names, Slave and Free: 1800-1864

Source List K: WHITE NAMES, GEORGIA, 1790-1818[51]

Most Common Given Names

The first list is alphabetical with frequency and rate per 100,000; the second list reflects frequency. The male list is followed by a female listing.

Male, Alphabetical

Aaron 50 420	George 222 1863	Nimrod 7 59
Abraham 66 554	Green 8 67	Obediah 7 59
Abram 6 50	Harrison 8 67	Owen 8 67
Absolem 13 109	Henry 272 2282	Patrick 15 126
Adam 24 201	Hezekiah 14 117	Peleg 6 50
Alexander 51 428	Hugh 26 218	Peter 126 1057
Allen 38 319	Isaac 117 982	Phillip 48 403
Amos 20 168	Isaiah 7 59	Pleasant 9 76
Anderson 6 50	Isham 22 185	Ralph 7 59
Andrew 60 503	Jacob 136 1141	Reuben 61 512
Anthony 13 109	James 825 6922	Richard 186 1560
Arthur 46 386	Jehu 6 50	Robert 283 2374
Augustus 5 42	Jeremiah 60 503	Sampson 17 143
Balaam 6 50	Jesse 192 1611	Samuel 261 2190
Bazil 8 67	Jethro 7 59	Shadrack 8 67
Benjamin 256 2148	Joab 7 59	Simon 14 117
Caleb 11 92	Job 16 134	Sion 5 42
Charles 130 1091	John 1610 13507	Solomon 53 445
Daniel 134 1124	Jordan 11 92	Stephen 82 688
David 210 1762	Joseph 313 2626	Theophilus 6 50
Dennis 9 76	Joshua 93 780	Thomas 607 5093
Dial 7 59	Josiah 31 260	Timothy 16 134
Ebenezer 5 42	Lawrence 7 59	Uriah 9 76
Edmo(u)nd 53 445	Leonard 11 92	Valentine 5 42
Edward 100 839	Levi 27 227	Vincent 9 76
Edwin 9 76	Lewis 103 864	Walter 11 92
Eli 10 84	Martin 23 193	Warren 6 50
Elias 15 126	Matthew 60 503	Washington 7 59
Elijah 46 386	Micajah 25 210	William 1254 10421
Elisha 43 360	Michael 36 302	Willis 31 260
Ethelred 8 67	Moses 83 696	Zachariah 32 268
Ezekiel 13 109	Nathan 58 487	Zadock 8 67
Francis 55 461	Nathaniel 69 579	Zechariah 8 67
Frederick 57 478	Nicholas 27 227	Zephaniah 6 50

Male, Frequency

John 1610	William 1254	James 825

---

[51]The lists come from 12,565 names from Georgia, Blair - Some Early Tax Digests of Georgia during the period 1790-1818; 11,919 males and 646 females.

Names, Slave and Free: 1800-1864 -- WHITE NAMES, GEORGIA, 1790-1818

Thomas 607	Phillip 48	Dennis 9
Joseph 313	Arthur 46	Edwin 9
Robert 283	Elijah 46	Pleasant 9
Henry 272	Elisha 43	Uriah 9
Samuel 261	Allen 38	Vincent 9
Benjamin 256	Michael 36	Basil 8
George 222	Ephraim 33	Ethelred 8
David 210	Zachariah 32	Green 8
Jesse 192	Josiah 31	Harrison 8
Richard 186	Willis 31	Owen 8
Jacob 136	Levi 27	Shadrack 8
Daniel 134	Nicholas 27	Zadock 8
Charles 130	Hugh 26	Zechariah 8
Peter 126	Micajah 25	Dial 7
Isaac 117	Adam 24	Jethro 7
Lewis 103	Martin 23	Joab 7
Edward 100	Isham 22	Lawrence 7
Joshua 93	Amos 20	Nimrod 7
Moses 83	Sampson 17	Obediah 7
Stephen 82	Job 16	Ralph 7
Nathaniel 69	Timothy 16	Washington 7
Abraham 66	Patrick 15	Abram 6
Reuben 61	Hezekiah 14	Anderson 6
Andrew 60	Simon 14	Balaam 6
Jeremiah 60	Absolem 13	Ebenezer 6
Matthew 60	Anthony 13	Isaiah 6
Nathan 58	Ezekiel 13	Jehu 6
Frederick 57	Elias 12	Peleg 6
Francis 55	Caleb 11	Warren 6
Edmo(u)nd 53	Jordan 11	Zephaniah 6
Solomon 53	Leonard 11	Theophilus 6
Alexander 51	Walter 11	Augustus 5
Aaron 50	Eli 10	Sion 5
		Valentine 5

Female, Alphabetical

Ann 41 6347	Frances 7 1084	Nancy 23 2167
Asia 5 774	Hannah 20 3096	Priscilla 6 929
Betsy 5 774	Jane 15 2322	Rach(a)el 6 929
C(K)atharine 14 2167	Lydia 7 1084	Rebecca 14 2167
Eliza 21 3251	Margaret 14 2167	Ruth 5 774
Elizabeth 64 9907	Martha 19 2941	Sally 6 929
Esther 5 774	Mary 90 13932	Sarah 49 7585

Female, Frequency

Mary 90	Eliza 21	Margaret 14
Elizabeth 64	Hannah 20	Rebecca 14
Sarah 49	Martha 19	Frances 7
Ann 41	Jane 15	Lydia 7
Nancy 23	C(K)atharine 14	Priscilla 6

Names, Slave and Free: 1800-1864 -- WHITE NAMES, GEORGIA, 1790-1818

Rach(a)el 6	Asia 5	Esther 5
Sally 6	Betsy 5	Ruth 5

Unusual Names

Male (Sample: 11,919)

Abednago	Boaz	Elphiston
Abednego	Bray	Enias
Abijah	Brazil	Enoch
Abisha	Britain	Enos
Abraham	Briton	Epaphroditus
Abram	Bud	Ephraim
Absalem	Cader	Ephrim
Absalom	Cain	Eps
Absolam	Caleb	Esaw
Absolem	Calep	Eseff
Absolom	Calip	Ethelred
Absolum	Calrup	Ezekial
Acey	Caneth	Ezekiel
Ancil	Charnel	Ezeliel
Ancram	Chislieu	Faddy
Anterine	Christian	Fielden
Appe	Church	Figures
Aqualla	Cloudless	Finney
Aquella	Coonrod	Finny
Archelaus	Dalphin	Galba
Archelause	Darling	Gedion
Archeless	Dempsy	Gehazai
Argygle	Diaclisten	Gideon
Arkelus	Dial	Gustavus
Arress	Dier	Hance
Asael	Dinkins	Hardress
Asaph	Dread	Henny
Azariah	Ebenezer	Hezekiah
Balaam	Eginiah	Hinchy
Bale	Ehud	Honour
Bannister	Ele	Hue
Baptis	Eleazer	Icabod
Barna	Eley	Ichabod
Barnaba	Eli	Ichabud
Barnabas	Eliakim	Ignatius
Barthemus	Elias	Instance
Batt	Elie	Instant
Bazel	Elijah	Irael
Bazil	Elinah	Iram
Beckum	Eliphilett	Isaac
Benajah	Elisas	Isaah
Bidcar	Elisha	Isaam
Bidkar	Elkanah	Isaiah
Bird	Elphinson	Isam

Names, Slave and Free: 1800-1864 -- WHITE NAMES, GEORGIA, 1790-1818

Isham	Malchijah	Pugh
Ishamel	Malicha	Rabun
Israel	Mallekiah	Ramson
Ithamer	Mansil	Ransom
Jabez	Marcator	Ranson
Jacklin	Massy	Rasen
Jain	Mastin	Rearcdon
Jehu	Matthias	Reason
Jeneper	Menoah	Record
Jephthah	Mescheck	Redach
Jeptha	Meshack	Reedy
Jepthy	Mesheck	Resdon
Jeremiah	Micader	Reuel
Jethro	Micajah	Rezon
Jiles	Michajah	Rhodum
Jilson	Millge	Right
Joab	Moab	Rix
Job	Mordecai	Rodolphos
Joday	Mordica	Rodolphus
Joeddy	Morning	Roister
Jonah	Moses	Roman
Jonas	Mountain	Royalbud
Joshua	Nahum	Saltrus
Josiah	Nehemiah	Sampson
Josias	New	Sands
Juniper	Newbell Waller	Sans
Kadish	Nimrod	Savage
Keader	Noble	Sevastian
Kesiah	Noel	Senor
Keziah	Non	Septemus
Kimbro	Obadiah	Septimus
Kimme	Obediah	Serenus
Kinchin	Obediruc	Shadrach
Kindred	Obednego	Shadrack
Laban	Olif	Shadrick
Labon	Olive	Sharp
Lamech	Orandatus	Shildrak
Land	Orendatus	Silvanous
Lazarous	Orren	Silvanus
Lazarus	Ozias	Sincinnatus
Lazerus	Par	Sion
Lemmon	Parsons	Solomon
Lequinio	Paschal	Spire
Leven	Peleg	Spivy
Levi	Pernol	Starling
Licum	Perygrene	Stith
Little	Pharis	Stokeley
Loamme	Philemon	Tabner
Maith	Phineas	Teekle
Major	Pleasant	Theaphilus
Malachi	Precious	Theny
Malachiah	Prior	Theofelus

Names, Slave and Free: 1800-1864 -- WHITE NAMES, GEORGIA, 1790-1818

Theophelous	Whiltmal	Zadock
Theophilus	Wimbon	Zebulon
Theopholis	Wormly	Zechariah
Tobias	Zac	Zedach
Ulysses	Zachariah	Zedkijah
Uriah	Zacharias	Zenes
Val	Zacherah	Zephaniah
Valentine	Zacheus	Zepheniah

Female (Sample: 646)

Abra	Deberah	Lurana
Ageniah	Desdemonia	Lurena
Aggy	Dicy	Mirada
Ailsey	Dosher	Moodic
Albra	Easter	Mourning
Aleny	Ebe	Penelope
Almira	Eve	Penina
Amelia	Faithy	Pheba
Anstacy	Feney	Priscilla
Aquila	Galba	Ruthy
Artemasia	Goodde	Sary
Asia	Habukuh	Scarlett
Ava	Hannah	Sophia
Avera	Hillerea	Sukey
Axeth	Jacinthe	Suzelle
Barbary	Jerutia	Tabitha
Barnaba	Juda	Tandy
Belitha	Lavina	Thene
Bershaby	Leah	Thusba
Bisha	Levina	Welcome
Charity	Littice	Winney
Cleon	Lovey	Zealah
Cordy	Lucretia	Zemila

Names, Slave and Free: 1800-1864

Source List L: SURNAMES, SOUTH, 1800-1860[52]

For convenience an alphabetical listing with the frequency of occurrence and rate per 100,000 will be followed by a frequency listing with the frequency number.

Free Blacks

Alphabetical (152 names)

Adams 17 122	Franklin 10 72	Jordon 38 272
Alexander 12 86	Freeman 81 580	Kelly 27 192
Allen 51 365	Fuller 13 93	Kennedy 11 79
Anderson 73 523	Gardner 5 36	Key 7 50
Atkins 5 36	Garner 8 57	King 43 308
Bailey 47 337	Gibson 19 136	Lawson 5 36
Baker 34 243	Gordon 17 122	Lee 20 143
Banks 42 301	Grant 9 64	Lewis 65 465
Bell 42 301	Gray 29 208	Lucas 51 365
Berry 10 72	Green 63 451	Marshall 10 72
Black 12 86	Griffin 38 272	Martin 56 401
Booker 14 100	Hall 24 172	Mason 25 179
Brooks 11 79	Hamilton 10 72	Miller 29 208
Brown 150 1074	Hammond 11 79	Mitchell 84 601
Bugg 7 50	Hampton 5 36	Montgomery 5 36
Butcher 18 129	Harper 14 100	Moore 73 523
Butler 18 344	Harris 135 967	Morgan 43 308
Campbell 22 158	Harrison 23 165	Morris 68 487
Carr 5 36	Harvey 15 107	Morse 7 50
Carter 99 709	Hawkins 25 179	Morton 6 43
Clark 23 165	Hayes 10 72	Murray 6 43
Clarke 13 93	Henderson 12 86	Nelson 15 107
Coleman 29 208	Henry 19 136	Owens 5 36
Collins 76 544	Hill 78 558	Pa(i)ge 9 64
Cook 29 208	Hoggatt 8 57	Parker 23 165
Cooper 48 344	Holland 10 72	Patterson 21 150
Cox 11 79	Holley 8 57	Payne 16 115
Cumbo 5 36	Holloway 17 122	Penn 7 50
Curry 8 57	Holmes 20 143	Phillips 16 115
Davis 57 408	Hopkins 8 57	Pierce 18 129
Dickerson 5 36	Howard 20 143	Pleasant(s) 17 122
Dixon 21 150	Hughes 15 107	Porter 17 122
Douglass 15 107	Hunter 9 64	Powell 20 143
Dunn 8 57	Jackson 148 1060	Price 22 158
Edwards 19 136	James 62 444	Randolph 9 64
Elliott 23 637	Jenkins 30 215	Reed 36 258
Evans 89 637	Johnson 185 1325	Reid 6 43
Ferguson 15 107	Johnston 49 351	Reynolds 13 93
Fields 12 86	Jones 239 1711	Richards 7 50

---

[52]See References in Source List A.

Names, Slave and Free: 1800-1864 -- SURNAMES, SOUTH, 1800-1860

Richardson 55 394	Stevens 12 86	Watts 14 100
Roberts 51 365	Stewart 59 422	Welch 10 72
Robertson 21 150	Taylor 41 294	West 31 222
Robinson 25 179	Tucker 11 79	White 78 558
Rogers 8 57	Turner 56 401	Williams 90 644
Russell 19 136	Walker 34 243	Willis 10 72
Sanders 10 72	Wallace 30 215	Wilson 107 766
Saunders 11 79	Ward 8 57	Winn 11 79
Scott 212 1518	Ware 5 36	Wood 19 136
Simmons 13 93	Washington 11 79	Wright 35 251
Simms 7 50	Watkins 18 129	Young 26 186
Smith 184 1317	Watson 8 57	

Frequency (152 names)

Jones 239	Bell 42	Russell 19
Scott 212	Taylor 41	Wood 19
Johnson 185	Griffin 38	Butcher 18
Smith 184	Jordan 38	Pierce 18
Brown 150	Reed 36	Watkins 18
Jackson 148	Wright 35	Adams 17
Harris 135	Baker 34	Gordon 17
Wilson 107	Walker 34	Holloway 17
Carter 99	West 31	Pleasant(s) 17
Williams 90	Jenkins 30	Porter 17
Evans 89	Wallace 30	Payne 16
Mitchell 84	Coleman 29	Phillips 16
Freeman 81	Cook 29	Douglass 15
Hill 78	Gray 29	Ferguson 15
White 78	Miller 29	Harvey 15
Collins 76	Kelly 27	Hughes 15
Anderson 73	Young 26	Nelson 15
Moore 73	Hawkins 25	Booker 14
Morris 68	Mason 25	Harper 14
Lewis 65	Robinson 25	Watts 14
Green 63	Hall 24	Clarke 13
James 62	Clark 23	Fuller 13
Stewart 59	Elliott 23	Reynolds 13
Davis 57	Harrison 23	Simmons 13
Martin 56	Parker 23	Alexander 12
Turner 56	Campbell 22	Black 12
Richardson 55	Price 22	Fields 12
Allen 51	Dixon 21	Henderson 12
Lucas 51	Patterson 21	Stevens 12
Roberts 51	Robertson 21	Brooks 11
Johnston 49	Holmes 20	Cox 11
Butler 48	Howard 20	Hammond 11
Cooper 48	Lee 20	Kennedy 11
Bailey 47	Powell 20	Saunders 11
King 43	Edwards 19	Tucker 11
Morgan 43	Gibson 19	Washington 11
Banks 42	Henry 19	Winn 11

Names, Slave and Free: 1800-1864 -- SURNAMES, SOUTH, 1800-1860

Berry 10	Austin 3	Abram
Franklin 10	Barrett 3	Bussey
Hamilton 10	Collier 3	Callaghan
Hayes 10	Foster 3	Callahan
Holland 10	Graham 3	Corley
Marshall 10	Hart 3	Crouch
Sanders 10	Jefferson 3	Davis
Welch 10	Lyons 3	Deas
Willis 10	Murphy 3	Elias
Grant 9	Perry 3	Fambro
Hunter 9	Ridgely 3	Gallagher
Pa(i)ge 9	Sullivan 3	Gambo
Randolph 9	Wade 3	Germany
Curry 8	Woods 3	Glover
Dunn 8	Barnes 2	Golphin
Garner 8	Cobb 2	Greene
Hoggatt 8	Cohen 2	Groves
Holley 8	Coles 2	Hair
Hopkins 8	Crawford 2	Lamar
Rogers 8	Daniels 2	Lampkin
Ward 8	Fletcher 2	Lark
Bugg 7	Gaines 2	McCarthy
Key 7	Malone 2	Mack
Morse 7	May 2	Mahoney
Penn 7	Procter 2	Murphey
Richards 7	Ross 2	Myers
Simms 7	Sharpe 2	O'Bryant
Morton 6	Vaughn 2	O'Connor
Murray 6	Webster 2	Pearre
Reid 6	Wigfall 2	Polk
Atkins 5	Abraham 1	Ramsey
Carr 5	Bennett 1	Redd
Cumbo 5	Benson 1	Riley
Dickerson 5	Burch 1	Robert
Gardner 5	Cummings 1	Rooney
Hampton 5	Fleming 1	Samuels
Lawson 5	Garrett 1	Sheahan
Montgomery 5	Levy 1	Shelton
Owens 5	McDonald 1	Simpkins
Ware 5	Parks 1	Stokes
Bradley 4	Pendleton 1	Tarver
Bryant 4	Ray 1	Tice
Burrell 4	Reese 1	Toole
Carr 4	Rice 1	Walsh
Fisher 4	Rivers 1	Walton
Vaughan 4	Tolbert 1	Weathers
Woodward 4	Tutt 1	Wren
		Youngblood

Names, Slave and Free: 1800-1864 -- SURNAMES, SOUTH, 1800-1860

Whites

Alphabetical (142 names)

Adams 23 181	Green 24 189	Parks 5 39
Alexander 11 87	Greene 6 47	Patterson 5 39
Allen 40 315	Griffin 25 197	Perry 15 118
Anderson 20 158	Hall 44 347	Phillips 32 252
Atkins 8 63	Hamilton 19 150	Porter 11 87
Bailey 17 134	Harper 20 158	Powell 40 315
Baker 29 229	Harris 61 481	Price 12 95
Banks 5 39	Harrison 33 260	Ray 6 47
Barnes 19 150	Hart 21 165	Reese 18 142
Bell 7 55	Harvey 5 39	Reid 10 79
Berry 14 110	Henderson 12 95	Reynolds 17 134
Bradley 10 79	Henry 10 79	Rice 8 63
Brooks 37 292	Hill 73 575	Richardson 15 118
Brown 72 567	Holland 10 79	Riley 5 39
Bryant 19 150	Holley 5 39	Roberts 39 307
Bugg 11 87	Hopkins 10 79	Robertson 23 181
Burch 6 47	Howard 20 158	Robinson 9 71
Bussey 7 55	Hughes 7 55	Rogers 38 299
Butler 13 102	Hunter 6 47	Ross 7 55
Campbell 10 79	Jackson 47 370	Sanders 8 63
Carr 6 47	James 11 87	Saunders 5 39
Carter 61 481	Jenkins 11 87	Scott 18 142
Clark 24 189	Johnson 63 496	Simmons 29 229
Clarke 7 55	Johnston 61 481	Simms 12 95
Coleman 10 79	Jones 180 1418	Smith 150 1182
Collins 18 142	Jordan 17 134	Stewart 19 150
Cook 13 102	Kelly 24 189	Stokes 5 39
Cooper 23 181	King 21 165	Tarver 5 39
Cox 30 236	Lawson 6 47	Taylor 56 441
Curry 15 118	Lee 20 158	Tucker 16 126
Davis 75 591	Lewis 37 292	Turner 36 284
Dixon 17 134	Lucas 6 47	Vaughn 5 39
Douglass 7 55	Lyons 9 71	Walker 58 457
Dunn 11 87	McDonald 5 39	Wallace 16 126
Edwards 30 236	Martin 30 236	Walton 16 126
Elliott 6 47	Mason 6 47	Ward 22 173
Evans 26 205	May 10 79	Ware 9 71
Fleming 6 47	Miller 32 252	Watkins 14 110
Fletcher 5 39	Mitc hell 27 213	Watson 13 102
Foster 12 95	Moore 74 583	Watts 10 79
Franklin 7 55	Morgan 16 126	White 25 197
Gardner 12 95	Morris 16 126	Williams 118 930
Gibson 19 150	Murphy 5 39	Willis 23 181
Glover 7 55	Murray 10 79	Wilson 25 197
Gordon 5 39	Nelson 14 110	Wood 24 189
Grant 10 79	Owens 13 102	Woodward 5 39
Gray 26 205	Parker 35 276	Wright 64 504
		Young 23 181

Names, Slave and Free: 1800-1864 -- SURNAMES, SOUTH, 1800-1860

Frequency (142 names)

Jones 180	Ward 22	Grant 10
Smith 150	Hart 21	Henry 10
Williams 118	King 21	Holland 10
Davis 75	Anderson 20	Hopkins 10
Moore 74	Harper 20	May 10
Hill 73	Howard 20	Murray 10
Brown 72	Lee 20	Reid 10
Wright 64	Barnes 19	Watts 10
Johnson 63	Bryant 19	Lyons 9
Carter 61	Gibson 19	Robinson 9
Harris 61	Hamilton 19	Ware 9
Johnston 61	Stewart 19	Atkins 8
Walker 58	Collins 18	Rice 8
Taylor 56	Reese 18	Sanders 8
Jackson 47	Scott 18	Bell 7
Hall 44	Bailey 17	Bussey 7
Allen 40	Dixon 17	Clarke 7
Powell 40	Jordan 17	Douglass 7
Roberts 39	Reynolds 17	Franklin 7
Rogers 38	Morgan 16	Glover 7
Brooks 37	Morris 16	Gordon 7
Lewis 37	Tucker 16	Hughes 7
Turner 36	Wallace 16	Ross 7
Parker 35	Walton 16	Burch 6
Harrison 33	Curry 15	Carr 6
Miller 32	Perry 15	Elliott 6
Phillips 32	Richardson 15	Fleming 6
Cox 30	Berry 14	Greene 6
Edwards 30	Nelson 14	Hunter 6
Martin 30	Watkins 14	Lawson 6
Baker 29	Butler 13	Lucas 6
Simmons 29	Cook 13	Mason 6
Mitchell 27	Owens 13	Ray 6
Evans 26	Watson 13	Banks 5
Gray 26	Foster 12	Fletcher 5
Griffin 25	Gardner 12	Harvey 5
White 25	Henderson 12	Holley 5
Wilson 25	Price 12	McDonald 5
Clark 24	Simms 12	Murphy 5
Green 24	Alexander 11	Parks 5
Kelly 24	Bugg 11	Patterson 5
Wood 24	James 11	Riley 5
Adams 23	Jenkins 11	Saunders 5
Cooper 23	Porter 11	Stokes 5
Robertson 23	Bradley 10	Tarver 5
Willis 23	Campbell 10	Vaughn 5
Young 23	Coleman 10	Woodward 5

Names, Slave and Free: 1800-1864

Source List M: FREED BLACKS, WASHINGTON, D.C., 1863-1864[53]

Surnames

Following are two lists: an alphabetical listing indicating the rate of use and a second number indicating the rate per 100,000; a frequency listing indicating the rate of use. No number indicates that the name was found only once with a rate per 100,000 of 36.

Alphabetical

Adams 12 435	Bennett 3 109	Brogden
Addison 7 254	Berkley	Broker
Adely	Berry 9 326	Bronaugh
Affutt	Beson 2 72	Brook 4 145
Alexander 2 72	Billings 2 72	Brooke 21 761
Alfred	Billingslee	Broom 7 254
Allen 16 580	Bird 3 109	Brotten 2 72
Ambush 4 145	Biscon	Brown 67 2429
Anderson 5 181	Black	Bruce 16 580
Arnold	Blackeston 2 72	Bryan
Ashton	Blackston	Bryant
Atkinson	Blackstone	Buchannan 4 145
Augustus	Blair	Bundy
Ayres	Blake	Burgess 11 399
Bacon	Blaney	Burley 3 109
Baker	Blaxton	Burnett
Banks	Blount	Burrell 2 72
Baltimore	Boarman	Butler 48 1740
Barber 3 109	Bodely	Butts
Barbour	Bond	Caesar
Barker 9 326	Booker	Calvert 3 109
Barley	Boone	Cammel
Barnes 3 109	Booth	Cambell
Bartey	Boston 2 72	Campbell 11 399
Barton 6 216	Bowen 3 109	Cane
Bass	Bowie 21 761	Carlton
Bateman 2 72	Bowles	Carmichael
Bateson	Bowman 7 254	Carpenter 5 181
Bayley 2 72	Bowyer	Carr 2 72
Bealle 14 507	Boyd 8 290	Carrol 23 834
Beander	Bradley	Carter 35 1269
Beckett 9 326	Bragden 3 109	Cartwright 4 145
Bedda	Brannon	Casey
Bell 24 870	Branson 6 216	Cass
Belt 4 145	Brant	Chambers 2 72
Bembrage 4 145	Brent 4 145	Champ 3 109
Bender	Brisco 13 471	Chandler

[53]From the 38th Congress, 1st Session (1863-64), House Executive Document No. 42, Vol. IX.

Names, Slave and Free: 1800-1864 -- FREED BLACKS, WASHINGTON, D.C., 1863-1864

Chapman 2 72	Diggs 14 507	Garner 3 109
Chase 7 254	Dines 9 326	Gassaway 2 72
Childes	Dixon 8 290	Gault
Chism 3 109	Dochet	Geary 2 72
Chisman	Dodson 14 507	Getter
Clarke 50 1813	Domer	Ghentt
Claxton	Doner	Gibson 8 290
Clements 2 72	Dorman	Gilbert
Coakley 8 290	Dorcey	Gillis
Coates 6 216	Doris 2 72	Gladden
Colbert	Dorsey 27 979	Goins 3 109
Cole 13 471	Douglas 3 109	Goodall 2 72
Coleman 15 544	Dover 3 109	Goodwin
Collins 6 216	Duchett	Gordan 12 435
Colvert 2 72	Duckett	Gover
Commodore 5 181	Duffin	Graham 8 290
Compton 7 254	Duglas	Grant 2 72
Coney	Duiell	Gray 20 725
Contee 6 216	Dulaney	Grayson 2 72
Cook 4 145	Duskin	Green 23 834
Coolidge	Duval	Greenfield 5 181
Coombes 5 181	Duviell	Greenleaf 2 72
Cooper 3 109	Dyer 7 254	Greenwell 6 216
Coquire 9 326	Dyson 10 363	Grey 5 181
Countee 2 72	Easton 5 181	Grinful 2 72
Covington 10 363	Edmonston 4 145	Gross 5 181
Cox 3 109	Edwards	Gunnell
Crawley	Elzey	Gustus
Crompton	Etchison 6 216	Guttridge 12 435
Cross 4 145	Evans 4 145	Guy
Crown	Erving	Hagan
Crowner	Fairfax 4 145	Hatton 6 216
Crumwell	Fauntleroy	Hall 17 616
Crusey 11 399	Fenwick	Hamilton 4 145
Crutis 15 544	Ferguson 4 145	Hammond 3 109
Cyrass	Finnick	Hampton 2 72
Dade 6 216	Fisher 2 72	Handy 5 181
Daines 2 72	Fletcher 20 725	Hanson 10 363
Dalcher	Ford 6 216	Harley 3 109
Dan	Foreman 2 72	Harper 9 326
Dangerfield	Forrest 21 761	Harris 11 399
Dant 7 254	Fortune	Harrison 8 290
Dashiel	Francis	Harrold
Davis	Freeman 2 72	Harwood 2 72
Day	Frisby	Hasson
Dean 2 72	Gains	Hatton
Delaney 2 72	Gale 3 109	Hawkins 28 1015
Delavan	Gantt 7 254	Hays
Dent	Gardiner 3 109	Hayes 3 109
Dickinson		Henderson 2 72
Didney		Hensley 2 72
Digges 5 181		Henson 5 181

Names, Slave and Free: 1800-1864 -- FREED BLACKS, WASHINGTON, D.C., 1863-1864

Henry 3 109	Leonard	Mulliken
Hepburn 3 109	Lewis 15 544	Munroe
Herbert 11 399	Lincoln	Munson
Hickman 2 72	Lineless 2 72	Murray
Hicks	Lloyd 5 181	Myers
Hill 10 363	Locke 3 109	McClelland
Hilleary	Loggins 3 109	McCubbins
Hinton 5 181	Lounds	McGrundy
Horden	Lourye	McKenny
Holmes 13 471	Lowe	McKenzie
Hollis 2 72	Lowndes 2 72	McKinsey 2 72
Hollyday	Lowrie 2 72	McLain
Honesty	Lowry	McPherson 4 145
Hopkins 9 326	Lucas 2 72	Napa
Hopp 3 109	Ludlow	Nash 8 290
Hoskin	Lyles 12 435	Naughton
Howard 11 399	Lynch	Nead
Howe	Macoy	Neale 2 72
Hudley	Mackall 2 72	Nelson 10 363
Hues 3 109	Maddox 5 181	Netter
Humphreys	Magruder 4 145	Newman
Hurd	Mahoney 3 109	Newton 3 109
Hutchins	Maize	Nichols
Hutchinson 16 580	Mann	Noble 3 109
Hutton 2 72	Mansfield	Nokes 3 109
Ingersoll	Marugder 3 109	Noland 5 181
Ingram 3 109	Marler	Norris 2 72
Jacks 2 72	Marlow 2 72	Norton 4 145
Jackson 41 1523	Mars	Ogle 3 109
Jamison 2 72	Marshal 5 181	Oliver 3 109
Jefferson 3 109	Marshall 3 109	Orem
Jenefer	Martin 11 399	Orme 2 72
Jenifer 6 216	Mason 14 507	Owen
Jenkins 7 254	Massi	Page 5 181
Jennefer	Mathews 15 544	Parker 4 145
Jennie	Mead	Parr
Johnson 65 2356	Mealy	Patrick 2 72
Jokey 2 72	Meekin	Patterson 3 109
Jones 38 1377	Meekins 4 145	Payne 6 216
Jordan 4 145	Meredith 13 471	Pearson
Jourdan	Middleton 3 109	Peck 2 72
Joyce 2 72	Miles 4 145	Peel 4 145
Juniors 9 326	Miller 2 72	Penn
Karna 5 181	Mills 3 109	Perry 4 145
Keffert	Minor 2 72	Peterson
Kepler	Mitchell 5 181	Phenix 4 145
Key 8 290	Mochabee 9 326	Pinkney 7 254
King 15 544	Montgomery 9 326	Pinkwood
Lancaster 15 544	Moore 12 435	Pipes
Lang	Morris	Pipsico 3 109
Lawson 2 72	Mudd 3 109	Pitts
Lee 62 2284	Mullican	Pleasants 6 216

Names, Slave and Free: 1800-1864 -- FREED BLACKS, WASHINGTON, D.C., 1863-1864

Plowden 5 181	Shields	Tippins
Polk	Shiles 3 109	Tolson 2 72
Pool 2 72	Shorter 29 1051	Toogood
Powell 2 72	Sidney	Toyer 7 254
Powers 3 109	Siebert	Trapnell
Prather 4 145	Sifas	Trusty 3 109
Price 7 254	Silvas 4 145	Truxson
Prior	Silvey 2 72	Turley 6 216
Proctor	Simms 33 1197	Turner 8 290
Prout 3 109	Singleton 3 109	Tyler 18 653
Pullison	Skinner 2 72	Upsher 2 72
Purnell	Slater 2 72	Vallis
Pymon	Slatten	Vandrey 2 72
Pynion	Smallwood 13 471	Vaugham
Quad	Smart 3 109	Verlinda
Quander 2 72	Smilo	Vigell 2 72
Queen 7 254	Smith 52 1885	Walker 8 290
Radcliffe 2 72	Snell 3 109	Wallace 16 580
Randoy	Snowden 16 580	Ward 8 290
Rawlings	Solomon 4 145	Ware 4 145
Raymond	Solomons	Warren 12 435
Reed 2 72	Somers	Warring 2 72
Reintzell	Somerville 2 72	Washington 17 616
Rendler	Soper	Waters 17 616
Reynolds 3 109	Speaks 2 72	Watkins 4 145
Rhodes 3 109	Spriggs 3 109	Watson 2 72
Richardson 2 72	Spriggs	Watts
Rideout	Stanford	Weaver 2 72
Ridgley 2 72	Statesman	Webb
Rigney 11 399	Stevens	Webster 3 109
Riley	Stevenson 2 72	Wedge 3 109
Ringold 3 109	Steward 30 1088	Weeks
Ritter	Stoddart	Weldon
Roberson	Stoddert 2 72	Wells 2 72
Robertson 2 72	Strabit	Welsh
Robinson 9 326	Stutley	Wesley
Rosier 5 181	Sutton	West 25 906
Ross 20 725	Sybolt	Wharton
Rousellas	Syphax	Wheeler 4 145
Rustin 9 326	Talbot	Whitaker 3 109
Sampson 6 216	Talbott	White
Sanders 7 254	Taney	Whiting 4 145
Savage 6 216	Tate	Whitney
Scifas (or Cephas)	Taylor 27 979	Widdecomb
Scipia	Tenney 2 72	Wilkinson
Scott 8 290	Teresa	Williams 30 1088
Seibert 3 109	Thomas 52 1885	Wilson 9 326
Selby	Thompson 3 109	Winston 2 72
Semmes	Thornton 2 72	Wood 5 181
Sepas 2 72	Tibbes 2 72	Woodland
Sewell 3 109	Tighlman 11 399	Woodley 2 72
Shaw 6 216	Tilman 4 145	Woodward

Names, Slave and Free: 1800-1864 -- FREED BLACKS, WASHINGTON, D.C., 1863-1864

Worthington 8 290	Wright 3 109	Yearby
Worthy	Yates 9 326	York
		Young 19 689

Frequency
(No number indicates that the name was found only once.)

Brown 67	Diggs 14	Gibson 8
Johnson 65	Dodson 14	Graham 8
Lee 62	Mason 14	Harrison 8
Smith 52	Brisco 13	Key 8
Thomas 52	Cole 13	Nash 8
Clarke 50	Holmes 13	Scott 8
Butler 48	Meredith 13	Turner 8
Jackson 42	Smallwood 13	Walker 8
Jones 38	Adams 12	Ward 8
Carter 35	Gordan 12	Worthington 8
Simms 33	Guttridge 12	Addison 8
Steward 30	Lyles 12	Bowman 7
Williams 30	Moore 12	Broom 7
Shorter 29	Warren 12	Chase 7
Hawkins 28	Burgess 11	Compton 7
Dorsey 27	Campbell 11	Dant 7
Taylor 27	Crusey 11	Dyer 7
West 25	Harris 11	Gantt 7
Bell 24	Herbert 11	Jenkins 7
Carrol 23	Howard 11	Pinkney 7
Green 23	Martin 11	Price 7
Bowie 21	Rigney 11	Queen 7
Brooke 21	Tighlman 11	Sanders 7
Forrest 21	Covington 10	Toyer 7
Davis 20	Dyson 10	Barton 6
Fletcher 20	Hanson 10	Branson 6
Gray 20	Hill 10	Coates 6
Ross 20	Nelson 10	Collins 6
Young 19	Barker 9	Contee 6
Tyler 18	Beckett 9	Dade 6
Hall 17	Berry 9	Etchison 6
Washington 17	Coquire 9	Ford 6
Waters 17	Dines 9	Greenwell 6
Allen 16	Harper 9	Hatton 6
Bruce 16	Hopkins 9	Jenifer 6
Hutchinson 16	Juniors 9	Payne 6
Snowden 16	Mochabee 9	Pleasants 6
Wallace 16	Montgomery 9	Sampson 6
Coleman 15	Robinson 9	Savage 6
Curtis 15	Rustin 9	Shaw 6
King 15	Wilson 9	Turley 6
Lancaster 15	Yates 9	Anderson 5
Lewis 15	Boyd 8	Carpenter 5
Mathews 15	Coakley 8	Commodore 5
Bealle 14	Dixon 8	Coombes 5

Names, Slave and Free: 1800-1864 -- FREED BLACKS, WASHINGTON, D.C., 1863-1864

Digges 5	Bennett 3	Snell 3
Easton 5	Bird 3	Sprigs 3
Greenfield 5	Bowen 3	Thompson 3
Grey 5	Bragden 3	Trusty 3
Gross 5	Burley 3	Webster 3
Handy 5	Calvert 3	Wedge 3
Henson 5	Champ 3	Whitaker 3
Hinton 5	Chism 3	Wright 3
Karna 5	Cooper 3	Alexander 2
Lloyd 5	Cox 3	Bateman 2
Maddox 5	Douglas 3	Bayley 2
Marshal 5	Dover 3	Beson 2
Mitchell 5	Gale 3	Billings 2
Noland 5	Gardiner 3	Blackeston 2
Page 5	Garner 3	Boston 2
Plowden 5	Goins 3	Brotten 2
Rosier 5	Hammond 3	Burrell 2
Wood 5	Harley 3	Carr 2
Ambush 4	Hayes 3	Chambers 2
Belt 4	Henderson 3	Clements 2
Bembrage 4	Henry 3	Colvert 2
Brent 4	Hensley 3	Countee 2
Brook 4	Hepburn 3	Daines 2
Buchannan 4	Hopp 3	Dean 2
Cartwright 4	Hues 3	Delaney 2
Cook 4	Ingram 3	Doris 2
Cross 4	Jefferson 3	Fisher 2
Edmonston 4	Locke 3	Foreman 2
Evans 4	Loggins 3	Freeman 2
Fairfax 4	Mahoney 3	Gassaway 2
Ferguson 4	Marshall 3	Geary 2
Hamilton 4	Marugder 3	Goodall 2
Jordan 4	Middleton 3	Grant 2
Magruder 4	Mills 3	Grayson 2
Meekins 4	Mudd 3	Greenleaf 2
Miles 4	Newton 3	Grinful 2
McPherson 4	Noble 3	Hampton 2
Norton 4	Nokes 3	Harwood 2
Parker 4	Ogle 3	Hickman 2
Peel 4	Oliver 3	Hollis 2
Perry 4	Patterson 3	Hutton 2
Phenix 4	Pipsico 3	Jacks 2
Prather 4	Powers 3	Jamison 2
Silas 4	Prout 3	Jokey 2
Solomon 4	Reynolds 3	Joyce 2
Tilman 4	Rhodes 3	Lawson 2
Ware 4	Ringold 3	Lineless 2
Watkins 4	Seibert 3	Lowndes 2
Wheeler 4	Sewell 3	Lowrie 2
Whiting 4	Shiles 3	Lucas 2
Barber 3	Singleton 3	Mackall 2
Barnes 3	Smart 3	Marlow 2

Black Names in America

Miller 2	Bass	Crown
Minor 2	Bateson	Crowner
McKinsey 2	Beander	Crumwell
Neale 2	Bedda	Cyrass
Norris 2	Bender	Dalcher
Orme 2	Berkley	Dan
Patrick 2	Billingslee	Dangerfield
Peck 2	Biscon	Dashiel
Pool 2	Black	Day
Powell 2	Blackston	Delavan
Quander 2	Blackstone	Dent
Radcliffe 2	Blair	Dickinson
Reed 2	Blake	Didney
Richardson 2	Blaney	Dochet
Ridgley 2	Blaxton	Domer
Robertson 2	Blount	Doner
Sepas 2	Boarman	Dorcey
Silvey 2	Bodely	Dorman
Skinner 2	Bond	Duchett
Slater 2	Booker	Duckett
Somerville 2	Boone	Duffin
Speaks 2	Booth	Duglas
Stevenson 2	Bowles	Duiell
Stoddert 2	Bowyer	Dulaney
Tenney 2	Bradley	Duskin
Thornton 2	Brannon	Duval
Tibbes 2	Brant	Duviell
Tolson 2	Brogden	Edwards
Upsher 2	Broker	Elzey
Vandrey 2	Bronaugh	Erving
Vigell 2	Bryan	Fauntleroy
Warring 2	Bryant	Fenwick
Watson 2	Bundy	Finnick
Weaver 2	Burnett	Fortune
Wells 2	Butts	Francis
Winston 2	Caesar	Frisby
Woodley 2	Cambell	Gains
Adely	Cammel	Gault
Affutt	Cane	Getter
Alfred	Carlton	Ghentt
Arnold	Carmichael	Gilbert
Ashton	Casey	Gillis
Atkinson	Cass	Gladden
Augustus	Chandler	Goodwin
Ayres	Childes	Gover
Bacon	Chisman	Gunnell
Baker	Claxton	Gustus
Baltimore	Colbert	Guttrich
Banks	Coney	Guy
Barbour	Coolidge	Hagan
Barley	Crawley	Harrold
Bartey	Crompton	Hasson

Names, Slave and Free: 1800-1864 -- FREED BLACKS, WASHINGTON, D.C., 1863-1864

Hatton	Myers	Sidney
Hays	McClelland	Siebert
Hicks	McCubbins	Sifas
Hilleary	McGrundy	Slatten
Hollyday	McKenny	Smilo
Honesty	McKenzie	Solomons
Horden	McLain	Somers
Hoskin	Napa	Soper
Howe	Naughton	Spriggs
Hudley	Nead	Stanford
Humphreys	Netter	Statesman
Hurd	Newman	Stevens
Hutchins	Nichols	Stoddart
Ingersoll	Orem	Strabit
Jenefer	Owen	Stutley
Jennefer	Parr	Sutton
Jennie	Pearson	Sybolt
Jourdan	Penn	Syphax
Keffert	Peterson	Talbot
Kepler	Pinkwood	Talbott
Lang	Pipes	Taney
Leonard	Pitts	Tate
Lincoln	Polk	Teresa
Lounds	Prior	Tippins
Lourye	Proctor	Toogood
Lowe	Pullison	Trapnell
Lowry	Purnell	Truxson
Ludlow	Pymon	Vallis
Lynch	Pynion	Vaugham
Macoy	Quad	Verlinda
Maize	Randoy	Watts
Mann	Rawlings	Webb
Mansfield	Raymond	Weeks
Marler	Reintzell	Weldon
Mars	Rendler	Welsh
Massi	Rideout	Wesley
Mead	Riley	Wharton
Mealy	Ritter	White
Meekin	Roberson	Whitney
Morris	Rousellas	Widdecomb
Mullican	Scifas (or Cephas)	Wilkinson
Mulliken	Scipia	Woodland
Munroe	Selby	Woodward
Munson	Semmes	Worthy
Murray	Shields	Yearby
		York

Names, Slave and Free: 1800-1864 -- FREED BLACKS, WASHINGTON, D.C., 1863-1864

Unusual Names

A number after a name indicates the frequency with which it was found; no number indicates it was found once.

Male

Abraham 4	Friday	Marshack
Abraham Dixie Gray	Gabriel 3	Matthais
Abr'm Lincoln	German	Moses 6
Aloysius 3	George Washington 3	Nace 7
Ananias 2	Gusty 4	Nebraska Bill Gray
Andrew Jackson	Hamlet	Noah
Basil 4	Hank	Noble
Boker	Hannibal 2	Orange
Bosquet H'y Shorter	Henny	Orpheus
Caddy	Hezekiah 2	Osceola 2
Caesar	Ignatius 2	Otho 2
Cagy	Isaac 16	Paris Green
Cato	James K. Polk	Protus
Colonel	Jeremiah 4	Resin
Columbus	John Wesley	Reverdy
Darkey	Josua 2	Rezin 2
Dominick 2	Judah	Romulus
Duke	Julius Caesar	Rozier
Eli	July	Sandy 7
Elias 4	Kaliski	Scy
Emanuel	Leander 2	Solomon
Esau	Lamertine	Stanislaus
Ezekiel	Levi 3	Steptoe
Feudal	Loretto	Tecumseh
Floreed	Marcellus	Tobias 2
		Washington

Female

Abigail	Charity 7	Gathy
Acquilla	Chia	Genora
Aldezena	Chissa	Ginnie 2
Aisey	Chloe 2	Hannah 19
Amanda 6	Clarissa	Henry 5
Amelia 8	Comfort	Hortensi
Arena	Crissina	Indiana
Ariana 3	Dallas	Jemima 3
Arilla	Darkey	Jereline
Ary	Delilah 4	Jinney 2
Avonia	Delozier	John Wesley
Belinda	Dinah 2	Jubah
Binah	Edmonia	Kessiah
Bohemia	Elvira	Landonina
California	Fatina	Lavinia 2
Camilla	Florida 3	Leathe 2

130

Names, Slave and Free: 1800-1864 -- FREED BLACKS, WASHINGTON, D.C., 1863-1864

Lethea	Melinda 3	Sophia 20
Lethe 3	Milla	Sophronia
Letitia	Minta 2	Sophy 2
Levinia	Minty 4	Tabitha
Lina	Miranda	Tempe
Linah 2	Narcissa	Treacy
Lishey	Paralle 2	Trecey
Lin	Penelope	Trecy
Louisiana	Phillis 6	Valinda
Lucinda 15	Priscilla 11	Veronica
Lucretia 3	Reny	Verlinda
Malinda 3	Rozetta	Violetta
Mandy	Sebra 2	Winna
Maranda	Selina 2	Winnean
Margella	Selima	Winny 6
Mariah 71	Serena	Zara
Matilda 14	Sillah	Zilphia
		Zora

CHAPTER III

Southern Cities: 1877 to 1937

In the year 1877, Augusta, Georgia, reflecting continued growth after the havoc of the Civil War period, possessed a population of approximately 19,933 Black and White citizens.[1] (In 1860, the population of Augusta was 12,493-- 8,444 White, 3,663 Black slaves and 386 free Blacks; in 1870 the population was 15,389 and in 1880 it had increased to 21,891.) Of these, 19,933 citizens in 1877, there were 5,426 White males and 5,501 White females, a total of 10,927 Whites, and there were 3,999 Black males and 5,007 Black females, totaling 9,006 Blacks.

These citizens could trade, if they read the advertisements, with J. D. Hahn and Bros. Wholesale Manufacturing Concern which made and sold Crackers as well as Plain Stick Candies. J. H. Trump dealt in Fancy Goods, Notions, Jewelry, Flowers, Straw Goods, etc.; Planter's Livery and Sale Stables were dealers in Horses and Mules, Carriages, Phaetons, Buggies and Saddle Horses for Hire. Stock dealers could be accommodated with lodging over the stable, free of charge. And the Grey Eagle Feed and Sale Stables took care of Funerals and Wedding Parties, etc., furnished in the Most Elegant Style with Carriages and Buggies. This was Augusta, Georgia in 1877.

Of the 9,006 Blacks in Augusta, this collection lists 2,766, almost one-third, and of the 10,927 Whites, 4,706 are listed, more than a third. Amongst Blacks and Whites, males reflect a very high percentage of the total lists. Of 3,999 Black males, 2,076 names were collected; of 5,426 White males, 3,535 names were gathered. Amongst females the samples are much smaller: of 5,007 Black females, 690 names are in this list; of 5,501 White females, 1,171 names are used. Nevertheless, the total sample is quite impressive: of the approximately 19,933 citizens of Augusta, Georgia in 1877, this discussion includes 7,474 names, slightly less than 40 per cent.

The Black surnames listed reflect exactly the total of male and female given names collected, 2,766; White surnames collected total 5,056, 350 more than White given names. This is due to the fact that only the first initial of some given names was recorded.

---

[1]These and subsequent census figures were taken from the U. S. Bureau of Census, 1860-1940.

Southern Cities: 1877 to 1937

The following lists show the twenty-five most popular
given names of Blacks and Whites in Augusta, Georgia in
1877 (see Source List N).   The number after the White
name indicates that name's position on the Black's list;
NL indicates that the White given name is not found amongst
the most popular twenty-five Black names. A female list
follows the male list.

Black Given Male Names

Henry	Edward	David
William	Joseph	Adam
John	Lewis	Frank
James	Samuel	Solomon
Robert	Peter	Daniel
Charles	Richard	Alfred
Thomas	Alexander	Jackson
George	Benjamin	Moses
		Isaac

White Given Male Names

John 3	Robert 5	David 17
William 2	Edward 9	Jacob NL
James 4	Frank 19	Andrew NL
Charles 6	Patrick NL	Peter 13
Thomas 7	Michael NL	Albert NL
George 8	Samuel 12	Richard 14
Henry 1	Daniel 21	Alexander 15
Joseph 10	Benjamin 16	Frederick NL
		Theodore NL

Black Female Given Names

Mary	Lizzie	Betsy
Sarah	Susan	Elizabeth
Harriet	Maria	Emily
Eliza	Fanny	Hannah
Jane	Frances	Lucy
Anna	Julia	Margaret
Louisa	Laura	Ellen
Martha	Nancy	Josephine
Emma		

White Female Given Names

Mary 1	Eliza 4	Julia 15
Sarah 2	Ellen 24	Nancy 17
Elizabeth 19	Susan 11	Mattie NL
Martha 8	Fanny 13	Ann NL
Jane 5	Margaret 23	Emma 9
Anna 6	Catharine NL	Amanda NL

BLACK NAMES IN AMERICA

Southern Cities: 1877 to 1937

Frances 14	Caroline NL	Harriet 3
Lucy 22	Alice NL	Lizzie 10
	Sally NL	

A very high correspondence exists between male Black and White given name usage; the first ten most popular names are the same amongst both groups although the order does change somewhat. Of the first twenty-five, seven White names are not found; they are: Patrick, Michael, Jacob, Andrew, Albert, Frederick and Theodore. Blacks use, instead: Lewis, Adam, Solomon, Alfred, Jackson, Moses and Isaac. Although Blacks do not show a great interest in Jacob, it appears that they employ a greater number of Old Testament names than do Whites.

Female name usage differs in seven out of the most popular twenty-five given names, but of the first ten names, White women use only six found amongst the first ten on the Black's list. Yet the first two most popular Black names, Mary and Sarah, are also, in the same order, the two most popular White names, a situation not found amongst males. There appears no discernible pattern in these differences. Both males and females of both races employ eighteen identical names from the lists of twenty-five most frequently used names.

Of the 2,076 Black male given names, 205 are unusual, but when we deduct those considered old-fashioned, 101 names, the amount drops from 9.9 per cent to 5 per cent. Of the 690 Black female given names, 117 are unusual, but 75 are merely old-fashioned, reducing the percentage from 17 per cent to 6.1 per cent. It appears that males used a slightly higher percentage of unusual names whereas females used a much higher percentage of old-fashioned names. Black men used five famous names; Black females, none.

Of the 3,535 White male given names, 140, or 4 per cent, are unusual. Of these, 78 are old-fashioned so that the percentage of unusual names is a very low 1.8 per cent. White females employed 114 unusual names, a 9.7 percentage, but 62 of these are old-fashioned, reducing the figure to 4.4 per cent. White females employ a greater percentage of unusual names than White males. In this case, unlike Black women, White females seem to be less conservative than their men. Like Blacks, White males employed five famous names and again, like Blacks, White females employed none.

Blacks of both sexes employed 11.6 per cent unusual names, or 322 of 2,766; 176 of these were old-fashioned, bringing the total down to 146, or 5.3 per cent. Whites used 254 unusual names from a list of 4,706, a much lower 5.4 per cent; 140 were old-fashioned, bringing the total of unusual names down to 114, or a very low 2.4 per cent. Thus, Blacks appear to be less conservative than Whites. This may be seen in the famous names used by Black and White males. Blacks were attracted to Bonaparte, Columbus, Garibaldi, Martin Van Buren and Osceola; Whites employed Washington three times and Columbus twice.

There are two "alley" names worth noting, both belonging to Blacks: Tin Cup Alley and Thank God Alley. The whole question of unusual names characteristic of Black Americans is pervaded by stereotyped prejudice and myth.

Southern Cities: 1877 to 1937

Unusual names listed earlier have pointed to the eccentric predilections of both races, and this is borne out here.

Following are lists of unusual White and Black names taken from the roles of Welfare clients in Richmond County.[2]

Male

Bannister	M.T.
Big-un	Mum
Boston	Peas Wash
Coot	Pedigree
Cootsie	Polasky Ryas
Handy	Professor Polite
Julius Caesar	Reason
King Solomon	Rolling Stone
Major	Royal
Messiah Golphin	Squire
	Zim

Female

Affie	Frezette
Angel	Kizziah
Brooksie	Lilly White
Easter Lily	Princess

Some Unusual Surnames

Jim Corker	Sam Possum
David B. Early	Hattie Sapp
Rosa Easter	Martha Trotty
	George Zie

Male

Cotton	Marcellus
Flanery Salter	Ools
Flake	Simmie Witt
George Washington Tudor	Sol Moog
Hapsey Hoover	Theophilus
King David Sullivan	Turley Pincard Blackstone
	Zedie Salter

Female

Army	Euphemia
Arzula	Falbia
Drucilla	Falkia Diligence

---

[2]Richmond County, Department of Public Welfare.

Southern Cities: 1877 to 1937

Florian	Orneita
Gyphene	Remmie
Ida Frost Green	Sabra
Letha	Samantha
Mary Magdalene	Signie
Musette	Ulie

It would be presumptuous for one to hazard a guess as to the racial identity of these names without some familiarity with the bearers of these names. And I would suspect that some readers will be surprised to learn that the male and female given names in the last two lists are those of Whites in Augusta, Georgia in 1877.

In the following list we see the differences in given name usage of Augusta, Georgia Blacks, in 1877, Black slaves in the South, 1800-1860 and free Blacks in the South, 1800-1860. A female list follows the male list. The number after the name indicates that name's position amongst Augusta, Georgia Blacks; NL indicates that the name was not found amongst the twenty-five most popular Augusta, Georgia given names (see Source Lists I, J, N).

Augusta, Georgia Black Males, 1877	Slave Black Males	Free Black Males, 1800-1860
Henry	John 3	John 3
William	Henry 1	William 2
John	George 8	James 4
James	Sam NL	Thomas 7
Robert	Tom NL	George 8
Charles	Charles 6	Henry 1
Thomas	Jim NL	Samuel 12
George	Jack NL	David 17
Edward	Peter 13	Charles 6
Joseph	William 2	Peter 13
Lewis	Joe NL	Joseph 10
Samuel	Bob NL	Isaac 25
Peter	Bill NL	Daniel 21
Richard	Moses 24	Richard 14
Alexander	Isaac NL	Robert 5
Benjamin	Ben NL	Benjamin 16
David	Dick NL	Jesse NL
Adam	James 4	Jacob NL
Frank	Harry NL	Moses 24
Solomon	Lewis 11	Stephen NL
Daniel	Jacob NL	Lewis 11
Alfred	Frank 19	Edward 9
Jackson	Ned NL	Billy NL
Moses	Daniel 21	Jack NL
Isaac	Stephen NL	Anthony NL

Southern Cities: 1877 to 1937

Augusta, Georgia Black Females, 1877	Slave Black Females	Free Black Females, 1800-1860
Mary	Mary 1	Nancy 17
Sarah	Maria(h) 12	Mary 1
Harriet	Nancy 17	Sally NL
Eliza	Sarah 2	Betsy 18
Jane	Lucy 22	Polly NL
Anna	Harriet 3	Lucy 22
Louisa	Elisa NL	Elizabeth 19
Martha	Jane 5	Jane 5
Emma	Hannah 21	Sarah 2
Lizzie	Martha 8	Hannah 21
Susan	Rach(a)el NL	Fanny 13
Maria	Caroline NL	Milly NL
Fanny	Ann NL	Rachael NL
Frances	(Anna 6)	Patsy NL
Julia	Sally NL	Peggy NL
Laura	Amy NL	Eliza 4
Nancy	Betsy 18	Ann NL
Betsy	Milly NL	(Anna 6)
Elizabeth	Fanny 13	Susan 11
Emily	Louisa 7	Maria 12
Hannah	Matilda NL	Rebecca NL
Lucy	Emily 20	Charlotte NL
Margaret	Margaret 23	Martha 8
Ellen	Rose NL	Margaret 23
Josephine	Susan 11	Catharine NL
	Charlotte NL	Judy NL

Of the first ten names employed by Augusta, Georgia Black males in 1877, only five appear amongst Black slaves in the South from 1800-1860. Indeed, four of the ten most frequently used Black slave names do not appear amongst the twenty-five most popular names of Augusta, Georgia Blacks. And of the first twenty-five most popular names in 1877, only eleven are to be found on the list of Black slaves. It should be noted that six of the slave names not found in 1877, Sam, Tom, Joe, Bob, Ben and Dick, are diminutives of names which do find great favor with Blacks in 1877. They are: Samuel (12th), Thomas (7th), Joseph (10th), Robert (5th), Benjamin (16th) and Richard (14th).

Free Blacks in the South from 1800-1860, as expected, show a closer relationship with Augusta, Georgia Blacks in 1877, than with slave Blacks in the South during the period 1800-1860; only six names from the pre-1860 list do not appear amongst the first twenty-five names on the 1877 list, and of the ten most popular names, seven are found amongst both groups of Blacks. This pattern does not hold true with females. It seems that slave females in the South used fifteen names which are duplicated by females in Augusta, Georgia in 1877, and of the ten most popular, these two groups have five in common. They both favor Mary most; and Sarah and Harriet, second and third in 1877, appear fourth and sixth amongst slave women in the 1800-1860 period.

BLACK NAMES IN AMERICA

Southern Cities: 1877 to 1937

On the other hand, free Black females in the South used fourteen names in common with their sisters in 1877, and of the first ten, only three find a place in the Augusta, Georgia group. Thus, contrary to their men, slave females before 1860 show a closer tie, in terms of given name usage, to Black women in Augusta, Georgia in 1877 than do the free Black women before 1860. This reinforces the idea that Black females generally tended to be more conservative in name usage than their men.

The following lists indicate the twenty-five most popular surnames of Blacks and Whites in Augusta, Georgia in 1877 (see Source List N). The number after the White surname indicates that name's position on the Black list; NL indicates that the name was not found amongst the most popular twenty-five surnames of Blacks.

Black Surnames, Augusta, Ga., 1877	White Surnames Augusta, Ga., 1877
Williams	Smith 4
Jones	Williams 1
Johnson	Johnson 3
Smith	Jones 2
Jackson	Brown 7
Thomas	Davis 9
Brown	Moore 16
Walker	Thompson NL
Davis	Miller 23
Green	Hill NL
Robinson	Walker 8
Scott	Baker NL
Harris	Clark 25
Turner	Wilson 17
Anderson	Parker NL
Moore	Simmons NL
Wilson	Anderson 15
Washington	Evans NL
Mitchell	Jackson 5
Cummings	Butler 21
Butler	Martin 22
Martin	Roberts NL
Miller	Thomas 6
Carter	Fleming NL
Clark	Scott 12

Of the twenty-five most popular surnames used by Blacks in Augusta, Georgia in 1877, only eight are not found amongst Whites in the same area. Green and Robinson, 10th and 11th, Harris and Turner, 13th and 14th, Washington, Mitchell and Cummings, 18th, 19th and 20th, and Carter, 24th, are eschewed by Whites in favor of Thompson, Hill, Baker, Parker, Simmons, Evans,

Southern Cities: 1877 to 1937

Roberts and Fleming, appearing on the White list 8th, 10th, 12th, 15th, 16th, 18th, 22nd and 24th, respectively.

And of the ten surnames most frequently used by Blacks, six are found amongst the first ten White surnames. Indeed, the first four Black surnames are identical, although not in the same order, to the first four White surnames. It appears that with seventeen out of the twenty-five most popular names appearing on both lists, at least in terms of surname usage, Blacks and Whites seem to be very much assimilated.

It is interesting to note that the surnames of some prominent slaveholders in Georgia find favor amongst Blacks. Sir James Wright and John Perry at least preceded, if indeed they were not connected in some way with, the six Black Wrights and Perrys. Butler (14), Carter (13), Hill (10), and Willis (7) also bear names prominent amongst slaveholders in Georgia of the period preceding the Civil War. Whites employed these names also: Wright (9), Butler (13), Carter (8), Hill (21) and Willis (4). Perry is not used by Whites in this listing. On the other hand, such names as Habersham, Morel, Spalding, Bissett, Bond, Dickson, Pope, Couper and Everett, prominent slaveholders all, found little or no favor with either Blacks or Whites.[3]

Four Black surnames of this period give special pause for conjecture, for they very well may be illustrative of universal practices whereby surnames evolve from given names. Benjamin, Pleasant, Julia and Nancy do not appear on the White surname list but do appear once each as Black surnames. Moreover, Benjamin appears twenty-eight times as a Black male given name and Pleasant four times. Julia appears on the female given name list twelve times and Nancy eleven times. It is possible, although there are of course other possibilities, that these four given names became surnames for Blacks after freedom. It is also possible that the more common slave name Ben was elongated after freedom to a surname Benjamin. And, just as it is possible that the female Black slaves Nanny and Judy were graced with the surnames Nancy and Julia, the Black slave called Pleasant may have taken that as his surname.

        The following lists indicate the twenty-five most popular surnames of Blacks in Washington, D. C., who were freed in 1863-64, as well as the twenty-five most popular surnames of Blacks and Whites in Augusta, Georgia in 1877. The number after the names of Augusta Blacks and Whites indicates that name's position amongst Washington Blacks; NL indicates that the name was not found amongst the most popular Washington names (see Source Lists M, N).

Washington, D. C. Surnames of Blacks Freed in 1863-1864	Augusta, Ga., 1877 Black Surnames	Augusta, Ga., 1877 White Surnames
Brown	Williams 13	Smith 4
Johnson	Jones 9	Williams 13

---

[3]Flanders, op. cit., p. 86.

Southern Cities: 1877 to 1937

Washington, D. C. Surnames of Blacks Freed in 1863-1864	Augusta, Ga., 1877 Black Surnames	Augusta, Ga., 1877 White Surnames
Lee	Johnson 2	Johnson 2
Smith	Smith 4	Jones 9
Thomas	Jackson 8	Brown 1
Clarke	Thomas 5	Davis 25
Butler	Brown 1	Moore NL
Jackson	Walker NL	Thompson NL
Jones	Davis 25	Miller NL
Carter	Green 21	Hill NL
Simms	Robinson NL	Walker NL
Steward	Scott NL	Baker NL
Williams	Harris NL	Clark 6
Shorter	Turner NL	(with an 'e')
Hawkins	Anderson NL	Wilson NL
Dorsey	Moore NL	Parker NL
Taylor	Wilson NL	Simmons NL
West	Washington NL	Anderson NL
Bell	Mitchell NL	Evans NL
Carrol	Cummings NL	Jackson 8
Green	Butler 7	Butler 7
Bowie	Martin NL	Martin NL
Brooke	Miller NL	Roberts NL
Forrest	Carter 10	Thomas 5
Davis	Clark 6	Fleming NL
	(with an 'e')	Scott NL

Of the twenty-five most popular surnames taken by Washington, D. C. Blacks in 1863-64, only twelve retained their standing amongst Blacks in Augusta, Georgia thirteen years later. And of the first ten, only six retained their standing. Of these same twenty-five surnames, only ten retained their standing amongst Whites in Augusta, Georgia, and only four continued in the first ten.

It seems that Blacks in Augusta, Georgia were much more prone to employ surnames comparable with those used by Whites in the same city than they were to follow the lead of Washington, D. C. Blacks. But when we compare the surnames employed in Augusta, Georgia with those used by free Blacks throughout the country in 1830 (see Footnote 47, Chapter II), we find that it is the Washington group which varies considerably from the pattern established by free Blacks throughout the nation in 1830. Indeed, it is interesting to note that Augusta, Georgia Whites in 1877 employ surnames closer to the national surname usage of Blacks in 1830 than do those freed Blacks in Washington, D. C. in 1864.

The following lists indicate the twenty-five most popular surnames of Blacks and Whites in the following groups: All Free Blacks, 1830; Washington, D. C. Free

Southern Cities: 1877 to 1937

Blacks, 1863-64; Augusta, Georgia, Blacks, 1877; and
Augusta, Georgia, Whites, 1877. The number after the name
indicates that name's position amongst all free Blacks,
1830; NL indicates that the name was not listed amongst
the most popular twenty-five surnames used by free Blacks
throughout the country in 1830 (see Source Lists M, N).

All Free Blacks 1830	Washington, D. C. Free Blacks	Augusta, Ga. Blacks, 1877	Augusta, Ga. Whites, 1877
Johnson	Brown 2	Williams 5	Smith 3
Brown	Johnson 1	Jones 6	Williams 5
Smith	Lee NL	Johnson 1	Johnson 1
Jackson	Smith 3	Smith 3	Jones 6
Williams	Thomas 10	Jackson 4	Brown 2
Jones	Clarke NL	Thomas 10	Davis 13
Thompson	Butler 17	Brown 2	Moore 18
Scott	Jackson 4	Walker NL	Thompson 7
Freeman	Jones 6	Davis 13	Miller 16
Thomas	Carter NL	Green 15	Hill 20
Harris	Simms NL	Robinson 25	Walker NL
Wilson	Steward NL	Scott 8	Baker NL
Davis	Williams 5	Harris 11	Clark NL
Anderson	Shorter NL	Turner NL	Wilson 12
Green	Hawkins NL	Anderson 14	Parker NL
Miller	Dorsey NL	Moore 18	Simmons NL
Butler	Taylor 23	Wilson 12	Anderson 14
Moore	West NL	Washington NL	Evans NL
White	Bell NL	Mitchell NL	Jackson 4
Hill	Carrol NL	Cummings NL	Butler 17
Roberts	Green 15	Butler 17	Martin NL
Hall	Bowie NL	Martin NL	Roberts 21
Taylor	Brooke NL	Miller 16	Thomas 10
Cooper	Forrest NL	Carter NL	Fleming NL
Robinson	Davis 13	Clark NL	Scott 8

Of the ten most frequently used Black surnames throughout the country in
1830, Washington, D. C. Blacks chose six as part of their most popular ten.
Of the remaining four, Lee (3rd), Clarke (6th) and Carter (10th) do not appear on the national list of twenty-five at all. And, of the first twenty-
five amongst Washington Blacks, fourteen names do not appear amongst the
twenty-five most frequently used surnames by Blacks throughout the country
in 1830.

In sharp contrast to this are the comparisons of Blacks and Whites in
Augusta, Georgia in 1877. The former lists seven names of their first ten
which correspond to those of the ten most popular names of all Blacks, and
only one name, Walker, of the first ten does not appear on the national list
of twenty-five. In addition, only eight of the first twenty-five most popular surnames are not duplicated on the national list. Of the White surnames
six out of ten of the most frequently used appear on the list of the ten most

Southern Cities: 1877 to 1937

popular free Black surnames throughout the country, and of even greater importance is the fact that not one name amongst the ten most popular White surnames is not found amongst the first twenty-five free Black surnames throughout the country. It is most interesting to note that of these groups, the
Washington Blacks freed in 1863-1864, the Augusta Blacks in 1877 and the
Augusta Whites in 1877, the Whites reflect the closest correspondence to free
Black surname usage throughout the country in 1830.

Between 1877 and 1899, the population of Augusta almost doubled, from
19,933 to 38,787, and the Black population reflected this growth. That is,
Blacks increased in number from 9,006 in 1877 to 18,226 in 1899, slightly more
than double. Males increased, amongst Blacks, from 3,999 to 8,224 and females
from 5,007 to 10,002. This collection deals with 6,457 Black males and 2,579
Black females. The sample is even more comprehensive than the earlier one.
In 1877, the Black male sample was more than 50 per cent and the Black female
sample about 14 per cent. In 1899, the Black male sample climbs to over 75
per cent, and the Black female sample reaches over 25 per cent. Of the 20,561
Whites in Augusta in 1899, this collection deals with 8,622 male names from a
total of 10,027 males and 2,743 female names from a total of 10,534 females.
Again, this sample is even more representative than the one in 1877. In the
earlier period, the White male sample dealt with a little less than 65 per
cent of the total White male population; in 1899 this sample rises to over
85 per cent. In 1877, the White female sample reflected approximately 21 per
cent of the White female population; in 1899, this sample rises to a little
over 26 per cent.

Typical ads in Augusta in 1899 come from The Grand Opera House which, for
some reason, sells Electric Fans (in the summer) and Steam Heat (in winter).
The Augusta Bicycle Exchange says that it has "an elegant line of Bicycles for
rent"; The Augusta Brewing Company handles Keg and Bottle Beer and always one
finds "money loaned on anything of value."

The total number of Black surnames in this collection is 9,184, 148 more
than the combined male and female given name lists. Thus, the surname sample
of the Black community reflects a little over 50 per cent of the entire Black
population. White surnames in this list include 11,840 names, 475 more than
the total of White male and female given names. This sample reflects over
55 per cent of the total White population.

The following lists represent the twenty-five most
popular given names of Blacks in Augusta, Georgia in 1899
(see Source List O). The numbers after each name indicate
that name's position amongst Blacks and Whites in 1877
(see Source List N). NL indicates the name was not found
amongst 1877 males. A female list follows the male list.

BLACK NAMES IN AMERICA

Southern Cities: 1877 to 1937

Male Black Given Names, 1899	1877	White Males, 1877	Male Black Given Names, 1899	1877	White Males, 1877
William	2	2	Benjamin	16	16
John	3	1	David	17	17
Henry	1	7	Alexander	15	23
James	4	3	Andrew	NL	19
George	8	6	Daniel	21	15
Charles	6	4	Albert	NL	21
Solomon	20	NL	Augustus	NL	NL
Robert	5	9	Jesse	NL	NL
Edward	9	10	Moses	24	NL
Joseph	10	8	Louis	NL	NL
Samuel	12	14	Peter	13	20
Frank	19	11	Alfred	22	NL
Richard	14	22			

Female Black Given Names, 1899	1877	White Females, 1877	Female Black Given Names, 1899	1877	White Females, 1877
Mary	1	1	Louisa	7	NL
Anna	6	6	Lucy	22	20
Sarah	2	2	Mattie	NL	15
Emma	9	17	Ella	NL	NL
Fanny	13	10	Alice	NL	22
Maria	12	NL	Laura	16	NL
Martha	8	7	Amanda	NL	18
Eliza	4	7	Hattie	NL	NL
Julia	15	13	Elizabeth	19	3
Jane	5	5	Sally	NL	23
Rosa	NL	NL	Carrie	NL	NL
Annie	NL	NL	Frances	14	19
Lizzie	10	25			

Of the twenty-five most popular given names of Black males in Augusta, Georgia, in 1899, twenty are found among the twenty-five most popular names of Blacks in 1877 and nineteen among Whites in 1877. Of the first ten in 1899, Blacks and Whites in 1877 used nine. Solomon, Samuel, Richard, Augustus, Jesse and Louis increase in popularity amongst Blacks in 1899 in relation to Black and White usage in 1877.

On the other hand, Henry, Robert, Alexander, Peter and Alfred drop in popularity amongst Blacks. All these shifts place these names in closer proximity to the degree of popularity these names enjoyed amongst Whites.

Of the twenty-five most popular given names of Black females in Augusta in 1899, sixteen are found amongst Black females in 1877 and seventeen among Whites in 1877. Of the first ten in 1899, Black and White women used seven.

144

BLACK NAMES IN AMERICA

Southern Cities: 1877 to 1937

The most dramatic shifts involve Emma, Maria, Rosa, Annie, Ella, Hattie, Elizabeth and Carrie, reflecting marked changes in popularity.

Although many shifts occur, there seems to be no discernible pattern emerging other than that Black men, unlike Whites, are attracted to the Biblical name Solomon and that Black women, again unlike their White counterparts, prefer the quasi-Biblical/foreign Maria, while rejecting Elizabeth.

Of the 6,457 male names, 646, or 10 per cent, are unusual; of these 304 are considered old-fashioned, leaving a total of unusual names of 342, or 5.3 per cent. Black males employed twenty-seven famous names. Of the 2,579 Black female names, 453, or 17.6 per cent, are unusual; of these 294 are old-fashioned, leaving a total of unusual names of 159, or 6.2 per cent. Black females used no famous names. It appears that Black females enjoy a slightly greater use of unusual names and a much greater use of old-fashioned names. Black females seem to be, on the one hand, more radical in their use of unusual names, and, on the other hand, more conservative in their use of old-fashioned names than their male counterparts. Of the 8,622 White male given names, 301, or 3.5 per cent, are unusual; deducting the 129 old-fashioned names leaves those unusual at 172, or 2 per cent. White males employ nine famous names. Of the 2,743 White female given names, 277, or 10.1 per cent, are unusual; of these, 112 are old-fashioned, leaving 165, or 6 per cent unusual. White females use four famous names.

White females employ a markedly greater percentage of unusual and old-fashioned names than do White males. Again, like Black females, White women appear more radical than their men in their use of unusual names and more conservative than their men in their employment of old-fashioned names.

Black males use the following famous names: Beauregard, Charlemagne, Columbus (9), Garfield (2), George Washington (7), Hannibal, Jefferson Davis, Napoleon (4) and Stonewall. White males' famous names are: Columbus (4), Cortez (2) and Napoleon (3). White females are graced with Jefferson Davis and Wilhelmina (3).

The following lists indicate the twenty-five most popular surnames of Blacks and Whites in Augusta, Georgia in 1899 from a total of 9,184 Black surnames and 11,840 White surnames. The number after the White surname indicates that name's position on the Black list; NL indicates that the name was not found amongst the most popular twenty-five surnames of Blacks (see List O).

Black Surnames Augusta, Ga., 1899	White Surnames Augusta, Ga., 1899
Williams	Smith 5
Johnson	Jones 3
Jones	Johnson 2
Brown	Williams 1

Southern Cities: 1877 to 1937

Black Surnames Augusta, Ga., 1899	White Surnames Augusta, Ga., 1899
Smith	Brown 4
Jackson	Davis 9
Thomas	Clark NL
Walker	Thomas 7
Davis	Young NL
Harris	Allen 19
Robinson	Taylor NL
Green	Hill NL
Scott	Miller NL
Wright	Moore 17
White	Hale NL
Wilson	King NL
Moore	Martin NL
Washington	Wilson 16
Allen	Thompson 8
Jenkins	Howard NL
Evans	White 15
Anderson	Wright 14
Carter	Lee NL
Cummings	Roberts NL
Collins	Green 12

Of the first ten Black surnames in 1899, seven appear amongst Whites; of the first twenty-five Black names, thirteen are the same on the White list. In 1877, six of the first ten and seventeen of the first twenty-five were identical. Allen, White and Wright do not appear amongst the first twenty-five Black or White surnames in 1877; interestingly enough, however, in the intervening twenty-two years they gained great popularity, appearing in both Black and White surname lists in 1899.

The following list represents the twenty-five most popular surnames used by Blacks in Augusta, Georgia in 1899. The number after the name indicates that name's position amongst 1877 Blacks in Augusta, Georgia; NL indicates that the name was not found amongst the first twenty-five Black surnames in 1877 (see Source Lists N, O).

Williams 1	Davis 9	Moore 16
Johnson 3	Harris 13	Washington 18
Jones 2	Robinson 11	Allen NL
Brown 7	Green 10	Jenkins NL
Smith 4	Scott 12	Evans NL
Jackson 5	Wright NL	Anderson 15
Thomas 6	White NL	Carter 24
Walker 8	Wilson 17	Cummings 20
		Collins NL

Black Names in America

Southern Cities: 1877 to 1937

Of the first ten Black surnames used in 1899, nine were amongst the first
ten used in 1877; of the first twenty-five in 1899, nineteen were equally
popular twenty-two years before. There appears no dramatic change in surname
popularity from 1877 to 1899 in Augusta, Georgia, amongst Blacks.

The following list represents the twenty-five most
popular surnames used by Whites in Augusta, Georgia, in
1899. The number after the name indicates that name's
position amongst 1877 Whites in Augusta, Georgia; NL indicates that the name was not found amongst the first
twenty-five White surnames in 1877 (see Source Lists N, O).

Smith 1	Young NL	Martin 21
Jones 4	Allen NL	Wilson 14
Johnson 3	Taylor NL	Thompson 8
Williams 2	Hill 10	Howard NL
Brown 5	Miller 9	White NL
Davis 6	Moore 7	Wright NL
Clark 13	Hale NL	Lee NL
Thomas 23	Kings NL	Roberts 22
		Green NL

Of the first ten in 1899, only six were the same in 1877, and of the first
twenty-five, only fifteen were the same. It appears that White surname practices were in a greater period of shift than Black surname practices in 1899.

Some interesting names possibly reflect universal naming practices; for
example, Son Phoeby, Black male, is the only Phoeby in the Augusta directory.
Is it possible that he is the "son of Phoebe?" An example of sex name switch-
ing is a White nurse in Augusta with the name Jessie. The name of a Black
man, Henry Kentucky, reflects a location operative in surname development.

Following is a list of women who bore male names. Mrs. Hill J. Davis,
widow of Walter, is Black; the list among Whites is more extensive: Mrs.
Harvie J. Smith, widow of William J.; Mrs. Bennie J. Swinler, widow of Monroe;
Misses Ezra C. Hoffman, Eddie R. May, Dickie Puryear, Joe Johnson, Perry
Johnson and Theodore Murphy. The number of Willies is high; twelve amongst
Blacks and ten amongst White females.

Twenty years later, in 1919, the population of Augusta numbered approximately 51,322: 22,158 Blacks and 29,164 Whites. Of these, there were approximately 9,772 Black males and 12,386 Black females and 14,192 White males
and 14,972 White females. By this time, advertisements announced "over
1,000,000 Fords in use." One could enter the Dreamland Moving Pictures
Theatre. The Kodak Man roamed the streets and Mazda lamps were available.
In addition, the United Detective Agency was at one's service and Coca-Cola
was on the scene.

Black Names in America

Southern Cities: 1877 to 1937

This collection includes the given names of 9,613 Black citizens of Augusta, almost 45 per cent of the entire Black community. There are 5,789 Black male given names listed, approximately 59 per cent, and 3,824 Black female given names, approximately 28 per cent. For Whites, the samples are larger, with 9,266 White male given names, approximately 65 per cent, and 10,136 White female names, approximately 70 per cent, included.

This collection lists 9,621 Black surnames, approximately 45 per cent of the entire Black community in Augusta, and 19,788 White surnames, approximately 67 per cent.

The following list represents the twenty-five most popular Black male given names in Augusta, Georgia, 1919 (see Source List P). The first number after the name indicates that name's position amongst Black males in Augusta in 1899; the second number indicates that name's position amongst Black males in Augusta in 1877; the third number indicates that name's position amongst White males in Augusta in 1877; NL indicates the name was not listed amongst the first twenty-five (see Source Lists N, O, P).

Black Male Given Names, 1919	1899	1877	Whites, 1877
William	1	2	2
John	2	3	1
James	4	4	3
George	5	8	6
Charles	6	6	4
Henry	3	1	7
Solomon	7	20	NL
Robert	8	5	9
Joseph	10	10	8
Edward	9	9	10
Samuel	11	12	14
Frank	12	19	11
Albert	19	NL	21
Benjamin	14	16	16
Richard	13	14	22
David	15	17	17
Arthur	NL	NL	NL
Walter	NL	NL	NL
Jesse	21	NL	NL
Andrew	17	NL	19
Moses	22	24	NL
Alexander	16	15	23
Louis	23	NL	NL
Clarence	NL	NL	NL
Peter	24	13	20

Southern Cities: 1877 to 1937

Black males in 1899 and 1919 appear highly consistent in their use of given names; of the first ten most popular names, both groups concur, although the order shifts slightly. Of the first twenty-five most popular given names, only three, <u>Arthur</u>, <u>Walter</u> and <u>Clarence</u>, are found in great use amongst Black males in 1919 but not amongst Blacks in 1899 or 1877.

Black males in 1919 employ nine names of their first ten which are found amongst the first ten in 1877. But the shifts among the first ten are relatively marked. Of the first twenty-five names, only seven on the 1919 list are not found in 1877.

The following list represents the twenty-five most popular Black female given names in Augusta, Georgia, 1919. The first number after the name indicates that name's position amongst Black females in Augusta in 1899; the second number indicates that name's position amongst Black females in Augusta in 1877; the third number indicates that name's position amongst White females in Augusta in 1877; NL indicates the name was not listed amongst the first twenty-five (see Source Lists N, O, P).

Black Female Given Names, 1919	1899	1877	Whites, 1877
Mary	1	1	1
Annie	12	NL	NL
Carrie	24	NL	NL
Emma	4	9	17
Sarah	3	2	2
Lizzie	13	10	25
Hattie	21	NL	NL
Fanny	5	13	10
Julia	9	15	13
Rosa	11	NL	NL
Ella	17	NL	NL
Lula	NL	NL	NL
Mamie	NL	NL	NL
Louise	NL	NL	NL
Eliza	8	4	7
Alice	18	NL	22
Amanda	20	NL	18
Laura	19	16	NL
Jennie	NL	NL	NL
Janie	NL	NL	NL
Martha	7	8	4
Clara	NL	NL	NL
Katy	NL	NL	NL
Minnie	NL	NL	NL
Susie	NL	NL	NL

BLACK NAMES IN AMERICA

Southern Cities: 1877 to 1937

Of the first ten names in 1919, only five are found in 1899. Of the first twenty-five names found in 1919, only sixteen are the same as in 1899.

In 1919, only four names of the most popular ten are to be seen on the list in 1877. It seems clear that the Black female given names were in a much greater period of shift during the years 1877-1919 than were Black male given names.

Of the 5,789 Black male names, 540, or 9.3 per cent, are unusual; of these, 234 are old-fashioned, leaving a total of 306 or 5.3 per cent unusual. Black males employ twenty-five famous names. Of the 3,824 Black female given names, 490, or 12.8 per cent, are unusual; of these, 292 are old-fashioned, leaving a total of 198, or 5.2 per cent, unusual. Black females employ a higher percentage of old-fashioned names than do Black males, but the difference in percentage of unusual names is insignificant: males, 5.3 per cent; females, 5.2 per cent.

Of the 9,266 White male given names, 357, or 3.8 per cent, are unusual; of these, 123 are old-fashioned, leaving a total of 243, or 2.5 per cent, unusual. White males employ fifteen famous names. Of the 10,136 White female given names, 740, or 7.3 per cent, are unusual. Of these, 230 are old-fashioned, leaving a total of 510, or 5 per cent, unusual. White females employ almost exactly twice the percentage of old-fashioned and unusual names as White males.

Black males employ these famous names: Columbus (5), Garfield (3), George Washington (6), Henry Clay, Horace Greely, Lincoln (2), Martin Van Buren, Napoleon (3), Roosevelt and Thomas Jefferson (2). Black females employ Wilhelmina. White males use these famous names: Columbus (4), Cortez (3), George Washington, Napoleon (3), Osceola, Roosevelt, Stonewall Jackson and Ulysses S. In addition, there are many Robert E's and Jefferson D's. White females use Wilhelmina (14).

There are some interesting name patterns amongst these citizens of Augusta, Georgia. Juliet emerges for the first time amongst Blacks in 1919. Rosie, popular amongst slave women as Rose and modern Black women as Rosa, appears also for the first time. Alliterative nomenclature appears in Katie Key, Lottie Lucky, Lula Loyd and Rosa Roe, and one wonders at the motivation behind Fields Wright. There appear numerous Guses, no doubt a shortened Augustus. William Williams appears twenty-five times in Augusta, Georgia in 1919 among Blacks; two of these appear with females as Willie Williams. Amongst White males, William Williams appears five times.

If the City Directory is correct, Whites exhibit a number of sex name changes. There are White males named Ebbie, Georgia and Florence and White females named Albert, Allen (2), Bertrand, Byron, Carrol, Chester, Claude, Clifford, Clyde, Earl, George, Joel, John, Jonnye, Lee, Leonard, Martin, Marvin, Otis, Reuben, Russell, Warren and Willis.

Black Names in America

Southern Cities: 1877 to 1937

The following lists represent the twenty-five most popular Black and White surnames in Augusta, Georgia, 1919 from a total of 9,621 Black, and 19,788 White surnames collected. The number after the White surname indicates that name's position on the Black surname list. "NL" indicates that the White surname was not among the most popular twenty-five Black surnames (see Source List P).

1919 Black Surnames	1919 White Surnames
Williams	Smith 6
Jones	Jones 2
Johnson	Johnson 3
Brown	Brown 4
Jackson	Williams 1
Smith	Miller NL
Thomas	Wilson 18
Walker	Wright 21
Harris	Davis 10
Davis	Morris NL
Robinson	Hill 24
Green	Moore 19
Scott	Hall NL
Glover	Walker 8
Butler	Murphy NL
Evans	Clark NL
White	Parker NL
Wilson	Allen 22
Moore	Martin NL
Jenkins	Jackson 5
Wright	Scott 13
Allen	Thomas 7
Young	White 17
Hill	Green 12
Mitchell	Owens NL

Of the first ten Black surnames in Augusta in 1919, it appears that Whites used the same six names. Of the first twenty-five surnames used by Blacks and Whites, seventeen are identical.

The following list represents the twenty-five most popular Black surnames in Augusta, Georgia, 1919. The first number after the name indicates that name's position amongst Blacks in Augusta in 1899; the second number indicates that name's position amongst Blacks in Augusta in 1877; the third number indicates that name's position amongst free Blacks throughout the country in 1830; NL indicates the name was not listed amongst the first twenty-five (see Source Lists N, O, P and Chapter II, Footnote 47).

Southern Cities: 1877 to 1937

1919	1899	1877	1830
Williams	1	1	5
Jones	3	2	6
Johnson	2	3	1
Brown	4	7	2
Jackson	6	5	4
Smith	5	4	3
Thomas	7	6	10
Walker	8	8	NL
Harris	10	13	11
Davis	9	9	13
Robinson	11	11	25
Green	12	10	15
Scott	13	12	8
Glover	NL	NL	NL
Butler	NL	21	17
Evans	21	NL	NL
White	15	NL	19
Wilson	16	17	12
Moore	17	16	18
Jenkins	20	NL	NL
Wright	14	NL	NL
Allen	19	NL	NL
Young	NL	NL	NL
Hill	NL	NL	20
Mitchell	NL	19	NL

Of the first ten surnames used in 1919, we find that the same ten were employed by Blacks in 1899, nine out of ten were used in 1877 and seven of ten in 1830. Of the twenty-five most frequently employed surnames in 1919, twenty were used in 1899, seventeen in 1877 and again seventeen in 1830. It seems that by 1877 surname usage amongst Blacks had become somewhat patterned and rigid.

By 1937, the population of Augusta had risen to 64,042: 26,159 Blacks and 37,883 Whites. Black males total 11,672; females, 14,487. White males number 18,572 and White females, 19,311. This collection includes the given and surnames of 20,020 Blacks, almost 80 per cent of the entire Black population. There are 8,677 Black male given names from the total of 11,672, a sample of more than 75 per cent; and 11,343 given names from the total population of 14,487 Black females, a sample of, again, close to 80 per cent. Of the 18,572 White male given names, this collection includes 13,740 given names, approximately 75 per cent. White female given names include 15,310 from a total of 19,311, a sample of just under 80 per cent. White male and female given names total 29,050.

The following list represents the twenty-five most popular Black male given names in Augusta, Georgia, 1937. The first number after the name indicates that name's

Southern Cities: 1877 to 1937

position amongst Black males in Augusta in 1919; the second
number indicates that name's position amongst Black males
in Augusta in 1899; the third number indicates that name's
position amongst Black males in Augusta in 1877; the fourth
number indicates that name's position amongst White males in
Augusta in 1877; NL indicates the name was not listed amongst
the first twenty-five (see Source Lists N, O, P, Q).

1937	1919	1899	1877	Whites, 1877
William	1	1	2	2
John	2	2	3	1
James	3	4	4	3
George	4	5	8	6
Robert	8	8	5	9
Charles	5	6	6	4
Henry	6	3	1	7
Thomas	NL	NL	7	5
Joseph	9	10	10	8
Edward	10	9	9	10
Frank	12	12	19	11
Samuel	11	11	12	14
Benjamin	14	14	16	16
Walter	18	NL	NL	NL
Albert	13	19	NL	21
Jesse	19	21	NL	NL
Arthur	17	NL	NL	NL
David	16	15	17	17
Fred	NL	NL	NL	NL
Andrew	20	17	NL	19
Ernest	NL	NL	NL	NL
Clarence	24	NL	NL	NL
Richard	15	13	14	22
Eugene	NL	NL	NL	NL
Alexander	22	16	15	23

The following list represents the twenty-five most
popular Black female given names in Augusta, Georgia in
1937. The first number after the name indicates that
name's position amongst Black females in Augusta in 1919;
the second number indicates that name's position amongst
Black females in Augusta in 1899; the third number indicates that name's position amongst Black females in Augusta
in 1877; the fourth number indicates that name's position
amongst White females in Augusta in 1877; NL indicates the
name was not listed amongst the first twenty-five (see
Source Lists N, O, P, Q).

BLACK NAMES IN AMERICA

Southern Cities: 1877 to 1937

1937	1919	1899	1877	Whites, 1877
Mary	1	1	1	1
Annie	2	12	NL	NL
Mattie	NL	16	NL	15
Carrie	3	24	NL	NL
Rosa	10	11	NL	NL
Lillie	NL	NL	NL	NL
Emma	4	4	9	17
Mamie	13	NL	NL	NL
Hattie	7	21	NL	NL
Sarah	5	3	2	2
Fanny	8	5	13	10
Louise	14	NL	NL	NL
Elizabeth	NL	22	19	3
Ella	11	17	NL	NL
Julia	9	9	15	13
Lula	12	NL	NL	NL
Lizzie	6	13	10	25
Marie	NL	NL	NL	NL
Susie	25	NL	NL	NL
Alice	16	18	NL	22
Janie	20	NL	NL	NL
Anna	NL	2	6	6
Maggie	NL	NL	NL	NL
Laura	18	19	16	NL
Frances	NL	25	14	19

Amongst Black males in Augusta, Georgia, there seem to be a remarkable consistency in the use of given names in the sixty years from 1877 to 1937. Of the first ten names all but Thomas are identical for all four groups. There are some minor shifts, to be sure; yet, considering the variety of possibilities, their given name preferences seem to be very consistent. Of the twenty-five most popular names in 1937, twenty-one are identical in 1919, eighteen in 1899 and sixteen in 1877. Henry is an interesting example of a pattern. This name was the most popular one in 1877 and has lost popularity consistently, dropping to third in 1899, sixth in 1919 and seventh in 1937.

The situation is quite different with Black females in Augusta, Georgia, during the same period, 1877 to 1937. Of the first ten given names in 1937, only seven were used in 1919 and three in 1899 and 1877. And of these ten in 1937, two in 1919 and 1899 and seven in 1877 do not appear on the lists of twenty-five at all.

Of the twenty-five most popular names in 1937, seven did not appear on the lists in 1919, eight did not appear in 1899, and fifteen did not appear on the list in 1877. Other than Mary, which retains the most popularity throughout this period, only Sarah seems to have an established pattern; it was most popular in 1877, appearing second; in 1899 it was third; in 1919

154

Southern Cities: 1877 to 1937

fifth; and in 1937 it appeared tenth. Females were, in terms of name usage, during this period much less consistent in their use of given names than males in Augusta, Georgia.

Of the 8,677 Black male given names, 854, or 9.8 per cent, are unusual; of these, 280 are old-fashioned, leaving a total of 574, or 6.6 per cent, unusual names. Black males used seventy-five famous names. Of the 11,343 Black female given names, 1,234, or 10.9 per cent, are unusual; of these, 372 are old-fashioned, leaving a total of 862, or 7.6 per cent, unusual names. Black females use only one famous name. Black females use a slightly higher percentage of unusual names than Black males.

Of the 13,740 White male given names, 624, or 4.5 per cent, are unusual; of these, 95 are old-fashioned, leaving a total of 529, or 3.9 per cent, unusual names. White males employ thirty-nine famous names. Of the 15,310 White female given names, 1,220, or 8 per cent, are unusual; of these, 165 are old-fashioned, leaving a total of 1,055, or 6.9 per cent, unusual names. White females use only two famous names. White females employ almost twice the percentage of unusual names than do White males.

The following lists indicate the twenty-five most popular surnames of Blacks and Whites in Augusta, Georgia in 1937. The number after the White surname indicates that name's position on the Black list. NL indicates that the name was not found amongst the most popular twenty-five surnames of Blacks (see Source List Q).

Black Surnames, Augusta, Georgia, 1937	White Surnames, Augusta, Georgia, 1937
Williams	Smith 5
Jones	Johnson 3
Johnson	Jones 2
Brown	Williams 1
Smith	Davis 10
Jackson	Brown 4
Thomas	Thompson NL
Walker	Anderson 24
Green	Clark NL
Davis	Wilson 17
Harris	Hall NL
White	Moore 18
Scott	Howard NL
Washington	Adams NL
Evans	Walker 8
Robinson	Phillips NL
Wilson	Taylor NL
Moore	Hill 21
Butler	Miller NL
Holmes	Crawford NL

Southern Cities: 1877 to 1937

Black Surnames Augusta, Georgia, 1937	White Surnames, Augusta, Georgia, 1937
Hill	Wright NL
Allen	Allen 22
Murray	Turner NL
Anderson	Martin NL
Carter	Owens NL

Of the first ten Black surnames in 1937, six appear amongst Whites; of the first twenty-five Black names, twelve are the same on the White list. In 1877, the correspondence was six of ten and seventeen of twenty-five; in 1899, seven of ten and thirteen of twenty-five; in 1919, six of ten and seventeen of twenty-five.

The following list represents the twenty-five most popular Black surnames in Augusta, Georgia, 1937. The first number after the name indicates that name's position amongst Blacks in Augusta in 1919; the second number indicates that name's position amongst Blacks in Augusta in 1899; the third number indicates that name's position amongst Blacks in 1877; NL indicates the name was not listed amongst the first twenty-five (see Source Lists N, O, P, Q).

Black Surnames, Augusta, Georgia, 1937	1919	1899	1877
Williams	1	1	1
Jones	2	3	2
Johnson	3	2	3
Brown	4	4	7
Smith	6	5	4
Jackson	5	6	5
Thomas	7	7	6
Walker	8	8	8
Green	12	12	10
Davis	10	9	9
Harris	9	10	13
White	17	15	NL
Scott	13	13	12
Washington	NL	18	18
Evans	16	21	NL
Robinson	11	11	11
Wilson	18	16	17
Moore	19	17	16
Butler	15	NL	21
Holmes	NL	NL	NL
Hill	24	NL	NL
Allen	22	19	NL
Murray	NL	NL	NL

Southern Cities: 1877 to 1937

Black Surnames, Augusta, Georgia, 1937	1919	1899	1877
Anderson	NL	22	15
Carter	NL	23	24

The ten most popular surnames amongst Blacks in Augusta, Georgia, in 1937 are identical with those used by Blacks sixty years previously in 1877. Indeed, with the exception of Brown, fourth in 1937 and seventh in 1877, and Green, ninth in 1937 but tenth in 1877, the two lists are identical in order as well. Of the twenty-five most popular in 1937, all but four are used in 1877. Of the twenty-five most popular in 1899, all but four are used in 1937, and in 1919 twenty of twenty-five are on the list in 1937. Of the first ten in 1937, the 1899 and 1919 lists use nine.

In addition to the fifteen surnames which appear amongst the twenty-five most popular Black surnames from 1877 to 1937, four other surnames are found in three of the four lists: Anderson, Butler, Carter and Washington.

The following list deals with White surnames in Augusta, Georgia from the same periods (see Source Lists N, O, P, Q).

White Surnames, Augusta, Georgia, 1937	1919	1899	1877
Smith	1	1	1
Johnson	3	3	3
Jones	2	2	4
Williams	5	4	2
Davis	9	6	6
Brown	4	5	5
Thompson	NL	19	8
Anderson	NL	NL	17
Clark	16	7	13
Wilson	7	18	14
Hall	NL	NL	NL
Moore	12	14	7
Howard	NL	20	NL
Adams	NL	NL	NL
Walker	14	NL	11
Phillips	NL	NL	NL
Taylor	NL	11	NL
Hill	11	12	10
Miller	6	13	9
Crawford	NL	NL	NL
Wright	8	22	NL
Allen	18	10	NL
Turner	NL	NL	NL
Martin	19	17	21
Owens	25	NL	NL

BLACK NAMES IN AMERICA

Southern Cities: 1877 to 1937

Only the first six White surnames appear to have the consistency of usage and order found amongst the first ten Black surnames. Indeed, of the first ten White surnames used in 1937, only seven are to be found in each of the other periods, and of the first twenty-five most popular White surnames in 1937, only fifteen are found in 1877, seventeen in 1899 and sixteen in 1919.

In addition to the twelve surnames which appear amongst the twenty-five most popular White surnames from 1877 to 1937, four other surnames are found in three of the four lists: <u>Thompson</u>, <u>Walker</u>, <u>Wright</u> and <u>Allen</u>.

The following table indicates the differences in consistency of surname usage between Whites and Blacks in Augusta, Georgia from 1877 to 1937. The figures relate to the first ten and first twenty-five names used in 1937.

Names Used in 1937	1877		1899		1919	
	Black	White	Black	White	Black	White
Out of First 10	10	7	9	7	9	7
Out of First 25	19	15	21	17	20	16

By examining the names of students in a school system, it is possible to suggest the trends in name usage for the immediate future. The Augusta, Georgia--i.e., Richmond County School Census of 1938 (<u>see</u> Source List R)-- (ages 6 to 18) indicates that of the 2,368 Black male given names, 188, or 7.9 per cent, are unusual; of these, thirty-one are old-fashioned, leaving a total of 157, or 6.6 per cent, unusual. Black males used twenty famous names. Of the 2,811 Black female given names, 336, or 11.9 per cent, are unusual; of these, forty-two are old-fashioned, leaving a total of 294, or 10.5 per cent, unusual. Black females used no famous names.

Of the 2,848 White male given names, 132, or 4.6 per cent, are unusual; of these, six are old-fashioned, leaving a total of 126, or 4.4 per cent, un- usual. White males use five famous names. Of the 3,039 White female given names, 254, or 8.4 per cent, are unusual; of these, twenty-three are old- fashioned, leaving a total of 231, or 7.6 per cent, unusual. White females use only one famous name.

In examining the rural schools in Richmond County (<u>see</u> Source List R), we find that of the 796 Black male given names, 85, or 10.6 per cent, are un- usual; of these, fifteen are old-fashioned, leaving a total of 70, or 8.8 per cent, unusual. Black males in rural schools employ six famous names. Of the 790 Black female given names, 109, or 13.8 per cent, are unusual; of these, fifteen are old-fashioned, leaving a total of 94, or 11.9 per cent, unusual. Black females use no famous names.

Of the 1,112 White given names in rural schools, 52, or 4.7 per cent, are unusual; of these, three are old-fashioned, leaving a total of 49, or 4.4 per cent, unusual. White males employ three famous names. Of the 1,131 White

BLACK NAMES IN AMERICA

Southern Cities: 1877 to 1937

female given names, 92, or 8.1 per cent, are unusual; of these, six are old-fashioned, leaving a total of 86, or 7.6 per cent, unusual. White females employ no famous names.

What emerges can be summarized by the following table (see Source Lists N, O, P, Q, R):

Augusta, Georgia		Male % Unusual	No. Famous	Female % Unusual	No. Famous
Blacks	1877	5.	5	6.1	0
	1899	5.3	27	6.2	0
	1919	5.3	25	5.2	1
	1937	6.6	75	7.6	1
City School	1938	6.6	20	10.5	0
Rural School	1938	8.8	6	11.9	0
Whites	1877	1.8	5	4.4	0
	1899	2.0	9	6.0	4
	1919	2.5	15	5.0	14
	1937	3.9	39	6.9	2
City School	1938	4.4	5	7.6	1
Rural School	1938	4.4	3	7.6	0

There appears to have been a small but steady increase in the use of un-usual names among both Whites and Blacks, and although Blacks start this se-quence with a higher percentage of unusual names, both groups seem to be equally sensitive to naming practice pressures and trends. More specifically, in 1919 Blacks and Whites used a smaller percentage of unusual names, but in 1937 both jumped past the 1899 level to resume the trend established in the nineteenth century. Although both groups show an increase in the use of un-usual names, Blacks tend to increase their usage a little faster; Black males, from 1877 to 1938, move from a usage of 5 per cent to 8.8 per cent; White males increase their usage from 1.8 per cent to 4.4 per cent. Black males increase 3.8 per cent; White males increase 2.6 per cent. Black females start at 6.1 per cent in 1877 and by 1938 their percentage is 11.9 per cent; White females move from 4.4 per cent to 7.6 per cent. Black females increase 5.8 per cent; White females increase 3.2 per cent.

Although the percentage of unusual names increased amongst Blacks, it does seem remarkable that, given the nature of their experience in America, Blacks seem to have acquired a very close approximation to White naming practices. For example, as White females consistently employ a greater percentage of un-usual names than White males, Black females do the same. And, as White males make a dramatically greater use of famous names than White females, so do Black males in comparison to Black females.

If there is one singular point of departure, it is suggested in the school records of 1938. White naming patterns seem very much the same in rural and

Southern Cities: 1877 to 1937

city schools; Black names indicate a greater percentage of unusual names in
rural schools than in city schools.

The relatively high level of consistency in the naming practices of Black
males in the South is not restricted to Augusta, Georgia. Montgomery, Alabama's Black citizenry in 1933 reflect patterns similar to those seen in
Augusta. The Black community in Montgomery in 1933 numbered 31,339. Of these,
13,620 were male and 17,719 female. Whites totaled 38,338, 18,561 male and
19,777 female. This collection lists 1,955 Black males and 3,063 Black females, much smaller samples than those of Augusta, Georgia (see Source List S).
However, the surname sample numbers an estimated 20,500, approximately two-
thirds of the total Black population. The White surname sample deals with an
estimated 29,500 names, more than three-quarters of the White population.

The following list reflects the twenty-five most
popular given names of Black males in Montgomery, Alabama,
in 1933. The first number after the name indicates that
name's position amongst Black males in Augusta, Georgia
in 1937; the second number indicates the name's position
amongst White males in Augusta, Georgia, in 1937; NL indicates the name was not among the first twenty-five given
names in Augusta (see Source Lists Q, S).

Black Males, Montgomery, Ala., 1933	Black Males, Augusta, Ga., 1937	White Males, Augusta, Ga., 1937
William	1	2
James	3	3
John	2	1
Charles	6	4
Robert	5	6
George	4	5
Joseph	9	8
Thomas	8	7
Henry	7	10
Samuel	12	14
David	18	17
Edward	10	11
Booker	NL	NL
Frank	11	9
Arthur	17	19
Jesse	NL	21
Louis	NL	NL
Walter	14	13
Albert	15	15
Lee	NL	NL
Nathaniel	NL	NL
Richard	23	NL
Alexander	25	NL
Alfred	NL	NL
Andrew	20	NL

BLACK NAMES IN AMERICA

Southern Cities: 1877 to 1937

Of the ten most popular Black male given names in Montgomery, Alabama in 1933, nine are identical with those used by Blacks in Augusta, Georgia in 1937. And of the first twenty-five used in Montgomery, nineteen are used in Augusta. Of the ten most popular Black given names in Montgomery, Alabama in 1933, nine are identical with those used by Whites in Augusta, Georgia in 1937. And of the first twenty-five, seventeen are used by Whites. It appears, then, that Montgomery, Alabama Black male given names reflect no great differences between Augusta, Georgia Blacks and Montgomery, Alabama Whites in the fourth decade of the twentieth century.

The following list reflects the twenty-five most popular given names of Black females in Montgomery, Alabama in 1933. Again, the number after each name indicates that name's position amongst Black and White females in Augusta, Georgia in 1937 (see Source Lists Q, S).

Black Females, Montgomery, Ala., 1933	Black Females, Augusta, Ga., 1937	White Females, Augusta, Ga., 1937
Mary	1	1
Annie	2	2
Mattie	3	20
Emma	7	18
Rosa	5	NL
Fanny	11	NL
Lula	16	NL
Elizabeth	13	4
Lizzie	17	NL
Hattie	9	NL
Ella	14	NL
Lillie	6	15
Anna	22	NL
Ida	NL	NL
Willie	NL	NL
Carrie	4	NL
Lucy	NL	NL
Rebecca	NL	NL
Sally	NL	NL
Bessie	NL	13
Sarah	10	8
Minnie	NL	11
Georgia	NL	NL
Susie	19	NL
Alice	20	16

Of the ten most popular Black female given names in Montgomery, Alabama in 1933, six are used by Black women in Augusta, Georgia in 1937. And of the first twenty-five used in Montgomery in 1933, seventeen are used in Augusta in 1937. Of the ten most popular Black female given names in Montgomery in 1933, only three are used by White females in Augusta, Georgia in 1937, and

Southern Cities: 1877 to 1937

of the twenty-five used in Montgomery, Alabama by Black females, White females
in Augusta in 1937 employ only ten.

   Black female given names in Montgomery, Alabama in 1933 show some di-
vergence from those used by Black females in Augusta, Georgia in 1937. Certainly, their men are more consistent. Nevertheless, six of the first ten
and seventeen of the first twenty-five reflect differences that seem less than
unusual.

        The following is a list of the twenty-five most common
        Black surnames used in Montgomery, Alabama in 1933. The
        numbers after each name indicate that name's position
        amongst the first twenty-five surnames in Augusta in 1937,
        Black and White and amongst Montgomery Whites. NL indicates
        that the surname was not located amongst the first twenty-
        five Black surnames in Montgomery (see Source Lists Q, S).

Black Surnames Montgomery, 1933	Blacks Augusta, 1937	Whites Augusta, 1937	Whites Montgomery, 1933
1. Williams	1	4	4
2. Johnson	3	2	3
3. Jackson	6	NL	17
4. Smith	5	1	1
5. Jones	2	3	2
6. Thomas	7	NL	18
7. Brown	4	6	6
8. Harris	11	NL	NL
9. Davis	10	5	5
10. Lewis	NL	NL	NL
11. Taylor	NL	17	7
12. Robinson	16	NL	NL
13. Green	9	NL	NL
14. Hall	NL	11	9
15. Lee	NL	NL	NL
16. Scott	13	NL	14
17. Wilson	17	10	8
18. Wright	NL	21	NL
19. Carter	25	NL	NL
20. Washington	14	NL	NL
21. Moore	18	12	10
22. Walker	8	15	12
23. Hill	21	18	15
24. Howard	NL	13	NL
25. White	12	NL	24

   Of the first ten Black surnames in Montgomery, Alabama in 1933, eight are
the same as those used by Augusta Blacks in 1937. Of the first twenty-five,
nineteen are the same. Of the first ten Black surnames in Montgomery, Alabama
in 1933, six are the same as those used by Whites in Augusta in 1937. Of the
first twenty-five, fourteen are the same. Montgomery, Alabama Blacks employed

Southern Cities: 1877 to 1937

surnames much more in common with those used by Blacks than those used by Whites in Augusta. In addition, of the first ten Black surnames in Montgomery, Alabama in 1937, six are identical with those used by Montgomery Whites. Of the first twenty-five, sixteen are the same. These comparisons suggest that Blacks in Montgomery, Alabama in 1933 employed surnames more in common with those used by Blacks in Augusta, Georgia in 1937 than with those used by Whites in their own community in the same year.

Some names are used with regularity by Blacks and avoided, to a great extent, by Whites. For example, Carter, Green, Harris, Robinson and Washington are among the twenty-five most popular Black surnames in Montgomery and Augusta; they are not found on the lists of most popular White surnames in these cities. Conversely, Adams, Clark, Martin, Miller and Thompson are quite popular with Whites in Augusta in 1937 and Montgomery in 1933 but less favored by Blacks.

In Montgomery, Blacks did not use Black as a surname, whereas forty-two Whites did. There was not one Black Blackman, although six Whites had that surname. Three hundred and eighteen Blacks were named Brown (177 Whites used Brown); 163 Blacks had the surname Green compared to 36 Whites. Blacks used White as a surname 103 times, Whites only 74 times; 40 Blacks were Gray; 27 Whites were, and 9 Blacks were Grey, compared to 3 Whites. Finally, 14 Blacks were Ivory but only one White reflected that hue.

In 1936, the population of Pine Bluff, Arkansas numbered 21,069. Of these, 6,667 were Black and 14,402 were White. The Black male population numbered 2,880 and the Black female population was 3,787. White males numbered 6,902; White females numbered 7,500. This collection represents a sample of 2,118 Black males and 2,994 Black female given names, 5,112 in all, almost 80 per cent of the entire population. The list of Black surnames totals 5,473, over 80 per cent of the Black community. White male given names number 3,754, and White female given names total 5,666, 9,420 in all, approximately 65 per cent of the entire population. The list of White surnames totals 11,624, like the Black sample, over 80 per cent of the White community (see Source List T).

The following list reflects the twenty-five most frequently used Black surnames in Pine Bluff, Arkansas in 1936. The first number after the name indicates that name's position amongst Blacks in Augusta, Georgia in 1937; the second number indicates that name's position amongst Blacks in Augusta, 1919; the third number, Blacks in Montgomery, Alabama, 1933. NL indicates that the name was not listed amongst the twenty-five most popular Black surnames (see Source Lists P, Q, S, T).

BLACK NAMES IN AMERICA

Southern Cities: 1877 to 1937

Black Surnames
Pine Bluff, Arkansas--1936

Most Frequently Used	Augusta 1937	Augusta 1919	Montgomery 1933
1. Williams	1	1	1
2. Johnson	3	3	2
3. Jones	2	2	5
4. Smith	5	6	4
5. Brown	4	4	7
6. Jackson	6	5	3
7. Davis	10	10	9
8. Harris	11	9	8
9. Thomas	7	7	6
10. Thompson	NL	NL	NL
11. Robinson	16	11	12
12. Moore	18	19	21
13. Green	9	12	13
14. Washington	14	NL	20
15. Lee	NL	NL	15
16. Anderson	24	NL	NL
17. Taylor	NL	NL	11
18. Walker	8	8	22
19. Sanders	NL	NL	NL
20. Holmes	20	NL	NL
21. Adams	NL	NL	NL
22. Scott	13	13	16
23. White	12	17	25
24. Clark	NL	NL	NL
25. Young	NL	23	NL

Of the ten most frequently used Black surnames in Pine Bluff in 1936, eight are the same in Augusta, Georgia in 1937, nine are identical with those in Augusta in 1919 and nine duplicate those used by Blacks in Montgomery, Alabama in 1933. Of the twenty-five most popular surnames in Pine Bluff, eighteen are identical with those used in Augusta in 1937 and Montgomery in 1933, and sixteen are identical with those used by Blacks in Augusta in 1919. There seems no discernible pattern of surname usage which can distinguish between Black and White usage.

The following list reflects the twenty-five most frequently used White surnames in Pine Bluff in 1936. The numbers reflect the name's position in Augusta, Georgia in 1937 and 1919 and Montgomery, Alabama in 1933, respectively. NL indicates the name was not located amongst the twenty-five most popular White surnames (see Source Lists P, Q, S, T).

Southern Cities: 1877 to 1937

White Surnames
Pine Bluff, Arkansas--1936

Most Frequently Used	Augusta 1937	Augusta 1919	Montgomery 1933
1. Smith	1	1	1
2. Johnson	2	3	3
3. Taylor	17	NL	7
4. Brown	6	4	6
5. Jones	3	2	2
6. Wilson	10	7	8
7. Williams	4	5	4
8. Davis	5	9	5
9. Harris	NL	NL	NL
10. Moore	12	12	10
11. Adams	14	NL	25
12. Allen	22	18	NL
13. Martin	24	19	16
14. Tucker	NL	NL	NL
15. Young	NL	NL	NL
16. Reed	NL	NL	NL
17. White	NL	23	24
18. King	NL	NL	NL
19. Mitchell	NL	NL	NL
20. Sanders	NL	NL	NL
21. Green	NL	24	NL
22. Evans	NL	NL	NL
23. Baker	NL	NL	NL
24. Robinson	NL	NL	NL
25. Gray	NL	NL	NL

Of the ten most frequently used White surnames in Pine Bluff in 1936,
seven are duplicated in Augusta in 1937 and 1919 and nine are the same as
those found in Montgomery, Alabama in 1933. Of the twenty-five most popular
surnames in Pine Bluff, twelve are identical with those found in each of the
other groups. It seems that Whites maintain a consistency in their use of
the ten most popular surnames equal to that seen amongst Blacks, but in terms
of the most popular twenty-five surnames, Whites do not demonstrate the consistency found amongst Blacks. The following table represents the contrast
in levels of continuity between Whites and Blacks.

	Augusta, 1937	Augusta, 1919	Montgomery, 1933
Blacks			
of 10 most popular	8	9	9
of 25 most popular	18	16	18
Whites			
of 10 most popular	7	7	9
of 25 most popular	12	12	12

Southern Cities: 1877 to 1937

The following list reflects the twenty-five most frequently used Black surnames in Pine Bluff, 1936. The number
after the name indicates that name's position amongst the
first twenty-five White surnames in Pine Bluff. NL indicates
that the name was not listed amongst the twenty-five most
popular White surnames (see Source List T).

Black Surnames Pine Bluff, 1936	White Surnames Pine Bluff, 1936
1. Williams	7
2. Johnson	2
3. Jones	5
4. Smith	1
5. Brown	4
6. Jackson	NL
7. Davis	8
8. Harris	9
9. Thomas	NL
10. Thompson	NL
11. Robinson	24
12. Moore	10
13. Green	21
14. Washington	NL
15. Lee	NL
16. Anderson	NL
17. Taylor	3
18. Walker	NL
19. Sanders	20
20. Holmes	NL
21. Adams	11
22. Scott	NL
23. White	17
24. Clark	NL
25. Young	15

Of the ten most frequently used Black surnames, seven are used by Whites and
of the twenty-five most popular Black surnames, fifteen are identical with
those in the White community. Pine Bluff Blacks show a slightly greater correspondence in naming usage to Blacks in Augusta and Montgomery in the
twentieth century than they do to Whites in their own community.

Of the 2,118 Black male given names, 221 were unusual, with fifty-one
old-fashioned by 1936 Arkansas standards, leaving a rate of unusualness of
8 per cent. Black female unusualness was 12.9 per cent. White male unusualness was 5.4 per cent and White female unusualness was 10.5 per cent.

BLACK NAMES IN AMERICA

Southern Cities: 1877 to 1937

The following table represents the percentage of unusual given names from the collected lists for Blacks and Whites in Augusta, Montgomery and Pine Bluff (see Source Lists N, O, P, Q, R, S, T).

	Augusta				City Schools Augusta	Rural Schools Augusta	Montgomery	Pine Bluff
	1877 %	1899 %	1919 %	1937 %	1938 %	1938 %	1933 %	1936 %
Black								
Males	5.0	5.3	5.3	6.6	6.6	8.8	7.7	8.0
Females	6.1	6.2	5.2	7.6	10.5	11.9	8.5	12.9
White								
Males	1.8	2.0	2.5	3.9	4.4	4.4		5.4
Females	4.4	6.0	5.0	6.9	7.6	7.6		10.5

Unusual name usage increases steadily, if slowly, amongst males and females of both races during the years 1877 - 1938.

Southern Cities: 1877 to 1937

Source List N: AUGUSTA, GEORGIA, 1877[4]

Most Common Given Names, Black

The first list includes the number of times the name was found, and a second number indicates the rate of usage per 100,000, with a rate of 48. The second list, a frequency listing, indicates with a number only the total of incidences.

MALE
Alphabetical

Aaron 9 434	Floyd 1	Matthew 5 241
Abraham 4 193	Frank 24 1156	Mingo 2 96
Abram 11 530	Fred 2 96	Moses 18 867
Adam 24 1156	Frederick 2 96	Nathan 6 289
Albert 12 578	George 57 2746	Nathaniel 1
Alexander 29 1397	Gilbert 2 96	Nelson 11 530
Alfred 20 963	Harrison 5 241	Oliver 6 289
Allen 4 193	Harry 2 96	Oscar 5 241
Alonzo 3 145	Harvey 3 145	Paul 7 337
Alvin 1	Henry 124 5973	Peter 32 1541
Amos 2 96	Howard 3 145	Phillip 6 289
Anderson 9 434	Isaac 17 819	Pleasant 4 193
Andrew 16 771	Isham 4 193	Pompey 2 96
Anthony 7 337	Jack 1	Prince 5 241
Arthur 7 337	Jackson 19 915	Reuben 4 193
Augustus 8 385	Jacob 16 771	Richard 32 1541
Benjamin 28 1349	James 80 3854	Robert 79 3805
Caesar 9 434	Jefferson 8 385	Robin 1
Calvin 4 193	Jerry 2 96	Sampson 1
Cato 1	Jesse 13 626	Samuel 38 1830
Charles 68 3276	John 109 5251	Sidney 1
Chester 2 96	Jordon 7 337	Simon 4 193
Daniel 21 1012	Joseph 50 2409	Solomon 22 1060
David 26 1252	Julius 5 241	Stephen 11 530
Dennis 9 434	Lawrence 4 193	Theodore 3 145
Edgar 1	Lee 9 434	Thomas 68 3276
Edmond 15 723	Leonard 2 96	Ulysses 1
Edward 54 2601	Lewis 40 1927	Walter 5 241
Edwin 3 145	Louis 1	Washington 10 482
Eli 2 96	Luther 2 96	Wesley 6 289
Ephraim 2 96	Madison 2 96	William 115 5540
Eugene 1	Martin 3 145	Willis 11 530

MALE
Frequency

Henry 124	John 109	Robert 79
William 115	James 80	Charles 68

[4]From the City Directory, Augusta, Ga., 1877.

Southern Cities: 1877 to 1937 -- AUGUSTA, GEORGIA, 1877

Thomas 68	Anderson 9	Harvey 3
George 57	Caesar 9	Howard 3
Edward 54	Dennis 9	Martin 3
Joseph 50	Lee 9	Theodore 3
Lewis 40	Augustus 8	Amos 2
Samuel 38	Jefferson 8	Chester 2
Peter 32	Anthony 7	Eli 2
Richard 32	Arthur 7	Ephraim 2
Alexander 29	Jordon 7	Fred 2
Benjamin 28	Paul 7	Frederick 2
David 26	Nathan 6	Gilbert 2
Adam 24	Oliver 6	Harry 2
Frank 24	Phillip 6	Jerry 2
Solomon 22	Wesley 6	Leonard 2
Daniel 21	Harrison 5	Luther 2
Alfred 20	Julius 5	Madison 2
Jackson 19	Matthew 5	Mingo 2
Moses 18	Oscar 5	Pompey 2
Isaac 17	Prince 5	Alvin 1
Andrew 16	Walter 5	Cato 1
Jacob 16	Abraham 4	Edgar 1
Edmond 15	Allen 4	Eugene 1
Jesse 13	Calvin 4	Floyd 1
Albert 12	Isham 4	Jack 1
Abram 11	Lawrence 4	Louis 1
Nelson 11	Pleasant 4	Nathaniel 1
Stephen 11	Reuben 4	Robin 1
Willis 11	Simon 4	Sampson 1
Washington 10	Alonzo 3	Sidney 1
Aaron 9	Edwin 3	Ulysses

FEMALE
Alphabetical
Rate per 100,000 = 145.

Adaline 3 435	Clarissa 3 435	Emily 8 1159
Addie 1	Cora 3 435	Eveline 2 290
Agnes 5 725	Delia 1	Eve 1
Alice 2 290	Dinah 3 435	Fanny 13 1884
Amanda 6 870	Dolly 3 435	Flora 3 435
Amelia 5 725	Dorcas 1	Florence 1
Amy 1	Edith 1	Frances 12 1739
Ann 5 725	Edna 1	Grace 3 435
Anna 19 2754	Eliza 21 3043	Hannah 8 1159
Betsy 9 1304	Elizabeth 9 1304	Harriet 23 3333
Betty 2 290	Ella 2 290	Henrietta 3 435
Carrie 1	Ellen 7 1015	Hester 2 290
Catharine 3 435	Elsie 3 435	Ida 3 435
Charity 1	Elvira 3 435	Isabella 4 580
Charlotte 6 870	Emiline 3 435	Jane 21 3043
Chloe 1	Emma 15 2174	Josephine 7 1015
Clara 5 725	Esther 2 290	Judy 2 290

Southern Cities: 1877 to 1937 -- AUGUSTA, GEORGIA, 1877

Julia 12 1739	Martha 18 2609	Patsy 1
Laura 11 1594	Maria(h) 14 2029	Pauline 1
Lavina 4 580	Marion 1	Phillis 2 290
Leah 2 290	Mary 50 7246	Phoebe 5 725
Lena 1	Matilda 5 725	Polly 3 435
Letty 1	May 1	Priscilla 4 580
Lizzie 15 2174	Mildred 1	Rachel 5 725
Louisa 18 2609	Milly 3 435	Rebecca 6 870
Louise 5 725	Minnie 1	Rhoda 1
Lucinda 4 580	Molly 2 290	Rosa 2 290
Lucy 8 1159	Minerva 1	Rose 4 580
Lydia 1	Nancy 11 1594	Sally 6 870
Maggie 1	Nanny 1	Sarah 35 5072
Malinda 5 725	Nelly 3 435	Sophia 6 870
Margaret 8 1159	Patience 2 290	Susan 15 2174
		Virginia 2 290

FEMALE
Frequency

Mary 50	Ann 5	Eveline 2
Sarah 35	Clara 5	Hester 2
Harriet 23	Louise 5	Judy 2
Eliza 21	Malinda 5	Leah 2
Jane 21	Matilda 5	Molly 2
Anna 19	Phoebe 5	Patience 2
Louisa 18	Rachel 5	Phillis 2
Martha 18	Isabella 4	Rosa 2
Emma 15	Lavinia 4	Virginia 2
Lizzie 15	Lucinda 4	Addie 1
Susan 15	Priscilla 4	Amy 1
Maria(h) 14	Rose 4	Carrie 1
Fanny 13	Adaline 3	Charity 1
Frances 12	Catharine 3	Chloe 1
Julia 12	Clarissa 3	Delia 1
Laura 11	Cora 3	Dorcas 1
Nancy 11	Dinah 3	Edith 1
Betsy 9	Dolly 3	Edna 1
Elizabeth 9	Elsie 3	Eve 1
Emily 8	Elvira 3	Florence 1
Hannah 8	Emiline 3	Lena 1
Lucy 8	Flora 3	Letty 1
Margaret 8	Grace 3	Lydia 1
Ellen 7	Henrietta 3	Maggie 1
Josephine 7	Ida 3	Marion 1
Amanda 6	Milly 3	May 1
Charlotte 6	Nelly 3	Mildred 1
Sally 6	Polly 3	Minerva 1
Sophia 6	Alice 2	Minnie 1
Rebecca 6	Betty 2	Nanny 1
Agnes 5	Ella 2	Patsy 1
Amelia 5	Esther 2	Pauline 1
		Rhoda 1

Southern Cities: 1877 to 1937   --   AUGUSTA, GEORGIA, 1877

Unusual Names, Black

The following lists reflect the unusual given names of Blacks in Augusta, Georgia in 1877. Alphabetical listings of male and female names follow with a number representing the frequency of use; no number indicates the name was found only once.

Male

Aberdeen	Glasgow	Moses 18
Abraham 4	Gus	Nace
Abram 11	Hage	Nassau
Alonzo	Handy	Nero 2
Americus	Harby	Noah 2
Antonio	Hector	Orange
Asa	Hosea	Osceola
Bird	Isaac 17	Ossie
Bonaparte	Isadore	Pleasant 4
Bony	Isaiah	Plunk
Boss	Isham 4	Pompey 2
Boston	Jabez 2	Porse
Brutus	January	Pournelle
Bunyan	Jeremiah 2	Prince 5
Caesar 9	Jonas 3	Reason
Captain 2	Joshua 2	Riley
Carlo 2	Josiah	Romeo
Carolina (Emery)	Judge	Rouse
Cassius	July	Ryas
Cato	Juni	Sambo
Cicero	Junius	Sampson
Columbus	Kilo (Sly)	Sancho 2
Cudjoe	Lafayette	Sandy
Cuffee	Lawyer	Sargent
Cuffie	Lazarus 2	Septimus
Cuffy	Leonidas	Shadrach 2
Cupid	Levi 2	Shadroch
Dallas	Lexius	Sharper
Doc	London	Sherley
Dublin	Major	Simeon
Dutch	Mange	Smart
Ebenezer	Manuel	Solomon 22
Edlow	Martin (Van Buren)	Squire
Eli 2	Micajah	Tip
Emanuel 2	Milo	Tobias 2
Ephraim 2	Mingo 2	Ulysses
Farmer	Monk	Uriah
Gabriel	Monmouth	Virgil
Garibaldi	Mordecai	Zach

Southern Cities: 1877 to 1937 -- AUGUSTA, GEORGIA, 1877

Female

Amanda 6	Gilsey	Narcisse
Amelia 5	Hagar	Nicey
Arey	Hannah 8	Patience 2
Chaney	Jerusha	Phillis 2
Charity	Lavinia 4	Phoebe 5
Cheney	Leanna	Priscilla 4
Chloe	Levira	Pyrinthia
Clarinda	Lorena 2	Queen
Clarissa 3	Lucilla	Rhoda
Daphne	Lucinda 4	Ritta
Dicey	Lucretia	Robinette
Dinah 3	Mahala 2	Rose 2
Dorcas	Malinda 5	Savannah
Drucilla	Malvina	Selina 2
Effie	Mariah 14	Sophia 6
Epsey	Matilda 5	Tamer
Eve	Melissa	Tamey
Florinda	Miranda	Terry
Georgiana	Mittie	Tina 3
		Vinne

Surnames, Black

The following lists are composed of 2766 surnames employed by Blacks in Augusta, Georgia, in 1877; the numbers after the name indicate the frequency of usage and the rate per 100,000. No number indicates the name was found once and has a rate per 100,000 of thirty-six. A frequency list indicating the rate of usage follows the alphabetical list.

Alphabetical

Adams 8 289	Carter 13 470	Foster 4 145
Alexander 9 325	Clark 13 470	Franklin 2 72
Allen 12 434	Coleman 8 289	Freeman 2 72
Anderson 20 723	Coles 7 253	Gaines 7 253
Atkins 3 108	Collins 5 180	Gardner 9 325
Bailey 9 325	Cooper 6 216	Gibson 2 72
Baker 7 253	Crawford 7 253	Gordon 10 362
Banks 3 108	Cummings 15 542	Grant 8 289
Barnes 8 289	Daniel 2 72	Gray 4 145
Bell 6 216	Davis 30 1085	Green 30 1085
Benjamin	Dixon 2 72	Griffin 11 398
Booker 3 108	Edwards 7 253	Hall 8 289
Bradley	Elliott 4 145	Hamilton 4 145
Brooks 8 289	Evans 8 289	Hammond 3 108
Brown 45 1627	Ferguson 3 108	Harper 6 216
Bryant 6 216	Fields 7 253	Harris 25 904
Butler 14 506	Fleming	Hawkins
Campbell 5 180	Fletcher 2 72	Henderson 5 180

Southern Cities: 1877 to 1937 -- AUGUSTA, GEORGIA, 1877

Henry 2 72	Morton 2 72	Simmons 8 289
Hill 10 362	Murray 10 362	Simms 6 216
Holloway	Myers 2 72	Smith 59 2132
Holmes 11 398	Nancy	Stevens
Hopkins	Owens	Stewart 13 470
Howard 11 398	Parker 4 145	Taylor 8 289
Hunter 3 108	Parks 3 108	Thomas 52 1880
Jackson 53 1916	Patterson 3 108	Thompson 6 216
James 3 108	Perry 4 145	Tucker
Jefferson 10 362	Phillips 3 108	Turner 22 795
Jenkins 11 398	Pierce	Wade
Johnson 65 2350	Pleasant	Walker 38 1374
Jones 66 2386	Polk 6 216	Ward 5 180
Jordon 4 145	Porter 8 289	Washington 17 615
Julia	Price 2 72	Watkins 13 470
King 10 362	Reed 5 180	Watson 2 72
Lee 10 362	Richardson 2 72	Webster
Lewis 11 398	Roberts 9 325	West 4 145
Martin 14 506	Robinson 29 1048	White 8 289
Mason 6 216	Rogers 4 145	Williams 115 4158
Miller 14 506	Ross 4 145	Willis 7 253
Mitchell 16 578	Russell 4 145	Wilson 20 723
Montgomery	Scott 26 940	Wright 6 216
Moore 20 723	Shelton 2 72	Young 11 398

Frequency

Williams 115	Stewart 13	Hall 8
Jones 66	Watkins 13	Porter 8
Johnson 65	Allen 12	Simmons 8
Smith 59	Griffin 11	Taylor 8
Jackson 53	Holmes 11	White 8
Thomas 52	Howard 11	Baker 7
Brown 45	Jenkins 11	Coles 7
Walker 38	Lewis 11	Crawford 7
Davis 30	Young 11	Edwards 7
Green 30	Gordon 10	Fields 7
Robinson 29	Hill 10	Gaines 7
Scott 26	Jefferson 10	Willis 7
Harris 25	King 10	Bell 6
Turner 22	Lee 10	Bryant 6
Anderson 20	Murray 10	Cooper 6
Moore 20	Alexander 9	Harper 6
Wilson 20	Bailey 9	Mason 6
Washington 17	Gardner 9	Polk 6
Mitchell 16	Roberts 9	Simms 6
Cummings 15	Adams 8	Thompson 6
Butler 14	Barnes 8	Wright 6
Martin 14	Brooks 8	Campbell 5
Miller 14	Coleman 8	Collins 5
Carter 13	Evans 8	Henderson 5
Clark 13	Grant 8	Reed 5

Southern Cities: 1877 to 1937 -- AUGUSTA, GEORGIA, 1877

Ward 5	Hunter 3	Watson 2
Elliott 4	James 3	Benjamin
Foster 4	Parks 3	Bradley
Gray 4	Patterson 3	Fleming
Hamilton 4	Phillips 3	Hawkins
Jordon 4	Daniel 2	Holloway
Parker 4	Dixon 2	Hopkins
Perry 4	Fletcher 2	Julia
Rogers 4	Franklin 2	Montgomery
Ross 4	Freeman 2	Nancy
Russell 4	Gibson 2	Owens
West 4	Henry 2	Pierce
Atkins 3	Morton 2	Pleasant
Banks 3	Myers 2	Stevens
Booker 3	Price 2	Tucker
Ferguson 3	Richardson 2	Wade
Hammond 3	Shelton 2	Webster

Most Common Given Names, White

The following lists reflecting white male nomenclature in Augusta, Georgia, in 1877, are composed of 4,706 names, 3535 male and 1171 female. The first list includes the number of times the name was found, and a second number indicates the rate of usage per 100,000 with a rate of 28.289. The second list, a frequency listing, indicates with a number only the total of incidences.

MALE
Alphabetical

Aaron 4 113	Carl 1 28	Eugene 10 283
Abraham 3 85	Charles 165 4668	Felix 2 57
Abram 2 57	Charley 1 28	Floyd 1 28
Adam 6 170	Chester 2 57	Francis 18 509
Albert 22 622	Clarence 4 113	Frank 57 1612
Alexander 19 537	Clifford 1 28	Fred 5 141
Alfred 15 424	Daniel 31 877	Frederick 19 537
Allen 3 85	David 30 849	George 135 3819
Alonzo 2 57	Dennis 7 198	Gilbert 2 57
Amos 3 85	Doc 3 85	Green 2 57
Anderson 2 57	Donald 2 57	Harrison 1 28
Andrew 23 651	Earl 1 28	Harry 1 28
Anthony 5 141	Edgar 1 28	Harvey 2 57
Archie 1 28	Edmond 8 226	Henderson 2 57
Arthur 4 113	Edward 76 2150	Henry 123 3480
August 5 141	Edwin 6 170	Herbert 1 28
Augustus 14 396	Eli 3 85	Herman 4 113
Barnard 7 198	Elias 1 28	Homer 2 57
Benjamin 30 849	Elijah 2 57	Hugh 12 339
Berry 1 28	Emanuel 1 28	Isaac 9 255
Caleb 1 28	Ephraim 1 28	Isaiah 1 28
Calvin 6 170	Ernest 6 170	Isham 4 113

Southern Cities: 1877 to 1937 -- AUGUSTA, GEORGIA, 1877

Jackson 6   170
Jacob 26   736
James 245   6931
Jasper 3   85
Jefferson 7   198
Jeremiah 11   311
Jerome 3   85
Jerry 3   85
Jesse 6   170
John 449   12,702
Jordan 1   28
Joseph 106   2999
Joshua 7   198
Julian 5   141
Julius 10   283
Lawrence 3   85
Leonard 2   57
Leroy 2   57
Levi 1   28
Lewis 14   396
Louis 18   509
Luther 3   85
Mack 3   85
Madison 3   85
Marshall 3   85

Martin 9   255
Matthew 11   311
Melvin 3   85
Michael 49   1386
Miles 1   28
Milton 3   85
Morris 3   85
Moses 6   170
Nathan 1   28
Nathaniel 4   113
Nelson 3   85
Nicholas 4   113
Oliver 6   170
Oscar 3   85
Otis 1   28
Owen 6   170
Patrick 55   1556
Paul 5   141
Peter 23   651
Phillip 15   424
Pleasant 2   57
Ralph 1   28
Reuben 6   170
Richard 20   566
Robert 77   2178

Roger 1   28
Sam 1   28
Sampson 1   28
Samuel 49   1386
Sidney 1   28
Simeon 8   226
Simon 1   28
Solomon 5   141
Stephen 8   226
Theodore 19   537
Thomas 162   4583
Timothy 18   509
Ulysses 1   28
Vernon 1   28
Wallace 1   28
Walter 7   198
Warren 5   141
Washington 4   113
Wesley 1   28
Wilbur 2   57
William 365   10,325
Willie 1   28
Willis 1   28
Zachariah 7   198

MALE
Frequency

John 449
William 365
James 245
Charles 165
Thomas 162
George 135
Henry 123
Joseph 106
Robert 77
Edward 76
Frank 57
Patrick 55
Michael 49
Samuel 49
Daniel 31
Benjamin 30
David 30
Jacob 26
Andrew 23
Peter 23
Albert 22
Richard 20
Alexander 19

Frederick 19
Theodore 19
Francis 18
Louis 18
Timothy 18
Alfred 15
Phillip 15
Augustus 14
Lewis 14
Hugh 12
Jeremiah 11
Matthew 11
Eugene 10
Julius 10
Isaac 9
Martin 9
Edmond 8
Simeon 8
Stephen 8
Barnard 7
Dennis 7
Jefferson 7
Joshua 7

Walter 7
Zachariah 7
Adam 6
Calvin 6
Edwin 6
Ernest 6
Jackson 6
Jesse 6
Moses 6
Oliver 6
Owen 6
Reuben 6
Anthony 5
August 5
Fred 5
Julian 5
Paul 5
Solomon 5
Warren 5
Aaron 4
Arthur 4
Clarence 4
Herman 4

Southern Cities: 1877 to 1937 --   AUGUSTA, GEORGIA, 1877

Isham 4	Chester 2	Floyd 1
Nathaniel 4	Donald 2	Harrison 1
Nicholas 4	Elijah 2	Harry 1
Washington 4	Felix 2	Herbert 1
Abraham 3	Gilbert 2	Isaiah 1
Allen 3	Green 2	Jordan 1
Amos 3	Harvey 2	Levi 1
Doc 3	Henderson 2	Melvin 1
Eli 3	Homer 2	Miles 1
Jasper 3	Leonard 2	Nathan 1
Jerome 3	Leroy 2	Otis 1
Jerry 3	Pleasant 2	Ralph 1
Lawrence 3	Wilbur 2	Roger 1
Luther 3	Archie 1	Sam 1
Mack 3	Berry 1	Sampson 1
Madison 3	Caleb 1	Sidney 1
Marshall 3	Carl 1	Simon 1
Milton 3	Charley 1	Ulysses 1
Morris 3	Clifford 1	Vernon 1
Nelson 3	Earl 1	Wallace 1
Oscar 3	Edgar 1	Wesley 1
Abram 2	Elias 1	Willie 1
Alonzo 2	Emanuel 1	Willis 1
Anderson 2	Ephraim 1	

FEMALE
Alphabetical
Rate per 100,000 = 85.

Adaline 5 427	Dolly 1	Hattie 7 598
Agnes 2 171	Dora 1	Helen 2 171
Alice 13 1110	Dorcas 1	Henrietta 2 171
Amanda 16 1366	Edith 2 171	Hester 1
Amelia 3 256	Eleanor 1	Ida 3 256
Ann 19 1623	Eliza 33 2818	Irene 2 171
Anna 37 3160	Elizabeth 62 5295	Isabella 5 427
Annie 10 854	Ella 9 769	Jane 39 3330
Belle 2 171	Ellen 30 2562	Jeannette 3 256
Betsy 2 171	Emily 7 598	Jennie 7 598
Betty 6 512	Emma 19 1623	Johanna 6 512
Beulah 1	Ernestine 2 171	Josephine 7 598
Bridget 8 683	Esther 2 171	Julia 21 1793
Caroline 14 1196	Eugenia 4 342	Kate 9 769
Carrie 6 512	Eunice 1	Katy 3 256
Catharine 25 2135	Fanny 29 2477	Kitty 1
Celia 1	Flora 2 171	Laura 9 769
Charity 1	Florence 1	Lavinia 4 342
Charlotte 3 256	Frances 15 1281	Lena 5 427
Christine 1	Georgia 10 854	Lizzie 11 939
Clara 1	Gertrude 1	Louisa 5 427
Clarissa 1	Hannah 3 256	Louise 3 256
Della 1	Harriet 11 939	Lucinda 6 512

Southern Cities: 1877 to 1937 -- AUGUSTA, GEORGIA, 1877

Lucy 15 1281	Milly 1	Rosa 4 342
Lula 7 598	Minerva 2 171	Rose 3 256
Lydia 1	Minnie 1	Ruth 2 171
Maggie 8 683	Miriam 1	Sally 13 1110
Malinda 2 171	Molly 5 427	Sarah 75 6405
Mamie 1	Nancy 21 1793	Savannah 3 256
Margaret 26 2220	Nelly 3 256	Silva 1
Maria 11 939	Pauline 1	Sophia 5 427
Marion 4 342	Polly 4 342	Susan 30 2562
Martha 54 4611	Priscilla 2 171	Susie 1
Mary 161 13,749	Rachel 9 769	Viola 2 171
Matilda 6 512	Rebecca 8 683	Virginia 3 256
Mattie 20 1708	Rhoda 2 171	Winney 1

FEMALE
Frequency

Mary 161	Emily 7	Edith 2
Sarah 75	Hattie 7	Ernestine 2
Elizabeth 62	Jennie 7	Esther 2
Martha 54	Josephine 7	Flora 2
Jane 39	Lula 7	Helen 2
Anna 37	Betty 6	Henrietta 2
Eliza 33	Carrie 6	Irene 2
Ellen 30	Johanna 6	Malinda 2
Susan 30	Lucinda 6	Minerva 2
Fanny 29	Matilda 6	Priscilla 2
Margaret 26	Adaline 5	Rhoda 2
Catharine 25	Isabella 5	Ruth 2
Julia 21	Lena 5	Viola 2
Nancy 21	Louisa 5	Beulah 1
Mattie 20	Molly 5	Celia 1
Ann 19	Sophia 5	Charity 1
Emma 19	Eugenia 4	Christine 1
Amanda 16	Lavinia 4	Clara 1
Frances 15	Marion 4	Clarissa 1
Lucy 15	Polly 4	Della 1
Caroline 14	Rosa 4	Dolly 1
Alice 13	Amelia 3	Dora 1
Sally 13	Charlotte 3	Dorcas 1
Harriet 11	Hannah 3	Eleanor 1
Lizzie 11	Ida 3	Eunice 1
Maria 11	Jeanette 3	Florence 1
Annie 10	Katy 3	Gertrude 1
Georgia 10	Louise 3	Hester 1
Ella 9	Nelly 3	Kitty 1
Kate 9	Rose 3	Lydia 1
Laura 9	Savannah 3	Mamie 1
Rachel 9	Virginia 3	Milly 1
Bridget 8	Agnes 2	Minnie 1
Maggie 8	Belle 2	Miriam 1
Rebecca 8	Betsy 2	Pauline 1

Southern Cities: 1877 to 1937 -- AUGUSTA, GEORGIA, 1877

Silvia 1   Susie 1   Winny 1

Unusual Names, White

Male

Abel	Emanuel	Levi
Abraham 4	Enoch	Mack 3
Abram 2	Ephraim	Madison 3
Alonzo 2	Erasmus 4	Malachi 2
Aloysius	Erastus	Marcellus 3
Alpheus	Essie	Marshall 3
Ardis	Ezekiel	Massilon
August 7	Ezra	Matthias
Basil	Fee	Moses 6
Berry	Fernandez	Obadiah
Buck	Green 2	Philemon
Cadmus	Harrison	Phineas
Caleb	Hezekiah 3	Pleasant 2
Calous	Hosea 2	Sampson
Christ	Isaac 9	Shadrach
Christian	Isaiah	Simeon 8
Christie	Isham 4	Solomon 3
Columbus 3	Jabez	St. John
Darling 2	Jeremiah 11	Ulysses
Datus	Job 2	Uriah
Delaware	Joshua 7	Valentine 2
Doc 4	Josiah 3	Washington 4
Dock	Juriah	Wink
Eli 3	Ker	Zaccheus
Elias	Leander	Zach
Elijah 3	Leebud	Zachariah 7
Elisha	Leonidas	Zephamiah

Female

Abigail	Delilah	Lucinda 6
Albenia	Dorcas	Lucretia 3
Alcenia	Druscilla	Mahala 2
Almeda	Elzara	Malinda 2
Amanda 16	Epsey	Mamie
Amelia 3	Eugenia 4	Maria 11
Anastasia	Francina	Marsena
Araminta	Gussie	Matilda 6
Ardella	Hannah 3	Melissa 3
Artemesia	Idella	Minerva 2
Bethina	Indiana	Minnie
Camille	Jemima	Mirabelle 2
Cassie	Johanna 6	Miranda
Charity	Lavinia 4	Missouri 2
Clarissa	Lina	Narcissa

Southern Cities: 1877 to 1937 -- AUGUSTA, GEORGIA, 1877

Priscilla 2	Savannah 3	Tursey
Rhoda 2	Selina	Velia
Robina	Sena	Vermille
Rosa 4	Silva	Viney
Salvena	Sophia 5	Viola 2
Samantha	Susannah 2	Winney
Saphronia 2	Tabina	Winnie

Surnames, White

The following lists reflect the use of surnames amongst 5,056 Whites in Augusta, Ga., 1877; the numbers after the name indicate the frequency of usage and the rate per 100,000. No number indicates the name was found once and has a rate per 100,000 of twenty. A frequency list indicating the rate of usage follows the alphabetical list. Four thousand, seven hundred and six given names of Whites were used, after dropping foreign names and initials from the list of 5,056 full names.

Alphabetical

Adams 8 158	Evans 15 297	Jackson 14 277
Alexander 4 79	Ferguson 5 99	James 2 40
Allen 11 218	Fields	Jefferson
Anderson 15 297	Fisher 2 40	Jenkins 4 79
Austin 3 59	Fleming 12 237	Johnson 34 672
Bailey 8 158	Fletcher 3 59	Jones 34 672
Baker 18 356	Foster 8 158	Jordon 7 138
Banks	Franklin 9 178	King 10 198
Barnes 9 178	Freeman 5 99	Lee 5 99
Bell 8 158	Fuller 3 59	Lewis 11 218
Brooks 3 59	Gaines 2 40	Martin 13 257
Brown 32 633	Gardner 3 59	Miller 23 455
Bryant 8 158	Gibson 3 59	Mitchell 5 99
Butler 13 257	Gordon 5 99	Montgomery
Campbell 7 138	Gray 8 158	Moore 28 554
Carter 8 158	Green 10 198	Morse
Clark 18 356	Griffin 7 138	Murray 9 178
Clarke 7 138	Hall 8 158	Myers 7 138
Coleman 8 158	Hamilton	Owens 4 79
Coles 2 40	Hammond 6 119	Parker 16 316
Collins 11 218	Harper 7 138	Parks 2 40
Cooper 8 158	Harris 5 99	Patterson 4 79
Cox	Hart 2 40	Payne 4 79
Crawford 4 79	Hayes 2 40	Penn
Cummings 2 40	Henderson 4 79	Phillips
Daniels	Henry 10 198	Pierce 5 99
Davis 31 613	Hill 21 415	Porter 3 59
Dixon	Holland	Price 7 138
Douglass	Holmes 9 178	Procter
Edwards 2 40	Hopkins 5 99	Randolph
Elliott 2 40	Howard 11 218	Reed 3 59

Southern Cities: 1877 to 1937 -- AUGUSTA, GEORGIA, 1877

Reid 5 99	Smith 61 1206	Watkins 4 79
Richardson 2 40	Stevens 5 99	Watson 4 79
Rivers 2 40	Stewart 6 119	West 3 59
Roberts 13 257	Taylor 8 158	White 11 218
Robinson 11 218	Thomas 13 257	Williams 35 692
Rogers 9 178	Thompson 24 475	Willis 4 79
Ross 5 99	Tucker	Wilson 17 336
Russell 10 198	Turner 11 218	Wood 3 59
Scott 12 237	Wade 3 59	Woods
Sharpe 3 59	Walker 20 396	Wright 9 178
Simmons 16 316	Ward 5 99	Young 7 138
Simms 4 79	Washington 3 59	

Frequency

Smith 61	Franklin 9	Ward 5
Williams 35	Holmes 9	Alexander 4
Johnson 34	Murray 9	Crawford 4
Jones 34	Rogers 9	Henderson 4
Brown 32	Wright 9	Jenkins 4
Davis 31	Adams 8	Owens 4
Moore 28	Bailey 8	Patterson 4
Thompson 24	Bell 8	Payne 4
Miller 23	Bryant 8	Simms 4
Hill 21	Carter 8	Watkins 4
Walker 20	Coleman 8	Watson 4
Baker 18	Cooper 8	Willis 4
Clark 18	Foster 8	Austin 3
Wilson 17	Gray 8	Brooks 3
Parker 16	Hall 8	Fletcher 3
Simmons 16	Taylor 8	Fuller 3
Anderson 15	Campbell 7	Gardner 3
Evans 15	Clarke 7	Gibson 3
Jackson 14	Griffin 7	Porter 3
Butler 13	Harper 7	Reed 3
Martin 13	Jordon 7	Sharpe 3
Roberts 13	Myers 7	Wade 3
Thomas 13	Price 7	Washington 3
Fleming 12	Young 7	West 3
Scott 12	Hammond 6	Wood 3
Allen 11	Stewart 6	Coles 2
Collins 11	Ferguson 5	Cummings 2
Howard 11	Freeman 5	Edwards 2
Lewis 11	Gordon 5	Elliott 2
Robinson 11	Harris 5	Fisher 2
Turner 11	Hopkins 5	Gaines 2
White 11	Lee 5	Hart 2
Green 10	Mitchell 5	Hayes 2
Henry 10	Pierce 5	James 2
King 10	Reid 5	Parks 2
Russell 10	Ross 5	Richardson 2
Barnes 9	Stevens 5	Rivers 2

Southern Cities: 1877 to 1937 -- AUGUSTA, GEORGIA, 1877

Banks	Hamilton	Phillips
Cox	Holland	Procter
Daniels	Jefferson	Randolph
Dixon	Montgomery	Tucker
Douglass	Morse	Woods
Fields	Penn	

Southern Cities: 1877 to 1937

Source List O: AUGUSTA, GEORGIA, 1899[5]

Most Common Given Names, Black

The following list concerns itself with the most common given names of Black males from a total of 6,457 persons. The first list includes the number of times the name was found, and a second number with a rate of fifteen, indicates the rate of usage per 100,000. The second list, a frequency listing, indicates with a number only the total of incidences.

MALE
Alphabetical

Aaron 16 248	Earl 1	Jasper 5 77
Abraham 14 217	Edgar 7 108	Jeff 12 186
Abram 11 170	Edmond 16 248	Jefferson 8 124
Adam 9 139	Edward 166 2571	Jeremiah 11 170
Albert 57 883	Edwin 1	Jerry 30 465
Alexander 61 945	Eli 3 47	Jesse 54 836
Alfred 41 653	Elias 3 47	Joe 2 31
Allen 34 527	Elijah 15 232	John 476 7372
Alonzo 8 124	Emanuel 17 263	Jonas 6 93
Amos 11 170	Ephraim 10 155	Jordon 13 201
Andrew 61 945	Ernest 3 47	Joseph 160 2478
Andy 4 62	Eugene 17 263	Joshua 16 248
Anthony 12 186	Felix 11 170	Julius 8 124
Arthur 30 465	Floyd 5 77	King 5 77
Augustus 55 852	Frank 101 1564	Lawrence 13 201
Benjamin 72 1115	Fred 6 93	Lee 17 263
Berry 13 201	Frederick 31 480	Leon 1
Caesar 3 47	Gabriel 10 155	Leonard 2 31
Caleb 3 47	George 243 3763	Leroy 1
Calvin 17 263	Gilbert 15 232	Lewis 16 248
Carl 1	Green 4 62	Lloyd 3 47
Cato 3 47	Harrison 12 186	Louis 52 805
Charles 230 3562	Harry 23 356	Luther 9 139
Charlie 3 47	Harvey 4 62	Mack 20 310
Chester 3 47	Henderson 1	Madison 11 170
Cicero 6 93	Henry 301 4662	Major 9 139
Clarence 23 356	Howard 6 93	Martin 4 62
Claude 2 31	Irwin 4 62	Matthew 11 170
Clifford 9 139	Isaac 41 635	Melvin 2 31
Clifton 1	Isaiah 24 372	Miles 5 77
Columbus 9 139	Isham 4 62	Milledge 7 108
Daniel 61 945	Jabez 5 77	Milton 6 93
David 62 960	Jack 20 310	Mingo 1
Dennis 25 387	Jackson 15 232	Moses 54 836
Dick 1	Jacob 38 589	Napoleon 6 93
Dock 15 232	James 330 5111	Nathan 17 263

[5]From the City Directory, Augusta, Ga., 1899.

Southern Cities: 1877 to 1937 -- AUGUSTA, GEORGIA, 1899

Nathaniel 10 155	Prince 15 232	Ulysses 1
Ned 4 62	Reuben 17 263	Wallace 5 77
Nelson 14 217	Richard 79 1223	Walter 35 542
Oliver 16 248	Robert 217 3361	Wash 2 31
Otis 4 62	Roy 1	Washington 18 279
Oscar 6 93	Sampson 1	Wesley 24 372
Paul 18 279	Samuel 124 1920	Will 1
Peter 50 774	Sidney 8 124	William 535 8286
Phillip 13 201	Simon 21 252	Willie 1
Pleasant 3 47	Solomon 224 3469	Willis 20 310
Pompey 1	Stephen 31 480	York 1
Primus 1	Theodore 4 62	Zachariah 9 139

MALE
Frequency

William 535	Dennis 25	Abram 11
John 476	Isaiah 24	Amos 11
Henry 301	Wesley 24	Felix 11
James 330	Clarence 23	Jeremiah 11
George 243	Harry 23	Madison 11
Charles 230	Simon 21	Matthew 11
Solomon 224	Jack 20	Ephraim 10
Robert 217	Mack 20	Gabriel 10
Edward 166	Willis 20	Nathaniel 10
Joseph 160	Paul 18	Adam 9
Samuel 124	Washington 18	Clifford 9
Frank 101	Calvin 17	Columbus 9
Richard 79	Emanuel 17	Luther 9
Benjamin 72	Eugene 17	Major 9
David 62	Lee 17	Zachariah 9
Alexander 61	Nathan 17	Alonzo 8
Andrew 61	Reuben 17	Jefferson 8
Daniel 61	Aaron 16	Julius 8
Albert 57	Edmond 16	Sidney 8
Augustus 55	Joshua 16	Edgar 7
Jesse 54	Lewis 16	George Washington 7
Moses 54	Oliver 16	Milledge 7
Louis 52	Dock 15	Cicero 6
Peter 50	Elijah 15	Fred 6
Alfred 41	Gilbert 15	Howard 6
Isaac 41	Jackson 15	Jonas 6
Jacob 38	Prince 15	Milton 6
Walter 35	Abraham 14	Napoleon 6
Allen 34	Nelson 14	Oscar 6
Frederick 31	Berry 13	Floyd 5
Stephen 31	Jordon 13	Jabez 5
Arthur 30	Lawrence 13	Jasper 5
Jerry 30	Phillip 13	King 5
	Anthony 12	Miles 5
	Harrison 12	Wallace 5
	Jeff 12	Andy 4
		Green 4

Southern Cities: 1877 to 1937 -- AUGUSTA, GEORGIA, 1899

Harvey 4	Elias 3	Henderson 1
Irwin 4	Ernest 3	Leon 1
Isham 4	Lloyd 3	Leroy 1
Martin 4	Pleasant 3	Mingo 1
Ned 4	Claude 2	Pompey 1
Otis 4	Leonard 2	Primus 1
Theodore 4	Melvin 2	Roy 1
Caesar 3	Wash 2	Sampson 1
Caleb 3	Carl 1	Ulysses 1
Cato 3	Clifton 1	Will 1
Charlie 3	Dick 1	Willie 1
Chester 3	Earl 1	York 1
Eli 3	Edwin 1	

FEMALE
Alphabetical
Rate per 100,000 = 39.

Adaline 11 427	Effie 2 76	Jane 50 1939
Addie 13 504	Eliza 52 2016	Jennie 14 543
Agnes 2 76	Elizabeth 32 1241	Jessie 3 116
Alice 35 1357	Ella 36 1396	Josephine 20 776
Amanda 33 1280	Ellen 25 969	Judy 1
Amelia 14 543	Elsie 4 155	Julia 52 2016
Amy 8 310	Elvira 2 76	Katy 13 504
Ann 3 116	Emily 7 271	Kitty 4 155
Anna 93 3606	Emma 74 2869	Laura 35 1357
Annie 45 1745	Esther 2 76	Leah 2 76
Bellah 1	Essie 1	Lena 11 427
Bertha 4 155	Ethel 1	Letty 2 76
Bessie 4 155	Eunice 1	Lillie 13 504
Betty 11 427	Eva 2 76	Lizzie 41 1590
Betsy 12 465	Evaline 3 116	Louisa 41 1590
Biddy 4 155	Evelyn 1	Louise 6 233
Blanche 1	Fanny 56 2171	Lucille 1
Caroline 14 543	Flora 9 349	Lucinda 19 737
Carrie 31 1202	Florence 4 155	Lucy 40 1551
Catharine 19 737	Frances 30 1163	Lula 17 659
Celia 10 388	Georgia 17 659	Lydia 5 194
Charity 12 465	Gertrude 1	Mabel 2 76
Charlotte 14 543	Grace 9 349	Maggie 17 659
Chloe 3 116	Hannah 17 659	Mahala 5 194
Clara 20 776	Harriet 23 892	Malinda 16 620
Cora 8 310	Hattie 33 1280	Mamie 10 388
Daisy 7 271	Hazel 1	Margaret 22 853
Delia 3 116	Henrietta 23 892	Marion 9 349
Dina(h) 9 349	Hester 5 194	Matilda 23 892
Dolly 4 155	Hetty 1	Mattie 37 1435
Dorcas 3 116	Ida 23 892	Maria(h) 56 2171
Easter 6 233	Indiana 5 194	Martha 56 2171
Edith 1	Irene 3 116	Mary 200 7755
Edna 3 116	Isabella 7 271	Maude 5 194

Southern Cities: 1877 to 1937 -- AUGUSTA, GEORGIA, 1899

May 1	Peggy 5 194	Sarah 85 3296
Milly 9 349	Phillis 7 271	Savannah 10 388
Mima 2 76	Phoebe 10 388	Silvey 2 76
Minerva 3 116	Polly 8 310	Sophia 12 465
Minnie 10 388	Priscilla 9 349	Susan 30 1163
Molly 6 233	Rachel 24 931	Susie 10 388
Nancy 29 1124	Rebecca 21 814	Venus 2 76
Nanny 1	Rhoda 3 116	Viola 3 116
Nelly 13 504	Rosa 46 1784	Violet 2 76
Patience 4 155	Rose 9 349	Virginia 13 504
Patsy 10 388	Ruth 2 76	Vivian 1
Pauline 1	Sadie 3 116	Willie 4 155
Pearl 3 116	Sally 32 1241	Winny 8 310

Female
Frequency

Mary 200	Clara 20	Milly 9
Anna 93	Josephine 20	Priscilla 9
Sarah 85	Catharine 19	Rose 9
Emma 74	Lucinda 19	Amy 8
Fanny 56	Georgia 17	Cora 8
Maria(h) 56	Hannah 17	Polly 8
Martha 56	Lula 17	Winn(e)y 8
Eliza 52	Maggie 17	Daisy 7
Julia 52	Malinda 16	Emily 7
Jane 50	Amelia 14	Isabella 7
Rosa 46	Caroline 14	Phillis 7
Annie 45	Charlotte 14	Easter 6
Lizzie 41	Jennie 14	Louise 6
Louisa 41	Addie 13	Molly 6
Lucy 40	Katy 13	Hester 5
Mattie 37	Lillie 13	Indiana 5
Ella 36	Nelly 13	Lydia 5
Alice 35	Virginia 13	Mahala 5
Laura 35	Betsy 12	Maude 5
Amanda 33	Charity 12	Peggy 5
Hattie 33	Sophia 12	Bessie 4
Elizabeth 32	Adaline 11	Bertha 4
Sally 32	Betty 11	Biddy 4
Carrie 31	Lena 11	Dolly 4
Frances 30	Celia 10	Elsie 4
Susan 30	Mamie 10	Florence 4
Nancy 29	Minnie 10	Kitty 4
Ellen 25	Patsy 10	Patience 4
Rachel 24	Phoebe 10	Willie 4
Harriet 23	Savannah 10	Ann 3
Henrietta 23	Susie 10	Chloe 3
Ida 23	Dina 9	Delia 3
Matilda 23	Flora 9	Dorcas 3
Margaret 22	Grace 9	Edna 3
Rebecca 21	Marion 9	Eveline 3

Southern Cities: 1877 to 1937 -- AUGUSTA, GEORGIA, 1899

Irene 3	Leah 2	Ethel 1
Jessie 3	Letty 2	Eunice 1
Minerva 3	Mabel 2	Evelyn 1
Pearl 3	Mima 2	Gertrude 1
Rhoda 3	Ruth 2	Hazel 1
Sadie 3	Silvey 2	Hetty 1
Viola 3	Venus 2	Judy 1
Agnes 2	Violet 2	Lucille 1
Effie 2	Bellah 1	May 1
Elvira 2	Blanche 1	Nanny 1
Esther 2	Edith 1	Pauline 1
Eva 2	Essie 1	Vivian 1

Unusual Names, Black

Alphabetical listings of male and female names follow with a number representing the frequency of use; no number indicates the name was found only once.

Male

Abraham 14	Caesar 3	Derris
Abram 11	Cage	Dillie
Agent	Caiaphas	Dink
Albentun	Cain	Dock 15
Altheus	Calcut	Dorpheus
Ambrus	Caleb 3	Dorse 2
Americus	Cap	Dozie
Anatimus	Captain	Dozier
Ankey	Carolina 2	Dublin
Asene	Cash 2	Duffy
Aug	Cass	Dwelle
August 2	Cato 4	Dy
Auvergne	Charlemange	Early
Babe 2	Cheeley	Ebenezer
Barto	Cicero 6	Elexzener
Beauregard	Codoza	Eli 3
Bonnie	Colie	Elias 3
Bosie	Colonel	Elizah 15
Boss	Columbus 9	Elisha
Bossie	Comie	Elza
Boston 2	Condas	Emanuel 17
Boyco	Consul 2	Enoch 3
Brazie	Council	Enos 2
Bright	Cordoza	Ephraim 10
Brister	Crueso	Esau 2
Brit	Cudger	Eustice
Bub	Cudgo 2	Ezekiel 2
Buck	Cuff	Fate
Bud	Cupid	Flanders
Buddie	Dace	Fortune
Burmah	Deedom	Gabe

Southern Cities: 1877 to 1937 -- AUGUSTA, GEORGIA, 1899

Gabriel 10	Kissar	Pop
Gad 3	Kit	Portion
Gadeous	Labron	Primus
Garfield 2	Lark	Prince 15
Gas	Lawyer	Prophet
Gazzie	Lazarus 2	Punch
General 4	Lenus	Ransom
Gentle	Leonidas	Renty
George Washington 7	Lethia	Rollie
German	Levi 3	Roman
Gideon	Levy	Royal
Gip	Lisbon 2	Sampson
Glasgow	London 3	Sandy 2
Glasker	Lore	Sanks
Golden	Lum	Scipio 3
Governor	Major 9	Shank
Hamp	Mange	Shadrach 4
Hannibal	Marcellus 4	Shaver
Happy	March	Shed
Hark	Marse	Silax
Hector 3	Maryland	Siva
Hezekiah 3	Milledge 7	Smart
Hix	Miner	Squire 3
Hosea	Mingo	Solomon 224
Hosey	Minor 2	Son
Hosia	Monk 3	Standard
Ignatius	Mose 3	Stonewall
Isaac 41	Moses 54	Tack
Isaiah 24	Mossy	Tapper
Isam	Nace	Team
Ishael	Napoleon 6	Telt
Isham 4	Nero 2	Tete
Israel 4	Ninrod	Theophilus
Jabe	Nitus	Tobias
Jabez 5	Noble 3	Toby 2
Jabus	Ockey	Toms
Jade	Oscie	Toomer
Jam	Ossie	Troop
Jeb	Otha	Uriah 3
Jefferson	Othello 3	Vedery
Jep	Ottimous	Ves
Jeremiah 11	Ousa	Vince
Jetus	Ovid	Virge
Jonas 6	Paris 3	Virgis
Joshua 16	Peer	Wash 2
Judge 4	Phoenix	Zach
Jule	Pleasant 3	Zachariah 9
July	Pledger	Zackery
Juriah	Plumie	Zeb
Ketter	Plunk	Zedekiah
Key	Pompey	Zemmie
King 5	Pony	

Southern Cities: 1877 to 1937 -- AUGUSTA, GEORGIA, 1899

Female

Alphonsine	Handsome (Ivey)	Mozelle 2
Alzarah	Hannah 17	Narcissus 2
Alzera	Hansie	Nazarene
Amanda 33	Harty	Nicie 2
Amelia 14	Hennie	Octavie
America	Idella	Odas
Anaky	Indiana 5	Orelia
Arberta	Inetta	Palmyra
Arie	Irena	Paris
Augustena	January	Parnie
Bertlina	Jestine	Parthenia
Camilla	Joycie	Patience 4
Cap	Jugie	Penda
Cassie	Kissie	Petunia
Ceny	Kizziah	Phillis 7
Chanie	Kizzie	Phoebe 10
Charity 12	Laney	Pinda
Chattie	Lear	Pinkie 3
Chloe 3	Letha	Priscilla 9
Clarennie	Lillie (White)	Queen
Clarentine	Liney	Rena 2
Clarion	Litha	Rhoda 3
Clarisy	Littie 3	Rhodie
Classy	Livia	Rita
Corena	Love	Salina 4
Cosey	Lou	Savannah 10
Croesie	Lourane	Sepher
Debie	Louvenia 2	Sibbie 2
Devy	Lucinda 19	Sila
Dilcie 2	Lucretia 2	Sina
Dilsey	Lulie	Sissy
Dilsy 2	Lurenia	Sophia 12
Dina 9	Mahala 5	Susannah
Docia	Mahaley 2	Tabitha 2
Donie	Mahalia 2	Tamer
Dorcas 3	Malinda 16	Tamo
Drucilla 2	Malissa	Telissa
Easter 6	Maria 56	Tena 3
Eathis	Marinda 2	Tennessee
Effie 2	Maroda	Tina
Essie	Masaline	Tisher
Floy	Massene	Tommie
Florida	Massina	Toma
Fluta	Matilda 23	Treacy
Fronie	Melvina 2	Tulie
Georgie	Minty 2	Ursula 2
Geralvine	Miranda	Venie
Gerryline	Missouri 3	Venus 2
Gillie	Mittie 4	Vernel
Gussie 3	Mosel	Viana

Southern Cities: 1877 to 1937 -- AUGUSTA, GEORGIA, 1899

| Vicey 2 | Viney | Winney 8 |
| Vina 4 | Viscus | |

Surnames, Black

The following lists are composed of 9,184 surnames employed by Blacks in Augusta, Ga., in 1899; the numbers after the name indicate the frequency of usage and the rate per 100,000. No number indicates the name was found once and has a rate per 100,000 of eleven. A frequency list indicating the rate of usage follows the alphabetical list.

Alphabetical

Adams 26 283	Fisher 11 120	Jones 207 2254
Alexander 6 65	Fleming	Jordon 9 98
Allen 47 512	Fletcher 2 22	King 31 338
Anderson 45 490	Foster 10 109	Lee 31 338
Atkins 3 33	Franklin 12 131	Lewis 39 425
Bailey 28 305	Freeman 24 261	Lucas 7 76
Baker 8 87	Fuller 6 65	Martin 35 381
Banks 13 142	Gaines 10 109	Mason 15 163
Barnes 27 294	Gardner 28 305	Matthews 16 174
Bell 21 229	Gibson 15 163	Miller 24 261
Bennett 23 250	Gordon 13 142	Mitchell 36 392
Berry 13 142	Grant 18 196	Montgomery 4 44
Booker 7 76	Gray 15 163	Moore 51 555
Bradley 7 76	Green 81 882	Morse 7 76
Brooks 15 163	Griffin 32 348	Morton 3 33
Brown 183 1993	Hale 21 229	Murray 29 316
Bryant 13 142	Hamilton 9 98	Myers 7 76
Burrell	Hammond 17 185	Owens 13 142
Butler 26 283	Harper 28 305	Paige
Campbell 20 218	Harris 103 1122	Parker 23 250
Carter 45 490	Hart	Parks 16 174
Clark 42 457	Harvey 6 65	Patterson 16 174
Coleman 24 261	Hawkins 6 65	Payne 12 131
Coles 10 109	Hayes 2 22	Penn 4 44
Collins 43 468	Henderson 15 163	Perry 14 152
Cooper 15 163	Henry 2 22	Phillips 11 120
Cox 2 22	Hill 31 338	Phoeby
Crawford 30 327	Holland 6 65	Pierce
Cummings 44 479	Holloway 20 218	Polk 2 22
Daniels 5 54	Holmes 33 359	Porter 22 240
Davis 103 1122	Hopkins 7 76	Price 2 22
Dickerson 4 44	Howard 27 294	Procter
Dixon 9 98	Hunter 3 33	Reid 27 294
Edwards 28 305	Jackson 142 1546	Richardson 17 185
Elliott 11 120	James 20 218	Ridgeley
Evans 46 501	Jefferson 15 163	Rivers 2 22
Ferguson 8 87	Jenkins 47 512	Roberts 16 174
Fields 8 87	Johnson 229 2494	Robinson 88 958

Southern Cities: 1877 to 1937 -- AUGUSTA, GEORGIA, 1899

Rogers 5 54	Taylor 37 403	Webster
Ross 11 120	Thomas 141 1535	West 13 142
Russell 10 109	Thompson 21 229	White 58 632
Scott 63 686	Tucker 5 54	Williams 406 4421
Sharpe 3 33	Turner 39 425	Willis 15 163
Shelton 2 22	Wade 4 44	Wilson 53 577
Simmons 25 272	Walker 123 1339	Wood 8 87
Simms 30 327	Ward 6 65	Woods 8 87
Smith 151 1644	Washington 48 523	Wright 61 664
Stevens 7 76	Watkins 27 294	Young 35 381
Stewart 21 229	Watson 13 142	

Frequency

Williams 406	Simms 30	Jefferson 15
Johnson 229	Murray 29	Mason 15
Jones 207	Bailey 28	Willis 15
Brown 183	Edwards 28	Perry 14
Smith 151	Gardner 28	Banks 13
Jackson 142	Harper 28	Berry 13
Thomas 141	Barnes 27	Bryant 13
Walker 123	Howard 27	Gordon 13
Davis 103	Reid 27	Owens 13
Harris 103	Watkins 27	Watson 13
Robinson 88	Adams 26	West 13
Green 81	Butler 26	Franklin 12
Scott 63	Simmons 25	Payne 12
Wright 61	Coleman 24	Elliott 11
White 58	Freeman 24	Fisher 11
Wilson 53	Miller 24	Phillips 11
Moore 51	Bennett 23	Ross 11
Washington 48	Parker 23	Coles 10
Allen 47	Porter 22	Foster 10
Jenkins 47	Bell 21	Gaines 10
Evans 46	Hale 21	Russell 10
Anderson 45	Stewart 21	Dixon 9
Carter 45	Thompson 21	Hamilton 9
Cummings 44	Campbell 20	Jordon 9
Collins 43	Holloway 20	Baker 8
Clark 42	James 20	Ferguson 8
Lewis 39	Grant 18	Fields 8
Turner 39	Hammond 17	Wood 8
Taylor 37	Richardson 17	Woods 8
Mitchell 36	Matthews 16	Booker 7
Martin 35	Parks 16	Bradley 7
Young 35	Patterson 16	Hopkins 7
Holmes 33	Roberts 16	Lucas 7
Griffin 32	Brooks 15	Morse 7
Hill 31	Cooper 15	Myers 7
King 31	Gibson 15	Stevens 7
Lee 31	Gray 15	Alexander 6
Crawford 30	Henderson 15	Fuller 6

Southern Cities: 1877 to 1937 -- AUGUSTA, GEORGIA, 1899

Harvey 6	Wade 4	Price 2
Hawkins 6	Atkins 3	Rivers 2
Holland 6	Hunter 3	Shelton 2
Ward 6	Morton 3	Burrell
Daniels 5	Sharpe 3	Fleming
Rogers 5	Cox 2	Hart
Tucker 5	Fletcher 2	Paige
Dickerson 4	Hayes 2	Pierce
Montgomery 4	Henry 2	Procter
Penn 4	Polk 2	Ridgeley
		Webster

Surnames, White

The following is a list of White surnames taken from 11,840 Whites in Augusta, Ga., in 1899; the numbers after the name indicate the frequency of usage and the rate per 100,000. No number indicates the name was found once and has a rate per 100,000 of eight. A frequency list indicating the rate of usage follows the alphabetical list.

Alphabetical

Adams 22 186	Daniels 3 25	Hawkins 2 17
Alexander 17 144	Davis 53 448	Hayes 8 68
Allen 39 329	Dixon 9 76	Henderson 10 84
Anderson 23 194	Douglass 2 17	Henry 13 110
Atkins 3 25	Edwards 18 152	Hill 36 304
Austin 5 51	Elliott 13 110	Holland 3 25
Bailey 11 93	Evans 19 160	Holloway 20 169
Baker 16 135	Ferguson 8 68	Holmes 7 59
Banks 10 84	Fisher 2 17	Hopkins 19 160
Barnes 25 211	Fleming 23 194	Howard 29 245
Bell 15 127	Fletcher 3 25	Hunter 5 42
Bennett 17 144	Foster 13 110	Jackson 25 211
Berry 11 93	Franklin 11 93	James 14 118
Booker	Freeman 8 68	Jefferson 2 17
Bradley 10 84	Fuller 15 127	Jenkins 8 68
Brooks 15 127	Gardner 6 51	Johnson 88 743
Brown 71 600	Gibson 6 51	Jones 94 794
Bryant 10 84	Gordon 9 76	Jordon 26 220
Butler 19 160	Grant 3 25	King 33 279
Campbell 26 220	Gray 9 76	Lee 28 236
Carter 13 110	Green 27 228	Lewis 11 93
Clark 43 363	Greene 2 17	Lucas
Clarke 7 59	Griffin 25 211	Martin 33 279
Coleman 8 68	Hale 33 279	Mason 4 34
Collins 17 144	Hamilton 6 51	Matthews 9 76
Cooper 14 118	Hammond 6 51	Miller 34 287
Cox 8 68	Harper 4 34	Mitchell 16 135
Crawford 19 160	Harris 20 169	Montgomery 8 68
Cummings	Hart	Moore 34 287

Southern Cities: 1877 to 1937 -- AUGUSTA, GEORGIA, 1899

Morse 2 17	Ridgeley 4 34	Tucker 9 76
Murray 17 144	Rivers 8 68	Turner 27 228
Myers 7 59	Roberts 28 236	Wade 5 42
Owens 17 144	Robinson 20 169	Walker 9 76
Parker 22 186	Rogers 19 160	Ward 13 110
Parks 11 93	Ross 10 84	Washington
Patterson 14 118	Russell 13 110	Watkins 16 135
Payne 4 34	Scott 19 160	Watson 17 144
Perry 8 68	Sharpe 2 17	Webster 2 17
Phillips 12 101	Shelton 2 17	West 6 51
Pierce 4 34	Simmons 14 118	White 29 245
Polk	Smith 151 1275	Williams 82 693
Porter 3 25	Stevens 10 84	Willis 11 93
Price 15 127	Stewart 4 34	Wilson 33 279
Reed 7 59	Taylor 38 321	Wood 13 110
Reid 13 110	Thomas 43 363	Woods 3 25
Richardson 11 93	Thompson 30 253	Wright 29 245
		Young 40 338

Frequency

Smith 151	Anderson 23	Carter 13
Jones 94	Fleming 23	Elliott 13
Johnson 88	Adams 22	Foster 13
Williams 82	Parker 22	Henry 13
Brown 71	Harris 20	Reid 13
Davis 53	Holloway 20	Russell 13
Clark 43	Robinson 20	Ward 13
Thomas 43	Butler 19	Wood 13
Young 40	Crawford 19	Phillips 12
Allen 39	Evans 19	Bailey 11
Taylor 38	Hopkins 19	Berry 11
Hill 36	Rogers 19	Franklin 11
Miller 34	Scott 19	Lewis 11
Moore 34	Edwards 18	Parks 11
Hale 33	Alexander 17	Richardson 11
King 33	Bennett 17	Willis 11
Martin 33	Collins 17	Banks 10
Wilson 33	Murray 17	Bradley 10
Thompson 30	Owens 17	Bryant 10
Howard 29	Watson 17	Henderson 10
White 29	Baker 16	Ross 10
Wright 29	Mitchell 16	Stevens 10
Lee 28	Watkins 16	Dixon 9
Roberts 28	Bell 15	Gordon 9
Green 27	Brooks 15	Gray 9
Turner 27	Fuller 15	Matthews 9
Campbell 26	Price 15	Tucker 9
Jordon 26	Cooper 14	Walker 9
Barnes 25	James 14	Coleman 8
Griffin 25	Patterson 14	Cox 8
Jackson 25	Simmons 14	Ferguson 8

Southern Cities: 1877 to 1937 -- AUGUSTA, GEORGIA, 1899

Freeman 8	West 6	Woods 3
Hayes 8	Hunter 5	Douglass 2
Jenkins 8	Wade 5	Fisher 2
Montgomery 8	Harper 4	Greene 2
Perry 8	Mason 4	Hawkins 2
Rivers 8	Payne 4	Jefferson 2
Clarke 7	Pierce 4	Morse 2
Holmes 7	Ridgeley 4	Sharpe 2
Myers 7	Stewart 4	Shelton 2
Reed 7	Atkins 3	Webster 2
Austin 6	Daniels 3	Booker
Gardner 6	Fletcher 3	Cummings
Gibson 6	Grant 3	Hart
Hamilton 6	Holland 3	Lucas
Hammond 6	Porter 3	Polk
		Washington

Unusual Names, White

The following lists indicate the unusual given names used by Whites in Augusta, Ga., 1899, from 8,622 males and 2,743 females. Alphabetical listings of male and female names follow with a number representing the frequency of use; no number indicates the name was found only once.

Male

Abdell	Blondel	Ebenezer 2
Abraham	Bub	Edgie
Abram	Buck	Eli 2
Absolom	Budd	Elias 2
Adiel	Cadmus	Elijah 5
Alonzo	Cajus	Elisha 7
Alpha	Caleb	Elmo
Alpheus	Caro	Emanuel 2
Altie	Cassius	Enoch 2
Andie	Cephalus	Ephie
Aquilla 2	Chaney	Ephraim 2
Arizona	Christian 3	Ephriam
Armine	Cicero	Erander 2
Army	Columbus 4	Erasmus 2
Artemus	Cortez 2	Euphrates
Artie	Cula	Ezekiel 3
Atticus	Damarcus	Ezrie
August 5	Darling	Fair
Auren	Demetrius	Fate
Ausier	Derry	Flavel
Azor	Devers	Flavius
Barzilla 2	Dionysius	Fook
Basil 2	Doc	Fountain
Batte	Dock	Gabriel
Bigue	Eben 2	Gideon 3

BLACK NAMES IN AMERICA

Southern Cities: 1877 to 1937 -- AUGUSTA, GEORGIA, 1899

Given
Goody
Gouveneur
Hammy
Hezekiah 3
Hosea
Hoy
Hub
Ignatius
Irenius
Isaac 9
Isaiah 2
Isham 3
Jabe
Jabez
Jabons
Jepha
Jeremiah 6
Jern
Jeru
Jethio
Jirael
Job 3
Jonah
Jophet 2
Josephus
Joshua 13
Josiah 2
Jules
June
Katon
Keff
Key
Kie
Laurel
Lazarus
Lebbeus
Leck
Lem
Leonidas 2
Levi 3

Levy 2
Lily
London
Loney
Lonnie 2
Loois
Lore
Lorick
Lorie
Lucilous
Malachi
Malary
Mallie
Manly
Marcellus 4
Mathia
Mathias 2
Milas
Milledge 3
Milus
Minor
Minus
Mont
Mood
Moses 6
Napoleon 2
Nehemiah
Noah 3
Noel 2
Ocram
Odas
Olley
Omer
Onan
Orchen
Orga
Philolgus
Pink
Pleas
Pleasant
Pliny

Range
Ransom
Ras
Reedie
Rhesa
Roff
Rowley
Royal
Salem
Sandy 3
Sebastian
Semps
Senie
Septimus
Sheppy
Solomon 6
Solon
Son
Theophilus
Theus
Tiden
Toucey
Ulver
Uriah
Vandy
Verdery
Wash
Wave
Wheelis
Woody
Worth
Wumble
Zach
Zachariah 5
Zacheus
Zeb
Zebulon
Zeke
Zell
Zirney

Female

Agatha
Agathia
Ahava
Alabama
Albertine
Alcena
Alesa
Almena

Almeta 2
Amanda 14
Amelia 5
Angie 2
Annas
Arabella 2
Army
Arrie

Artie
Artimisse
Asenith
Atha
Athanasius
Avalitha
Avis
Bashiba

Southern Cities: 1877 to 1937 -- AUGUSTA, GEORGIA, 1899

Basil	Gabrella	Narcissus 2
Berena	Gelina	Nicy
Bethamy	Georgian	Nodie
Birtie	Colillia	Nonie
Boodie	Gussie 3	Olivette 2
Burmah	Hannah 3	Oneda
Caddie	Hassie	Onie
Camilla	Hinorah	Orgey
Cassandra	Huld	Ori
Cassie	Ila	Orrie 2
Cedecia	Indiana	Ottie
Celestia	Iola	Ozella
Charity 2	Irena	Pallie
Chessie	Izara	Phenice
Christian	Izie	Phoebie
Cleora	J. Davis	Pinkey
Clorie	Jose	Priscilla
Colie	Larisa	Queen
Crommelin	Larissa	Renice
Datie	Laronia	Rhoda
Deb	Launa	Rhode
Delila	Lesia	Salina
Dessa	Letetia	Samantha 2
Dessie 4	Lether	Saphronia 3
Dicie	Lethie	Savannah 11
Dillie	Lisette	Selena
Docia	Lomie	Serepta
Donie	Lontie	Serilda
Donna	Lorenia	Seva
Dorie	Lorie 3	Sina
Dru	Louraney 2	Sonita
Drucilla 2	Lucinda 5	Sophia 5
Earlle	Lucretia 4	Sophie 2
Effie 3	Ludie	Tabytha
Elitha	Luta	Teace
Elsara	Luthenia	Tempie
Endora	Macie 2	Tena
Enola	Malinda 3	Tenie
Epsie	Malissa 4	Terrie
Epsy	Malissy	Therusther
Essa 2	Malzey	Tincy
Essie 2	Maria 3	Turley
Euphratia	Mariah 3	Ursula
Ezra	Matilda 8	Vader
Falba	Medora	Vancie
Fameriah	Melley	Vandie
Flewellyn	Mercedes	Vastile
Florida 2	Miley	Venice
Floride	Mittie 2	Vicy
Frederick	Missouri 4	Viney
Fronie	Mozelle 3	Wilhelmina 3
Furlena	Narcissa	Wrennie

195

Southern Cities: 1877 to 1937 -- AUGUSTA, GEORGIA, 1899

Zada	Zeborah	Zoe
Zay	Zibonia	Zonna
		Zora

Southern Cities: 1877 to 1937

Source List P: AUGUSTA, GEORGIA, 1919[6]

Most Common Given Names, Black

The first number after the name indicates the rate per 100,000 on the basis of 1 = 17.274. This alphabetical list is followed by a frequency listing indicating the number of times the name was used. Then follows an alphabetical and frequency listing for Black females, with a rate per 100,000 on the basis of 1 = 26.15. There are 5,789 males and 3,824 females.

MALE
  Alphabetical

Aaron 11 190	Dennis 9 155	Irwin 3 52
Abraham 10 173	Dock 12 207	Isaac 28 484
Abram 8 138	Earl 1	Isaiah 17 294
Adam 6 104	Edgar 6 104	Isham 3 52
Albert 67 1157	Edmond 5 86	Jack 7 121
Alexander 38 656	Edward 155 2677	Jackson 8 138
Alfred 25 432	Edwin 6 104	Jacob 23 397
Allen 17 294	Eli 5 86	Jake 1
Alonzo 11 190	Elias 3 52	James 355 6132
Alvin 5 86	Elijah 20 345	Jasper 9 155
Amos 4 69	Elmer 1	Jeff 4 69
Anderson 18 311	Emanuel 5 86	Jefferson 6 104
Andrew 44 760	Ephraim 5 86	Jerome 5 86
Anthony 7 121	Ernest 17 294	Jerry 25 432
Arthur 49 846	Eugene 26 449	Jesse 45 777
Augustus 12 207	Ezekiel 5 86	Joe 1
Ben 1	Felix 7 121	John 460 7946
Benjamin 63 1088	Floyd 3 52	Jordan 3 25
Berry 1	Frank 104 1796	Joseph 171 2954
Caesar 5 86	Fred 27 466	Joshua 12 207
Caleb 2 35	Frederick 15 259	Julius 5 86
Calvin 18 311	George 229 3956	Lawrence 16 276
Carl 1	George Washington 6 104	Lee 16 276
Cato 2 35	Gilbert 6 104	Leon 1
Charles 213 3679	Green 6 104	Leonard 3 52
Charlie 2 35	Harold 2 35	Leroy 8 138
Chester 7 121	Harrison 11 190	Leslie 2 35
Clarence 34 587	Harry 23 397	Levi 7 121
Claude 11 190	Harvey 4 69	Lewis 30 518
Clifford 13 225	Henderson 2 35	Lloyd 5 86
Clifton 1	Henry 208 3593	Lonnie 5 86
Clyde 1	Herbert 20 345	Louis 35 605
Columbus 5 86	Herman 5 86	Lucius 14 242
Curtis 1	Hosea 5 86	Luther 19 328
Daniel 31 535	Howard 1	Mack 16 276
David 60 1036	Hubert 1	Madison 6 104

_____
[6]From the City Directory, Augusta, Ga., 1919.

Southern Cities: 1877 to 1937 -- AUGUSTA, GEORGIA, 1919

Major 7 121	Otis 12 207	Sidney 7 121
Martin 6 104	Paul 33 570	Simon 5 86
Matthew 14 242	Phillip 7 121	Solomon 192 3317
Melvin 5 86	Pleasant 2 35	Stephen 19 328
Miles 4 69	Peter 34 587	Theodore 3 52
Milledge 13 225	Prince 6 104	Ulysses 1
Milton 2 35	Ralph 1	Wallace 10 173
Mingo 1	Raymond 4 69	Walter 48 829
Moses 42 726	Reuben 18 311	Wash 6 104
Nat 3 52	Richard 63 1088	Washington 5 86
Nathan 12 207	Robert 183 3161	Wesley 15 259
Nathaniel 12 207	Roscoe 1	Wilbur 2 35
Ned 7 121	Roy 1	William 533 9207
Nelson 9 155	Sampson 4 69	Willie 4 69
Oliver 12 207	Samuel 108 1866	Willis 18 311
Oscar 14 242	Sandy 5 86	

MALE
  Frequency

William 533	Jerry 25	Alonzo 11
John 460	Harry 23	Claude 11
James 355	Jacob 23	Harrison 11
George 229	Elijah 20	Abraham 10
Charles 213	Herbert 20	Wallace 10
Henry 208	Luther 19	Dennis 9
Solomon 192	Stephen 19	Jasper 9
Robert 183	Anderson 18	Nelson 9
Joseph 171	Reuben 18	Abram 8
Edward 155	Willis 18	Jackson 8
Samuel 108	Allen 17	Leroy 8
Frank 104	Calvin 17	Anthony 7
Albert 67	Ernest 17	Chester 7
Benjamin 63	Isaiah 17	Felix 7
Richard 63	Lawrence 16	Jack 7
David 60	Lee 16	Levi 7
Arthur 49	Mack 16	Major 7
Walter 48	Frederick 15	Ned 7
Jesse 45	Wesley 15	Phillip 7
Andrew 44	Lucius 14	Sidney 7
Moses 42	Matthew 14	Adam 6
Alexander 38	Oscar 14	Edgar 6
Louis 35	Clifford 13	Edwin 6
Clarence 34	Milledge 13	George Washington 6
Peter 34	Augustus 12	Gilbert 6
Paul 33	Dock 12	Green 6
Daniel 31	Joshua 12	Jefferson 6
Lewis 30	Nathan 12	Madison 6
Isaac 28	Nathaniel 12	Martin 6
Fred 27	Oliver 12	Prince 6
Eugene 26	Otis 12	Wash 6
Alfred 25	Aaron 11	Alvin 5

Southern Cities: 1877 to 1937 -- AUGUSTA, GEORGIA, 1919

Caesar 5
Columbus 5
Edmond 5
Eli 5
Emanuel 5
Ephraim 5
Ezekiel 5
Herman 5
Hosea 5
Jerome 5
Julius 5
Lloyd 5
Lonnie 5
Melvin 5
Sandy 5
Simon 5
Washington 5
Amos 4
Harvey 4
Jeff 4

Miles 4
Raymond 4
Sampson 4
Willie 4
Elias 3
Floyd 3
Irvin 3
Isham 3
Leonard 3
Nat 3
Theodore 3
Caleb 2
Cato 2
Charlie 2
Harold 2
Henderson 2
Jordan 2
Leslie 2
Milton 2
Pleasant 2

Wilbur 2
Ben 1
Berry 1
Carl 1
Clifton 1
Clyde 1
Curtis 1
Earl 1
Elmer 1
Howard 1
Hubert 1
Jake 1
Joe 1
Leon 1
Mingo 1
Ralph 1
Roscoe 1
Roy 1
Ulysses 1

FEMALE
Alphabetical

Adaline 9   235
Addie 22   575
Agnes 6   157
Alberta 8   209
Alice 44   1151
Alma 4   105
Amanda 44   1151
Amelia 14   366
Amy 4   105
Ann 1
Anna 18   471
Annie 135   3530
Beatrice 7   183
Bellah 3   78
Bernice 1
Bertha 24   628
Bessie 33   863
Betsy 2   52
Betty 8   209
Biddy 1
Blanche 2   52
Caroline 10   262
Carolyn 1
Carrie 98   2563
Catharine 12   314
Celia 4   105
Charity 8   209
Charlotte 17   445

Chloe 1
Clara 38   994
Cleo 5   131
Cora 21   549
Daisy 20   523
Delia 3   78
Dina 3   78
Dolly 3   78
Dorcas 1
Dorothy 2   52
Edith 7   183
Edna 4   105
Effie 3   78
Eliza 48   1255
Elizabeth 24   628
Ella 58   1517
Ellen 30   785
Elouise 3   78
Elsie 4   105
Elvira 1
Emma 98   2563
Ernestine 1
Emiline 3   78
Emily 5   131
Essie 18   471
Esther 6   157
Ethel 21   549
Eunice 3   78

Eva 12   314
Eveline 1
Evelyn 6   157
Fanny 75   1961
Flora 4   105
Florence 11   288
Frances 30   785
Geneva 2   52
Georgia 34   889
Gertrude 23   601
Gladys 3   78
Grace 9   235
Hannah 8   209
Harriet 19   497
Hattie 76   1987
Hazel 3   78
Helen 4   105
Henrietta 28   732
Hester 5   131
Hetty 3   78
Ida 33   863
Inez 5   131
Irene 18   471
Isabella 6   157
Jane 10   262
Janie 42   1098
Jennie 43   1124
Jessie 9   235

Southern Cities: 1877 to 1937 -- AUGUSTA, GEORGIA, 1919

Josephine 21 549	Margaret 24 628	Phoebe 8 209
Juanita 4 105	Maria(h) 29 758	Pinkie 5 131
Judy 1	Marie 35 915	Polly 8 209
Julia 74 1935	Martha 40 1046	Priscilla 8 209
Katy 38 994	Mary 229 5988	Queen 5 131
Kitty 3 78	Matilda 19 497	Rachael 26 680
Laura 44 1151	Mattie 27 706	Rebecca 26 680
Leah 1	Maude 5 131	Rena 7 183
Lena 15 392	May 6 157	Rosa 73 1909
Leola 5 131	Mildred 1	Rose 6 157
Letty 1	Milly 9 235	Ruby 4 105
Lillian 2 52	Minerva 3 78	Ruth 19 497
Lillie 28 732	Minnie 36 941	Sadie 8 209
Lizzie 77 2014	Molly 7 183	Salby 34 889
Louisa 4 105	Mozelle 6 157	Sarah 79 2066
Louise 52 1360	Myrtle 1	Savannah 12 314
Lucille 8 209	Nancy 29 758	Silvey 1
Lucinda 16 418	Nanny 1	Sophia 12 314
Lucy 28 732	Naomi 4 105	Susan 12 314
Lula 58 1517	Nelly 16 418	Susie 36 941
Lydia 2 52	Patience 3 78	Thelma 5 131
Mabel 4 105	Patsy 2 52	Viola 16 418
Maggie 34 889	Pauline 4 105	Virginia 14 366
Malinda 11 288	Pearl 26 680	Willie 14 366
Malissa 12 314	Peggy 5 131	Willie Mae 8 209
Mamie 57 1491	Phillis 4 105	Winney 6 157

FEMALE
Frequency

Mary 229	Katy 38	Margaret 24
Annie 136	Minnie 36	Gertrude 23
Carrie 98	Susie 36	Addie 22
Emma 98	Marie 35	Cora 21
Sarah 79	Georgia 34	Ethel 21
Lizzie 77	Maggie 34	Josephine 21
Hattie 76	Sally 34	Daisy 20
Fanny 75	Bessie 33	Harriet 19
Julia 74	Ida 33	Matilda 19
Rosa 73	Ellen 30	Ruth 19
Ella 58	Frances 30	Anna 18
Lula 58	Maria(h) 29	Essie 18
Mamie 57	Nancy 29	Irene 18
Louise 52	Henrietta 28	Charlotte 17
Eliza 48	Lillie 28	Lucinda 16
Alice 44	Lucy 28	Nelly 16
Amanda 44	Mattie 27	Viola 16
Laura 44	Pearl 26	Lena 15
Jennie 43	Rachael 26	Amelia 14
Janie 42	Rebecca 26	Virginia 14
Martha 40	Bertha 24	Willie 14
Clara 38	Elizabeth 24	Catharine 12

Southern Cities: 1877 to 1937   --   AUGUSTA, GEORGIA, 1919

Eva 12	Mozelle 6	Elouise 3
Malissa 12	Rose 6	Emiline 3
Savannah 12	Winney 6	Eunice 3
Sophia 12	Cleo 5	Gladys 3
Susan 12	Emily 5	Hazel 3
Florence 11	Hester 5	Hetty 3
Malinda 11	Inez 5	Kitty 3
Caroline 10	Leola 5	Minerva 3
Jane 10	Maude 5	Patience 3
Adaline 9	Peggy 5	Betsy 2
Grace 9	Pinkie 5	Blanche 2
Jessie 9	Queen 5	Dorothy 2
Milly 9	Thelma 5	Geneva 2
Alberta 8	Alma 4	Lillian 2
Betty 8	Amy 4	Lydia 2
Charity 8	Celia 4	Patsy 2
Hannah 8	Edna 4	Ann 1
Lucille 8	Elsie 4	Bernice 1
Phoebe 8	Flora 4	Biddy 1
Polly 8	Helen 4	Caroline 1
Priscilla 8	Juanita 4	Chloe 1
Sadie 8	Mabel 4	Dorcas 1
Willie Mae 8	Louisa 4	Elvira 1
Beatrice 7	Naomi 4	Ernestine 1
Edith 7	Pauline 4	Eveline 1
Molly 7	Phillis 4	Judy 1
Rena 7	Ruby 4	Leah 1
Agnes 6	Bellah 3	Letty 1
Esther 6	Delia 3	Mildred 1
Evelyn 6	Dina (h) 3	Myrtle 1
Isabella 6	Dolly 3	Nanny 1
May 6	Effie 3	Silvey 1

Unusual Names, Black

The following lists represent unusual male and female Black names from the list of 5,789 male and 3,824 female names available. The number after the name indicates the frequency of usage; no number indicates that the name was found once.

Male

Abraham 10	Aquilla	Bose
Abram 8	Aroyal	Boss
Alcurine	Athis	Bossie
Almous	August	Boston 2
Amaziah	Bee	Boyzie
Ananias	Bizzell	Bunyon
Ance	Boisey 2	Caesar 5
Antone	Boisie	Caleb 2
Antonio 2	Boisy	Cape

Southern Cities: 1877 to 1937 -- AUGUSTA, GEORGIA, 1919

Cardoza	Gustave	Lucious
Carlos 2	Ham	Lum
Cash	Hancy	Lummie
Cass	Hasty	Maceo 2
Cast	Henry Clay	Mahue
Cates	Hezekiah 2	Major 7
Cato 2	Hobsy	Mal
Champ	Horace Greeley	Malachi
Chaney	Hosea 5	Mally
Cogie	Iley	Mancy
Colie	Isaac 28	Manny
Columbus 5	Isadore 2	Mars
Cuggo	Isaiah 17	Martin
Damon	Isham 3	Media
Dandy	Ishmael	Memphis
Darius	Isom 3	Milledge 13
Dash	Israel 2	Mingle
Divelle 2	Jabe	Mingo
Dixie	Japham	Monnie
Dock 12	Jeremiah	Mordecai
Drue	Jestine	Moses 42
Dub	Jett	Napoleon 3
Duffy	Jip	Nazaris
Dutch	Jonah	Nevada
Early 3	Jonas	Nias
Ebb	Joshua 12	Nimrod
Eli 5	Judge 2	Noah
Elias 3	Jule	Noble
Elijah 20	Junior	Obadiah
Elisha	Junius 4	Obie
Emanuel 5	King 3	Ocilla
Ennis 2	Kit	Odie
Enoch 2	Laney	Ollie 4
Ephraim 5	Lany	Omie
Esau	Lark 2	Onery
Esli	Lawyer 2	Orelian
Essage	Leb	Ormul
Euel	Leffy	Orrie
Euliss	Lemmie	Orsie
Ezekiel 5	Lemmon	Osie 2
Ezra	Lemon	Ossie
Fate 2	Lennie	Otha
Ferba	Lessie	Ozzie
Focus	Levi 7	Palestine
Gabe 2	Levy 2	Paris 3
Gabriel 3	Lexius	Parson
Gardelle	Limus	Pashmon
Garfield 3	Lincoln 2	Peddix
General 4	Link	Pick
George Washington 6	Linious	Pink
Governor 2	Lisbon	Pleas 2
Gustav 2	Lonnie 5	Pleasant 2

Southern Cities: 1877 to 1937 -- AUGUSTA, GEORGIA, 1919

Potrust	Sanco	Troupe
Press 3	Sandy 5	Truly
Prince 6	Sapho	Tunis
Quintus 2	Scipio 3	Ulysses
Rafe 2	Semmie	Uriah 2
Ransom 4	Shedrich 2	Valley
Rap	Shug	Visker
Rightaway	Simmie	Wash 6
Roman 3	Sip	Wave
Romeo	Skip	Woody
Romie	Socrates	Zaccharias
Roosevelt	Solomon	Zach
Royal	Somer	Zack 2
Rulus	Son 2	Zan
Saltus	Squire 3	Zannie
Saluda	Tee	Zeak
Sampson 4	Thomas Jefferson 2	Zeph
Sancho	Toby	Zonnie
		Zulean

Female

Alivan	Charity 8	Florine 2
Almena	Cherry	Florrie 2
Alzarah	Clarie	Fronie
Alzora	Claudie	Gensy
Amanda 44	Cleobelle	Hagar
Amelia 14	Cogy	Hannah 8
Aray	Commer	Hattiebell
Arie	Cylla	Hennie
Arminta	Deborah	Hessie
Arrabella	Dicy 2	India
Artimichian	Dilsy	Indiana 2
Aurora	Dinah 3	Inetha
Azaline	Dona	Ionia
Azore	Dorcas	Iris
Bedelia	Dove 2	Jencie
Belinda	Easter 4	Jenilene
Berta	Eddie	Keziah
Bina	Effie 3	Kizzie 3
Birdie	Elvira	Larcenie
Camilla 4	Eola	Lavena
Camille 2	Essie 18	Lavina
Cammie	Essielee	Lavinia 2
Candice	Etoy	Lavona
Caola	Eulalie	Leitha
Cassie 2	Euphemia	Leonnie
Celina	Facilla	Lethia
Chaine	Fairy 2	Levina
Chainey	Fancie	Lindy
Chaney 3	Fara	Little
Chanie	Fletta	Liza

Southern Cities: 1877 to 1937 -- AUGUSTA, GEORGIA, 1919

Louvenia 4	Nicey	Rosina 3
Lovie	Nicy	Rozell
Lucinda 16	Nona 2	Rubena
Luckie	Odessa	Sabina
Ludelle	Omie	Sabra
Ludie	Orie 3	Sapher
Luethel	Oro	Saphronia
Lutisia	Orrie 2	Saras
Luvernia	Oscieola	Saster
Madelle	Ossie	Savannah 12
Magnolia	Parmela	Selena 2
Mahala 2	Parmie	Sena
Mahale	Paris 2	Sinie
Mahaley	Parthenia	Sollie
Maide	Patience 3	Sophia 12
Malinda 11	Phillis 4	State
Malissa 12	Phoebe 8	Sunie
Manda 2	Pinder	Tabitha 3
Mandy 3	Pinkie 5	Tamer
Manilla	Plumie	Tansy
Manola	Priscilla 8	Tena
Maria(h) 29	Prudence	Theodocia
Matilda 19	Prudie 2	Tyra
Maydelle	Queen 5	Ursula 2
Maxie	Queenie	Vassar
Mazie 2	Rebie 2	Vicie
Melissa 2	Rena 7	Victory
Melvira	Rene	Vina
Merodia	Rhoda	Vinnie
Minola	Rica	Vonder
Minta	Richardine	Wardelle
Missouri	Rilla	Wilhelmina
Mittie 2	Rissie	Winney 6
Mozelle 6	Rita	Zana
Myrterious	Ritta	Zelene
Myrtis	Robena	Zell
Narcissa	Robertha	Zelna
Narcissus	Rolanda	Zena
Nealie	Rosella 2	Zerilda

Surnames, Black

The number of Blacks represented in this list is 9,621; the rate per 100,000 is 1 = 10.394. The first number indicates the number of times the surname was used; the second number reflects the rate per 100,000. A frequency list follows the alphabetical listing.

Alphabetical

Abraham 1	Adams 20 208	Allen 49 509
Abram 6 62	Alexander 9 94	Anderson 41 426

Southern Cities: 1877 to 1937 -- AUGUSTA, GEORGIA, 1919

Atkins 5 52	Fleming 6 62	Lampkin 10 104
Austin 4 42	Foster 15 156	Lark 18 187
Bailey 31 322	Franklin 10 104	Lawson 13 135
Baker 18 187	Freeman 37 385	Lee 44 457
Banks 12 125	Fuller 13 135	Levy 1
Barnes 26 270	Gaines 9 94	Lewis 43 447
Barrett 1	Gardner 26 270	Lucas 4 42
Bell 20 208	Garrett 24 249	Lyons 7 73
Bennett 30 312	Germany 10 104	McCarthy 2 21
Benson 2 21	Gibson 20 208	McDonald 1
Berry 21 218	Glover 69 717	Mack 18 187
Black 1	Golphin 23 239	Mahoney 3 31
Booker 3 31	Gordon 12 125	Malone 4 42
Bradley 3 31	Graham 7 73	Marshall 19 197
Brooks 41 426	Grant 16 166	Martin 32 333
Brown 198 2058	Gray 11 114	Mason 25 260
Bryant 16 166	Green 73 759	May 1
Bugg 11 114	Greene 13 135	Miller 19 197
Bussey 23 239	Griffin 43 447	Mitchell 45 468
Butler 66 686	Hall 29 301	Montgomery 4 42
Callahan 3 31	Hamilton 8 83	Moore 55 572
Campbell 14 146	Hammond 12 125	Morgan 16 166
Carr 12 125	Hampton 26 270	Morris 20 208
Carter 36 374	Harper 27 281	Morse 6 62
Clark 27 281	Harris 96 998	Morton 6 62
Clarke 1	Harrison 37 385	Murphey 3 31
Cobb 25 260	Hart 2 21	Murphy 5 52
Cohen 11 114	Harvey 9 94	Murray 28 291
Coleman 42 437	Hawkins 10 104	Myers 11 114
Coles 5 52	Hayes 8 83	Nelson 9 94
Collier 34 353	Henderson 14 146	O'Bryant 13 135
Collins 44 457	Henry 5 52	O'Connor 1
Cooper 22 229	Hill 47 489	Owens 14 146
Corley 1	Holland 2 21	Parker 19 197
Cox 2 21	Holloway 17 177	Parks 9 94
Crawford 30 312	Holmes 44 457	Patterson 16 166
Cummings 37 385	Hopkins 7 73	Payne 5 52
Curry 32 333	Howard 23 239	Pendleton 4 42
Daniels 4 42	Hughes 34 353	Penn 3 31
Davie 14 146	Hunter 7 73	Perry 11 114
Davis 90 935	Jackson 155 1611	Phillips 5 52
Dickerson 3 31	James 13 135	Pierce 3 31
Dixon 8 83	Jefferson 18 187	Polk 2 21
Douglass 3 31	Jenkins 52 540	Porter 15 156
Dunn 24 249	Johnson 224 2328	Powell 4 42
Edwards 38 395	Jones 229 2380	Price 6 62
Elliott 11 114	Jordan 16 166	Ramsey 23 239
Evans 61 634	Kelly 11 114	Randolph 1
Fambro 1	Kennedy 4 42	Ray 4 42
Ferguson 14 146	Key 29 301	Redd 2 21
Fields 15 156	King 28 291	Reed 18 187
Fisher 10 104	Lamar 12 125	Reese 10 104

Southern Cities: 1877 to 1937 -- AUGUSTA, GEORGIA, 1919

Reid 25 260	Simms 7 73	Ward 5 52
Reynolds 16 166	Simpkins 12 125	Ware 8 83
Rice 2 21	Smith 155 1611	Washington 41 426
Richards 2 21	Stevens 5 52	Watkins 26 270
Richardson 18 187	Stewart 22 229	Watson 15 156
Riley 6 62	Stokes 11 114	Watts 11 114
Rivers 5 52	Sullivan 20 208	Webster 2 21
Roberts 10 104	Tarver 3 31	Welch 5 52
Robertson 16 166	Taylor 27 281	West 15 156
Robinson 89 925	Thomas 150 1559	White 60 624
Rogers 9 94	Tolbert 18 187	Wigfall 11 114
Ross 18 187	Tucker 6 62	Williams 395 4106
Russell 15 156	Turner 23 239	Willis 17 177
Samuels 13 135	Tutt 15 156	Wilson 58 603
Sanders 17 177	Vaughn 1	Winn 3 31
Saunders 6 62	Wade 5 52	Wood 6 62
Scott 72 748	Walker 108 1123	Woods 3 31
Sharpe 7 73	Wallace 11 114	Woodward 4 42
Shelton 2 21	Walsh 1	Wright 52 540
Simmons 31 322	Walton 33 343	Young 49 509
		Youngblood 9 94

Frequency

Williams 395	Griffin 43	Gardner 26
Jones 229	Lewis 43	Hampton 26
Johnson 224	Coleman 42	Watkins 26
Brown 198	Anderson 41	Cobb 25
Jackson 155	Brooks 41	Mason 25
Smith 155	Washington 41	Reid 25
Thomas 150	Edwards 38	Dunn 24
Walker 108	Cummings 37	Garrett 24
Harris 96	Freeman 37	Bussey 23
Davis 90	Harrison 37	Golphin 23
Robinson 89	Carter 36	Howard 23
Green 73	Collier 34	Ramsey 23
Scott 72	Hughes 34	Turner 23
Glover 69	Walton 33	Cooper 22
Butler 66	Curry 32	Stewart 22
Evans 61	Martin 32	Berry 21
White 60	Bailey 31	Adams 20
Wilson 58	Simmons 31	Bell 20
Moore 55	Bennett 30	Gibson 20
Jenkins 52	Crawford 30	Morris 20
Wright 52	Hall 29	Sullivan 20
Allen 49	Key 29	Marshall 19
Young 49	King 28	Miller 19
Hill 47	Murray 28	Parker 19
Mitchell 45	Clark 27	Baker 18
Collins 44	Harper 27	Jefferson 18
Holmes 44	Taylor 27	Lark 18
Lee 44	Barnes 26	Mack 18

Southern Cities: 1877 to 1937 -- AUGUSTA, GEORGIA, 1919

Reed 18	Wallace 11	Welch 5
Richardson 18	Watts 11	Austin 4
Ross 18	Wigfall 11	Daniels 4
Tolbert 18	Fisher 10	Kennedy 4
Holloway 17	Franklin 10	Lucas 4
Sanders 17	Germany 10	Malone 4
Willis 17	Hawkins 10	Montgomery 4
Bryant 16	Lampkin 10	Pendleton 4
Grant 16	Reese 10	Powell 4
Jordan 16	Roberts 10	Ray 4
Morgan 16	Alexander 9	Woodward 4
Patterson 16	Gaines 9	Booker 3
Reynolds 16	Harvey 9	Bradley 3
Robertson 16	Nelson 9	Callahan 3
Fields 15	Parks 9	Dickerson 3
Foster 15	Rogers 9	Douglass 3
Porter 15	Youngblood 9	Mahoney 3
Russell 15	Dixon 8	Murphey 3
Tutt 15	Hamilton 8	Penn 3
Watson 15	Hayes 8	Pierce 3
West 15	Ware 8	Tarver 3
Campbell 14	Graham 7	Winn 3
Davie 14	Hopkins 7	Woods 3
Ferguson 14	Hunter 7	Benson 2
Henderson 14	Lyons 7	Cox 2
Owens 14	Sharpe 7	Hart 2
Fuller 13	Simms 7	Holland 2
Greene 13	Abram 6	McCarthy 2
James 13	Fleming 6	Polk 2
Lawson 13	Morse 6	Redd 2
O'Bryant 13	Morton 6	Rice 2
Samuels 13	Price 6	Richards 2
Banks 12	Riley 6	Shelton 2
Carr 12	Saunders 6	Webster 2
Gordon 12	Tucker 6	Abraham 1
Hammond 12	Wood 6	Barrett 1
Lamar 12	Atkins 5	Black 1
Simpkins 12	Coles 5	Clarke 1
Bugg 11	Henry 5	Corley 1
Cohen 11	Murphy 5	Fambro 1
Elliott 11	Payne 5	Levy 1
Gray 11	Phillips 5	May 1
Kelly 11	Rivers 5	McDonald 1
Myers 11	Stevens 5	O'Connor 1
Perry 11	Wade 5	Randolph 1
Stokes 11	Ward 5	Vaughn 1
		Walsh 1

Southern Cities: 1877 to 1937   --   AUGUSTA, GEORGIA, 1919

Surnames, White

The number of Whites represented in this list is 19,788; the rate per 100,000 is 1 = 5.054. The first number indicates the number of times the surname was used; the second number reflects the rate per 100,000. A frequency list follows the alphabetical listing.

Alphabetical

Adams 50 253	Daniels 4 20	Harvey 6 30
Alexander 27 136	Davis 87 440	Hawkins 6 30
Allen 63 318	Deas 41 207	Hayes 11 56
Anderson 46 232	Dickerson 5 25	Henderson 15 76
Atkins 7 35	Dixon 16 81	Henry 16 81
Austin 10 51	Douglass 3 15	Hill 84 425
Bailey 27 136	Dunn 22 111	Holland 8 40
Baker 40 202	Edwards 36 182	Holley 42 212
Banks 24 121	Elias 1	Holloway 2 10
Barnes 50 253	Elliott 25 126	Holmes 26 131
Barrett 23 116	Evans 43 217	Hopkins 5 25
Bell 52 263	Ferguson 12 61	Howard 47 238
Bennett 24 121	Fields 1	Hughes 26 131
Benson 27 136	Fleming 29 147	Hunter 5 25
Berry 12 61	Fletcher 5 25	Jackson 62 313
Black 20 101	Foster 21 106	James 26 131
Booker 1	Franklin 9 45	Jefferson 1
Bradley 12 61	Freeman 16 81	Jenkins 16 81
Brooks 15 76	Fuller 23 116	Johnson 167 844
Brown 130 657	Gaines 6 30	Johnston 28 142
Bryant 23 116	Gallagher 3 15	Jones 188 950
Bugg 13 66	Gardner 17 86	Jordan 18 91
Burch 22 111	Garner 25 126	Kelly 51 258
Bussey 15 76	Garrett 16 81	Kennedy 33 167
Butler 41 207	Gibson 14 71	Key 13 66
Callahan 10 51	Glover 45 227	King 46 232
Campbell 44 222	Gordon 14 71	Lamar 18 91
Carr 15 76	Graham 11 56	Lampkin 9 45
Carter 33 167	Grant 3 15	Lawrence 2 10
Clark 65 329	Gray 15 76	Lee 45 227
Clarke 23 116	Green 55 278	Levy 23 116
Cobb 7 35	Greene 34 172	Lewis 42 212
Cohen 26 131	Griffin 46 232	Lyons 24 121
Coleman 21 106	Groves 2 10	McCarthy 25 126
Collier 16 81	Hair 18 91	McDonald 37 187
Collins 39 197	Hall 75 379	Mack 3 15
Cooper 33 167	Hamilton 15 76	Mahoney 4 20
Corley 16 81	Hammond 23 116	Malone 14 71
Cox 17 86	Hampton 4 20	Marshall 26 131
Crawford 37 187	Harper 17 86	Martin 63 318
Crouch 29 147	Harris 33 167	Mason 5 25
Cummings 5 25	Harrison 22 111	May 21 106
Curry 22 111	Hart 9 45	Miller 93 470

Southern Cities: 1877 to 1937 -- AUGUSTA, GEORGIA, 1919

Mitchell 27 136	Reynolds 49 248	Toole 23 116
Montgomery 26 131	Rice 17 86	Tucker 12 61
Moore 80 404	Richards 23 116	Turner 38 192
Morgan 51 258	Richardson 27 136	Tutt 1
Morris 86 435	Riley 26 131	Vaughn 11 56
Morse 3 15	Rivers 10 51	Wade 14 71
Murphey 14 71	Robert 1	Walker 72 364
Murphy 70 354	Roberts 32 162	Wallace 30 152
Murray 14 71	Robertson 44 222	Walsh 18 91
Myers 10 51	Robinson 43 217	Walton 28 142
Nelson 10 51	Rogers 34 172	Ward 21 106
O'Connor 38 192	Rooney 7 35	Ware 6 30
Owens 54 273	Ross 6 30	Washington 4 20
Parker 65 329	Russell 16 81	Watkins 28 142
Parks 20 101	Samuels 1	Watson 20 101
Patterson 21 106	Sanders 29 147	Watts 6 30
Payne 2 10	Saunders 4 20	Weathers 48 243
Pearre 19 96	Scott 62 313	Webster 7 35
Pendleton 4 20	Sharpe 2 10	Welch 6 30
Perry 7 35	Sheahan 15 76	West 11 56
Phillips 22 111	Shelton 7 35	White 57 288
Pierce 10 51	Simmons 11 56	Williams 122 617
Polk 2 10	Simpkins 1	Willis 19 96
Porter 2 10	Smith 246 1243	Wilson 89 450
Powell 52 263	Stevens 21 106	Winn 1
Price 13 66	Stewart 12 61	Wood 22 111
Ramsey 19 96	Stokes 6 30	Woods 8 40
Randolph 1	Sullivan 39 197	Woodward 43 217
Ray 8 40	Tarver 10 51	Wren 24 121
Redd 38 192	Taylor 54 273	Wright 88 445
Reed 11 56	Thomas 58 293	Young 43 217
Reese 39 197	Tice 12 61	Youngblood 35 177
Reid 25 126	Tolbert 1	

Frequency

Smith 246	Parker 65	Reynolds 49
Jones 188	Allen 63	Weathers 48
Johnson 167	Martin 63	Howard 47
Brown 130	Jackson 62	Anderson 46
Williams 122	Scott 62	Griffin 46
Miller 93	Thomas 58	King 46
Wilson 89	White 57	Glover 45
Wright 88	Green 55	Lee 45
Davis 87	Owens 54	Campbell 44
Morris 86	Taylor 54	Robertson 44
Hill 84	Bell 52	Evans 43
Moore 80	Powell 52	Robinson 43
Hall 75	Kelly 51	Woodward 43
Walker 72	Morgan 51	Young 43
Murphy 70	Adams 50	Holley 42
Clark 65	Barnes 50	Lewis 42

Southern Cities: 1877 to 1937 -- AUGUSTA, GEORGIA, 1919

Butler 41	Levy 23	Price 13
Deas 41	Richards 23	Berry 12
Baker 40	Toole 23	Bradley 12
Collins 39	Burch 22	Ferguson 12
Reese 39	Curry 22	Stewart 12
Sullivan 39	Dunn 22	Tice 12
O'Connor 38	Harrison 22	Tucker 12
Redd 38	Phillips 22	Graham 11
Turner 38	Wood 22	Hayes 11
Crawford 37	Coleman 21	Reed 11
McDonald 37	Foster 21	Simmons 11
Edwards 36	May 21	Vaughn 11
Youngblood 35	Patterson 21	West 11
Greene 34	Stevens 21	Austin 10
Rogers 34	Ward 21	Callahan 10
Carter 33	Black 20	Myers 10
Cooper 33	Parks 20	Nelson 10
Harris 33	Watson 20	Pierce 10
Kennedy 33	Pearre 19	Rivers 10
Roberts 32	Ramsey 19	Tarver 10
Wallace 30	Willis 19	Franklin 9
Crouch 29	Hair 18	Hart 9
Fleming 29	Jordan 18	Lampkin 9
Sanders 29	Lamar 18	Holland 8
Johnston 28	Walsh 18	Ray 8
Walton 28	Cox 17	Woods 8
Watkins 28	Gardner 17	Atkins 7
Alexander 27	Harper 17	Cobb 7
Bailey 27	Rice 17	Perry 7
Benson 27	Collier 16	Rooney 7
Mitchell 27	Corley 16	Shelton 7
Richardson 27	Dixon 16	Webster 7
Cohen 26	Freeman 16	Gaines 6
Holmes 26	Garrett 16	Hawkins 6
Hughes 26	Henry 16	Ross 6
James 26	Jenkins 16	Stokes 6
Marshall 26	Russell 16	Ware 6
Montgomery 26	Brooks 15	Watts 6
Riley 26	Bussy 15	Welch 6
Elliott 25	Carr 15	Cummings 5
Garner 25	Gray 15	Dickerson 5
McCarthy 25	Hamilton 15	Fletcher 5
Reid 25	Henderson 15	Hopkins 5
Banks 24	Sheahan 15	Hunter 5
Bennett 24	Gibson 14	Mason 5
Lyons 24	Gordon 14	Daniels 4
Wren 24	Malone 14	Hampton 4
Barrett 23	Murphey 14	Harvey 4
Bryant 23	Murray 14	Mahoney 4
Clarke 23	Wade 14	Pendleton 4
Fuller 23	Bugg 13	Saunders 4
Hammond 23	Key 13	Washington 4

Southern Cities: 1877 to 1937   --   AUGUSTA, GEORGIA, 1919

Douglass 3	Lawson 2	Jefferson 1
Gallagher 3	Payne 2	Randolph 1
Grant 3	Polk 2	Robert 1
Mack 3	Porter 2	Samuels 1
Morse 3	Sharpe 2	Simpkins 1
Groves 2	Elias 1	Tolbert 1
Holloway 2	Fields 1	Tutt 1
		Winn 1

Unusual Names, White

MALE
   (Sample: 9,266)

Abe	Bright	Elijah 6
Abraham 6	Brue	Elisha 5
Abram 2	Brutus	Elmo 3
Acquilla	Bud	Emanuel
Adoniram	Budd	Emerald
Alaska	Buist	Enid
Alexis	Caesar	Enoch 2
Aloysius	Cajus	Enos
Alpha 2	Cake	Ephraim 3
Alpheus 3	Carlos 2	Erastus
Alphia	Casnova	Eule
Antone	Cephelie	Eunon
Aquilla	Cheethain	Evander
Archilles	Cicero 2	Ezra
Aris	Cleon	Faith
Arrie	Cluese	Fountain
Artemus	Colonel	Foy
Aruna	Columbus 4	Garien
Ashira	Cord	Gasaway
Asia	Cordie	Gassie
Atticus	Corker	Gelo
August	Cortez 3	George Washington
Avice	Counts 2	Gideon 2
Azar 2	Covey	Gulian
Bade	Cyprian	Gusta
Barzilla	Dadie	Gustav
Bash	Damascus	Hezekiah 5
Basil 3	Darling 3	Hie
Batte	Davie	Hinchie
Battie	Deeb	Hosea 2
Batty	Dibble	Hydie
Baultie	Dock	Ignatius 2
Beachie	Druid	Ireaneus
Bonnie	Early	Isaac 13
Boozer	Eben 2	Isiah 3
Boster	Eli 5	Isham 2
Braudie	Elias 3	Jabe

Southern Cities: 1877 to 1937 -- AUGUSTA, GEORGIA, 1919

Jabes	Mordie	Sailor
Jabez 2	Mosco	Sandy
Jams	Moses 9	Schabie
Jep	Napoleon 3	Sebe
Jeptha 2	Noah 6	Shivers
Jeremiah 4	Noel 2	Solomon 8
Joshua 5	Obie 2	Son
Josiah 2	Odelle	Spires
Jouett	Olice	Starlie
Jules	Ollie	St. John
Jumell	Omer	St. Pierre
Junius 2	Onan	Stonewall Jackson
Kiser	Oreste	Texas
Laban	Ortie	Toccoah
Lanie	Osceola	Tyrus
Lazarus	Otha	Ulis
Leck	Othello	Ulmo
Leonidas 3	Oza	Ulysses 3
Lethur	Pallie	Uphire
Levi 3	Paris	Urban
Levy	Perley	Usher
Linder	Petrona	Venda
Loney	Philander	Venice
Lonnie 15	Phineas	Vines
Looney	Pleasant	Wash
Luckie	Pliny	Wave 2
Maduell	Primus	Weems
Manilla	Purlee	Whirley
Mannie	Ras	Wingo
Manzie	Refo	Wistar
Marcellus 2	Rem	Woodie
Menarda	Remer	Zach
Mettie	Remi	Zachariah
Mezie	Renaldo	Zachrias
Milledge 3	Robert E. Lee	Zack
Millwee	Roman	Zeb 2
Mindorse	Rome 3	Zebulon
Mingle	Roosevelt	Zell
Montreal	Rozzie	Zem
Moragne	Russie	Zenoph

FEMALE
   (Sample: 10,136)

Abigal	Alfreda	Amanda 16
Adgie	Alida	Amandtine
Agatha	Alledes	Amazon
Ala	Alletba	Amelia 9
Albertina	Almeda 3	Ammie
Aleitha	Almena	Ancie
Alema	Almeta	Angelest
Alesa	Alpharatte	Aquilla

212

Southern Cities: 1877 to 1937 -- AUGUSTA, GEORGIA, 1919

Arca	Cleva	Estoria
Armenia	Cloatie	Eulalia
Arrie	Coline	Eulalie 4
Artie	Cootosa	Euphemie
Aselee	Coppie	Eusie
Asie	Coren	Faby
Athelin	Creecy	Fanneyelu
Athma	Cressie	Ferol
Audie	Dahlia	Fernande
Austelle	Damie	Fleta
Avice	Daralee	Fletta
Avis	Datie	Florida 3
Avaha	Davie	Floride 3
Avonia	Dawn	Florie
Azalee 2	Deicy	Florien
Bartie	Delgracia	Florine
Bartow	Delilah 2	Florrie 3
Bennie	Dennie	Flossie 8
Berdie	Derena	Floy 4
Berdye	Derry	Floye
Berma	Deryle	Francina
Berta	Dessa	Frankie 4
Bertie	Dessie 7	Gennevine
Bertis	Desser	Georgebell
Berto	Dicey	Gesina 2
Betheny	Dicie	Golda
Betra	Dillie	Goldie 2
Birda	Docia 4	Grusaie
Birdie 3	Dolores	Gussie 12
Bobbie	Doni	Hannah 10
Bonnie	Donie	Hanora
Bonnylu	Dosia	Hapsey
Brezelia	Dovie 2	Haseltine
Bromah	Drucilla 2	Hassie 2
Buena	Ebbie 2	Hennie
Burma	Eddie 3	Hollie
Burmah	Edmonia	Icy
Calene	Effie 17	Imogene 3
Calola	Ega	India 3
Camilla 4	Elemena	Ineita
Camille 5	Elender	Iola
Carlos	Elinden	Iradelle
Carola	Elva	Iris 2
Cassie 7	Elvira	Isadora 2
Cattie	England	Izetta
Champia	Enise	Jenelle
Charity 2	Enola 2	Jewel
Chessie	Epsie 3	Josela
Chloe	Ermine	Jossie
Clementina 2	Ersula	Kella 2
Clemie	Eryth	Kellah
Clercie	Essie 44	Kerlie

Southern Cities: 1877 to 1937 -- AUGUSTA, GEORGIA, 1919

Kinnie	Malissa	Onida 2
Kizzie	Manie	Onie 2
Laila	Mannie 3	Oregon
Lanie	Manolia	Orlean 2
Laretto	Marcella 2	Orrie
Lavinia	Maria 5	Osa
Leatha	Mariah 2	Othella
Lellie	Marina	Ottilie
Lennie	Martina	Oveda
Leo	Marzie	Ozena
Leonie 2	Mathilda 3	Pallie
Leoris	Matilda 9	Panie
Lessie 2	Mauritius	Parmie 2
Lethea	Medora	Patria
Letitia	Melissa 2	Petrony
Leventa	Melvina	Phillippa
Levi	Mena 3	Philomena 2
Levie	Mercedes	Pinkie
Levina	Mersa	Pluma
Lexie	Meta 7	Priscilla
Linda	Mexie	Prue
Liney	Milledge	Queen
Linnie 2	Milo	Queenie
Linola	Minardi	Quilla 2
Lisa	Missouri 2	Quinnie
Livy	Mittie 2	Rae
Loamay	Monica	Rassie
Lodie 2	Monnie	Rea
Lolie	Mono	Rebie
Lolita	Montine	Redolia
Lollie	Moselle 2	Reeva
Loma	Mozell 3	Remie
Lonnie 2	Mozelle 2	Rena 5
Lorie	Nada	Rennis
Lovenia	Nanaline	Reva
Lovie 2	Narcissa	Rheta
Loy	Narvelle	Richardine 3
Lucinda 5	Nataline	Richie
Lucretia	Nealie	Rina
Lullie	Nelure	Rissie
Luma	Nodie 2	Robbie
Luna	Noena	Robertelle
Lurania	Nonie	Roma 2
Lurina	Nonnie	Rusha
Lutheney	Obelia	Sabra Jo
Lutie 2	Obera	Sabry
Lyde	Odelia	Salantha
Magda	Odressa	Samantha 2
Magadalena	Offie	Samella
Magnolia	Oma	Samuella
Mahala	Omega	Savannah 6
Malinda	Ones	Sedonie

Southern Cities: 1877 to 1937   --   AUGUSTA, GEORGIA, 1919

Selecta	Theodosia 2	Versie
Selenia	Thomasine	Vesta
Sennie 2	Tina	Victory
Senora	Tincy	Vida
Seppie	Tiney	Vidue
Serepta	Tinie	Vilandie
Simmie	Tiveetie	Vinvie
Sina 2	Tracey	Vurnia
Solie	Trizille	Wilhelmina 14
Sophia 5	Truedell	Willa
Sophie 15	Tulla	Williebill
Sophronia 6	Tullie	Wilthy
Subrina	Tullulah	Winnie 8
Sudie	Uline	Wylena
Sunie	Ulla	Wynona 2
Surella	Vallie	Zadelle
Tallulah 2	Vander	Zahade
Talulah 2	Vannie	Zaidee
Tannie	Varie	Zeara
Tassia	Varina	Zella
Teckla	Varnetta	Zeloma
Teedie	Vashti 2	Zena
Telotha	Vasie	Zenie 2
Tempie	Vela	Zenobia 2
Tena	Venie 2	Zillah 2
Tessie 3	Verlee	Zona
Tetia	Vernie	Zuna
Theodocia	Verona 2	Zylpha

Southern Cities: 1877 to 1937

Source List Q: AUGUSTA, GEORGIA, 1937

Most Common Given Names, Black

The first number after the name indicates the number of times the name was used; the second number indicates the rate per 100,000 on the basis of 1 = 11.513. This alphabetical list is followed by a frequency listing indicating the number of times the name was used. Then follows an alphabetical and frequency listing for Black females with a rate per 100,000 on the basis of 1 = 8.816. There are 8,677 males and 11,343 females.

MALE
Alphabetical

Aaron 12 138	Daniel 49 564	Herbert 29 334
Abraham 18 207	David 77 887	Herman 14 161
Abram 7 81	Dennis 15 173	Hezekiah 9 104
Adam 5 58	Doc(k) 19 219	Homer 6 69
Albert 85 979	Donald 1	Horace 18 207
Alexander 51 587	Douglas 2	Hosea 11 127
Alfred 31 357	Earl 14 161	Howard 12 138
Allen 25 288	Eddie 3	Hubert 5 58
Alonzo 20 230	Edgar 11 127	Hugh 5 58
Alvin 14 161	Edward 185 2130	Irvin 7 81
Amos 11 127	Edwin 4	Isaac 32 368
Anderson 21 242	Eli 5 58	Isaiah 29 334
Andrew 70 806	Elias 2	Isham 1
Anthony 7 81	Elijah 29 334	Jack 18 217
Archie 13 150	Emanuel 5 58	Jackson 4
Arthur 77 887	Ephraim 4	Jacob 18 207
August 3	Ernest 62 714	Jake 1
Augustus 20 230	Eugene 52 599	James 539 6206
Benjamin 110 1266	Felix 7 81	Jasper 11 127
Berry 8 92	Floyd 21 242	Jeff 3
Bishop 6 69	Francis 2	Jefferson 7 81
Booker 11 127	Frank 151 1738	Jeremiah 1
Caesar 12 138	Fred 76 875	Jerry 35 403
Caleb 1	Frederick 27 311	Jesse 81 933
Calvin 13 150	Garfield 8 92	John 622 7161
Carl 4	George 291 3350	Joseph 215 2475
Cato 1	Gilbert 9 104	Joshua 20 230
Cecil 1	Governor 5 58	Julian 21 242
Charles 284 3270	Green 4	Julius 19 219
Chester 10 115	Gus 19 219	Junius 6 69
Clarence 61 702	Guy 5 58	Kenneth 1
Claude 20 230	Harold 12 138	King 6 69
Clifford 10 115	Harrison 11 127	Lamar 5 58
Clifton 1	Harry 30 345	Lawrence 24 276
Clyde 5 58	Harvey 10 115	Lee 28 322
Columbus 7 81	Henderson 2	Leon 9 104
Curtis 11 127	Henry 254 2924	Leonard 21 242

Southern Cities: 1877 to 1937   --   AUGUSTA, GEORGIA, 1937

Leroy 48 553	Nathan 18 207	Sampson 6 69
Leslie 4	Nathaniel 27 311	Samuel 145 1669
Lester 8 92	Ned 4	Sandy 7 81
Levi 11 127	Nelson 14 161	Sidney 20 230
Lewis 44 507	Nicholas 1	Simeon 1
Lloyd 7 81	Obie 5 58	Simon 8 92
Lonnie 20 230	Oliver 12 138	Solomon 25 288
Louis 30 345	Oscar 25 288	Stanley 1
Lucius 21 242	Otis 28 322	Stephen 12 138
Luther 27 311	Owen 1	Theodore 14 161
Mack 29 334	Patrick 6 69	Thomas 230 2648
Madison 8 92	Paul 31 357	Timothy 9 104
Major 9 104	Percy 6 69	Ulysses 9 104
Marshall 15 173	Peter 26 299	Vernon 6 69
Martin 1	Phillip 18 207	Virgil 4
Marvin 4	Primus 1	Wade 6 69
Matthew 19 219	Prince 8 92	Wallace 10 115
McKinley 7 81	Ralph 8 92	Walter 90 1036
Melvin 8 92	Raymond 8 92	Warren 19 219
Michael 5 58	Reginald 2	Wash 1
Miles 1	Reuben 17 196	Washington 8 92
Milledge 9 104	Richard 57 656	Wesley 16 184
Milo 5 58	Robert 287 3304	Wilbur 8 92
Milton 10 115	Roger 10 115	Willard 3
Morris 7 81	Roosevelt 17 196	William 831 9567
Mose 9 104	Roscoe 1	Willie 22 253
Moses 39 449	Roy 9 104	Willis 14 161
Napoleon 5 58	Russell 3	York 2
		Zachariah 3

MALE
  Frequency

William 831	Andrew 70	Mack 29
John 622	Ernest 62	Lee 28
James 539	Clarence 61	Otis 28
George 291	Richard 57	Frederick 27
Robert 287	Eugene 52	Luther 27
Charles 284	Alexander 51	Nathaniel 27
Henry 254	Daniel 49	Peter 26
Thomas 230	Leroy 48	Allen 25
Joseph 215	Lewis 44	Oscar 25
Edward 185	Moses 39	Solomon 25
Frank 151	Jerry 35	Lawrence 24
Samuel 145	Isaac 32	Willie 22
Benjamin 110	Alfred 31	Anderson 21
Walter 90	Paul 31	Floyd 21
Albert 85	Harry 30	Julian 21
Jesse 81	Louis 30	Leonard 21
Arthur 77	Elijah 29	Lucius 21
David 77	Herbert 29	Alonzo 20
Fred 76	Isaiah 29	Augustus 20

Southern Cities: 1877 to 1937 -- AUGUSTA, GEORGIA, 1937

Claude 20	Roger 10	Guy 5
Joshua 20	Wallace 10	Hubert 5
Lonnie 20	Gilbert 9	Hugh 5
Sidney 20	Hezekiah 9	Lamar 5
Doc(k) 19	Leon 9	Michael 5
Gus 19	Major 9	Milo 5
Julius 19	Milledge 9	Napoleon 5
Matthew 19	Mose 9	Obie 5
Warren 19	Roy 9	Carl 4
Abraham 18	Timothy 9	Edwin 4
Horace 18	Ulysses 9	Ephraim 4
Jack 18	Berry 8	Green 4
Jacob 18	Garfield 8	Jackson 4
Nathan 18	Lester 8	Leslie 4
Phillip 18	Madison 8	Marvin 4
Reuben 17	Melvin 8	Ned 4
Roosevelt 17	Prince 8	Virgil 4
Wesley 16	Ralph 8	August 3
Dennis 15	Raymond 8	Eddie 3
Marshall 15	Simon 8	Jeff 3
Alvin 14	Washington 8	Russell 3
Earl 14	Wilbur 8	Willard 3
Herman 14	Abram 7	Zachariah 3
Nelson 14	Anthony 7	Douglas 2
Theodore 14	Columbus 7	Elias 2
Willis 14	Felix 7	Francis 2
Archie 13	Irvin 7	Henderson 2
Calvin 13	Jefferson 7	Reginald 2
Aaron 12	Lloyd 7	York 2
Caesar 12	McKinley 7	Caleb 1
Harold 12	Morris 7	Cato 1
Howard 12	Sandy 7	Cecil 1
Oliver 12	Bishop 6	Clifton 1
Stephen 12	Homer 6	Donald 1
Amos 11	Junius 6	Isham 1
Booker 11	King 6	Jake 1
Curtis 11	Patrick 6	Jeremiah 1
Edgar 11	Percy 6	Kenneth 1
Harrison 11	Sampson 6	Miles 1
Hosea 11	Vernon 6	Nicholas 1
Jasper 11	Wade 6	Owen 1
Levi 11	Adam 5	Primus 1
Chester 10	Clyde 5	Roscoe 1
Clifford 10	Eli 5	Sampson 1
Harvey 10	Emanuel 5	Simeon 1
Milton 10	Governor 5	Stanley 1
		Wash 1

Southern Cities: 1877 to 1937 -- AUGUSTA, GEORGIA, 1937

FEMALE
Alphabetical

Adaline 11 97	Dorcas 1	Jane 14 123
Addie 49 432	Doris 1	Janie 126 1111
Aggy 1	Dorothy 53 467	Jeanette 2
Agnes 28 247	Easter 7 62	Jennie 60 529
Alberta 61 538	Edith 22 194	Jessie 53 467
Albertha 5 44	Edna 19 168	Jewel(1) 3
Alice 126 1111	Effie 19 168	Jimmie 1
Alma 24 212	Eleanor 8 71	Joan 1
Almeta 6 53	Eliza 77 679	Josephine 62 547
Alzora 5 44	Elizabeth 149 1314	Juanita 24 212
Amanda 42 370	Ella 147 1296	Julia 147 1296
Amelia 20 176	Ellen 34 300	Kate 24 212
Amy 15 132	Eloise 21 185	Kathleen 4
Ann 8 71	Elsie 8 71	Katy 59 520
Anna 116 1023	Emily 16 141	Kitty 1
Annie 432 4809	Emma 198 1746	Laura 108 952
Aurelia 3	Ernestine 5 44	Lavinia 2
Beatrice 63 555	Essie 72 635	Leah 1
Belle 39 344	Estelle 63 555	Lelia 13 115
Bernice 5 44	Esther 18 159	Lena 46 406
Bertha 69 608	Ethel 101 890	Leola 28 247
Bessie 95 838	Eugenia 9 79	Lessie 12 106
Betsy 6 53	Eunice 17 150	Letty 7 62
Betty 9 79	Eva 49 432	Lillian 39 344
Beulah 39 344	Eveline 4	Lillie 204 1798
Blanche 14 123	Evelyn 29 256	Lizzie 136 1199
Bridget 2	Fairy 5 44	Lois 6 53
Caroline 8 71	Fanny 166 1463	Louisa 8 71
Carolyn 4	Flora 11 97	Louise 157 1384
Carrie 282 2486	Florence 29 256	Lovie 10 88
Cassie 5 44	Florine 14 123	Lucille 80 705
C(K)atharine 58 511	Flossie 6 63	Lucinda 23 203
Celia 5 44	Frances 104 917	Lucy 87 767
Charity 18 159	Frankie 8 71	Lula 138 1217
Charlotte 28 247	Geneva 24 212	Luvenia 10 88
C(h)loe 18 159	Georgia 101 890	Lydia 4
Christine 17 150	Gertrude 69 608	Mabel 37 326
Clara 84 741	Gladys 34 300	Maggie 109 961
Clary 1	Grace 39 344	Malinda 10 88
Cleo 13 115	Gussie 23 203	Mamie 194 1640
Cora 74 652	Hannah 14 123	Margaret 69 608
Cornelia 29 256	Harriet 13 115	Marguerite 20 176
Daisy 95 838	Hattie 191 1684	Maria(h) 28 247
Delia 8 71	Hazel 7 62	Marian 7 62
Della 26 229	Henrietta 37 326	Marie 127 1120
Dinah 4	Hester 7 62	Marion 8 71
Docia 5 44	Hetty 3	Marjorie 5 44
Dolly 13 115	Inez 44 388	Martha 71 626
Dora 40 353	Isabella 6 53	Mary 720 6348

Southern Cities: 1877 to 1937 -- AUGUSTA, GEORGIA, 1937

Matilda 25 220	Ophelia 26 229	Sadie 44 388
Mattie 285 2513	Patience 1	Sally 92 811
Maude 33 291	Patsy 8 71	Sarah 190 1675
May(e) 22 194	Pauline 25 220	Savannah 18 159
Mildred 17 150	Pearl 66 582	Silvia 11 97
Milly 8 71	Phillis 5 44	Sophia(e) 20 176
Minerva 2	Ph(o)ebe 8 71	Sue 2
Minnie 103 908	Pinkie 9 79	Susan 9 79
Miriam 4	Polly 7 62	Susie 127 1120
Mittie 5 44	Priscilla 8 71	Tessie 5 44
Molly 25 220	Queen 14 123	Thelma 39 344
Mozelle 32 282	Rach(a)el 27 238	Tommie 1
Myra 1	Rebecca 42 370	Vera 5 44
Myrtle 2	Rena 7 62	Viola 81 714
Nancy 61 538	Reva 5 44	Violet 3
Nanny 8 71	Rhoda 3	Virginia 28 247
Naomi 16 141	Roberta 16 141	Vivian 6 53
Nelly 40 353	Rosa 238 2098	Willie 55 485
Nona 5 44	Rose 11 97	Willie Mae 90 793
Nora(h) 33 291	Ruby 59 520	Winn(e)y 11 97
Norma 7 62	Ruth 92 811	

FEMALE
Frequency

Mary 720	Georgia 101	Willie 55
Annie 432	Bessie 95	Dorothy 53
Mattie 285	Daisy 95	Jessie 53
Carrie 282	Ruth 92	Addie 49
Rosa 238	Sally 92	Eva 49
Lillie 204	Willie Mae 90	Lena 46
Emma 198	Lucy 87	Inez 44
Mamie 194	Clara 84	Sadie 44
Hattie 191	Viola 81	Amanda 42
Sarah 190	Lucille 80	Rebecca 42
Fanny 166	Eliza 77	Dora 40
Louise 157	Cora 74	Nelly 40
Elizabeth 149	Essie 72	Belle 39
Ella 147	Martha 71	Beulah 39
Julia 147	Bertha 69	Grace 39
Lula 138	Gertrude 69	Lillian 39
Lizzie 136	Margaret 69	Thelma 39
Marie 127	Pearl 66	Henrietta 37
Susie 127	Beatrice 63	Mabel 37
Alice 126	Estelle 63	Ellen 34
Janie 126	Josephine 62	Gladys 34
Anna 116	Alberta 61	Maude 33
Maggie 109	Nancy 61	Nora(h) 33
Laura 108	Jennie 60	Mozelle 32
Frances 104	Katy 59	Cornelia 29
Minnie 103	Ruby 59	Evelyn 29
Ethel 101	C(K)atharine 58	Florence 29

Southern Cities: 1877 to 1937 -- AUGUSTA, GEORGIA, 1937

Agnes 28	Harriet 13	Alzora 5
Charlotte 28	Lelia 13	Bernice 5
Leola 28	Lessie 12	Cassie 5
Maria(h) 28	Adaline 11	Celia 5
Virginia 28	Flora 11	Docia 5
Rach(a)el 27	Rose 11	Ernestine 5
Della 26	Silvia 11	Fairy 5
Ophelia 26	Winn(e)y 11	Marjorie 5
Matilda 25	Lovie 10	Mittie 5
Molly 25	Luvenia 10	Nona 5
Pauline 25	Malinda 10	Phillis 5
Alma 24	Betty 9	Reva 5
Geneva 24	Eugenia 9	Tessie 5
Juanita 24	Pinkie 9	Vera 5
Kate 24	Susan 9	Carolyn 4
Gussie 23	Ann 8	Dinah 4
Lucinda 23	Caroline 8	Eveline 4
Edith 22	Delia 8	Kathleen 4
May(e) 22	Eleanor 8	Lydia 4
Eloise 21	Elsie 8	Miriam 4
Amelia 20	Frankie 8	Aurelia 3
Marguerite 20	Louisa 8	Hetty 3
Sophia(e) 20	Marion 8	Jewel(l) 3
Edna 19	Milly 8	Rhoda 3
Effie 19	Nanny 8	Violet 3
Charity 18	Patsy 8	Bridget 2
C(h)loe 18	Ph(o)ebe 8	Jeanette 2
Esther 18	Priscilla 8	Lavinia 2
Savannah 18	Easter 7	Minerva 2
Christine 17	Hazel 7	Myrtle 2
Eunice 17	Hester 7	Sue 2
Mildred 17	Letty 7	Aggy 1
Emily 16	Marian 7	Clary 1
Naomi 16	Norma 7	Dorcas 1
Roberta 16	Polly 7	Doris 1
Amy 15	Rena 7	Jimmie 1
Blanche 14	Almeta 6	Joan 1
Florine 14	Betsy 6	Kitty 1
Hannah 14	Flossie 6	Leah 1
Jane 14	Isabella 6	Myra 1
Queen 14	Lois 6	Patience 1
Cleo 13	Vivian 6	Tommie 1
Dolly 13	Albertha 5	

Surnames, Black

The number of Blacks represented in this list is 20,020; the rate per 100,000 is 1 = 4.995. The first number indicates the number of times the surname was used; the second number reflects the rate per 100,000. A frequency list follows the alphabetical listing.

Southern Cities: 1877 to 1937   --   AUGUSTA, GEORGIA, 1937

Alphabetical

Adams 55 275	Grant 53 265	Patterson 36 180
Alexander 32 160	Gray 39 195	Payne 15 75
Allen 102 509	Green 191 954	Penn 9 45
Anderson 98 490	Greene 26 130	Perry 33 165
Atkins 6 30	Griffin 96 480	Phillips 11 55
Austin 3	Groves 1	Pierce 7 35
Bailey 45 225	Hall 89 445	Polk 5 25
Baker 24 120	Hamilton 13 65	Porter 19 95
Banks 14 70	Hammond 27 135	Price 33 165
Barnes 66 330	Harper 34 170	Randolph 2
Bell 67 335	Harris 180 899	Reed 33 165
Booker 14 70	Hart 8 40	Reid 72 370
Bradley 11 55	Harvey 10 50	Richardson 26 130
Brooks 57 285	Hawkins 26 130	Rivers 7 35
Brown 401 2003	Hayes 12 60	Roberts 27 135
Bryant 65 325	Henderson 36 180	Robinson 139
Butler 107 534	Henry 7 35	Rogers 15 75
Campbell 22 110	Hill 103 514	Ross 45 225
Carter 98 490	Holland 5 25	Russell 22 110
Clark 56 280	Holloway 14 70	Scott 144 719
Clarke 3	Holmes 105 524	Sharpe 2
Coleman 98 490	Hopkins 10 50	Shelton 5 25
Coles 5 25	Howard 42 210	Simmons 59 295
Collins 82 410	Hunter 14 70	Simms 6 30
Cooper 37 185	Jackson 288 1439	Smith 351 1753
Cox 11 55	James 50 250	Stevens 15 75
Crawford 88 440	Jefferson 36 180	Stewart 51 255
Cummings 57 285	Jenkins 77 395	Taylor 82 410
Daniels 17 85	Johnson 466 2328	Thomas 282 1409
Davis 190 949	Jones 497 2483	Thompson 46 230
Dickerson 7 35	Jordan 49 245	Tucker 15 75
Dixon 41 205	King 37 185	Turner 70 350
Douglass 1	Lee 82 410	Wade 13 65
Edwards 59 295	Lewis 88 440	Walker 255 1274
Elliott 14 70	Lucas 4	Ward 15 75
Evans 142 608	Martin 35 175	Washington 144 618
Ferguson 37 185	Mason 37 185	Watkins 31 155
Fields 15 75	Miller 57 285	Watson 65 325
Fisher 9 45	Mitchell 57 285	Webster 11 55
Fleming 4	Montgomery 20 100	West 32 160
Fletcher 2	Moore 112 559	White 145 724
Foster 21 105	Morse 9 45	Williams 725 3756
Franklin 20 100	Morton 21 105	Willis 22 110
Freeman 97 485	Murray 100 500	Wilson 133 664
Fuller 22 110	Myers 23 115	Wood 3
Gaines 15 75	Owens 34 170	Woods 13 65
Gardner 44 220	Pa(i)ge 10 50	Wright 98 490
Gibson 48 240	Parker 43 215	Young 70 350
Gordon 22 110	Parks 46 230	

BLACK NAMES IN AMERICA

Southern Cities: 1877 to 1937   --   AUGUSTA, GEORGIA, 1937

<u>Frequency</u>

Williams 752	Clark 56	Daniels 17
Jones 497	Adams 55	Fields 15
Johnson 466	Grant 53	Gaines 15
Brown 401	Stewart 51	Payne 15
Smith 351	James 50	Rogers 15
Jackson 288	Jordan 49	Stevens 15
Thomas 282	Gibson 48	Tucker 15
Walker 255	Parks 46	Ward 15
Green 191	Thompson 46	Banks 14
Davis 190	Bailey 45	Booker 14
Harris 180	Ross 45	Elliott 14
White 145	Gardner 44	Holloway 14
Scott 144	Parker 43	Hunter 14
Washington 144	Howard 42	Hamilton 13
Evans 142	Dixon 41	Wade 13
Robinson 139	Gray 39	Woods 13
Wilson 133	Cooper 37	Hayes 12
Moore 112	Ferguson 37	Bradley 11
Butler 107	King 37	Cox 11
Holmes 105	Mason 37	Phillips 11
Hill 103	Henderson 36	Webster 11
Allen 102	Jefferson 36	Harvey 10
Murray 100	Patterson 36	Hopkins 10
Anderson 98	Martin 35	Pa(i)ge 10
Carter 98	Harper 34	Fisher 9
Coleman 98	Owens 34	Morse 9
Wright 98	Perry 33	Penn 9
Freeman 97	Price 33	Hart 8
Griffin 96	Reed 33	Dickerson 7
Hall 89	Alexander 32	Henry 7
Crawford 88	West 32	Pierce 7
Lewis 88	Watkins 31	Rivers 7
Collins 82	Hammond 27	Atkins 6
Lee 82	Roberts 27	Simms 6
Taylor 82	Greene 26	Coles 5
Jenkins 77	Hawkins 26	Holland 5
Reid 72	Richardson 26	Polk 5
Turner 70	Baker 24	Shelton 5
Young 70	Myers 23	Fleming 4
Bell 67	Campbell 22	Lucas 4
Barnes 66	Fuller 22	Austin 3
Bryant 65	Gordon 22	Clarke 3
Watson 65	Russell 22	Wood 3
Edwards 59	Willis 22	Fletcher 2
Simmons 59	Foster 21	Randolph 2
Brooks 57	Morton 21	Sharpe 2
Cummings 57	Franklin 20	Douglass 1
Miller 57	Montgomery 20	Groves 1
Mitchell 57	Porter 19	

Southern Cities: 1877 to 1937 -- AUGUSTA, GEORGIA, 1937

Unusual Names, Black

MALE
   (Sample: 8,677)

Abraham 18	Cash	Dorus
Abram 7	Cato	Dosier
Adolphus 3	Cebrien	Dozier
Adger	Cephas	Drelly
Alfester	Cephus	Duce
Algernon	Chaftie	Dutch
Aloysius	Champ	Dwelle
Alphonso	Chance	Early 3
Alphonzo 3	Chapel	Ebb
Americus	Chessie	Ebenezer 2
Ansel	Chiman	Elgy
Arcy 2	Christian	Eli 5
Ardis	Cicero 4	Elias 2
Artance	Clanton	Elijah 29
Artie	Claret	Ellie
Artis	Clemmie 2	Emanuel 5
Athus	Cleophus	Enoch 4
Atrey	Clever	Ephesus
Attaway	Clovest	Ephraim 4
August	Cluese	Erasmus
Bagie	Cluster	Esau
Beady	Cobe	Essage
Beauregard	Cobie	Essex
Berain	Cody	Ethon
Bishop 6	Cogie	Eulice
Boisey 3	Coley	Euliss
Boisie 2	Colonel	Ezra 4
Boisy	Columbus 7	Ezekiel 4
Booker 11	Comer	Fate
Boose	Commodore	Fest
Bose	Corinthian	Florrie
Boston 3	Coty	Flurely
Boysie 2	Council	Foshen
Brisco	Crim	Futhey
Brodus	Cris	Gabriel
Brooksie	Curley 2	Gadis
Brother	Cuylas	Garfield 8
Buck 2	Dakota	Garlin
Bud 2	Dallas 2	General 3
Buddy	Darius	Golden 3
Cabe	Dee	Goliath
Caesar 12	Delmon	Gooden
Cain	Denigo 2	Governor 5
Caleb	Devotus	Gustave
Capers	Dillie 2	Hammie 2
Capus	Doc(k) 19	Handy 3
Carlos 2	Dogie	Hansom

Southern Cities: 1877 to 1937 -- AUGUSTA, GEORGIA, 1937

Hansport	Lem	Nazario
Harvest	Lemmie	Neamon
Hercules	Lemon	Neeley
Hestus	Lennie	Neilus
Hezekiah 9	LeRoy	Nero
Hoke	Levi 11	Nias
Honor 2	Levie	Nish
Hood	Lief	Nitrus
Hosea 11	Lincoln	Noah 4
Hosey	Lisbon	Noble
Jurie	Loin	Noe
Ignatius	Lonnie 20	Nollie
Isaac 32	Lonzie	Nonas
Isadne 2	Loverte	Noy
Isaiah 29	Luff	Obediah
Isham	Lukie	Obie 5
Isom 2	Lum	Orange 2
Israel 4	Lunie	Orle
Jabie	Mace	Ossian
Jabus	Maceo 2	Ossie
Jeremiah 2	Major 9	Otho
Jeter	Mal	Overn
Jett 2	Malachi 2	Ozzie 4
Jetter	Malkie	Paris 2
Jonah	Maluce	Pashmon
Jonas 3	Mannie	Peletier
Jorored	Manse 2	Pen
Josh	Marcellus	Perliey
Joshua 20	March	Phocian
Judge 2	Martinez	Prestine
Jule	McKinley 7	Preview
Jules 2	Mell	Primus
Junior 2	Memphis	Prince 8
Junius 6	Menor	Professor
Juriah	Mid	Pulaski
Key	Milleaget	Rainey
King 6	Milledge 9	Rance
Kit	Milo 5	Ransom 2
Lafayette 3	Miner	Reamer
Lance	Mingle	Renil
Lancie	Minus	Rias
Landres	Moggie	Richmond 3
Landsley	Monnie	Right
Laney	Montean	Rilens
Lanis	Montrie	Rockefeller
Lank	Moose	Roman 4
Lark 3	Moot	Romie
Larney	Mose 9	Roneny
Leamon	Moses 39	Roosevelt 17
Leander	Mount	Rossie
Leanious	Namon	Royal
Ledoscer	Napoleon 5	Rube

Southern Cities: 1877 to 1937 -- AUGUSTA, GEORGIA, 1937

Rudell	Spurgeon	Wade 6
Saltas	Squire 2	Wash
Sampson 6	Starling	Wations
Sandy 7	Stonewall	West
Scipio 3	Stonewall Jackson 2	Witelaw
Seabron	Sumlar	Winder
Sellers	Teal	Wise
Serions	Theron	Woodrow Wilson
Session	Theus	Yewston
Shady	Tinner	York
Shedrie	Titus	Zach
Shedrick	Tobe	Zachariah 3
Shellie 2	Tobias	Zachary
Shubrick	Tobie	Zack
Silver	Toles	Zebedee
Sim	Tump	Zeke
Smalley 2	Twiggs	Zendell
Smart	Ulus	Zeno
Solomon 25	Ulysses 9	Zick
Son	Usher 2	Zollie
Sonny 2	Vander	Zone
Special	Verdery	

FEMALE
(Sample: 11,343)

Adakar	Arizona	Birdie
Adrena 2	Armita	Blandina
Adrenia	Armissie	Blendina
Aggy	Arpie	Blossom
Ailese	Arra	Bluma
Albertha 5	Arrie 2	Boisie 2
Aletha	Artie 3	Bonnie 3
Alfair 2	Austine	Brinie
Allene	Artholia	Callena
Almeta 6	Arveolla	Camella
Alpha	Auzie	Camilla 2
Alzora 5	Avada	Camille 2
Alzota 2	Azalee	Cammie
Angelie	Azaline	Candasy
Anona	Azelia 2	Candes
Amanda 42	Azeline 3	Canute
Amelia 20	Azzie 2	Carleen
Ammie	Babe	Carolina
Aquilla	Banna	Casino
Ara	Bassar	Cassie 5
Aralee	Beaury	Cenie
Arcelia	Bennie	Ceola 2
Ardella 2	Berta 2	Chaney 3
Aretha	Bertie 4	Chanie
Aria	Biddie	Charity 18
Arie	Biney	Charlene

Southern Cities: 1877 to 1937 -- AUGUSTA, GEORGIA, 1937

Charlie	D'ora	Florine 14
Charline	Dorcas	Florrie
Charlsie	Dorus	Flossie 6
Cherry 3	Dovie	Fluter
Chloria	Duella	Focie
Chlorine	Earlese	Freddie
Cindie	Easter 7	Frankie 8
Cintilla	Ebbie 2	Fronnie
Cissie	Edmonia	Gaynelle 2
Claricia	Effie 19	Gena
Clarisse	Elbertha	General
Classie 2	Elesta	Genola
Claudine	Elester	Gertie
Clay	Elexenia	Girlie
Clementine 2	Elfletta	Golden
Clemmie 2	Eliease	Goldie
Clenderline	Elkie	Golie
Cleola	Elmina 2	Gratha
Cloreand	Elmira	Gussie 23
Clouise 2	Elvie	Hadessa
Cloye	Emerlyn	Hages
Colie	Emmie	Handsome
Columbia	Endie	Hannah 14
Connie	Epsie	Hassie 3
Cordie	Esserlena	Hassolaba
Corines	Essie 72	Hazeline
Corrie 2	Estellar	Hessie
Cozie 3	Estine	Hope
Creacy	Ethelene	Hurtha
Cresye	Ethelyne	Icelea
Dalsese	Etoy	Icie
Daner	Eudora	Icybell
Darcas	Eufaula	Idelia
Delphene	Eulah 2	Idella 2
Delphine 2	Eulie	Idonia
Delcie	Eura 2	Idozier
Dementris	Eureka	Ila
Dennie	Eurice	Ina
Dessa	Evadern	India 3
Dessie	Evalena	Indiana 2
Dicie 2	Evangeline	Ionia
Dilcey	Evelee	Isadora
Dilcie	Evena	Isedora
Dilla	Everlena	Isolene
Dilsie	Fairy 5	Iuka 2
Dimeda	Felicia 4	Ivory 3
Dina	Fenezie	Izetta
Dinah 4	Finney	Izzie
Docia 5	Fleta	Janeva
Docie	Florida 3	Jayma
Donie	Florette	Jeffie
Donnie 2	Florie 2	Jerolin
		Jettie 2

Southern Cities: 1877 to 1937 -- AUGUSTA, GEORGIA, 1937

Jetty	Louvenia 2	Mazie 3
Jimmie	Louisiana 3	Mazillie
Jocelia	Lourena	Meta 3
Joetta	Lourie	Matabell
Johnnie	Love 4	Melinda
Josabell	Lovey	Melissa 3
Jovie	Lovie 10	Melvenia
Junie	Lovine	Melvina
Justine	Lucinda 23	Mercedes
Juvel	Lucendia	Mickie
Kaola	Luchia	Mintia
Katrina	Lucretia 2	Miranda
Kettie	Ludie 3	Missie
Keziah	Lueneal 2	Missomi 2
Kissiah	Lugenia	Mittie 5
Kiziah	Lunette	Montilla
Kizzie 3	Lukie	Mozelle 32
Laborgia	Lurania	Murine
Lackey	Lurina	Murtice
Laddie	Lurla	Musia
Ladora	Lurline	Myrtie
Lamar	Lusina	Myrtis 2
Laney 3	Lutetia	Nadine
Larcenia	Lutis	Narcissus 2
Lavenia 2	Luvenia 10	Natalie
Lavinia	Luvinia 3	Nazarine
Lavonia	Luvernice	Nazrinie
Lawuna	Luverna	Neola
Leanell	Lyncha	Nezzie
Leaver	Madelle	Nollie
Ledora	Madie 2	Nona 5
Lemon	Maecile	Nonie 2
Lenola	Magdalene	Norean
Leola	Magdaline 2	Normia
Leolaw	Magnolia 2	Novella
Lessie 12	Mahala	Novia
Letetia	Malinda 10	Noylee
Letha 3	Malissa	Ocie 2
Lethia	Malvenia 2	Octoria
Leverta	Manilla	Odessa 4
Levessie	Manola 2	Ola
Lina 3	Maonie	Omega 2
Linnie	Marcella	Omelia
Lisha	Margree	Ommie
Lissie	Mariah 28	Oneita
Littie	Marovia	Onie
Lodie	Marstella	Ora 4
Lona 3	Matilda 25	Orietta 2
Lonia	Maxie	Orine 2
Lonie	Maxine 4	Orttie
Lonnie	Maydelle	Osceola
Lorine 2	Mayoso	Osia

Southern Cities: 1877 to 1937 -- AUGUSTA, GEORGIA, 1937

Osie	Riller	Surilla
Otelia 2	Rivanna	Susannah
Oveen	Robena	Syphronia
Ozie	Rochelle	Tabitha
Pallie 2	Rolanda	Talulah 2
Pamela	Romelia	Tama
Para	Rorie	Tamar
Parmie	Rosebud	Tamer 2
Parthene	Rosenia	Tanzie
Parthenia 3	Rosella 2	Taz
Patience	Rovina	Telia 2
Pauleta	Rozena 2	Tena
Pearline 3	Rozelia	Tessie 5
Pecola	Rozella 2	Tettie
Pecolia	Rozetta	Texana
Pennie	Rozzie	Theodocia
Penny 2	Rupertee	Theodosia 4
Phenie	Ryans	Theola
Phillis 5	Sabra	Thomasina
Philor	Sabre	Tilda
Phoebe	Saconia	Tilla
Piccola	Saffie	Tina
Pink	Salena 3	Tinnie
Pinkie 9	Salina	Tiny
Pollie	Saloni	Tivernia
Plumer	Salonia	Tomasina
Plummie 2	Sammie	Tomasino
Precious 2	Samuella	Tommie
Priscilla 8	Sannie	Tressie
Prudence	Saphronia 3	Trudie
Prudie	Savanis	Trudell
Prunella	Savannah 18	Tula
Pruttie	Scylla	Uevaha
Queen 14	Selena	Ursula 2
Queenie 4	Selina	Vallie 4
Reather	Sena	Valine
Rebie 2	Senia	Vandella
Redolger	Sephronia	Vannie
Redolia	Serena	Varcissus
Remell	Sheldonia	Vashti
Rena 7	Sillah	Velleen
Rener	Sillie	Verda
Reola	Simmie 2	Verma
Reta	Singie	Vertie
Retha 3	Snola	Veta
Reva 5	Solomie	Vianna
Rezolla	Solonia	Vicie 2
Rhea	Sophenia	Villie
Rhiner	Sophia 20	Viney 2
Rhoda 3	Stately	Vinie
Rhodie	Stephania	Viny
Richardine	Sudie	Virgil

Southern Cities: 1877 to 1937   --   AUGUSTA, GEORGIA, 1937

Virgis	Zadie 2	Zellean
Vonciel	Zady	Zelma
Vossie	Zannie	Zena
Wahlena	Zeffie	Zenia
Whurria	Zelean	Zenobia 2
Winney 11	Zelene	Zepora
Wylona	Zeline	Zeta
Wylene	Zella 2	Zora 2
		Zorata

Most Common Given Names, White

The first number after the name indicates the number of times the name was used; the second number indicates the rate per 100,000 on the basis of 1 = 7.278. This alphabetical list is followed by a frequency listing indicating the number of times the name was used. Then follows an alphabetical and frequency listing for White females with a rate per 100,000 on the basis of 1 = 6.531. There are 13,740 males and 15,310 females.

MALE
Alphabetical

Aaron 3	Carl 33 240	Elmer 12 87
Abraham 7 51	Cecil 20 146	Emanuel 7 51
Abram 1	Charles 371 2700	Ernest 93 677
Adam 3	Charley 2	Eugene 57 415
Albert 105 764	Chester 18 131	Felix 2
Alexander 51 371	Clarence 71 517	Floyd 24 175
Alfred 34 247	Claude 51 371	Francis 18 131
Allen 39 284	Cleon 5 36	Frank 230 1674
Alonzo 7 51	Clifford 40 291	Fred 74 539
Alton 3	Clifton 3	Frederick 44 320
Alvin 19 138	Clyde 26 189	George 367 2671
Amos 2	Columbus 5 36	Gerald 6 44
Anderson 8 58	Curtis 23 167	Gilbert 6 44
Andrew 33 240	Dan 2	Gus 9 66
Andy 1	Daniel 63 459	Guy 16 116
Anthony 9 66	David 98 713	Harold 41 328
Archie 11 80	Dennis 4	Harrison 1
Arthur 93 677	Dick 3	Harry 125 910
August 5 36	Doc(k) 2	Harvey 28 204
Augustus 17 124	Donald 13 95	Henderson 1
Ben 1	Douglas 7 51	Henry 199 1448
Benjamin 103 750	Earl 43 313	Herbert 56 408
Berry 6 44	Eddie 5 36	Herman 24 175
Bill 2	Edgar 28 204	Hoke 7 51
Billy 1	Edmo(u)nd 7 51	Homer 21 153
Bob 1	Edward 193 1405	Horace 19 138
Caesar 3	Edwin 18 131	Howard 24 175
Caleb 1	Eli 3	Hubert 14 102
Calvin 4	Elijah 5 36	Hugh 30 218

Southern Cities: 1877 to 1937 -- AUGUSTA, GEORGIA, 1937

Irvin 13 95	Louis 61 444	Richard 62 451
Isaac 14 102	Lucius 7 51	Robert 328 2387
Isham 3	Luther 36 262	Roger 11 80
Jack 43 313	Mack 10 73	Roscoe 8 58
Jackson 8 58	Madison 4	Roy 55 400
Jacob 24 175	Major 1	Russell 24 175
Jake 3	Malcolm 5 36	Sam 2
James 548 3988	Marshall 10 73	Sampson 1
Jasper 10 73	Martin 17 124	Samuel 108 786
Jeff 4	Marvin 24 175	Sidney 10 73
Jefferson 9 66	Matthew 11 80	Simeon 3
Jeremiah 5 36	Melvin 17 124	Simon 3
Jerome 8 58	Michael 7 51	Solomon 12 87
Jerry 10 73	Miles 1	Stanley 8 58
Jesse 73 531	Milledge 7 51	Stephen 9 66
Jim 1	Milton 17 124	Theodore 27 197
Joe 3	Morris 16 116	Theron 8 58
John 817 5946	Moses 10 73	Thomas 288 2096
Jordan 2	Nathan 12 87	Timothy 5 36
Joseph 297 2031	Nathaniel 11 80	Tom 2
Joshua 4	Neil 3	Ulysses 5 36
Julian 39 284	Nelson 4	Vernon 15 109
Julius 33 240	Nicholas 5 36	Victor 6 44
Junius 7 51	Oliver 19 138	Virgil 8 58
Kenneth 6 44	Oscar 27 197	Wade 10 73
Lamar 9 66	Otis 66 480	Wallace 15 109
Lawrence 47 342	Owen 5 36	Walter 121 881
Lee 38 277	Patrick 24 175	Washington 1
Leland 2	Paul 65 473	Warren 19 138
Leon 23 167	Perey 10 73	Wendell 1
Leonard 30 218	Peter 15 109	Wesley 14 102
Leroy 36 262	Phil 6 44	Wilbur 17 124
Leslie 9 66	Phillip 21 153	Will 1
Lester 26 189	Prince 1	Willard 6 44
Levi 2	Ralph 39 284	William 676 4920
Lewis 49 357	Raymond 36 262	Willie 9 66
Lloyd 21 153	Reginald 4	Willis 15 109
Lonie 22 160	Reuben 8 58	Woodrow 5 36

MALE
Frequency

John 817	Edward 193	Jesse 73
William 676	Harry 125	Clarence 71
James 548	Walter 121	Otis 66
Charles 371	Samuel 108	Paul 65
George 367	Albert 105	Daniel 63
Robert 328	Benjamin 103	Richard 62
Thomas 288	David 98	Louis 61
Joseph 279	Ernest 93	Eugene 57
Frank 230	Arthur 93	Herbert 56
Henry 199	Fred 74	Roy 55

Southern Cities: 1877 to 1937   --   AUGUSTA, GEORGIA, 1937

Alexander 51	Milton 17	Milledge 7
Claude 51	Wilbur 17	Berry 6
Lewis 49	Guy 16	Gerald 6
Lawrence 47	Morris 16	Gilbert 6
Frederick 44	Peter 15	Kenneth 6
Earl 43	Vernon 15	Phil 6
Jack 43	Wallace 15	Victor 6
Harold 41	Willis 15	Willard 6
Clifford 40	Hubert 14	August 5
Allen 39	Isaac 14	Cleon 5
Julian 39	Wesley 14	Columbus 5
Ralph 39	Donald 13	Eddie 5
Lee 38	Irvin 13	Elijah 5
Leroy 36	Elmer 12	Jeremiah 5
Luther 36	Nathan 12	Malcolm 5
Raymond 36	Solomon 12	Nicholas 5
Alfred 34	Archie 11	Owen 5
Andrew 33	Matthew 11	Timothy 5
Carl 33	Nathaniel 11	Ulysses 5
Julius 33	Roger 11	Woodrow 5
Hugh 30	Jasper 10	Calvin 4
Leonard 30	Jerry 10	Dennis 4
Edgar 28	Mack 10	Jeff 4
Harvey 28	Marshall 10	Joshua 4
Oscar 27	Moses 10	Madison 4
Theodore 27	Percy 10	Nelson 4
Clyde 26	Sidney 10	Reginald 4
Lester 26	Wade 10	Aaron 3
Floyd 24	Anthony 9	Adam 3
Herman 24	Gus 9	Alton 3
Howard 24	Jefferson 9	Caesar 3
Jacob 24	Lamar 9	Clifton 3
Marvin 24	Leslie 9	Dick 3
Patrick 24	Stephen 9	Eli 3
Russell 24	Willie 9	Isham 3
Curtis 23	Anderson 8	Jake 3
Leon 23	Jackson 8	Joe 3
Lonie 22	Jerome 8	Neil 3
Homer 21	Reuben 8	Simeon 3
Lloyd 21	Roscoe 8	Simon 3
Phillip 21	Stanley 8	Amos 2
Cecil 20	Theron 8	Bill 2
Alvin 19	Virgil 8	Charley 2
Horace 19	Abraham 7	Dan 2
Oliver 19	Alonzo 7	Doc(k) 2
Warren 19	Douglas 7	Felix 2
Chester 18	Edmo(u)nd 7	Jeremiah 2
Edwin 18	Emanuel 7	Jordan 2
Francis 18	Hoke 7	Leland 2
Augustus 17	Junius 7	Levi 2
Martin 17	Lucius 7	Sam 2
Melvin 17	Michael 7	Tom 2

Southern Cities: 1877 to 1937 -- AUGUSTA, GEORGIA, 1937

Abram 1	Caleb 1	Miles 1
Andy 1	Harrison 1	Prince 1
Ben 1	Henderson 1	Sampson 1
Billy 1	Jim 1	Washington 1
Bob 1	Major 1	Wendell 1
		Will 1

FEMALE
Alphabetical

Addie 28 183	Dahlia 5 33	Frances 117 764
Agnes 39 255	Daisy 34 222	Frankie 11 72
Alberta 12 78	Delia 3	Geneva 16 104
Alice 88 575	Della 10 65	Georgia 48 313
Alma 45 294	Dessie 14 91	Gertrude 41 268
Amanda 42 274	Dolly 10 65	Gladys 53 346
Amelia 9 59	Dora 26 170	Goldie 7 46
Amy 7 46	Doris 19 124	Grace 51 333
Ann 35 229	Dorothy 104 679	Gussie 15 98
Anna 52 340	Dovie 5 33	Gwendolyn 2
Annie 298 1946	Edith 33 216	Hannah 4
Arrie 5 53	Edna 60 392	Harriet 14 91
Aurelia 1	Effie 39 255	Hattie 57 372
Beatrice 34 222	Eleanor 39 255	Hazel 36 235
Bellah 1	Eliza 13 85	Helen 97 634
Belle 29 189	Elizabeth 195 1274	Henrietta 20 131
Bernice 24 157	Ella 52 340	Hester 2
Bertie 19 124	Ellen 34 222	Hetty 3
Bertha 64 418	Eloise 27 176	Ida 53 346
Bess 2	Elsie 18 118	Inez 23 150
Bessie 98 640	Elvira 3	Irene 36 235
Betsy 1	Emiline 3	Irma 9 58
Betty 29 189	Emily 28 183	Isabella 3
Beulah 21 137	Emma 84 549	Jane 22 144
Birdie 6 39	Ernestine 5 33	Janie 25 163
Blanche 21 137	Essie 21 137	Jean(ne) 14 91
Bonnie 8 52	Estelle 32 209	Jeannette 12 78
Bridget 2	Esther 25 163	Jennie 39 255
Camille 7 46	Ethel 78 509	Jessie 45 294
Caroline 10 65	Eugenia 13 85	Jewel(1) 20 131
Carolyn 21 137	Eunice 22 144	Jimmie 4
Carrie 57 372	Eva 57 372	Jinn(e)y 7 46
Cassie 6 39	Eve 1	Joan 3
C(K)atharine 136 888	Eveline 1	Johannah 1
Celia 3	Evelyn 69 451	Josephine 38 248
Charlotte 4	Fanny 55 359	Juanita 14 91
Christine 5 53	Flora 4	Judy 2
Clara 56 366	Florence 54 353	Julia 69 451
Clary 1	Florie 6 39	Kate 27 176
Cleo 6 39	Florine 8 52	Kathleen 20 131
Cora 39 255	Florrie 17 111	Katy 50 327
Cornelia 14 91	Flossie 12 78	Kitty 3

Southern Cities: 1877 to 1937 -- AUGUSTA, GEORGIA, 1937

Laura 44 287	Mary 534 3488	Phillis 3
Leah 2	Matilda 3	Ph(o)ebe 4
Lelia 5 33	Mattie 78 509	Priscilla 2
Lena 37 242	Maude 55 359	Rach(a)el 15 98
Leola 9 59	Maurine 1	Rebecca 29 189
Lessie 14 91	May(e) 63 411	Rena 6 39
Letty 2	Meta 7 46	Roberta 8 52
Lillian 72 470	Mildred 76 496	Rosa 61 398
Lillie 91 594	Minerva 3	Rose 27 176
Lizzie 23 150	Minnie 107 699	Ruby 120 1306
Lois 38 248	Miriam 8 52	Ruth 135 882
Lollie 6 39	Molly 15 98	Sadie 32 209
Lora 3	Mozelle 4	Sally 59 385
Louisa 2	Myra 3	Sarah 132 862
Louise 171 1117	Myrtie 5 33	Savannah 2
Lucille 88 575	Myrtis 16 104	Sophia 9 59
Lucinda 1	Myrtle 46 300	Sudie 5 33
Lucy 37 242	Nancy 15 98	Sue 18 118
Ludie 6 39	Nanny 11 72	Susan 13 85
Lula 55 359	Naomi 7 46	Susie 51 555
Lydia 5 33	Natalie 5 33	Tessie 8 52
Mabel 34 222	Nelly 57 372	Thelma 61 398
Maggie 49 320	Nona 6 39	Tommie 2
Mamie 67 438	Nora(h) 31 202	Vera 23 150
Margaret 210 1372	Norma 8 52	Viola 28 183
Marguerite 11 72	Odessa 6 39	Violet 5 33
Maria(h) 2	Ophelia 13 85	Virginia 71 464
Marian 16 104	Ouida 5 33	Vivian 21 137
Marie 74 483	Patsy 3	Willie 53 346
Marion 46 300	Pauline 41 268	Winn(e)y 5 33
Marjorie 15 98	Pearl 59 385	Zona 5 33
Martha 69 451	Peggy 1	Zora 5 33

FEMALE
<u>Frequency</u>

Mary 534	Lucille 88	Edna 60
Annie 298	Emma 84	Pearl 59
Margaret 210	Ethel 78	Sally 59
Elizabeth 195	Mattie 78	Carrie 57
Louise 171	Mildred 76	Eva 57
C(K)atharine 136	Marie 74	Hattie 57
Ruth 135	Lillian 72	Nelly 57
Sarah 132	Virginia 71	Clara 56
Ruby 120	Evelyn 69	Fanny 55
Frances 117	Julia 69	Lula 55
Minnie 107	Martha 69	Maude 55
Dorothy 104	Mamie 67	Florence 54
Bessie 98	Bertha 64	Gladys 53
Helen 97	May(e) 63	Ida 53
Lillie 91	Rosa 61	Willie 53
Alice 88	Thelma 61	Anna 52

Southern Cities: 1877 to 1937   --   AUGUSTA, GEORGIA, 1937

Ella 52	Beulah 21	Goldie 7
Grace 51	Blanche 21	Jinn(e)y 7
Susie 51	Carolyn 21	Meta 7
Katy 50	Essie 21	Naomi 7
Maggie 49	Vivian 21	Birdie 6
Georgia 48	Henrietta 20	Cassie 6
Marion 46	Jewel(l) 20	Cleo 6
Myrtle 46	Kathleen 20	Florie 6
Alma 45	Bertie 19	Lollie 6
Jessie 45	Doris 19	Ludie 6
Laura 44	Elsie 18	Nona 6
Amanda 42	Sue 18	Odessa 6
Gertrude 41	Florrie 17	Rena 6
Pauline 41	Geneva 16	Arrie 5
Agnes 39	Marian 16	Christine 5
Cora 39	Myrtis 16	Dahlia 5
Effie 39	Gussie 15	Dovie 5
Eleanor 39	Marjorie 15	Ernestine 5
Jennie 39	Molly 15	Lelia 5
Josephine 38	Nancy 15	Lydia 5
Lois 38	Rach(a)el 15	Myrtie 5
Lena 37	Dornelia 14	Natalie 5
Lucy 37	Dessie 14	Ouida 5
Hazel 36	Harriet 14	Sudie 5
Irene 36	Jean(ne) 14	Violet 5
Ann 35	Juanita 14	Winn(e)y 5
Beatrice 34	Lessie 14	Zona 5
Daisy 34	Eliza 13	Zora 5
Ellen 34	Eugenia 13	Charlotte 4
Mabel 34	Ophelia 13	Flora 4
Edith 33	Susan 13	Hannah 4
Estelle 32	Alberta 12	Jimmie 4
Sadie 32	Flossie 12	Mozelle 4
Nora(h) 31	Jeanette 12	Ph(o)ebe 4
Belle 29	Frankie 11	Celia 3
Betty 29	Marguerite 11	Delia 3
Rebecca 29	Nanny 11	Elvira 3
Addie 28	Caroline 10	Emiline 3
Emily 28	Della 10	Hetty 3
Viola 28	Dolly 10	Isabella 3
Eloise 27	Amelia 9	Joan 3
Kate 27	Irma 9	Kitty 3
Rose 27	Leola 9	Lora 3
Dora 26	Sophia 9	Matilda 3
Esther 25	Bonnie 8	Minerva 3
Janie 25	Florine 8	Myra 3
Bernice 24	Miriam 8	Patsy 3
Inez 23	Norma 8	Phillis 3
Lizzie 23	Roberta 8	Bess 2
Vera 23	Tessie 8	Bridget 2
Eunice 22	Amy 7	Gwendolyn 2
Jane 22	Camille 7	Hester 2

Southern Cities: 1877 to 1937 -- AUGUSTA, GEORGIA, 1937

Judy 2
Leah 2
Letty 2
Louisa 2
Maria(h) 2
Priscilla 2

Savannah 2
Tommie 2
Adaline 1
Aurelia 1
Bellah 1
Betsy 1

Clary 1
Eve 1
Eveline 1
Johanna 1
Lucinda 1
Maurine 1
Peggy 1

Surnames, White

The number of Whites represented in this list is 29,050; the rate per 100,000 is 1 = 3.442. The first number indicates the number of times the sur-name was used; the second number reflects the rate per 100,000. A frequency list follows the alphabetical listing.

Alphabetical

Adams 102   531
Alexander 22   76
Allen 85   293
Anderson 130   447
Atkins 12   41
Austin 14   48
Bailey 61   210
Baker 64   220
Banks 22   76
Barnes 64   220
Bell 65   224
Booker 5   17
Bradley 15   52
Brooks 18   62
Brown 149   513
Bryant 31   107
Burrell 1
Butler 33   114
Campbell 30   103
Carter 67   231
Clark 122   420
Clarke 10   34
Coleman 18   62
Collins 45   155
Cooper 51   176
Cox 32   110
Crawford 91   313
Cummings 3
Daniels 12   41
Davis 150   516
Dickerson 1
Dixon 36   124
Douglass 2
Edwards 45   155

Elliott 32   110
Evans 51   176
Ferguson 11   38
Fields 4
Fisher 10   34
Fleming 27   93
Fletcher 11   38
Foster 18   62
Franklin 28   96
Freeman 19   65
Fuller 20   69
Gaines 9   31
Gardner 11   38
Gibson 33   114
Gordon 19   65
Grant 10   34
Gray 11   38
Green 69   237
Greene 40   138
Griffin 42   145
Hall 113   389
Hamilton 35   120
Hammond 15   52
Harper 25   86
Harris 63   217
Hart 1
Harvey 5   17
Hawkins 6   21
Hayes 18   62
Henderson 37   127
Henry 27   93
Hill 93   320
Holland 19   65
Holloway 9   31

Holmes 37   127
Hopkins 12   41
Howard 106   365
Hunter 11   38
Jackson 77   265
James 67   231
Jenkins 31   107
Johnson 308   1060
Jones 258   888
Jordan 52   179
King 74   255
Lee 37   127
Lewis 64   220
Lucas 5   17
Martin 80   275
Mason 17   59
Miller 92   317
Mitchell 47   163
Montgomery 33   114
Moore 107   368
Morse 2
Morton 7   24
Murray 29   100
Myers 16   55
Owens 79   272
Pa(i)ge 19   65
Parker 64   220
Parks 23   79
Patterson 23   79
Payne 13   45
Perry 12   41
Phillips 97   334
Pierce 17   59
Polk 1

236

Southern Cities: 1877 to 1937 -- AUGUSTA, GEORGIA, 1937

Porter 9 31
Price 56 193
Procter 7 24
Randolph 4
Reed 12 41
Reid 25 86
Richardson 18 62
Ridgely 5 17
Rivers 17 59
Roberts 60 207
Robinson 45 155
Rogers 42 145
Ross 25 86
Russell 32 110
Saunders 16 55

Scott 71 244
Sharpe 14 48
Shelton 10 34
Simmons 21 72
Simms 2
Smith 353 1215
Stevens 27 93
Stewart 43 148
Taylor 96 330
Thomas 70 241
Thompson 148 509
Tucker 10 34
Turner 84 289
Wade 17 59
Walker 99 341

Ward 37 127
Washington 13 45
Watkins 59 203
Watson 15 52
Webster 6 21
West 22 76
White 37 127
Williams 190 654
Willis 27 93
Wilson 114 392
Wood 47 163
Woods 9 31
Wright 88 303
Young 79 272

Frequency

Smith 353
Johnson 308
Jones 258
Williams 190
Davis 150
Brown 149
Thompson 148
Anderson 130
Clark 122
Wilson 114
Hall 113
Moore 107
Howard 106
Adams 102
Walker 99
Phillips 97
Taylor 96
Hill 93
Miller 92
Crawford 91
Wright 88
Allen 85
Turner 84
Martin 80
Owens 79
Young 79
Jackson 77
King 74
Scott 71
Thomas 70
Green 69
Carter 67
James 67
Bell 65

Baker 64
Barnes 64
Lewis 64
Parker 64
Harris 63
Bailey 61
Roberts 60
Watkins 59
Price 56
Jordan 52
Cooper 51
Evans 51
Mitchell 47
Wood 47
Collins 45
Edwards 45
Robinson 45
Stewart 43
Griffin 42
Rogers 42
Greene 40
Henderson 37
Holmes 37
Lee 37
Ward 37
White 37
Dixon 36
Hamilton 35
Butler 33
Gibson 33
Montgomery 33
Cox 32
Elliott 32
Russell 32

Bryant 31
Jenkins 31
Campbell 30
Murray 29
Franklin 28
Fleming 27
Henry 27
Stevens 27
Willis 27
Harper 25
Reid 25
Ross 25
Parks 23
Patterson 23
Alexander 22
Banks 22
West 22
Simmons 21
Fuller 20
Freeman 19
Gordon 19
Holland 19
Pa(i)ge 19
Brooks 18
Coleman 18
Foster 18
Hayes 18
Richardson 18
Mason 17
Pierce 17
Rivers 17
Wade 17
Myers 16
Saunders 16

Southern Cities: 1877 to 1937 -- AUGUSTA, GEORGIA, 1937

Bradley 15	Gray 11	Booker 5
Hammond 15	Hunter 11	Harvey 5
Watson 15	Clarke 10	Lucas 5
Austin 14	Fisher 10	Ridgely 5
Sharpe 14	Grant 10	Fields 4
Payne 13	Shelton 10	Randolph 4
Washington 13	Tucker 10	Cummings 3
Atkins 12	Gaines 9	Douglass 2
Daniels 12	Holloway 9	Morse 2
Hopkins 12	Porter 9	Simms 2
Perry 12	Woods 9	Burrell 1
Reed 12	Morton 7	Dickerson 1
Ferguson 11	Procter 7	Hart 1
Fletcher 11	Hawkins 6	Polk 1
Gardner 11	Webster 6	

Unusual Names, White

MALE
  (Sample: 13,740)

Abraham 7	Athel	Bud
Abram	Aubin	Bunyan
Ace	Azor	Bynum
Acey	Basil 2	Byrtis
Acree	Baron	Caesar 4
Albra	Barto	Caleb
Alcander	Basie	Cardon
Aldolphus 3	Bazz	Carlos 2
Allone	Bear	Carmel
Alonza	Beauford	Carmon
Aloysuis 2	Beaufort 2	Carthen
Alpheus	Berteau	Caudell
Alphonse	Bevil	Chafee
Alphonso	Birmah	Champion
Alver	Bishop	Charlcie
Amon 2	Blight	Chavers
Ancelan	Bloom	Chief Justice
Antonia	Blue	Christian 2
Antonio	Bonita	Cicero 2
Ashal	Bonnie	Clean
Archillis	Botie	Cleary
Archelaus	Boudre	Cleo
Argie	Boykin 3	Cleon 5
Arial	Brad	Cluese 3
Arlie	Bright	Cluies
Armie	Broadus	Coad
Arno	Brood	Cody
Artie 2	Brue 2	Coker
Artis	Brutus	Colar
Atticus	Buck	Colden

Southern Cities: 1877 to 1937 -- AUGUSTA, GEORGIA, 1937

Colon 2	Emile 2	Ire
Columbus 5	Emperor	Ireland
Comer 2	Enoch 4	Isadore
Cortez 3	Enos 3	Isaac 14
Council	Erastus	Isham 3
Covunio	Erbie	Jabe
Czirnez	Erlie	Jabeus
Dallas 3	Estee	Jabus
Damascus	Etral	Jap
Danzel	Eudelle	Jay
Danzil	Evel	Jelles
Darcy	Eulez	Jeptha
Darling	Eulie	Jeremiah 5
Day	Euly	Jethro 2
Deal	Euriah	Jobie
Dee 2	Evander	Jodie
Dell	Ezra 2	Johah
Denzil	Fabian	Josh
Detroit	Fernie	Joshua 4
De Votie 2	Ficken	Josiah
Dino	Florian	Jule
Diomead	Floy	Jules
Dock 2	France	Junior
Doctor	Frankie	Junius 7
Dolphus	Gardelle	Keren
Donnie 2	Gartrue	King
Dorroh 2	General 2	Kiser
Dow	Gideon	Lablon
Duffy	Gideons	Lafayette 3
Duke	Hance	Lake
Duluth	Haven	Lally
Dumah	Havie	Lance 2
Dyce	Hayman	Laurie
Ealy	Haze	Lavoisuer
Eaves	Healon	Lawtis
Eben	Heinie	Lazarus
Echols	Hercules	Leaser
Eel	Hezekiah	Leck
Egie	Hezzie 2	Leibun
Elbee	Himsell	Leoline
Elexis	Hogrefe	Leonidas 3
Eli 3	Hoke 7	Lem
Elijah 5	Holland 3	Le Roy
Elisha 2	Hollice	Levi 2
Ell	Hoyt	Lightning
Ellube	Hydie	Linnie
Elmo 3	Hymie	Lomie
Elvie	Iber	Lonie 22
Elza	Idale	Lorie
Elzie	Idis	Lorne
Emanuel 2	Inus	Loron
Emel	Iram	Luckey

Southern Cities: 1877 to 1937   --   AUGUSTA, GEORGIA, 1937

Lum	Osbie	Sig
Lundy	Osie	Sim
Lunus	Osteen	Solomon 12
Mace	Othello	Spivey
Mahola	Othor	Spurgeon 2
Major 2	Ottmar	Starlie
Manin	Ozern	Starling
Marcell	Ozzie 2	Steely
Marcellus 4	Pearre	St. Elmo
Maxino	Penland	Stonewall
McKinley	Perk	St. Pierre
Mell	Philomena	Taft
Menanda	Pierre 2	W. H. Taft
Meral	Pinkie	Tampa
Milas 2	Pleas	Tandy
Milledge 7	Postelle	Tarver
Milwee 2	Prince 2	Teague
Milo 4	Quince	Thearo
Minick	Rainy	Theolu
Minus	Ransom 2	Theron 8
Monica	Ras	Tobe
Montezz	Rasho	Tobias 2
Mood	Raub	Toby
Mordecai	Reb	Tolly
Moscoe	Reedy	Trammel
Moses 10	Refo	Troup
Mugar	Reggie	Troy 2
Mundy	Reguile	Truette
Napoleon	Remer	Tuccoah
Nette	Remus	Tyre
Nezzie	Respess	Tyrus
Nivars	Restees	Ubie
Noah	Rhomell	Ulie 2
Noble	Rocie	Ulysses 5
Noel 3	Rolling Stone	Uriah
None	Roma	Usher
Obediah 2	Romeo	Vadis
Obie 3	Romie	Valentine
Ocie	Roosevelt	Vanderbult
Ocram	Royal	Verdie
Olee	Ruel	Verdis
Olim	Russie	Verlie
Omar	Sandy 3	Verne
Omer 2	Sampson	Verner
Omri	Saul	Vezzie
Oran	Seabron	Vlrick
Oreste	Seck	Vonell
Orie	Seelye	Vydell
Orion 2	Shade	Wade 10
Oris	Shier	Walena
Orrie	Shire	Wave
Orris	Shivers	Welcome

Southern Cities: 1877 to 1937 -- AUGUSTA, GEORGIA, 1937

Weltz	Yankee	Zemmie
Windom	Youles	Zeno
Wingo	Zachariah	Zeph
Worth 2	Zack	Zinn
Worthin	Zavel	Zoe
Woodrow 5	Zebulon	Zuscha
Yale	Zellick	

FEMALE
(Sample: 15,310)

Abertine	Angie	Birdiejell
Abiah	Aquilla 3	Blenie
Abiatha	Arabella	Blonnie
Absye	Archia	Bloom
Adgie	Ardella	Bobbie 3
Aeria	Ardis	Bonnie 8
Agatha	Argine	Bright
Agnold	Arilla	Bronnie 2
Ahava	Armenia	Brunie
Aire	Armie	Buena
Aimee	Arnie	Burma
Alocoque	Arrie 5	Butys
Aletha	Artie 2	Byrdie 2
Alexia	Arvelle	Cadence
Algia	Arvonia	Calene
Allee	Atha	Camilla 4
Allue	Atossa	Camille 7
Allyn	Audie	Candace
Almeda 4	Auline	Cannie
Almena 2	Avice 3	Carlene
Almeta	Avis 2	Carole
Alpheus 2	Avise	Carolee
Altha 2	Azalee 2	Carrie
Alvena	Azaline	Cassie 6
Alvertine	Azie	Celesta
Alyerine	Azilee 2	Chessie 2
Alzona	Beachy	Chlotilde
Amanda 42	Bena	Cissie
Amandtine	Benita	Clarina
Amarinthia	Bennie 4	Claudie
Ambra	Benola	Claudine 3
Amelia 9	Bennola	Clemenette
America	Berdie 2	Clementena
Americus	Berma	Clemmie 3
Ammie 2	Bernie	Clennice
Amina	Berta 5	Cleonis
Anastasia 2	Bertie 19	Cleopatra
Andre	Berto	Cless
Angele	Bicie	Cleta
Angelle	Billie 4	Clewouise
Angelus	Birdie	Clover

Southern Cities: 1877 to 1937 -- AUGUSTA, GEORGIA, 1937

Clovies	Dove 3	Fielda
Codis	Dovie 5	Fleta
Coke	Drucilla 3	Flewellyn
Columbia	Duella	Flordie
Cootosa	Duffie	Floreid
Constance 3	Dulce	Florida
Constania	Ealer	Floride 4
Constantine	Ebbie	Florie 6
Cordelia	Edie	Floriede
Cordie 2	Edmunda	Florine 8
Coxie	Edria	Florrie 17
Christdale	Edtha	Flossie 12
Cressida	Effie 39	Floy 2
Dahlia 5	Eglah	Fluiter
Dallas	Electa	Fonella
Darcy	Eliphus	Fontelle
Darralee	Elis	Francesca
Deborah	Elma 2	Frankelene
Deanie	Elthalia	Frankie 11
Decca	Elva	Freddie
Dedie	Emmagene	Frederica
Dee	Emmie	Fredericka 3
Delanie	Enise	Fronnie
Delcia	Ennis	Gabrella
Delorine	Enola	Ganell
Delphia	Eolion	Gaynelle
Delsie	Epsie	Genesta
Dena	Era	Germaine
Dene	Esseline	Gerome
Denna	Essie 21	Gertie
Dennie	Ethelyn	Gesina 2
Deona	Etholene	Gippie
Deryl	Ettie 4	Glencie
Dess	Eufaula	Golden
Dessie 14	Eulah	Goldie 7
Dicey	Eulala 2	Guessela
Dicie	Eulalie 3	Gussie 15
Dicy	Eulaween	Hannah 4
Dilly 2	Evalena	Hannie
Docia 4	Eve	Haroldine
Dolores	Evell	Harrydele
Donie 2	Evelle	Hassel
Donna	Evie	Hassie 2
Doreen	Ezzie	Hennie
Doretta	Fairest	Hermie
Dorine	Fairy 3	Hessie 2
Dorne	Faith	Holland
Doroselle	Falbia	Hope 2
Dosia	Fallie	Hutchie
Dosie	Fate	Icey
Dottie	Fathie	Icy
Dova	Felta 2	Idella

Southern Cities: 1877 to 1937 -- AUGUSTA, GEORGIA, 1937

Ila 3	Lauree	Lovey
Ilma	Lavada	Lovie 3
Ima	La Vada	Loyola 2
Imelda	La Verne 3	Lucinda
Imogene 2	Lavina	Lucretia
Imond	Lavonia	Luda
India 4	Lazelle	Ludie 6
Ineita	Lear	Lueisa
Iness	Leda 2	Luerane
Inis	Lee	Lulline
Iola	Leeda	Luna 3
Iona	Lema	Lunda
Iowa	Lenna	Lundine
Iree	Lennie 2	Lunette 2
Irvena	Leoma	Luouida
Isadora	Leonie 2	Lurie
Isma	Leontine	Lurlene
Isolene	Leoris	Lurline
Ities	Leose	Luthie
Ivalene	Lera	Lutrelle
Izola	Lerline	Luvenia 2
Izora 3	Lessie 14	Lyndall
Jadie	Letha 3	Macie 2
Jamesetta	Lethea	Madell
Janetta	Lethia	Madena
Jena	Letitia	Madolon
Jenia	Levancie	Magnolia
Jerrie	Levy 2	Maidie
Jetta 2	Lilla	Mailland
Jettie 2	Lillyetta	Maitress
Jewelene	Lilyon	Malene
Jhonnie	Linda	Mallie
Jimmie 4	Linna 2	Manilla
Jodie	Linnetta	Mantine
Joelena	Linnie 4	Marcella 3
Joellen	Lisa	Margolese
Johnnie 2	Lissie	Margorene
Jordie	Littoria	Maria 2
Julie	Liverty	Marjel
Junnie	Lizzette	Martine
Katrine	Lochie	Marvilla
Kella	Loisy	Maryan
Laddieree	Lolita	Maryland
La Fils	Lollie 6	Mathilde 2
Lalla	Lona 3	Matilda 3
Lamie	Londine	Maudel
La Nelda	Lonie 2	Mavis 3
Lanie	Loree	Maxine 4
Lannie	Lorie	Maydelle
Lanora	Loueseba	Maynie
Laree	Louree	Mazel
Launa	Lourene	Mazie

Southern Cities: 1877 to 1937 -- AUGUSTA, GEORGIA, 1937

Mealie	Nellavease	Parmella
Medie	Neva 2	Parmie 2
Medora 2	Nevada	Patia
Mehlena	Noelle	Pattie
Melanie	Nolia	Pearlie
Melissa 2	Nomina	Pensacola
Melrose	Nona 6	Permelia
Melvina	Nonie	Perthenia
Mena 2	Obelia	Phillippa
Mercedes 2	Obie	Phillis 3
Mercine	Ocie	Piccola
Merial	Oda	Pinkie
Mersine	Odelia	Pretto
Mertie	Odena	Priscilla 2
Meta 7	Odessa 6	Prue
Mettie	Odette	Queen 3
Mexie	Ofie	Queenie 2
Milbra	Ogarietta	Quilla 2
Mina	Ogle	Quinnie 2
Minna	Oleater	Radie
Minnie	Olena	Rama
Minta	Olvet	Ranie
Mintie	Oma	Rebie 2
Miskel	Omeda	Reda
Missouri	Omelia	Reine
Mitchie	Omie 2	Rema
Mittie 4	Ona	Remmie
Modesta	Onie	Rena 6
Moina	Onnie	Rentha
Montie	Ora	Ressie 2
Montina	Orelle	Rennis
Montine 3	Orene	Reta
Moselle	Oretta	Retta 2
Mozelle	Orie 4	Reva 3
Mozie	Orlena	Reville
Myrdie 2	Orma	Rhetta
Myrtice 4	Orneita	Rhoda
Myrtie 5	Orphia	Rhodie
Myrtis 16	Orrie 3	Richardine
Myrtrie	Osa 2	Rilla
Nadean	Osceola	Rissie
Nana	Oscie 2	Robbie 4
Nanaline	Othella	Robelle
Nanie	Ottie 3	Roena 2
Nalure	Ouida 5	Roma
Nassie	Ouraleen	Roselle
Natalie 5	Ozell 2	Rosena
Nathalee	Ozelle	Rossie
Nathalene	Ozie	Rozell
Nealie 2	Pallie 3	Ruchia
Needia	Paloma	Ruedell
Neela	Parmelia	Runette

Southern Cities: 1877 to 1937 -- AUGUSTA, GEORGIA, 1937

Sabina	Theola 2	Vienna
Sabra	Theopia	Virginius
Sabry	Thomascine	Visions
Sadonia	Thomasine	Vista
Saffrona	Thyra	Vivienne
Samantha 2	Tincy	Vixie
Sammie	Tiny 4	Volumnia
Santippe	Tommie 4	Voncille
Saphronia 2	Trennie	Vondell 2
Sarafrances	Tressie 2	Voula
Saree	Tula	Wadine
Savannah 2	Tulamaye	Wannie
Seabie	Tullie 2	Welda
Sedonie	Tullulah	Wildella
Seibelle	Tululah	Willene
Selena	Turley	Willianna
Senie	Una 2	Willodene
Seppie	Ursula	Willyne
Shadie	Vada	Wilmoth
Shellie	Valeree	Winney 5
Sighnie	Valerie	Winona
Sigma	Vanella	Wylena
Silverbud	Vannie	Wynona 2
Simmie	Varie	Zadah
Simmye	Varina	Zadie
Sivvie	Varnie	Zaidee 2
Sophia 9	Vashti	Zailease
Sudie 5	Velara	Zelime
Sula 3	Velves	Zellamae
Swanee	Velvie	Zellie
Sylvania	Venera 2	Zelma
Taliela	Venia	Zenia
Tallu	Venice	Zennie
Taltha	Venie	Zenoba
Talulah	Vennie	Zeta
Teckla	Verdelle	Zillah
Tekla	Verdie	Ziller
Tempie	Vergie	Zilphie
Tennie	Vernell	Zimmie
Tensie	Vernie 2	Zohde
Tessie 8	Veronica 3	Zola
Thea	Veta	Zona 5
Theadocia	Vianah 2	Zora 5
Theodosia 2	Vicie	Zoretta
		Zula 3

Southern Cities: 1877 to 1937

Source List R: SCHOOL BOYS AND GIRLS, UNUSUAL NAMES[7]

Black School Boys
(1 = 13 per 100,000)

Abraham 4 53	Athens	Boots
Abram 2 26	Atlas	Bosh
Abraman	Attis	Boston
Add	Audry	Boyce
Adie	Autral	Boykin
Advert	Axwood	Brother 2 26
Alburnion	Baby Ray	Brou Minnow
Alchester	Barn	Brownie 2 26
Alfonso 3 39	Battle	Bubber
Alphonsis 2 26	Beauford	Buck
Alphonso	Beaugard	Buddie
Annias 2 26	Bee	Buddy
Aquila	Benjamin Franklin	Bunch
Arbon	Bennis	Buniest
Ardric	Bilbo 3 39	Burl
Arfenly	Bircy	Burlie
Arion	Bishop	Caesar 4 53
Arizona	Bland	Caleb
Arlandera	Bobe	Calfric
Arlias	Boise	Caliph
Artese	Boohter	Camen
Artie	Booker 8 105	Cap 2 26
Astric	Booster	Captain

_____

[7]Combined list taken from:

Richmond County (Georgia) School Census, 1938

Black Males	Augusta, City	2,368
	Richmond County, Rural	796
	Total	3,164

Black Females	Augusta, City	2,811
	Richmond County, Rural	790
	Total	3,601

White Males	Augusta, City	2,848
	Richmond County, Rural	1,112
	Total	3,960

White Females	Augusta, City	3,039
	Richmond County, Rural	1,131
	Total	4,170

Lowndes County (Mississippi) School Census, 1935

Black Males	Columbus, Mississippi	4,435
Black Females	Columbus, Mississippi	4,759
White Males	Columbus, Mississippi	2,401
White Females	Columbus, Mississippi	2,271

246

Southern Cities: 1877 to 1937 -- SCHOOL BOYS AND GIRLS, UNUSUAL NAMES

Cathney	Eldie	Heiday
Cato	Elester 2 26	Hence
Cebon	Elfish	Henry Clay
Cefer	Elijah 7 92	Herbert Hoover
Celester	Elisha 2 26	Hezekiah 4 53
Celine	Elmo	Hill
Cellus 2 26	Elonia	Hizer
Central	Emanuell	Holland
Cephus	Emerald	Honey
Chapel	Enzie	Hood Wood
Chartie	Ephram	Hoover
Cicero 7 92	Ephesians	Horade
Citzo	Erge Lee	Horal
Claret	Erise	Hosea 2 26
Claudell	Erlie	Hosie
Claudius	Esdra	Hossie
Clemmie	Ethells	Hot 2 26
Cleofus	Etroy	Hot Ash White
Cleopus	Eulin	Hozie 2 26
Cluese	Eulon	Hubbie
Cogie 2 26	Excel	Hudie
Columbus	Exekiel	Hulion
Commodore	Febber	Husberry
Coot 2 26	Fed	Ignatius
Cornizia	Finest	Immanuel
Corn Wallace	Flemon	Inman
Cozie	Flex	Irvan
Critzo	Floris	Isaac 19 250
Curley 5 66	Floyzell	Isaaca 2 26
Dallas	Flozel	Isadore
Dane 2 26	Flu	Isiah
Danzy	Foashee	Isaiah 8 105
Del	Free	Isom
Detroit	Frenchman	Israel 2 26
Devaughn	Gardells	Ivory 3 39
Dewillie 2 26	Garfield 3 39	Jabbo
Dimber 2 26	Garita	Jakie
Dizzie	Garnalie	Jauier
Dob Brad	Garo	Jeremiah
Doc 2 26	General 3 39	Jesse James 5 66
Dock 5 66	George Washington 3 39	Jesseline
Dodid	Gilester	Jethro
Dolphus	Ginger	Jethrow
Dome	Golitha	Jigg
Donnie	Governor	Jobe
Dosie	Grant Lee	Jolia
Doucious	Gull	Jonah
Dutch	Guyle	Jordan
Earlie 11 145	Habor	Jorrett
Early 2 26	Hannaball	Josh 3 39
Echols	Heams	Joshua 4 53
Edwon	Heck	Josuway

247

Southern Cities: 1877 to 1937 -- SCHOOL BOYS AND GIRLS, UNUSUAL NAMES

Juanal Valley	Lonzee	Osiola
Juber	Lorenza 2 26	Ovidas
Judge 3 39	Loy	Ozell 2 26
Jule	Lucious	Ozy
Jules	Lureery	Paris
July	Lurgin	Paza
Junior 22 290	Lutheral	Peara
Junius 2 26	Lymore	Persia
Kaiser	Maceo	Pervia
Kekey	Machine	Phinizy 3 39
Kind	Magor	Picola
King 4 53	Major 6 79	Pilate
Lalaris	Malachi	Pink 3 39
Lanie	Manero	Plato
Lansey	Manner	Pleas
Larmy	Manuel	Please
Layhew	Marcellus 5 66	Pournelee
Lazelle	Mathis	Precious Legion
Leaby	McKinley 8 105	Prince 3 39
Lebra	Mertin	Prinelle
Ledger	Mick	Purstine
Leflatte	Mid	Quina
Leger	Midas	Quincy
Lem	Milledge 2 26	Raleigh
Lemon	Miller	Rallie
Lenaz	Milo	Ransom
Lennie	Milredge	Red
Lent Gaudy	Miner	Reddie
Lepolian	Misery	Remus 2 26
Leslus	Mock Smith	Renzo
Levander	Mond	Revelation
Levenee	Monzella	Roman
Levi 2 26	Mose 16 211	Romie
Levorgia	Moses 17 224	Rommel
Levy	Movre	Romolo
Lieutenant	Murch	Roosavelt
Limm	Mutt	Roosevelt 33 434
Lin	Nantee	Rosevelt 3 39
Linn	Napoleon 4 53	Royal 3 39
Lincoln 2 26	Neg	Rube 2 26
Linzie	Newick	Ruddie
Litt	Nong	Rudelle
Little Boy	Nook	Rugee
Little Freeman	Oddias	Sampson 2 26
Little Nigh	Oddis	Sampton
Litus 2 26	Odia	Sandy 5 66
Llewellyn	Odie 3 39	Saul 2 26
Logi	Olea	Schene
Londsa	Oleo	Seafus
Lonie 2 26	Opello	Sebion
Lonnie 4 53	Ordell	Sebron
Lonsy	Oscella	Selvin 2 26

Southern Cities: 1877 to 1937 -- SCHOOL BOYS AND GIRLS, UNUSUAL NAMES

Sessard	Theola	Vatus
Setrick	Temnit	Vaughty
Shang	Thattis	Velvet
Shelman	Theodus	Verdery
Show	Theron	Veus
Si	T. Homey	Virgis
Silent	Thirkel	Vrige
Simp	Thymon	Wade
Singer	Tig	Walsie
Slim 2 26	Titus 2 26	Wash
Snowball	Tobe	Washington
Sol	Todie	Wee Baby
Solomon 7 92	Tola	Wencus
Son	Tollie	Wes
Sonnie 2 26	Trandus	West
Sonny 2 26	Tyrus	Wildie
Sonny Boy	Uleses	William McKinley 2 26
Sonnia	Uley	Wise
Sox	Ulipes	Woodie 3 39
Spanish 2 26	Ulysses 2 26	Woodrow Wilson 4 53
Squire	Union	Wortea
Stayzola	Urgie	Yoke
Sug	Useless Sykes	Zachary
Taff	Uster	Zack
Talty	Valee	Zavilain
Teat	Van Clain	Zeppes
Theady	Vandy	Zollie

Black School Girls
  (1 = 12 per 100,000)

Addassa	Almeta 2 24	Armecia
Addyne	Almetta	Arnesa
Adesta	Alodoil	Arnetha
Adina	Alta	Arsenia
Adrena	Alvernia	Artent
Adrener	Alzora	Artheria
Agala	Amanda 8 96	Artorio
Agulla	Amoyda	Arvester
Albene	Anavester	Ary 2 24
Albertina	Andrens	Asilene
Al Chester	Araletha	Ater
Aldia	Arbelia	Audella
Alfra	Ardella	Aura 2 24
Alfreddie	Ardelia	Augustan
Alfredia	Ardell	Autree
Alfreeda	Ardena	Aza Belle
Alfresa	Argellan	Azalle
Algie	Arie	Azarene
Allegia	Arlee	Azeline
Alloivisa	Arlelia	Babie
Almary	Arlena	Baby 5 60

Southern Cities: 1877 to 1937 -- SCHOOL BOYS AND GIRLS, UNUSUAL NAMES

Ballencia	Climmie	Elester
Bamma	Clolelia	Elissa Jane
Bantie	Clorine	Ellabelle
Beaurina	Cloteal	Ellaneese
Beauty	Clotine	Elnada
Beechie	Clouise	Elvada
Belessa	Clydena	Elvira
Berk Esta	Clydester	Elvise 2 24
Bernadette	Clytee	Elzena
Berrens	Colia	Elzina
Berta	Collins	Enelean
Bertie	Commeare	Ennis
Bethine	Cordie 2 24	Erly Mae
Birdester	Costella 2 24	Erra
Birdie 3 36	Cotie	Ertha
Bobbie	Creasie	Esater
Bubber	Crecilla	Essie 30 359
Buddy Mae	Creola	Esterine 2 24
Burdelle	Cresa	Etha 2 24
Calsie	Curley 10 120	Eudora
Caralla	Daily	Eulalie 2 24
Cardina	Danula	Euline
Carrelean	Dealla	Eura
Carzella	Debirdie	Eurdie
Cassie	Deedie	Evalina 2 24
Castalla	Delias	Evangeline 2 24
Castella 2 24	Delita	Evergreen 3 36
Castilla	Delois	Ever Leana
Celestine	Deloria	Everleaner
Central	Delphine	Everline
Charity 3 36	Delphis	Evlamoy
Charlene	Delvin	Ezeka
Charline 3 36	Dennie	Fausteen
Cherokee	Dera	Flonteen
Cherry 2 24	Desmar	Floria
Christian 2 24	Dessie	Florine 5 60
Christiana	Dicie	Flossie
Christie	Dinah 2 24	Fly Kate
Christinia	Doak	Fosteria
Cidda Lou	Docile	Francena
Cile	Dollina	Frankie 13 155
City	Donnie	Frederica
Clagee	Dorazelle	Fredima
Clar	Doria	Frozee
Clarissa	Dwellie	Gelester
Clarisse	Eartha	Genia
Classie 3 36	Easter 8 96	Georgene 2 24
Classy	Ednelia	Geralyn
Claudie	Ednola	Gertis 2 24
Clemmie	Edvenia	Gexana
Cleony	Effie 3 36	Gillie Will
Cleopatra	Eldra	Girlee 2 24

Southern Cities: 1877 to 1937 -- SCHOOL BOYS AND GIRLS, UNUSUAL NAMES

Girtie	Josiello	Louvenia 3 36
Gladiola	Joy	Love
Glorie	Julie	Lovella
Gold	Junie	Loventrice
Gonzola	Juraby	Lovie 3 36
Gordea	Kansas	Luberta 10 120
Gozy	Karine	Lubertha
Gracy	Kizzie	Lucinda 11 132
Gussie 7 84	Lady Dell	Lucky
Gutha	La June	Lucretia
Gwince	Lalee	Ludeen
Gynell	Lassie	Luders
Haddie	Lavenia 2 24	Ludia 2 24
Halla	Lavina	Ludie 2 24
Hanna	Lavonia	Ludina
Hannah 4 48	Leany	Luetta
Hancy	Leatha 2 24	Lugesta
Hassie	Leavie	Lulila
Hellena	Ledosia	Lullia
Icy	Leedie	Lybertia
Idelia	Leitha 2 24	Lura
Idella 3 36	Leittia	Lurine
Idena	Lenie	Lurline 3 36
Ifella 2 24	Lenuel	Luvena
Ilene	Leria	Luvenia 3 36
Imogene 5 60	Lerona	Luvina 3 36
Inell	Lessie 2 24	Lysbeth
Iola	Lestine	Mackamo
Iowa	Letha	Macie Lee
Isadora	Letitia	Madena
Isletta	Leu Dosia	Madera
Isie	Levenia	Madesta
Isodora 3 36	Levinia	Madine
Isola 2 24	Levora	Magalina
Isolene	Lexie	Magella
Issie	Lisha	Magilene
Ivella	Little Ann	Magnolia 28 335
Ivery	Lolo	Magnotia
Ivory 2 24	Lona	Maida
Izell	Loneday	Maisie
Izola	Lonely	Malinda 3 36
Jammie	Lonie	Malissie
Jeddie	Lonnie	Malissa
Jelma	Lonzella	Mammie
Jenesa	Loree	Manda 2 24
Jenlee	Lorie	Mandeva
Jerusha	Lorine	Mandy 6 72
Jestina	Louberta 5 60	Manelle
Jettie	Louetta	Manzellie
Johnnie 2 24	Louia	Maple
Johnniee	Louisiana	Marcella
Josia	Lounett	Margree
		Maria 12 144

Southern Cities: 1877 to 1937 -- SCHOOL BOYS AND GIRLS, UNUSUAL NAMES

Mariah	Oceline	Phylis
Marire	Ocie	Piciola
Marjoe	Odelia	Picola
Marline	Odell	Pinkie
Mary Hell	Odella	Pinky 2 24
Mary Magdeline	Odeso	Pneufolia
Marria	Odessa 10 120	Pocahontas 2 24
Martini	Odesta 2 24	Priscilla
Marzetta	Odetta	Queen 15 179
Matilda 8 96	Offie	Queenella
Matilde	Olalee	Queenesta
Matteen	Olena	Queen Esta 5 60
Mauline	Olene	Queen Esther 8 96
Mavis 2 24	Oletha	Quillia
Maychell	Olia	Quitha
Mayola	Olymphia	Ramah
Mel Rosa	Onie Lee	Ramona
Melinda	Ora 4 48	Rammie
Melvina	Orange Lean	Readia
Memphis 2 24	Oremia	Rebia 2 24
Mendora 3 36	Oreta	Rebie
Menergh	Oria	Redell
Menora 2 24	Orlena	Redessa
Mercedes 2 24	Ormee	Reena
Mercides	Orpha	Renoyner
Missouri	Ortharia	Remal
Mittie	Osa	Remel
Mobile	Ossa	Rena 5 60
Mohilia	Ossie 2 24	Renees
Moline	Ote	Renfoe
Monia	Otelia	Reselle
Morena	Otha Dell	Rether
Moselle 3 36	Ovein	Reva
Mossy	Ozela	Rheolia
Mozelle 2 24	Ozella 5 60	Rivilne
Muvina	Pally	Rixie
Myrtis 3 36	Pandora 2 24	Robbiesteen
Nadine 3 36	Paza	Rocky
Nanon	Pearlie 3 36	Rosabud
Natine	Pearlina	Rosella 2 24
Navey Lee	Pearline 6 72	Roselle
Nazlee	Pearly 3 36	Rosena 2 24
Neba Bell	Pecola 3 36	Rozell
Nellon	Penney	Rubie
Neoma	Pensacola	Rubena
Net	Perarlie	Rubenia
Nezzie	Percila	Rubina
Nobie	Perlia	Rufa
Nona	Pernall	Ruthie
Nute	Philda	Sabina
Nutie	Phillica	Saffie
	Phillis	Saline

252

Southern Cities: 1877 to 1937 -- SCHOOL BOYS AND GIRLS, UNUSUAL NAMES

Samalla	Teretha 2 24	Verenous
Sammie 2 24	Tessie 2 24	Verlie Lee
Samuella	Texanna	Vernice 2 24
Santilla	Theatrice	Vertille
Saphronia	Theodora	Viana
Sarata	Theodosia 2 24	Vicie 2 24
Savannah 5 60	Thessia	Victory
Savilla	Thomasena 2 24	Viddlia 2 24
Sciney	Thomasine 8 96	Videlle
Sebana	Thongual	Virdas
Sema	Tiny	Virginial
Sennie	Tommie	Virlee
Shelldonia	Tommisteen	Virtula
Sigmy	Tommy	Wander
Simia	Tota	Warthie
Sina	Treasie	Weeder
Sister 2 24	Tredda	Willie
Sophia	Trendenner	Winnie
Sophie 3 36	Tryphenise	Winona 6 72
Sree	Unite	Worcester
Steveanna	Uovella	Yandell
Susiella	Urada	Yvonne
Sybel	Vacilla	Zaddie
Sylvilla 2 24	Vallie	Zella 2 24
Synestine	Vanda	Zellena
Synthia	Vandella 4 48	Zena
Syretha	Vaudella	Zenaby
Tack	Veatrice	Zeola
Teacake	Venella	Zettee
Tecora	Veneller	Zettie Lee
Tempia	Verdell	Zil
Tena	Verdery	Zola

White School Boys
(1 = 16 per 100,000)

Abe	Beamus	Cato
Abram	Beasie	Ceyphus
Agee 2 31	Bemie	Charlsey
Aloysius	Bronzelle	Chevis
Alter	Budd	Chuton
Alvin	Buddie 3 47	Clelon
Aril	Buddy	Cleon
Arlo	Burnie	Cloris
Arnel	Buyn	Cloud
Arno	Calax	Cluese
Astroin	Candacy	Cluff
Autey	Cap	Cluise
Auvin	Caple	Cogar
Barns	Captain	Colden
Baron	Carvlee	Colon
Basil 2 31	Casius	Columbus

Southern Cities: 1877 to 1937   --   SCHOOL BOYS AND GIRLS, UNUSUAL NAMES

Cordie	Frontis	London
Cordon	Ganus	Lonnie 3 47
Corine	Gavil	Loria
Cortez	Gaylor	Loucious
Coy Lee	George Washington 2 31	Loyal
Daliss	Gettis	Loyce 2 31
Danzell	Gillian	Lubie
Darwin	Givezester	Lurid
Dee	Glinn	Marcelle
Delan	Govde	Mavice
Delvyn	Goya	McKinley
Delys	Gully	Medie
Denver	Gussy	Mefrin
Deron	Halcon	Meliun
Derwine	Harlee	Mell
Detroy	Haroland	Mertis
Dini	Heard	Milledge
Donne	Heubel	Milo
Donsil	Hilary 2 31	Minous
Dosier	Holdutch	Minus
Dugger	Hosia	Minvial
Durie	Hulet	Monte
Earlie 2 31	Hulow	Mose
Earlie Lee	Idis	Moses
Early	Ignatius	Napoleon
Earvan	Ike	Nay Lee
Ederin	Isaiah	Netrill
Edgert	Jeptha	Nimrod
Edries	Jeremiah	Noah 3 47
Edwon	Jock	Noble
Efton	Josh 2 31	Nuell
Eli	Josiah	Odelle
Elijah	Jule 2 31	Oertel
Ellonine	Julese	Ohio
Elmo 4 63	Julus	Omer
Elvon	Junior 13 204	Onesa
Elzy	Keeble	Oris
Emil	Kersine	Orwel
Emile 2 31	Laddie	Ostell
English	Lance	Other
Erbie	Lando	Ottie
Erby	Layel	Ovid
Eris	Lecie	Ozie
Esker	Le Corge	Ozy
Eulie	Le Garde	Ped
Eulon	Lessey	Pera
Ewell	Lessier	Plum
Exam	Libon	Quay
Exra	Lindberg	Rabon
Fairest	Lindy	Ramie
Flint	Linol	Rastus
Floy	Lion	Roamie

Southern Cities: 1877 to 1937 -- SCHOOL BOYS AND GIRLS, UNUSUAL NAMES

Rolly	Tanzie	Vavire
Rome	Tavelyan	Veatch
Royal	Terrace	Verelle 2 31
Rube	Tharion	Verner
Ruel	Thermon	Vernie
Sandy 2 31	Theron 5 79	Vestis
Secar	Tip	Virdel
Shivers	Tobin	Wade 5 79
Shorty	Toby	Wales 2 31
Sol 2 31	Troy 7 110	Wetlie
Solomon 2 31	Truxton	Woodie
Sonny 3 47	Tyras	Woodrow Wilson
Sonny Boy	Vadis	Worth
Starling 2 31	Valdee	Zack 3 47
		Zenus

White School Girls
(1 = 16 per 100,000)

Adeen	Authena	Clinia
Adeon	Avella	Cressie
Aderade	Avie	Dalhia
Agatha	Avonel	Dalma
Albertine	Baby	Dardanell
Aletha	Balzora	Darlyn
Alita	Benita	Darrah
Allena	Bertie	Delaine
Aloris	Biddie	Delores
Althes	Billy	Deloris
Alyne	Birdie	Delphin
Amcely	Birmah	Deryl
Amelia	Bobbie	Desire
Amilee	Bonetta	Diana
Anastalia	Bonita	Deloise
Andreinna	Bonnie 8 124	Doloras
Andrina	Brazalee	Donie
Anjadell	Bunnie	Dorise
Annell	Camilla 2 31	Dosha
Anulee	Camille 4 62	Dovie
Areminta	Carlene	Drixie
Aretta	Carmel	Drucilla
Armenia	Cecetia 2 31	Dutha
Aronell	Cele	Earthlee
Artemisia	Charlene 3 47	Easline
Asalee	Cherry 3 47	Effie 2 31
Athalee	Clarissa 3 47	Eildmeda
Athens	Clarvina	Elbira
Atta Ruth	Claudie	Eldina
Audice	Claudine 3 47	Eliranda
Audine	Cleavie	Elner
Audrene	Clementine	Emmaline
Auriebell	Clemmie	Emogene 2 31

Southern Cities: 1877 to 1937 -- SCHOOL BOYS AND GIRLS, UNUSUAL NAMES

Emola	Illa	Manda
Endora	Imogene 10 155	Marcel
Enid	Indiana	Marcella 2 31
Eris	Irdelle	Marcia 2 31
Essie 4 62	Irvena	Margene
Etoy	Ivylyn	Marlene
Ettall	Jamelle	Marthilda
Eucese	Janelle 3 47	Martina
Eudelle	Jeddie	Matine
Eudora	Jenora	Maudeen
Eulalie	Jestine	Mauline
Eulatie	Jolie	Maureen
Eumice	Joy 2 31	Maurine
Evell	Justine	Mava
Ezzie	Ladine	Mavis 2 31
Florice	Lady Betty	Maxine 5 76
Florie	Laudice	Maytrel
Florine 4 62	Lavada	Meara
Florrie	Lavertice	Melideen
Flossie 4 62	Lazile	Mellie
Foresteen	Leda	Mellouise
Fostine 3 47	Leelia	Melissa 2 31
Frankie 9 140	Leilou	Mellvina
Fredericker	Lerna	Melvira
Freeda	Lessie	Meme
Freidi	Levie	Merceree
Freva	Lexie	Merline
Gabie	Lida	Mertie
Gabrella	Liddy	Mimi
Gaynelle 3 47	Lidwena	Mirial
Gayril	Linda 2 31	Mittie
Genell	Lodema	Mona
Genevia	Lodessa	Monita
Gertie 2 31	Loleta	Montez
Ginia	Lollie	Montine 7 109
Gladiola	Lonnie	Montyne 2 31
Glendora	Loreda	Morma
Glendoris 2 31	Lorie	Moselle
Goldie	Lossie	Mozzell
Gussie 3 47	Loutrell	Mural
Hannah 2 31	Loventrice 2 31	Murlene
Hanoris	Lucretia	Myrtice
Harryette	Lulyanne	Myrtis 17 264
Hassierne	Lura	Nadine 2 31
Hermine	Lurline 4 62	Nathalene
Hildrathe	Luverina 2 31	Natilee
Hildyer	Lylette	Nelda 3 47
Hilmer	Madetine	Neldor
Honor	Malinda	Neola
Icy Ree	Malura	Neva
Idelle	Mamai	Neville
Ignell	Mammie	New

Southern Cities: 1877 to 1937 -- SCHOOL BOYS AND GIRLS, UNUSUAL NAMES

Nomina	Quillar	Uline
Norice	Ramona	Ullaimee
Novis	Rebe	Uni
Nucia	Rebie	Vadis
Nuzzie	Rebion	Valeria
Nyree	Rella	Valley
Odelle	Relta	Vallusia
O'Desa	Remona	Vandola
Odessa 5 76	Rena 2 31	Vannette
Olear	Renina	Vaudine
Oleta 3 47	Rhodom	Vaurice
Oletia	Rhuea	Ventral
Omar Dell	Rippi Jean	Ventrice
Omeda	Robbie	Verdria
Omega	Roma	Verla
Onell	Ronie	Vernell
Onella	Roudine	Vernice
Onerta	Rozzie	Vertlee
Onida	Rusha	Vesta
Ophie	Sammie	Vinnie
Opie	Saphronia 2 31	Vridell
Orena	Savannah	Vista
Orene	Sebelle	Vivin
Oretha	Seleta	Voncine
Orie	Sible	Vonzie
Ormie Bell	Silvernia	Vylen
Orzell	Sunie	Wanda 3 47
Ossie	Syddie	Wander
Oteli	Teckla	Warrenette
Otheal 2 31	Telma	Weda
Oueida	Tempie	Williine 2 31
Patience	Tena	Willons
Paulee	Tera	Winnie
Pearlie	Terasa	Winona 4 62
Pemie Lee	Tessie	Wylene 3 47
Penny	Thalia	Wyndall
Perrigene	Theola	Wynell
Phillis	Thomasine 3 47	Yale
Phyllis 2 31	Tiney	Yvonne 4 62
Pinkey	Toby	Zaides
Ponder 2 31	Tommie	Zela
Primrose	Tressie 2 31	Zoe
Priscilla 2 31	Tula	Zola 2 31
Quay	Twa	Zona
Quila	Undelle 2 31	Zora
		Zuandry

Southern Cities: 1877 to 1937

Source List S: MONTGOMERY, ALABAMA (AND COLUMBUS, MISSISSIPPI)[8]

Most Common Given Names, Black, 1933

MALE
Alphabetical (Sample: 1,955)

Aaron 5	Eugene 9	Melvin 3
Abraham 6	Floyd 2	Milton 2
Abram 1	Frank 30	Moses 5
Adam 5	Fred 10	Nathan 8
Albert 17	Frederick 7	Nathaniel 14
Alexander 12	George 60	Ned 2
Alfred 12	Green 4	Nelson 5
Allen 5	Harold 2	Oliver 5
Alonzo 3	Harvey 2	Oscar 11
Amos 2	Henry 43	Otis 8
Andrew 12	Herbert 7	Paul 5
Andy 1	Herman 2	Peter 9
Anthony 2	Howard 2	Philip 4
Arthur 25	Hubert 1	Pleasant 1
Augustus 7	Irwin 1	Primus 1
Berry 2	Isaac 11	Prince 1
Booker 30	Isham 5	Ralph 8
Caesar 1	Jack 9	Raymond 5
Caleb 3	Jacob 8	Reuben 3
Calvin 2	James 128	Richard 13
Carl 1	Jeff 2	Robert 64
Cecil 1	Jefferson 4	Roy 2
Charles 66	Jerome 1	Sam 1
Chester 1	Jerry 5	Sampson 2
Clarence 4	Jesse 22	Samuel 40
Claude 7	Joe 2	Sidney 2
Clifford 2	John 126	Simon 2
Clifton 1	Johnnie 2	Solomon 1
Curtis 1	Joseph 55	Stephen 3
Daniel 7	Julius 4	Thomas 50
David 38	Lawrence 4	Ulysses 1
Dennie 1	Lee 15	Wallace 2
Earl 1	Leon 12	Walter 18
Eddie 3	Leroy 2	Washington 5
Edgar 1	Leslie 1	Wesley 4
Edward 37	Lewis 6	Wilbur 3
Eli 1	Lloyd 2	Will 1
Elijah 5	Louis 19	Willie 5
Elmer 3	Madison 2	Willis 6
Ernest 5	Matthew 7	William 177

_____

[8]From the City Directory, 1899, 1920, 1933.

Southern Cities: 1877 to 1937 - MONTGOMERY, ALABAMA (& COLUMBUS, MISSISSIPPI)

MALE
Frequency

William 177	Herbert 7	Harold 2
James 128	Matthew 7	Harvey 2
John 126	Abraham 6	Herman 2
Charles 66	Lewis 6	Howard 2
Robert 64	Willis 6	Jeff 2
George 60	Aaron 5	Joe 2
Joseph 55	Adam 5	Johnnie 2
Thomas 50	Allen 5	Leroy 2
Henry 43	Elijah 5	Lloyd 2
Samuel 40	Ernest 5	Madison 2
David 38	Isham 5	Milton 2
Edward 37	Jerry 5	Ned 2
Booker 30	Moses 5	Roy 2
Frank 30	Nelson 5	Sampson 2
Arthur 26	Oliver 5	Sidney 2
Jesse 22	Paul 5	Simon 2
Louis 19	Raymond 5	Wallace 2
Walter 18	Washington 5	Abram 1
Albert 17	Willie 5	Andy 1
Lee 15	Clarence 4	Caesar 1
Nathaniel 14	Green 4	Carl 1
Richard 13	Jefferson 4	Cecil 1
Alexander 12	Julius 4	Chester 1
Alfred 12	Lawrence 4	Clifton 1
Andrew 12	Philip 4	Curtis 1
Leon 12	Wesley 4	Dennis 1
Isaac 11	Alonzo 3	Earl 1
Oscar 11	Caleb 3	Edgar 1
Fred 10	Eddie 3	Eli 1
Eugene 9	Elmer 3	Hubert 1
Jack 9	Melvin 3	Irwin 1
Peter 9	Reuben 3	Jerome 1
Jacob 8	Stephen 3	Leslie 1
Nathan 8	Wilbur 3	Pleasant 1
Otis 8	Amos 2	Primus 1
Ralph 8	Anthony 2	Prince 1
Augustus 7	Berry 2	Sam 1
Claude 7	Calvin 2	Solomon 1
Daniel 7	Clifford 2	Ulysses 1
Frederick 7	Floyd 2	Will 1

FEMALE
Alphabetical (Sample: 3,063)

Adaline 5	Alma 8	Annie 104
Addie 7	Amanda 24	Beatrice 21
Agnes 3	Amelia 11	Bernice 4
Alberta 20	Amy 3	Bertha 17
Alice 28	Anna 34	Bessie 31

Southern Cities: 1877 to 1937 - MONTGOMERY, ALABAMA (& COLUMBUS, MISSISSIPPI)

Betty 8	Grace 6	May 13
Blanche 2	Hannah 4	Margaret 13
Caroline 8	Harriet 2	Martha 25
Carolyn 2	Hattie 37	Mary 225
Carrie 32	Hazel 1	Mildred 7
Catharine 20	Helen 2	Milly 11
Celia 7	Henrietta 8	Minerva 3
Charity 4	Hester 3	Minnie 30
Charlotte 8	Ida 33	Molly 15
Clara 17	Inez 5	Myrtle 6
Cleo 4	Irene 12	Nancy 16
Cora 12	Irma 5	Nanny 3
Daisy 13	Isabelle 2	Nelly 20
Delia 5	Jane 9	Patience 1
Dorothy 8	Jessie 13	Patsy 8
Edith 2	Josephine 21	Pauline 6
Edna 11	Juanita 7	Pearl 24
Effie 9	Katy 15	Peggy 3
Eleanor 3	Laura 22	Phillis 4
Ella 36	Lavinia 2	Polly 7
Eliza 25	Lena 9	Priscilla 5
Elizabeth 40	Leola 10	Rachel 11
Ellen 23	Lillian 12	Rebecca 32
Eloise 5	Lillie 36	Rosa 56
Elsie 5	Lizzie 40	Rose 11
Elvira 1	Lois 1	Ruby 11
Emily 7	Louisa 5	Ruth 12
Emma 56	Lucille 20	Sadie 9
Ernestine 1	Louise 20	Sally 32
Essie 18	Lucy 32	Sarah 31
Esther 2	Lula 47	Sophia 3
Ethel 24	Mabel 7	Susan 4
Eunice 1	Maggie 20	Susie 29
Eva 2	Malinda 5	Thelma 2
Evelyn 6	Mamie 23	Venus 1
Fanny 49	Marguerite 5	Viola 20
Florence 18	Maria 7	Violet 2
Frances 18	Marie 15	Virginia 14
Geneva 5	Marion 1	Vivian 2
Georgia 29	Matilda 5	Willie 33
Gertrude 12	Mattie 76	Willie Mae 16
Gladys 4	Maude 2	Winney 5

FEMALE
Frequency

Mary 225	Lula 47	Anna 34
Annie 104	Elizabeth 40	Ida 33
Mattie 76	Lizzie 40	Willie 33
Emma 56	Hattie 37	Carrie 32
Rosa 56	Ella 36	Lucy 32
Fanny 49	Lillie 36	Rebecca 32

Southern Cities: 1877 to 1937 - MONTGOMERY, ALABAMA (& COLUMBUS, MISSISSIPPI)

Sally 32	Gertrude 12	Malinda 5
Bessie 31	Irene 12	Marguerite 5
Sarah 31	Lillian 12	Matilda 5
Minnie 30	Ruth 12	Priscilla 5
Georgia 29	Amelia 11	Bernice 4
Susie 29	Edna 11	Charity 4
Alice 28	Milly 11	Cleo 4
Louise 28	Rachel 11	Gladys 4
Eliza 25	Rose 11	Hannah 4
Martha 25	Ruby 11	Phillis 4
Amanda 24	Leola 10	Susan 4
Ethel 24	Effie 9	Agnes 3
Pearl 24	Jane 9	Amy 3
Ellen 23	Lena 9	Eleanor 3
Mamie 23	Sadie 9	Hester 3
Laura 22	Alma 8	Minerva 3
Beatrice 21	Betty 8	Nanny 3
Josephine 21	Caroline 8	Peggy 3
Alberta 20	Charlotte 8	Sophia 3
Catharine 20	Dorothy 8	Winney 3
Lucille 20	Henrietta 8	Blanche 2
Maggie 20	Patsy 8	Carolyn 2
Nelly 20	Addie 7	Edith 2
Viola 20	Celia 7	Esther 2
Essie 18	Emily 7	Eva 2
Florence 18	Juanita 7	Harriet 2
Frances 18	Mabel 7	Helen 2
Bertha 17	Mildred 7	Isabella 2
Clara 17	Polly 7	Lavinia 2
Nancy 16	Evelyn 6	Maude 2
Willie Mae 16	Grace 6	Thelma 2
Katy 15	Myrtle 6	Violet 2
Marie 15	Pauline 6	Vivian 2
Molly 15	Adaline 5	Elvira 1
Lucinda 14	Delia 5	Ernestine 1
Virginia 14	Eloise 5	Eunice 1
Daisy 13	Elsie 5	Hazel 1
Jessie 13	Geneva 5	Lois 1
Margaret 13	Inez 5	Marion 1
May 13	Irma 5	Patience 1
Cora 12	Louisa 5	Venus 1

Surnames, Black, 1933

Alphabetical (Sample: 20,500)

Abercrombie 8	Andrews 27	Bailey 47
Adams 55	Armstrong 23	Baker 27
Alexander 29	Arrington 41	Baldwin 16
Allen 74	Atkins 8	Bandy 16
Anderson 55	Austin 9	Banks 31

Southern Cities: 1877 to 1937 - MONTGOMERY, ALABAMA (& COLUMBUS, MISSISSIPPI)

Barnes 26	Evans 69	Judkins 36
Barnett 32	Farris 19	Kelly 31
Beasley 26	Felder 66	Kennedy 24
Bell 69	Fields 19	King 41
Bennett 13	Fisher 5	Knight 20
Berry 38	Flowers 29	Lawrence 18
Bibb 57	Floyd 24	Lee 131
Bilser 28	Foster 48	Lewis 214
Bimbo 5	Franklin 47	Long 24
Blackman 11	Freeman 42	Lucas 30
Booker 6	Fuller 10	Mack 26
Boyd 41	Gaines 9	Marshall 34
Bradley 12	Gardner 31	Martin 64
Brooks 32	Garrett 25	Mason 11
Brown 318	Gibson 29	Matthews 45
Bryant 28	Goodwin 10	May 36
Burch 23	Gordon 14	McCall 45
Burke 23	Graham 56	McDonald 16
Burrell 9	Grant 31	McQueen 47
Burton 14	Gray 40	Miller 42
Bush 18	Green 163	Mitchell 68
Butcher 6	Grey 9	Montgomery 11
Butler 20	Griffin 25	Moore 104
Byrd 26	Hall 135	Morgan 34
Calhoun 51	Hamilton 51	Morris 23
Calloway 36	Hammond 5	Moss 26
Campbell 28	Hardy 46	Murphy 44
Carter 116	Harper 7	Murray 23
Clark 31	Harris 283	Myers 14
Clayton 28	Harrison 19	Nelson 33
Cobb 32	Harvey 31	Nichols 15
Coleman 43	Hawkins 18	Oliver 38
Collins 38	Hayes 25	Owens 26
Cook 29	Henderson 76	Parker 28
Cooper 32	Henry 18	Parks 23
Cotton 24	Hicks 27	Patterson 38
Cox 12	Hill 103	Payne 23
Crawford 23	Holmes 22	Perry 27
Cummings 5	Holt 22	Phillips 38
Daniels 39	Hooks 17	Pickett 55
Dawson 22	Hopkins 6	Pierce 17
Davis 253	Howard 103	Porter 26
Day 15	Hudson 16	Powell 74
Dean 18	Hunter 48	Price 29
Demus 7	Ivory 14	Randolph 6
Dickerson 17	Jackson 394	Ray 11
Dillard 22	James 72	Reed 39
Dixon 15	Jefferson 23	Reese 39
Dudley 18	Jenkins 44	Reid 6
Edwards 58	Johnson 452	Reynolds 30
Ellis 36	Jones 326	Richardson 34
Ephriam 24	Jordon 79	Rivers 13

Southern Cities: 1877 to 1937 - MONTGOMERY, ALABAMA (& COLUMBUS, MISSISSIPPI)

Roberts 11	Smith 341	Watson 61
Robertson 50	Stephens 14	Ward 21
Robinson 164	Stevens 7	Warren 35
Rogers 38	Stewart 44	Washington 106
Ross 42	Stokes 28	Watts 27
Russell 16	Taylor 196	Webb 31
Sanders 59	Thomas 326	Webster 13
Scott 121	Thompson 49	West 10
Sellers 39	Thornton 8	White 103
Sharp 27	Tucker 10	Williams 702
Sharpe 18	Turner 65	Willis 31
Shelton 7	Vaughan 16	Wilson 117
Simmons 37	Wade 11	Wood 11
Simms 5	Walker 104	Woods 25
Singleton 25	Wallace 32	Wright 117
Sippial 8	Watkins 48	Young 71

Frequency

Williams 702	Mitchell 68	Boyd 41
Johnson 452	Felder 66	King 41
Jackson 394	Turner 65	Gray 40
Smith 341	Martin 64	Daniels 39
Jones 326	Watson 61	Reed 39
Thomas 326	Sanders 59	Reese 39
Brown 318	Edwards 58	Sellers 39
Harris 283	Bibb 57	Berry 38
Davis 253	Graham 56	Collins 38
Lewis 214	Adams 55	Oliver 38
Taylor 196	Anderson 55	Patterson 38
Robinson 164	Pickett 55	Phillips 38
Green 163	Calhoun 51	Rogers 38
Hall 135	Hamilton 51	Simmons 37
Lee 131	Robertson 50	Calloway 36
Scott 121	Thompson 49	Ellis 36
Wilson 117	Foster 48	Judkins 36
Wright 117	Hunter 48	May 36
Carter 116	Watkins 48	Warren 35
Washington 106	Bailey 47	Marshall 34
Moore 104	Franklin 47	Morgan 34
Walker 104	McQueen 47	Richardson 34
Hill 103	Hardy 46	Nelson 33
Howard 103	Matthews 45	Barnett 32
White 103	McCall 45	Brooks 32
Jordon 79	Jenkins 44	Cobb 32
Henderson 76	Murphy 44	Cooper 32
Allen 74	Stewart 44	Wallace 32
Powell 74	Coleman 43	Banks 31
James 72	Freeman 42	Clark 31
Young 71	Miller 42	Gardner 31
Bell 69	Ross 42	Grant 31
Evans 69	Arrington 41	Harvey 31

Southern Cities: 1877 to 1937 - MONTGOMERY, ALABAMA (& COLUMBUS, MISSISSIPPI)

Kelly 31	Murray 23	Ray 11
Webb 31	Parks 23	Roberts 11
Willis 31	Payne 23	Wade 11
Lucas 30	Dawson 22	Wood 11
Reynolds 30	Dillard 22	Fuller 10
Alexander 29	Holmes 22	Goodwin 10
Cook 29	Holt 22	Tucker 10
Flowers 29	Ward 21	West 10
Gibson 29	Butler 20	Austin 9
Price 29	Knight 20	Burrell 9
Bilser 28	Farris 19	Gaines 9
Bryant 28	Fields 19	Grey 9
Campbell 28	Harrison 19	Abercrombie 8
Clayton 28	Bush 18	Atkins 8
Parker 28	Dean 18	Sippial 8
Stokes 28	Dudley 18	Thornton 8
Andrews 27	Hawkins 18	Demus 7
Baker 27	Henry 18	Harper 7
Hicks 27	Lawrence 18	Shelton 7
Perry 27	Sharpe 18	Stevens 7
Sharp 27	Dickerson 17	Booker 6
Watts 27	Hooks 17	Butcher 6
Barnes 26	Pierce 17	Hopkins 6
Beasley 26	Baldwin 16	Randolph 6
Byrd 26	Bandy 16	Reid 6
Mack 26	Hudson 16	Bimbo 5
Moss 26	McDonald 16	Cummings 5
Owens 26	Russell 16	Fisher 5
Porter 26	Vaughan 16	Hammond 5
Garrett 25	Day 15	Simms 5
Griffin 25	Dixon 15	Fleming 4
Hayes 25	Nichols 15	Fletcher 4
Singleton 25	Burton 14	Hart 4
Woods 25	Gordon 14	Morse 4
Cotton 24	Ivory 14	Paige 4
Ephriam 24	Myers 14	Saunders 4
Floyd 24	Stephens 14	Coles 3
Kennedy 24	Bennett 13	Elliott 3
Long 24	Rivers 13	Ferguson 3
Armstrong 23	Webster 13	Holland 3
Burch 23	Bradley 12	Polk 3
Burke 23	Cox 12	Clarke 2
Crawford 23	Blackman 11	Greene 2
Jefferson 23	Mason 11	Holloway 2
Morris 23	Montgomery 11	Morton 2

Southern Cities: 1877 to 1937 - MONTGOMERY, ALABAMA (& COLUMBUS, MISSISSIPPI)

Surnames, White, 1933

Alphabetical (Sample: 29,500)

Abercrombie 10	Coker 27	Griffin 44
Adams 73	Coleman 28	Groves 1
Alexander 16	Collins 51	Hall 112
Allen 73	Cook 84	Hamilton 30
Anderson 76	Cooper 64	Hammond 11
Andrews 46	Cotton 14	Hardy 18
Armstrong 40	Cox 62	Harper 27
Arrington 16	Crawford 33	Harris 54
Atkins 2	Cummings 9	Harrison 55
Austin 14	Daniels 10	Hart 9
Baggett 35	Davis 208	Harvey 12
Bailey 50	Dawson 25	Hawkins 40
Baker 36	Day 25	Hayes 19
Baldwin 13	Dean 51	Haynie 20
Banks 10	Dickerson 8	Henderson 39
Barnes 54	Dillard 22	Henry 9
Barnett 35	Dixon 19	Hicks 26
Beasley 52	Donovan 18	Hill 90
Bell 57	Douglass 9	Holland 16
Bennett 9	Dudley 14	Holloway 22
Berry 21	Edwards 59	Holmes 20
Bibb 8	Elliott 20	Holt 35
Bilser 11	Ellis 35	Hopkins 10
Black 42	Evans 54	Howard 61
Blackman 6	Farris 18	Hudson 53
Boyd 58	Felder 7	Hunter 11
Bradley 21	Ferguson 8	Jackson 89
Brooks 57	Fields 7	James 36
Brown 177	Fisher 11	Jefferson 3
Bryant 37	Fleming 11	Jenkins 37
Burch 13	Fletcher 10	Johnson 242
Burke 15	Flowers 22	Jones 328
Burrell 1	Floyd 17	Jordan 56
Burton 18	Foster 57	Judkins 10
Bush 28	Franklin 24	Katy 19
Butler 39	Freeman 26	Kelly 42
Byrd 22	Fuller 72	Kennedy 28
Calhoun 10	Gaines 9	King 66
Callahan 9	Gardner 81	Knight 40
Calloway 10	Garrett 22	Lawrence 40
Campbell 56	Gibson 10	Lewis 70
Carrigan 8	Goodwin 32	Loeb 39
Cauthen 23	Gordon 25	Long 31
Clark 74	Graham 32	Lucas 14
Clarke 14	Grant 35	Marshall 25
Clayton 19	Gray 27	Martin 90
Cobb 22	Green 36	Mason 17
Cohen 15	Greene 20	Matthews 21

Southern Cities: 1877 to 1937 - MONTGOMERY, ALABAMA (& COLUMBUS, MISSISSIPPI)

Max 29	Price 48	Stewart 53
McCall 11	Procter 4	Stokes 19
McDonald 41	Randolph 7	Sullivan 40
McQueen 14	Ray 44	Taylor 153
Miller 97	Reed 7	Thomas 86
Mitchell 47	Reese 20	Thompson 106
Montgomery 13	Reid 14	Thornton 47
Moore 106	Reynolds 69	Tucker 31
Morgan 62	Richardson 27	Turner 62
Morris 42	Ridgeley 3	Vaughan 44
Moss 9	Rivers 9	Wade 10
Murphy 34	Roberts 43	Walker 99
Murray 22	Robertson 39	Wallace 35
Myers 13	Robinson 41	Ward 46
Nelson 38	Rogers 49	Warren 32
Nichols 39	Ross 29	Washington 6
O'Connor 12	Russell 34	Watkins 14
Oliver 28	Sanders 23	Watson 53
Owens 25	Saunders 14	Watts 32
Paige 5	Scott 94	Webb 36
Parker 76	Sellers 55	Webster 6
Parks 13	Sharp 13	Weil 38
Patterson 25	Sharpe 10	West 26
Payne 25	Shelkofsky 15	White 74
Penn 2	Shelton 12	Williams 218
Perry 63	Simmons 29	Willis 15
Phillips 27	Simms 4	Wilson 145
Pickett 37	Singleton 27	Wood 35
Pierce 15	Smith 338	Woods 35
Porter 18	Stephens 26	Wright 53
Powell 67	Stevens 17	Young 53

Frequency

Smith 338	Cook 84	Howard 61
Jones 328	Gardner 81	Edwards 59
Johnson 242	Anderson 76	Boyd 58
Williams 218	Parker 76	Bell 57
Davis 208	Clark 74	Brooks 57
Brown 177	White 74	Foster 57
Taylor 153	Adams 73	Campbell 56
Wilson 145	Allen 73	Jordan 56
Hall 112	Fuller 72	Harrison 55
Moore 106	Lewis 70	Sellers 55
Thompson 106	Reynolds 69	Barnes 54
Walker 99	Powell 67	Evans 54
Miller 97	King 66	Harris 54
Scott 94	Cooper 64	Hudson 53
Hill 90	Perry 63	Stewart 53
Martin 90	Cox 62	Watson 53
Jackson 89	Morgan 62	Wright 53
Thomas 86	Turner 62	Young 53

Southern Cities: 1877 to 1937 - MONTGOMERY, ALABAMA (& COLUMBUS, MISSISSIPPI)

Beasley 52	Watts 32	Burton 18
Carter 52	Long 31	Donovan 18
Collins 51	Tucker 31	Farris 18
Dean 51	Hamilton 30	Hardy 18
Bailey 50	May 29	Porter 18
Rogers 49	Ross 29	Floyd 17
Price 48	Simmons 29	Mason 17
Mitchell 47	Bush 28	Stevens 17
Thornton 47	Coleman 28	Alexander 16
Andrews 46	Kennedy 28	Arrington 16
Ward 46	Oliver 28	Holland 16
Griffin 44	Coker 27	Burke 15
Ray 44	Gray 27	Cohen 15
Vaughan 44	Harper 27	Pierce 15
Roberts 43	Phillips 27	Shelkofsky 15
Black 42	Richardson 27	Willis 15
Kelly 42	Singleton 27	Austin 14
Morris 42	Freeman 26	Clarke 14
McDonald 41	Hicks 26	Cotton 14
Robinson 41	Stephens 26	Dudley 14
Armstrong 40	West 26	Lucas 14
Hawkins 40	Dawson 25	McQueen 14
Knight 40	Day 25	Reid 14
Lawrence 40	Gordon 25	Saunders 14
Sullivan 40	Marshall 25	Watkins 14
Butler 39	Owens 25	Baldwin 13
Henderson 39	Patterson 25	Burch 13
Loeb 39	Payne 25	Montgomery 13
Nichols 39	Franklin 24	Myers 13
Robertson 39	Cauthen 23	Parks 13
Nelson 38	Sanders 23	Sharp 13
Weil 38	Byrd 22	Harvey 12
Bryant 37	Cobb 22	O'Connor 12
Jenkins 37	Dillard 22	Shelton 12
Pickett 37	Flowers 22	Bilser 11
Baker 36	Garrett 22	Fisher 11
Green 36	Holloway 22	Fleming 11
James 36	Murray 22	Hammond 11
Webb 36	Berry 21	Hunter 11
Baggett 35	Bradley 21	McCall 11
Barnett 35	Matthews 21	Abercrombie 10
Ellis 35	Woods 21	Banks 10
Grant 35	Elliott 20	Calhoun 10
Holt 35	Greene 20	Calloway 10
Wallace 35	Haynie 20	Daniels 10
Wood 35	Holmes 20	Fletcher 10
Murphy 34	Reese 20	Gibson 10
Russell 34	Clayton 19	Hopkins 10
Crawford 33	Dixon 19	Judkins 10
Goodwin 32	Hayes 19	Sharpe 10
Graham 32	Katy 19	Wade 10
Warren 32	Stokes 19	Bennett 9
		Callahan 9

267

Southern Cities: 1877 to 1937 - MONTGOMERY, ALABAMA (& COLUMBUS, MISSISSIPPI)

Cummings 9	Dickerson 8	Paige 5
Douglass 9	Ferguson 8	Procter 4
Gaines 9	Felder 7	Simms 4
Hart 9	Fields 7	Jefferson 3
Henry 9	Randolph 7	Ridgeley 3
Moss 9	Reed 7	Atkins 2
Rivers 9	Blackman 6	Penn 2
Bibb 8	Washington 6	Burrell 1
Carrigan 8	Webster 6	Groves 1

Unusual Names, Black

Male, 1899

Abe	Duke	Kit
Abram	Dummy	Lawyer
Adam	Dutch	Leak
Adolphus	Early	Lem
Alex	Eleazar	Levi
Americus	Eli	Leviticus
Ananias	Elijah	Link
Artee	Enon	Linsy
Asa	Ephraim	Lonnie
August	Fate	Loveless
Bamma	Florida	Major
Booker	Freeman	Mamsa
Bose	Frenchy	Mando
Brogg	Gabe	Manoc
Buck	Gable	Manse
Burly	Gabriel	Mat
Caesar	Gallilee	Minger
Cain	General	Mingo
Caleb	Gib	Mordecai
Calep	Givy	Mose
Calip	Hamp	Napoleon
Canvas	Handy	Nat
Cap	Heard	Ned
Cape	Hercules	Nero
Captain	Horace	Neuda
Cedar	Isaiah	Noah
Cicero	Isham	Nub
Cloddy	Jailus	Nun
Columbus	January	Orange
Crede	J C	Osceola
Creed	Jed	Paris
Cupid	Jerdie	Patron
Dink	Josh	Peter
Dock	Joshua	Philandus
Doke	Josiah	Pious
Dublin	Judge	Pleas
Duffie	King	Pleasant

Southern Cities: 1877 to 1937 - MONTGOMERY, ALABAMA (& COLUMBUS, MISSISSIPPI)

Pompey	Shadrach	Talls
Primus	Shedrick	Tanny
Primus, Jr.	Sigh	Tap
Prophet	Silas	Titus
Rafe	Simmie	Tobe
Rapie	Singer	Tobias
Reedy	Sip	Vassar
Rias	Smart	Verine
Rome	Soloman	Victor
Sandy	Sonny	Virgil
Scipio	Sparrow	Wash
Sebe	Square	Wesley
Seve	Squire	Xerxes
Shack	St. Paul	Zeb

Male, 1920

Aaron	Dungu	Kiah
Abe	Early	King
Ace	Eleaver	Kit
Acie	Eli	Lazarus
Adam	Eliza	Leak
Alabama	Emanuel	Lemon
America	Enoch	Lemuel
Americus	Ephraim	Levi
Ananias	Eprezel	Lige
Argo	Erin	Lisbon
Bloom	Ermine	Lonnie
Booker	Esau	Lum
Bose	Europe	Major
Bruga	Ezekiel	Malachi
Buck	Ezra	McKinley
Caesar	Festus	Mercy
Caffa	Fortune	Milo
Cap	Gaddie	Monk
Capitola	Garfield	Morrisette
Captain	General	Moses
Cathie	Gentle	Napoleon
Cato	Glouchester	Nat
Charming	Green	Neater
Cicero	Handsome	Nehemiah
Clonezer	Handy	Nero
Cola	Hercules	Noah
Colonel	Hezekiah	Ocie
Columbus	Ihady	Ocy
Cupid	Isaac	Ozie
Curley	Isaiah	Parlor
Daddy	Isom	Pet
Demp	Jettie	Peyton
Doc	Jonas	Pink
Dock	Joshua	Pleasant
Dub	Kence	Pliney

Southern Cities: 1877 to 1937 - MONTGOMERY, ALABAMA (& COLUMBUS, MISSISSIPPI)

Plute	Shack	Tilly
Pompey	Shed	Tobe
Primus	Silas	Tobias
Prince	Smart	Tullis
Professor	Sol	Ulysses
Quinter	Solomon	Vassar
Ransom	Squire	Velvet
Rasmus	Sug	Vohn
Rizz	Tampa	Wade
Roman	Tap	Zachary
Romie	Tapey	Zeb
Roosevelt	Teacher	Zebron
Sandy	Thearthur	Zek
Sank	Theophilus	Zeke
		Zimmie

Male, 1933

Abe Abram	Ebb	Lafayette
Alabama 2	Elcana	Lazarus
Aladin	Eldra	Laze
Alduffie	Elzy	Leak
Alfonzia	Erastus	LeGrand
Alto	Esco	Lennie
Andre 2	Eskiview	Lexiux
Angelo	Essie	Lige
Antonio 2	Ezzie	Lisbon
Artesius	Fate	Lock
Arvelle	Fenna	Lon
Bark	Fester	Lonzie
Bleu	Freeny	Love
Bodie	Gabel	Loveless
Bosie	Gabre	Malachi
Bout	Gadis	Manuel
Boysie	General Jackson	Miley
Bragie	Gentile	Milo
Bride	Glydon	Modiste
Brutus	Goin	Monk
Cathey	Hammie	Naaman
Cephus	Handy	Naulbert
Champ	Hence	Nehemiah
Cleophas	Hercules	Nemroy
Cread	Hula	Nero
Creek	Israel 2	Nimmie
Culasket	Italy	Noah
Curley	J. P.	Nolie
Cute	Jethro	Ocie 2
Dade	Jett	Ossie
Dedie	Jobe	Otho
Derry	Jonas	Ozy
Dunge	Josh	Parlor
Dunk	Jupiter	Parse

Southern Cities: 1877 to 1937 - MONTGOMERY, ALABAMA (& COLUMBUS, MISSISSIPPI)

Phamous	Shack	Toby
Pherrie	Shade	Tyree
Pirmous	Shadrack	Urias
Pleasant	Sicily	Valentine
Plent	Silver	Vashti
Pluie	Smilie	Vesty
Quintus	Social	Vice
Rad	Sol 2	Waddie
Raspberry	Son	Wade
Real	Sonnie	Waery
Roman	Squire	Wrazie
Roosevelt	Suite	Zebe
Rovine	Tampie	Zebedee
Rozelle	Tiny	Zebulon
Saul	Tip	Zid
		Zore

Female, 1899

Adelpha	Eveline	Obie
Amanda	Florida	Paralee
Amity	Fredonia	Patience
Anezer	Gussie	Patient
Artamissa	Hulda	Pennie
Barnella	Jette	Pet
Beckie	Judia	Petronia
Bird	Kisia	Philis
Birdie	Lizzie	Phoebe
Brandona	Letha	Phyliss
Camilla	Lettia	Pink
Candis	Lida	Pinkie
Captora	Lina	Posie
Carlina	Littie	Priscilla
Cassie	Lizinkle	Pruty
Cely	Lolo	Queen
Charity	Love	Rantha
Cherry	Lovenia	Rena
Cicely	Lucinda	Rhoda
Clarisy	Ludie	Rhodie
Crecy	Luvenia	Savannah
Daphne	Lyda	Savilla
Delpha	Mahala	Selina
Dicie	Malissa	Serena
Dilcy	Mariah	Silena
Dinah	Matilda	Silla
Donie	Missouri	Sina
Easter	Mittie	Spinkey
Elvira	Moaning	Stina
Elzora	Moddie	Sylvania
Emeline	Nervy	Tamar
Epsy	Nica	Tempie
Erin	Novie	Tena

Southern Cities: 1877 to 1937 - MONTGOMERY, ALABAMA (& COLUMBUS, MISSISSIPPI)

Tina	Verbena	Winnie
Tinkie	Vinie	Zela
		Zilpha

Female, 1920

Adelphia	Frona	Otilie
Alabama	Forney	Ovetta
Alto	Gabrella	Parthenia
Amanda	Gussie	Patience
Angeline	Hager	Pearlie
Arizona	Hermenia	Pennie
Arminta	Hinnie	Phenie
Arriana	Jense	Phyllis
Artu	Kansas	Pinkey
Azalie	Keziah	Priscilla
Babe	Kiah	Queen
Bama	Kizzie	Quenetta
Bazille	Lavonia	Rhetta
Binah	Ledger	Robenia
Callie	Le Grand	Rosebud
Camilla	Leota	Saphronia
Caressa	Lettia	Scrappy
Cassie	Louisiana	Selina
Charity	Love	Septha
Chistee	Lovie	Sigurna
Clarissa	Lucinda	Silla
Cormilla	Mahala	Sudie
Dahlia	Maisie	Tabbie
December	Malinda	Tannie
Deva	Mandy	Tatie
Diana	Maria	Tempie
Dicie	Matilda	Tena
Dillie	Mealy	Texas
Dilsie	Melinda	Tina
Dinah	Melvina	Truzella
Dovey	Meta	Vashti
Easter	Missie	Venus
Eliza	Missouri	Viney
Elmetta	Mittie	Winnie
Ermine	Murilla	Wottie
Essaline	Myrtaline	Zannie
Eva	Narcissus	Zelma
Evalina	Nicey	Zidie
Exie	Nicola	Zilplyon
Florida	Nonie	Zollie
Flossie	Odelia	

Female, 1933

Addis	Alabama 7	Alflorence
Agah	Alethia	Alinez

Southern Cities: 1877 to 1937 - MONTGOMERY, ALABAMA (& COLUMBUS, MISSISSIPPI)

Almeda	Donella	Kissie
Almetta	Dorie	Lavenia
Alwilder	Doshia	Leasure
Amertine	Dumpie	Lellie
Anona	Earsie	Lemmie
Antoinette	Eddie	Leontine
Ardelia	Elgartha	Lessie
Areta	Elgirtha	Lessio
Arie 2	Epsie	Letitia
Arlie	Era 2	Levonia
Arrie	Erminie	Linda
Arsula	Ersie	Littie
Arta	Ettie	Lonia
Arthurine 2	Eulene	Lorella
Arwolds	Evangeline	Loretha
Australia	Evelena	Louisiana
Azalie	Evergreen	Louvenia
Bama	Fair	Love
Bela	Fizar	Lovey
Berla	Florene	Lovie 3
Bethalena	Flozell	Luana
Birda	Flutsie	Lucine
Bloom	Fredonia	Luckie
Bloxie	Fronnia	Lugenia
Brondina	Gabriella	Lurline
Camillo	Gillie	Luwenia
Candas	Girlie	Luvenia
Candie	Goldbeam	Luverne
Canneta	Gurseal	Luvina
Cannie	Habie	Luvira
Caponia	Havannah	Luvisa
Caressa	Haysal	Luwilla
Ceola	Hermenia	Lyzola
Cindy	Hiawatha	Macedonia
Chaddie	Honey	Macie
Charlene	Hoxie	Marcella
Classie	Hyacinth	Marossie
Clementine	Irazetta	Mattline
Cloybelle	Isephense	Mavis
Collie	Isophine 2	Miril
Columbiana	Izola	Missie
Creasy	Janetta	Modelle
Cressie	Jeffie	Monnie
Dahlia	Jenna	Mosetta
Darnella	Jensie	Mozetta
Decie	Jerusha	Nanetta
Delphine	Jettie	Naomia
Dequilla	Jewette	Nathia
Dicey	Joy	Nerissa
Dickie	Jule	Nicie
Dilcie	Kansas	Noma
Doll	Kinnie	Nona

Southern Cities: 1877 to 1937 - MONTGOMERY, ALABAMA (& COLUMBUS, MISSISSIPPI)

Nonie	Quentine	Tex
Norval	Reaver	Thenie
Nurcie	Rellie	Tina 2
Octave	Rena	Tinie
Ole	Renna	Tizzer
Onada	Retha	Tobie
Orellie	Richetta	Topsie
Oriah	Rilla	Tossie
Ornee	Rillia	Truzelle
Osa	Rita	Tusie
Oshell	Rochelle 4	Twilda
Ossie	Rozena	Veldora
Othelia	Salina	Velsoria
Otillia	Samella	Venus
Ottie	Sanella	Verdelle
Pansy	Savilla	Vic
Paralee	Segeina	Vicie
Pastorie	Selena	Victorice
Pecola 2	Selina	Vida
Penny 2	Sennia	Vina
Percilla	Shady	Vinia
Petronella	Shula	Vinnie
Phenia	Smithie	Vinus
Philandi	Sophie	Virgin
Philippa	Sudie 4	Wealthy
Phoebe	Surener	Willola
Pixie	Sweet	Wymon
Plessie	Sweetie 2	Zelia
Pocohantas	Sylvania	Zilla
Portalie	Tabitha	Zora
Predensie	Talitha	Zore
Prevelle	Tannie	Zova 2
Primrose	Tarsher	Zula
		Zuline

Unusual Names, White

Male, 1899

Aaron	Eli	Leander
Abe	Elijah	Lemuel
Abraham Behr	Elisha	Leonidas
Absalom	Emanuel	Lorenzo
Cad	Enoch	Luke
Capus	Ephraim	Malachi
Cephas	Ezra	Marcellus
Christian	Green	Michigan
Darling	Isaac Block	Mose
Dilmos	Jeremiah	Moses
Dionysius	Josiah	Moses Behr
Dock	Laban	Moses Block

Southern Cities: 1877 to 1937 - MONTGOMERY, ALABAMA (& COLUMBUS, MISSISSIPPI)

Nimrod	Ransom	Timothy
Noa	Royal	Valentine
Noble	Rush	Wade
Osceola	Sherry	Zachariah
Peyton	Shy	Zacharias
Phares	Solomon Behr	Zadoc
Pleasant	Tinie	

Male, 1920

Aaron	Gathra	Philemon
Atlas	Gensie	Phillipa
Atticus	Gideon	Pleasant
August	Hazzy	Ral
Berto	Israel	Reedy
Bijie	Jeptha	Romeo
Bird	Joshua	Romulus
Bodie	Jude	Rufus
Buck	Judge	Singer
Cato	Junie	Sol
Cephas	Junius	Spurgeon
Chelsea	Justus	Stork
Columbus	Laxie	Tandy
Cosette	Leonida	Urie
Crescent	Leonidas	Urquhart
Darius	Lexie	Valentine
Dolos	Lonnie	Vanezzer
Early	Lot	Velatta
Eldno	Low	Virgil
Eli	Malachi	Wanda
Eliza	Micajah	Zeddie
Elzy	Nimrod	Zeka
Entha	Noah	Zemmie
Exa	Orlando	Zeno
Ezekial 2	Osceola	Zeo
Fonda	Peak	Zeltbie
		Zolly

Male, 1933

Alabama	Bijie	Cy
Alex	Bluff	Denzie
Almond	Bog	Devotion
Alto	Cairo	Diamond
Amangus	Cave	Dock
Argo	Chellie	Duffie
Arvid	Cicero	Early
Arzo	Cobie	Echo
Asa	Colon	Elisha 2
Atlas	Commodore	Ellie
Bela	Coon	Ellmaevous
Beniah	Coy	Elly

Southern Cities: 1877 to 1937 - MONTGOMERY, ALABAMA (& COLUMBUS, MISSISSIPPI)

Elmo	Kolie	Polie
Elonza	Koran	Potice
Emanuel	Labon	Pride
Ennis	Lanoyd	Pyron
Ephraim	Latona	Romeo
Ephy	Lavarius	Romulus
Era	Lemon	Royal
Erastus	Lenia	Simeon
Etowah	Lexie	Smiley
Eural	Love	Sol
Eureka	Lucious	Squire
Ezra	Lummie	Tandy
Fate	Lussie	Teddis
Floy	Magnus	Tobias
Fonza	Malachi	Toledo
Gideon	Mallie	Toofie
Hercules	Menza	Truss
Hobbie	Mirileau	Ulysses
Holland	Moses	Uriah
Inzer	Napoleon	Vasco
Ivie	Nimrod 2	Velatti
Jabe	Nobie	Vonceil
Jepsy	Noble	Vonnie
Jeptha	Nollie	Welcome
Jodie	Oce	Wice
Jonah 2	Onie	Zary
Judge	Oroon	Zeddie
Jules	Osce	Zedekiah
Junior	Other	Zell
Justice	Oyer	Zema
Kaga	Pennie	Zerrel
Ketto	Pick	Zid
King	Pliny	Zollie

Female, 1899

Abarena	Dazell	Leah
Agatha	Deborah	Leta
Aletha	Delena	Lovie
Alief	Desdemona	Lucinda
Almarine	Doica	Lucretia
Amangus	Donie	Malinda
Arcada	Easter	Marina
Aurora	Elvie	Matilda
Birdie	Evalina	Melissa
Camilla	Florida	Melvina
Cassie	Frankie	Mena
Celina	Hettie	Minerva
Clarissa	Inda	Missouri
Claytonia	Kiziah	Mittie
Corinthy	Ladie	Musidora
Cottie	Lavonia	Ora

Southern Cities: 1877 to 1937 - MONTGOMERY, ALABAMA (& COLUMBUS, MISSISSIPPI)

Pari Lee	Rotha	Valeria
Parolee	Salina	Venie
Parthenia	Sammie	Willie
Patience	Saphronia	Zara
Penelope	Serima	Zillie
Philippa	Semiramis	Zilpah
Prinnie	Sophia	Zula
Rosine	Tabitha	

Female, 1920

Alima	Jettie	Rozelle
Alpha	Johness	Salatha
Alta	Lerah	Salemma
Aroezena	Liberia	Samuella
Babette	Liona	Serena
Bamma	Lulleane	Sophia
Birdie	Luna	Sophie
Blondina	Lunetta	Sudie
Buna	Lurline	Theodosia
Celena	Lutie	Topie
Clauselle	Lynette	Trasilla
Clementina	Macedonia	Typhene
Cleone	Malinda	Una
Clerah	Matelenis	Venetia
Consuelo	Melissa	Vida
Cullie	Menla	Watha
Dera	Minerva	Wilhemina
Dimple	Minnesota	Willula
Dorinda	Mozelle	Winnie
Dressa	Nadine	Winona
Eizette	Nealtha	Wynona
Etruria	Nevada	Wyolene
Eulalia	Nozelle	Zara
Exa	Odesso	Zelena
Flossie	Oella	Zellee
Frankie	Omie	Zena
Gera	Ottillie	Zerline
Hannah	Ozella	Zoe
Icie	Ovie	Zora
Imogene	Pamela	Zorra
Jeilee	Permelia	Zudie
		Zula

Female, 1933

Abrena	Alpha	Annala
Aili	Althea	Annulette
Alazanah	Alzie 2	Ardelia
Albur	Amanda	Artemesia
Aleana	Amber	Artie
Alfrances	Ammie	Attie

Southern Cities: 1877 to 1937 - MONTGOMERY, ALABAMA (& COLUMBUS, MISSISSIPPI)

Ava	Frankie	Mineola
Avis	Fredanna	Modelle
Azzie	Genoa	Modest
Bama 2	Glycine	Mona
Bina	Goldie 3	Monzora
Birdie	Gussie	Motine
Blondina	Hassie	Musette
Bonnie 2	Hixie	Myrteline
Brina	Icye	Nadie
Brittie	Idelia	Nadine
Buena	Idonia 2	Nannie
Cammie	Imena	Narcissa
Capitola	Imer	Natala
Cappie	India	Nelder
Cassie	Inee	Nep
Chebis	Isla	Neva
Clauselle	Isophine	Nevada
Cleona	Izora	Nitus
Clotilde	Jimetta	Nob
Clydie	Josia	Norine
Cudella	Juelda	Ocy
Dannie	Kimmie	Odessa
Debbie	Lantie	Odette
Deda	Lavada	Oella
De Vera	Lavolia	Omera
Dewilda	Lennie	Omie
Doll	Le Noir	Onzelle
Dollie	Leota	Opieree
Donnie	Lessie	Osie
Dorinda	Levada	Othera
Effie 2	Levis	Ouida
Elaline	Linzkey	Ozola
Eldessa	Loie	Persia
Elphie	Lorita	Philippa
Elzona	Lovie	Pinkie
Enola	Lowa	Pluma
Epatha	Lozetta	Prude
Erta	Luna	Quennie
Essie	Lura	Randy
Etheldra	Lurline	Reatha
Etruila	Luta	Rhondabelle
Eulalia	Mabla	Rinsie
Eulania	Madonna	Rodella
Eurena	Malah	Roma
Evie	Malinda	Sabina
Exa 2	Malissa	Sala
Exer	Malvina	Sammye
Exie	Marillia	Segusta
Fanellen	Mathilde	Settie
Fena	Mazelle	Sola
Filie	Meda	Sophia
Florida	Mignon	Sudie

Southern Cities: 1877 to 1937 - MONTGOMERY, ALABAMA (& COLUMBUS, MISSISSIPPI)

Swan	Ula	Voncile
Swannie	Ulva	Willula
Sydna	Vadah	Winona
Tannie	Valla	Wortie
Tennie	Valsie	Zabie
Tenolia	Vashti	Zadie 2
Texas	Venetia	Zellah
Thomasine	Venetta	Zenia
Tinnie	Vennie	Zenobia
Tinsie	Verabel	Zilpah
Totsie 2	Verbye	Zipporah
Toy	Vetella	Zoa
Tracie	Vinnie	Zoe
Trudie	Virdie	Zora
Tula	Vonceil	Zula

Unusual Names[9]

Black Male

Aguinaldo	Elzie	Litt
Amzi 2	Fance	Lizander
Antonio	Febel	London
Artie	General	Lum
Atress	Gid	Lumie
Atrus	Gillie	Major 3
Aug	Glee	Maecellus
Beatrice	Gold	Mint
Bee	Governor	Mose 4
Berry	Hamp	Moses 6
Bishop 2	Handy	Napoleon 4
Bloom	Hezekiah 2	Norvell
Borus	Isaiah	Orgie
Brass	Isham 2	Ozie
Buck 2	Ishmon	Phylis
Caesar 4	Isom	Pink 3
Cammie	Izera	Pinkey 2
Captain	Izfy	Pleas
Cato	Jaise	Plenn
Columbus	Jepthro	Pond
Constance	Jonah	Prince
Dillie	Jonas	Quince
Doc	Josh	Roosevelt 3
Dother	Jude	Saul
Early	Judge	Seal
Eli 2	King	Sennie
Elias	Laselle	Shadrach
Elijah 4	Lemon	Shed 2
Elisha	Lennie	Smella

[9]From the City Directory, Columbus, Mississippi, 1926.

Southern Cities: 1877 to 1937 - MONTGOMERY, ALABAMA (& COLUMBUS, MISSISSIPPI)

St. Elmo 2
Tass
Theodoric 2
Thursday

Titus
Tobias
Vallie
Warn

Washington
Watsie
Zeb

Black Female

Abanda
Almeda
Amenthie
America
Aminda 2
Ara
Aretha
Arkansas
Arsie
Arta
Artesia
Attie
Baina
Biddie
Bird
Buena
Candice
Cassie 2
Castella
Celina
Charity
Cherry 4
Claretes
Classy
Claudie 2
Colin
Connie
Corilla
Cressie
Curley 3
Dallie
Delena
Delilah 2
Delsie
Denkie
Dessie 2
Dinah
Dolena
Dotsie
Dovie
Dumpsie
Eadie
Easter 3
Edmonia
Elma

Elvira
Epsey
Evaline
Eveler
Evelina 2
Frankie 2
Gillie
Girley
Glassie
Golden
Gussie 2
Hannah 5
Icie
Idella 2
Izella
Janine
Jeffie
Jency
Jerrusha
Joehanna
Joella
Jola
Kissie
Lahalia
Leanna
Lendie
Lemona
Lera
Lessie
Letha 2
Lina 2
Loda
Lovey
Luberta 7
Lucinda 5
Luda
Ludie
Luella
Lugenia 2
Lum
Lurena 2
Lurine
Lutie
Luvendia
Luvenia 2

Luvina
Magnolia 5
Malinda 2
Malissa 8
Mandy 2
Manassas
Marcella 4
Maria 2
Marinda
Matilda 6
Mellie
Melvina 2
Mida
Minta
Mirina
Misher
Missouri 2
Mug
Myria
Nadine
Narcissa
Narsisus
Nola
Oletha
Orece
Osie
Otie
Ozella
Ozema
Pallee
Paralee 2
Parthenia
Patience
Patrina
Peach
Perarla
Perlara
Pernella
Phoebe 2
Phoney
Pink
Pinkie 2
Queen 2
Queenie
Quilla

Southern Cities: 1877 to 1937 - MONTGOMERY, ALABAMA (& COLUMBUS, MISSISSIPPI)

Rena
Reva
Regina
Retha
Rhoda
Rhode
Rosalle
Rosebud
Rosella
Rosetta 2
Ruberta
Salone
Samantha
Savannah 7

Savilla
Senna
Serena
Sevilla
Silla 2
Siller
Silley
Soloda
Sonette
Syvilla
Tempie 2
Tennessee
Tennie 3
Tildie

Timpie
Tisha 2
Tissie
Tissue
Trilla
Trudie
Valeria
Veola
Vergia
Vina 2
Vistula
Wide
Zana
Zeldia
Zella

White Male

Acy
Adoniram
Adrown
Alma
Almond 2
Almus 2
Anizo
Audie
Battle
Bell
Berry
Bonnie 2
Bunyon
Cicero 2
Cirt
Clanie
Claugh
Clovis
Covie
Crit
Damon
Danzy
Dess
Donnie
Duff

Dunk
Elam
Elder
Eltraney
Elrie
Elzey 2
Enoch
Festus
Finas
Flagus
Fonda
Gailar
Gay
General
Hick
Horan
Hosea
Jule
Junius 2
Kedar
Lathaddious
Ledyard
Liliburn
Major
Manly

Mertie
Moses
Napoleon
Neva
Nim
Noah 3
Nona
Nova
Orange
Pink 2
Pleasant
Prince
Robin
Rush
Salathiel
Shula
Square
Tharon
Thomasian
Tobe
Toxey
Troy 2
Ular
Verna
Woody 2
Zebedee

White Female

Addill
Altha
Alvina
Arie
Aubie

Aubra
Audie
Azalee
Bartee
Bena

Bevie
Birdie 4
Blannie
Blondie
Blumie

Southern Cities: 1877 to 1937 - MONTGOMERY, ALABAMA (& COLUMBUS, MISSISSIPPI)

Bonnie 3	Lallaiegh	Ordalia
Burma	La Perle	Ottie
Calara	Laudice	Ozell
Cappia	Laudie	Ozzie 3
Chebie	Laveella	Parrie
Chlora	Leanna	Perla
Claudius	Lecie	Perlila
Clemmie	Lell	Queenie
Clevie	Lennie	Quejette
Clytee	Leota	Rama 2
Cutie	Lerah	Ramie
Dee	Letha 2	Reava
Dena	Lilla	Rebie
Desdie	Linda	Rennie
Dewdrop	Lissette	Rewa
Dezzie	Lizette	Rieveland
Ditha	Loa	Rilla
Docia 2	Lockie	Rinda
Donia	Loel	Romie
Donnie	Lonnie	Rowa
Dovie	Lorinne	Samantha
Easter	Loudie 2	Sammie
Ecklee	Lowel	Sudie
Edwoina	Lucenda	Tempie
Eldra	Ludie	Tennie
Emergine	Luna 2	Tezzie
Ennie	Lura 3	Tildie
Eppie	Lurid	Tisha
Era	Lutie	Trannie 2
Erdeal	Luvenia	Trudie
Erroldine	Luvil	Tula
Eulis	Lynie	Orella
Faith	Mace	Vada
Fletta	Madie	Vadiel
Florine	Magaline	Vana
Floy 4	Maidelle	Vannie
Flute	Matilda	Vashti
Gabie	Melanie	Vella
Gabrella 2	Mellie 3	Vervie
Georgia	Mignon	Vinia
Gertha	Minnett	Vonnie
Getha	Mittie	Weenonah
Goldie 3	Moina	Wessar
Habbo	Morrah	Wildie 3
Hastine	Moselle	Willard
Hypatia	Nemy	Willeda
India	Nera	Woodie
Iuna	Nola	Yona
Jala	Nylodine	Zada
Jemima	Odette 2	Zelda 2
Jodie	Olline	Zella
Johntie	Ona	Zilla
Kansas	Onie	Zilpah

Southern Cities: 1877 to 1937

Source List T: PINE BLUFF, ARKANSAS, 1936[10]

Surnames, Black

Alphabetical

Adams 28	Ferguson 13	Jones 117
Alexander 15	Fields 4	Jordan 6
Allen 17	Fisher 6	Kelly 9
Anderson 31	Fleming 2	King 7
Andrews 13	Fletcher 13	Lee 32
Atkins 1	Foster 11	Lewis 12
Atkinson 2	Franklin 20	Long 12
Austin 8	Freeman 21	Martin 12
Bailey 17	Fuller 2	Mason 8
Baker 8	Gaines 1	Matthews 5
Banks 8	Gardner 18	McDonald 2
Barnes 7	Garner 5	Meeks 3
Bayliss 2	Gibson 3	Miller 23
Bell 13	Gordon 3	Mitchell 20
Bennett 6	Grant 6	Montgomery 2
Benson 4	Gray 5	Moore 41
Berry 3	Green 36	Morgan 17
Bradley 12	Griffin 13	Murphy 8
Brooks 15	Hall 9	Murray 6
Brown 84	Hamilton 3	Myers 3
Bryant 4	Hammond 1	Nelson 19
Burrell 1	Harper 11	Nichols 10
Butler 10	Harris 59	Owen 3
Campbell 4	Harrison 5	Owens 6
Carr 6	Hart 1	Parker 18
Carter 18	Harvey 8	Parks 3
Clark 27	Hawkins 5	Patterson 7
Clarke 2	Hayes 9	Payne 5
Coleman 22	Henderson 26	Perry 10
Collins 11	Henry 11	Phillips 7
Cook 7	Hill 25	Pierce 1
Cooper 11	Holland 2	Polk 2
Cox 1	Holloway 12	Porter 3
Crawford 1	Holmes 29	Price 16
Cummings 2	Hopkins 2	Randolph 1
Daniels 14	Howard 3	Ray 6
Davis 61	Hughes 15	Reed 16
Dickerson 4	Hunter 15	Reynolds 2
Douglas 7	Jackson 84	Rice 5
Dixon 8	James 19	Richardson 16
Edwards 16	Jefferson 14	Riley 4
Elliott 3	Jenkins 18	Roberts 9
Evans 8	Johnson 118	Robertson 7
		Robinson 48
		Rogers 5

[10]From the City Directory, Pine Bluff, Arkansas, 1936.

Southern Cities: 1877 to 1937 -- PINE BLUFF, ARKANSAS, 1936

Ross 15	Taylor 31	Watson 15
Sanders 30	Thomas 59	Watts 6
Saunders 7	Thompson 49	Welch 5
Scott 28	Tucker 2	West 9
Shelton 15	Turner 19	White 28
Simms 3	Wade 3	Williams 152
Simmons 16	Walker 31	Willis 16
Sims 26	Wallace 13	Wilson 26
Smith 92	Ward 6	Woods 11
Stevens 9	Washington 36	Wright 11
Stewart 18	Watkins 4	Young 27

Frequency

Williams 152	Gardner 18	Henry 11
Johnson 118	Jenkins 18	Woods 11
Jones 117	Parker 18	Wright 11
Smith 92	Stewart 18	Butler 10
Brown 84	Allen 17	Nichols 10
Jackson 84	Bailey 17	Perry 10
Davis 61	Morgan 17	Hall 9
Harris 59	Edwards 16	Hayes 9
Thomas 59	Price 16	Kelly 9
Thompson 49	Reed 16	Roberts 9
Robinson 48	Richardson 16	Stevens 9
Moore 41	Simmons 16	West 9
Green 36	Willis 16	Austin 8
Washington 36	Alexander 15	Baker 8
Lee 32	Brooks 15	Banks 8
Anderson 31	Hughes 15	Dixon 8
Taylor 31	Hunter 15	Evans 8
Walker 31	Ross 15	Mason 8
Sanders 30	Shelton 15	Murphy 8
Holmes 29	Watson 15	Barnes 7
Adams 28	Daniels 14	Cook 7
Scott 28	Jefferson 14	Douglas 7
White 28	Andrews 13	King 7
Clark 27	Bell 13	Patterson 7
Young 27	Ferguson 13	Phillips 7
Henderson 26	Fletcher 13	Robertson 7
Sims 26	Griffin 13	Russell 7
Wilson 26	Hamilton 13	Saunders 7
Hill 25	Wallace 13	Bennett 6
Miller 23	Bradley 12	Carr 6
Coleman 22	Holloway 12	Fisher 6
Freeman 21	Lewis 12	Grant 6
Franklin 20	Long 12	Jordan 6
Mitchell 20	Martin 12	Murray 6
James 19	Collins 11	Owens 6
Nelson 19	Cooper 11	Ray 6
Turner 19	Foster 11	Ward 6
Carter 18	Harper 11	Watts 6

Southern Cities: 1877 to 1937 -- PINE BLUFF, ARKANSAS, 1936

Garner 5	Elliott 3	Holland 2
Gray 5	Gibson 3	Hopkins 2
Harrison 5	Gordon 3	McDonald 2
Hawkins 5	Howard 3	Montgomery 2
Matthews 5	Meeks 3	Polk 2
Payne 5	Myers 3	Reynolds 2
Rice 5	Owen 3	Tucker 2
Rogers 5	Parks 3	Atkins 1
Welch 5	Porter 3	Burrell 1
Benson 4	Simms 3	Cox 1
Bryant 4	Wade 3	Crawford 1
Campbell 4	Atkinson 2	Gaines 1
Dickerson 4	Bayliss 2	Hammond 1
Fields 4	Clarke 2	Hart 1
Riley 4	Cummings 2	Harvey 1
Warkins 4	Fleming 2	Pierce 1
Berry 3	Fuller 2	Randolph 1

Surnames, White

Alphabetical

Adams 56	Collins 13	Green 43
Alexander 31	Cook 37	Griffin 7
Allen 54	Cooper 8	Groves 6
Anderson 25	Cox 6	Hall 38
Andrews 10	Crawford 11	Hamilton 13
Atkins 6	Culpepper 27	Hammond 12
Atkinson 33	Cummings 2	Harper 11
Austin 6	Daniels 17	Harris 57
Bailey 22	Davis 71	Harrison 14
Baker 40	Dixon 7	Hart 13
Banks 3	Douglas 6	Harvey 4
Barnes 14	Edwards 11	Hawkins 16
Bayliss 14	Elliott 14	Hayes 7
Bell 15	Evans 42	Henderson 11
Bennett 5	Ferguson 31	Henry 19
Benson 15	Fisher 3	Hill 22
Berry 23	Fleming 4	Hogan 19
Bradley 10	Foster 8	Holland 3
Brooks 8	Franklin 5	Holloway 3
Brown 91	Freeman 27	Holmes 9
Bryant 13	Fuller 2	Hopkins 10
Butler 10	Gaines 2	Howard 12
Campbell 19	Gardner 13	Hughes 17
Carr 11	Garner 12	Hunter 13
Carter 13	Gibson 15	Jackson 23
Clark 28	Glover 19	James 4
Clarke 3	Gordon 13	Jefferson 3
Coleman 11	Grant 2	Jenkins 14
Coles 3	Gray 38	Johnson 101

Southern Cities: 1877 to 1937 -- PINE BLUFF, ARKANSAS, 1936

Jones 82	Parker 18	Simms 4
Jordan 14	Parks 1	Sims 11
Kelly 11	Patterson 19	Smith 212
Kennedy 16	Payne 14	Stevens 10
King 45	Perry 13	Stewart 26
Laminack 10	Phillips 32	Stone 23
Lee 36	Pierce 9	Taylor 98
Lewis 9	Porter 4	Thomas 25
Long 22	Price 13	Thompson 32
Lucas 2	Puddephatt 14	Tucker 53
Martin 53	Randolph 2	Turner 20
Mason 12	Ray 14	Wade 6
Matthews 30	Reed 47	Walker 36
McCain 27	Reid 15	Wallace 19
McDonald 24	Reynolds 36	Ward 23
Meeks 24	Rice 12	Washington 4
Miller 31	Richardson 7	Watkins 8
Mitchell 44	Riley 12	Watson 8
Montgomery 15	Rivers 4	Watts 16
Moore 57	Roberts 21	Webster 1
Morgan 23	Robertson 16	Welch 11
Morton 1	Robinson 39	West 24
Murphy 15	Rogers 34	White 47
Murray 7	Ross 28	Williams 72
Myers 9	Russell 16	Willis 33
Nelson 13	Sanders 44	Wilson 82
Nichols 33	Scott 15	Wood 13
Owen 34	Shelton 3	Woods 6
Owens 25	Simmons 17	Wright 29
		Young 53

Frequency

Smith 212	Sanders 44	Ferguson 31
Johnson 101	Green 43	Miller 31
Taylor 98	Evans 42	Matthews 30
Brown 91	Baker 40	Wright 29
Jones 82	Robinson 39	Clark 28
Wilson 82	Gray 38	Ross 28
Williams 72	Hall 38	Culpepper 27
Davis 71	Cook 37	Freeman 27
Harris 57	Lee 36	McCain 27
Moore 57	Reynolds 36	Stewart 26
Adams 56	Walker 36	Anderson 25
Allen 54	Owen 34	Owens 25
Martin 53	Rogers 34	Thomas 25
Tucker 53	Atkinson 33	McDonald 24
Young 53	Nichols 33	Meeks 24
Reed 47	Willis 33	West 24
White 47	Phillips 32	Berry 23
King 45	Thompson 32	Jackson 23
Mitchell 44	Alexander 31	Morgan 23

Southern Cities: 1877 to 1937 --   PINE BLUFF, ARKANSAS, 1936

Stone 23	Carter 13	Watkins 8
Ward 23	Collins 13	Watson 8
Bailey 22	Gardner 13	Dixon 7
Hill 22	Gordon 13	Griffin 7
Long 22	Hamilton 13	Hayes 7
Roberts 21	Hart 13	Murray 7
Turner 20	Hunter 13	Richardson 7
Wallace 19	Nelson 13	Austin 6
Campbell 19	Perry 13	Cox 6
Glover 19	Price 13	Douglas 6
Henry 19	Wood 13	Groves 6
Hogan 19	Garner 12	Wade 6
Patterson 19	Hammond 12	Woods 6
Parker 18	Howard 12	Bennett 5
Daniels 17	Mason 12	Franklin 5
Hughes 17	Rice 12	Atkins 4
Simmons 17	Riley 12	Fleming 4
Hawkins 16	Carr 11	Harvey 4
Kennedy 16	Coleman 11	James 4
Robertson 16	Crawford 11	Porter 4
Russell 16	Edwards 11	Rivers 4
Watts 16	Harper 11	Simms 4
Bell 15	Henderson 11	Washington 4
Benson 15	Kelly 11	Banks 3
Gibson 15	Sims 11	Clarke 3
Montgomery 15	Welch 11	Coles 3
Murphy 15	Andrews 10	Fisher 3
Reid 15	Bradley 10	Holland 3
Scott 15	Butler 10	Holloway 3
Barnes 14	Hopkins 10	Jefferson 3
Bayliss 14	Laminack 10	Shelton 3
Elliott 14	Stevens 10	Cummings 2
Harrison 14	Holmes 9	Fuller 2
Jenkins 14	Lewis 9	Gaines 2
Jordan 14	Myers 9	Grant 2
Payne 14	Pierce 9	Lucas 2
Puddephatt 14	Brooks 8	Randolph 2
Ray 14	Cooper 8	Morton 1
Bryant 13	Foster 8	Parks 1
		Webster 1

Unusual Names

Black Male

Abraham 4	Antwine	Broker
Adolphus	Arbiet	Bud
Alfine	Avis	Butch
Allcird	Baron	Cagill
Alcoe	Boires	Caleb
Allmra	Booker 4	Cash

Southern Cities: 1877 to 1937 -- PINE BLUFF, ARKANSAS, 1936

Christie	Hap	Mose 12
Cicero	Hezzy	Napoleon 12
Claddie	Hiawatha	Nehemiah
Cledie	Highie	Nimit
Cleophas	Iriot	Nimroy
Clondie	Isaac 7	Nohanner
Columbus 2	Isador	Noah 3
Coot	Ishadol	Olie
Cortez 2	Israel 3	Ollie
Coy	Ivey	Orlee
Creed	Ivy	Ossie
Crettis	Jeremiah	Othell
Curly	Jetco	Painter (Green)
Dallas	Jethra	Pink
Dane	Joan	Pleas
Dee	Job	Press
Demis	Jody	Prince
Deris	Jonas 2	Red
Dero	Jube	Renault
Doc(k) 4	Judge	Rim
Dutchie	Junius	Roosevelt 4
Early	Justine	Roso
Eli 3	King 2	Sandy 2
Elihu	Laivious	Selorn
Elijah	Lasher	Semmial
Elisha	Lawyer	Shead
Elmo	Lenis	Sol 2
Employ	Leolus	Solomon
Era	Levis	Suel
Essex	Lessie	Tal
Essie	Levi 4	Tardy
Ezekiel	Lew	Theopolis
Fad	Link	Tyree 2
Fate	Lodge	Tyrie
Fed	Lonnie 5	Uriah
Firie	Lutrell	Veo
Fleeter	McAdoo	Vugal
Foti	Major 4	Wash
Frax	Mal	Wess
Gabriel	Malson	Whell
General 2	Mannesset	Wilberforce
Gentle	Mars	Witha
Gentry 2	Maryland	Zack 2
Gep	Massadonia	Zachariah
Gilliam 2	Mebane	Zak
Gillie	Mee	Zeb
Gillion	Mile	Zen
Girt	Mirles	Zinka
Gurley	Modie	

Southern Cities: 1877 to 1937 -- PINE BLUFF, ARKANSAS, 1936

Black Female

Abie	Burline	Elezar
Adelia	Calonthe	Ellease
Alcenia	Camille	El Nora
Aldora	Carlodena	Elnoria
Aleaser	Charity 2	Elphanie
Alerine	Charlene	Elverta
Alfreda	Charlie 2	Elvira
Almeda	Chatnee	Elzaner
Almeta	Chattie	Ema
Alphi	Cherubina	Emelia
Altha 2	Christy	Ersaline
Altoria	Claudine 2	Erseline
Alvira	Clementine	Esabelle
Alzada	Clencie	Esnold
Amanda 3	Cleophia	Essie 10
Amelia	Cleotha	Esta
Amendo	Colena	Etah
Annielou	Creedie	Ethelean
Aquilla	Crenie	Eulalah
Arber	Crocha 2	Euther
Ardelia	Dassie	Evangeline
Ardella	Davidica	Ezetta
Ardis	Delliana	Fairy
Arena 2	Dellie	Favoretta
Aretha	Delphine	Favorite
Arky	Detie	Felicia
Arlinza	Dessie 2	Florene
Armanda	Dicy	Florenza
Armantha	Dimple 2	Florida
Armentie	Dinah	Flossie 2
Armina	Dinna	Floy 2
Armintha	Divine	Fontana
Artis	Dochie	Frankie 2
Artesia	Docia	Freda
Arzola	Dolemia	Freddie 3
Aslina	Donie	Future
Assie	Doshie	Golda
Astria	Dot	Goldie
Attie	Dovie	Gussie 3
Azalina	Drucilla	Guyoria
Azzie	Drunetta	Hannah 3
Bama	Drissa 2	Hassie
Bee	Dymple	Hertha
Belinda	Eariest	Hessie
Bertie 3	Eartha	Hytorria
Bennie	Easter	Icie
Birdia	Edda	Icky
Birdie 2	Eddie 2	Idama
Birtie	Effie 8	Idell
Brunette	Elereen	Idella

289

Southern Cities: 1877 to 1937 -- PINE BLUFF, ARKANSAS, 1936

Indiana	Lycille	Onida
Irener	Machie	Onie
Irewilla	Macie	Ora
Ivie	Madie	Oralee
Ivory	Mahaley	Ossie
Ivy	Magnolia 3	Otha
Jerussia	Malinda 5	Ottie
Jettie	Malissa 4	Ovene
Jimmie	Manda	Ozie
Joe	Mande	Palmyra
Johnny	Mandester	Paralee 2
Lady	Mandy 4	Parthena
Lannie	Margo	Parthenia
Lasella	Mariah 4	Pastoria
Laural	Maryland	Pearlee
Lee	Matilda 10	Pearlie 2
Lennie 3	Mayleen	Pecola 2
Lephis	Meddie	Penny
Letha 4	Meledia	Penola
Lethia	Melia 2	Peola
Levada	Melinee	Permealia
Levenia	Melvina	Pernella
Levina	Melzore	Petrola
Levinia 2	Mercy	Phillis
Lima	Merdie	Pilvia
Lina	Mettie	Pinkie 6
Lindy	Mineola	Precious
Lissie	Miranda	Pricie
Liza 2	Mirream	Priscilla 6
Linnie	Missie	Queen 2
Lobertha	Missouri	Queenie
Lonnie 2	Mittie 2	Reola 5
Lonnie Mae	Modelia	Ressie
Lonteshia	Mohaley	Restena
Love	Morzillor	Reta
Lucetta	Mossie	Revivian
Lucienda	Mozelle	Rheola
Lucinda 16	Nadine	Roda 3
Ludea	Narcissus	Rollee
Ludella	Nevada	Rosada
Ludessa	Nicie	Rosia
Ludie	Nittie	Rosilla
Ludine	Nodie	Safronie
Luna	Noca	Salinda
Luoda	Novella	Samantha
Lura	Obria	Samentha
Lurline	Ocelia	Sammie
Lussie	Odessia	Sarella
Lutie 2	Omera	Savannah 8
Luvada	Omizell 2	Scenna
Luvenia 4	Onia	Scottie

Southern Cities: 1877 to 1937 -- PINE BLUFF, ARKANSAS, 1936

Sefronia	Thenie	Vianna
Sis	Thersia	Viessa
Sissie	Timezena	Werda
Sophia 3	Tommie	Winnie 4
Stafine	Tressa	Winona
Suarade	Trudelle	Zada
Sula	Trudy	Zalphan
Sussie	Truzella	Zanie
Taretha	Tyra	Zella
Telitha 2	Ulebelle	Zenia
Tempy	Valentine	Zenobia
Tennessee	Vashti	Zetha
Tensie	Vee	Zilpha
Textie	Verline	Zola
Theodosia	Versa	Zora 2
Theola	Versie	

White Male

Abraham 2	Chavis	French
Ace	Chieftan	Garnol
Agens	Columbus	Genio
Albro	Coy 4	Gevin
Almos	Daglen	Gillam
Alvis 2	Dasey	Given
Alvy	Devine	Gratis
Aneil	Dink	Gust
Antonia	Docia	G. Washington
Arengus	Dock 4	Havis 6
Arkansas	Donat	Hebe
Arnie	Dutch	Huel
Artie	Early	Iddo
Arvie	Elijah	Isaac
Arvil	Elisha	Ivy
Ary	Either	Jefferson Davis
Athol	Elmo 5	Jentry
Benoy	Elvis	Jet
Bonnie 2	Emrie	Jett 2
Brek	Era	Jettie
Brunie	Erlie	Josh 3
Buck	Esca	Junior
Bud	Esso	Karvin
Buddy 5	Eulis	Kaybon
Bunyon 3	Everion	La Clede
Burl	Ezekiel	Law
Butch	Ezra	Leander
Cage	Famon	Leniel
Cam	Fate	Lexie
Care	Finis 2	Lonnie 6
Carman	Floy	Luck 2
Carrancy	Fortune	Magness
Cenie	Fount	Major 2

291

Southern Cities: 1877 to 1937 -- PINE BLUFF, ARKANSAS, 1936

Malachi 2	Otha	Tull
Malee	Othal	Tuney
Marce	Otho	Ulysses
Meador	Ozy	Valder
Merel	Pink	Valorous
Met 2	Pleas	Valve
Milosh	Poley	Vanard
Miner	Prince	Veljean
Minor 3	Red	Veo 3
Montie	Reno	Vestel
Mose	Rimmer	Vetall
Navel	Rollie	Vetol
Neddo	Romaine	Virgie
Noah 5	Rozzel	Voy
Noble	Ruel	Waddie
Noel	Saul	Wallend 2
Norvelle	Scottie	Woodrow Wilson
Ollest	Shorty	Wroe
Oma	Sol 2	Wyvwin
Orby	Tenny	Zach
Orien	Thermon	Zedic
Orral	Tobey	Zollie
Orval	Treber	Zenno
Osey	Trinidad	Zeno
Osye	Troy 4	Zettie

White Female

Adda	Ardesia	Belva
Addilou	Argie	Bennie
Adiabelle	Arrie	Bera
Aldah	Arris	Bertia
Alethia	Arta	Bertie 14
Alfie	Artelia	Bethenie
Alamlene	Artis	Beuria
Almaretta 2	Athelene	Billie 5
Almeda	Audie 2	Birdie 4
Alneta	Ava 5	Birtie
Alpha 3	Avalon	Bobby
Alta 8	Avice	Bonnie 10
Althea	Avie	Brittie
Alvena	Avil	Brownie
Alvenia 2	Avis 2	Buna
Alyn	Avo	Cabelle
Amanda 2	Avra	Caley
Amber 2	Azzie	Camilla
Amelia 5	Bama	Camille
America	Baydie	Canada
Amil	Bazetis	Carmelita
Amoree	Bea	Caro
Anthesia	Bee	Cassie 2
Ardecia	Belma	Charity

Southern Cities: 1877 to 1937 -- PINE BLUFF, ARKANSAS, 1936

Charlene 2	Elah	Garcia
Charlie	Electa	Gay
Chatnee	Electra	Gazette
Chenetta	Elija	Gilley
Cherry 2	Elitha 2	Golden
Chloe	Ellice	Goldia
Chlorene	Elmo	Goldie 4
Chlothilde	Elowea	Gretha
Clamance	Elphia	Gussie 6
Claralie	Eltine	Gwennie
Clata	El Vada	Hannah 4
Claudie	Elvane	Harmel
Claurie	Elvera	Hessie
Cloma 2	Elvise	Hethie
Clova 2	Elzetta	Hinda
Comer	Enid	Hope 2
Cordia	Eolian	Hyacinth
Cordie	Eppie	Icy
Cozie	Era 2	Idella
Cressie	Eritta	Idora
Cyrena	Erla	Ileva
Cula	Erminie	Illeen
Dallas	Essie 5	Imogene 3
Darlene	Etha	Isala
Davie	Ethie	Isalee
Dee 2	Etty	Isla
Delca	Eulalie 3	Ivory
Delloh	Eunie	Izora
Delorese	Eura 2	Jeffie 5
Delta	Evene	Jerene
Dema	Exa	Jettie 3
Dena	Exielee	Jemima
Dessie 3	Fairy 2	Jimmie
Dinah	Faith	Jimmy
Divena	Fanie	Joe Nita
Docie	Fannalee	Joueta
Donal	Fanola	Kibble
Dorline	Faytie	Kirks
Dorlis	Felcia	Kosa
Dovie 3	Fenny	La Delle
Drucie	Fern 6	Lala
Drucilla 2	Fleta	La Lelle
Dulie	Florine	Laroma
Eafee	Flossie 6	Latishia
Easter	Floy 7	Laurine
Eberene	Francilia	Laverne
Ebolein	Frankie 4	Laverta
Eddie 2	Freda	Lavetra
Eddye	Freddie	Lavonne
Edrie	Fredericka	Leano
Effie 18	Fronia	Lee
Ela	Fuchsia	Leiron

293

Southern Cities: 1877 to 1937 -- PINE BLUFF, ARKANSAS, 1936

Leither	Maria	Obera
Lemma	Marnette	Ocele
Lemmer	Marue	Ocey
Lenova	Matilda 5	Ocie
Lera	Maudine	Oddie
Lessie	Maysel	Odessa
Lestina	Mazie	Odie
Leta 2	Melissa	Odom
Letha 3	Melisse	Oleta
Levenia	Mellie	Olta
Lexie 2	Mena 2	Oma 2
Lidda	Mennie	Omega
Lima	Merele	Ona 2
Lina	Merlie	Oneta 2
Linda	Mertie 2	Ora 9
Linna 2	Metrol	Orene
Linnie 2	Metta	Orpha 2
Lise	Mettie	Osie
Liza 2	Midge	Ossie
Lizula	Mina 2	Ottilia
Lockie	Minett	Ouida
Lon	Minta	Ouita
Lorine	Missouri	Ova
Louana	Mittie 4	Ozelle 2
Loulie	Modie 3	Penny
Louvenia	Mona 2	Pernie
Love	Monia	Phillis 2
Lovie	Monie 2	Philomena
Loy	Monnie	Placida
Lucinda 3	Moree	Popless
Lucretia	Mortina	Queen
Lucyhearn	Mozelle 3	Queenie
Ludie	Mozeta	Rada
Luedna	Myrle	Radie
Ludy	Myrth	Ratie
Luna	Myrtie	Rea 2
Lurelene	Myrtis	Readie
Lutie 6	Nacy	Reatha
Lycille	Nadine	Rellus
Maeten	Narcis	Rena 6
Mahalia	Natalie	Reta 2
Malinda	Naudine	Retta
Malissa	Nealia	Reva
Malisse	Negie	Rhoda 2
Mama 2	Neva 2	Rilda
Mandie	Nevelyn	Robie
Mandy	Nixie	Roma
Manie 3	Norene	Ruffie
Marcella 2	Nova 2	Rusha
Marcelline	Novaline	Sannie
Mardice	Novel	Saphronia
Marjoria	Novella	Seney

Southern Cities: 1877 to 1937 -- PINE BLUFF, ARKANSAS, 1936

Selina	Ursel	Victory 2
Shelba	Ursula	Vida
Sophia 6	Vadia	Vina
Stacia	Valda	Vinnie
Stevie	Valia	Vir
Storia	Valla	Voy
Sucie	Valrie	Wanda 4
Sula 2	Vanita	Wetta
Sunny	Varner	Wilkina
Sunshine	Vashti	Willene 3
Sybino	Vaudie	Willine
Tallulah	Veda	Wilmoth
Tandy	Vee	Winney 16
Tankie	Velera	Wirta
Tempy	Velma	Wordna
Tennie 2	Velta	Zada 2
Terrah	Vena	Zelda
Tessie	Venie	Zella
Thedro	Venne	Zellia
Theola	Vennie	Zelma
Theta	Veoma 2	Zemma
Tina	Verdia	Zeola
Tiney	Verea	Zeph
Tommie	Verla	Zetha
Toy	Verna	Zethar
Tressie	Vernona	Zetta 2
Tura	Vessie	Zettie 2
U-Bell	Vevi	Zona
Una	Vicie	Zora

CHAPTER IV

Conformity in College vs. Individuality

In 1935, the Black population of the United States numbered approximately 12,378,500, and a large majority, approximately 78 per cent, or 9,655,230 Black Americans lived in the Southern States. At that time, only 35 per cent of the Southern Black population lived in urban areas.[1] That means that approximately 3,379,331 Blacks were urban dwellers.

Billingsley points out that even up to 1965 "the overwhelming majority (85 per cent) of Negro adults on farms have had no high school education."[2] We can assume, therefore, that Black College students were drawn, primarily, from the 3,379,331 Southern Black urban dwellers, since with few exceptions the list of Black college student names is drawn from Southern Black Colleges (see Source List U). In the South in 1950, 4.1 per cent of the Black population had some college experience.[3] On the basis of a 3 per cent approximation for 1935, it would seem that approximately 101,379 Southern Blacks had attended college by that date. And on the basis of 20,212 given names of Black male and female college students in 1935, this collection reflects a sample of more than 20 per cent, since a number of the 101,379 Blacks with college experience must have attended college before the 1930-1940 period.

Furthermore, since these college students came from such urban areas as Augusta, Georgia, we might expect that their names would be relatively similar to those we have seen already.

The following list represents the twenty-five most popular Black male college students' names from a list of 9,064 (see Source List U). The numbers following the name indicate that name's position amongst the first twenty-five given names in Augusta during the years indicated. "NL" means that the name was not listed amongst the twenty-five most popular given names (see Source Lists N, O, P, Q, U).

---

[1] Reynolds Farley, Growth of the Black Population (Chicago, Ill.: Markham Publishing Company, 1970), pp. 22, 43 and 50.

[2] Andrew Billingsley, Black Families in White America (New York: Prentice-Hall, Inc., 1968), p. 81.

[3] Ibid., pp. 79-80.

Conformity in College vs. Individuality

Black Male College Students	1937	1919	1899	1877
1. James	3	3	4	4
2. William	1	1	1	2
3. John	2	2	2	3
4. Charles	6	5	6	6
5. Robert	5	8	8	5
6. George	4	4	5	8
7. Edward	10	10	9	9
8. Thomas	8	NL	NL	7
9. Joseph	9	9	10	10
10. Henry	7	6	3	1
11. Samuel	12	11	11	12
12. Willie	NL	NL	NL	NL
13. Walter	14	18	NL	NL
14. Arthur	17	17	NL	NL
15. Clarence	22	24	NL	NL
16. Albert	15	13	19	NL
17. Frank	11	12	12	19
18. Richard	23	15	13	14
19. David	18	16	15	17
20. Benjamin	13	14	14	16
21. Jesse	16	19	21	NL
22. Ernest	21	NL	NL	NL
23. Eugene	24	NL	NL	NL
24. Lawrence	NL	NL	NL	NL
25. Leroy	NL	NL	NL	NL

Of the twenty-five most popular given names used by Black males attending college in the 1930's, fifteen are found in 1877, sixteen in 1899, nineteen in 1919 and twenty-two in 1937. Of greater significance is the fact that of the first ten most popular names amongst college males, the same ten are used in 1877, nine out of ten in 1899 and 1919 and the same ten in 1937. Only Thomas is not found on the lists in 1899 and 1919. There appears a very strong consistency, bespeaking a conservative attitude on the part of Black males; their given name usage seems to have established and maintained a pattern over this sixty year span.

Of the twenty-five most popular given names of White males attending college in the 1930's, fourteen are found amongst Blacks in 1877, fifteen in 1899 and seventeen in 1919 and 1937. Of the ten most popular White college names, nine are found amongst Blacks in 1877, eight in 1899 and 1919 and nine in 1937 (see Source Lists N, O, P, Q, U). The trend is remarkably consistent amongst Augusta Black males; their names correspond with White nomenclature. As it is to be expected, there exists a slightly greater correspondence between Black college student names and Augusta, Georgia Black names. For example, Willie, twelfth, amongst college Blacks, Lawrence, twenty-fourth and Leroy, twenty-fifth, do not appear at all amongst the most popular names of Augusta Blacks.

Conformity in College vs. Individuality

The following list represents the twenty-five most popular Black female college students' given names from a list of 11,148. The numbers following the names indicate that name's position amongst the first twenty-five given names in Augusta, Georgia, during the years indicated. "NL" means that the name was not listed amongst the twenty-five most popular given names (see Source Lists N, O, P, Q, U).

Black Female College Students	1937	1919	1899	1877
1. Mary	1	1	1	1
2. Annie	2	2	12	NL
3. Ruth	NL	NL	NL	NL
4. Helen	NL	NL	NL	NL
5. Dorothy	NL	NL	NL	NL
6. Thelma	NL	NL	NL	NL
7. Louise	12	14	NL	NL
8. Lillian	NL	NL	NL	NL
9. Alice	20	16	18	NL
10. Elizabeth	13	NL	22	19
11. Mildred	NL	NL	NL	NL
12. C(K)atharine	NL	NL	NL	NL
13. Ethel	NL	NL	NL	NL
14. Carrie	4	3	24	NL
15. Emma	7	4	4	9
16. Gladys	NL	NL	NL	NL
17. Ruby	NL	NL	NL	NL
18. Sarah	10	5	3	2
19. Marie	18	NL	NL	NL
20. Evelyn	NL	NL	NL	NL
21. Edna	NL	NL	NL	NL
22. Grace	NL	NL	NL	NL
23. Margaret	NL	NL	NL	23
24. Rosa	5	10	11	NL
25. Mattie	3	NL	16	NL

Of the twenty-five most popular given names used by Black females attending college in the 1930's, only five are found in 1877, nine in 1899, eight in 1919 and eleven in 1937. Of equal significance is that of the first ten most popular names amongst college females, only one is found in 1877 and in 1899 and only two are found in 1919 and in 1937. Black females attending college favored names markedly different than those, with the exception of Mary and Annie, employed by those of their sisters not attending college or those of an earlier generation.

Of the twenty-five most popular given names used by White females attending college in the 1930's, seven are found amongst Blacks in 1877, eight in 1899, six in 1919 and seven in 1937. Of the first ten most popular White female college student names, two are found amongst Black females in 1877 and in 1899, and one in 1919 and in 1937.

Conformity in College vs. Individuality

This situation is remarkably different from that amongst males. Black female naming patterns are far from orderly. There is somewhat of a movement over the years in Augusta, Georgia toward a correspondence with Black female naming practices amongst college students, but only amongst the twenty-five most popular names; of the ten most popular names amongst their sisters in college, Black females in Augusta seem to take no notice. Indeed, Black females in Augusta seem just as unaffected by naming practices of White female college students.

The correspondence between Black and White female college students is greater (of the twenty-five most popular, fourteen are identical; of the ten most popular, five are the same) than the correspondence between Black female college students and Black Augusta, Georgia females during any period from 1877 to 1937. This suggests, once again, that Black female naming practices remained in a much more flexible state than did the highly patterned and, in this sense, conservative practices of their men. At the same time, Black female naming practices were less affected by White female naming usage, in terms of popularity, than were the practices of their men.

The following list represents the twenty-five most popular surnames of Black college students. The numbers following the name indicate that name's position among the first twenty-five in Augusta during the years indicated. "NL" means that the name was not listed amongst the twenty-five most popular surnames (see Source Lists N, O, P, Q, U).

Black College Students	Position Among 25 Most Popular Names in Augusta			
	1937	1919	1899	1877
1. Johnson	3	3	2	3
2. Williams	1	1	1	1
3. Jones	2	2	3	2
4. Smith	5	6	5	4
5. Brown	4	4	4	7
6. Jackson	6	5	6	5
7. Davis	10	10	9	9
8. Robinson	16	11	11	11
9. Harris	11	9	10	13
10. Taylor	NL	NL	NL	NL
11. Thomas	7	7	7	6
12. Wilson	17	18	16	17
13. Thompson	NL	NL	NL	NL
14. Walker	8	8	8	8
15. Washington	14	NL	18	18
16. Moore	18	19	17	16
17. White	12	17	15	NL
18. Scott	13	13	13	12
19. Lewis	NL	NL	NL	NL
20. Anderson	24	NL	22	15
21. Hill	21	24	NL	NL
22. Martin	NL	NL	NL	22

Conformity in College vs. Individuality

Black College Students	Position Among 25 Most Popular Names in Augusta			
	1937	1919	1899	1877
23. Lee	NL	NL	NL	NL
24. Carter	25	NL	23	24
25. Green	9	12	12	10

Of the twenty-five most popular surnames used by Blacks attending college in the 1930's, nineteen are found in Augusta, Georgia in 1877 and 1899, seventeen in 1919 and twenty in 1937. Of the first ten, seven are used in 1877, eight in 1899 and in 1919, and seven in 1937. Williams, the perennial favorite, drops to second place, as Johnson, previously second or third, becomes the most favorite surname. Of the twenty-five most popular surnames used by White college students in the 1930's, sixteen are used by Blacks in Augusta, Georgia in 1877, fourteen in 1899, twelve in 1919 and fourteen in 1937. Of the ten most popular White college student surnames, six are used by Blacks in Augusta, Georgia in each period from 1877 to 1937. Black surname usage parallels closely Black male given name usage: consistent patterns of popularity, generation after generation.

It appears that Black males are very consistent in name usage, in terms of the twenty-five most popular names, from 1877 to 1937 in Augusta, Georgia and in colleges throughout the South, whereas Black female name shifting is much more dramatic. Surname usage is relatively stable throughout this period. As one might have predicted, Black college student naming practices, with the exception of those of the females, coincide with urban Black naming practices.

An examination of all names in this collection indicates definite patterns of change. For example, by omitting those thirty-seven names found on both the slave and college student 100 most frequently used name lists (see Source List V), we see that 13.8 per cent of all Black male given names in Augusta in 1877 were found amongst the sixty-three remaining names on the slave list and only 5.5 per cent on the college list. In Augusta in 1899, 9.5 per cent were identical with those of slave names and 7.7 per cent amongst Black college students. In 1919, 7 per cent were found amongst slaves and 10.1 per cent amongst Black college students and, finally in 1937, only 3.8 per cent of the names of male Blacks in Augusta, Georgia were found on the list of 100 most popular slave names, whereas 13.4 per cent were found amongst Black college students. The trend is toward a closer identification with Black college student names and a greater rejection of slave names.

The shift amongst Black females is similar but even more dramatic (see Source List V). In 1877, 42.5 per cent of Black females in Augusta, Georgia had names identical with those of slave female names, and only 5.9 per cent of the names reflected Black female college student usage. In 1899, the percentages shift to 28.9 per cent and 18.7 per cent. By 1919, only 13.8 per cent were identical with slave names and 36.6 per cent reflected Black college student usage. Finally, Augusta, Georgia, 1937 sees Black females employing only 5.8 per cent names common to slave usage and 45.5 per cent common to Black college student usage.

The following table represents these shifts.

Conformity in College vs. Individuality

	Black Female Names		Black Male Names	
	% Slave	% College	% Slave	% College
1877	42.5	5.9	13.8	5.5
1899	28.9	18.7	9.5	7.7
1919	13.8	36.6	7.0	10.1
1937	5.8	45.5	3.8	13.4

On the other hand, omitting those thirty-seven names common to both the 100 most frequently used slave and college student name Black lists, White male given names in Augusta, Georgia in 1877 reflect 4.6 per cent identification with slave names and 6.2 per cent identification with Black college sutdent names. By 1937, the identification moves to 1.1 per cent with slave names and 13.1 per cent with Black male college student names. Amongst females, the 1877 figures show 28.2 per cent identification with slave names and 11.7 per cent with Black female college student names to, in 1937, 2.7 per cent similarity with slave names and 26 per cent identification with Black female college student names.

The following table represents these shifts.

	White Female Names		White Male Names	
	% Slave	% College	% Slave	% College
1877	28.2	11.7	4.6	6.2
1937	2.7	26.0	1.1	13.1

It appears, then, that Augusta, Georgia Blacks move away from an identification with slave names and employ names similar to those used by Black college students more and more from one generation to another. Whites move in this direction as well, but more slowly, and again, males, White and Black, appear more conservative in shifting than do their females.

This trend can be illustrated in another way. By omitting those thirty-eight of the 100 most common to slaves and White college students (see Source List V), we find that amongst Black males in Augusta, Georgia in 1877, 14.8 per cent had names common to the sixty-two of the 100 most common slave names and 3.8 per cent had names common to the sixty-two of the 100 most popular White male college student names. By 1937, the correspondence had shifted to a 5.9 per cent identification with slave names and an 11.2 per cent identification with White college student names. Amongst Black females in Augusta, the shift is again more dramatic. In 1877, 23 per cent of Augusta females had names identical to those sixty-seven slave names not shared by White college female students and 4.2 per cent had names identical with those of White female college students (see Source List V). By 1937, 5.8 per cent of Black women had names identical to the same sixty-seven most common slave names and 23.8 per cent had names identical to those used by White female college students.

The following table represents these shifts.

Conformity in College vs. Individuality

	Black Female Names		Black Male Names	
	% Slave	% College	% Slave	% College
1877	23.0	4.2	14.8	3.8
1899	19.7	9.8	13.3	5.1
1919	10.0	18.0	11.2	7.0
1937	5.8	23.8	5.9	11.2

Black males seem much more constant than Black females in the employment of given names. This also holds true for Whites. However, Black surname usage seems somewhat more constant than White surname usage.

The following lists represent the twenty-five most popular given names of male college students, Black and White. The number after the name indicates that name's position amongst the most popular given names of the other race. "NL" means that the name was not listed among the most popular twenty-five given names (see Source List U).

Black Male College Students		White Male College Students	
James	3	William	2
William	1	John	3
John	2	James	1
Charles	5	Robert	5
Robert	4	Charles	4
George	6	George	6
Edward	9	Thomas	8
Thomas	7	Joseph	9
Joseph	8	Edward	7
Henry	17	Frank	17
Samuel	21	Richard	18
Willie	NL	Jack	NL
Walter	13	Walter	13
Arthur	18	Paul	NL
Clarence	NL	Harry	NL
Albert	22	David	19
Frank	10	Henry	10
Richard	11	Arthur	14
David	16	Harold	NL
Benjamin	NL	Joe	NL
Jesse	NL	Samuel	11
Ernest	NL	Albert	16
Eugene	NL	Donald	NL
Lawrence	NL	Fred	NL
Leroy	NL	Louis	NL

Black and White college male students employ very similar given names. Of the first ten, nine are identical; of the first twenty-five, seventeen are the same.

Conformity in College vs. Individuality

The following lists represent the twenty-five most popular given names of female college students, Black and White. The number after the name indicates that name's position amongst the most popular given names of the other race. "NL" means that the name was not listed among the most popular twenty-five given names (see Source List U).

Black Female College Students		White Female College Students	
Mary	1	Mary	1
Annie	25	Margaret	23
Ruth	7	Dorothy	5
Helen	8	Frances	NL
Dorothy	3	Elizabeth	10
Thelma	NL	C(K)atharine	12
Louise	14	Ruth	3
Lillian	NL	Helen	4
Alice	23	Virginia	NL
Elizabeth	5	Martha	NL
Mildred	15	Betty(ie)	NL
C(K)atharine	6	Sarah	18
Ethel	NL	Marjory	NL
Carrie	NL	Louise	7
Emma	NL	Mildred	11
Gladys	NL	Jean(ne)	NL
Ruby	NL	Evelyn	20
Sarah	12	Jane	NL
Marie	NL	Eleanor	NL
Evelyn	17	Sara	NL
Edna	NL	Doris	NL
Grace	24	Edith	NL
Margaret	2	Alice	9
Rosa	NL	Grace	22
Mattie	NL	Annie	2

Black and White female college students employ less similar given names than do males. Of the first ten most popular female given names, only five are the same for both races; of the first twenty-five, only fourteen are the same.

The following lists represent the twenty-five most popular surnames employed by Black and White college students. The number after each name indicates that name's position amongst the most popular surnames of the other race. "NL" means that the name was not listed among the most popular twenty-five surnames (see Source List U).

Black College Students Surnames		White College Students Surnames	
1. Johnson	2	1. Smith	4
2. Williams	6	2. Johnson	1

BLACK NAMES IN AMERICA

Conformity in College vs. Individuality

Black College Students Surnames		White College Students Surnames	
3. Jones	3	3. Jones	3
4. Smith	1	4. Davis	7
5. Brown	5	5. Brown	5
6. Jackson	17	6. Williams	2
7. Davis	4	7. Moore	16
8. Robinson	NL	8. Taylor	10
9. Harris	19	9. Martin	22
10. Taylor	8	10. Wilson	12
11. Thomas	NL	11. Thompson	13
12. Wilson	10	12. Miller	NL
13. Thompson	11	13. White	17
14. Walker	16	14. Adam	NL
15. Washington	NL	15. Anderson	20
16. Moore	7	16. Walker	14
17. White	13	17. Jackson	6
18. Scott	NL	18. Campbell	NL
19. Lewis	NL	19. Harris	9
20. Anderson	15	20. Carter	24
21. Hill	NL	21. Hall	NL
22. Martin	9	22. Turner	NL
23. Lee	NL	23. Bell	NL
24. Carter	20	24. King	NL
25. Green	NL	25. Phillips	NL

Of the twenty-five most popular surnames used by Black and White college students, seven of the first ten, and seventeen of the first twenty-five, are identical. It appears that Black surname nomenclature amongst college students is similar to that amongst White college students.

Black male college students employ seventeen of those most popular twenty-five given names of White male college students and of the ten most frequently used Black male college student names, nine are identical with White names. Amongst females, in terms of earlier trends the identification is much more dramatic. Of the twenty-five most popular Black female college student names, fourteen are identical with White female college student names, but only eleven are the same as Black female names in Augusta in 1937. And of the ten most popular Black female college student names, five are identical with those names used by White female college students, but only two are the same as those used by Augusta Black females in 1937.

The latter tends to support the belief that, despite marked consistency in Black male given name usage and Black surname usage from 1877 to 1937 in Augusta, Georgia and amongst Black male college students in 1937, and despite marked inconsistency in female given name usage over this same period, Blacks of both sexes in college came from homes which reflected a sensitivity to and a predilection for White name usage.

We can assume that in 1935 Blacks attending college constituted the portion of the Black community most fully attuned to White values and most able to participate in activities which reflected White values. Whatever arguments

Conformity in College vs. Individuality

may be voiced in 1974 questioning the desire for a college education as reflective of White values, all indications suggest that in 1935 a college education represented a major value for White America. Thus, most Blacks de-
sirous and able to attend college must have been highly attracted toward some
aspects of the White value system. Name usage reinforces this assumption.

Nevertheless, Black college students employ not only a greater percentage
of unusual names but also a great many more famous and old-fashioned names
than do White college students. Of the 9,064 Black college male given names
collected (see Source List U), 776 are unusual, 225 are famous and 221 are
old-fashioned. The percentage of unusual given names is 8.6 per cent. Of the
11,148 Black college female given names, 1,715 are unusual, 70 are famous and
191 are old-fashioned. The percentage of unusual names is 15.4, almost twice
that of the males. The totals for both groups is: of 20,212 names, 2,491 unusual, 295 famous and 412 old-fashioned. The total percentage of unusual
names is 12.3.

In contrast, of the 17,373 White college male given names collected, only
837 are unusual, 77 famous and 67 old-fashioned. The percentage of unusual
names is 4.8. Of the 10,750 White college female given names, 1,066 are unusual, 11 are famous and 101 are old-fashioned. The percentage of unusual
female names is 9.9 and, like that of the Black female student population,
approximately twice that of males. The totals for both White males and females is: of 28,123 names, 1,903 unusual, 88 famous and 168 old-fashioned.
The total percentage of unusual names is 6.8.

Women of both races used a markedly greater percentage of unusual names
than men. Black women employed a very high 15.4 per cent unusual names; White
women 9.9 per cent. Black men used 8.6 per cent; White men a very low 4.8 per
cent. Male and female Blacks totaled 12.3 per cent unusual names; this is much
higher than the 6.8 per cent used by Whites.

To review a previous discussion, in the eighteenth century 25.36 per cent
of Black male slave names were unusual; 13.64 per cent of free Black male
names were unusual. Female slaves with unusual names numbered 18.09 per cent;
15.23 per cent of free Black females used unusual names. All Black slaves
used 22.47 per cent unusual names; all free Blacks used 14.25 per cent unusual
names.

In the period 1800-1860, 9.52 per cent of Black male slaves had unusual
names; 16.10 per cent of free Blacks chose unusual names. Female slaves in
this period employed 9.79 per cent unusual names and free Black females used
22.31 per cent unusual names. All Black slaves used 9.66 per cent unusual
names; all free Blacks used 18.28 per cent unusual names. In Augusta, Georgia,
Black males used unusual names in the years 1877-1937 as follows: 5 per cent,
5.3 per cent, 5.3 per cent and 6.6 per cent. School records in 1938 reflect
a 6.6 per cent usage of unusual names in city schools and 8.8 per cent usage
in rural schools amongst boys. Black females in the same period in Augusta
employ unusual names as follows: 6.1 per cent, 6.2 per cent, 5.2 per cent and
7.6 per cent. Girls in city schools use 10.5 per cent unusual names in 1938
and in rural schools, 11.9 per cent.

BLACK NAMES IN AMERICA

Conformity in College vs. Individuality

In Montgomery, Alabama in 1933, Black males employ 7.7 per cent unusual names; Black females use unusual names at a rate of 8.5 per cent. And in Pine Bluff, Arkansas in 1936, Black males use unusual names at a rate of 8 per cent and Black females at a rate of 12.9 per cent.

Initially, then, Black slaves were given considerably more unusual names than those used by free Blacks, but in the nineteenth century free Blacks used apparently twice as many unusual names as did slaves. And, initially, male slaves used more unusual names than female slaves, whereas free males used fewer unusual names than free females. However, again by the nineteenth century, females, whether slave or free, employed a greater percentage of unusual names than did males.

In Augusta, Montgomery and Pine Bluff, Black females consistently employ a greater percentage of unusual names than do Black males, albeit the slimness of the differences. And the percentage of unusual names used by all Blacks in these cities is considerably lower than that used by Blacks in the pre-Civil War periods. There appears to have been a drastic reduction in the percentage of unusual names employed by Blacks immediately after emancipation. The percentages of unusual names consistently but slowly increase from 1877 on, paralleling a pattern exhibited by White naming usage, although Whites do consistently employ a slightly lower percentage of unusual names than do Blacks.

By the 1930's amongst Black college students, male unusual name usage rose from a low of 5 per cent in Augusta, Georgia in 1877 to 8.6 per cent. This is still a far cry from the 16.10 per cent usage amongst free Black males one hundred years previously. Black female college students employ 15.4 per cent unusual names: still not as extensive as the 22.31 per cent used by free females one hundred years previously, but quite a climb from the low of 6.1 per cent in Augusta in 1877. Black females, by refusing to be influenced by White naming usage or patterns established by earlier generations of Black women, enjoy a degree of freedom to experiment and be eccentric not known to Black men.

White male naming practices reflect unusual usage along lines parallel to Black males. A 1.8 per cent unusual rate in Augusta in 1877 gradually rises to a 4.8 per cent amongst White college students. White female naming patterns also parallel those seen amongst Black females. A 4.4 per cent unusual rate in Augusta in 1877 climbs steadily to a 9.9 per cent amongst White college women.

Although 8.6 per cent of Black male college student given names are unusual, the overwhelming majority of Black males attending college in the 1930's employ names in a most consistent manner. For example, the twenty-five most frequently used names total 4,104 incidences; 45.2 per cent of the entire Black male college student sample. The fifty most frequently used names total 5,048, 55.5 per cent of the entire sample, and the 100 most frequently used names total 6,034 incidences, 66.5 per cent of the entire sample.

Black female college students use 15.4 per cent unusual names. This propensity for individual eccentricity is sanctioned by group practices as evidenced in the cluster patterns of those names most popular with Black women.

Conformity in College vs. Individuality

For example, the twenty-five most frequently used names total 3,260 incidences, 29.2 per cent of the entire Black female college student sample; this is considerably less than the 45.2 per cent seen amongst Black males. The fifty most frequently used female names total 4,952, 44.4 per cent of the entire sample. Males had gone well over 50 per cent of the total number of names in their most frequently used fifty names. The 100 most frequently used female names total 6,945 incidences, 62.2 per cent of the entire sample (see Source List U). Thus, although Black female naming practices allow for a greater degree of imaginative variation in coining new and fanciful names, in terms of the 100 most frequently used names Black females are only slightly less consistent than males (62.2 per cent for females; 66.5 per cent for males) in their preferences.

Like Black male students, White males attending colleges in the 1930's used names which clustered overwhelmingly amongst the most frequently employed names. The twenty-five most frequently used names total 8,525 incidences, 49 per cent of the entire White male college student sample. The fifty most frequently used names total 10,500, 60.4 per cent of the entire sample and the 100 most frequently used names total 12,294 incidences, 70.7 per cent of the entire sample. Indeed, White male name usage consistency is remarkably similar to that seen amongst Black males.

The twenty-five most frequently used names amongst White female college students total 4,901 incidences, 45.5 per cent of the entire White female college student sample (see Source List U). The fifty most frequently used names total 6,263, 58.3 per cent of the entire sample, and the 100 most frequently used names total 7,586 incidences, 70.5 per cent of the entire sample. White female name clusters are only slightly less inclusive than that of White men and only slightly more inclusive than that of Black men.

The following table illustrates the remarkable consistency of Black naming practices amongst college students in relation to White college student naming practices, albeit the tendency of Black females toward greater freedom in name usage.

College Students	% of the 1st 25	% of the 1st 50	% of the 1st 100
Black			
Male	45.2	55.5	66.5
Female	29.2	44.4	62.2
White			
Male	49.0	60.4	70.7
Female	45.5	58.3	70.5

It must be apparent, then, that by the 1930's, Black and White name usage, for the most part, had developed similar patterns in terms of growth of percentages of unusual names. Black name usage starts in the post-Civil War period with a slightly higher percentage of unusual name usage amongst males

Conformity in College vs. Individuality

and females; however, this percentage difference remains, remarkably, very much the same through the nineteenth and into the twentieth century.

Furthermore, what at first appear to be significant departures on the part of Black females from patterns maintained by Whites and Black males, on closer examination, turn out to be less than dramatic. Indeed, despite the highest percentage of unusual names and the variations amongst the first twenty-five names, Black females in college employ, of the 100 most popular, seventy-one which are identical with those found amongst the 100 most frequently used White female college student names. By comparison, Black males, who have thus far shown very high correspondence with White males, employ, of the 100 most popular, seventy-two names which are also found on the list of those 100 most popular names used by White male college students. There seems no appreciable difference.

The following lists reflect those names from the 100 most frequently used Black male and female college student lists which do not correspond with White college student usage. The number after the name indicates the position of popularity of that name amongst Black males and females (see Source List U).[+]

MALE

Willie 12	Luther 61	Ulysses 88
Nathaniel 29	Curtis 64	Cecil 89
Johnnie 42	Solomon 68	Clifford 90
Booker 48	Aaron 69	Floyd 91
Eddie 49	Calvin 71	Roscoe 93
Isaac 50	Isaiah 73	Wesley 94
Oliver 52	Clifton 83	Charley 95
Matthew 58	Reginald 84	Franklin 97
Alonzo 60	Moses 87	Reuben 98
		Abraham 99

FEMALE

Carrie 14	Mamie 50	Alberta 80
Rosa 24	Cora 60	Essie 81
Hattie 33	Minnie 63	Geneva 83
Beatrice 35	Daisy 64	Irma 87
Willie 41	Lula 65	Beulah 91
Inez 43	Esther 66	Ernestine 92
Fanny 44	Susie 69	Janie 94
Lillie 47	Addie 72	Willie Mae 95
Maggie 48	Naomi 78	Katy 96
Sadie 49	Viola 79	

[+]See the selected list of unusual names in Source List U and the complete list in the Index.

Conformity in College vs. Individuality

However strong the pressures of social life, however powerful the demands upon an individual to accept the values, tastes and judgments of his culture, human beings have always managed to somehow avoid complete subjection to group desires and whims. Indeed, one of the most exciting qualities of the human experience is just this refusal to be totally devoid of individual singularity. And one of the most interesting and humorous ways man has devised of announcing to the world that he is, in spite of everything, a unique being is by selecting a name that defies group sanctions. The bearer of the eccentric name may or may not wear his name with pride in its singularity; social disapproval may force him to petition for a new name: witness the number of Adolphs or, more to the point, Hitlers in the United States in the late 1930's and early 1940's who felt the need to have their name changed legally. Aside from these inopportune, to say the least, coincidences, unusual names offer a somewhat irreverent and often needed antidote to the solemnity with which we usually view life. They are fun; they bespeak a sense of humor and proportion; they reflect wit and vitality and imagination, and they are a legacy belonging to all people.

The following combinations speak for themselves:

Lemon Pinkney	Truie Blue	Sun Beam Chaney
Thinkie Black	Shade Sparrow	America Shoemaker
Handsome Lockett	Tiney Bugg	The Prodical Homes
Man Wise	Brown Roache	Hope Lord
Undine Salad	Meat Cook	Plesant Feelings
Pleasure Bird	Early Guest	Virginia Ham
Mance Pie	Little Bit White	Ship Stewart
Fuller Booze	Strong Man	Choice Cook
Good Price	Cement Church Powell	Hazzie Head
Precious Glass	Secret Hand	Luke Tea Orange
Ernestenburnesyalonia	Come Potts	Tiny Little
Stell	Kansas Scales	Hoover Depression
Be Careful McGee	Love Wright	Clark
Crystal White	Sin Hall	Pan Quick
Pink Green	Waxes Merry	Darling Self
Wash Saturday	Thigpen Truelock	King Solomon
Golden Day	Parka Doreman	Hangabook
Sunya Moon	Teapot Hill	Alice Self Boss
Rolling Church	Lent Bride	Professor Works
Extra White	Southern East Myers	Money May Rumph
(a Black Child)	Butter Still	Handful Grist
Precious Person	Asia Minor	Baker Cook
Clear Blue	More Payne	Duck Pool
Mollie Wollie	Cain Oliver ⎫	Vinch Finch
Rude Usher	Able Oliver ⎭ Twins	Rose Dew
Mark Price	See Strong	Lovie P. Honey
U. R. Low	Gracious King	April Shivers
Evergreen Ford	Sugar Blanks	Gasielene Allen
Iser Cow Green	Early Flowers	Since Wynn
Moses Law	Education Thomas	America Music
Etta Apple	Constant Bitting	Jack Frost
John B. A. Angel	Georgia Farmer	Queen Aster Birth

Conformity in College vs. Individuality

Wash Black
Normal Cherry
P. Parker Peppers
Juicy M. Love
Prince Knight
Perley Gates
Righteous Butts
Choice Herring
Silver Spoon
Count Forty Lee
Heart Green
Della Short Speed
Pearl Green Stone
Classie Bell
Grant Freelove
May B. Dunn
Shade Green
Vicy Laugh
Love Bonds
Trouble White
   (Illegitimate Black Child)

Brunet Person
Stoney House Glass
Fair Swann
Green Wood
June Weed
Market Hill
Clay Street
June Burg
Free Chambers
Lean Lawyer
Sappie Farmer
Curl Burner
Poke Cole
Gadget Kitchens
William Thrower
   Fitts, Jr.
Son Gunn
Cora Apple
Letcher Goforth
Bettie Love Bacon

Dock Pass
Toll Shank
European Hill
Grant Free Love
Sophy Greene Meadows
See Bright Sea
Pink Green
Payed Cash
June May March
Top Roe
Lock Gates
Pound Shy
Late Night Mann
Joyful Nations
Love Spooner
Ford Rider
Pink Sunset
Wilder Person
Charity Booth
Fancy Herrin

Conformity in College vs. Individuality

Source List U: COLLEGE STUDENTS, 1930's

Most Common Given Names, Black

The following is an alphabetical list of the twenty-seven Colleges and catalogues from which Black male and female given names were taken.

1. Agricultural and Technical College of North Carolina, Greensboro, North Carolina, 1930-1931 and 1935-1936.

2. Alcorn Agricultural and Mechanical College, Alcorn, Miss., 1932-1933.

3. Allen University, Columbia, South Carolina, 1935-1936.

4. Arkansas State College, Pine Bluff, Ark., 1930-1935.

5. Benedict College, Columbia, S. C., 1935-1936.

6. Chaflin College, Orangeburg, S. C., 1934-1935.

7. Clark University, Atlanta, Ga., 1935-1936.

8. Colored Agricultural and Normal University, Langston, Okla., 1932-1936.

9. Dillard University, New Orleans, La., 1935-1936.

10. Dunbar Junior College, Little Rock, Ark., 1931-1936.

11. Fisk University, Nashville, Tenn., 1934-1935.

12. The Florida A. and M. College, Tallahassee, Fla., 1932-1936.

13. Florida Normal and Industrial Institute, St. Augustine, Fla., 1935-1936.

14. Hampton Institute, Hampton, Virginia, 1935-1936.

15. Howard University, Washington, D. C., 1935-1936.

16. Knoxville College, Knoxville, Tenn., 1935-1936.

17. Morgan College, Baltimore, Maryland, April, 1936.

18. Morris College, Sumter, S. C., 1935-1936.

19. Prairie View State Normal and Industrial College, Prairie View, Texas, 1935-1936.

Conformity in College vs. Individuality -- COLLEGE STUDENTS, 1930's

20. Southern University and A. and M. College, Baton Rouge, La., 1935-1936.

21. State A. and M. College, Orangeburg, S. C., 1935-1936.

22. Tennessee Agricultural and Industrial State College, Nashville, Tenn., 1935-1936.

23. Tougaloo College, Tougaloo, Mississippi, 1935-1936.

24. Tuskegee Normal and Industrial Institute, Tuskegee, Alabama, 1935-1936.

25. Virginia State College for Negroes, Ettrick, Va., 1935-1936.

26. Virginia Union University, Richmond, Va., 1935-1936.

27. Voorhees Institute, Denmark, S. C., 1935-1936.

MALE
Alphabetical (Sample: 9,064)
Rate per 100,000 = 11.

Aaron 20 221	Cecil 16 177	Francis 14 154
Abraham 14 154	Charles 238 2736	Frank 84 927
Adam 11 121	Charley 15 165	Franklin 14 154
Albert 85 938	Chester 18 199	Fred 47 519
Alexander 30 331	Clarence 92 1015	Frederick 40 441
Alfred 34 375	Claude 18 199	George 238 2626
Allen 18 199	Clifford 16 177	Gerald 11 121
Alonzo 23 254	Clifton 18 199	Gilbert 6 66
Alton 11 121	Clyde 22 243	Gus 3 33
Alvin 19 210	Curtis 22 243	Guy 8 88
Amos 8 88	Daniel 30 331	Harold 48 530
Anderson 6 66	David 73 805	Harrison 8 88
Andrew 30 331	Dennis 3 33	Harry 46 508
Anthony 6 66	Doc(k) 3 33	Harvey 14 154
Archie 11 121	Donald 12 132	Henderson 6 66
Arthur 94 1037	Douglas 17 188	Henry 148 1633
Augustus 13 143	Earl 48 530	Herbert 39 430
Ben 3 33	Eddie 27 298	Herman 38 419
Benjamin 64 706	Edgar 31 342	Homer 8 88
Bernard 20 221	Edmo(u)nd 14 154	Horace 42 463
Berry 3 33	Edward 161 1776	Howard 47 519
Bill 6 66	Edwin 12 132	Hubert 12 132
Billy 6 66	Elias 3 33	Hugh 17 188
Booker 27 298	Elijah 11 121	Irvin 14 154
Caesar 3 33	Elmer 13 143	Irving 6 66
Caleb 6 66	Ernest 59 651	Isaac 27 298
Calvin 20 221	Eugene 58 640	Isaiah 20 221
Carl 20 221	Felix 6 66	Jack 20 221
Cato 3 33	Floyd 16 177	Jackson 8 88

Conformity in College vs. Individuality -- COLLEGE STUDENTS, 1930's

Jacob 14   154
Jake 3   33
James 604 6664
Jasper 10   110
Jeff 3   33
Jefferson 11   121
Jeremiah 6   66
Jerome 12   132
Jerry 6   66
Jesse 61   673
John 445   4910
Johnnie 32   252
Joe 20   221
Joseph 157   1732
Julian 14   154
Julius 22   243
Kenneth 16   177
Lamar 3   33
Lawrence 52   574
Lee 27   298
Leland 3   33
Leo 6   66
Leon 35   386
Leonard 26   287
Leroy 52   574
Leslie 15   165
Lester 3   33
Levi 6   66
Lewis 25   276
Lloyd 13   143
Louis 34   375
Lucius 14   154
Luther 23   254

Madison 3   33
Major 3   33
Malcolm 3   33
Marshall 3   33
Martin 14   154
Marvin 6   66
Matthew 24   265
Melvin 24   265
Milton 25   276
Morris 28   309
Moses 17   188
Nathan 11   121
Nathaniel 48   530
Nelson 11   121
Norman 14   154
Oliver 27   298
Oscar 25   276
Otis 11   121
Patrick 6   66
Paul 43   474
Percy 6   66
Peter 8   88
Phil 3   33
Phillip 25   276
Pleasant 3   33
Prince 3   33
Ralph 23   254
Ray 3   33
Raymond 41   452
Reginald 18   199
Reuben 14   154
Richard 74   816
Robert 248   2736

Roger 6   66
Roscoe 16   177
Roy 22   243
Russell 20   221
Sam 8   88
Samuel 127   1401
Sidney 11   121
Simon 6   66
Solomon 21   232
Stanley 3   33
Stephen 8   88
Theodore 52   574
Thomas 159   1754
Timothy 11   121
Tom 6   66
Ulysses 17   188
Vernon 20   221
Victor 8   88
Virgil 6   66
Wallace 14   154
Walter 97   1070
Warren 22   243
Washington 3   33
Wendell 11   121
Wesley 16   177
Wilbur 19   210
Will 3   33
Willard 3   33
William 522   5759
Willie 102   1125
Willis 11   121
Woodrow 6   66
Zachariah 3   33

MALE
Frequency

James 604
William 522
John 445
Charles 248
Robert 248
George 238
Edward 161
Thomas 159
Joseph 157
Henry 148
Samuel 127
Willie 102
Walter 97
Arthur 94
Clarence 92

Albert 85
Frank 84
Richard 74
David 73
Benjamin 64
Jesse 61
Ernest 59
Eugene 58
Lawrence 52
Leroy 52
Theodore 52
Earl 48
Harold 48
Nathaniel 48
Fred 47

Howard 47
Harry 46
Paul 43
Horace 42
Raymond 41
Frederick 40
Herbert 39
Herman 38
Leon 35
Alfred 34
Louis 34
Johnnie 32
Edgar 31
Alexander 30
Andrew 30

Conformity in College vs. Individuality -- COLLEGE STUDENTS, 1930's

Daniel 30	Roscoe 16	Anderson 6
Morris 28	Wesley 16	Anthony 6
Booker 27	Charley 15	Bill 6
Eddie 27	Leslie 15	Billy 6
Isaac 27	Franklin 14	Caleb 6
Lee 27	Reuben 14	Felix 6
Oliver 27	Abraham 14	Gilbert 6
Leonard 26	Edmo(u)nd 14	Henderson 6
Lewis 25	Francis 14	Irving 6
Milton 25	Harvey 14	Jeremiah 6
Oscar 25	Irvin 14	Jerry 6
Phillip 25	Jacob 14	Leo 6
Matthew 24	Julian 14	Levi 6
Melvin 24	Lucius 14	Marvin 6
Alonzo 23	Martin 14	Patrick 6
Luther 23	Norman 14	Percy 6
Ralph 23	Wallace 14	Roger 6
Clyde 22	Augustus 13	Simon 6
Curtis 22	Elmer 13	Tom 6
Julius 22	Lloyd 13	Virgil 6
Roy 22	Donald 12	Woodrow 6
Warren 22	Edwin 12	Ben 3
Solomon 21	Hubert 12	Berry 3
Aaron 20	Jerome 12	Caesar 3
Bernard 20	Adam 11	Cato 3
Calvin 20	Alton 11	Dennis 3
Carl 20	Archie 11	Doc(k) 3
Isaiah 20	Alijah 11	Elias 3
Jack 20	Gerald 11	Gus 3
Joe 20	Jefferson 11	Jake 3
Russell 20	Nathan 11	Jeff 3
Vernon 20	Nelson 11	Lamar 3
Alvin 19	Otis 11	Leland 3
Wilbur 19	Sidney 11	Lester 3
Allen 18	Timothy 11	Madison 3
Chester 18	Wendell 11	Major 3
Claude 18	Willis 11	Malcolm 3
Clifton 18	Jasper 10	Marshall 3
Reginald 18	Amos 8	Phil 3
Douglas 17	Guy 8	Pleasant 3
Hugh 17	Harrison 8	Prince 3
Moses 17	Homer 8	Ray 3
Ulysses 17	Jackson 8	Stanley 3
Cecil 16	Peter 8	Washington 3
Clifford 16	Sam 8	Will 3
Floyd 16	Stephen 8	Willard 3
Kenneth 16	Victor 8	Zachariah 3

Conformity in College vs. Individuality -- COLLEGE STUDENTS, 1930's

FEMALE
    Alphabetical (Sample: 11,148)
    Rate per 100,000 = 8.97

Addie 40 359	Eloise 39 350	Julia 80 718
Agnes 35 314	Elsie 29 260	Kathleen 13 117
Alberta 37 332	Elvira 4 36	Katy 30 269
Alice 122 1094	Emily 17 152	Laura 50 449
Alma 44 395	Emma 104 933	Lavinia 9 81
Amanda 7 63	Ernestine 31 278	Lelia 11 99
Amelia 9 81	Essie 37 332	Lena 23 206
Amy 4 36	Estelle 15 135	Leola 24 215
Ann 4 36	Esther 45 404	Letty 4 36
Anna 70 628	Ethel 106 951	Lillian 123 1103
Anne 28 251	Eugenia 17 152	Lillie 58 520
Annie 239 2144	Eunice 22 197	Lizzie 11 99
Aurelia 2 18	Eva 47 422	Lois 32 287
Beatrice 70 628	Evelyn 93 834	Louise 124 1112
Bernice 73 655	Fanny 59 526	Lucille 75 673
Bertha 69 617	Flora 13 117	Lucinda 9 81
Bessie 78 700	Florence 47 422	Lucy 53 475
Betty 22 197	Frances 69 617	Lula 46 413
Beulah 31 278	Geneva 36 323	Lydia 15 135
Blanche 41 368	Georgia 31 278	Mabel 81 727
Caroline 4 36	Gertrude 40 359	Maggie 58 520
Carolyn 20 179	Gladys 99 888	Malinda 7 63
Carrie 104 933	Grace 88 789	Mamie 57 511
C(K)atharine 111 996	Gwendolyn 24 215	Margaret 88 789
Celia 2 18	Hannah 7 63	Marguerite 34 305
Charity 2 18	Harriet 24 215	Maria(h) 9 81
Charlotte 28 251	Hattie 71 637	Marian 22 197
Christine 22 197	Hazel 76 682	Marie 95 852
Clara 58 520	Helen 149 1337	Marion 56 502
Clarissa 9 81	Henrietta 21 188	Marjorie 33 296
Clary 4 36	Hester 2 18	Martha 79 709
Cleo 18 161	Hetty 2 18	Mary 444 3983
Cora 47 422	Ida 61 547	Matilda 4 36
Cornelia 24 215	Inez 61 547	Mattie 84 753
Daisy 46 413	Irene 40 359	Maude 27 242
Delia 2 18	Irma 33 296	May(e) 35 314
Della 4 36	Isabel 2 18	Mildred 113 1014
Dolly 4 36	Isabella 7 63	Milly 9 81
Dora 15 135	Jane 7 63	Minerva 2 18
Dorothy 145 1301	Janie 31 278	Minnie 47 422
Edith 70 628	Jeanette 11 99	Miriam 11 99
Edna 90 807	Jennie 24 215	Molly 24 215
Effie 23 206	Jessie 53 475	Mozelle 4 36
Eleanor 44 395	Jewel(l) 17 152	Myra 4 36
Eliza 17 152	Jimmie 7 63	Myrtle 37 332
Elizabeth 120 1076	Joan 4 36	Nancy 26 233
Ella 55 493	Josephine 49 440	Nanny 20 179
Ellen 22 197	Juanita 58 520	Naomi 38 341

Conformity in College vs. Individuality -- COLLEGE STUDENTS, 1930's

Norma 4 36	Roberta 26 233	Susan 7 63
Nelly 32 314	Rosa 85 762	Susie 42 377
Nina 7 63	Rose 26 233	Thelma 137 1229
Nora(h) 9 81	Ruby 99 888	Tommie 15 135
Ophelia 11 99	Ruth 200 1794	Vera 39 350
Patsy 2 18	Sadie 58 520	Viola 38 341
Pauline 51 457	Sally 41 368	Violet 4 36
Pearl 69 617	Sara 39 350	Virginia 68 610
Phillis 4 36	Sarah 98 879	Vivian 50 449
Polly 2 18	Savannah 2 18	Willie 66 592
Priscilla 4 36	Silvia 15 135	Willie Mae 31 278
Rach(a)el 20 179	Sophia(e) 17 152	Winn(e)y 7 63
Rebecca 48 431	Sue 7 63	

FEMALE
Frequency

Mary 444	Edith 70	Sally 41
Annie 239	Bertha 69	Addie 40
Ruth 200	Frances 69	Gertrude 40
Helen 149	Pearl 69	Irene 40
Dorothy 145	Virginia 68	Eloise 39
Thelma 137	Willie 66	Sara 39
Louise 124	Ida 61	Vera 39
Lillian 123	Inez 61	Naomi 38
Alice 122	Fanny 59	Viola 38
Elizabeth 120	Clara 58	Alberta 37
Mildred 113	Juanita 58	Essie 37
C(K)atharine 111	Lillie 58	Myrtle 37
Ethel 106	Maggie 58	Geneva 36
Carrie 104	Sadie 58	Agnes 35
Emma 104	Mamie 57	May(e) 35
Gladys 99	Marion 56	Marguerite 34
Ruby 99	Ella 55	Irma 33
Sarah 98	Jessie 53	Marjorie 33
Marie 95	Lucy 53	Lois 32
Evelyn 93	Pauline 51	Nelly 32
Edna 90	Laura 50	Beulah 31
Grace 88	Vivian 50	Ernestine 31
Margaret 88	Josephine 49	Georgia 31
Rosa 85	Rebecca 48	Janie 31
Mattie 84	Cora 47	Willie Mae 31
Mabel 81	Eva 47	Katy 30
Julia 80	Florence 47	Elsie 29
Martha 79	Minnie 47	Anne 28
Bessie 78	Daisy 46	Charlotte 28
Hazel 76	Lula 46	Maude 27
Lucille 75	Esther 45	Nancy 26
Bernice 73	Alma 44	Roberta 26
Hattie 71	Eleanor 44	Rose 26
Anna 70	Susie 42	Cornelia 24
Beatrice 70	Blanche 41	Gwendolyn 24

Conformity in College vs. Individuality -- COLLEGE STUDENTS, 1930's

Harriet 24	Flora 13	Caroline 4
Jennie 24	Kathleen 13	Clary 4
Leola 24	Jeanette 11	Della 4
Molly 24	Lelia 11	Dolly 4
Effie 23	Lizzie 11	Elvira 4
Lena 23	Miriam 11	Joan 4
Betty 22	Ophelia 11	Letty 4
Christine 22	Amelia 9	Matilda 4
Ellen 22	Clarissa 9	Mozelle 4
Eunice 22	Lavinia 9	Myra 4
Marian 22	Lucinda 9	Norma 4
Henrietta 21	Maria(h) 9	Phillis 4
Carolyn 20	Milly 9	Priscilla 4
Nanny 20	Nora(h) 9	Violet 4
Rach(a)el 20	Amanda 7	Aurelia 2
Cleo 18	Hannah 7	Celia 2
Eliza 17	Isabella 7	Charity 2
Emily 17	Jane 7	Delia 2
Eugenia 17	Jimmie 7	Hester 2
Jewel(l) 17	Malinda 7	Hetty 2
Sophia(e) 17	Nina 7	Isabel 2
Dora 15	Sue 7	Minerva 2
Estelle 15	Susan 7	Patsy 2
Lydia 15	Winn(e)y 7	Polly 2
Silvia 15	Amy 4	Savannah 2
Tommie 15	Ann 4	

Surnames, Black

The following list represents the 100 most common surnames of Black College students. The rate per 100,000, using a sample of 22,081 Black students, is 1 = 4.528. A frequency list follows the alphabetical listing.

Black surnames were taken from the same college catalogues used to derive given names with the following exceptions:

1. Colored Agricultural and Normal University, Langston, Okla., was not used.

2. The following catalogues were added:

    a. Wilberforce University, Wilberforce, Ohio, Alumni lists after 1900 and the catalogue of 1935-1936.

    b. West Virginia State College Institute, West Va., 1935-1937.

    c. Lincoln University, Jefferson City, Missouri, 1920-1930.

    d. Armstrong High School, Richmond, Va., 1936.

Conformity in College vs. Individuality -- COLLEGE STUDENTS, 1930's

Alphabetical

Adams 47 213	Gordon 35 158	Parker 50 226
Alexander 47 213	Grant 26 118	Patterson 43 195
Allen 67 303	Gray 26 118	Payne 25 113
Anderson 99 448	Green 78 353	Perry 37 168
Austin 26 118	Greene 45 204	Phillips 26 118
Bailey 38 172	Hall 60 272	Porter 30 136
Baker 51 231	Hamilton 33 149	Price 34 154
Banks 44 199	Harris 156 706	Reed 37 168
Barnes 38 172	Harvey 27 122	Reid 37 168
Bell 49 222	Hawkins 25 113	Richardson 63 285
Booker 25 113	Hayes 41 186	Roberts 59 267
Bradley 28 127	Henderson 51 231	Robinson 196 887
Brooks 51 231	Hill 83 376	Rogers 41 186
Brown 275 1245	Holmes 38 172	Ross 48 217
Bryant 48 217	Howard 62 281	Scott 103 466
Butler 27 122	Jackson 206 933	Simmons 39 177
Campbell 48 217	James 66 299	Smith 306 1386
Carter 81 367	Jefferson 27 122	Stewart 55 249
Clark 58 263	Jenkins 41 186	Taylor 155 702
Clarke 30 136	Johnson 422 1911	Thomas 138 625
Coleman 69 312	Jones 362 1639	Thompson 123 557
Collins 38 172	Jordon 58 263	Turner 56 254
Cooper 44 199	King 67 303	Walker 115 521
Crawford 41 186	Lee 82 371	Ward 31 140
Daniels 26 118	Lewis 100 453	Washington 112 507
Davis 200 906	Martin 83 376	Watkins 39 177
Dixon 40 181	Mason 29 131	Watson 47 213
Edwards 46 208	Miller 71 321	West 26 118
Evans 56 254	Mitchell 76 344	White 106 480
Foster 46 208	Moore 107 484	Williams 389 1761
Franklin 39 177	Murray 36 163	Wilson 133 602
Freeman 31 140	Myers 27 122	Wood 26 118
Gibson 28 127	Owens 31 140	Wright 72 326
		Young 65 294

Frequency

Johnson 422	Walker 115	Wright 72
Williams 389	Washington 112	Miller 71
Jones 362	Moore 107	Coleman 69
Smith 306	White 106	Allen 67
Brown 275	Scott 103	King 67
Jackson 206	Lewis 100	James 66
Davis 200	Anderson 99	Young 65
Robinson 196	Hill 83	Richardson 63
Harris 156	Martin 83	Howard 62
Taylor 155	Lee 82	Hall 60
Thomas 138	Carter 81	Roberts 59
Wilson 133	Green 78	Clark 58
Thompson 123	Mitchell 76	Jordon 58

Conformity in College vs. Individuality -- COLLEGE STUDENTS, 1930's

Evans 56	Crawford 41	Owens 31
Turner 56	Hayes 41	Ward 31
Stewart 55	Jenkins 41	Clarke 30
Baker 51	Rogers 41	Porter 30
Brooks 51	Dixon 40	Mason 29
Henderson 51	Franklin 39	Bradley 28
Parker 50	Simmons 39	Gibson 28
Bell 49	Watkins 39	Butler 27
Bryant 48	Bailey 38	Harvey 27
Campbell 48	Barnes 38	Jefferson 27
Ross 48	Collins 38	Myers 27
Adams 47	Holmes 38	Austin 26
Alexander 47	Perry 37	Daniels 26
Watson 47	Reed 37	Grant 26
Edwards 46	Reid 37	Gray 26
Foster 46	Murray 36	Phillips 26
Greene 45	Gordon 35	West 26
Banks 44	Price 34	Wood 26
Cooper 44	Hamilton 33	Booker 25
Patterson 43	Freeman 31	Hawkins 25
		Payne 25

Most Common Given Names, White

The following is an alphabetical list of the nineteen Colleges and catalogues from which White male and female names were taken.

1. The College of the Ozarks, Clarksville, Ark., 1936-1937.

2. Florida State College for Women, Tallahassee, Fla., June, 1938.

3. Mississippi State College, State College, Miss., 1935-1936.

4. Mississippi State College for Women, Columbus, Miss., 1934-1935.

5. Mississippi Woman's College, Hattisburg, Miss., 1935-1936.

6. Oklahoma City University, Oklahoma City, Okla., 1936-1937.

7. Texas Christian University, Fort Worth, Texas, 1937-1938.

8. Tulane University, New Orleans, La., 1936-1937.

9. University of Alabama, Tuscaloosa, Ala., 1932-1933.

10. University of Arkansas, Fayetteville, Ark., 1937-1938.

11. University of Mississippi, Oxford, Miss., 1935-1936.

12. University of North Carolina, Chapel Hill, N. C., 1937-1938.

Conformity in College vs. Individuality -- COLLEGE STUDENTS, 1930's

13. University of South Carolina, Columbia, S. C., 1936-1937.

14. University of Tennessee, Knoxville, Tenn., 1937-1938.

15. University of Tulsa, Tulsa, Okla., 1938-1939.

16. University of Virginia, Charlottesville, Va., 1937-1938.

17. Vanderbilt University, Nashville, Tenn., 1937-1938.

18. Woman's College of Alabama, Montgomery, Ala., 1935-1936.

19. The Woman's College of the University of North Carolina, Greensboro, N. C., 1936-1937.

MALE

Alphabetical (Sample: 17,373)
Rate per 100,000 = 5.756

Albert 124 714	Fred 115 662	Louis 115 662
Alexander 37 213	Frederick 87 501	Martin 31 178
Alfred 67 386	George 478 2751	Marvin 46 265
Allen 32 184	Guy 31 178	Melvin 30 173
Alvin 31 178	Harold 137 789	Michael 30 173
Andrew 43 248	Harry 184 1059	Milton 55 317
Arthur 149 858	Harvey 30 173	Morris 34 196
Ben 53 305	Henry 174 1002	Norman 62 357
Benjamin 70 403	Herbert 85 489	Oscar 32 184
Bernard 61 351	Herman 66 380	Paul 186 1071
Bill 48 276	Horace 30 173	Phillip 90 518
Billy 32 184	Howard 113 650	Ralph 112 645
Bob 29 167	Hugh 70 403	Ray 32 184
Carl 96 553	Irving 28 161	Raymond 89 512
Charles 609 3505	Jack 223 1284	Richard 226 1301
Chester 29 167	James 931 5359	Robert 758 4363
Clarence 71 409	Jesse 56 322	Roger 31 178
Claude 54 311	Jim 28 161	Roy 82 472
Clyde 50 288	Joe 134 771	Russell 43 248
Daniel 62 357	John 1112 6401	Sam 55 317
David 175 1007	Joseph 308 1773	Samuel 125 720
Donald 118 679	Julius 33 190	Sidney 53 305
Douglas 29 167	Kenneth 73 420	Stanley 37 213
Earl 79 455	Lawrence 72 414	Stephen 29 167
Earnest 97 558	Lee 32 184	Theodore 42 242
Edgar 47 271	Leo 31 178	Thomas 373 2147
Edmo(u)nd 33 190	Leon 43 248	Tom 35 201
Edward 283 1629	Leonard 77 443	Vernon 32 184
Edwin 91 524	Leroy 29 167	Walter 197 1134
Elmer 31 178	Leslie 30 173	Warren 36 207
Eugene 92 530	Lester 35 201	Wilbur 31 178
Francis 35 201	Lewis 43 248	Willard 29 167
Frank 241 1387	Lloyd 42 242	William 1150 6619
		Woodrow 28 161

Conformity in College vs. Individuality -- COLLEGE STUDENTS, 1930's

MALE
    Frequency

William 1150	Frederick 87	Warren 36
John 1112	Herbert 85	Francis 35
James 931	Roy 82	Lester 35
Robert 758	Earl 79	Tom 35
Charles 609	Leonard 77	Morris 34
George 478	Kenneth 73	Edmo(u)nd 33
Thomas 373	Lawrence 72	Julius 33
Joseph 308	Clarence 71	Allen 32
Edward 283	Benjamin 70	Billy 32
Frank 241	Hugh 70	Lee 32
Richard 226	Alfred 67	Oscar 32
Jack 223	Herman 66	Ray 32
Walter 197	Daniel 62	Vernon 32
Paul 186	Norman 62	Alvin 31
Harry 184	Bernard 61	Elmer 31
David 175	Jesse 56	Guy 31
Henry 174	Milton 55	Leo 31
Arthur 149	Sam 55	Martin 31
Harold 137	Claude 54	Roger 31
Joe 134	Ben 53	Wilbur 31
Samuel 125	Sidney 53	Harvey 30
Albert 124	Clyde 50	Horace 30
Donald 118	Bill 48	Leslie 30
Fred 115	Edgar 47	Melvin 30
Louis 115	Marvin 46	Michael 30
Howard 113	Andrew 43	Bob 29
Ralph 112	Leon 43	Chester 29
Earnest 97	Lewis 43	Douglas 29
Carl 96	Russell 43	Leroy 29
Eugene 92	Lloyd 42	Stephen 29
Edwin 91	Theodore 42	Willard 29
Phillip 90	Alexander 37	Irving 28
Raymond 89	Stanley 37	Jim 28
		Woodrow 28

FEMALE
    Alphabetical (Sample: 10,750)
    Rate per 100,000 = 9.302.

Agnes 35	326	Betty(ie) 155	1442	Edith 80	744
Alice 79	735	Blanche 25	233	Edna 72	670
Alma 31	288	Caroline 24	223	Eleanor 95	884
Ann 55	512	Carolyn 50	465	Elizabeth 261	2428
Anna 66	614	C(K)atharine 254	2363	Ella 23	214
Anne 52	484	Charlotte 50	465	Ellen 27	251
Annie 77	716	Christine 32	298	Eloise 34	316
Bernice 24	223	Clara 35	326	Elsie 24	223
Bertha 25	233	Doris 85	791	Emily 39	363
Bessie 18	167	Dorothy 283	2632	Emma 44	409

Conformity in College vs. Individuality -- COLLEGE STUDENTS, 1930's

Estes 28 260	Josephine 45 419	Miriam 47 437
Ethel 41 381	Juanita 22 205	Myrtle 28 260
Eugenia 18 167	Julia 59 549	Nancy 60 558
Eva 22 205	Kathleen 41 381	Nelly 20 186
Evelyn 107 995	Laura 36 335	Norma 21 195
Florence 74 688	Lillian 64 595	Peggy 30 279
Frances 263 2446	Lois 71 660	Pauline 43 400
Georgia 17 158	Louise 131 1219	Pearl 21 195
Gertrude 28 260	Lucille 64 595	Phillis 19 177
Gladys 53 493	Lucy 35 326	Rach(a)el 25 233
Grace 78 726	Mabel 33 307	Rebecca 23 214
Harriet 44 409	Majorie 143 1330	Roberta 22 205
Hazel 50 465	Margaret 371 3451	Rose 25 233
Helen 225 2093	Marguerite 42 291	Ruby 55 512
Ida 35 326	Marie 60 558	Ruth 236 2195
Irene 22 205	Marian 30 279	Sally 22 205
Isabel 17 158	Marion 60 558	Sara 91 846
Jane 104 967	Martha 212 1972	Sarah 145 1349
Jeanette 20 186	Mattie 22 205	Sue 31 288
Jean(ne) 116 1079	Maude 21 195	Susan 28 260
Jessie 39 363	Mary 974 9060	Thelma 36 335
Jewel(1) 22 205	May(e) 31 288	Vera 24 223
Joan 24 223	Mildred 122 1135	Virginia 214 1991
		Vivian 30 279

FEMALE
Frequency

Mary 974	Annie 77	Ethel 41
Margaret 371	Florence 74	Kathleen 41
Dorothy 283	Edna 72	Emily 39
Frances 263	Lois 71	Jessie 39
Elizabeth 261	Anna 66	Laura 36
C(K)atharine 254	Lillian 64	Thelma 36
Ruth 236	Lucille 64	Agnes 35
Helen 225	Marie 60	Clara 35
Virginia 214	Marion 60	Ida 35
Martha 212	Nancy 60	Lucy 35
Betty(ie) 155	Julia 59	Eloise 34
Sarah 145	Ann 55	Mabel 33
Majorie 143	Ruby 55	Christine 32
Louise 131	Gladys 53	Alma 31
Mildred 122	Anne 52	May(e) 31
Jean(ne) 116	Carolyn 50	Sue 31
Evelyn 107	Charlotte 50	Marian 30
Jane 104	Hazel 50	Peggy 30
Eleanor 95	Miriam 47	Vivian 30
Sara 91	Josephine 45	Estes 28
Doris 85	Emma 44	Gertrude 28
Edith 80	Harriet 44	Myrtle 28
Alice 79	Pauline 43	Susan 28
Grace 78	Marguerite 42	Ellen 27

Conformity in College vs. Individuality -- COLLEGE STUDENTS, 1930's

Bertha 25	Ella 23	Maude 21
Blanche 25	Rebecca 23	Norma 21
Rach(a)el 25	Eva 22	Pearl 21
Rose 25	Irene 22	Jeanette 20
Bernice 24	Jewel(1) 22	Nelly 20
Caroline 24	Juanita 22	Phillis 19
Elsie 24	Mattie 22	Bessie 18
Joan 24	Roberta 22	Eugenia 18
Vera 24	Sally 22	Georgia 17
		Isabel 17

Surnames, White

The following is an alphabetical list of the thirteen Colleges and catalogues from which White surnames were taken.

1. Louisiana State University, Baton Rouge, La.

2. Mississippi State College, Starksville, Miss.

3. Mississippi State College for Women, Columbus, Miss.

4. Mississippi Women's College, Hattisburg, Miss.

5. University of Alabama, Tuscaloosa, Ala.

6. University of Arkansas, Fayetteville, Ark.

7. University of Georgia, Athens, Ga.

8. University of Mississippi, Oxford, Miss.

9. University of North Carolina, Chapel Hill, N. C.

10. University of South Carolina, Columbia, S. C.

11. University of Virginia, Charlottesville, Va.

12. Vanderbilt University, Nashville, Tenn.

13. Woman's College of Alabama, Montgomery, Ala.

Alphabetical
Rate per 100,000 = 7.998

Adam 47 376	Baker 29 232	Bryant 11 88
Alexander 16 128	Bell 37 296	Butler 22 176
Allen 35 280	Barnes 19 152	Campbell 41 328
Anderson 47 376	Bradley 11 88	Carter 40 320
Austin 11 88	Brooks 18 144	Clark 34 272
Bailey 17 136	Brown 89 712	Coleman 27 216

Conformity in College vs. Individuality -- COLLEGE STUDENTS, 1930's

Collins 21 168	Hopkins 16 128	Robinson 29 232
Cooper 27 216	Howard 12 96	Rogers 34 272
Cox 21 168	Jackson 43 344	Ross 15 120
Crawford 24 192	James 17 136	Russell 20 160
Davis 98 784	Jenkins 15 120	Scott 36 288
Edwards 31 248	Johnson 110 880	Shelton 11 88
Elliott 12 96	Jones 101 808	Simmons 14 112
Evans 29 232	Jordon 32 256	Smith 195 1560
Ferguson 12 96	King 36 288	Stevens 16 128
Fleming 13 104	Lee 28 224	Stewart 23 184
Fisher 10 80	Lewis 22 176	Taylor 56 448
Franklin 16 128	Martin 55 440	Thomas 36 288
Freeman 10 80	Miller 50 400	Thompson 52 416
Gardner 13 104	Mitchell 33 264	Tucker 17 136
Gordon 15 120	Montgomery 14 112	Turner 38 304
Green 19 152	Moore 75 600	Wade 13 104
Greene 13 104	Myers 19 152	Walker 44 352
Griffin 16 128	Parker 33 264	Watkins 10 80
Hall 38 304	Patterson 20 160	Watson 19 152
Hamilton 15 120	Perry 14 112	West 11 88
Harper 15 120	Phillips 36 288	White 50 400
Harris 41 328	Porter 11 88	Williams 84 672
Hart 13 104	Price 18 144	Willis 12 96
Hawkins 14 112	Reed 14 112	Wilson 54 432
Hayes 11 88	Reid 12 96	Wood 36 288
Henderson 19 152	Richardson 22 176	Wright 33 264
Hill 31 248	Roberts 33 264	Young 30 240

Frequency

Smith 195	Bell 37	Coleman 27
Johnson 110	King 36	Cooper 27
Jones 101	Phillips 36	Crawford 24
Davis 98	Scott 36	Stewart 23
Brown 89	Thomas 36	Butler 22
Williams 84	Wood 36	Lewis 22
Moore 75	Allen 35	Richardson 22
Taylor 56	Clark 34	Collins 21
Martin 55	Rogers 34	Cox 21
Wilson 54	Mitchell 33	Patterson 21
Thompson 52	Parker 33	Russell 20
Miller 50	Roberts 33	Barnes 19
White 50	Wright 33	Green 19
Adam 47	Jordon 32	Henderson 19
Anderson 47	Edwards 31	Myers 19
Walker 44	Hill 31	Watson 19
Jackson 43	Ward 31	Brooks 18
Campbell 41	Young 30	Price 18
Harris 41	Baker 29	Bailey 17
Carter 40	Evans 29	James 17
Hall 38	Robinson 29	Tucker 17
Turner 38	Lee 28	Alexander 16

Conformity in College vs. Individuality -- COLLEGE STUDENTS, 1930's

Franklin 16	Perry 14	Reid 12
Griffin 16	Reed 14	Willis 12
Hopkins 16	Simmons 14	Austin 11
Stevens 16	Fleming 13	Bradley 11
Gordon 15	Gardner 13	Bryant 11
Hamilton 15	Greene 13	Hayes 11
Harper 15	Hart 13	Porter 11
Jenkins 15	Wade 13	Shelton 11
Ross 15	Elliott 12	West 11
Hawkins 14	Ferguson 12	Fisher 10
Montgomery 14	Howard 12	Freeman 10
		Watkins 10

Unusual Names, White

MALE
(Sample: 17,373)

Abraham 9	Aran	Bobbie Welma
Abram	Ardis	Bonito
Acy	Argyle	Bonnie 2
Adna	Arkie	Brutus
Adron	Arlie	Buchel
Albin	Armand	Buck
Alcide 2	Arromanus	Bunn
Aldo	Artemus	Bunyan
Aljo	Arvine	Byrl
Allie	Asa	Caesar
Almon	Asbill	Caleb
Alnus	Ashamed	Cambrai
Almyra	Athel	Camillus
Alney	Aundee	Cammie
Aloysius	Ausmon	Capers 2
Alpa	Azad	Captain
Alpheus	Azile	Caredo
Alphonse 3	Balmer	Caris
Alphonso	Balsorah	Carleslie
Alto 2	Banner	Carlo
Altona	Barto	Carlos 2
Alvah	Basil 3	Carmel
Alvan	Battle 2	Casimir 3
Alvie 3	Beamon	Casmus
Amalveno	Benjamin Franklin 3	Cerf
Amedie	Bertel	Chad
Americus	Benjamin Harrison	Challie
Ancel 2	Bestor	Chapel
Ander	B'Ho	Charles Wesley
Andre	Bion 2	Chestmir
Andrew Jackson 6	Bird	Cheves
Angelo 2	Birnie	Chivous
Anselm	Blaize	Chock

326

Conformity in College vs. Individuality -- COLLEGE STUDENTS, 1930's

Cicero	Eason	Fes
Cleatus 2	Einar 2	Finfred
Cleberne	Elexis	Finis 2
Cleed	Elgar	Fleet
Clelan	Elgey	Flinn
Cleodus 2	Eli 5	Floy
Cleon 2	Elias 5	Foi
Cleophus	Elijah 2	Foy
Cletus	Elisha 3	France
Clody	Elm	Francis Xavier
Clovis	Elmo 5	Frantz
Cloyce	Elmou	French 4
Cloyd 2	Elmus	Frenchie
Clytus	Elroy	Gabe
Collie	Elzie	Gallie
Colon	Emanuel 4	Gar
Colonel	Emelious	Garden
Columbus	Emil	Garrie Lee
Coram	Emile 6	Gayle 2
Cosmas	Emilius	Gedney
Council	Emit	General
Coy 5	Emmanuel 3	George Washington 6
Crete 2	Emmette	Gerd
Criddle	Ennis	Gerry
Crysup	Enoch 2	Gervaise
Cy	Enos	Geilcin
Cyrace	Enrique	Gillie
Dallas 2	Enzo	Glathan
Damaris	Ephraim 2	Glendy
Damon	Erastus	Goah
Dana 2	Erb	Gradie
Daniel Webster 2	Erdice	Greck
Davine	Eris	Griff
Dee 2	Ervell	Grover Cleveland
Del	Ervil	Guido 3
Demetrius	Escar	Guion
Denver	Estus	Gurley
Denzil	Ethelred	Gustaf
Derry	Etol	Gustave 2
Devanie	Euel	Gustavus Adolphus
Dial	Eulan 2	Guss
Dimitry	Eulis	Guy
Dolfo	Evander	Gynne
Dominic 2	Evon	Hallum
Dominick	Ewel	Haman
Donal	Ezra 2	Hans
Doyle	Fain Pink	Happy 2
Duffel	Fendol	Harle
Duke	Ferdi	Harlos
Du Val	Ferdie	Harva
Earon	Fernando	Harvel
Early 2	Ferreol	Hastel

Conformity in College vs. Individuality -- COLLEGE STUDENTS, 1930's

Haze	John Alden	Levi
Heard	John Jacob Astor	Levis
Hector	John Milton	Lieutelle
Heman	John Randolph	Lilius
Henry Clay 4	John Westly	Linus
Henry Grady	Jose	Loather
Herbert Spencer	Josiah	Lon 2
Hercules	Josua 2	Lonas
Herlong	Judge	Lonie
Hi	Jule	Lonnie 5
Hickory	Jules 3	Lorin
Hilah	Junius 4	Lovick
Hillrie	Justino	Loyal
Hilmar	Kaleb	Loyce
Hodby	Karin	Lucious
Hoke	Kiah 2	Luman
Holland	Kile	Macagal
Hosmer	Kimber	Mace
Hoy	Kincer	Major 3
Huel	Kinch Exam, Jr.	Manah
Hugo	King 2	Mannie
Hulette Noah	Kip	Marcellus 3
Huss	Kirt	Marcel
Hyle	Kitt	Marcus
Ignacio	Kleber	Marie 4
Ignatius	Krank	Marius
Iloff	Kusher	Marne
Irbing	Label	Marte
Isaac 10	Ladislav	Martin Luther
Isadore 3	Lafayette	Marvilee
Isham	Lamb 2	Marzine
Isidore 2	La Monte	Mathias
Isiah	Lance	Matter
Israel 2	Lancelot	Mauldin
Ivan 2	Lavada Frenchie	Maunsel
Jabus	Lavelle	Mel
Jac	La Verne 2	Melvan
Jack Dempsey	Lazard	Melzar
Jacques 2	Lazarus	Meron
James Pershing 2	Lynt	Mert
Jan	Leander	Meubern
Jarmie	Lecil	Milam
Jay 3	Leize	Mildin
Jay Gould	Lelie	Milledge
Jay Tee	Len	Moe
Jefferson Davis	Leno	Moise 2
Jehu	Lent	Monette
Jeptha 2	Leonidas 2	Mortie
Jere	Leoncie	Mose 2
Jess Willard 2	Leron	Moses 3
Joab	Leve	Mose Law
Joffre Pershing	Le Vere	Myra

Conformity in College vs. Individuality -- COLLEGE STUDENTS, 1930's

Myron	Pichegree	Selix
Narvin	Piercy	Senate
Nath	Pierre 4	Serbetus
Neo	Pincus	Sereno
Nicolaos	Polie	Sharon
Nim	Pompeo	Shed
Noah	Porcher	Shed Hill
Noah Webster	Pleasant	Sherlock Holmes
Noble 2	Prieth	Shiprah
Noel 4	Prime	Shirl
Nollie	Quillin	Shoal
Nonie	Quint	Socrates
Normal	Rabon	Solomon 3
Norval	Ralsa	Solon
Obadiah	Ralston	Spurgeon
Obed	Ramelle	Spurgeon Bonaparte
Odie	Ransom	Squire
Odus	Rapheal 2	Sy
Offa	Readue	Tasso
Ogie	Reagon	Te Wyatt
Olaf	Reh	Thea
Omar 5	Rene	Theron 4
Omer	Reno 2	Therron
Ople	Reufine	Thetus
Oran 2	Revis	Theus
Ord	Robert E. Lee	Thomas Jefferson 3
Oren 4	Roby	Thomas Nelson Page
Orel	Roddy	Tiffin
Orgie	Roelof	Tivey
Orlan 2	Rollo	Tobias
Orle	Roman	Toxey 3
Orrie	Rome	Tracie
Orris 2	Romuel	Trez
Orval 2	Romulus	Trice
Orvis 2	Rooney	Troas
Otha	Rosendo	Trois
Othel	Roupen	Trosper
Othmiel	Royal 9	Trox
Otho	Royd	Troy 10
Otus	Ruel	Truxton
Ovid 2	Russian	Tuckey
Ovis	Sabin	Tullis
Ozmus	Salvador	Tyne
Pardue	Salvatore 2	Tyree
Partee	Sandy	Ual
Pascal	Saul 3	Ulain
Paschal 2	Saverine	Urath 2
Pasquale	Savey	Uriah
Pedro 3	Seah	Val
Pershing	Seavy	Valgean
Pharris	Sebron	Varley
Phineas	Seisel	Varon

Conformity in College vs. Individuality -- COLLEGE STUDENTS, 1930's

Vasil	Virgis	Woodie
Vasser	Voen	Woodrow Wilson 16
Veit Avel	Volney	Woody
Veldon	Vondas	Word
Venancio	Vonno	Worth
Venetia	Waitus 2	Wray
Verne	Waldemar	Yale
Verner	Walter Scott 3	Yuille
Vernie	Washington Irving 2	Zash
Versie Luke	Weeber	Zearl
Vester	Welch	Zelle
Victor Emmanuel	Wendall Holmes	Zenas
Victor Hugo	Willied	Zeno 2
Villie Pique Shivers	Wishard 2	Ziv
Vim	Wiltz	Zolomon
		Zygrfied

FEMALE
(Sample: 10,750)

Abigail	Amelia 7	Basha
Adnen	Amret	Bee 2
Adrian	Andra	Belva 2
Adriana	Andrea	Bennie
Adris	Andromedia	Bera
Aenard	Angela	Bernadette
Aina	Angelo 2	Bernadine
Alba	Ara	Bernedene
Alda	Arianna	Bershe
Aleta	Ardis	Berta 2
Aletha	Ariette	Bertie 2
Alethea	Arlita	Bethel 4
Alexandra	Armanda	Billie 7
Alfredina	Armenia	Billy
Alieze	Arnette	Billie Burke
Alisa	Arthemise 2	Billy Burke
Alisia	Artie	Birdie 3
Allefair	Arystine	Bitsy
Almarine	Astrid	Bleaca
Almeda	Athalie	Bliss
Almeta	Attant	Blondelle
Alpha	Audley	Bob 2
Alst	Audrin	Bobbie 2
Alta 3	Aulsie	Bobbye
Althea 4	Ava 2	Bonita 4
Altie	Ava Rae	Bonny
Alto	Avalee	Brenelle
Alva	Avis 5	Brownie 2
Alvah	Azelea	Brown, Cascilla
Alvina	Babette	Brya
Ama	Barney	Buena
Amanda 5	Barrier	Burdette

Conformity in College vs. Individuality -- COLLEGE STUDENTS, 1930's

Butroyce	Crissy	Elmo
Byrdie Opal	Crystal	Elodie 2
Cajetine	Dallas Belle	Elspeth
Caledonia	Dallia	Elta
Calista	Dallila	Elton
Camilla 6	Damora	Elva 4
Camille 9	Daphna	Elvera
Capitola	Daphyne 2	Elvia
Carese	Darma	Elvira
Carlee 2	Darrah	Elviretta
Carlene	Dartha	Elvis
Carlota	Darween	Elvita
Carmela	Davida	Elvy
Carmelite	Dawn 2	Emajean
Carnele	Dea	Emerald
Carnie	Deborah	Emile
Caro	Delene	Emilia
Caro Beth	Delma	Emogene 2
Cecil	Delphine	Emozene
Celestia	Delta 2	Ena
Celine	Dimples	Enal
Ceola	Ditty	Endeana 2
Charlene 3	Dola	Enola
Charles	Donis	Erika
Charlette	Dorlene	Erladean
Charline 2	Dorthea	Ermile
Cherrie	Dottie	Ermine
Cherry 2	Dove 2	Erminie
Chettie	Dovie	Erna
Chloe 2	Drusilla	Erva
Christiana	Duane 3	Essie 4
Christme	Dulcie 2	Estamae
Civia	Dulcie Lee	Esthma
Clarabeth	Earcy	Estie
Clarissa	Ebie	Ethelvest
Clela	Ebbie	Ethelwyn
Cleolene	Edda	Ethelyne
Clementeene	Eddie	Eudena
Clemmie	Edelle	Eudora
Cleona	Edith Cavelle	Eulalie 3
Cleta	Edmonia	Eulila
Clio	Edra	Ever
Clothilde	Effie 5	Evetta
Clova	Elba 2	Faith 3
Clytee	Elda	Farra
Coleene	Elen	Faustine
Conchetta	Elflaeda Brunhilde	Fay
Congetta	El Fleda	Felicia 2
Coral	Ellaree	Felicie
Cozie	Ellagene	Felma
Creo	Ellemena	Fern 4
Crenola	Elly	Fernande

Conformity in College vs. Individuality -- COLLEGE STUDENTS, 1930's

Ferna Faye	Hettilu	Kasimir
Fillette	Hil	Katibel
Flavia	Hildur	Katurah
Flavil	Hira	Kennette
Fleda	Homer	Lady 2
Fleurette	Honor	Lalage
Floe	Hope 5	Lalla 2
Floread	Hyacinth	Lallie
Foreine	Idalane	Lalouise
Florida	Idella	Lamar
Florine 2	Idelle 2	Lamora
Florita 2	Idena	La Nette
Florrie 2	Iderstine	La Rue 2
Flossie 3	Ika	Lauree
Floy 4	Ila 6	Laurita
Fortuna	Ilene	La Verda
Frank	Illa 2	La Vere
Frankie 2	Ilma	Laverne
Freda 2	Ilse	La Vida
Gail	Ima 2	Lavine
Gails	Imogene 11	Lavinia
Gaithel	Ina	Lavonia 2
Gatsye	Inda	Lawles
Gaynelle 2	India	Lea
Genelle	Ineta	Learline
George 2	Inetha	Le Claire
Georgenia 2	Irby	Lee 3
Georgie 2	Isla	Leita
Geral Dean	Istalena	Lemora
Garda	Iuka	Lenamae
Gerry	Iva	Lenna
Gillie	Iveene	Leoline
Giralda	Jacque	Le Noir
Glatha	Jacqueline 5	Leota
Glenda	James	Lera
Glynda	Jamesina	Lessie
Golda 2	Janella	Lestle
Goldie 3	Jaxie	Leta 2
Gowdylock	Jenelle	Letha
Gralande	Jenny Wren	Letitia 2
Gratia	Jere	Letta
Grosie	Jessamine	Lexey 2
Gussie	Jettie	Liddie
Guynelle	Jewel	Lili
Gwendoyn	Johnnie 2	Lima
Hanna	Johnnie Lou	Linda
Hannah 3	Johnsie	Linnea
Harryette	Joe	Lizette
Hasseltine	Joy 3	Lloyd
Hazie	Joseph	Lolla
Henri Motte	Juana	Lollie
Hermoine	Jule	Loma

Conformity in College vs. Individuality -- COLLEGE STUDENTS, 1930's

Lonnie	Maruvilburn	Nadine 5
Lonnie Belle	Marjean	Nan
Loree	Mar Letta	Nanie
Lorelle	Marshlea	Nannie
Lorna Doone	Martel	Narcie
Loten	Marthajean	Natalee
Louessie	Martha Washington	Natalie 4
Louie 2	Marvel	Nathalie 2
Lourie	Marylois	Neata
Love	Masquelette	Needa
Lovie	Mathilda	Nelda 4
Loyce	Matilda	Nelia
Luana	Matilie	Nello 2
Luanne	Mauree	Nelwyn
Lucerne	Mavine	Nena
Lucretia	Mavis 3	Neola
Lurline 4	Mavolyn	Neppie
Lu Mar 2	Maxine 9	Neta
Luna 2	Mazie	Netta
Lura	Meaze	Neva 4
Lutrelle	Meida	Nevada
Lyal	Melinda	Newrie
Lyall	Melissa	Ninette
Lyle	Melna	Nona 3
Lyn	Mercedes	Nona Lurleen
Lynelle	Meriba	Noreen
Lyra	Merita	Noreene
Lyrabeth	Merlee	Norine
Mabry	Meta 2	Nubye
Magda	Metha	Nula
Magdalena 2	Mignon	Nyleen
Maida	Mignonne 2	Odette
Malinda 3	Mimi	Odia
Manda	Minda	Odie Dee
Manine	Mindel	Ola 2
Manerva	Mirial	Olene
Mansleat	Missouri	Olneta
Maoma	Mittie	Omah
Maple	Modena	Oma 2
Maradele	Modene	Omega 3
Marcella	Modest	Ona 3
Marcelynn	Mona 5	Ona Gazelle
Mardelle	Monette	O'Neal
Mardite	Monita	Ora 3
Margel	Montine	Orra
Marene	Morene	Othma
Mariada	Moselle	Ottie
Marigayle	Mossie	Ouida 6
Mariella	Mozell	Ouita 2
Marina 3	Mozelle 3	Oval
Marinelle	Myrtie	Ozalea
Marionette	Nadia	Ozane

Conformity in College vs. Individuality -- COLLEGE STUDENTS, 1930's

Ozell
Ozella
Pamela 2
Parma
Patti Gee
Penelope 2
Perci Mae
Petrea
Phala Marie
Pharos
Phil
Phylis
Phyllis 14
Pinkey
Portia
Priscilla 7
Q'Milla New
Rabbye
Ramelle
Ramona 2
Rayanna
Re
Ree
Regine
Rela
Rema
Remie
Rena 2
Renah
Renee
Renna
Renna Europa
Reta
Retha 2
Retta
Reva
Reverie
Rhea
Rheata
Rhetta
Rheufina
Rhoba
Rhoda 2
Rhonda 2
Rhonwynn
Rilla 2
Rita
Riva
Robens 2
Roma 4
Romayne
Rose Marie

Rothe
Roxilu
Roy Elizabeth
Rozelle
Rudine
Rufie
Runette
Rutha
Salome
Sammie 2
Sammye
Santa
Saphronia
Sarabel
Saralen
Sarah Bernhardt
Selene
Seraphim
Serita
Shoshana
Sicily Sallis
Sidney
Sidonie 2
Sina
Sonia
Sophia 2
Sophie 5
Sophronia
Sophronie
Sula
Sunshine
Sureen
Sydette
Sydney
Talish
Tempe
Terah
Tex
Thais 3
Thea
Theola
Thermal
Theron
Thowasine
Thresse
Thyra 2
Tillye
Tivis
Trugen
Twila
Tybell
Una

Ursula 2
Urlyne
Valerie 2
Valoris
Vanescel
Vardaman
Vastine
Vaulda
Velda
Velora
Vena
Venda
Venita
Verd
Verlia
Verlin
Vermal
Verna
Verner
Vernie 2
Verona
Veryl 2
Vesta
Vida
Vilda
Vineta
Vinnie
Virgia
Virginia Dare
Visa
Vista
Vivienne 2
Volita
Vonceil 2
Voncile 2
Vonnie
Vontese
Voris 2
Vyande
Wade
Waldeen
Wallie
Walterine
Walterrene
Wanda 7
Waverlyn
Welcome
Welda
Weleska
Whit
Wilda 4
Willadene

Conformity in College vs. Individuality -- COLLEGE STUDENTS, 1930's

Willard	Wylodine 2	Zelinda
Willardine 2	Wynette	Zella 4
Willilou	Xymena	Zelma
Willyne	Yetta	Zettie
Wilmanell	Yola	Zilpah
Wimbreth	Yolanda	Zita
Winnie 10	Yvette 2	Zoe
Winona 4	Yvonne 3	Zona 2
Winta	Zaidee	Zorada
Woddy	Zanola	Zovira
Wrenella	Zelda	Zula
Wrennie	Zelia	Zulieme
		Zulma

Unusual Black Names Used by Whites

MALE

The following list reflects some unusual Black male given names found amongst White males. There are 398 names in all; however, many others are omitted either due to variant spellings such as Alex/Allex or due to another name added such as King/King Aguppa.

Abraham	Atlas	Cage	Comer
Abram	August	Cam	Commodore
Absalom	Babe	Cap	Coon
Ace	Baron	Capers	Cord
Acquilla	Barto	Captain	Cortez
Adolphus	Battle	Carlos	Council
Alabama	Bear	Carmel	Coy
Alaska	Beauford	Carthen	Creed
Almon	Benjamin	Cash	Dallas
Aloysius	Franklin	Cephas	Daniel
Alto	Benjamin	Chapel	Webster
Alvah	Harrison	Charles	Dante
Americus	Bishop	Wesley	Darius
Andre	Blue	Christian	Darling
Andrew	Bluff	Cicero	Darwin
Jackson	Bodie	Claudius	Dee
Angelo	Bonnie	Cleophus	Del
Antone	Boykin	Cleotus	Demetrius
Antonio	Brutus	Cletus	Denver
Aquilla	Buck	Cloud	Derry
Ardis	Bud	Clovis	Detroit
Argo	Buddie	Cluese	Diamond
Ariel	Buddy	Cobie	Dink
Arkansas	Bunyon	Cody	Doc(k)
Arkie	Burl	Collie	Doctor
Artie	Butch	Colonel	Dolphus
Artis	Caesar	Columbus	Donnie

335

Conformity in College vs. Individuality -- COLLEGE STUDENTS, 1930's

Dozier	Haze	Lamb	Noel
Duffy	Hector	Lance	Nollie
Duke	Heman	Lazarus	Normal
Dutch	Hence	Le Roy	Norval
Earlie	Henry Clay	Leander	Obed
Early	Hercules	Lem	Obediah
Echo	Hezekiah	Lemon	Obie
Echols	Hiawatha	Len	Ocie
Edwon	Hoke	Leonidas	Odie
Elam	Holland	Levi	Olee
Eli	Hosea	Levis	Olin
Elias	Hulet (Hood)	Levy	Ollie
Elijah	Ignacio	Lige	Omar
Elisha	Ignatius	Lightning	Omega
Ellie	Ike	Lon	Oral
Elmo	Ireland	London	Oran
Emanuel	Isaac	Lonie	Orie
Emile	Isadore	Lonnie	Orion
English	Isaiah	Looney	Orlando
Ennis	Isham	Love	Orrie
Enoch	Isiah	Lucious	Orval
Enos	Israel	Lum	Osceola
Ephraim	Ivy	Lummie	Otha
Era	Jabe	Mace	Othal
Erasmus	Jabus	Major	Othello
Erastus	Jan	Malachi	Otho
Erlie	Jay	Mannie	Ozie
Esco	Jay Gould	Manzie	Ozy
Estus	Jeptha	Marcel	Ozzie
Euel	Jeremiah	Marcellus	Paris
Eulon	Jess Willard	Marcus	Paschal
Eureka	Jeter	McKinley	Pee Wee
Evander	Jethro	Mell	Perk
Evon	Jett	Micajah	Pershing
Ezekiel	Jettie	Milledge	Philander
Ezra	Jock	Milo	Pick
Fate	Jodie	Miner	Pierre
Finis	John Milton	Mingle	Pink
Floy	John Wesley	Minor	Plato
Fountain	Jonah	Minus	Pleas
French	Josh	Monte	Pleasant
Gabe	Joshua	Mordecai	Poley
Gardelle	Josiah	Mose	Primus
Garden	Jude (Moore)	Moses	Prince
General	Judge	Nando	Quintus
George	Jule	Napoleon	Ralston
Washington	Junior	Nebraska	Rance
Gid (Davis)	Junius	Nias	Ransom
Gideon	Justice	Nimrod	Raphael
Gillie	Kiah	Noah	Ras
Gurley	King	Noah Webster	Red
Gustave	Kip	Noble	Reedy
	Laddie		

336

Conformity in College vs. Individuality -- COLLEGE STUDENTS, 1930's

Remus	Sim	Tip	Wade
Robert E. Lee	Singer	Tobe	Walter
Rollie	Socrates	Tobias	Scott
Roman	Solon	Toby	Wash
Romeo	Son	Toledo	Washington
Romie	Sonny	Toy	Irving
Romulus	Sonny Boy	Troy	Wave
Romus	Spurgeon	Tullis	Welcome
Roosevelt	Squire	Tyree	Woodie
Royal	Stonewall	Tyrus	Woodrow
Rube	Stonewall	Ulysses	Wilson
Rufus	Jackson	Urban	Woody
St. Elmo	Sug	Uriah	Yankee
Samp	Taft	Urie	Zachariah
Sampson	Tampa	Usher	Zack
Sandy	Tandy	Valdee	Zeb
Sank	Texas	Valentine	Zebulon
Saul	Theophilus	Vanderbilt	Zell
Sebron	Theopolis	Veo	Zema
Selix	Theron	Ves	Zeno
Shade	Theus	Vester	Zeph
Shed	Thomas	Virgis	Zid
Shorty	Jefferson	Waddie	Zollie

FEMALE

The following list reflects some unusual Black female given names found amongst White females. There are 703 names in all; however, many others are omitted either due to variant spellings such as Abia/Abiah or due to another name added such as Icy/Icy Blizzard.

Abigail	America	Aubra	Bennie
Adda	Ammie	Auline	Bera
Agatha	Aquilla	Australia	Berdie
Albertina	Ara	Avalon	Berma
Aletha	Ardelia	Avice	Bernadette
Alethea	Ardella	Avie	Berta
Alethia	Ardis	Avis	Bertie
Alfreda	Arie	Azalee	Biddie
Allee	Arizona	Azaline	Bina
Almeda	Armanda	Azie	Binah
Almena	Armenia	Azzie	Birda
Almeta	Arnette	Babe	Birdie
Alpha	Arrie	Baby	Birtie
Alpheus	Arris	Bama	Blondelle
Alta	Arta	Bamma	Bloom
Altha	Artelia	Beauty	Blumie
Althea	Artie	Bee	Bobbie
Alva	Asia	Bela	Brownie
Amanda	Athalia	Belva	Buena
Amelia	Attie	Benita	Camille

337

Conformity in College vs. Individuality -- COLLEGE STUDENTS, 1930's

Cammie	Delphine	Erninie	Glenda
Candace	Delsie	Erna	Golda
Cannie	Delta	Essie	Golden
Carmel	Dena	Estoria	Goldie
Cassandra	Dennie	Etha	Gussie
Cassie (Fell)	Dera	Etheldra	Hanna
Celestia	Desire	Ethelwyn	Hannah
Ceola	Dessa	Ethelyne	Harryette
Charity	Dessie	Etoy	Hassie
Charlene	Dicey	Ettie	Hennie
Charlie	Dicie	Eudora	Hepsie
Charline	Dicy	Eufaula	Hessie
Cherrie	Dillie	Eulah	Honor
Cherry	Dimple	Eulalia	Hope
Chessie	Dinah	Eulalie	Hulda
China	Docia	Eulila	Hyacinth
Chloe	Docie	Euphemia	Icie
Christiana	Doll	Eura	Icy
Cindy	Dollie	Evalena	Idelia
Cissie	Dona	Evetta	Idella
Clarine	Donie	Exie	Idelle
Clarissa	Donnie	Fairy	Idena
Claudie	Doreen	Faith	Idonia
Claudine	Doretha	Felicia	Ila
Clementina	Dorinda	Fern	Ilene
Clementine	Dove	Fleta	Ima
Clemmie	Dovie	Fletta	Imogene
Clennice	Duella	Florene	Ina
Cleopatra	Easter	Floria	India
Clinia	Ebbie	Florida	Indiana
Clio	Edda	Floride	Inetha
Clotilde	Eddie	Florie	Iowa
Clover	Edmonia	Florine	Isadora
Clytee	Edria	Florita	Isola
Columbia	Effie	Florrie	Isolene
Consuelo	Eldra	Flossie	Isoline
Cordie	Electa	Floy	Isophine
Cozie	Electra	Fostine	Isora
Creola	Elmo	Frankie	Iva
Cressie	Elvira	Freda	Ivory
Cullie	Elvise	Freddie	Izella
Dahlia	Emerald	Frederica	Izetta
Dallas	Ena	Fredericka	Janelle
Datie	Enid	Fronia	Jeddie
Davie	Ennis	Fronnie	Jeffie
Dawn	Enola	Garcia	Jemima
Deborah	Eppie	Genoa	Jenelle
Dee	Epsie	Georgie	Jerusha
Delilah	Era	Gertha	Jestine
Deloria	Eris	Gertis	Jetta
Delphia	Erla	Gillie	Jettie
Delphin	Ermine	Gladiola	Jewel

Conformity in College vs. Individuality -- COLLEGE STUDENTS, 1930's

Jimmie	Lida	Mandy	Myrtie
Joe	Lima	Manilla	Myrtis
Johnnie	Lina	Mannie	Nadine
Johnsie	Linda	Marcella	Nannie
Josia	Linnie	Marcelline	Narcie
Joy	Lissie	Maria	Narcissa
Juana	Liza	Mariella	Natalee
Jule	Lodie	Marionette	Natalie
Juno	Loleta	Martha	Nealie
Justine	Lolita	Washington	Neola
Kansas	Lollie	Maryland	Nevada
Katrine	Lona	Marzie	Nobie
Kinnie	Lonie	Mathilda	Nodie
Kissie	Lonnie	Matilda	Nola
Kizzie	Loree	Maudine	Nolia
La Perle	Lorelle	Mauline	Nona
La Vada	Lorine	Mavis	Nonie
La Verne	Lossie	Maxine	Nonnie
Lady	Louana	Maydelle	Norene
Lady Bird	Lourie	Mazie	Norice
Lannie	Louvenia	Medora	Norine
Larceny	Love	Melinda	Novel
Lavella	Lovenia	Melissa	Obelia
Laverta	Loventrice	Melvina	Obera
Lavina	Lovey	Melvira	Obie
Lavinia	Lovie	Memory	Ocie
Lavonia	Lucinda	Mercedes	Oda
Lazelle	Lucretia	Merlee	Odelia
Lea	Ludie	Merline	Odelle
Learline	Luna	Mertie	Odessa
Leatha	Lunette	Meta	Offie
Lecie	Lura	Mettie	Ofie
Leda	Lurania	Mignon	Ola
Lee	Lurlene	Minda	Olena
Leeda	Lurline	Mineola	Olene
Leitha	Luster	Minta	Oma
Lellie	Lutie	Missouri	Omeda
Lennie	Luvenia	Mittie	Omega
Leoma	Lycille	Modelle	Omelia
Leontine	Lynette	Modena	Omera
Leota	Macedonia	Modest	Omie
Lera	Macie	Monia	Ona
Lerline	Madie	Monica	Oneida
Lessie	Madonna	Monnie	Onida
Letha	Magdalena	Montez	Onie
Lethia	Magnolia	Mortina	Ora
Letitia	Mahala	Moselle	Orena
Levada	Maida	Mosetta	Oretha
Levenia	Malinda	Mossie	Oria
Levina	Malissa	Mozelle	Orie
Lexie	Mallie	Mozie	Orlena
Lexine	Manda	Musette	Orpha

Conformity in College vs. Individuality -- COLLEGE STUDENTS, 1930's

Orrie	Reva	Tecora	Vernice
Osa	Rhea	Telitha	Verona
Osceola	Rhetta	Tella	Veronica
Osie	Rhoda	Tempie	Versie
Ossie	Rhodie	Tempy	Vertlee
Otella	Richardine	Tena	Veta
Otha	Rilla	Tennesee	Vicie
Ottie	Rissie	Tennie	Victory
Ouida	Rita	Tensie	Vida
Oval	Riva	Tera	Vienna
Ozane	Robena	Tessie	Vina
Ozell	Roda	Tex	Vinia
Ozella	Rodella	Texas	Vinie
Ozelle	Roma	Texie	Vinnie
Ozena	Rosebud	Thalia	Wander
Ozie	Roselle	Theodosia	Welcome
Ozola	Rosena	Theola	Wessie
Pallie	Rozell	Thomasine	Wildie
Pamela	Rozella	Thursa	Willa
Paralee	Rozelle	Thyra	Willene
Parmie	Rozzie	Tildy	Willianna
Patience	Sabina	Tina	Winnie
Pattie	Sabra	Tinie	Winona
Pearlie	Salena	Tinnie	Woody
Penelope	Salome	Tommie	Wortie
Penny	Samantha	Topie	Wrennie
Pensacola	Samella	Tressie	Wylena
Pernie	Sammie	Trudie	Wylene
Philippa	Sannie	Tula	Yvonne
Phillis	Saphronia	Twila	Zada
Phylis	Savannah	Una	Zadie
Piccola	Selena	Ursula	Zelda
Pink	Selina	Vada	Zella
Pinkey	Sennie	Valda	Zelma
Pinkie	Senora	Valeria	Zena
Pluma	Serena	Valerie	Zenia
Portia	Simmie	Vallie	Zenobia
Primrose	Sina	Vandola	Zeola
Princess	Sophia	Vandora	Zerline
Priscilla	Sophie	Vanella	Zeta
Prue	Sophronia	Vannie	Zetha
Queen	Sudie	Vashti	Zettie
Queenie	Sula	Vastine	Zilla
Quinnie	Sunie	Vee	Zillah
Rama	Sunny	Vella	Zilphie
Ramona	Sunshine	Venera	Zipporah
Rebie	Swannie	Venetta	Zola
Reena	Sylvania	Verdelle	Zollie
Rena	Tabitha	Verdie	Zona
Renna	Talulah	Verla	Zora
Ressie	Tamar	Verlee	Zula
Reta	Tannie	Vernell	Zylpha

Black Names in America

Conformity in College vs. Individuality

Source List V: COLLEGE AND SLAVE NAMES

One hundred most common Black Male College Student names not found amongst 100 Slave Males.

Willie	Louis	Carl
Walter	Johnnie	Isaiah
Clarence	Edgar	Russell
Benjamin	Morris	Vernon
Ernest	Booker	Alvin
Eugene	Eddie	Wilbur
Lawrence	Oliver	Chester
Leroy	Leonard	Claude
Theodore	Milton	Clifton
Earl	Oscar	Reginald
Harold	Matthew	Douglas
Nathaniel	Melvin	Hugh
Fred	Alonao	Ulysses
Howard	Luther	Cecil
Paul	Ralph	Clifford
Horace	Clyde	Floyd
Raymond	Curtis	Kenneth
Frederick	Julius	Roscoe
Herbert	Roy	Charley
Herman	Warren	Leslie
Leon	Bernard	Franklin

One hundred most common Slave Male names not found amongst 100 College Students.

Sam	Phil	Cato
Tom	Dave	Hardy
Jim	Will	Jake
Peter	Caesar	Madison
Bob	Davy	Elias
Bill	Dennis	Elijah
Ben	Ephraim	Isham
Dick	Nathan	Lem
Jacob	Prince	Nat
Ned	Anderson	Pompey
Stephen	Green	York
Abram	Jeff	Harrison
Jerry	Amos	Joshua
Washington	Jackson	Martin
Billy	Jordon	Robin
Simon	Primus	Spencer
Anthony	Gilbert	Cyrus
Nelson	Henderson	Eli
Willis	Pleasant	Gabriel
Ellick	Sampson	Jefferson
Adam	Andy	Wash

Conformity in College vs. Individuality -- COLLEGE AND SLAVE NAMES

Thirty-seven names common to slave and Black College lists, Male.

John	Frank	Reuben
Henry	Daniel	Thomas
George	Alfred	Edward
Charles	Andrew	Solomon
Jack	David	Alexander
William	Jesse	Richard
Joe	Robert	Joseph
Moses	Allen	Samuel
Isaac	Edmond	Arthur
James	Aaron	Phillip
Harry	Abraham	Wesley
Lewis	Albert	Calvin
		Lee

One hundred most common Black Female College Student names not found amongst 100 Slave Females.

Ruth	Pearl	Addie
Annie	Virginia	Gertrude
Helen	Willie	Irene
Dorothy	Ida	Eloise
Thelma	Inez	Sara
Louise	Juanita	Vera
Lillian	Lillie	Naomi
Mildred	Maggie	Viola
Ethel	Sadie	Alberta
Carrie	Mamie	Essie
Gladys	Marion	Myrtle
Ruby	Ella	Geneva
Marie	Jesse	May(e)
Evelyn	Pauline	Marguerite
Edna	Vivian	Irma
Rosa	Josephine	Marjorie
Mattie	Cora	Lois
Mabel	Eva	Beulah
Bessie	Florence	Ernestine
Hazel	Minnie	Georgia
Lucille	Daisy	Janie
Bernice	Lula	Willie Mae
Hattie	Alma	Katy
Beatrice	Eleanor	Elsie
Edith	Susie	Anne
Bertha	Blanche	Maude

One hundred most common Slave Female names not found amongst 100 College Students.

Maria(h)	Elisa	Rach(a)el
Nancy	Jane	Caroline
Harriet	Hannah	Ann

Conformity in College vs. Individuality -- COLLEGE AND SLAVE NAMES

Amy	Winn(e)y	Jinn(e)y
Betsy	Lydia	Nanny
Milly	Becky	Sylvia
Louisa	Celia	Dorcas
Matilda	Patsy	Edy
Emily	Ph(o)ebe	Minerva
Rose	Silvey	Molly
Susan	Venus	Priscilla
Phillis	Caty	Henrietta
Peggy	Chloe	Letty
Betty	Flora	Sary
Judy	Kate	Mima
Lucinda	Aggy	Elsey
Ellen	Hester	Leah
Polly	Emiline	Nan
Kitty	Sukey	Amelia
Charity	Violet	Charlotte
Adeline	Delia	Cynthia
Amanda	Penny	Peg
Bet	Dolly	Sophia
Malinda	Patience	Bella(h)
Clarissa	Elvira	Clary
Dinah	Isabella	Eve

Twenty-two names common to slave and Black College lists, female.

Mary	Charlotte	Grace
Sarah	Frances	Rebecca
Lucy	Nelly	Emma
Martha	Elizabeth	Anna
Sally	Julia	Alice
Fanny	Catharine	Laura
Margaret	Esther	Clara
		Agnes

One hundred most common White Male College Student names not found amongst 100 Slave Males.

Walter	Herbert	Sidney
Paul	Roy	Clyde
Harold	Earl	Edgar
Donald	Leonard	Marvin
Fred	Kenneth	Leon
Louis	Lawrence	Russell
Howard	Clarence	Lloyd
Ralph	Benjamin	Theodore
Earnest	Hugh	Stanley
Carl	Herman	Warren
Eugene	Norman	Francis
Edwin	Bernard	Lester
Raymond	Milton	Morris
Frederick	Claude	Julius

Conformity in College vs. Individuality -- COLLEGE AND SLAVE NAMES

Oscar	Roger	Chester
Ray	Wilbur	Douglas
Vernon	Harvey	Leroy
Alvin	Horace	Willard
Elmer	Leslie	Irving
Guy	Melvin	Woodrow
Leo	Michael	

One hundred most common Slave Male names not found amongst 100 White College Students.

Peter	Caesar	Jake
Moses	Davy	Madison
Isaac	Dennis	Elias
Dick	Ephraim	Elijah
Jacob	Nathan	Isham
Ned	Prince	Lem
Abram	Anderson	Nat
Jerry	Green	Pompey
Washington	Jeff	York
Simon	Amos	Harrison
Anthony	Solomon	Joshua
Nelson	Jackson	Robin
Willis	Jordan	Spencer
Ellick	Primus	Wesley
Adam	Gilbert	Calvin
Phil	Henderson	Cyrus
Dave	Pleasant	Eli
Aaron	Sampson	Gabriel
Abraham	Andy	Jefferson
Reuben	Cato	Wash
Will	Hardy	

Thirty-eight names common to Slave and White College Lists, Male.

John	James	Edmond
Henry	Harry	Albert
George	Lewis	Thomas
Sam	Frank	Edward
Tom	Daniel	Alexander
Charles	Stephen	Richard
Jim	Billy	Joseph
Jack	Alfred	Samuel
William	Andrew	Arthur
Joe	David	Martin
Bob	Jesse	Phillip
Bill	Robert	Lee
Ben	Allen	

Conformity in College vs. Individuality -- COLLEGE AND SLAVE NAMES

One hundred most common White Female College Student names not found amongst 100 Slave Females.

Dorothy	Gladys	Gertrude
Ruth	Anne	Myrtle
Helen	Carolyn	Bertha
Virginia	Hazel	Blanche
Marjorie	Miriam	Bernice
Louise	Josephine	Elsie
Mildred	Pauline	Joan
Jean(ne)	Marguerite	Vera
Evelyn	Ethel	Ella
Eleanor	Kathleen	Eva
Sara	Jessie	Irene
Doris	Thelma	Jewel(1)
Edith	Ida	Juanita
Annie	Eloise	Mattie
Florence	Mabel	Roberta
Edna	Christine	Maude
Lois	Alma	Norma
Lillian	May(e)	Pearl
Lucille	Sue	Jeannette
Marie	Marian	Bessie
Marion	Vivian	Eugenia
Ruby	Estes	Georgia
		Isabel

One hundred most common Slave Female names not found amongst 100 White Female College Students.

Maria(h)	Matilda	Bet
Elisa	Judy	Malinda
Hannah	Lucinda	Clarissa
Amy	Polly	Dinah
Betsy	Kitty	Winn(e)y
Milly	Charity	Esther
Fanny	Adeline	Lydia
Louisa	Amanda	Becky
Celia	Delia	Henrietta
Patsy	Penny	Letty
Ph(o)ebe	Dolly	Sary
Silvey	Patience	Mima
Venus	Elvira	Elsey
Caty	Isabella	Leah
Chloe	Jinn(e)y	Nan
Flora	Nanny	Amelia
Kate	Sylvia	Charlotte
Aggy	Dorcas	Cynthia
Hester	Edy	Peg
Emiline	Minerva	Sophia
Sukey	Molly	Bella(h)
Violet	Priscilla	Clary
		Eve

Conformity in College vs. Individuality -- COLLEGE AND SLAVE NAMES

Thirty-three names common to Slave and White College Lists, Female.

Mary	Emily	Elizabeth
Nancy	Margaret	Julia
Sarah	Rose	Catharine
Lucy	Susan	Grace
Harriet	Charlotte	Rebecca
Jane	Phillis	Emma
Martha	Peggy	Anna
Rach(a)el	Betty	Alice
Caroline	Ellen	Laura
Ann	Frances	Clara
Sally	Nelly	Agnes

CHAPTER V

Dictionary of African Origins

There was a time, not too terribly distant, when those involved in Black studies faced the task of overcoming a number of inaccurate assumptions. Although not all the debris of eighteenth and nineteenth century misconceptions have been carted off, the ground has been cleared a bit. Thanks to scholars such as Melville Herskovits[1] and Lorenzo Turner[2] no one questions any longer the understanding that, despite conscious and often vicious attempts on the part of slave-holding white Americans and despite unconscious but often just as vicious attempts on the part of a society whose traditions lie in Northwestern Europe, Black Americans, slave and free, have retained Africanisms, "even though the degree of purity of these Africanisms varies widely with locality, socio-economic class and religious affiliations."[3]

The question now concerns the "degree of purity of these Africanisms." More particularly, our concern is with the degree and purity of these Africanisms. The material in this collection suggests an almost complete rejection of Africanisms in terms of name usage. The greatest percentage occurred amongst slave males in the eighteenth century (9.25 per cent); by the mid-nineteenth century less than one-half of one per cent of all names collected suggest the possibility of African origin.

These considerations resist use as evidence to suggest insignificant African influence; for one, we need merely refer to Turner's discussion of "basket names" and naming practices in general[4] and, for another, Herskovits shows clearly enough that vocabulary items are most easily substituted in a language.[5]

With this in mind, the following is an alphabetical listing of all the names used by Blacks, slave and free, and Whites in this country which suggest African origin. The symbols for race, B and W, indicate whether the name was first found among Blacks or Whites. M and F refer to the gender. Each name

---

[1]Melville J. Herskovits, ed. by Frances S. Herskovits, The New World Negro (Bloomington, Ind.: Indiana University Press, 1966).

[2]Lorenzo D. Turner, Africanisms in the Gullah Dialect (Chicago, Ill.: The University of Chicago Press, 1949).

[3]Herskovits, op. cit., pp. 13-14.

[4]Turner, op. cit., pp. 40-43.

[5]Herskovits, op. cit., pp. 60, 171.

347

Dictionary of African Origins

is identified by those African languages or dialects from which it seems to
have derived, or at least resembles strongly. The form, if different, and
meaning of the word in that language is indicated.

NAME	RACE & SEX	LANGUAGE & DEFINITION	
Abah	B, F	Bobangi	(aba) conj. if, provided that
		Hausa	(aba) a thing, thing of, thing for, property, that which, the affair
		Bini	(aba) seeds hung up on a stick that is used in divination and when feeding witches; gives knowledge of the secrets of witchcraft
		Bini	(aba) an old word for the anklet worn by the drummers
		Bini	(abã) originally: native handcuff, nowadays a witch doctor's implementation, used to press a medicine against the ground while a prayer is said. - a protective spell is cast
		Congo	(aba) obj. pronoun 3 per. pl. them
		Efik	(aba) n. hole, cave
		Efik	(aba) adj. hollow
		Efik	(aba) adv. more, again
		Efik	adj. (Iba) forty, fortieth
		Arabic	(abã) become father, call someone father, take for a father
Abb	B, F	Arabic	(ab) father, patriarch
Abana	W, F	Efik	(ábana) the point called East Head, at the entrance of Calabar River
Abanna	B, F	See Abana	
Abba	B, F	See Abah	
Abia	B & W, F	Hausa	(abiya) "Katsina Hausa" f. female, friend of man or woman
		Efik	(abiya) n. small bird, migratory
		Efik	(abia) n. practitioner; professor
Abiah	W, F	See Abia	
Accoo	B, F	Mende	(aako) conj. in order that, so that, cf. kɔɔ, akɔɔ
		Hausa	Akū m.f. parrot
		Hausa	(acca) f. the cereal grass
		Bini	(ako) a tree, its fruit is like hot peppers

Dictionary of African Origins

NAME	RACE & SEX	LANGUAGE & DEFINITION	
Accoo (cont.)		Bini (cont.)	(ako) place encircled by hunters
			(ako) a shrine moved through the streets at second burials
			(ako) a position in the Ogwega - divination
		Efik	(aku) v. debt of retribution; or requittal of good or evil; reciprocity, retribution; companionship, mutual friendship
		Congo	(aku) poss. pron. 2nd per. sing., they, thine, your, yours
Acha	W, F	Kele	(acha) be rent
		Swahili	(acha) let, permit
		Hausa	(aka) anything
			(acca) See Accoo
		Congo	(aka) adv., always, ceaselessly, constantly, only, directly, solely
		Bini	(akā) pain in the side, probably due to pneumonia or pleurisy
			(aka) grass-snake, bite not very harmful to man
			(aka) rack for drying meat, with a fire underneath
		Efik	(aka) adj., sour, heady, brittleness, brittle roof mats; a fisherman, a trade, craft, profession, employment
		Bobangi	(ākā) vin. to arrive, become, come to be, grow
Acque	W, M	Bini	(ake) a growth on the thighbone
		Hausa	(akē) when
Ada	B, F	Hausa	(ada) f. custom, manner, order
			(adda) f. matchet, leper's fingerless handstump
			(adda āmi) "derived from Arabic" food
		Bini	(ada) state-sword, worn by chiefs & priests of Osa
			(adã) family-representatives at a burial
			(ada) junction; crossroads
		Arabic	(adã) paying, requital, fulfilling a duty
			(adã) assist
			(ada) coagulate (milk); be many; abundant
			(âda) better paying

Dictionary of African Origins

NAME	RACE & SEX	LANGUAGE & DEFINITION	
Ada (cont.)		Efik	(ada) n. a room, an apartment in a house; a ship's cabin; an excavation, forming part of the grove in which the body of a chief is put; an equal; barrenness, sterile
Adah	B, F	See Ada	
Adakar	B, F	Hausa	(adak<u>a</u>) f. wooden or metal case, trunk, etc.; any large load, type of short gun
Adda	B, F	See Ada	
Addill	W, F	Hausa	(addila) (<u>a</u>dīl<u>a</u>) f. any large load
Adgie	W, F	Hausa	(aji) m. school class, heap, loading up a pack animal
Adina	B, F	Hausa	(addīnī) "derived from Arabic-Hebrew" m. any religion pl. addinai (adīni) n. religion, the profession of religion
Affa	B, F	Hausa Efik	(af<u>a</u>) threw into one's mouth (afa) adj. (new) new
Affee	B, F	Hausa Hausa	(afi) courage-endowing medicine for hunter, warrior, hunting dog. Pagan's putting ashes on heads in obeisance (affi) to make obeisance
Affey	B, F	See Affee	
Affiah	B & W, F	Efik Bini	(afia) n. snare, trap, gin; the lot; ordeal of the lot; white, pale, clear, cloudless (afiã) chisel, an insect affecting the yam-creepers
Affie	B, F	See Affee	
Affy	B, F	See Affee	
Agah	B, F	Hausa Bini Swahili	(agā) f. possessing much of (aggā) "Yoruba word" m. leader(s) (agã) a chair (with rest); cane-chair (aga) barren woman Cf. Yoruba aga (aga) take leave

350

Dictionary of African Origin

NAME	RACE & SEX	LANGUAGE & DEFINITION	
Agala	B, F	Hausa	(agāla) i.q. n. rope
Agga	B, F	See Agah	
Ahava	W, F	Bini	(ahavā) n. akpa inflammation of breasts
Ahma	W, F	Hausa	(ammā) "derived from Arabic" but
		Bini	(ama) sign, mark, omen, symptom, brass-figure or plaque as a souvenir, an oracle, wound
		Arabic	(amâ) intestines; bowels
			(amma) stupid, dull, weak of character
			(amah) promise; stipulate, recommend; oblivion
			(amâ) become, make, buy a female slave
		Efik	(ama) n. one loving or beloved; a friend; a lover
			(ama) n. friendship
		Soko	(ama) exclaim
		Ngala	(ama) to press, squeeze
		Kele	(ama) compress, exclaim, squeeze
		Poto	(ama) to press, to squeeze
Akbar	B, M	Hausa	(akbar) "derived from Arabic" used in Allāhu Akbar - God is the Greatest (prayer formula)
Ala	B & W, F	Hausa	(ala) anything
			(ala) used at times for Alla (God)
		Lolo	(ala) gaze at, look; scrape
		Ngombe	(ala) rend, be rent
		Arabic	(allâh) God
			(alah) adore
			(alâ) be not equal to a thing or person
Alcoe	B, M	Hausa	(alkō) m. weak person, poor quality
Alena	B, F	Hausa	(alēnā) "Katsina Hausa" you bloody blind person there!
Aley	B, F	Bobangi	(āle) (french) are (metric measure)
Allena	B, F	See Alena	
Alipha	W, F	Hausa	alif m.pl. alafai "derived from Arabic" the letter Aleph, thousand

351

Dictionary of African Origin

NAME	RACE & SEX	LANGUAGE & DEFINITION	
Alkana	W, F	Hausa	(alkáma) n. wheat
Allee	B & W, F	Hausa	(ali) adv. very much (alli) n. some kind of white earth or stuff used by women in serving instead of bee's wax
		Hausa	(allī) m. chalk from lime or burnt bones (āli) m. man's name (originally name of son-in-law of the Prophet) (ali̱) m. the index finger
		Soko	(alī) admirable, good
Alli	B, F	See Allee	
Allie	W, M	See Allee	
Ally	B, F	See Allee	
Almos	W, M	Hausa	(almōsa) derived from Arabic word, Sokoto Hausa F. any knife
Alyema	B, F	Kongo	(alimau) n. (Port. Alemao) A German
Alzena	B, F	Hausa	(Alžena) spirits
Ama	B & W, F	See Ahma	
Amangus	W, F, M	Hausa	(amaŋgá) m. type of black and white cloth
Amasa	W, F	Hausa	(amasa) "derived from Arabic" became large; attained full strength; became abundant; became important, became serious
Amaziah	B, F	Hausa	(amāzayā) place of resort, went off at a tangent
Amaziah	W, M	See Amaziah	
Ambo	B, F	Hausa	(ambō) "Sokoto Hausa" m. anything stinking
		Kele	(ambo) if
Amina	W, F	Hausa	(amina) anything - women's name, the Prophet's foster-mother

Dictionary of African Origin

NAME	RACE & SEX	LANGUAGE & DEFINITION	
Amina (cont.)		Mende	(amina) interj. Amen, so be it
Amoree	W, F	Hausa	(amōre) Northern Filani bowmen - highwaymen; Ya amore
Anaca	B, F	Hausa	(annākīyā) f. sweatness of face, neck, and shoulders and its effect on clothing (annakō) "Sokoto Hausa" m. type of small hare
Anada	B, F	Hausa	(anāde) part. perf. rolled together, twisted, entangled
Anaka	B, F	See Anaca	
Anaky	B, F	See Anaca	
Aneca	B, F	See Anaca	
Aneky	B, F	See Anaca	
Anika	B, F	See Anaca	
Anikee	B, F	See Anaca	
Ankque	B, M	Efik	(anka) n. name of a family EGBO
Annaka	B, F	See Anaca	
Annaky	B, M	See Anaca	
Annica	B, F	See Anaca	
Annika	B, F	See Anaca	
Aphnah	B, F	Hausa	(afno) mf. Kanuri term for a Hausa(s)
Ara	B, M	Hausa Bini Arabic	(ara) anything, borrowed, lent (ara) a very small worm (caterpillar?), living on leaves, affects hunters; very irritating to skin (arǎ) opinions (ara) fitter, more appropriate (arâ) pastures (ara) make honey; drive the clouds and bring rain; to eat from the same manger with another animal; tie up, fasten; conceal

Dictionary of African Origin

NAME	RACE & SEX	LANGUAGE & DEFINITION	
Ara	B & W, F	See Ara	
Araam	B, M	Hausa	(árāme) lean, emaciated
		Arabic	(aram) spotted white and black
			(ârâm) stones to indicate the road in the desert
Arah	B, F	See Ara	
Aralee	B, F	Bini	(arale) interference with other people's talk, etc.; name of a deity, also called Arale
Areta	B, F	Bini	(areta) a charm used to make someone reveal a secret
Aretta	B, F	See Areta	
Aria	B, F	See Ara	
Arra	B, F	See Ara	
Arria	B, F	See Aria	
Arrie	B, F	Bini	(ari) next reincarnation
Arzata	B, F	Hausa	(arzuta) (is) prosperous, (was)
Asa	B & W, M	Hausa	(asa) anything
			(asā̱-asā̱) m. restlessness
		Bini	(asa) whip
			(asa) shield, wing-covert of beetle or cricket
		Efik	(asa) family name; ATA-family name
		Lolo	(asa) seek
		Poto	(asa) say
		Ngala	(asa) seek
		Ngombe	(asa) take
		Arabic	(asâ) grief
			(asâ) nurse, cure, make peace
			(asa) reserve
Asalee	W, F	Bini	(asɛlɛ) a cricket
Ashira	W, M	Hausa	(āshūrā) "derived from Arabic" f. devotions done on 19th Muharram
Asma	B, F	Arabic	(azmâ) rivulets, valleys, calamity
			(as̱maẖ) brave, bold

354

Dictionary of African Origin

NAME	RACE & SEX	LANGUAGE & DEFINITION	
Asma (cont.)		Arabic (cont.)	(asma) ascending, vivacious, bold; sword (azmâ) thirst (aẕma) brown; bloodless; fleshless; blackish
Assa	W, M	<u>See</u> Asa	
Atha	W, F	Arabic	(adâ) field of pebble ground
Atossa	W, F	Hausa	(ātĭsa) intra. v. to sneeze
Atta	W, F	Hausa Bini	(attā) a man's name (atâ) a tree, from it medicine is prepared
		Efik	(ata) adj. real, very, exceedingly n. a practitioner; one skilled in a thing; n. A wager, a competing, emulation; bravado, obstinacy, dourness, persistency, a tree producing edible fruit, used as medicine; a black ant said to sting not bite; a spot, place flood tide; a flood, name of a dish, calabas chop
		Kele Ngala Poto Arabic	(ata) rend, split (ata) split (ata) rend, be rent, split (atah) panting of one who carries a burden (atâ) arrive (after a prosperous journey), visit, meet; come plentifully (ata) come; bring, give, give birth
Ava	W, F	Bini	(ava) wooden or iron wedge used to split wood (avǎ) thunder and lightning, thunderbolt (avǎ) daytime
Aza	B, F	Hausa Bini	(aza) put on another (aza) storeroom in the house; long bell always found hanging over the image of a god; a creeper chewed by "doctors" to enable them to tell the future
		Swahili Arabic	(aza) think (azâ) grow short (shadow when the sun is high)

Dictionary of African Origin

NAME	RACE & SEX	LANGUAGE & DEFINITION	
Azalee	W, F	Hausa	(aẑálạ) pl. azalai, n. wheel (azạlīyạ) "derived from Arabic" misfortune
Azuba	B, F	Hausa	(aẑ̌ibi) n. Monday
Azzma	B, M	See Asma	
Azzy	B, F	Hausa	(aẑe or aẑ̌ie) to put, place, lay, lay aside, to keep, keep back, preserve, to lay, hold on, to hold fast
		Bini	(azi) adze (used for smoothing wood) (Engl.?)
Baina	B, F	Hausa	(baina) anything f. dearness; the back, backwoods
		Bobangi	(baima) vs. to blink, move (gills), quiver (eyes or leaves), twinkle
Balla	B, M	Hausa	(ɓalla) hooked up; secured by pulling knotted end through loop (balle) conj. except, otherwise, else
		Mende	(bala) n. calabash
		Bobangi	(bala) vt. to marry, wed (bala) vin. to break out or come out bright (of light or sun after a cloudy sky or in a morning about 7 o'clock (bāla) vt. to count, enumerate (bāla) vt. to trim (fronds from palm)
		Kongo	(bala) v. to grow, be hard, firm, tough, to harden (bala) n. hardness, firmness, toughness (bala) v. to be sour, strong (of palm wine) (bala) n. excessive sourness (of old palm wine) (bala) v.i. to be dear (in price) (bala) p. costly (bala) n. cassava root steeped in water, peeled and dried in the sun
		Poto	(bala) marry
		Ngombe	(bala) say, speak, talk
		Arabic	(balâ) visitation; affliction; calamity; sorrow; trouble; bravery (bala) swallow; pierce

Dictionary of African Origin

NAME	RACE & SEX	LANGUAGE & DEFINITION	
Balla (cont.)		Arabic (cont.)	(balah) stupidity, idiotry, loutishness
			(balâ) try; probe, test, put to severe trials; grieve
		Bangi	(bala) marry
		Bobangi	(mbālā) n. artificial article, counterfeit, fiction, fraud, imitation, retained information, sham, shaft of spear
		Hausa	(gballa) tr. v. to fasten, to tie a knot; to button
		Kongo	(mbala) n. sweet potato, the portion of the coast between the mouth of the Kongo River and Ambrigette, where until quite recently nearly all the trade with Europeans was carried on; leopard-cat, pipe-bead (red, large) a hardening
		Mende	(mbala) n. sheep
Bama	B & W, F	Hausa	(ɓamā) f. vibrating tongue of flute - flute player
		Kongo	(bama) v. to speak angrily; scold
		Mende	(baama) n. cheek, jaw
		Kongo	(mbama) n. girdle, scolding, a tightening
		Efik	(mbäma) n. a kind of cloth made in Ibo
		Bobangi	(mbamba) n. kind of light-colored crocodile
Bamba	B, M	Mende	(bambo) n. leaves of raffia palm sewn together for thatching; a broad head-covering worn as a protection against rain
		Bangi	(bamba) mend, repair
		Kongo	(bamba) v. to tie well, n. middleman (in trade)
		Bobangi	(bamba) vin. to develop into a clever person
			(bamba) vin. to crack (sound)
			(bãmba) vt. to mend, patch, remedy, repair
		Ngala	(bamba) mend, repair
Bambara	B	Hausa	(ɓamɓarạ) broke off; separated
Bame	B, M	Hausa	(ɓame) closed; opened
Bamma	B & W, F	See Bama	

357

Dictionary of African Origin

NAME	RACE & SEX	LANGUAGE & DEFINITION	
Bamma	W, M	See Bama	
Bann	B, M	Hausa	(ba̲n) anything, ban ci ba I've not eaten
		Efik	(ban) v.tr. to sharpen, to grind on tools, to have as a razor
		Arabic	(bann) stand, remain, stay, settle (bân) be separate, distinct, far, distant (bân) the Egyptian willow
Banna	B, F	Hausa	(bana) anything; this year, the current year; year of age of cattle
		Efik	(bana) v.tr. to dress; adorn; ornament
		Kongo	(bana) dem. & rel. pron. i. I pl. that, those
		Hausa	(gbánna) n. the process of spoiling, decaying of anything; corruption, decay, ruin, devastation, desolation, destruction
		Efik	(mbana) n. adornment, ornament
Bannaka de oblay		Mende	(banaku) n. variety of yellowish cassava
Bantie	B, F	Hausa	(ɓantí) cloth
Bap	B, M	Hausa	(bappa̲) m. paternal uncle
		Efik	(mbap) n. an expression of contempt
Barna	W, M	Hausa	(barna̲) f. wearing white and black turbans together (ɓa̲rnā) f. damage
Barsha	W, M	Hausa	(ɓarshē) "Katsina Hausa" uncooked (rambo̲) m. a food of uncooked flour with Rama-leaves and water (Rama - Indian hemp)
Barte	B, M	Hausa	(ba̲rtī) "Katsina Hausa" m. returning to school; Filani migration from wet-season grounds to dry-season grazing
Bartee	B, M	See Barte	
Bartee	W, F	See Barte	
Bartie	W, F	See Barte	

358

Dictionary of African Origin

NAME	RACE & SEX	LANGUAGE & DEFINITION	
Barto	B & W, M	Hausa	(bartō) name given to girl to avert the evil eye
Barto	B, F	See Barto	
Bartow	W, F	See Barto	
Basha	W, F	Hausa	(bāshā) a game
Bassar	B, F	Hausa	(bāsara) n. summer, the finest part of the dry season, or just before the rains begin (bāsa) person of the Bassa tribe of Kabba and Niger provinces
Bat	B, F & W, M	Efik	(bât) v.tr. to number, count, reckon, to esteem (mbat) n. dirt, mud, sludge, clay; adv. dirtily, filthily adj. flat or flatish; muddy; miry; dirty; impure; filthy
		Arabic	(bat) pass the night (batt) cut, lop, decide (batt) hood, wrapped rope, coarse piece of dress to cover the head (bâtt) cutting, breaking, weakening; foolish, drunk; lean, thin
		Mende	(bat) conj. perhaps
Batt	B & W, M	See Bat	
Battah	B, F	Bobangi	(bata) vt. to ascend, climb, scale, soar, get up (a tree), give raised tone (to a vowel) (bāta) vt. to bite, sting
		Hausa	(bata) anything (bātā) "Sokoto Hausa", f. bundle of thatching grass (batta) a small receptacle of hide, metal or wood for snuff, tobacco, etc.; very short
		Swahili	(bata) duck
		Soko	(bata) steer
		Poto	(mbata) noun, seat
		Lolo	(mbata) noun, chair, plank
		Bangi	(mbata) sheep (bata) ascend, bite, climb
		Arabic	(bata) remain, stay (batâ) goods, property (used as a

Dictionary of African Origin

NAME	RACE & SEX	LANGUAGE & DEFINITION	
Battah (cont.)		Arabic (cont.)	possessive adjective) (bata) prepare the wine
		Kongo	(mbata) n. prequisite, commission, brokerage, a blow with the open hand, above, on top of, over
		Efik	(mbata) adj. all the sixty; and so on
		Mende	(gbato) n. whip, molar, pre-molar
		Bobangi	(mbata) n. chair, form, seat, stool
			(mbātā) n. sheep
			(mbātā) n. blow with the palm of the hand
Batte	W, M	Hausa	(bate) a mushy food of flour and onions (Katsina Hausa)
Battie	W, M	Mende	(bati) n. area which is flooded every rainy season when a river overflows its banks; grassy swamp, dry in the dry season
		Bobangi	(bāti) Eng. n. pl. bath
		Hausa	(batti) anything; collision, attack, charge, battle
		Kongo	(mbati) n. trousers
Batty	W, M	See Battie	
Bayna	B, F	Hausa	(beyéna) int. v. to appear, to spread
Bazilla	B, F	Kongo	(bazula) v. to ache (spoken only of the head)
Bazz	W, M	Arabic	(bahz) burden; weight; importance (bâz) grow thin after being stout (bazz) capture; rob; plunder (bazz) fine linen, silk; clothing, armour; drapery; superiority; victory; end (bazz) tune and touch the strings of an instrument; exert one's self zealously; excel, grow fast (bâz) perish or live on
Bebb	B, M	Hausa	(bebe) a person dumb and deaf
		Mende	(bɛbɛ) n. a small flat dish
		Bini	(bebe) to be naughty, of boys; it implies acts like touching what must not be touched

360

Dictionary of African Origin

NAME	RACE & SEX	LANGUAGE & DEFINITION	
Becae	B, F	Hausa	(bēkē) m. surprise
		Mende	(beke) n. maggot, a child's game (beke wulɔ)
		Efik	(bekhe) v. intr. to arrive at port; come to land; to beach, to land upon the beach; to sift; to belch, to engage, employ, give business to
		Bobangi	(beke) vt. to break (limb), snap (bones of limbs)
		Mende	(mbeke) n. limb, branch (of tree, river)
		Bobangi	(mbëkë) n. curse, refusal to restore borrowed goods
			(mbekē) n. piece of broken pot, potsherd
Becca	B, F	Bobangi	(bëka) vt. to forecast, foretell, predict
			(bëka) vt. to growl at, to bark at
			(bêka) vt. to borrow
		Kongo	(beka) v. to wait for, delay, stop, stay, await
		Soko	(beka) say, speak, talk
		Ngala	(beka) borrow, call
		Ngombe	(beka) borrow
		Bobangi	(mbêka) n. abrupt fall of ground on bed of river, gully
			(mbêkā) n. borrowed article or money
			(mbêkā) n. kind of monkey
		Kongo	(mbeka) n. precipice, cliff
Beck	B, F	Efik	(bek) v.tr. to crumble as bread; to pick or press off piecemeal as clay off a wall, corn off its cob; to chip off
		Efik	(mbek) n. a chipping off of a small piece; a chip; a chapping of the lips, as in cold, after a fever
Beckum	W, M	Bobangi	(bēkuma) vs. to jump backwards, start backwards
Bek	B, F	See Beck	
Bela	B & W, F B, M	Mende Bobangi	(bele) n. trousers (bëla) vt. to call to or for (bëla) vin. to be cooked, be healed (bêla) vt. to border (a basket, shield, etc.)

Dictionary of African Origin

NAME	RACE & SEX	LANGUAGE & DEFINITION	
Bela (cont.)		Bobangi (cont.)	(bɛlɛ) adv. long ago, long since (bele) vt. to kill (insect) between finger nail (bēle) vin. to be aggravated, be annoyed
		Kongo	(bela) v. to perch, settle (as a bird)
		Lolo	(bela) draw, tow
		Kongo	(mbela) n. near at hand (mbela) n. a sickness, a being ill, a perching
		Mende	(mbela) n. father-in-law, brother-in-law, male relative of one's wife (mbela) neut. split, break, thrash
Bem	B, M	Efik	(bem) v.tr., to precede; be, or get before another; to anticipate; to select beforehand
		Mende	(bɛmɛ) id. (of people) thickset squat; n. gently sloping land, a style of haircut - only top of head left un-shaved
Bena	B & W, F	Hausa Poto	(bēna) f. hide with adverent hair (benā epolo) to hurt
Benah	B, F	See Bena	
Bendo	B, M	Mende Kongo	(benda) n. a person who seeks fame (benda) v.i. to be crooked (benda-benda) v. to prevaricate; equivocate, be fickle, unreliable, to quibble
Benola	W, F	Bobangi	(bẽnöla) vt. to lever along with paddle resting on canoe, lift on to hip, scull
Bennola	W, F	See Benola	
Bera	B & W, F	Hausa	(ɓērā) rat, mouse; a girl whose breasts are not yet formed
Bero	B, F	Hausa	(béro) to leave at some place
Betta	B, F	Bobangi	(bëta) vt. to challenge, gamble, game, lay down stakes

Dictionary of African Origin

NAME	RACE & SEX	LANGUAGE & DEFINITION	
Betta (cont.)		Bobangi (cont.)	(béta) vt. to bear, carry, sustain
			(bete) vt. to beat, strike
		Kongo	(beta) vt. to hit, strike
		Ngombe	(kbeta) ripen
		Mende	(bete) n. cooked leaves with oil, meat, etc., cooked vegetables
		Hausa	(bete) m. a mushy food of flour and onions
Bial	W, M	Hausa	(bial) dive
Bijah	B, F	Hausa	(bijā-bijā) anything; scatterbrained
		Mende	(mbijɛ) neut. flatter, cajole
		Kongo	(mbiji) n. an animal whose flesh is eaten for food; meat (uncooked), "beef"
Bijie	B & W, M	Hausa	(biji-biji) anything; scatterbrained; feckless work
		Kongo	(mbiji) meat
Bilah	B, F	Hausa	(bila) anything; deceitfully
			(bilā) "derived from Arabic" without
		Bobangi	(bíla) vt. to appoint (to office), depose, depute, draw (knife), extract, ordain, pick up, take out, pluck out, pull out or up, unscrew
			(bīla) vin. to be as deep as required
			(bīla) vt. to aim at, appeal (to another authority), go after, go in search of, pursue, run after, trace
		Lolo	(bila) extract, pull out
		Poto	(bila) draw, pull along, hoist, haul, tow
		Ngala	(bila) extract, pull out
		Bangi	(bila) chase, extract, pick up, pull out
		Ngombe	(bila) (noun) battle
		Kongo	(mbila) n. a summons, a call
		Mende	(gbili) neut. grow dark, become overcast, cloudy, neap tide
Bimba	B, M	Bobangi	(bimbabimba) vs. to shake one's self violently
		Kongo	(bimba) v.i. to be clapped to by someone who is about to perform a salute
		Bobangi	(mbimbā) n. flat side of blade
			(mbimbā) n. diameter, trunk of body or tree

363

Dictionary of African Origin

NAME	RACE & SEX	LANGUAGE & DEFINITION	
Bina	B & W, F	Bobangi	(bina) to dance
		Bangi	(bina) dance
		Lolo	(bina) dance
		Soko	(bina) dance, gambol
		Ngala	(bina) dance
		Arabic	(bina) building, structure; vault, form
		Bini	(gbíni) to fight; to wage war; to seek shelter with somebody
Binah	B & W, F	See Bina	
Bing	B, M	Mende	(biŋ) id. (of falling) with a thud
		Hausa	(bingi) n. male donkey
Binga	B, M	Kongo	(binga) v.i. to take up room, occupy space
		Soko	(binga) roll up, wrap, to fold
		Bobangi	(mbinga) n. thickness in size; colq., glorious
Bingo	B, M	Bobangi	(bingö) pron. them, they
Birma	W, F	Hausa	(burma) anything; deceived, tricked; grass bag for storing clothes; caved in
Birmah	W, M & F	See Birma	
Bis	B, F	Hausa	(bis) "Sokoto Hausa" on; onto; conj. according as
Bisha	W, F	Hausa	(bishe) anything; "Katsina Hausa" buried
Boce	B, M	Kongo	(bosa) v.t. to break, smash, crush
		Lolo	(boci) noun, star
Boohter	B, M	Hausa	(būter) m. Maria Theresa dollar
Boomy	B, M	Hausa	(bumi) reinforcement with grass matting
		Efik	(bumi) v.intr. to grope about like a blind man, to be handless, inept, to be stupid, shiftless, to wander about from place to place not knowing where to go
		Lolo	(boomi) husband
		Kongo	(mbumi) n. a low tree bearing fruit with a woody rind, resembling an orange in size and colour

364

Dictionary of African Origin

NAME	RACE & SEX	LANGUAGE & DEFINITION	
Boomy (cont.)		Efik	(mbumi) n. stupidity; shiftlessness; a wandering from house to house; un-settledness; a vagabond
Boose	B, M	Soko	(boose) day
Boylee	B, M	Soko	(boili) mother-in-law
Boyyas	B, M	Bobangi	(boyásu) n. lightness in weight
		Hausa	(bōyā) "Sokoto Hausa" f. slave girl
		Mende	(mboya) n. soup; small present given in return for a present
			(gboya) n. sea
Bromah	W, F	Mende	(braima) n. the bush spirit
Buda	B, F	Hausa	(buda) n. snow, frost
			(buda) tr.v. to open
		Kongo	(buda) (v.t. to puff, to smoke)
Bulalla	B, M	Hausa	(bulala) n. whip made of hippopotamus skin
		Bobangi	(bulola) vt. to push on one side
			(bulola) vt. to examine (a cloth), rummage
Bumbo	B, M	Bobangi	(bumba) vt. to clasp, grasp, grip, hold fast, seize
		Kongo	(bumba) vt. to mould; make pottery
			v.i. to get mouldy or rusty; to corrode
			v.t. to draw up the earth around the roots of anything; to make a mound
		Mende	(mbumbu) n. fish trap made of cane, a plant
			(mbumbu) neut. take, pick up, elect, choose, flap the wings
Buna	W, F	Mende	(buna) n. a tree related to kola, with seeds one inch long, surrounded by a fleshy covering which is edible
		Bobangi	(buna) vt. to break, break off, click, full, snap
			(buna) vt. to contend, fight with fists
		Hausa	(ɓūnā) cantankerous; vicious ox
			(ɓūnā) m. farm already worked where soil is therefore fertile
		Kongo	(buna) v. to strip off (bark)

Dictionary of African Origin

NAME	RACE & SEX	LANGUAGE & DEFINITION	
Buna (cont.)		Bangi	(buna) break, fight
		Lolo	(buna) break, fight, war
		Poto	(buna) fight, to price, strive
		Soko	(buna) break, to price
		Ngala	(buna) fight, strive, war
		Ngombe	(buna) to price, fight
		Mende	(mbuna) n. a tree with scarlet edible fruit
Bungoh	B, M	Bobangi	(bunga) vt. to add, bring or put together
		Kongo	(bunga) v. to squander, waste
		Hausa	(bunga) thing or woman of poor appearance or little value
		Bobangi	(mbungā) n. common fund or stock
		Efik	(mbunō) n. brokenness; lameness; a lame man
		Mende	(mbɔngɛ) n. a species of rattan palm
Burma	W, F	See Birma	
Burmah	B, M & W, F	See Birma	
Burrah	B, M	Hausa	(būra) n. penis (būra hanci) m. large green caterpillar (būrā kăi) the white ant (Būrā kōgō) m. hawk
Cabe	B, M	Hausa	(cabe) anything; boy's game of striking sickle edges together (kaɓe) to shake (something off)
Caffa	B, M	Hausa	(caffa̱) served (cafa) caught a thing thrown; clutched at a moving thing; crocodile, dog, etc., snapped at (kafa) anything; small hole; chance; built (kafa̱) f. foot, leg (kaffa) tr.v. to build a house (kaffe) int.v. to subside
		Mende	(kafa) neut. to be almost finished, have very little left (kafa) neut. cheating, deception, defraud (kafa) n. several species of skunk, some of which yield a red-brown dye

Dictionary of African Origin

NAME	RACE & SEX	LANGUAGE & DEFINITION	
Caffee	B, M	Hausa	(kaffi) n. gate; stockade, barrier (kafi) n. & adj. plural blind persons (kafi) m. hut of cornstalks; stockade; to reinforce
		Kongo	(nkafi) noun, oar
		Swahili	(kafi) noun, paddle
Caggie	B, M	Mende	(kaji) id. emaciated, very thin (kaji) neut. strict, severe, unsympathetic
		Hausa	(cāji) Eng. m. charging a person criminally; type of drum beaten by priest-drummer
		Kongo	(kaji) n. Haematuria
Cagie	B, M	See Caggie	
Calola	W, F	Lolo	(kalola) to snore
Cam	W, M	Efik	(kam) v.intr. to be accustomed; used to; to prefer or think better to do; (always used with another verb)
		Hausa	(Kam) dried rigidly (kam) anything; securely; indeed; slapped
Camma	B, F	Hausa	(kāma) tr.v. to catch, to lay hold on, to seize, to hold fast (káma) as, like (káma) n. likeness; one like myself, hence companion, associate, fellow, partner, friend (kama) anything; seized hold of; arrested; included
		Mende	(kama) n. Poro bush (kama) conj. in order to (kama) n. marvel, astonishment, wonder (kama) n. whereabouts, place in question
		Efik	(kama) v.tr. to hold in the hand; to have, possess; to owe; to have absolute power over
		Kongo	(kama) v. to press, press out, squeeze, squeeze out, wring, wring out
		Soko	(kama) to press
		Kele	(kama) to press
		Swahili	(kama) as

Dictionary of African Origin

NAME	RACE & SEX	LANGUAGE & DEFINITION	
Canna	B, F	Mende	(kana) id. clear
		Kongo	(kana) v. to intend, resolve, propose, plan, mean
		Swahili	(kana) deny; if
		Hausa	(cānā) that
			(kana) thou
			(kana) adv. before, then
			(kana) anything; then; in addition
Cara	B, M	Hausa	(kāra) tr.v. to add to, to increase
			(kāra) f.n. reed, stalk or stem of plants
			(kára) tr. v. to call upon
			(cara) anything; crowing of cock
			(ƙara) anything; f. being screened off; m. stalk, esp. corn stalk
			(kara) anything; cried out; complaining; increased
		Efik	(kara) v. tr. to encompass; encircle; to have absolutely in the grasp; to master, understand
Carfy	W, F	Hausa	(ƙarfī) m. strength
Caro	W, F	Hausa	(karo) anything; m. collision; attack; parent's entrusting bringing up of children to another
			(ƙārō) m. gum (from trees)
Carra	B, F	See Cara	
Casiah	B, F	Hausa	(kášia) some kind of grass, perhaps dry grass or hay
			(kašie) to bring one over to his side, to convince one
			(kaúsie) to remove something, to take away
		Swahili	(kasia) noun, oar
Casina	B, F	Hausa	(kasina) town in Hausa
Cassa	B, F	Hausa	(cassá) f. bow-leggedness
			(kāsa) n. earth, land, ground; prep. down
			(kāsa) n. fowl
			(kasa) anything; arranged in small heaps; fell short; garment worn out; an inferior in ability; puff adder
			(ƙasa) anything; earth, soil; on the

Dictionary of African Origin

NAME	RACE & SEX	LANGUAGE & DEFINITION	
Cassa (cont.)		Hausa (cont.)	ground; bother!; fancy! (ƙassā) bones
		Kongo	(kasa) v.t. to tighten, draw tight; to chew
		Kongo	(nkasa) poison ordeal
Cata	B, M	Mende	(kata) n. physic nut, fig nut, the commonest hedge plant (kata) neut. compound, wall linking buildings together, to confine (kata) n. catfish
		Kongo	(kata) n. the penis (kata) v. to pull, stretch, extend, straighten out
		Hausa	(kata) anything; in broad daylight; girl employee in milk trade; small, shallow calabash used by sellers of milk or honey; circular salt cake; "Katsina Hausa" broad, thin section of kola-nut
		Bangi	(kata) grasp, hold, seize
		Swahili	(kata) carve, cut, fell, saw
		Ngombe	(kata) lizard
Cate	B, M	Hausa	(kate) "Katsina Hausa" m. gambling by a person who has already lost all his money
Catte	B, M	See Cate	
Catura	B, F	Hausa	(kátara) n. hip, haunch (kā turāṛa) m. kind of dumpling of millet made in times of scarcity
Cavannah	B, M	Kongo	(kavama) v. to be put (into a bottle, of a stopper)
Chia	B, F	Ngombe	(chia) escape
Chilla	B, F	Mende	(chila) id. assemble (with gom)
		Poto	(chila) run away, flee, escape
Chima	B, F	Poto	(chima) to hoe, dig (hoe)
China	B & W, F	Poto	(nchina) (noun) root
Chitt	B, M	Mende	(chitɔ) id. it is rather big, heavy (with kulo)

Dictionary of African Origin

NAME	RACE & SEX	LANGUAGE & DEFINITION	
Chitta	B, F	See Chitt	
Ciah	B, M	Mende	(kia) conj. as
		Hausa	(kiá or kiya) with difficulty, much exertion
Cidda	B, F	Hausa	(cīda) anything; rumbling of thunder; name given to child born at time of harvest
Cille	B, F	Hausa	(cila) "Katsina Hausa" f. tapeworm (cile) fag-end of cassava, cigarette, sugarcane
Clagee	B, F	Mende	(klaki) n. clerk, literate person
Coatsie	B, F	Hausa	(kōatsĕ) to commit a blunder or mistake
Coba	W, F	Mende	(koba) n. African Tragacanth
		Kongo	(koba) v. to climb a palm
		Ngala	(koba) again
Cobe	B, M	Efik	(kobi) v.tr. to fasten by the insertion of something; to lock; to chain, button, buckle; to fix, set, as a net for fish; to hook
Cobie	B & W, M	See Cobe	
Cock	B, M	Efik	(kok) v. tr. to grind by rubbing on a stone; to turn up, to cause to turn up; to overlap; to expectorate
Cof	B, M	Hausa	(kuf) m. type of rosary
Coffee	B, M	Hausa	(kōfī) English m. coffee; type of European cloth (kofi) anything; m. inspiring feeling of helpless fear
Coffie	B, M & F	See Coffee	
Cogie	B, M	Hausa	(kōgi) n. any large collection of water, lake, large river (kōgī) m. river
		Lolo	(nkoji) crocodile

Dictionary of African Origin

NAME	RACE & SEX	LANGUAGE & DEFINITION	
Cogy	B, F	See Cogie	
Cola	B, M & F	Hausa	(Kōlạ) double-spouted ewer; soldier's water bottle; bandolier, collar; cigarette holder
		Kongo	(kola) v.t. to pull out, draw out (nails), knock out or extract (a tooth); to unfasten; to shed (kola) v.i. to grow hard, be hard, be tough, to grow strong, mature, ripen, be intoxicating
		Lolo	(kola) take, obtain, get, gain
		Poto	(nkola) (noun) feast
Coley	B, M	Hausa	(koli) anything; m. peddling small wares (ḱoli) anything; m. top (kolli) n. a preparation made of lead and used by women to tinge the eyelids with
		Bangi	(nkoli) (noun) crocodile
		Ngala	(nkoli) crocodile
Colee	B	See Coley	
Colie	B, F	See Coley	
Colie Demus	B, F	See Coley	
Collia	B, F	Poto	(kolia) steer, repair
Comas	B, M	Mende	(koma) n. cheek (koma) neut. refuse a request, be mean, eat without sharing
Comba	B, F	Kongo	(komba) v. to sweep, clear out
		Ngala	(komba) sweep
		Lolo	(komba) shut
Comie	B, M	Hausa	(komi) indef. pron. anything, something, everything; whatever, whatsoever (komi) anything; m. any native boat; boat-shaped trough for cattle; bed for crops in irrigated field
Commenie	B, M	Hausa	(kōmine) indef. pron. whatsoever
		Kongo	(komena) v. to press, urge, persuade, exhort, insist upon

371

Dictionary of African Origin

NAME	RACE & SEX	LANGUAGE & DEFINITION	
Commo	B, M	Hausa	(kōmō) "old hand"; returning caravan; calabash which has buckled elliptically after removal of pulp; ellipse
			(kōmo) intr. v. to come back to the place where one wishes to be, i.e., to return from
		Kongo	(komo) n. heaviness
		Kele	(komo) cap, hat
			(koma ya litindi) heel
Condy	B, M	Mende	(kondi) n. sugar plum, red cedar
		Ngala	(nkondi) (noun) favour
Congo	B, M	Mende	(kongo) in the compounds
			(kongo) n. extension to a house, annex
		Kongo	(kongo) n. Kongo Country
			(kongo) interj. respectful answer to a call
			(a kongo) adj. reddish brown (the colour of a cosmetic)
		Efik	(kōno) v. tr. to hang anything over the shoulder as a sash; be hung, to hang
		Bangi	(kongo) strain (filter)
		Poto	(kongo) brass
		Ngala	(nkongo) (noun) hoe
		Kele	(kongo) alone, only
		Ngombe	(kongo) brass
Conney	B, F	Hausa	(kōne) tr. v. to burn down, to destroy by fire
			(kōni) "Sokoto Hausa" come, come! now, behave yourself
Conny	B, F	See Conney	
Coke	W, F	Hausa	(coke) anything m. play (game)
			(kōkē) m. plaint, complaint
			(ƙoƙe) "Katsina Hausa" faded
Coose	B, F	Hausa	(kusé) n. fly
			(kúsa) prep. & adv. near
Coot	B, M	Efik	(kṳt) v. tr. to call; to summon; to denominate
			(kút) v. tr. to hand up; to hoist up, or on board; to hitch up

Dictionary of African Origin

NAME	RACE & SEX	LANGUAGE & DEFINITION	
Coram	W, M	Hausa	(koráma) n. river (korámi) n. valley, dale (ɓōrama) f. large stream; head of women-traders in cereals and foodstuffs sold by measure
Cotta	B, F	Hausa Kongo Lolo Soko Ngala Kele	(ɓōta) f. haft (kota) v. to enter, go in, come in, pass in, penetrate, stick in, set (of the sun), flow in, sink (kota) write (kota) to adze (kota) scratch (kota) endeavor; taste; to try
Coty	B, M	Mende	(koti) n. court; coat
Coy	B, M	Hausa	(koi) i.q. kwoi n. egg
Cuba	B, F	Hausa Kongo Efik	(kūba) f. Joron door lock for outside; lock inside door of European house (kubba) f. "derived from Arabic dome" mausoleum (kúbe) n. sheath (kuba) v. to weave (kuba) v. to be shut down, as the lid of a box; to be turned mouth downward, to be capsized; to be shut, as the mouth; to lie or fall down on the belly; to crouch; to roost; to stoop much
Cubah	B, M	See Cuba	
Cubbah	B, M	See Cuba	
Cudah	B, M	Hausa	(cuɗa) anything; kneaded; massaged (ɓudā) m. fly; flies; painful (kūda masuhálbi) stinging flies or insects, and bees
Cuddy	B, F	Hausa	(kuɗɗi) "Katsina Hausa" m. bugs (kudī) m. black-bordered, red cotton material (kudī) money; cowries
Cudge	B, M	See Cudjoe	
Cudgo	B, M	See Cudjoe	

373

Dictionary of African Origin

NAME	RACE & SEX	LANGUAGE & DEFINITION	
Cudjo	B, M	See Cudjoe	
Cudjoe	B, M	Jamaica	(kwadjo) Monday.
Cuff	B, M & F, W, M	Hausa	(Kofa) n. the door-hole, or the opening in the wall for the door
Cuffe	B, M	Hausa	(kufi) anything; m. black dye for leather; food vessel left unwashed overnight (kufi) m. couldn't sleep through hunger, etc. (kufai) ruins of a place; desolated and dilapidated town
		Jamaica	(kofi) Friday.
		Kongo	(kufi) n. shortness; very short, too short; too near
Cuffee	B, M & F	See Cuffe	
Cuffey	B, M & F	See Cuffe	
Cuffie	B, M	See Cuffe	
Cuffy	B, M & F	See Cuffe	
Cula	W, M & F	Mende	(kula) n. cloth (kula) neut. knock down, thrown down (kula gula) fall down
		Hausa	(kula) anything; paid attention; didn't care; place name (kulla) tr. v. to care for one or something; to be concerned about; to mind or take notice of
		Kongo	(kula) v. to drive, frighten, chase away, banish, exile, expel, repulse, put to flight, disperse; to grow (in

Dictionary of African Origin

NAME	RACE & SEX	LANGUAGE & DEFINITION	
Cula (cont.)		Kongo (cont.)	stature or height); to buy back, redeem, ransom (kula) n. redemption (kulà) at too great a distance, too far, too distant
		Poto	(koola) to snore
		Lolo	(kula) daub; acquire
		Bangi	(kula) acquire, to gain, get, obtain; rub on
		Kongo	(kula) free, liberate; grow; to ransom
		Ngala	(kula) daub; rub on; smear
Cumba	B, F	Mende	(kumba) n. short skirt of country cloth, a garment
		Hausa	(kúmba) n. cockle; the scales of fish (kúmbe) n. slime (Kumbā) mussel-shell; talon of wild animal or bird of prey; "Katsina Hausa" fingernail
		Kongo	(kumba) v. to make a noise, to roar, rumble, grunt; to marvel, to be amazed, astonished, surprised; to wonder; to talk behind one's back, slander, vilify, calumniate, scandalize
		Lolo	(kumba) catch
		Kongo	(nkumba) navel
		Poto	(kumba) ward off; parry
		Ngala	(kumba) curse; parry; ward off
		Ngombe	(kumba) parry; ward off
Cumbo	B	Hausa	(kumbọ) m. calabash basin; cutting gourd to make calabash basin
Cumi	W, F	Hausa	(Kumi) anything; m. conceit; what a hard blow
		Kongo	(kumi) adj. ten
		Soko	(kumi) chief
Cusha	W, F	Hausa	(kushe) anything; found fault with
		Kele	(kucha) chastise
Dab	B, M	Hausa	(dab) close up to
		Arabic	(da'b) push back; repudiate, expel (dab') pest; beat, cudgle (da'b) matter, object of exertion; state, condition
		Mende	(ndabo) n. small bird that weaves a

Dictionary of African Origin

NAME	RACE & SEX	LANGUAGE & DEFINITION	
Dab (cont.)		Mende (cont.)	nest in grass (ndabu) n. genitals
Dage	B, M	Hausa	(dagà) prep. in, at, to, from, within (dage) anything; m. type of wild feline; cantankerous person; behaved mulishly; took a firm stand
Dago	B, M	See Dage	
Dalma	W, F	Hausa	(dalma) lead; tin (Darma) (dalma) n. lead (metal: my note)
Dalomba	B, F	Mende	(ndaloma) n. significance, relevance
Danula	B, F	Hausa	(danūwa) n. the child of my mother, associate, companion, intimate friend, elder brother, first born
Darma	W, F	Hausa Arabic	(darma) f. tin, lead (darmā) f. well rounded, fleshy
Darrah	W, F	Hausa	(dara) anything; game like draughts played on a board; granted something to a person for the rest of his life (darā-darā) fine and big (re: writing, eyes, stripes) (dāra) to laugh, to deride
		Efik	(dara) v. intr. to rejoice; exult; v. tr. to congratulate; wish joy to; to make a public rejoicing; triumph, jubilation; to set by; trust in
		Arabic	(darah) ward off; protect; attack; fall upon (darâ) know; know by experience; see through, learn; comprehend (darā) push back, repel, drive from; stray; shine, flicker, sparkle (darā) skin; cut off the neck; be partly eaten
Daz	B, M	Arabic	(da'z) fill; worry, strangle, choke (dazz) push aside; tear; doubt (da'z) push, push back; lie with
Debo	W, M	Hausa	(dēbō) removed; set aside; exception; extracted
		Bobangi	(ndêbö) n. fan palm

Dictionary of African Origin

NAME	RACE & SEX	LANGUAGE & DEFINITION	
Decca	W, F	Kongo	(deka) v. to cut up small, gnaw, nibble (deka) v. to trim (the hair from forehead) (deka) v.i. to crackle (deka) adv. sooner, rather
Deda	W, F	Kongo Bini Hausa	(deda) v.t. to peel (dede) to embrace (dedé) lingered, tarried, a long time
Dedemiah	W, F	Hausa Kongo	(ded<u>a</u>mī) m. Filani leather apron (dedema) v.i. to shake, tremble, shiver
Deedom	B, M	Hausa	(didum) pitch dark; stone blind
Delloh	W, F	Hausa Bangi Poto Ngala Mende Bobangi	(delā) n. numbness (ndelo) noun, limit, boundary (ndelo) noun, limit, boundary (ndelo) boundary, limit (ndelo) n. Southern Cross (ndêlô) n. bound, boundary, goal, frontier, limit, paragraph, verse
Dema	W, F	Mende	(ndema) neut. forgetting
Demeca	B, F	Kongo	(ndemoka) n. a jump
Demmy	B, M	Hausa Mende	(demmi) pl. demma, n. sheaf (demia) n. brother-in-law, a familiar term of address between men
Dena	B & W, F	Hausa	(dena) ceased doing something (dena) i.q. daina, to cease
Dene	W, F	Mende	(dɛnɛ) n. water lily
Denkie	B, F	Hausa	(déngi) n. kindred, family, tribe
Denna	W, F	See Dena	
Dessa	W, F	Mende Hausa	(dɛsɛ) id. the land is flat, sitting without showing animation (dessa) n. herbs, plants
Deva	B, F	Mende	(ndeve) neut. take off, flying off from the ground for a short hop (ndɛvɛ) n. house bat

377

Dictionary of African Origin

NAME	RACE & SEX	LANGUAGE & DEFINITION	
Deva (cont.)		Mende (cont.)	(ndɛvu) neut. life, rest
Dia		Kongo	(ndia) n. eating, a manner of eating
			(ndia) n. intestine, viscera, bowels, entrails
		Mende	(ndia) middle, among, in the middle of
		Efik	(ndia) n. the marrow of a bone
Diah	W, M	Mende	(diadia) n. a small rice-eating bird
		Hausa	(diá and dīya) collective noun, offspring; both male and female
		Bini	(dia) to become, be straight; to menstruate
		Kongo	(dia) prep. of, about, concerning
			(dia) v.t. to eat, feed, devour, subsist on, consume, spend; to use (as currency)
			(dia) n. food, victuals, nourishment, provisions
		Efik	(dia) v.tr. to eat; partake of food; to absorb; to inherit; to oppress
		Kongo	(dia) eat, food
			(ndia) bowels
		Ngombe	(dia) abide, acquire, be, food, labour
			(ndea) sew
			(dea) stab
Dibb	B, F	Kongo	(ndiba) n. pudding of cassava meal
		Mende	(ndibɔ) n. a "medicine" used for protecting crops
		Efik	(ndibe) n. secrecy; hiddenness; v. hidden; secret; underhand
Dibby	B & W, F	Hausa	(dībi) "Sokoto Hausa" m. fortune-telling
			(dībī) "Zaria Hausa" m. thing placed on another; surplus
Dibe	B, M	Hausa	(dībɛ) "Sokoto Hausa" looked completely
			(diba) tr. v. to offend
		Efik	(dibe) v. intr. to conceal, to hide one's self; to be hidden; to hide from
Dilla	B, F	Hausa	(dilā) m. jackal; "Sokoto Hausa" form of a game "Dara"
		Kongo	(dila) v. (form of dia) to eat in,

Dictionary of African Origin

NAME	RACE & SEX	LANGUAGE & DEFINITION	
Dilla (cont.)		Kongo (cont.)	off, with (dila) v. to weep, cry, mourn, fret, bewail (dila) n. capital (in trade); a large sum or pile of goods
		Kongo	(ndila) n. border (of farm, etc.) in process of extension, a manner of weeping, a lamentation
		Mende	(ndile) n. python; mythical creature in the shape of a python that is believed to attack children at night
Dimber	B, M	Kongo Mende	(dimba) n. direction (towards) (ndimba) neut. twist (thread), spin
Dini	W, M	Hausa	(dīnī) "Katsina Hausa" the one in question
Dinky	B, M	Hausa	(diŋki) m. being occupied in sewing; young leaves eaten as food
Dinna	B, F	Mende	(dina) n. a broad-leaved plant that grows in swamps (dina) n. religion "Kristimabla ti dinei"
		Bini Hausa	(dîna) to reach; to arrive (dina) English-dinner
Dochie	B, F	Hausa	(doshi) anything; set out for; went by direct route; hefted (a tool); set at a task; kept on doing; type of girl's dance; type of cloth (doshe) anything; m. short-cut, direct road (dotši) i.q. datši to be bitten
Doke	B, M	Hausa	(dṑ ɛ) surpassed (dŏka) n. plaiting of the hair, or the method of brushing it so as to make it stand erect on the head (dŏka) n. law; what is commanded (dōke) tr. v. to beat, strike, flog (dōki) n. horse
		Kongo	(doka) v.t. to click, crack (the fingers)
		Bobangi	(ndŏkā) n. punch (ndŏka) n. father's namesake
		Mende	(ndoke) n. a rope used for lowering containers of palm wine from the top

Dictionary of African Origin

NAME	RACE & SEX	LANGUAGE & DEFINITION	
Doke (cont.)		Mende (cont.)	of the tree (ndoke) neut. (of water) clearness, cleanness, purity
Dola	W, F	Mende Bobangi	(ndolaa) neut. growth (ndolaa) n. baby (ndolē) n. kind of bird
Dolos	W, M	Hausa Mende	(dōlō) m. fool (ndolo) n. African satinwood, yellow satinwood
Dona	B & W, F	Hausa Kongo	(dona) "Katsina Hausa" to put lips deeply into something to drink (dōne) tr. v. to hang up; to shut up a hole against rats (ndona) (Port. dona) names of women are prefixed by Ndona
Donna	W, F	See Dona	
Donnah	B, F	See Dona	
Dorroh	W, M	Hausa Efik Efik	(dōra) put thing or person on something or person; set (broken limb); helped person load (dōra and dōri) t.v. to join together, to heap up, to increase, to add to, to place, to put, to arrange (doro) v. to be viscous, glutinous (ndŏrŏ) n. viscidity, greed; glutinousness, covetousness
Dub	B, M	Hausa	(dub) m. noise of rat's step
Dube	B, M	Hausa	(dūbe) looked thoroughly, looked at all of (dúbā) intra. v. behold; trans. v. to look for, to search after (dúbi) tr. v. to look upon, to visit
Duce	B, M	Hausa	(duci) "Sokoto Hausa" m. stone
Ducko	B, M	Hausa Kongo	(dúka) adj. all, everyone, whole (dūka) intr. and refl. v. to stoop down, bend one's self (duka) v. to root about (as a pig), make a hole (as a rat)

Dictionary of African Origin

NAME	RACE & SEX	LANGUAGE & DEFINITION	
Dug	W, M	Mende	(dugba) n. cannon
Dula	B, F	Poto	(dula) pull
		Hausa	(dulu) n. bottle
		Mende	(ndula) neut. rottenness, rotting, decay
Dumah	W, M	Hausa	(duma) m. generic name for gourds and pumpkins; type of beer; rustic Hausa name for man called Audu (dumā-dumā) m.f. short, thick-set person
		Mende	(dumale) n. a large earthenware water pot
Dunah	B, M	Hausa	(duna) anything; m. very slack person or thing
		Kongo	(duna) v. to pull out
		Mende	(ndunya, dunya) n. world
Dunge	B, M	Hausa	(dungū) m. stump of maimed arm (dunge) m.f. short person; addled egg (dungi) m. giraffe-hide shield, adult giraffe
		Kongo	(dunga) n. a fool
		Kongo	(ndumba) n. porcupine, a moulding of pottery
Dungee	B, M	See Dunge	
Dungu	B, M	Kongo	(ndungu) pepper
		Bobangi	(ndungu) n. jar, vessel for fetching water, waterpot
		Kongo	(ndungu) n. war drum (ndungu) n. pepper, soup
Dura	B, F	Hausa	(ɗura) anything; poured liquid through narrow orifice (dura) i.q. dora tr. v. to feed, to stuff
Durah	B, F	See Dura	
Durrah	B, M	See Dura	
Eba	B, F	Mende	(eba, ebɛ) interj. introduces an emphatic statement, "I shall certainly not agree." eba ng luma

Dictionary of African Origin

NAME	RACE & SEX	LANGUAGE & DEFINITION	
Eba (cont.)		Bobangi	(ebá) n. kind of crocodile, light-skinned and cannibal
		Bini	(eba) a timber-tree; red tail feather of the grey West African parrot
			(ebã) nakedness
			(ebã́) now
		Kongo	(eba) n. palm tree; oil palm
		Efik	(eba) n. the breast; the udder; the paps
		Ngala	(eba) understand
Ebbie	W, F	Bini	(ebi) darkness
Ebby	B, F	See Ebbie	
Ebe	W, F	Bini	(ɛbe) danger, harm
			(ebe) leaf; herb; special herbs, paper, book
			(ebɛ) wine-tapping
			(ebē) boundary between farms of owners sharing the same plot
			(ebɛ) pointed iron rods or broken glass serving to keep people off from farm land
			(ebɛ̂) a ceremonial sword worn by chiefs; it does not show as high a rank as the ada
			(ebɛ̃) a tree, found near water; planks are used to build ceilings
		Hausa	(ebe) "Kano Rustic Hausa" removed; set aside
		Efik	(ēbē) n. a husband; an insect or grub which burrows in the yam; a glutton; a circle used as a mark to shoot at in a game of archery
Ebo Roben	B, M	Bobangi	(ebō) n. long barrelled gun with small bore
			(ebǒ) n. history, narrative
		Efik	(ebo) n. a tree which is frequently split to make boards
		Lolo	(ebo) flint of a gun
		Ngombe	(ebo) noun, arm, hand (arm) fathom
		Bini	(ebo)(Roben) European; white man; the Governor
			(ɛbo) a kind of sedge growing on river banks; the leaves have saw-like edges; used by women to make a kind of mat
			(ɛbo) any charm of powdery substance

382

Dictionary of African Origin

NAME	RACE & SEX	LANGUAGE & DEFINITION	
Ebo Roben (cont.)		Bini (cont.)	with which people wash themselves . . . or rub their foreheads or chests
Ecklee	W, F	Bobangi	(ekili) n. chair, form, seat, stool (ekīli) n. hip
Eda	B, F	Bini	(eda) rain-water (ede) buffalo; bush-cow; a strong creeper consisting of many threads (edε) gray hair; gray (ɛda) leucorrhoea (ɛde) native crown; bead-cap
Edda	W, F	See Eda	
Ega	W, F	Bini	(ega) main part of a cult known to adult men only (ega) a fence across the bush on which traps are set
Ege	B, F	See Ega	
Elel	B, M	Bobangi	(elēlē) n. clandestineness (elĕlĕ) n. cyclone, gale, gust, hurricane, squall, tornado
Elem	B, M	Bobangi	(elêmā) n. fool, idiot, stupid person (elēmā) n. limb
Elinah	W, M	Bobangi	(elima) n. awestriking thing, awful thing, idol, object of dread
Elitea	B, F	Bobangi	(elītô) n. weight (for scales)
Ellube	W, M	Bobangi	(elūbwa) n. general term for fishing traps
Elonza	W, M	Bobangi	(elönza) n. double bell or gong
Elowea	W, F	Kongo Hausa	(elowa) n. dew (elawu) perf. of Kwenda, to go (elawa) "Northern Hausa" i.e. Damagaram, Gobi, etc.; rope, string
Emola	W, F	Bini Poto	(emila) cow (emola) lift
Ena	W, F	Hausa	(enna) adv. where, whence

Dictionary of African Origin

NAME	RACE & SEX	LANGUAGE & DEFINITION	
Ena (cont.)		Efik	(ena) n. a kind of long white bead, worn as an ornament of the loins
		Soko	(ena) see
Epa	W, F	Bobangi	(epā) faint report of gun, small charge of powder
			(epā) field, nest of driver ants
Eppa	W, F	See Epa	
Eppe	W, F	See Epa	
Eppy	W, F	See Epa	
Equilla	W, F	Bobangi	(ekwālé) n. kind of bird, partridge
Erah	W, F	Bini	(era) ganglion
Erika	W, F	Efik	(erika) n. a going; proceeding on
Eritta	W, F	Efik	(erita) n. a planting; cultivating; a hitting, striking by a sudden, smart blow; shooting
			(erita) n. an eating, devouring, a consuming, as by fire
Essa	B & W, F	Bini	(esa) side taken by somebody who is not concerned in a quarrel, palaver, etc.; share in some enterprise, plot of ground, etc.
			(εse) well, properly; goodness, favor
		Kongo	(esa) n. maize
			(ese) n. father
		Efik	(esa) n. an inner yard, a private court; a very small species of antelope, bay coloured, found in Ibibio
		Poto	(esa) salute
		Kele	(esa) fetch
Esso	W, M	Bobangi	(esō) n. saw
		Bini	(eso) some
Etah	B, F	Bini	(eta) act of talking (also of parrots)
		Bobangi	(etai) n. kind of small edible frog
		Lolo	(eta) call
		Poto	(eta) (noun) war
		Soko	(eta) pass
		Kele	(eta) pass

Dictionary of African Origin

NAME	RACE & SEX	LANGUAGE & DEFINITION	
Eulah	W, F	Bobangi	(eula) n. cassava root
Evetta	W, F	Kongo	(eveta) n. a hunt (with dogs)
Ewa	B, F	Bini	(ewa) sleeping-mat; act of giving food to witches
		Mende	(ɛwo) n. lover, mistress
		Efik	(ewa) n. custom; manner; a species of yam
			(ewa) n. the dog
			(ewa) family name
		Poto	(ewa) know
Exa	W, F	Bini	(ɛxe) quiver, a curved tooth or bone which, in native opinion, the viper flings at its prey, out of the mouth
Ezeka	B, F	Bini	(ezikɛ̆) a musical instrument made of a long, thin calabash (a flute)
Ezema	B, F & M	Bini	(ezima) the senior chief at Uhɛ̆; he is said to have been the first Bini man to grow oil palms
Eziker	B, M	See Ezeka	
Faby	W, F	Mende	(fabo) n. parrot
Facilla	B, F	Mende	(fasele) id. fit, well, in good condition
		Arabic	(fâsila-T) intervening space, interstice, interval; distinction, difference
			(fasîla-T) palm-shoot
Fait	B, M	Hausa	(fate-fate) anything; "Zaria Hausa" m. a mushy food of flour and onions; thin and flimsy
		Arabic	(fâit) passing, passing by, escaping; lost
Fambro	B	Mende	(fambo) n. junior member of Wunde society
Fance	B & W, M	Hausa	(fansĭ) to redeem
Fara	B, F	Hausa	(fāra) n. locust; swarm of locusts

Dictionary of African Origin

NAME	RACE & SEX	LANGUAGE & DEFINITION	
Fara (cont.)		Hausa (cont.)	(fāra) tr. v. to begin, to attempt something, to begin to turn (farāa) n. joy; "yi faraa" to rejoice, be glad (fara) anything; began to; began by; was the first to do; white
		Arabic	(fará) wild ass or its grown foal (fará) mount; descend; brandish a cadgel above one's head (farrâ) line with fur, fur (fara) cut, cleave, sever; fashion; wander about a country; forge lies
		Efik	(fara) v. intr. to desist; give over; leave off; have done; to be moderate, temperate; to slip on or over one's self; to dress
Farih	B, F	Hausa	(farí) m. fara adj. white, light, bright (fāri) first (fari) anything; beginning; first; eldest; whiteness
		Efik	(fari) v. tr. to slip over; put on another person or thing; to cover over; envelope
		Arabic	(fârĭ') ally, confederate (farih) be brisk, agile and playful (fârĭ') high, towering (fârih) skillful, active, brisk, running well (farî) be astonished, perplexed, confused; admire one's self
		Efik	(mfari) n. an embrace
Faro	B, M	Hausa	(farō-farō) m. negative, water containing little flour; small numbers
Farra	W, F	See Fara	
Farry	B, F	See Farih	
Fassiah	B, F	Arabic	(fâsiyâ) a beetle (fâsiya-T) cattle, property
Fate	B & W, M W, F	See Fait	
Fate			

Dictionary of African Origin

NAME	RACE & SEX	LANGUAGE & DEFINITION	
Fatima	B, F	Arabic	(fâtima-t) mother weaning her child; female proper name
Fato	B, M	Hausa	(fātō) blow one's nose
Fenny	W, F	Hausa	(fēni) English m. penny
Feta	B, M	Soko Kele	(feta) float; refuse (feta) float
Finas	W, M	Kongo	(fina) v. a witch is said to Fina his victim; it infers the use of his black art (fina) vt. to draw something between a knife and a board or between two bars or finger and thumb or through a gauge hole
Flawilla	B, F	Mende	(flawa) n. flower, general name for the reproductive part of a plant
Fobola	B, F	Kongo	(fobola) vt. to batter in, indent, knock a hole in, drive in, crush in (fobolo) n. old, dilapidated or deserted house, a ruin, a thing which is falling to pieces
Foi	W, M	Efik	(foi) v. tr. to strike, but not a full blow; to graze; to take off a little at a time, as in eating, in order to make the most of a thing; to injure slightly, as a smart touch might do; to give a secret sign to by touching; to nudge
Fonda	B & W, M W, F	Mende Lolo	(fonde) neut. asthma; suffocation, difficult breathing (fonda) rot
Fook	W, M	Efik Mende	(fuk) v. tr. to cover; to spread a covering over; disguise; to blow the blacksmith's bellows; move up and down; to flutter (fuka) neut. grind, powder (fuke) neut. crisp, friable, crumbly (fuke) n. rat trap, bird trap

Dictionary of African Origin

NAME	RACE & SEX	LANGUAGE & DEFINITION	
Fook (cont.)		Mende (cont.)	(fuko) neut. head-pad, to coil, to form into a head-pad
		Hausa	(fuka) "Na yi fuka "I breathe hard
		Efik	(mfuk) n. the cheek
Foy	W, M	See Foi	
Fugaboo	B, M	Mende	(fugbu) id. (of the pulling) of a rope very quickly
Fute	B, M	Efik	(fut) v. tr. to fold as a cloth; v. intr. to swell; thrive; to boil; ferment; bubble up; foam; to make large; distend
		Kongo	(futa) v. to pay, repay, reward, compensate; to bathe, wash a wound with hot water (futa) n. grass
		Hausa	(fūta) intr. v. to rest, n. rest (fúta) tr. v. to take off
		Efik	(mfut) n. shade, mould; dark
Gabe	B, M	Hausa	(gābē) m. vicious top-playing
Gabi	B, M & F	Hausa	(gabi) anything; "Katsina Hausa" Bateleur Eagle; epithet of City of Daura (gabi) n. executioner
		Arabic	(gabî) fail to understand, to conceive; be concealed, obscure, unintelligible; escape; faint
Gabie	B, M & W, F	See Gabi	
Galba	W, M & F	Hausa	(galbi) "Filami word" m. wet season pasturage of cattle (galbali) "Katsina Hausa" m. a food of flour with boiling water and milk
Galma	B, F	Hausa	(galmā) "Sokoto Hausa" f. hoe
Gamba		Kongo	(ngamba) n. hired servant, labourer, porter, carrier

Dictionary of African Origin

NAME	RACE & SEX	LANGUAGE & DEFINITION	
Gamba (cont.)		Mende	(ngamba) neut. spying (ngambu) n. space between hills, the face
Gambo	B, M	Hausa	name for child born after twins (gámba) n. pl. gambobi; some kind of reed or rough grass
Gamby	B, M	Hausa	(gumbī) m. name of several thorny plants
Ganibo	B, M	Mende	(gani) n. old, rancid palm oil (gani gbongbo) old, rancid palm oil (gani) n. food cooked for girls in Bundu bush
Ganza	B, M	Arabic	(ganza) revile; talk obscenely
Gar	W, M	Arabic	(gâr) caves; lair; socket of the eye; a measurement; army; jealousy, envy (garr) deceive with empty hopes, delude (garr) fold, wrinkle; rent (gâr) descend into a valley; disappear in the ground; sink (gâr) be jealous; feel jealously, envy
Garah	B, F	Arabic	(garâ) glue (garâ) smear with glue or paste; adhere; wonder at
		Hausa	(gāra) inpers. v. it is better, preferable; conj. rather (gāra) n. ants; wood-ants (gará) tr. v. to prepare (gara) anything; f. wedding presents given bride by her parents; it would be better to; scorpion, lizard; white ant; rolled something rapidly along; drove quickly
Gatha	B, F	Arabic	(gadâ) be dark and cover everything (gada) wood
Gathra	W, M	Arabic	(gadrâ) plenty, abundance of; ease
Gato	B, M	Hausa	(gáto) n. foundation (gata) n. spy, intr. v. to be strong (gato) m. vagina; "Sokota Hausa" base of anything

Dictionary of African Origin

NAME	RACE & SEX	LANGUAGE & DEFINITION	
Gato (cont.)		Mende	(ngatε) neut. set (a trap, a fire), slice, chop up (ngati) n. pain, feeling
Gaza	B, M	Hausa	(gaza) anything; fell short; failed; "Katsina Hausa" f. yelling while working with others
		Arabic	(gazâ) strive for, intend, purpose, wish (gazâ) feed, nourish; be nutritious, invigorate, strengthen
Gera	W, F	Hausa	(gēra) tr. v. to prepare, to make ready; to mend; to amend (gērā-gērạ) f. flowering spikes of a reed; bird-snare on cornstalks; laying trap for person
Gerda	W, F	Hausa	(gerdawa) n. charmer of serpents
Gena	B, F	Bobangi	(gena) n. transliteration of gehenna, hell
Gesina	W, F	Hausa	(gēsa) pl. gesuna n. the ears of corn, rice or wheat
Gibby	W, F	Hausa	(gībi̱) n. tooth-gapping (gi̱bī) "Katsina Hausa" m. meddlesomeness (gībi̱) m. gap from loss of two or more teeth
Gill	B, M	Arabic	(gill) secret hatred, deep grudge
Gilla	B, F	Hausa	(gillạ) did excessively (gillạ-gillạ) m. small girl's cloth (from navel to knee)
		Soko	(ngila) law
		Arabic	(gilâ) dear, scarce
		Bobangi	(ngila) n. a game, a deep-seated abscess
Gilly	B, M & F	Mende	(gili) id. (with no stand) erect, rigid, stiffly (gili) n. kidney, termite, beeswax (gili) id. silent, quiet
		Hausa	(gilli̱) m. covert hatred; what a whopper!

390

Dictionary of African Origin

NAME	RACE & SEX	LANGUAGE & DEFINITION	
Gincy	W, F	Swahili	(ginsi) (noun) sort
Goah	W, M	Swahili	(ngoa) pull out; shield
Goffe	B, M	Hausa	(gōfī) m. nick at end of arrow (gōbe) tomorrow n.
Gola	W, M	Mende	(gula) n. bird with a big crest and long neck
		Hausa	(gōlā-gōla) "Sokoto Hausa" m. trousers made from uncut cloth
		Bangi	(ngola) noun, camwood
		Poto	(ngola) camwood
		Ngala	(ngola) camwood
		Ngombe	(gola) satisfied
		Bobangi	(ngölā) n. ground camwood used as a cosmetic
		Lolo	(ngola) camwood
		Kongo	(ngola) n. the bagre or cat-fish
		Mende	(ngola) neut. unite, join (ngola) n. forest (ngolaa) n. a small tree, with bluish-purple or pink flowers
Golie	B, F	Bangi	(ngoli) sheep
		Bobangi	(ngoli) n. cane string; sleep, repose
		Mende	(ngoli) n. ear, tail, urine
		Soko	(ngoli) noun, bell
		Ngombe	(ngoli) noun, snore
Gonde	W, M	Mende	(gonda) id. big, flat (gondo) id. large, big
		Bobangi	(ngōnde) n. kind of crocodile said to eat fish only
		Hausa	(gōnda) n. pawpaw tree, or fruit (gondo) n. a town near the Hausa country
		Kongo	(ngonde) n. moon, time, season (vaguely), month, "moon"
		Poto	(ngonde) noun, moon; crocodile
		Ngala	(ngonde) maiden
		Ngombe	(ngonde) crocodile
		Kele	(ngonde) crocodile
Goobey	B, M	Hausa	(gubbi) "Katsina Hausa" m. molar tooth (guba) n. a poison

391

Dictionary of African Origin

NAME	RACE & SEX	LANGUAGE & DEFINITION	
Goya	W, M	Hausa	(goya) anything; carried on one's back; helped; influence (góyo) tr. v. to tie up, together, to bear in the ear, as corn
Gozy	B, F	Swahili	(ngozi) noun, skin
Gulliah	B, M	Hausa	(gullīyā) f. dislocation, sprain
Gully	W, M	Hausa	(gullī) m. a small, striped gourd
Gumba	B, M	Mende	(ngumba) n. top, roof (gɔmba) n. small tree with rough nettle-like leaves, used for posts and roof poles or rafters
		Hausa	(gumbā) f. pounded bulrush-millet with water; "Katsina Hausa" mixed clay, used for building before matured; white head; saliva churned in the mouth and then spat out by boys playing; "Sokoto Hausa" type of white mat (gumɓā) f. the stinking soup base made from putrid meat, bones (gumbe) m. short person; short donkey
Gumbo	B, M	Mende	(ngumbu wulu) n. wooden head-rest
Habacuck	W, M	Hausa	(haɓaka) anything; rice, fire, river, etc.; expanded; swelled; caused to swell
Habukkuk	B, M	See Habacuck	
Habukuh	W, F	See Habacuck	
Habbo	W, F	Hausa	(haɓo) m. bleeding from the nose (habbo) n. bleeding of the nose
Habie	B, F	Hausa	(haɓi) m. swelling of domestic animal's udder just prior to giving birth
		Arabic	(hâbî) covered or filled with dust; grave-dust
Habis	B, M	Arabic	(habis) be brisk, nimble; lie in ambush for game, eat greedily
Hadessa	B, F	Hausa	(haddasā) started (haddace) memorized; is expert in

Dictionary of African Origin

NAME	RACE & SEX	LANGUAGE & DEFINITION	
Hage	B, M	Hausa	(hage) anything; m. getting something on credit
		Mende	(haga) neut. lazy
Hagur	B, F	Hausa	(haguri̅) m. type of epilepsy
Halla	B, F	Mende	(hala) n. light brown eel-shaped fish, unexpected gift
		Hausa	(hala̅) possibly
		Soko	(hala) scrape
		Ngombe	(hala) swell
		Arabic	(halâ) come!; come here
			(hallâ) why not?; is not?; has not?
			(hala') restlessness and discouragement
Hamet	B, M	Hausa	(hamutta) anything; armpit; inside bend of elbow
			(hamata̅) f. same as hamutta
Hamutt	B, M	See Hamet	
Hanna	W, F	Hausa	(hana) anything; prevented; forbid; regarded as illegal; refused
		Arabic	(hana') smear a camel with pitch; wish health to one, congratulate
			(hannâ) here
			(hana') bend together; submit; be bent
			(hana) do, make
Hannah	W, F	See Hanna	
Harby	B, M	Hausa	(harbi) m. act of shooting or kicking
Hattoe	B, F	Mende	(hatai) n. desire
		Soko	(hato) forest
Hilah	W, M & F	Hausa	(hi̅la) "derived from Arabic" f. guile
Hinda	W, F	Mende	(hinda) n. place, affair, business, matter
			(hindo) n. man, male
Hira	W, F	Hausa	(hira) anything; chatting
		Arabic	(hirâ) young palm-shoot; decay, destruction, putrefaction

Dictionary of African Origin

NAME	RACE & SEX	LANGUAGE & DEFINITION	
Hoke	B & W, M	Mende	(hoke) n. guinea-fowl (hoki) n. week
		Hausa	(hōke̲) m. work not profiting the doer
Hoodoo	B, F	Hausa	(hudu͡) f. four; hu u biyar f. tribal marks consisting of 5 cuts on right cheek and 4 on left (húdu) four
Hora	B, F	Hausa	(ho̲rā̲) disciplined; trained; punished
Huk	W, M	Mende	(hɔka) n. a big, broad-bladed hoe
Hula	B, M & F	Mende	(hu̲lā̲) neut. decide, make up one's mind, plan, arrange, straighten
		Hausa	(hula) f. a cap
		Ngombe	(hula) come from, return
		Arabic	(hulâ) discouragement, impatience (hûla) more frightful
Hulow	W, M	Mende	(hulo) neut. leave the inside in a certain condition
Hushia	W, M	Hausa	(hūs̆i) int. v. to be vexed, annoyed
Ibby	B, F	Bini	(ibi) charcoal, soot
		Hausa	(ibi̍) anything; type of Kola-nut known to Hausa kola-dealers in Yoruba land; place near Wukari so called
Ica	W, M	Bini	(ikã͡) a small-sized variety of (beads) (coral necklace for chiefs); spur of a cock (ika) a creeper, bow string
		Kongo	(ika) interj. an interjection a respectful person makes and adds to any remark made to a superior; a respectful assent
		Efik	(ika) a word; an articulated utterance; a speech; a language; an address, discourse, harangue; a sentence, paragraph discourse in a book; an argument; a statement; an advice; a palaver, a controversy; sentence, judgement; a message; a kind of spearmint or peppermint a kind of whistle used by boys; a meteor; a falling star; a large, broad

Dictionary of African Origin

NAME	RACE & SEX	LANGUAGE & DEFINITION	
Ica (cont.)		Efik (cont.)	knife or short two-edged sword (shaped like some meteors)
		Lolo	(ica) noun, fire
		Poto	(ika) abide, be, live
		Ngombe	(ika) feel, hear
		Kele	(icha) bite
Iddo	W, M	Bini	(ido) loom, cobweb
		Hausa	(ido) m. eye
Ika	W, F	See Ica	
Ila	B & W, F	Bini	(ile) (the) bet
		Hausa	(ila) "derived from Arabic" f. "Katsina Hausa" sudden misfortune (illa) anything; "derived from Arabic" f. blemish; crime, fault; except
		Ngombe	(ila) split
		Kele	(ila) hoist, lift
Illa	W, F	See Ila	
Ima	W, F	Bini	(ima) disjunctive pronoun of the first person plural
		Efik	(ima) n. love; affection; liking; preference; approval; approbation; esteem; an object of affection; one beloved (ima) slave name capriciously given by owner
		Ngombe	(ima) to press, squeeze
		Kele	(ima) groan; rebuke
Imena	W, F	Hausa	(imāna) n. protection, especially such as is given by a chief to a messenger sent to him
		Bini	(imina) dream
Ina	B & W, F	Hausa	(ina) anything; f. stuttering; where; how can that be!; "Northern Hausa" yes! (ina) pron. I (inna) n. mother (?)
		Mende	(ina) conj. if
		Kongo	(ina) dem. and rel. pron. cl. 2, sing.; 5 & 6 pl. 3 pos. that which, those which, which, that, those
		Efik	(ina) n. a place to lie down in; a sleeping place; a recess for a bed; a rendezvous; camp; encampment (ina) family name

Dictionary of African Origin

NAME	RACE & SEX	LANGUAGE & DEFINITION	
Ina (cont.)		Poto	(ina) dance
		Lolo	(ina) despise
		Ngala	(ina) hate
		Ngombe	(ina) sow, plant
		Kele	(ina) dance, gambol
Inee	W, F	Bini	(inyi) the sasswood tree; bark used as a taboo for witches
		Efik	(ine) n. a small temporary hut; an animal; a rodent
		Swahili	(ini) liver
Iree	W, F	Hausa	(īri) n. seed of plants, of men and creatures, offspring, kind, sort; stock, race, tribe, family
		Bini	(iri) rope; rope as part of a trap, creeper
Isah	B, M	Hausa	(isa) Jesus (issa) to be enough; sufficient; to reach to, or to arrive at; arrival; tr. v. can, to be able, to be equal to
		Bini	(isâ) faeces
		Efik	(isa) n. a thing, a person; hardhead-edness; regardlessness; impertinence
		Poto	(isa) pour (decant)
		Soko	(isa) lay down; put (place); set down
		Ngombe	(isa) pour (decant); put into; kindle
		Kele	(isa) conceal, hide
Isalee	W, F	Hausa	(īsalī) "Katsina Hausa" cause
		Kele	(isali) artery
Iva	B & W, F	Bini	(ive) promise (to give something) (ive) a proverb given as a hint in conversation; allusion
		Swahili	(iva) ripen
Izara	W, F	Hausa	(izārā) f. section of split tree
Jabe	W, F	Hausa	(jaɓe) put very heavy load on; put aside for sale what is not used; abundantly
		Mende	(jabe yia) n. saying things about a person without mentioning his name
Jabus	B & W, M	Arabic	(jabûs) mean person; vine branch

Dictionary of African Origin

NAME	RACE & SEX	LANGUAGE & DEFINITION	
Jaise	B, M	Arabic	(jâzi) quarrelsome (jâzî) sufficient, equivalent (jazi') sufficient
Jala	W, F	Mende	(jala) n. a large fresh-water fish; lion
		Hausa	(jalla) anything; bad luck; Glory to God; epithet of Kano; type of girl's name
		Poto	(njala) (noun) hunger
		Ngala	(jala) abide; n. farm; n. garden; n. plantation; sit; live (njala) n. hunger
		Arabic	(jala') throw down, throw away, pelt (jalâ) emigration; exile; splendor, brightness, polish (jala) be naked; strip; be open; be impudent (jalah) remove; prevent; divert; put away; uncover (jalâ) disclose, reveal, communicate, polish (jala) polish
		Mende	(njala) n. small leaved indigo, West African wild indigo (njala, jala) n. lion
Jamis	W, M	Arabic	(jamis) shaved smooth; hair remover
Janna	B, F	Mende	(njano) id. faded
		Hausa	(jā nā bāyā) m. baby acquired at same time as its slave mother; cord from woman's temples to back of head to fasten plaits (jannā) "Katsina Hausa" m. a row of reaped corn laid down on farm before heads cut off
		Arabic	(jana') fall on the face; bend over (janâ) plucked fruit; fruit of trees; harvest (jana) small plants
Jasie	B, M	See Jaise	
Jawn	B, M	Arabic	(jaun) red; white; black; day
Jazie	B, M	See Jaise	

Dictionary of African Origin

NAME	RACE & SEX	LANGUAGE & DEFINITION	
Jeilee	W, F	Mende	(jeilomɔ) n. the person who "interprets" for the Poro devil when he comes to town at night (jele) id. (with kpou red) bright (jeli) n. story, tale (njela) n. a tall tree used in furniture making, sapele mahogany
Jeller	W, M	See Jeilee	
Jena	W, F	Mende Kongo	(jɛnɛ) n. a small bird (jena) v. to urinate, make water
Jenna	B, F	See Jena	
Jetta	B & W, F	Kongo	(jeta) v.t. to form a ring around; go around; surround; encircle; pass or revolve round (jeta) v.t. to revolve, rotate, turn, twist, spin, go round (njeta) n. a revolution, circuit
Jette	B, F	See Jetta	
Jobah	B, M	Mende	(jɔbɔ) n. a variety of rice
Jobe	B, M	See Jobah	
Jola	B, F	Mende	(jolaa) id. very tall (njolaa) n. sweet potato leaf (njola) neut. dirtiness, filth, slovenliness (njola) neut. any tool, etc., with which a person can do good work; be of unusual skill
Joo	B, M	Mende Arabic Ngala	(joo) id. (of shouting) loudly, aloud (jû) hunger (ju) clan
Jub	B, M	Hausa	(juɓa) f. anthill (jubba) "derived from Arabic" f. kind of sleeveless gown
Juba	B, M & F	See Jub	
Jubah	B, F	See Jub	

Dictionary of African Origin

NAME	RACE & SEX	LANGUAGE & DEFINITION
Jube	B, M & F	See **Jub**
Juber	B, M	See Jub
Jubice	B, M	See Jub
Jubie	B, F	See Jub
Jubis	B, M	See Jub
Juby	B, M & F	See Jub
Jumbo	B, M	Mende	(jumbu) n. serious crime, sin
Kadish	W, M	Arabic	(kadîs) horse of a low breed; cart horse
Kaga	W, M	Hausa	(ƙaga) anything; f. "the pick of the bunch"; invented; lied; to move up in the world (kaga) that is it, it is done (?) (ƙage) anything; became temporarily stiff or permanently paralyzed; invented
Kaleb	W, M	Arabic	(kâlib) breeder of dogs
Kanuce	B, F	Bobangi	(kanisa) vt. to consider, estimate, reason, regard, surmise, think, wonder
		Arabic	(kanîs) synagogue; temple of an idol (kânis) hiding in its den or lair
Kanko	B, M	Hausa	(kánka) thyself (male) (kánki) thyself (female) (kánku) yourself (kaŋko̱) to imagine being able to do something
Kanze	B, M & F	Bobangi	(kānza) vin. to ache (of body), be troubled (of water), rage or raven (of wild beast)
		Kongo	(kanza) v. to snap (as a dog)

Dictionary of African Origin

NAME	RACE & SEX	LANGUAGE & DEFINITION	
Kaola	B, F	Kongo	(koala) vo kadi conj. forasmuch, as, because, since
Karna	B	Hausa	(karna) f. cord used by Arabs for tying up loads; cord covered with leather for stirrup-leathers
Karuma	B, F	Hausa	(karumba) f. struggle, collision (kārum) n. wine
Kata	B, F	Bobangi	(kata) vt. to apprehend, arrest, capture, grapple, hold, keep, lay hold of, occupy, reserve, retain, seize, sustain, take in hand, use, wield
			(kāta) vin. to be bulky, be corpulent, be stout, become large, dilate, expand, get fat, grow great, thrive, wax (of moon)
			(kātā) n. a kind of fish which becomes mokonga
			(nkatā) n. coil (of wire, tobacco), nest of fowl made in grass
			(nkāta) n. kind of small bird, hornbill
		Arabic	(katá) go away with, escape with; rob; be always active and ready for work
			(katâ) female slave, maid-servant (katâ) walk with short steps
		Kongo	(nkata) n. pad (of leaves, etc.), to place under a load carried on the head or shoulder, lap
		See Cata	
Katta	B, F	See Cata	
Katura	W, F	See Catura	
Kauchee	B, F	Hausa	(kōši) intr. v. to be satisfied (kóšia) n. wooden spoons
Kazee	B, M & F	Swahili	(fanya kazi) labour, work
Kea	B, F	Mende	(ke) id. openly, frankly, plainly (kea be) conj. although (ki) n. draughts
		Bobangi	(nki) pron. interrog. which, what (kī) ind. with a crack on the ground

Dictionary of African Origin

NAME	RACE & SEX	LANGUAGE & DEFINITION	
Kea (cont.)		Bobangi (cont.)	(with verb to fall), abiding, long (with verb to abide), delay, be (nke) n. light side of lobesi, a counter in a gambling game (nki) ind. deaf
		Hausa	(ke) thou (ke) v. to be (ki) thee, thy (kī) tr. v. to hate, to dislike; to refuse; to neglect, to disregard; to abhor; to be unwilling or obstinate (ki) you fem. singular and many verbal variations; e.g., refused; disliked; thrived; abundantly
		Bini	(ke) to be near, this verb used to indicate local relationship (ke) an auxiliary that links up events (ke) to come from a certain place (ke) to be suitable; to be the result of something (kɛ) to remain, to be left; to be quick (kī) to look for fruit at the base of a tree; to inspect (traps) (kī) to tie tightly; to dazzle; to coil - of snakes, caterpillars, centipedes (kie) to open; e.g., door, window
		Kongo	(ke) he, she, no, not, exactly, alike (ke) n. smallness, narrowness, littleness, fineness (ke) adj. very small, too small
		Poto	(ke) go
		Soko	(kea) go
		Ngombe	(ke) go
Keas	B, M	See Kea	
Kee See	B, F	Mende	(kisi) neut. restrain, prevent, stop (kisi) n. kitchen (kisi) adv. real, actual (kɛsi) n. pins and needles
		Bobangi	(nkīsa) n. favorite, pet
		Hausa	(kisse) n. fat (animal or vegetable fat - my note)
		Bini	(kisi) a descriptive adverb with the verb sa
		Kongo	(nkisi) noun, charm

401

Dictionary of African Origin

NAME	RACE & SEX	LANGUAGE & DEFINITION	
Kekey	B, M	Mende	(keke) n. a breed of dog that never becomes fully domesticated
		Bobangi	(kēke) n. accumulated tartar on teeth
			(kēke) vin. to be decayed (of cassava roots)
			(kê-kê) ind. loud (used with calling, challenge)
			(nkēkē) n. king of large water snake, said to be poisonous, and devours fish and fowl
		Bini	(keke) to push (in a crowd), to jostle
Kella	W, F	Mende	(kele) n. type of tall loom; thatch palm
			(kele) neut. strong tasting, pungent, bitter, hot
			(kele) n. a variety of pepper
			(kele) n. Diana's guenon
		Bobangi	(kêla) vt. to act, behave, commit, construct, contrive, do, exert, make, manufacture, operate, perform, produce, render, transact
		Kongo	(kela) v. to cut up to pieces (of grass, paper, leaves), to nibble, tear with the teeth; to strain, filter, pour through a sieve, direct the flow of a liquid
			(kela) n. cassava peeled and dried in the sun and used to make beer
			(nkela) n. box
		Soko	(kela) lihua labour, work
			(kela) lokila play
			(kela) kololi to snore
			(kela) do, make
		Poto	(kela) make, do
		Kele	(kela) do, make
			(kela kasi) labour
			(kela isa) play
			(kela likua) work
		Lolo	(kela) say, make, do
		Bangi	(kela) do, make
		Ngala	(nkela) bed
			(kela) do, make
Kellah	W, F	See Kella	
Kesia	B & W, M & F	Kongo	(nkesia) noun, sneeze
		See Kee See	

402

Dictionary of African Origin

NAME	RACE & SEX	LANGUAGE & DEFINITION	
Kessiah	B, F	See Kesia	
Ket	B, M	Efik	(ket) v. tr. to look along a thing to see whether it be straight, on a level, in a line; to aim, to point to or at; to peer, to look for; to aim, to plan; to scheme
Ketter	B, M	Bobangi	(kete) vt. to cut, elide, restrict
		Hausa	(kēta) n. mischief, cruelty, any kind of evil
			(kēta) tr. v. to cut or rip; to make a split, to split
Kettera	B, F	Hausa	(ketara) anything; stepped over something; crossed border; skin disease; slave who has escaped soon after being bought
Ketto	W, M	Hausa	(kētơ) verb. from earliest dawn; sunrise
			(kētu) n. steel, to strike fire on a flint
		Bobangi	(kēto-kēto) ind. waddling
			(nkëtu) n. enemy, enmity, foe, hostility
Key	W, M	See Kea	
Keyah	B, F	Mende	(keya) id. looking well, fit, in good health
		Hausa	(kēya) n. back part of the head
Kiah	B & W, M, B, F	Bobangi	(kīā) ind. abreast, tick (of clock)
			(kīā) ind. spread and laid out
			(kia-kia) ind. torn (of clothes)
			(kīa-kīa) ind. always, constant, continual, incessant, invariable, perpetual, usual
			(kiya) vin. to peel off (of skin)
		Kongo	(kia) n. to dawn, brighten, clear up (as weather); grow light; to commence (of the season)
			(nkia) interrog. pron. which, what
		Swahili	(mkia) tail

403

Dictionary of African Origin

NAME	RACE & SEX	LANGUAGE & DEFINITION	
Kiar	B, M	<u>See</u> Kiah	
Kie	W, M	<u>See</u> Kea	
Kile	W, M	Mende	(kile) id. (of tying) tightly
Kilo	B, M	Bobangi	(kīlö) adv. never until now
Kimber	W, M	Mende	(kimba) n. plant whose leaves are used for sauce
		Hausa	(kimba) n. some kind of pepper
Kimbro	W, M	Mende	(kimbo) n. giant anteater, big cricket
			(kimbo) neut. belch
Kimme	W, M	Mende	(kimi) n. Krim country
		Bobangi	(kima) vin. to alight (of bird)
		Hausa	(kim<u>e</u>) slightly; any medium-sized thing (f.); sat aloof or silent in company through disdain or vexation
		Kongo	(kīma) n. value
			(kime) n. dew
		Efik	(kim<u>e</u>) v. intr. to be pierced; to pierce or impale one's self by stepping or falling on a sharp pointed thing
Kinah	B, F	Bobangi	(kīna) vt. to be inattentive to a call, be unmindful of, disobey, be indifferent to, be refractory, disregard, ignore, make light of, neglect, put up with, set at naught, slight
		Hausa	(kin<u>a</u>) you (f.) are coming; imitation musk
		Kongo	(kina) dem. and rel. pron. cl. 5 & 6 sing. 3 pers. pos. that, which, that which
		Lolo	(kina) another
			(nkina) other, more
		Kongo	(kina) dance
Kinck	B, M	Bobangi	(nkinki) n. entirety, haleness, healthiness, immovableness, robustness, soundness, sturdiness, wholeness
Kinnie	B, F	Mende	(kinii) id. exactly, just enough
		Hausa	(kinī) m. one like; those like
		Kongo	(kini) n. shadow
		Efik	(kini) adv. at times; occasionally; seldom

Dictionary of African Origin

NAME	RACE & SEX	LANGUAGE & DEFINITION	
Kiseah	W, M	Hausa	(kiśia) n. jealously, the name given to the second wife of the polygamist, who is always represented as the rival of the first
Kisia	B, F	See Kiseah	
Kish	B, F	Hausa	(kiši) n. refusal, opposition
Kissar	B, M	See Kee See (Bobangi)	
Kissee	B, F	See Kee See	
Kissiah	B, F	See Kiseah	
Kissie	B, F	See Kee See	
Kit	B & W, F B, M	Efik	(kit) v. tr. to make a noise with the mouth; to show contempt for anyone or anything; to cluck at; to see
Kitt	B & W, M	See Kit	
Kiziah	B & W, F B, M	Bini See Kiseah	(kiza) to be foolish, senseless
Kizziah	B, F	See Kiziah	
Kizzie	B & W, F	See Kiziah	
Kizzy	B & W, F	See Kiziah	
Kof	B, M	See Cof	
Koma	B, F	Bobangi	(koma) (Eng.) n. comma (köma) vt. to tie (kôma) vt. to cut, engrave, smite (with knife or cutting instrument) (kôma bondêkô kwi) to make blood-brotherhood, make friendship (kōmo) vin. to be adequate, be applicable, avail, be befitting, be comfortable, be competent, be eligible, be favourable, be fitting, be good for, be legitimate, be mature, be perfect,

Dictionary of African Origin

NAME	RACE & SEX	LANGUAGE & DEFINITION	
Koma (cont.)		Bobangi (cont.)	be proper, be qualified, be right, serve, be successful, be suitable, be worthwhile, be worthy
		Hausa	(komā) n. louse
			(kōma) intr. v. to go back from the place where one is, or to return to
			(koma) anything; returned (in that direction); small fishing net
		Kongo	(koma) v. to put more, to add to; to nail up, fix, fasten by nailing, drive in a nail, hammer a nail; to put up (a calabash to catch palm wine)
		Soko	(koma) pick up
		Swahili	(koma) stop (cease)
		Ngala)	(koma) write
Kondo	B, M	Mende	(kondo) n. secret society which claims to be able to free children from witches
			(kondo) n. jumping fish, mud fish
			(kondo) neut. sound of water running over rocks; death rattle; war (of lion)
			(kondo) locust
		Bobangi	(kŏnda) vt. to reward, fee
		Hausa	(kóndo) n. basket, hamper
		Kongo	(nkondo) n. the baobab or calabash tree, adansonia; the upper part of the foreleg of an animal
Kongulay	B, M	Mende	(kongol) id. be short and stooping
			(kongolo) id. emaciated, with bones showing
			(kongolo) n. a stick bent in (part of a trap)
		Bobangi	(kôngóla) vt. to cast or shed (leaves) glance off (of an arrow), hop, jaunt, iterate, skirt a shore (on land)
			(kongolo) vt. to accumulate, gather up little by little, gather up fragments, skim
			(kŏngôlô) ind. alone, one, simple
			(kŏngôlô) adj. alone, only, by itself, solitary
Kora	B, F	Hausa	(kŏra) n. baldness such as is produced by shaving the head, or coming of itself
			(kōra) tr. v. to pursue, to run after one, to drive away
			(kora) anything; act of driving away;

Dictionary of African Origin

NAME	RACE & SEX	LANGUAGE & DEFINITION	
Kora (cont.)		Hausa (cont.)	drink water on the sly during Fast; ringworm
Kosa	W, F	Bobangi	(kôsa) vt. to be cruel to, be harsh to, maltreat, oppress, torture, treat unkindly (kŏsa-kŏsa) ind. fidgety, restless (kôsô-kôsô) ind. parched
		Hausa	(kōsa) intr. v. to be ripe (kōsa) pancakes (kōsa) m. type of chalk got by burning clay; epithet of any Sarkin Dawaki (ƙosa) anything; negative; appetite satisfied; trouble; enriched; become ripe
		Kongo	(kosa) v.t. to crush to pieces in or under the hand or foot
		Lolo	(kosa) smear, rub on
		Swahili	(kosa) err
Kosey	W, M	Mende	(kosi) n. carriage, coach (of a train) (kosi) n. trousers reaching to the knees
		Bobangi	(nkosī) n. lion; instrument of music consisting of a drum with a piece of string attached to skin inside which is drawn through the fingers
Kosse	B, F	See Kosey	
Kouba	B, F	Bobangi	(kūba) vph. to castrate
		Kongo	(nkuba) n. yaws (pian, framboesia) childhood disease
Kui	W, M	Bini	(kui) to splash water on something or somebody
		Efik	(kui) v. to slide along in a groove, or on the side; to shut anything sliding so; to shut out; to shut out from view by interposing something; v. tr. to bail, to ladle; to fill a pitcher or any vessel by thrusting it under the liquid
Kumba	B, M	Bobangi	(kūmbā) vt. to bend (knees)
		Kongo	(nkumba) n. track (of beasts) (nkumba) n. navel
		Bobangi	(nkumba) n. tortoise, hunchback, block and pully

407

Dictionary of African Origin

NAME	RACE & SEX	LANGUAGE & DEFINITION	
Kusher	W, M	See Cusha	
Laban	B & W, M	Arabic	(labân) chest, breast, bosom; breast-piece (labbân) brick-maker; seller of sour milk (laban) eat much; beat violently; beat or bruise the breast
Lafe	W, M	Hausa	(lāfe) thin and flimsy (lāfi) n. hem
Lala	W, F	Mende	(lala) n. oar, paddle; spade (in playing cards)
		Bobangi	(lala) vt. to exaggerate, increase (price), spread
		Hausa	(lala) anything; f. indolence; "Katsina Hausa" f. boy's whooping cough
		Kongo	(lala) v.i. to become less, reduced in size, wear away, wear out; be consumed, diminished, to evaporate, dissolve, flow away, ebb, decrease (lala) v. to sleep, slumber
		Arabic	(lálá) seller of pearls; shine, glitter, light, sparkle; ogle; wag the tail; shed tears (lálá) break (lálá) mirage; wolf
Lalage	W, F	Hausa	(lallagē) m. act of tapping; leaf budlets and branch tips
Lalee	B, F	Mende	(lali) neut. heed, take notice of
Lalla	W. F	See Lala	
Lallah	W, F	See Lala	
Lalu	B, F	Kongo	(lalu) n. a raft
Laman	B, M	Arabic	(lâmân) ignoble, vile, miserly
Lando	B & W, M	Mende Hausa	(lando) n. distilled palm wine (lando) n. skink-lizard; name for boy or girl born on a Sunday
Lango	B, M	Mende	(lango) neut. meet, discharge (responsibilities) (lango) n. string hammock, made of local cloth

Dictionary of African Origin

NAME	RACE & SEX	LANGUAGE & DEFINITION	
Lango (cont.)		Swahili	(mlango) gate, door
Langulo	B	Kongo	(langula) v.t. to knock down or get down or get down with something; to knock down and break something that was high up, or far off; hence to kill (a beast) at a long range
Lavuna	B, F	Kongo	(lavuna) v. to touch (so as to call attention)
Lawuna	B, F	See Lavuna	
Laze	B, M	Arabic	(lazî) blaze, flare
Lea	W, F	Mende	(lɛ) adv. yet, still
		Poto	(le) eat, to gain
		Soko	(lea) eat
		Kele	(le) be
		Lolo	(lea) know, understand
Leaby	B, M	Bobangi	(lēbe) vt. to lament, mourn for
		Hausa	(leɓe) m. lip; dewlap of cow; lobe of ear
		Bangi	(lebe) mourn
		Ngala	(lebe) mourn
Leba	B, M	Kongo	(leba) v. to allure, tempt, entice, persuade, induce, woo, coax
Lebe	W, M	See Leaby	
Lebo	B, M	Hausa	(lēbo) pl. lēba n. lip
Leboo (surname)	B, M	See Lebo	
Lema	W, F	Mende	(lema) n. palm wine tapped - stronger than ordinary palm wine
		Bobangi	(lêma) v. in. to be a fool or idiot
		Hausa	(lēma̱) f. dampness of ground or house; flattery with a view to swindling
			(lēma) n. tent
		Kongo	(lema) v. to glow, gleam, glare, blaze, burn, flare, shine (as a light)
Lemma	B, F	See Lema	
Leno	W, M	Bobangi	(lēno) n. today

409

Dictionary of African Origin

NAME	RACE & SEX	LANGUAGE & DEFINITION	
Lenna	W, F	Lolo	(lena) see
		Ngombe	(lena) cut, saw
			(lena eganda) circumcise
Lera	W, F	Hausa	(lerē) f. town in Bauchi Province; type of horse; girth-strap
Leta	W, F	Kongo	(leta) v.t. to lap (as a dog); to lick (abusive)
Letta	W, F	See Leta	
Leu Dosia	B, F	Bini	(lɛu) describes the fall of a heavy object having corners or a flat side
Leva	W, F	Kongo	(leva) n. flexibility, pliability
Libe	B, F	Mende	(libi) n. wood ashes mixed with water, then boiled till water evaporates, the residue being mixed with tobacco to make snuff, and also in soap-making
		Ngombe	(libe) udder
Lilla	W, F	Bobangi	(līla) vt. to await, remain for, stay for, wait for
			(lilé) n. a meal
			(lilé) n. prospect, view, wide land or waterscape
		Poto	(lila) await, wait for
		Soko	(lila) ascend, climb
		Kele	(lila) ascend, climb
Lima	B & W, F	Mende	(līma) neut. file, to file
		Bobangi	(līma) vt. to buy on credit, to sell on debit
		Lolo	(lima) keep back; come from; leave a place
		Poto	(lima) extinguish; quench
		Soko	(lima) extinguish
		Swahili	(lima) to hoe
		Arabic	(limâ) why?, what for?
Lina	B & W, F	Bobangi	(linā) n. name, noun, term, colq. superiority. In asking a person's name the natives do not use the interrogative what (nde) but who (na). lina li yo na? lit. Who is your name?
		Bangi	(lina) name
		Lolo	(lina) pour (decant)

410

Dictionary of African Origin

NAME	RACE & SEX	LANGUAGE & DEFINITION	
Lina (cont.)		Poto	(lina) noun, name
		Soko	(lina) name
		Kele	(lina) name
Linah	W, F	See Lina	
Lingo	B, M	Bobangi	(lingô) n. tiny thing (appearing tiny on account of distance)
Linna	B & W, F	See Lina	
Lisha	B, M & F	Hausa	(līshā) "derived from Arabic" f. period of darkness till towards midnight
Lishe	B, M	See Lisha	
Lissa	W, F	Bobangi	(lisa) vc., vt. to consume, eat, levy, partake of
		Hausa	(līsa) tr. v. to lick
		Lolo	(lisa) conceal, hide
Loa	W, F	Kongo	(loa) v.t. to catch with a hook
Loasbe	W, F	Bobangi	(loāsī) n. eighty
Lobelia	W, F	Bobangi	(lobëlā) n. loud call
			(lobēle) n. something connected with the liver, sweetbread
			(lobilā) n. palm nut, fat near tail of catfish
Loda	B, F	Hausa	(lǫdā) m. a plant
Lodee	B, M & F	Hausa	(lōdi) English m. load (for lorry, etc.)
Lodie	B & W, F	See Lodee	
Lokey	B, M	Bobangi	(lôki-lôki) ind. rusted, etc.
Lolo	B, F	Mende	(lolo) n. (obsolescent) cat
		Kongo	(lolo) dem. pron. cl. 10 & 11 sing.

411

Dictionary of African Origin

NAME	RACE & SEX	LANGUAGE & DEFINITION	
Lolo (cont.)		Kongo (cont.)	2nd poss. emphatic, that (lolo) n. a low tree the wood of which is of a bright yellow colour; a bush yielding a yellow edible fruit
		Bobangi	(lôla) vin. to be aflame, blaze, flame, flash (of gun)
Loma	W, F	Bobangi	(loma) n. arrogance, base, desire, cheek, evil intention, fault, impertinence, impudence, proposed wrongdoing, willfulness
		Hausa	(loma) f. mouthful of
		Ngombe	(loma) send
Loos	B, F	Arabic	(luss) thief, robber
Loosa	B, F	Kongo	(lusa) v. to prowl about
		Lolo	(lusa) throw
		Soko	(loosa) noun, garden
		Ngombe	(lusa) bore; burst; pierce
Lottee	B, F	Bobangi	(loti) n. piece cut off dog's tail, docked tail, kind of small shell
Lowa	W, F	Kongo	(lowa) v. to fish with a hook
		Ngala	(lowa) death
Lube	B, M	Hausa	(lube) "Katsina Hausa" m. type of tree
		Lolo	(lube) evil
Luby	B, M & F	See Lube	
Luff	B, M	Hausa	(luf) anything; peaceful, docile, quiet
Lum	B & W, M	Hausa	(lum) to move away; to vanish
Luma	W, F	Mende	(luma) n. a large number, a crowd
			(luma) neut. handful, give a handful
		Kongo	(luma) v.i. to emit semen
Luman	W, M	Arabic	(lu man) who deserve blame
			(lu man) abject, vile, cowardly; niggardly

Dictionary of African Origin

NAME	RACE & SEX	LANGUAGE & DEFINITION	
Luna	B & W, F	Kongo	(luna) dem. and rel. pron. cl. 10 & 11 sing. 3rd pron. that, which, that which
Lunana	W	Lolo	(lunama) bend
Lunda	W, F	Kongo	(lunda) v.t. to guard, keep, take care of, protect, watch, look after, reserve, preserve, hide, put away, lay by, set aside, save up, store, hoard
Lura	W, F	Hausa	(lura) paid attention; realized that: carefulness (lurra) "Zaria Hausa" f. "derived from Arabic"; necessity; living expenses (lura) n. wisdom, knowledge, understanding, good sense
Lurah	W, F	See Lura	
Luta	W, F	Bobangi Kongo Bangi Lolo Soko Kele	(luta) vt. to blow bellows (luta) v.t. to pass, go beyond, by, past, exceed, surpass, excel, come past, flow past, by, go further than, roll by, to pass, elapse, be more than, to outdo, gain, make a profit (luta) blow, bellows (luta) come back (luta) draw; haul; pull; pull along; tow (luta) draw; haul; pull; tow
Lutie	W, F	Bobangi	(luti) n. dirt or mud stirred up in water
Luuwah	B, M	Mende	(luwa) n. hernia
Luvata	B, F	Kongo	(luvati) n. rib, side (of body), also a pain in the side, a "stitch"
Mabla	W, F	Mende Arabic	(mabla) neut. cut into (but not through) (mabla) gullet; sink hole; drain
Macaree	B, M	Hausa	(makari) anything; m. antidote; epithet of warrior or chief; means of escape; to crease; love-philtre; boundary, limit, end; act of strangling (makari) n. shield (makeri) n. blacksmith

413

Dictionary of African Origin

NAME	RACE & SEX	LANGUAGE & DEFINITION	
Macaree (cont.)		Efik	(makara) n. a European; a white man - white men generally
Mace	B & W, M	Hausa	(mace) anything; f. woman; wife; died; "Katsina Hausa" m. the stirrups; cooked sorrel leaves
Macie	B & W, F	Mende Hausa	(masi) n. matches (m̲a̲sī) m. vowel points in Arabic script (maci) anything; m.f. eaten; English m. act of marching; marching people along
Madie	B, F	Mende Hausa Arabic	(madi) n. zeal, diligent effort (mádi) some kind of molasses (madɗi) m. sweet drink made from juice of sugar cane (madî̂) who adopts (mâdih) who praises (mâdî̂) passed; past, dead; quick, nimble; penetrating, sharp, effective; successful; lion
Mado	B, M	Hausa Efik	(madō) m. she (virgin) has been violated; abbreviation of name amadu (mädo) conj. therefore; wherefore
Mafus	B, M	Hausa	(mafusára) n. bladder
Magda	W, F	Arabic	(magda) morning walk
Mage	W, F	Hausa	(m̲a̲gē) f. cat
Mahale	W, F	Hausa Swahili	(m̲ahalli) "derived from Arabic"; place; place of residence (mahali) place
Mahaley	W, F	See Mahale	
Mahalia	B & W, F	Hausa	(m̲ahālīy̲a̲) f. "derived from Arabic" lie; craftiness; dishonesty
Mahalie	B, F	See Mahale	
Mahaly	B, F	See Mahale	
Mahola	W, M	Mende	(mahola) neut. filter, strain

Dictionary of African Origin

NAME	RACE & SEX	LANGUAGE & DEFINITION	
Mahue	B, M	Mende	(mahu) n. top, up-country
Mahuo	B, M	See Mahue	
Maida	B & W, F	Hausa	(maida) tr. v. to turn, turn back, to turn into, to be changed into something, to turn, return, send back, restore, to treat one as something, to reduce in value
Maide	B & W, F	See Maida	
Main	B, F	Arabic	(maîn) water flowing over a surface; source, spring
Maina	B, F	Hausa	(maina) East Hausa; name for son of chief
		Ngala	(maina) pus
Maisa	B, F	See Mace	
Maize	B, F	Hausa	(máiši) n. owner, proprietor
Makamo (Mackamo)	B, F	Hausa	(makāma) what is laid hold on, hence the handle of anything (makāmi) what is laid hold on, hence the handle of anything (makami) anything; m. person who seizes; any weapon
Makamo (variation of Mahala)	B, F	See Makamo	
Malacha	W, F	Hausa	(mallaka) possessed; ruled over (malāka) tr. v. to rule, to reign, to govern
Malachi	B & W, M	Hausa	(maláiki) n. angel
Malachia	W, F	Hausa	(mālikāwā) follower of the Maliki sect
Malachiah	W, M	See Malachia	
Malah	W, F	Mende	(mala) neut. increase, add to, exaggerate; to thatch (mala) n. a variety of rice (mala) neut. state the price
		Hausa	(mala) anything; type of satchel;

Dictionary of African Origin

NAME	RACE & SEX	LANGUAGE & DEFINITION	
Malah (cont.)		Hausa (cont.)	"Zaria Hausa" vanished; was intoxicated
		Arabic	(malâ) desert without vegetation
			(malaʿ) skin a sheep from the neck downwards
Malakiah	W, M	See Malachia	
Malchia	W, F	Hausa	(málka) n. gentle rain
Malee	W, M	Mende	(mali) neut. rub grease on the skin, anoint
			(mali) n. force, vigor, energy
		Bobangi	(māli) n. fat, grease, oil
		Bangi	(mali) oil, fat
			(mali) noun, palm oil
		Ngala	(mali) oil, palm oil
		Arabic	(malî) vast and bare tract, desert; full rich surfeit; cold; rheum
Malekiah	W, M	See Malachia	
Malicha	W, M	Mende	(malika) n. angel
		Hausa	(maliki) anything; the angel in charge of hell-fire; name of the founder of the Malikiyya, School of Muslim Law
Malichia	W, M	See Malachia	
Malkie	B, M	See Malchia	
Mallekiah	W, M	See Malachia	
Mallica	B, M	See Malicha	
Mally	B, F	See Malee	
Malsa	B, F	Arabic	(malsâ) sour milk mixed with sweet; afternoon; month of Safar
Malura	W, F	Mende	(maluwa) neut. frightening, frightful
Mamai	W, F	Mende	(mamai) n. lightning
		Hausa	(máma) n. breast
		Bini	(mama) to stick together; to press; to massage
Mana	W, F	Mende	(mana) n. plantation; cowpox; a banana-shaped earring

Dictionary of African Origin

NAME	RACE & SEX	LANGUAGE & DEFINITION	
Mana (cont.)		Bobangi	(māna) vin. to engage in fight, fight, make war
		Hausa	(mana) anything; to us; well, indeed
		Kongo	(mana) v.t. to perfect, finish, stop, consume, spend, exhaust, bring to an end, settle (a palaver)
			(mana) v.i. to be finished, to come to an end, end, cease
			(mana) n. produce, merchandise
			(mana) dem. & rel. pron. cl. 7, 8, 9 & 13 pl. 3rd pos. those, those which, which
		Efik	(mana) v. intr. to be born; to be related to by blood, to unite in brotherhood
			(mana) v. tr. to continue or repeat any action; add to what is done or given
			(manã) v. to love; to finish
		Bangi	(mana) to war
		Poto	(mana) wine
		Ngombe	(maɲa) consider; meditate; think; wine
		Arabic	(mána) sense, meaning; intrinsic nature and value; spirit of a thing, reality; opinion, thought, idea
			(maná) refuse; hinder, prevent, repel; defend, forbid
			(maná) message of death; prevention; hindrance; abstention
			(manå) put to the test, try, visit, afflict
			(mana) put to the test, try, visit, be visited from God; be tempted by, wish for
			(mana) destroy, fate, death; measure, quantity
			(maná) soak a skin to be tanned
			(mana) death
			(mannä) who hinders, prevents, refuses
Manah	B, F & W, M	See Mana	
Manda	B & W, F	Mende	(manda) id. (of tying) tightly
		Hausa	(mandā) f. a dark Bornu salt used medicinally
		Kongo	(manda) n. web, net, hammock; cobweb
Manga	B, M	Bobangi	(mangö) pron. they

417

Dictionary of African Origin

NAME	RACE & SEX	LANGUAGE & DEFINITION	
Manga (cont.)		Hausa	(manga) anything; "Sokoto Hausa" f. the plaits; name for boy or girl born soon after the mother's return home after longish absence
		Kongo	(manga) n. sting, venom (manga) v. to object to, disapprove, refuse, decline
		Ngala	(manga) wine
Mange	B, M	Bobangi	(mangēī) n. awe, horror, terror
Manima	B, F	Efik	(manima) n. a small musical instrument used in Ibibio. It is made of metal, and beaten with a stick.
Manna	B, F	See Mana	
Manse	B, M	Hausa	(mántše) to forget, to err, to make a mistake (mantšiē) tr. v. to forget someone (manzo) n. messenger i.q. manso
Manza	B, F	See Manse Arabic	(manzá) place from which anything is pulled out, from which one withdraws
		Bobangi	(manzā) n. instrument of music consisting of one piece of iron beaten with another, triangle
Manzey	B, F	Bobangi Bangi	(mānzī) n. a mat (manzi) noun, mat
Manzy	B, F	See Manzey	
Marma	W, M & F	Arabic	(marma) place where one throws to; shoots at, aim, target, game
Maroda	B, F	Mende	(marodi) n. Moslem Mutual Aid Club
Marue	W, F	Hausa	(māru) recalled forgotten detail
Maso	B, M	Hausa	(maso) (must be followed by another word) anything; one who likes, loves; north, south, east, west
Massa	B, F & W, M	Hausa	(māsa) n. males, men, husbands (māsa) n. pancake

418

Dictionary of African Origin

NAME	RACE & SEX	LANGUAGE & DEFINITION	
Massa (cont.)		Hausa (cont.)	(masa) to him, for him
			(massa) n. bread
		Kongo	(masa) n. maize, Indian corn, wheat (port and maize)
		Ngala	(masa) twins
		Arabic	(masaʿ) talk or act inconsiderately; keep in the middle of the road; tarry, hesitate, delay, cheat
			(masâ) evening
			(masa) emaciate; draw the sword; clear the uterus of a camel from sperm
			(maṣaʾ) flash; wag the tail and beat with it; strike with the sword of a whip; beat slightly, hit; hurry by, run fast; drop excrement, lose courage
Massey	B, M & F	Arabic	(maŝiʾ) harming, hurtful; sinner; rebel
			(masiʾ) eager for combat; bellicose, reckless fighter
Massi	B	See Massey	
Massie	B, F	See Massey	
Masue	B, F	Bobangi	(māsu) ind. vt., to cast, hit, put forth rapidly, recite, relate
		Hausa	(masu) anything; "Sokota Hausa" to them, spear; put something in its place; changed into
Massy	B, F	See Massey	
Matta	B, F	Mende	(mata) neut. praise, praise song, be ostentatious
		Hausa	(mata) f. to her, for her
			(māta) n. woman, wife
		Kongo	(mata) n. yaws (a disease of childhood)
		Soko	(mata) touch
		Kele	(mata) touch
		Arabic	(maʿtā) appearance, aspect; opposite side; place which one comes from; place of meeting
			(maṭa) lie with
			(mata) back; protection; yawning;

Dictionary of African Origin

NAME	RACE & SEX	LANGUAGE & DEFINITION	
Matta (cont.)		Arabic (cont.)	rope of palm-fibre (mata) depart and disappear; chew with the fore-part of the mouth (matâ) walk apace, hasten; travel far; stretch, extend (mata') beat, cadgel; stretch (matâ) property, possessions; goods, merchandise; furniture, utensils, household things, clothes; penis; metals; profit, gain (mata') enjoy, derive advantage from (matah) draw or pull up (the bucket out of the well) (matâ) stride apace; stretch (mata) when? at what time?
Mauree	W, F	Hausa	(mori) anything; m. type of white, hard-grained guinea corn; stable; a favorite
Mava	W, F	Mende Bobangi	(mava) neut. exploration; preface (māwā) n. grief, sadness, sorrow
Meck	W, F	Efik	(mek) v.tr. to choose, to prefer; to make a motion backward with hand or head, as a salutation of one at a distance
Meena	W, F	Bobangi Hausa	(mīna) vt. to appropriate, consume, detain, keep for one's self, embezzle, swallow (minā) pl. of lina, name, noun, term (mina) anything; "Sokoto Hausa" what is it; f. the town Minna
Mema	B, F	Hausa Kongo	(mēmā) f. the kola-nuts have internal blemish (mema) v. to make the daily cut in the palm for palm wine, to cut a slice
Meme	B & W, F	Mende Bobangi Soko	(mɛmɛ) id. holding up the hand as a sign to halt (mɛmɛ) n. mirror, glass (meme) vt. to cut irregular parts of the edge of anything to make such edge straight (mēme) vt. to bear, carry, sustain (meme) goat, sheep

Dictionary of African Origin

NAME	RACE & SEX	LANGUAGE & DEFINITION	
Mena	W, F	Bobangi	(mēne) vin. to grow, shoot up, sprout (menye) vt. to disparage
		Kongo	(mean) v.i. to grow, spring up, sprout, vegetate, germinate, cut (the teeth)
Menia	B, F	Kongo	(menia) n. malt, malted maize (beer)
Meta	B & W, F	Bobangi Bini	(mêta) n. metre (m-ɛtī) to take up, to carry (m-eto) to plait one's hair
		Kongo	(mete) n. saliva, spittle, expectoration
Metta	W, F	See Meta	
Miah	B, M	Mende	(mia) adv. yonder, there, over there (mia va) for that reason (mia) part. nya mia it's me (miamia) n. lightning
		Bobangi Bini	(mḗya) n. fire (miɛ) to see, to have, to obtain something from somebody
		Hausa Kongo	(mīa) n. soup, broth, sauce (mia) cl. 3, 4 pl. prep. of, about, concerning, from (mia) v.i. to dissolve, to melt (mia) n. capillary attraction
		Efik	(mia) v. to beat, to flog in any way or with anything; to be struck, to be caught by a trap
		Arabic	(miʼa) gut, intestines; irrigation canal
Mial	B, M	Arabic	(miʼâl) meadow; mill; wheel of a mill (miʼâl) meadow
Micah	W, M	Hausa	(mika) tr. v. to stretch forth, as the hands (miƙa) anything; stretched out; extended, one pace; ornament for baby's loins (miƙe) anything; independent; unrolled mat; overcharged; became stretched out; anything handed over fence or through doorway or window
		Kongo	(mika) n. wool, fur, hair

Dictionary of African Origin

NAME	RACE & SEX	LANGUAGE & DEFINITION	
Mida	B, F	Arabic	(mîdá') cloth bag, wardrobe; sufficient living (mîdâ) basin for ablutions
Mikay	W, M	See Micah	
Mila	B, F	Hausa	(mi̱lā) "Katsina Hausa" anything; well, I'll tell you the answer! (milla̱) travelled far; projected far
		Arabic	(milâ) full
Milah	B, F	See Mila	
Milla	B, F	See Mila	
Mima	B, F	Bobangi	(mimwa) vs. to be demure, be grave, be morose, be sedate, be sombre, be staid, be taciturn
Mimi	W, F	Kongo	(mimi) dem. pron. cl. 3 & 4 pl. these
		Swahili	(mimi) I
Mina	B & W, F B, M	Bobangi	(mi̱nyā) n. urine (mi̱nya) vt. crumple (mi̱nyā) n. account, announcement, message, mouth, nipple, orifice, report, rumour, sharp point
		Bini	(mina) to dream
		Kongo	(mina) dem. & rel. pron. cl. 3 & 4 pl. 3rd pos. those, those which, which (mina) to swallow (v.t.)
		Soko	(mina) allow, let, permit; stop (cease)
		Arabic	(mîna) harbor, anchorage (mînâ) glass bead
Minda	B & W, F	Hausa	(minda̱) f. English medal
Mingo	B, M	Bobangi	(minga) vt. to refuse to honour or obey, infringe, transgress (mingo) pron. they
Minna	B & W, F	See Mina	
Minty	B, F	Hausa	(minti̱) English; m. mint; minute of time

Dictionary of African Origin

NAME	RACE & SEX	LANGUAGE & DEFINITION	
Mira	B, F	Arabic	(mirâ) quarrel; dispute; doubt
Mirah	B, F	See Mira	
Mish	B, M	Hausa	(mīsì) n. male, man, husband, pl.masa
Misha	B, F	See Mish	
Misher	B, F	See Mish	
Missomi	B, F	Mende	(misimi) n. Moslem
Moddie	B, F	Hausa	(mōdí) n. gambling (mōda) n. mug, jug
Mohaley	B, F	Soko	(mohali) noun, wife
Mola	B, F	Bobangi Hausa	(molā) n. long and narrow cloth (mōlo) n. music
Monah	B, F	Kongo Soko	(mona) v.t. to see, observe, view, notice, feel, find, experience, witness, suffer, to sight (mona) n. vision, sight, light (mona) child (mona moke) boy (mona obota) freeman
Mono	W, F	Bobangi Efik Kongo Poto Ngali	(mono) n. drug, medicine, poison, remedy (mönö) v. tr. to see (mono) I (mono) hill (mono) medicine
Mont	W, M	Bobangi	(monta) (Fr.) n. watch (montö) n. bone in pectoral fin of catfish
Monta	B, F	See Mont	
Monte	B & W, M	See Mont	
Montoe	B, M	See Mont	
Moogie	B, M	Hausa	(mugīa) n. owl (mūgu) adj. bad (mūgu) n. wicked person

Dictionary of African Origin

NAME	RACE & SEX	LANGUAGE & DEFINITION	
Moose	B, M	Bobangi	(moōsī) n. curl
		Hausa	(muse) n. cat
Moree	W, F & B, M	Hausa	(morōri) n. pl. of mora, stomaches or waists (?)
			(mōra) n. stomach or waist (?)
			(mora) anything; made use of person or thing
Morrah	W, F	See Moree	
Mosetta	W, F	Bobangi	(mosētō) n. funeral dance
Motta	B, F	Bobangi	(motō) n. star
			(môtô) n. anyone, human being, person
		Hausa	(mōta̱) f. English; motor-car
		Kongo	(mote) n. beautiful, handsome, good-looking person
Moza	W, F	Bobangi	(mozö) n. death due
		Hausa	(mōsa) tr. v. to shake or move something
Mozelle	W, F	Bobangi	(mosēle) adj. out of square
Muke	W, M	Bobangi	(muka) vt. to call, gather, harvest, pluck, reap
		Hausa	(muka) we
			(mūke̱) I hit him with a stick
		Swahili	(muke) wife, female
Murriah	B, F	Hausa	(mūrīya̱) f. anus
			(múria) n. voice
		Efik	(murua) n. the name of an officer possessed by the highest grades in Egbo
Musa	B, F	Bobangi	(musa) n. pl. of busa, day, eventually
		Hausa	(mūsa) Moses
			(mūsa) n. cat
			(musa) "derived from Arabic" m. Moses
		Poto	(musa̅) throw
		Arabic	(mûsa̷) rich, powerful; Moses
Naab	W, F	Arabic	(nab) superiority, victory, success
			(nab̷) source, origin
			(nâb) dog-tooth, tusk, molar, tooth; ivory

Dictionary of African Origin

NAME	RACE & SEX	LANGUAGE & DEFINITION	
Naab (cont.)		Arabic (cont.)	(na'ab) croak and augur evil; crow; call out the hour for prayer
Naaman	B, M	Hausa	(nāamāa) n. some kind of sweet herbs (nāma) n. flesh, meat
Nace	B, M	Mende Hausa	(nasii) id. very small, tiny (nāsa) pron. m. his, his own (nēsa) n. distance (nássa) tr. v. to put in (nāce) persevered, persisted
Nada	W, F	Hausa Arabic	(nada) anything; wound (put on) tur- ban; put forth effort; severely whipped; heavily laden; ate much (nāda) adv. before, already (nāde) tr. v. to roll together, to spin; to wind up a watch (nada') put on coals or in the hot ashes; stir up the ashes; feel aversion, loathe (nadah) urge on camels, drive them away; call (nadâ) call, call out, call upon or to, assemble (nada) moisture, dampness; dew; rain, fresh food
Naise	B, M	See Nace	
Namon	B, M	See Naaman	
Nando	B & W, M	Mende	(nande) n. a variety of okra
Napa	B	Mende	(napi) id. moist and sticky, tacky, viscous
Nara	W, F	Arabic	(na'ra) clamorous woman
Narra	B, F	See Nara	
Nath	W, M	Arabic	(nádd) easily executed; money (nadd) ooze out, exude, flow out slowly; be doled out; burst; make known, publish
Nazara	W, F	Hausa	(nassāra) n. victory, success, good luck (nazarī) "derived from Arabic" m. looking at

Dictionary of African Origin

NAME	RACE & SEX	LANGUAGE & DEFINITION	
Nease	B, M	See Nace	
Neata	W, F	Mende	(nɛtɛ) n. door, diaphram
Neela	W, F	Mende	(nili) n. cicada (nili) id. pitch dark
Nemo	W, M	Mende Hausa	(nɛmu) neut. hurt, injure (seriously) (nēma) tr. v. to seek, to look for; to search (nēmō) anything; looked for; courting; fornicates
Nemy	W, F	Mende	(nimi) id. sweet
Nena	W, F	Mende Bobangi Hausa Kongo	(nɛnɛ) n. a plant with hard fruit and black seeds (nɛnɛ) n. shadow, picture, photograph; n n m : a spy (nɛnɛ) id. very young, new born (nēna) vt. to bend (a bow), drill stretch body, make taut, make tense, stretch elastic (nēna ndi) to strain, make very tense (nēna) tr. v. to cook, to boil (nena) v. to go to stool, to ease the bowels
Neta	W, F	See Neata	
Netta	W, F	See Neata	
Nias	B & W, M	Hausa	(nīa) intern. pron. Is it I - you mean me?
Nica	B, F	Mende Hausa Kongo	(nika) n. cow, ox (nika) ripened (fruit by storing); he is perspiring freely from the heat of the sun (niƙa) anything; ground up; being oc- cupied in grinding (nika) v. to grind, to crush on a stone, pound, rub and pound in washing
Nilla	B, F	Mende	(nɔlɔ) neut. glory, be glorious
Nim	W, M	Efik	(nïm) v. tr. to put; to place; to keep; to make good; v. intr. to drive

Dictionary of African Origin

NAME	RACE & SEX	LANGUAGE & DEFINITION	
Nish	B, M	Hausa	(nīsi) n. groaning
Nissa	W, F	Hausa	(nisa) anything; groaned; (wall) cracked; thought about dead or absent person; distance (nīso) intr. v. to dive, to immerse
Noa	W, M	Soko Swahili Ngombe	(noa) drink (noa) sharpen (noa) pass, surpass
Noca	B, F	Mende Kongo Lolo	(nɔkɔ) n. elbow (noka) v. to rain, pour, fall (as rain) (noka) pluck
Noe	B, M	See Noa	
Nola	B, F	See Nilla	
Noma	B, F	Hausa	(nōma) tr. v. to work with the hoe; to till the ground; to do the work of a husbandman (noma) anything; m. farming
Nona	B, F	Mende Hausa Kongo	(nɔnɔ) n. milk of goat or cow (nɔnnā) m. sour milk; milk; breast; udder; fins below head of a fish (nōno) n. milk, breast (nona) v. to pick up
Nong	B, M	Bobangi	(nönga) vin. to be homesick, be restless (of rats or fowl hopping about)
Numa	B, F & W, M	Arabic Hausa Mende	(nummā) somebody, anybody (nu'mā) ease, affluence, riches; pleasure (nūna) to be ripe (nūna) tr. v. to show, to point out (numu) n. person (numu) neut. disable
Nute	B, M	Mende Hausa	(notɔ) n. a small shellfish (nūtā) "Sokoto Hause"; (wind, trouble) abated; penetrated; vanished (núta) intr. v. to dive, to dip under water; to sink

427

Dictionary of African Origin·

NAME	RACE & SEX	LANGUAGE & DEFINITION	
Nutie	B, M	See Nute	
Nutta	B, F	See Nute	
Oba	W, M	Hausa	(obā) n. father
		Bini	(oba) a pattern similar to a chain
			(ba) the ruler of Bini
Obelia	W, F	Bini	(obɛlɛ) track cut through the bush with a machete, not cleared; mostly a casual track not destined to be used as a path
Obry	W, M	Efik	(obri) n. name of an object of worship; a black substance kept in a calabash
Ocele	W, F	Bini	(osele) rope or tree put up horizontally seven or eight feet high as a rack for drying corn
			(ɔsɛlɛ) (F) an insect similar to a locust said to appear during the dry season
Ockey	B, M	Bini	(oke) hill
			(oke) name of a Bini village
			(okī) giddiness, dazzle; pirouetting continuously, as in a dance
			(oki) a feat performed at the festival of Osu: a man who has a special charm is struck with machetes without a wound being inflicted
Oda	B & W, F	Bini	(odã) heel
			(odɛ) general term for way, road; a cleared bush path; manner of doing something
		Hausa	(ōda) f. English; order, command; forbidden; term of imprisonment; dilatoriness
Offa	W, M	Hausa	(ōfa) East Hausa f. doorway; breach in fence; hole; intermediary
		Soko	(ofa) blow, horn
		Bini	(ofe) rat, mouse
Ofie	W, F	Bini	(ofi) yaws
Ogie	W, M	Mende	(ogi) n. a preparation of maize foo-

Dictionary of African Origin

NAME	RACE & SEX	LANGUAGE & DEFINITION	
Ogie (cont.)		Mende (cont.)	foo, uncooked, eaten with sugar in the form of a porridge, a preparation of beniseed which may be added to palaver sauce
		Bini	(ogi) a creeper (ogie) a ruling chief, or hereditary village head; senior, headman; main, chief, principal, of animals, plants, objects (ogie) laughter
Ohma	B, F	Bini	(oma) a large tree; wood used for planks (omɛ) unopened palm branches tied as a fringe over a village gate or the gate of the shrine of a deity (omɛ) sorrow, affliction
		Kele	(oma) beat, blow, horn, fire (a gun)
		Soko	(oma) recover
		Poto	(oma) kill
Ojetta Azalee	B, F	See Azalee	
Ola	B & W, F	Bini	(ola) menorrhoea
		Kongo	(ola) n. (Port. ora) hour (of time)
		Kele	(ola) kill
Olee	B & W, M	Kongo	(ole) adj. two, a pair
Olie	B, M	See Olee	
Ollie	B & W, M	See Olee	
Olly	B, F	See Olee	
Oma	B & W, F & W, M	See Ohma	
Omah	W, F	See Ohma	
Omie	B, M & F	Bini	(omi) a kind of white yam
		Ngombe	(omi) (mo-omi) male
Ona	W, F	Bini	(ona) sketch, pattern (ɔna) this (one), these
		Kongo	(ona) dem. & rel. pron. cl. 1 sing., 3rd pos. he, who, he that, he who

Dictionary of African Origin

NAME	RACE & SEX	LANGUAGE & DEFINITION	
Ona (cont.)		Poto	(ona) plant; sow; so (thus)
		Swahili	(ona) feel; see
Ooman	B, F	Efik	(uman) n. bringing forth, birth; labour; birth pangs; family, race; female (applied to animals and vegetables); womanish, soft, quiet and modest; generation
Ora	B & W, F	Bini	(ora) stain, spot (ore) acquaintances (all the people a man knows) (orɛ) pillar (ore) town or Benin city; bright side of a cloud (ɔra) the ra country (ɔra) Ocro cut and dried, then pounded to powder; thus it lasts from three to five months (ɔra) a God of the ba (ora) a village situated on the Ifon Road, ten miles from Benin City (ɔre) a particle emphasizing the word it follows (ɔre) possessive pronoun 3rd pers. sing. "his, her, its"
Oree	B, M	Binee	(ori) corncake (usually wrapped in a big leaf)
Ori	W, F	See Oree	
Orie	B, F & W, M	See Oree	
Oro	B, F	Bini	(oro) a coral bead hat, pointed in the middle (oro) secret practices (referring to witchcraft and the worship of gods) (oro) world of the dead
Orra	W, F	See Ora	
Orrie	B & W, M & F	See Oree	
Osa	B & W, F	Bini	(osa) debt (osa) the Bini high god, creator of

Dictionary of African Origin

NAME	RACE & SEX	LANGUAGE & DEFINITION	
Osa (cont.)		Bini (cont.)	the world (ose) beauty; a position in the Ogwega divination (Ɔsã) a kind of creeper; the root is about as big as a yam (Ɔsa) title of a chief (Ɔsa) a big ape (chimpanzee?) (Ɔse) friend; mistress, lover
Ossa	B, F	<u>See</u> Osa	
Ote	B, F	Efik	(oti) n. the heart; daring, daunt-lessness; recklessness, hardihood; a musical instrument made of metal, with a stick inside to act in the manner of a bell
		Poto	(ote) as
		Swahili	(ote) all
Ova	W, F	Hausa	(ovo) n. January
		Bini	(ovɛ̃) sunshine
		Kongo	(ova nsi) down
Oza	W, M	Bini	(oze) lead (metal) (Ɔza) a strip of cloth used to fasten
		Swahili	(oza) rot
Pala	B, M	Mende	(pala) n. parlour, sitting room, central room with bedrooms leading off it (pala) id. be mad (kpela) neut. maturity (kpela) pp. near, beside
		Bobangi	(pala) vin. to bawl, shout (mpala) n. race; bela mpala, to race
		Kongo	(mpala) n. rival
		Soko	(pala) seek
		Ngombe	(pala) covet, like, love, want (desire)
Pateloe	B, M	Bini	(kpatalɛ) to defecate
Paya	B	Kongo	(mpaya) n. the curved protuberance on the base of the upper lip of the cat-fish of baghre
		Mende	(kpeya) neut. stand aside, get out of the way (kpia) neut. take out, pull, remove, extract

Dictionary of African Origin

NAME	RACE & SEX	LANGUAGE & DEFINITION	
Pecola	B, F	Mende	(pekulu) n. long-nosed mongoose, kusimanse (hioŋdo pekulu) a man with many wives
		Bobangi	(pekolo) vt. to break edge of vessel, to chip out, notch, strike off
Pecolia	B, F	See Pecola	
Penda	B, F	Mende	(penda) n. trigger of·a gun (kpondo) neut. squeeze hard, squash, a fall trap for rats
		Swahili	(penda) admire, like, love
Phena	W, F	Mende	(fɛnɛ) n. thick, slimy substance
Phola	B, F	Mende	(fole) neut. froth, lather (fole) n. resin (fole) neut. whistle (folo) n. sun, day, a tree with hard compact, durable wood, sometimes called West African walnut (folo) n. a plant, the seeds of which stick to clothing and skin
Piccola	B & W, F	See Pecola	
Piciola	B, F	See Pecola	
Picola	B, M & F	See Pecola	
Pinda	B, F	Kongo Mende	(mpinda) n. ground-nut (pindɛ) neut. jump, jumping
Pinder	B, F	See Pinda	
Pinna	B, M & F	Bini	(kpĩnya) to dig yams and cut their "heads" off which are used as seed-yam; to cut one's self (or somebody else) in shaving
		Mende	(kpini) neut. twist
Pisa	B	Mende	(pisu) n. a grass that grows in swamps
		Poto	(pisa) hide, conceal
Polie	W, M	Mende	(poli) n. a big fish (pole) neut. a condition in which the skin becomes dull and greyish, often as a result of anaemia, be dried up and lifeless

Dictionary of African Origin

NAME	RACE & SEX	LANGUAGE & DEFINITION	
Polie (cont.)		Bobangi	(kpoli) n. worm (kpoli) n. part of a river that branches from the main stream (mpoli) n. thing found and which it is necessary according to custom to bring to the owner of the part of land or river where it is found, or to chief if the finder be a slave
Poovey	B, M	Mende	(puve) n. a grass used for thatching (puvɛ) id. big, protruding
Pummie	B, M	Mende	(pumu) neut. blindness
Qua	B, M	Hausa	(kwā) you (kwā) f. slag; plucky
		Kongo	(kwa) n. sweet potatoes; how much, how many, what quantity (nkwa) n. fellow, comrade, mate, associate, colleague, companion, friend, partner; a game, like "hockey" (kwa monso) left arm (kwa nene) right arm (nkwa) labourer
		Efik	(quä) v. tr. & intr. to sing; to chant
		Poto	(kwa) to acquire; fall; obtain, receive, take, tumble
		Kele	(kwa) as, fall, tumble (kwa nda) embark (kwa otili) flee (kwa se) to land
		Ngala	(kwa) fall, tumble
		Ngombe	(kwa) fall, fall (as rain), to rain, tumble (kua) play (kue) short
		Swahili	(kua) grow
		Lolo	(kwa) fall, tumble (nkwa) excrement
Quack	B, M	Efik	(quak) v. tr. to beat as a drum; to beat together, to clap, as the hands; to cackle, as a hen
Quaccoo	B, M	Kongo	(kwaku) thyself, yourself; this
Quaco	B, M	Hausa	(kwakko) "Katsina Hausa" m. gruel (Kwaku) Wednesday.
		Poto	(kwaka) to hoe

Dictionary of African Origin

NAME	RACE & SEX	LANGUAGE & DEFINITION	
Quaco Minisee	B, M	See Quaco	
Quah	B, M	See Qua	
Quam	B, M	Hausa	(kwam) anything; m. it stinks; I heard axe blows
Quamana	B, M	See Quamin	
Quamin			(kwame) Saturday.
Quamina	B, M	See Quamin	
Quaminah	B, M	See Quamin	
Quaminy	B, M	See Quamin	
Quamino	B, M	See Quamin	
Quarco	B, M	Hausa	(kwarkọ) m. yellow Mexican poppy, used for staining teeth
Quas	B, M	Hausa	(kwas-kwas) he looks clean and tidy
Quash	B, M	See Quashey	
Quashey	B, M	Hausa	(kwashe) anything; dipped out; collected and removed; type of button-hole stitch in embroidery (kwāshī) anything; dipped out some of; bailed out (the boat)
Quashie			(kwasi) Sunday.
Quashoo	B, M	See Quashey	
Quawk	B, M	See Quaco	
Quay	B & W, M W, F	Bini Hausa Efik Ngala Swahili Poto	(kwe) an auxiliary verb indicating doubt in a question (kwɔ) to feather an arrow (kwăi) m. egg (quai) v. tr. to make thin (kue) short (mkwe) mother-in-law (kwe) short

Dictionary of African Origin

NAME	RACE & SEX	LANGUAGE & DEFINITION	
Quico	B, M	Kongo	(kwika) to kindle
Quomana	B, M	See Quamin	
Quominy	B, M	See Quamin	
Rada	W, F	Hausa	(radá) tr. v. to whisper, to speak secretly (radá) anything; beat with stick; whispered; slandered
		Arabic	(rada') prop a wall; give a support to; assist, help; pelt (rada) stamp the ground; go away; hop, walk in hops; grow, increase
Rahumah	W	Hausa	(rahūma) "Katsina Hausa" f. odds and ends
Rama	B & W, F	Hausa	(rāma) tr. v. to pay, repay; to revenge; to make restitution; to restore (rāma) intr. v. to be or to become lean (ráma) n. a reed or shrub from which the rind is taken to make ropes (rama) anything; repaid; took revenge; emaciation; Indian hemp
		Arabic	(rammâ) white (rama') tremble; beckon; nod the head (rama) throw; shoot arrows; shoot, fling (rama') stop, remain, abide; surpass in number (ramâ) usury; increase
Ramah	B, F	See Rama	
Rambo	B, M	Hausa	(rambo) m. a food of uncooked flour with rama-leaves and water; ya sha rambo: he jumped into shallow water thinking it was deep, and so hurt himself
Ramie	W, F	Hausa	(rāmi) m. "Katsina Hausa" hole in the ground, wall or earth floor; rustic (town)
		Arabic	(râmî) who throws, flings, hits; archer; saggitarius mocker, scoffer

435

Dictionary of African Origin

NAME	RACE & SEX	LANGUAGE & DEFINITION	
Rance	W, M	Hausa	(rance) anything; borrowed all of
Ras	W, M	Hausa	(ras) anything; snapped with crashing sound; the tree is dried up
		Arabic	(rass) dig a well; bury the dead; conceal, keep secret
			(rass) prelude; beginning
			(raśś) sprinkle, shed, strew, sow
			(râs) step along haughtily; carry away offal; eat well or much
			(râs) grow wise
			(râs) walk pompously with violent movements of the body
Razin	B, M	Arabic	(razîn) grave, dignified; heavy, weighty; dignity
			(razzîn) wild maize
Reda	W, F	Hausa	(rēdā) "Sokoto Hausa" ground; scrape meat from bone; pared (shavings)
Reena	W, F	Hausa	(rina) anything; dyed with indigo; slandered; type of hornet; type of embroidery
			(rina and rini) tr. v. to dye, to tinge
Refo	W, M	Hausa	(rēfo) as in the phrase (refon-itse), branch of a tree
Regga	W, M	Hausa	(rega) anything; shook (corn, rice, etc.) with water to rid it of sand, etc. "Sokoto Hausa" peeped into
			(réga) n. rags
			(regge) to diminish, to want
Rema	W, F	Hausa	(rēmā) m. coney, hyrax
			(rēme) n. a mouse, breeding in rocky ground
Rena	B & W, F	Hausa	(rēna) anything; despised; looked after
			(rena) tr. v. to slight, to neglect, to disregard, to refuse
Renah	W, F	See Rena	
Renee	W, F	Hausa	(rēni) m. contempt

Dictionary of African Origin

NAME	RACE & SEX	LANGUAGE & DEFINITION	
Renna	B & W, F	See Rena	
Resha	W, F	Hausa	(rēshe̠) m. branch
Reta	B & W, F	Hausa	(rēto) to shake, to swing
Retta	B & W, F	See Reta	
Rheata	W, F	See Reta	
Rheba	B, F	Hausa	(reba) to divide, to part with, to separate
Rheta	W, F	See Reta	
Rhetta	B & W, F	See Reta	
Rhina	B, F	See Reena	
Rhoba	W, F	Hausa	(roba) anything; f. type of all tall marsh-grass; English: rubber, India rubber; tire; sealing wax
Rhuea	W, F	Hausa	(rūa) pl. ruāyé, n. water, also used for rain (rūa) n. care, attention, thought, concern, business (rūa-alla) n. rainbow
Rias	B, M	Arabic	(riâs) pommel of a sword
Rica	W, F	Hausa	(riƙa) anything; kept on doing; become full grown, prosperous (rike) tr. v. to keep, to hold, to hold fast, to hold in mind
Rihna	B, F	See Reena	
Ritta	B, F	Arabic	(ritâ) pasturing freely
Roba	B, F	See Rhoba	
Robah	B, M	See Rhoba	
Roco	W, M	Hausa	(rōko) tr. v. to stand bail, to bail, to offer to pay, surity (róko) tr. v. to beg, to ask for alms (rōkō) m. beseeching, begging; requesting

Dictionary of African Origin

NAME	RACE & SEX	LANGUAGE & DEFINITION	
Rolla	B, M & F	Hausa	(rolla, na i rolla) I threw myself down in prayer
Rollo	W, M	See Rolla	
Roma	B & W, F	Hausa	(rōma) f. Rome; Byzantium
Roos	B, M & F	Hausa	(rus) the tree became dried up (rusa) thrashed, crunched, cried bitterly
Rowa	W, F	Hausa	(rōwa) f. miserliness (rōwa) adj. hard, illiberal, greedy n. greediness
Rufa	B, F	Hausa	(rufa) anything; covered; roofed; concealed; deceived; wrapped
Rusha	B & W, F	Hausa	(rūshe) demolished, caused to collapse; collapse (rushi) How huge!
Ryas	B, M	See Rias	
Saba	B, M	Mende	(saaba) n. wick, binding (in phases like) may we be alive tomorrow
		Bobangi	(saba) vt. vin. to swim rolling on each side alternately and with hand on same side taking stroke
		Hausa	(sābe) to choose (sába) choice (saba) tr. v. to rub (saba) anything; become accustomed (saɓa) anything; missed one another; quarrelled; varied; sloughed-off skin of snake or lizard; heat, air, liquor had overpowering effect on a person
		Bini	(saba) to be able
		Kongo	(saba) n. hut, shelter, cover, house (a temporary dwelling)
		Arabic	(saba') buy; neglect; take by the hand; skin; flay; scourge so as to tear the skin; scorch and cause to shrink (sabâ') driftwood; (sabbâ) wine merchant

Dictionary of African Origin

NAME	RACE & SEX	LANGUAGE & DEFINITION	
Saba (cont.)		Arabic (cont.)	(saba) complete the number of seven; twist sevenfold; shoot; frighten; bite; fall year (saba) make prisoner, lead into captivity or slavery; inf. saby: send into distant foreign lands, into captivity (saba) change from one religion to another (saba) east wind, zephyr, vernal breeze (saba) point at (contemptuously); point out (saba) be childish
Saba Quaico	B, M	See Saba	
Sabaloo	B, F	Bobangi	(sabala) n. Saturday
Sabarah	B, F	Hausa	(sābarā) f. a plant (pounded, dried leaves used for piles); its wood-smoke keeps flies off cattle; from roots comes decoction for nursing mothers and infants
Sabina	B & W, F	Bobangi	(sābinya) vt. to absolve, condone, forgive, pardon
Sabour	W, M	Hausa	(sábura) intr. v. to start up (sáburo) n. gnat, fly
Saby	B, F	Bobangi Hausa Kongo Ngombe Arabic	(sabi) n. kind of pot herb (sābi) anything; new; new ground-nuts; familiarity with; on account of; sinning (saɓi) anything; m. wickedness; mats of stalk; cubit; act of measuring; act of soaping; act of throwing dice (nsabi) n. (Port. chave) key (nsabi) key (saby) captivity (sâbi') seventh
Sack	B, F	Hausa Efik	(sak) due (direction) (sak) v. tr. to laugh at; to make sport of; to ridicule; to deride, to mock; v. intr. to laugh; to blame; to flame, as a fire; to give forth radiance;

Dictionary of African Origin

NAME	RACE & SEX	LANGUAGE & DEFINITION	
Sack (cont.)		Efik (cont.)	to be lustrous; to reflect or radiate light; to glitter; to evaporate; to be evaporated, by boiling; to be scorched; v. tr. to shake up and down a plaything, like a rattle; to riddle
		Arabic	(sakk) stop, bar, obstruct; chop excrement (şakk) beat violently; lock; judicial act, signed sentence; deed, document; slip, false step (sâk) rub, clean the teeth
Sackoe	B, M	Hausa	(sako) anything; m. one's next younger brother or sister by the same mother; dense undergrowth (sāko) to cast down, to cast one's self down, to let down (sāko) n. errand, message
		Bini	(s-akɔ̄) to break; to split; to file teeth
Sala	W, F	Mende	(sala) n. bush left standing between a farm and a road in order to give shade to the road
		Bobangi	(sala) vt. to be employed in, manipulate, serve, work (sāla) vin. to sell (of merchandise)
		Hausa	(sala) anything; f. long, thin slice of raw meat (sallạ) f. "derived from Arabic" each of the five Muslim daily series of prayers (sállạ) to worship, to pray
		Kongo	(sala) v.i. to do, act, work, toil, labour, execute (a work), to profit, be of use, be industrious, to prosper (sala) n. industry, work, labor (sala) v. t. to reap, cut, gather (corn) (sala) v. to remain, be left, dwell, abide (sala) n. a dance, characterized by rapid oscillation of the hips; fin, tail of fish (nsala) n. plumage, feathers, down, wing of insect; crawfish, shrimp, lobster; a manner of working
		Lolo	(sala) labour, work
		Poto	(sala) labour, work

440

Dictionary of African Origin

NAME	RACE & SEX	LANGUAGE & DEFINITION	
Sala (cont.)		Bangi	(sala) work, labour
		Ngala	(sala) labour, work
		Arabic	(sala) purify the butter; press sesame-oil; clean the palms free from thorns; beat; pay promptly
			(sala') split, cleave; be chopped; be leperous
			(salâ) console one's self about a thing and forget it
			(ṣa'lâ) bald
			(ṣalâ) beat on the middle of the back
Saleh	B, M	Hausa	(sale) anything; peeled, on abraded thing
		Mende	(sale) n. proverb, parable
		Bobangi	(salële) to serve, work for
Saliva Bungay	B, M	Hausa	(buŋge-buŋgē) m. petty, cadging
Sama	B, F	Mende	(sama) n. a person of high social standing, aristocrat
		Hausa	(sama) anything; chanced on; ransomed himself (slave); managed to; "derived from Arabic" sky, heavens; rain; top
			(sáma) to be
			(sáma) n. sky, heaven
			(same) tr. v. to get, to receive, to find, to happen, to meet with
		Bini	(s-amɛ) same as s-uma
		Kongo	(sama) same as sema
		Kele	(sama) love
		Arabic	(samã') heaven; firmament; roof
			(samâ) heaving, listening(s); reputation; dance and music of the dervishes
			(samah) run unwearyingly; be as if thunderstruck; dumbfounded
			(samâ) be high, elevated, sublime
Samba	B, M	Mende	(samba) n. a broad, open basket, wooden sandal with four points underneath
			(samba) neut. gift brought by a visitor, bring a gift
		Bobangi	(samba) vin. to sound (of gun)
			(samba mbalaka) vph. to pay death dues
			(sāmba) vt. to beat down (grass)
			(sāmba mwêtë) to beat or strike heavily with a stick
			(sāmba piô-piô) to lash

Dictionary of African Origin

NAME	RACE & SEX	LANGUAGE & DEFINITION	
Samba (cont.)		Kongo	(samba) v. to pray, entreat, supplicate, worship (used only in reference to God); to squall (as an infant) (nsamba) n. eaves, an offering of prayer, a prayer; parting (of hair), grass beaten down on each side of the road; tribal mark, cicatrices, tattoo; an ascent, a climbing
		Lolo	(samba) mend, sew
		Soko	(samba) buy
		Kele	(samba) poison ordeal
		Ngombe	(samba) accuse
		Arabic	(sambâ) podex (ṣamba') shrink, shrink back
Sambo	B, M & F	Mende	See also Chapter V, Footnote 7
		Bobangi	(sambo) n. example, an instance
		Hausa	(sambo) neut. disgrace (sāmböö) pind. long (sambọ) name for any man called Muhammadu; name given to second son; the Bori-spirit, Sambo
Samboe	B, M	See Sambo	
Saminy	B, M	Hausa	(saminī) "derived from Arabic" m. price; type of sweet tama-rind
Sanco	B, M	Hausa	(saŋkō) m. baldness; bald patch; shaving hair over eyes in v-shape (sankaī) n. thistles
Sango	B, M	Mende	(sanga) n. an ornament worn by Sande girls during the open part of their training (sanga) n. black-and-white kingfisher (sange) adv. soon, presently, just now (sango) n. all three
		Bobangi	(sangöö) n. father, sire
		Hausa	(saŋgo) m. elephant harpoon; name of Yoruba idol
		Lolo	(nsango) news
		Poto	(sango) father (nsango) news
		Ngala	(nsango) news
		Ngombe	(sango) father
		Kele	(sango) father

Dictionary of African Origin

NAME	RACE & SEX	LANGUAGE & DEFINITION	
Sanina	B, F	Hausa	(saŋ inna) insincere friendship
Sanney	B, M	Mende	(sani) n. bottle, jar, jam jar
		Hausa	(sani) anything; knew, knew that; knowledge; that thing (food) which has lost its flavor
			(sáni) tr. v. to know
			(sāne) n. spots, dots, lines
		Arabic	(sanih) have existed for many years; be advanced in age
			(sanî) of beautiful proportions, symmetry
			(sâni') artisan, artist; workman, apprentice
			(ṣânî) always sewing
			(ṣanî') made more pliable by use, inured; well kept and fed; skillful; prepared food
Sanny	B, M	See Sanney	
Sarata	B, F	Hausa	(sarauta) anything; f. being the ruler, having sovereignty; official position
			(sáráti) n. harm, hurt
Saree	W, F	Hausa	(sari) anything; m. chestnut horse
			(sārī) n. moth
			(sari) to accuse
			(sari) from which occurs
			(sāre) tr. v. to twine, to spin
			(sāre) n. thread; used also of wire
			(sarē) v. tr. to sting, to bite
			(sāre) tr. v. to cut down, to hew: to fell wood, to cut
			(sāre) to accuse
		Efik	(sari) v. tr. to scratch, as a hen in searching for food; to search diligently; to neglect; to pass over, or exclude; to speak to, or act towards one so as to treat him as an inferior
			(sari) v. intr. to act selfishly; to bode, forebode
			(nsari) n. a slight, a keeping outside, at a distance
		Arabic	(sârî) night-traveller
			(sarî) the most noble, best, swiftest horse
			(sarî) hastening, hasty, hurried, quick

Dictionary of African Origin

NAME	RACE & SEX	LANGUAGE & DEFINITION	
Saree (cont.)		Arabic (cont.)	(ṣarî̂) thrown to the ground; epileptic; hostage (ṣârî̂) sailor
Saria	W, F	Hausa	(sária) as sarian-zuri n. ant-hill (sārīyā) f. shaving front of head from ear to ear
Sariah	B, F	See Saria	
Satera	B, F	Hausa	(saṭṭārạ) f. ornamented saddle cover
Sawney	B, M	Hausa	(saŭna) to dwell, sit down (saúni) n. mountain, hill
		Bini	(sɔnɔ) to grieve, anger, annoy; to disgust, be disgusting
Seabie	W, F	Hausa	(sebbi) ina sebbi (I spin yarn)
Seafus	B, M	Hausa	(sēfa) liver-complaint (sēfa) n. gall
Seah	W, M	Hausa	(sāye) n. root (sayé) to buy and to sell
Seasess	B, M & F	Mende	(sɛsɛ) neut. cut into chips (sɛsɛ) n. a small green squirrel
Seba	B, M	Bobangi	(sêba) vt. to edge a tool, grind or file sharp (sêba) to ascend palm trees or rapids, gather palm wine, stem a current
		Ngala	(seba) know, understand
		Ngombe	(seba) sharpen
Sebana	B, F	Mende	(sefana) n. a ceremony performed about 40 days after burial
		Bobangi	(sebene) vs. to be helpless, be needing help
Sebany	B, F	See Sebana	
Sebe	B & W, M	Mende	(sɛbɛ) n. large paper amulet sewn into leather sachet, and worn round the neck; it is made by Moslems
		Kongo	(sebe) n. obstinacy (in children)
		Bini	(s-ebɛ̃) same as s-uma

444

Dictionary of African Origin

NAME	RACE & SEX	LANGUAGE & DEFINITION	
Secar	W, M	Hausa	(sēka) tr. v. to let down, to drop something (sēke) adv. openly, clearly
Selah	B & W, F	Mende	(sola) neut. a smell of fish, filthy behavior (sɔlɔ) id. long and thin (sɛlɛ) n. banana
		Bobangi	(sëla) vin. to be dying (sêla) see sila
		Kongo	(sela) v.t. same as sena (sela) n. (Port. cera) wax
		Soko	(sela) vomit
		Poto	(sela) bewitch
		Ngombe	(sela) bewitch
Sella	B, F	See Selah	
Sem	B, M	Efik	(sem) v. tr. to speak a language; to interpret (sem) v. intr. to shine; to glisten; to glitter; to flash, as lightning; to be lustrous; to be brilliant
Sema	B, F	Mende	(sema) n. "Ikoko", a tree with wood suitable for furniture making
		Bobangi	(sêma) vt. to admire
		Hausa	(sēmā) f. receptacle made of laced corn stalks
		Kongo	(sema) v. to gleam, shine, glow, be bright or clean, to flash as lightning, to lighten, to have shooting pain (nsema) n. a flash, a flashing, as of lightning
		Soko	(sema) noun, dream
		Swahili	(sema) say, speak, talk
Sena	B & W, F	Bobangi	(sëna) to bend (a bow), drill, stretch body, make taut, make tense, stretch elastic
		Kongo	(sena) v.t. to gird up loose robes, to tuck up one's cloth, to gird the loins
Seney	W, F	Mende	(sɛnɛ) interj. exclamation of appreciation and approval; ex. "well done" (sɛnɛ) n. a dish prepared from rancid shrimps and beniseed

Dictionary of African Origin

NAME	RACE & SEX	LANGUAGE & DEFINITION	
Senie	W, M	Mende	(seni) n. mite which causes a skin disease resembling craw-craw (seni) n. male infant not yet able to walk
		Hausa	(sēnị) (ala) long life to you
Senna	B, F	See Sena	
Sennie	B & W, F	See Senie	
Sessee	B, M	Bobangi	(sēse) vt. to carve meat, cut up, dismember
		Poto	(sese) carve
		Soko	(sese) alarm, down, land
		Ngala	(sese) carve; take leave
Seva	W, F	Kongo	(seva) v. to laugh, smile, grin, giggle, laugh at, to ridicule, deride, scoff, jeer, taunt, make fun of
Seve	B, M	Kongo	(nseve) n. heel of hoofed animal
Sheeba	B, F	Hausa	(shiɓa) m. cotton teased with small bow for preparing it for spinning; to tease cotton for this purpose
Shib	B, M	See Sheeba	
Sib	B, F	Bobangi Arabic	(siba) vin. to copulate (siba) satiation (sibah) similarity, resemblance (siba) satiety (siba) satiated, full
Sibb	B, F	See Sib	
Sibbie	B, F	Mende	(sibi) n. sweetheart, boy or girl friend
		Hausa	(sĩbi) to perspire
Sibby	B, M & W, F	See Sibbie	
Siby	B, F	See Sibbie	
Sifas	B	Mende	(sifa) n. a wild cat
		Hausa	(siffạ) f. "derived from Arabic" likeness; picture; photo; description; details

446

Dictionary of African Origin

NAME	RACE & SEX	LANGUAGE & DEFINITION	
Sila	B, F	Bobangi	(sīla) vin. to finish, be carried through, be complete, be done, exhaust, expire, stop, terminate (sila) vt. to curse, imprecate, wish (spoken) person ill
		Hausa	(sila) "derived from Arabic" f. intermediary (sile) money (silla) she made fine tuwo, i.e., the staple N. P. food, made from flour of guinea-corn, bulrush mullet or rice and served with butter (sille) m. wearing gown without trousers or loin-cloth; top section of corn-stalk
		Lolo	(sila) finished
		Poto	(sila) finished
		Soko	(sila) acquire, marry
		Ngala	(sila) finished
		Kele	(sila) finished
		Arabic	(si'lâ) a female demon; hag, fury (silâ') heat of the sun
Silla	B, F	See Sila	
Sillah	B, F	See Sila	
Siller	B, F	See Sila	
Silley	B, F	Hausa	(sillī) "Sokoto Hausa"; "Katsina Hausa"; m. foreskin; uncircumcised penis
Sim	B & W, M	Efik	(sïm) v. tr. to reach; to arrive at; to overtake; to touch, to affect. v. intr. to groan as in sickness or under oppression (nsim) n. a fish pot; a fish trap; a groan
Simbo	B, M	Efik	(nsimbo) n. the ape
Simboh	B, F	See Simbo	
Sina	B & W, F	Mende	(sina) n. tomorrow, near future, soon
		Bobangi	(sina) vt. to block, plug, stanch, stop up
		Hausa	(sina) tr. v. to pick up, to bewitch
		Kongo	(sina) depth

Dictionary of African Origin

NAME	RACE & SEX	LANGUAGE & DEFINITION	
Sinah	B & W, F	<u>See</u> Sina	
Sirar	B, M	Arabic	(sirâr) lines in the hand or on the forehead
Sive	B, M	Bini	(s-ivĩ) same as s-ak (sivĩ) to claim something by force or tricks (sivĩ) to be next of kin to somebody (sivĩ) to cure; to protect, e.g. in prayers
Sola	W, F	Bobangi	(sôla) vin. to be full grown, be mature, be of full stature, be ripe
		Kongo	(sola) v.t. to select, choose, pick, sort, prefer, look out (sola) v. to make a clearing (in a wood), make a farm on forest land (nsola) n. a choosing, choice (the act)
		Bangi	(sola) ripen
		Lolo	(sola) cleanse; pick (select); select; wash
		Kele	(sola) cleanse, wash
Sooh	B, F	Mende	(su) n. Moslem fast, a root used for dying (su wubu) n. a tree whose heartwood is used for making slit-drums (soo) id. (of itching, smarting) intensely, acutely
		Bobangi	(su) ind. nearly (with verbs denoting catching, hitting, etc.)
		Hausa	(su) they, them, their (su) anything; m. fishing; they; them
		Bini	(su) to be powdery, of ground or pounded foodstuffs like corn or soup herbs
		Poto	(nsu) noun, fish
		Kongo	(su) n. mortar (for pounding)
		Efik	(su) v. intr. to lie, to tell lies; v. tr. to convict of falsehood; v. intr. to happen, to occur, to come to pass (sü) intr. pron. what? (nsu) n. a lie, a falsehood: a liar
		Ngala	(nsu) noun, fish
		Ngombe	(su) smell
		Arabic	(sûh) courtyards

Dictionary of African Origin

NAME	RACE & SEX	LANGUAGE & DEFINITION	
Soudon	B, M	Hausa	(sudan) anything; "derived from Arabic"; black ones f. the Sudan
Soumah	W, F	Hausa	(súma) int. v. to faint (suma) int. v. to faint, to swoon; to become insensible (súma) n. rags (suma) anything; fainted; speechless from fear; withered; hair of the head; "Katsina Hausa" shaving baby's head on naming day
		Bini	(s-uma) to reach; to come true; to be enough; to visit
		Arabic	(summah) thunderstruck, bewildered
Suck	B, M	Efik	(suk) v. tr. to bring down; to bring low; to reduce; v. intr. to descend; to go down; v. tr. to leave; to omit; v. intr. to remain; to stay behind; to be left (nsuk) n. a descending; a relaxing, a moderation
Sudie	B & W, F	Hausa	(sudi) m. remains of food left in vessel for dependents
		Kongo	(nsudi) n. stench, stink, bad odour or smell
		Efik	(sudi) v. tr. to disgrace; to dishonour; to affront; to put to shame
Suke	W, F	Mende	(suka) n. a "medicine" used by chiefs to increase their fame; also used to enable the owner to go from place to place at great speed (suka) neut. loss, squander, waste
		Bobangi	(suka) vin. to come to an end, culminate, terminate
		Hausa	(sukē) they (suke) was speechless with rage; dead tired (suka) they (sūka) tr. v. to gallop; to make an attack upon an enemy
		Kongo	(nsuki) n. hair
Sula	B & W, F	Bobangi	(sūla) vin. to be afraid, to run away (sūla) vt. to poke (sula) vin., vs. to alter from proper condition to a worse one, be blighted,

Dictionary of African Origin

NAME	RACE & SEX	LANGUAGE & DEFINITION
Sula (cont.)		Bobangi (cont.) — fail in spirit, be overcome, be over-powered, paralyzed with fear, quail, be stunned
		Kongo — (sula) vt. to press the pulp of palm nuts in the hand with the thumb against the palm of the hand
		(sula) n. shell of a nut, ascites, dropsy, electric fish
		(nsula) n. electric fish
		Lolo — (soola) converse
		Ngala — (sula) betray
		Arabic — (ṣullâ') broad hard stone; deficient in vegetation
Sunna	B, M	Hausa — (suna) anything; they are; a name; any grain about a year or more old
		(súna) n. name, character, reputation
		Arabic — (sun'a) skillful man
Susa	W, F	Bobangi — (susa) vin., vs. to approach, or pro-ceed to any indicated place, budge, shift
		Hausa — (sūṣa) f. act of scratching (one's self)
		(sūsa) tr. v. to scratch
		Kongo — (susa) v. to urinate, make water
		Poto — (susa) another, cleanse, wash
		Ngombe — (susa) cleanse
Tabina	W, F	Bobangi — (tābinya) vc. to condole with, con-sole with, sympathize with
		Hausa — (tabi'īna) "derived from Arabic" Mu-hammad's companions and followers
Tabor (surname)	B	Bobangi — (ntābā) n. goat
		Hausa — (tabo) n. lunacy
		(tabo) n. mud, dirt
Tal	B, M	Hausa — (tal) anything; only, m. sound of dripping
		Arabic — (tâl) be long, stretch to a great ex-tent, last long; be tall; surpass in length or tallness; overcome finally; benefit; be able to reach with one's hands
		(ṭall) moisten slightly the ground; grant a delay of payment; hurt, injure
		(ṭall) slight rain, shower, dew; milk; beautiful, charming, lovely; very old man

Dictionary of African Origin

NAME	RACE & SEX	LANGUAGE & DEFINITION	
Tallu	W, F	Mende	(talu) n. nine
		Bobangi	(ntālô) n. meaning, value
		Kongo	(ntalu) n. value, price, worth, cost, amount, charge, expense, proceeds
Tama	B, F	Mende	(tamɔ) n. middle-aged man, mature male
			(tamɔ) id. cautious, deep
			(tama) n. fecklessness, inefficiency and carelessness; trouble which cannot be overcome
		Bobangi	(táma) vin. to be greased, be oiled
		Hausa	(tama) ore; type of cheap sword "Sokoto Hausa" helped
			(tammā) f. one-franc piece
		Kongo	(tama) v. to measure (length, distance), measure by paces, pace, space, fathom
			(ntama) n. distance, remoteness; a span; a stride, a distance measured, a measuring
		Efik	(tama) v. intr. to jump; to leap
		Arabic	(tama') greed, covetousness; ambition
			(tamâ') desire, eagerness, greed
Tamar	B & W, F	Arabic	(tamar) dig under, bury; conceal; fill; swell
Tamba	B, M	Mende	(tamba) n. a large rattan palm, an open space in a town or in front of a house, a stretch of bare ground, a musical instrument consisting of a strip of metal suspended between the first two fingers and beaten with a ring on the thumb
		Bobangi	(tamba) vt. to catch
		Hausa	(tamba) f. a type of grass
			(támba) n. tares
			(támbo) n. spot, mark
		Kongo	(tamba) v. to hold out in the hand, offer, show, hold, put, reach out, extend (the hand or arm); to tie, fix or fasten roughly, to baste, run, sew roughly
		Poto	(tamba) embark
		Soko	(tamba) await, guard, protect, wait for, ward off
		Kele	(tamba) ward off
		Ngala	(tamba) catch

Dictionary of African Origin

NAME	RACE & SEX	LANGUAGE & DEFINITION	
Tamba (cont.)		Ngombe	(tamba) embark
		Swahili	(tambaa) crawl
		Arabic	(tambâ') having a long back, weak legs
Tamey	B, F	Hausa	(tāmi) "Sokoto Hausa" m. help
Tampa	B & W, M	Hausa	(tampā) keen desire; remained mum; branch of date or banana tree
Tamzy	B, F	Hausa	(tamzā) f. tapeworm
Taney	B	Mende	(tani) neut. stand bail, go bail
			(tani) id. (of shutting) completely
		Hausa	(tani) name for girl born on a Monday
		Ngala	(tani) white
		Arabic	(tanî) buy palm trees, buy dates by the weight, persist in fornication
			(tany) suspicion; extinguished; illness, disease
			(tani') strong and corpulent
Tango	B, F	Mende	(tanga) n. cassava
		Bobangi	(tanga) vt. to call by name, call name, denominate, name, peruse, read, scandalize, slander
			(tānga) vin. to distill, dribble, drip, drop, fall in drops, flow, leak, ooze, percolate, roll down (of tears)
Tanoe	B, M	Bobangi	(tanô) five
		Kele	(tano) white
Tara	B, F	Hausa	(tara) anything; collected; added up; shared in; being finicky; nine; ninth; went to meet someone; intercepted
			(tára) tr. v. to gather, to collect, to assemble, to multiply
			(tāra) int. v. to wade through the water or stream
			(tāra) tr. v. to be in need of, to want
			(tāre) adv. together
		Efik	(tara) v. intr. to be loose; to open; to be unfurled; to spread, open; to melt; to spread out; to relax; to release from constraint; to gladden
			(ntără) n. a voiding of excrement; having a stool
		Arabic	(tara') fall upon unexpectedly; appear

Dictionary of African Origin

NAME	RACE & SEX	LANGUAGE & DEFINITION	
Tara (cont.)		Arabic (cont.)	suddenly; arise (tarâ) come from afar (tarrâ) filling the basin or channel; door keeper (tara) keep off; keep at a distance; full
Tarba	B, F	Hausa Arabic	(tarba) anything; "Sokoto Hausa" collected (tarbâ) earth, ground
Tarenah	W, F	Hausa	(tarēnīyā) f. constantly bustling to and fro
Tarsher	B, F	Hausa	(tarshē) "Sokoto Hausa" abundantly
Tasso	W, M	Hausa	(taso) anything; his; metal bowl or basin; placed
Tatie	B, F	Hausa	(tātī) used in rabo tati rabo yati: Luck comes and goes. "derived from Arabic" comes
Taynay	B, M	Mende Hausa	(tɛnɛ) n. Monday (tɛnɛ) n. thick nasal mucus (tainyo) tr. v. to help, to assist (tainye) tr. v. to help, to assist
Taz	B, F	Arabic	(ta'az) inf. ta'z close, come to close quarters (tâz) be thick, coarse, rude (ta'z) push back; lie with
Tecomia Uzee	B, F	Swahili	(uzi) thread
Teena	B, F	Kongo Bobangi Arabic Efik Bini	(tina) v. to run, scamper or run away, to flee, escape, abscond, decamp, abandon, leave, desert, shun, shrink from, to fear, be afraid of (ntinā) n. base of palm nuts, basis, cause, explanation, foot, import, meaning, object, principle, purpose, reason, root, sake, sense, signification, source, stand, theory (tînâ) (preceded by tur) Mount Sinai (ntinya) n. a tree or shrub used in medicine (tinɛ) very small; tiny, of babies and things

Dictionary of African Origin

NAME	RACE & SEX	LANGUAGE & DEFINITION	
Tella	B, F	Mende	(tele) n. very white rice flower made from new rice
			(tele) n. lalang grass
		Bobangi	(tele) vt. to enclose, infuse, instil, load (a breechloader), put in, insert
		Kongo	(tela) v.t. to add, put a little more, to put a little more than was bargained for
			(ntela) n. the measure or extent of height; height, stature (of persons only); tallness, height, size, stature (of persons only); a climbing fern
		Lolo	(tela) grow (spring up)
		Poto	(tela) enter
		Soko	(tela) betray
		Kele	(tela) ripen
Temba	B, M	Mende	(tɛmbɛ) n. drum which summons Moslems to prayer
		Hausa	(timbar) n. nakedness
Tena	B & W, F	Bobangi	(tĕna) vt. to burst (gun), snap
		Kongo	(tena) v. to retract the prepuce
		Lolo	(tena) cut, saw
		Poto	(tena) (mombondo) circumcise; cut, saw
		Soko	(tena) cut (tena ndola) carve
		Ngala	(tena) cut, saw (tena nsonge) circumcise
		Kele	(tena) cut, saw (tena nsonge) circumcise
		Swahili	(tena) again
Tenah	B, F	See Tena	
Tene	B, F	See Taynay	
Tenola	B, F	Bobangi	(tĕnŭla) vt. to abbreviate by degrees, pluck tops off cassava bushes to fatten roots, reduce by a small portion
Tete	B, M	Mende	(tete) n. vulva, vagina
			(tɛtɛ) neut. hatch (eggs), crack (nuts), hammer into shape
			(tɛtɛ) adv. early
		Bobangi	(ntetē) n. prophet, witness
		Bini	(tete) to save, to be economical with something
		Hausa	(tētē) m. baby's first stages in walking

Dictionary of African Origin

NAME	RACE & SEX	LANGUAGE & DEFINITION	
Tete (cont.)		Kongo	(teta) v.t. to peel, pare; break or crack (the shell of eggs, nuts, etc.) (ntete) n. a load, burden, bundle
		Bangi	(ntete) witness
Tias	B, M	Mende	(tia) combining pronoun he and/or she and/or it and they; also disjunctive pronoun
		Kongo	(tia) v. to copulate
Tibe	B, M	Bobangi	(ntībā) n. calabash pipe for hemp smoking
		Kongo	(tiba) n. the banana tree, also the fruit
		Efik	(tïbe) v. intr. to spring forth, burst forth; to sprout, to bud; to arise, begin, originate; v. tr. to cause to spring; to put forth; produce; to break forth, come out on; to be pierced, perforated; to be dug, thrust out; to break out; to come out; to give, make a contribution
		Arabic	(tibâ) succession of things, continuation
Tilla	B, F	Mende	(tila) n. gangosa, a disease in which the nose is destroyed
		Bini	(tila) to despise
		Hausa	(tila) anything; heaped up, piled up, earth thrown up by a rodent (tillo) n. heap
		Soko	(tila) flee, run away
		Kele	(tila) run away
		Arabic	(tilâ) what serves to fill up; what is smeared upon (salve, ointment, etc.)
Tiller	B, F	See Tilla	
Tina	B, F	See Teena	
Tinah	B, F	See Teena	
Tingo	B, M	Mende	(tingo) n. a mangrove tree, a semi-translucent, elongated bead (tingoi) n. a water spirit in the shape of a woman with long hair. If a person succeeds in obtaining the comb with which this spirit combs her hair, he can ask anything he likes in exchange

Dictionary of African Origin

NAME	RACE & SEX	LANGUAGE & DEFINITION	
Tingo (cont.)		Mende (cont.)	for it, but he must not return the comb or else he will lose everything
		Hausa	(tiŋga) f. obduracy; Nupe small hamlet of hunters, fishermen, etc.
Tip	B, M	Efik	(tip) v. tr. to blunt, make blunt; to dull; to hinder; to impede; to keep behind; to dwarf; to condemn; to continue unclean with; to fail, miss
Tippo	B, M	Bobangi	(tipô) (Eng.) n. type
Tisha	B & W, F	Hausa	(tishe) ground (condiments) on grinding stone; thrashed
Toccoah	W, M	Bobangi	(ntokō) n. professional ability, dexterity, means (ntōkō) n. charge against enemy in battle
Tola	B, M	Mende	(tola) interj. response given when called by a superior (tola) n. the split seeds of a tree, resembling the kola tree, used as a condiment (tola, tola) n. funnel, commonly made from a leaf (tola) n. a rat trap
		Bobangi	(tôlê) n. constellation which has not yet been identified
		Kongo	(tola) v. to be or get or grow fat, corpulent, plump, great, large, to increase (size) (tola) n. growth (in size)
		Lolo	(tola) curse
		Soko	(tola) carry, be clothed, dress, put on clothes, wear
		Kele	(tola) carry
Toma	B, F	Mende	(toma) n. meaning, significance (toma) n. a Sherbo secret society
		Bobangi	(ntöma) n. messenger
		Kongo	(toma) v. to be good, pleasant, sweet, nice, ornamented, pretty, beautiful, to taste nice, to taste; well, carefully, nicely, properly, correctly; to stir (a pipe)
		Bangi	(ntoma) messenger
		Lolo	(toma) food; send

Dictionary of African Origin

NAME	RACE & SEX	LANGUAGE & DEFINITION	
Toma (cont.)		Poto	(toma) educate; food; satisfied; send
		Soko	(toma) send
		Ngala	(toma) send
		Kele	(toma) pick up, send
Tomba	B	Mende	(tomba) n. a climber, the leaves of which are used as a laxative
			(tɔmba) n. foretelling ill of some-one, gloomy prophecy about someone
		Bobangi	(tomba) .vin. to fall or pour (of rain), hail (of hailstones)
		Hausa	(tómbo) n. scar
		Kongo	(tomba) v. to look for, search for, seek, desire, want
		Poto	(tomba) carry
		Lolo	(tomba) carry
		Bangi	(tomba) buy
		Ngala	(tomba) carry
		Ngombe	(tomba) carry
Tomma	B, M & F	See Toma	
Toofay	B, M	Mende	(tufe) n. a tree from which planks may be obtained
		Hausa	(túfe) itse ya tufe, the tree is in blossom
			(tufe) excrement; mucus
Toofie	W, M	See Toofay	
Toosh	B, M	Hausa	(tūša) int. v. to sneeze
			(tūše) n. a large bird, lives on ground, lives on frogs
			(tūše) int. v. to be loose, slack; to come off or fall off
Tucco	W, M	Bobangi	(ntuka) n. pawn, pledge, security
		Hausa	(tūƙō) "Katsina Hausa" sprouted; buds
			(tuke) sania na tuke, the cow in ruminating
Tuccoah	W, M	See Toccoah	
Tuck	B, M	Efik	(tuk) v. tr. to touch; to feel; to affect; to regard; to refer to; to de-fraud; to cheat; to oppress; to push over; to cant

457

Dictionary of African Origin

NAME	RACE & SEX	LANGUAGE & DEFINITION	
Tuck (cont.)		Efik (cont.)	(ntŭk) n. a peg; a pin fixed in the wall of a house; the half burnt sticks remaining after burning the bush cut down in clearing a plantation; a spasmodic sensation in some part of the body; a warning
Tuckey	W, M	Mende	(tɔki) n. a child's top spun with a whip
		Hausa	(tuk<u>i</u>) m. external apex of round thatch roof
Tula	B & W, F	Bobangi	(tula) vt. to beat, beat against, bump, collide with, forge, strike the foot against, weld (tūla) vin. to have no sale, be below standard, remain unsold
		Bini	(t-ulɛ mu) to start running
		Hausa	(tula) anything; "Sokoto Hausa" f. children's game of pelting each other with ragballs; the Tula pagans of Gombe (tulla) pierced
		Kongo	(tula) v.t. to butt, toss (tula) v. to arrive at, come to, get to, reach; to put, lay, set, place (ntula) n. size, height
		Kele	(tula) to blacksmith
		Soko	(tula) to blacksmith; chastise
		Poto	(tula) to blacksmith
		Bangi	(tula) to blacksmith (tula libaku) stumble
		Ngala	(tula) to blacksmith
		Arabic	(tûla) longer, taller; high rank; the (seven) long chapters of the Koran (tûlã) misfortune, calamities
Tull	W, M	Arabic	(tull) get moistened; urge on the camels
Tulla	W, F	See Tula	
Tullie	W, F	Hausa	(tul<u>i</u>) m. heap, crowd; abundantly
Tura	W, F	Hausa	(tura) anything; pushed; incited; persuaded; routed; lumbar spinal curvature; knocked against (túre) tr. v. to push down (túre) ba-túre, an Arab or European; white man

Dictionary of African Origin

NAME	RACE & SEX	LANGUAGE & DEFINITION	
Tura (cont.)		Efik	(tŭră̆) v. to keep insisting on one to do a thing; trouble; tease; to reprove, correct or coax; to admonish
		Arabic	(ṭurrâ) coming up suddenly (ṭur'â) coming up suddenly (ṭurra) chased she-ass
Tut	B, M	Hausa Efik	(tūta) n. flag, standard (tut) v. tr. push, shove, to push out; to be regardless; to disregard what is said; to shift one's self; to be forward; to be tough (ntut) n. a thrusting; a pushing out
		Arabic	(ṭût) long, tall; small; strong and courageous; quarrelsome; cotton (tût) mulberry; mulberry tree
Tutt	B & W	See Tut	
Twa	W, F	Mende Bobangi Kongo	(tuwa) n. black and white colobus (twa) vt. to abuse, inviegle, bite (twa) we; to strike; to ram, to poke, to stab; to thrust; to have an edge, be sharp
		Poto Soko Kele	(twa) bite (twa) curse (twa) gather (pluck) (twa bilungo) to sweat
		Swahili	(twaa) aim, take
Ula	W, F	Bini Hausa Kongo	(ulɛ) running away (ʉllē) f. cat (ula) v.t. to shatter, crush, break, smash
		Soko Ngala	(oola) laugh (ula) blow, horn; grow, ripen
Ulac	B, M	See Ula	
Ulla	W, F	See Ula	
Ulo Bobo	B, F	Bini Hausa	(bobo) to move to and fro (bō̠bō̠) "Sokoto Hausa" m. type of insect; m. small twigs for firewood
Una	B & W, F	Kongo	(una) that; that which, those, those which; as soon as, immediately, at that time, when, just when

459

Dictionary of African Origin

NAME	RACE & SEX	LANGUAGE & DEFINITION	
Uzee Tecomia	B, F	See Tecomia, Uzee	
Vama	W, F	Kongo	(vama) v.t. to strike or beat with (used by women only)
Vana	W, F	Kongo	(vana) that, that which; to give, grant, render, present, provide, subscribe, spend, surrender up (vana o nkalu) refuse
Vanda	B, F	Mende Kongo	(vanda) neut. (of rain) fall lightly (vanda) v.t. to plait (the hair), to braid, interweave (mvanda) n. a braid, plait, the springbok
Vela	W, F	Kongo	(vela) v. to gather, pick, pluck, call, strip off fruit or leaves, to pick (a bone) (vela) n. a hut in the compound where people are initiated into the mystery of a fetish (Ndembo) (mvela) n. (Port. vela) candle
Venda	W, M & F	Mende Kongo	(venda) neut. be full (venda) v. to lick, lap; to miss
Vennah	B, F	Kongo	(vena) v.t. to gird up the loin cloth very tightly, to tuck up one's cloth
Veo	B, M	Mende	(vio) id. quickly, in a flash
Veta	B, F	Kongo	(veta) v.t. to throw, cast, fling, heave away, to cast out; to hunt with dogs (veta) n. gable, gable end, the veranda
Vi Siba	B, F	Mende	(siba) n. onion, shallot
Villa	B, F	Kongo	(vila) v.t. to bind strongly the edge of a basket; to set the edges of a button hole (vila) v.i. to be lost, go out of sight, to vanish, disappear, perish (mvila) n. clans, border

Dictionary of African Origin

NAME	RACE & SEX	LANGUAGE & DEFINITION	
Visa	B, M	Kongo	(visa) v.t. to cause to be thoroughly cooked, to cook well, sufficiently
Wahwah	B, M	Bobangi	(wŏ-wŏ) ind. garrulous (wôwô) ind. vs. to be dissipated, spent
		Hausa	(wawa) anything; fool; crowd (wawa) n. fool (wāwa) adj. foolish, vain
		Ngala	(wawa) here
		Arabic	(wa'wa') stir up, excite, agitate; scream, bark, yelp (wa'wa') eloquent; fox, jackal; desert; guard; weak (wa'wa') cry of the jackal
Wanda	W, M B & W, M, F	Hausa	(wanda) who; which; that which he who...; wherein, whence
		Kongo	(wanda) n. web, net, hammock; spider's web, cobweb (wanda) v.t. to beat, strike, lash
Wann	B, M	Hausa	(wān-šēkari) the day before
		Efik	(wan) n. (Eng.) wine
		Arabic	(wann) weariness, tiredness, weakness; castanets (wahn) be weak, too weak (wahn) weakness, want of power (wa'n) hard white and bare ground; refuge, asylum (wa'n) short and thickset, broad
Warrah	B, M	Bini	(warha) describes a man with big buttocks sitting
		Hausa	(wara) separated out; is separate
		Efik	(wara) v. intr. to make haste; to be speedy, quick; to be ready; apt to do a thing; v.tr. to hasten, make haste with; interj. a form of Thanksgiving
		Arabic	(wara') turn off, refuse, hinder; surfeit (warâ) what is out of sight; back-part; buttocks, grandson; progeny (warâ) timidity, cautiousness, fear of sin (wara') abstinence from what is unlaw-ful; chastity; self-restraint; piety;

Dictionary of African Origin

NAME	RACE & SEX	LANGUAGE & DEFINITION	
Warrah (cont.)		Arabic (cont.)	timidity, cowardice (wara) corrode the inner parts of the body (pus); injure in the lungs
Watha	W, F	Arabic	(waḍa') surpass in cleanliness, tidiness, brightness (waḍḍâ) collector, compiler (waḍa') put down, put, set; degrade, render, contemptible; give birth, miscarry; compose
Wetta	W, F	Kongo	(weta) v.t. to beat, strike
Whurria	B, F	Bini	(weriε) to roll; to turn, change
Wice	W, M	Bobangi	(wisa) vc. to bewail, grieve over, mourn (wīsa) vt. to be able, can, have a right to do, be likely, be liable, bear with, tolerate
		Kongo	(wisa) v.t. to cause to hear (wisa) n. the power to make people hear and obey; authority, influence, power, mastery, control
Willa	B & W, F	Arabic	(wilâ) unbroken succession; continuation
Winna	B, F	Kele Arabic	(wina) friend (winâ) relaxedness, weakness
Witha	B, M	Arabic	(widâ) cleanly, tidy, neat, handsome of face
Wray	W, M	Bini	(re) to be in a certain place; to live at a certain place; to come; be far; to be a long time (ago); to tread mud of palm-kernels; to knot together; to make a noose; to eat, to be, to hide (something)
		Hausa	(rē) m. going hither and thither
Wroe	W, M	Bini	(ro) to be durable, of any breakable thing, e.g. a pot (rho) to praise somebody for some achievement (ro) to overflow; to inundate; to think

Dictionary of African Origin

NAME	RACE & SEX	LANGUAGE & DEFINITION	
Yamboo	B, M	Mende	(yambu) neut. show one's face (yambo, lambo, jambo) n. a society of snake dancers (yambobla) snake dancers
		Bobangi	(yāmbô) ind. first, former, heretofore, old, previous, prior
		Hausa	(yámbu) n. potter's clay
		Arabic	(yambû') spring, fountain; brook
Yanaky	B, F	Hausa	(yanaka) ya yanaka ga barim mutane: he has isolated himself
Yangey	B, M	Mende	(yangeyange) id. able to stand up to anyone, able to look after one's self, not afraid to speak one's mind (yaunga) n. Yalunka country
Yanikae	B, F	Kongo	(yanika) v. to dry, put, spread out, to air, warm (in the sun)
Yankee	B & W, M	Hausa	(yanki) m. piece cut off; district
Yaumah	B, M	Arabic	(yauma' iz-in) on that very day, just then
Yearie	B, M	Bini	(y-erhɛ̃) to set fire (to farmland only)
Yenty	B, M	Bobangi	(yende) vt. to be destitute of, go without, lack, need, be needy, stand in need of, be without, not possess
Yoke	B, M	Bobangi	(yŏka) vt. to apprehend, comprehend, feel, hear, understand, realize
		Efik	(yok) C. F. yuk (yok) n. (Eng.) a yoke; a tiller
Yola	W, F	Mende	(yola) neut. be filthy, dirty (yola) id. swollen, protruding
		Bobangi	(yöla) vin. to grow
		Hausa	(yōla) f. yola; f. fire fly
		Bangi	(yola) grow
Yook	B, M	Efik	(yük) v.tr. to tell lies; to lie; v. intr. to be unsteady; fidgety; to change position often; v. tr. to cause to roll; to make unsteady
		Arabic	(yûk) lumber-room (masculine)

Dictionary of African Origin

NAME	RACE & SEX	LANGUAGE & DEFINITION	
Zach	B, M	Hausa	(záka) int. v. to come (zāka) n. thou art about to go (zāka) m. measure (zāki) n. lion (zāki) f. thou art about to go (zāki) n. sweetness; flavour; that which is savory (zāku) ye are about to go
		Arabic	(zâk) strut with swinging shoulders (zâk) walk proudly with violent movements of the body
Zack	B & W, M	See Zach	
Zacko	B, M	Hausa	(zāko) f. pulled cassava which after two-three months becomes very sweet; type of bean
Zada	B & W, F	Hausa	(zāda) "derived from Arabic" f. exaggeration
		Arabic	(zada') sleep with (zadâ) play at holes (with nuts)
Zadah	W, F	See Zada	
Zado (surname)	B	Hausa	(zado) "Katsina Hausa" tall and handsome person
Zahde	W, F	Kongo	(nzadi) n. a brother or sister-in-law; a great river, the river Congo
Zak	B, M	See Zach	
Zana	B, F	Hausa	(zana) anything; drew; ornamented; cut tribal marks on; counted up (persons or things); mat made of one of the grasses; sloughed off skin of snake or lizard (zāna) n. a rough kind of mat made of grass or reeds with which the outside of houses is covered, and partitions made within (zanna) "Hadejiya Hausa"; sat down; settled; remained; line drawn; cloth
		Kongo	(zana) v.t. to take between or pull off with finger and thumb
		Arabic	(zanâ) be quick, alert; hasten; be merry (zanâ) be narrow

Dictionary of African Origin

NAME	RACE & SEX	LANGUAGE & DEFINITION	
Zana (cont.)		Arabic (cont.)	(zana) fornicate, commit adultery
Zanga	B, M	Bobangi	(zangā) n. frond
			(zāŋga) ind. armed with spear only
			(nzanga) n. noon, mid-day
			(nzāŋga) n. brave or savage person
		Hausa	(zánga) hundred
			(za̲nga) m. dirty trick
		Kongo	(zaŋga) v.t. to dirty, to make a mess, defecate (of babies only)
			(nzanga) n. large marimba; a mess
Zango	B, M	Bobangi	(zangô) n. perforated bowl, steamer for cooking
			(nzangö) n. clyster, enema
			(nzāngô) n. kind of bird
		Hausa	(zaŋgo) anything; m. camping place of caravan; lodging place of travellers on route; distance between two camping or lodging places; long-headed bulrush-millet
Zank	B, M	Hausa	(zanka) n. tuft of hair
Zanza	B, M	Kongo	(zanza) v.t. to cast, put, set or throw down violently or heavily, to cause to fall heavily, to dash to the ground
			(nzanza) n. a stand, foot of basket, etc.; plateau-level, flat hill tops, table land; a feathery marsh grass; arrow, harpoon; a throwing down heavily to the ground
Zara	B & W, F	Hausa	(zara) anything; f. snatching; grabbing; red-bellied tree starling; solely
			(zāra) tr. v. to accuse, to report, to inform against
			(zāra) tr. v. to fell trees
		Arabic	(zara') sow, scatter seed; let the seed grow or thrive, give strength for
			(zara) scold; blame; blacken, slander
			(za'rá) having thin hair
			(za̲ra) flow; have the diarrhoea
Zaro	B, M	Hausa	(zārō) unsheathed (sword); disengaged; a thread

Dictionary of African Origin

NAME	RACE & SEX	LANGUAGE & DEFINITION	
Zary	W, M	Hausa	(zari) m. jangling rings, etc., used for musical accompaniment; greed
			(zārį) int. v. to sneeze
		Arabic	(zarî) prepared for sawing
			(zârį) sower, planter, peasant
			(zârî) who scolds, inveighs
			(zârî) given to biting; mordacious
Zash	W, M	Arabic	(zaśś) rugged, stony place
Zattu	W	Bobangi	(zāta) vt. to crush, tread
		Hausa	(zāta) she is about to go
			(zatto) n. hope
Zay	W, F	Bobangi	(ze) ind. vs. to gyrate, spin, swirl, twirl
		Bini	(ze) to be hard, stiff; to be strong, powerful
			(zɛ) to choose; to select; to be proud; to speak a certain language
Zaza	W, F	Hausa	(zāzā) f. "Sokoto Hausa" (vulgar) pubic hair; well watered pasture land; prosperity
		Kongo	(zaza) v. to dash, jerk off (by a violent motion), to sprinkle
			(nzaza) n. a sailing ship or vessel, boat, sores, sore gums
		Poto	(zaza) fast, quickly
		Arabic	(zaza) move, shake; inspire with fear, frighten
			(za'zâ') hurricane-like
			(za'za') shake violently
			(za'za') shaking violently, stormy, tempest
			(za'za') speak with a lisp and indistinctly
Zebiah	B, M	Bobangi	(nzēbī) n. quick glance
		Bini	(zɛbi) to be guilty
		Kongo	(zeba) v. to play, to mess about with one's food
Zebe	B, M	See Zebiah	
Zeka	W, M	Bobangi	(zêka) n. grey clay for moulding pots
		Hausa	(zīka) n. bladder
		Kongo	(zeka) v. to twist, to turn or wring round, to screw

Dictionary of African Origin

NAME	RACE & SEX	LANGUAGE & DEFINITION	
Zeke	B, M	Bobangi	(zēke) vt. to laugh at; also vin. to laugh (zëkë) ind. awry (nzeke) n. bandy-leggedness
		Bangi	(zeke) laugh
Zela	W, F	Bobangi	(zëlā) n. no lack (nzela) n. footpath, path, road, way, route
		Bangi	(nzela) road, path, way
Zella	B & W, F	See Zela	
Zellah	B, F	See Zela	
Zeta	B & W, F B, M	Bobangi	(zëta) n. crop of bird
Ziba	W	Arabic	(z̲ibā) gazelles, mountain goats, marks by branding; name of a star
Zie	B, F	Bini	(zi) to bear, to endure
		Swahili	(zee) old
Zila	B, F	Hausa	(zilai) f. zilla (woman's name) (zill a̲) f. "derived from Arabic" oppression
Zilla	B & W, F	See Zila	
Zillah	B & W, F	See Zila	
Zina	W	Hausa	(zina) "derived from Arabic" f. adornment; adultery, fornication (zina zōzi dobi mayi) to bewitch (zinna) n. whoring
Zinda	B, F	Hausa	(zinder) a town in Hausa land
Zingo	B, M	Bobangi	(zinga) n. blue pigment
Zinka	B, M	Bobangi	(zinka) (Engl.) n. zinc
		Hausa	(zinke) pl. zinka n. fork
Zira	W, F	Hausa	(zira) tyranny; lowered (bucket into well)
Zoa	W, F	Bobangi	(zö) ind. vt. to be around, beset,

Dictionary of African Origin

NAME	RACE & SEX	LANGUAGE & DEFINITION	
Zoa (cont.)		Bobangi (cont.)	circumscribe, compass, be confused (of eyes), be dizzy (of eyes), inattentive (of eyes), be round about, surround
		Hausa	(zo) intr. v. to come
		Kongo	(zoa) (zowa) n. foolishness, folly, idiocy, lunacy
			(zoa) (zowa) v.t. to knead, to make a paste of, work up (clay, etc.)
			(nzo) abode, home, house
Zody	B, F	Hausa	(zōdi) n. ring
		Kongo	(nzodi) n. one who loves, likes, desires, a lover
Zoe	W, M	See Zoa	
Zoe	W, F	See Zoa	
Zola	B & W, F	Bobangi	(zölô) n. nose; colq. quick to smell
		Kongo	(zola) v. to love, to like, choose, desire, prefer, wish
			(zola) n. love, affection, fondness, desire
			(nzola) n. (act) love, a manner of love
Zooa	B, M	Hausa	(zuá) infin. to go, to be about to go
			(zuá) n. journey
		Bini	(zuã) to watch a man eating, in the hope of obtaining food (or usually some more food) by this silent appeal
		Kongo	(zua) v. to dash, or jerk off (by a violent motion)
			(nzua) n. (act) scolding, frowning
		Swahili	(zua) bore, pierce
Zoomm	B, M	Hausa	(zuma) honey; bee, bees
			(zumá) n. rag(s)
			(zūma) int. v. to faint; to swoon; to become insensible
Zora	B & W, F	Hausa	(zōra) n. bargain
Zorra	W, F	See Zora	
Zuma	B, F	See Zoomm	

Dictionary of African Origin

NAME	RACE & SEX	LANGUAGE & DEFINITION	
Zuna	W, F	Bobangi	(nzunā) n. abundance
		Kongo	(zuna) v.t. to cut off a small piece (of something edible)

INDEX OF UNUSUAL NAMES

<u>Black Males</u>

Aavin
A. B.
A. B. & S.
Abe Abram
Abedmege
Abraham
Abraham Lincoln
Abram
Abron
Absalom
A. C.
Ace
Acie
Acquilla
Acre
Activelt
A. D.
Adamize
Adamon
Add
Adger
Adie B.
Adjecenton Foster
Admiral Dewey
Adolp
Adolphus
Adomijah
Adonis
Advert
Aemilius
Aepheus
Aeroplane
Afric
Agen
Aguinaldo
Aguinaldo Hughes
Agward
Ahart
Airwood
Ajay

A. K.
Akbar
Akron
Al Smith
Alabama
Aladin
Alamo
Alaska
Alburnion
Alcavis
Alce Abercrombie
Alchester
Alcibiades
Alcoe
Alcurine
Aldero
Alduffie
Alduphus
Aleson Whitmice
Alexandra
Alexton
Alfalfa
Alfester
Alfine
Alfonzia
Alfrin
Algee G.
Algenal
Algernon
Algie
Alifar
Ailmenta Lawrence
Aljay
All
Allcird
Allex
Allmra
Alls Well
Almo
Almon

Almous
Alois
Alonzer
Aloysius
Alpha Omega (Jones)
Alpheus
Alphondus
Alphonsis
Alphonze
Alquill
Alrutheus Ambush
                (Taylor)
Alto
Altus
Alvah
Alverado
Alvester
Alvie Antonio
Alzena
Alzo
A. M.
Aman
Amaziah
Ambros
Ambus
A. M. C.
Ambush
A. M. E. Church
Amen
America
Americus
Ammon
Amas
Amoil
Amzi (Love)
Ananias
Anar Dulin
Anatole Longfellow
Ance
Andre

471

Index of Unusual Names

Andrew Jackson
Androcles
Angel
Angelo
Angrus
Annanias
Annias
Ansel
Anthracite
Antone
Antonio
Antwine
Anvy
Apostle
Appendicites
Apple
April
Aquilla
Aquila
Araby
Arbiet
Arcelious
Archangel
Arcy
Ardis
Ardric
Areciter
Areeties
Arena
Arent Lee
Arfenly
Argo
Ariel
Arien
Arion
Aristide Francisco
        Rodriquez
Aristotle
Arizona
Arkansas
Arkie
Arland
Arlanders
Arlandis Eastern
Arlester
Arlias
Arlion
Armistice
Armer
Armucto
Arntie
Arol

Arom
Arozel (Williams)
Arqueus
Arrice
Arselus Topalouski
        (West)
Artance
Artelesis
Artemius
Artesius
Artess
Artie
Artificial Flowers
Artillery
Artis
Arvanell
Arvelle
Arvil
Asenatle
Ashbury Falls
Asiah
Aslan
Aspirin
Astric
Athens
Athis
Athus
Atlanta Bryant
Atlantic City Joe
Atlas
Atney
Atress Brooks
Atreus
Atrus Harris
Attaway
Attis
Auditorium
Audy
Aug Johnson
August
Augustus Caesar
Aurelions
Aurelius
Aurlias
Australia (Booker)
Australia (Lightfoot)
Autopsy
Autral
Ave
Average
Avid
Avis

Axwood
A. Z.
Azeal
Azel
Azon
Azielee (Smoote)
Azzma
Baalam
Babe
Baby
Baby Face Nelson
Bacchus
Badger
Bailus
Baise
Balaam
Bales
Balthis
Bame
Bannaka DeOblay
Bannister
Barn
Barber Gene
Bark
Baron
Barto
Basco Knuckles
Base
Bashaner
Bass
Battle
Batty Price
B. C.
Beach
Beady
Bear
Beat the World
Beatrice Hill
Beauces
Beauford
Beaugard
Beauregard
Bee
Beef Loaf
Bellfield
Belt
Bem
Benjamin Franklin
Benjamin Harrison
Bennis
Bent Moore
Benzol

Index of Unusual Names

Index of Unusual Names

Caffa	Cast	Chassis
Cage	Caster	Chastisement
Caggie	Castor	Chat
Cagie	Castor Oil	Chattie Lazelle
Cagill	Castor Ulif	Chauncey Depew
Cain	Cata	Chavous
Calarous	Cate	Cherry
Caleb	Cates	Cherry Bush
Calfric	Catching	Chessie
Califern	Cathey	Chestnut White
Caliph	Cathie	Chicago Rucker
Calmay	Cathney	Chicken
Cam	C. C.	Chief Jones
Camen	Cessar	Chilan
Cammie Willaims	Cebon	Child
Canara	Cebrien	Chiman
Candas	Cefer	Chipso Greene
Candy Edwards	Cehelland	Chloroform
Cane	Celester	Choicy
Caneater	Celestus	Christ
Canly	Celine	Christian
Canute	Cellus	Christie
Canvis Ivey	Celophus Adolphus	Christmas
Cap	Celphanzo	Christe
Cape	Celsus	Christopher Columbus
Capers	Centennial	Christopher Columbus
Caprus (Hendrux)	Center	St. John
Captain	Central	Cicero
Capus	Century	Ciphus Bell
Cara	Ceolar	Cistitus
Carani	Ceotis	Citzo
Cardeza	Cephas	City Boy
Cardinal Gibbons	Cephas Salary	C. J.
Cardos	Cephus	Claddie
Cardoza	Cervera	Claitor
Carlos	Cevera	Clanton
Carlyle	Chaftie	Clar
Carmel	Chain	Claret
Carnegie	Chain Lightning	Clars
Carnie	Champ	Claster
Carothouse	Champagne	Claudius
Carranza	Chance	Claus
Carrol	Chancellor	Clay Henry
Cartelyon	Chancie	Cleaphres
Carthen	Chaney	Clearness
Carvy	Chapel	Clebot
Cash	Chardie Lee	Cledie
Cash Money	Charles Wesley	Clemencean McAdoo
Cashius	Charleston	Clemmie
Cass	Charming	Clenzo
Cassey	Charrience	Clenzy
Cassius	Chartie	Cleofus

Index of Unusual Names

Index of Unusual Names

Decline	Dizzie	Dunk
Dedie	Doc(k)	Dupree Ely
Dee	Doc T. B.	Duris
Dee Dee Fredien	Doctor	Durns
Dekato	Doctor Alice (Roberts)	Dusky
Del	Doctor Munyon Wineberry	Durrah
Delmon	Doctor Root Beer	Dutch
Delmus	Docroy Shepherd	Dutchie
Delone	Doe	Duty
Deluxe	Doggie	Duvoille
Demetresse Sebree	Doggywood	Dwelle
Demetrius	Dogie	Dynioush
Demis	Dollar	Ealem
Demosthenew	Dollarbill Johnson	Ean Lee
Demous	Dollar Bill Jones	Earlie
Demp	Dollars	Earlie Leizure
Demus Demacy	Dolph	Early
Denigo	Dolphus	Early Bird Jr.
Dense	Dome	Early Cook
Denver	Don Albert	Early Frost
Deodolphus	Doncious	Earth
Deodorus Blunt	Donnie	Easeman
Depression	Dorus	Easie
Deris	Dosier	Eashter
Derius	Dother Salter	East Virginia
Dero	Double O Two	Easter
Derry	Dove Tee	Eathon
Desmal	Doxey	Ebb
Deso Cater	Dozey	Ebbie
Detroit	Dozier	Ebenezer
Devaughn	Drane	Ebony
Dever	Dreadwell	Ecclesiastes Turner
Devotee War	Drelly	Echo
Devotus	Drewie	Echols
Dewillie	Drue	Ecriss
Dewey Meadows	Dub	Edel
Dexter	Dubro	Edinboro
Diamond	Duce	Edinburgh
Diaphragm	**Duck**	Edison
Dillie	Dude	Edram
Dilly	Duel	Edsel
Dimber Cannon	Duet	Edwon
Dink	Duffy	Eggie
Dinky	Duga	Egypt Abercrombie
Dionysius	Duke	Ejusten Bomden
Dious	Duke Prosper	Elacy
Diploma	Duly	Elam
Dipper	Dump	Elby Stays-Freeman
Distemper	Dunbar	Elbo
Divelle	Duncas Hymen	Elcana
Dixie	Dunge	Elder
Dixie Bell	Dungee	Eldie

476

Index of Unusual Names

Eldiest	Ennals	Essich
Eldra	Ennie	Essie
Eleazer	Ennis	Essig Adams
Electric Floyd	Enoch	Esterly
Electricity	Enos	Estern
Elel	Enzie	Estiemat
Elem (Little)	Enzy	Estil
Elemuel	Eon	Estras
Elester	Ephesians	Estus
Elevee	Ephesus	Ethbert
Elfish	Ephraim	Ethells
Elgie Morris	Ephram	Etholis
Elgin	Ephus	Ethon
Elgy	Epluribus	Etroy
Eli	Epp	Euel
Eli Whitney	Eprezel	Eulice
Elias	Equal	Eulin
Eliasha	Equinoxial	Euliss
Elihu	Era	Eulon
Elijah	Erasmus	Eulyssee
Elijah Donkey	Erastus	Eunice
Elisha	Ercell	Euphrates
Elius	Erdeal Blalock	Euphrey Tankersly
Eljay Valentine	Erge Lee	Eureka
Eljey	Erias (Bernadette)	Euric
Ellariz	Erie Canal Jackson	Europe
Ellie	Erin	Evan
Ellius	Erise	Evander
Elmo	Eristus	Evergreen
Elon Lavonia	Erlie	Every Payne
Elonia	Ermine	Evie Lemon
Elos	Eros	Evil
Elric	Erroneus	Evon
Elvahow	Ersell	Exczema
Elvern	Ervie	Excel
Elymais	Esaac	Exell Stribling
Emancipation	Esau	Exermas Mathes
Emancipation	Esau Redd	Exit Walker
Proclamation	Escamead	Exodus Jones
Freedom	Escel	Extra
Emanuel	Esco	Eza
Emanuel Jr.	Esdra	Ezea
Emanuell	Eskiview	Ezeele
Embry	Esli	Ezekiah
Emerald	Esnold	Ezekiel
Emile	Esophagus	Ezema
Emmual	Esprit Thompson	Eziker
Employ	Esque	Ezra
Enamel	Esquire	Ezzie
Endel	Essage	F. A.
Eneas Africanus	Essex	Fad
English	Essex Choice	Fairy

Index of Unusual Names

Famous	Fleeter	Gables
Famous Napoleon	Fleetwood	Gabre
Fance Nance	Flex	Gabriel
Farbest	Flemmie Mann	Gaddie
Farfus	Flemon	Gadis
Farmer Brady	Flim	Galen
Farmhouse Bentley	Flonnie	Galiton White
Farron	Flood	Gallistions
Fate	Floy	Galveston
Fato	Flozel	Gamabel Hezekial
Fatray	Flozelle Pippin	Gardelle
Fatty	Flu	Garden
Fauney	Fluker	Garfield
Fauntelroy	Flunely	Garita
Fea	Flunkey	Garlic
Feable	Fluten	Garnic
Fearfield	Foashee	Garlin
Feaster	Focus	Garnalie
Feb.	Follus	Garno
Febber	Fortune	Gary Cooper
Febel McCoy	Fortunat	Gasoline
Feby	Foshen	Gaspie Pryor
Fed	Foti	Gassaway
Federal	Fountain	Gastave
Felan (Capers)	Fox	Gat
Feldo	Francis Scott Key	Gatsey
Felisco	Franklin Delano	Gaza
Fenna	Roosevelt	Gee-Whizz
Ferba	Franklin Roosevelt Jr.	Gelicas
Ferble	Frax	General
Ferdinia	Frederica	General Baby
Fernonzo	Frederick Douglass	General Battle
Fertilizer	Fredericus	General Geo.
Fest	Fredonia	Washington Lee
Fester	Free	General Gideon
Festus	Freeny	General Lafayette
Feta	Freight Train	General Lee
Filmore	Frelin Howard	General Pershing
Filthy McNasty	French	Battle
Finance	Frenchman	General Price
Fineas Chinishia Roland	Frost	General Scott
Finest Moore	Frisco	Generator
Finis	Friday	Genesis
Finish	Fugaboo	Gentile
Fink	Fujabro	Gentle
Firecracker	Fulgency	Gentle Boy
Firie	Funro	Gentle Judge McEachera
Fitzburg	Futhey	Gentry
Flat Foot Floogie	Gabbel	Genus
Flavious	Gabbie	George Washington
Flayzell	Gabe	George Washington
Fleet Elmus	Gabel	Carver Davis

Index of Unusual Names

Gep	Gurley	Hector
German	Gue Thankful	Heck
German King	Gustan	Heck Moon
Germany	Gustave	Heiday
Ghilenar	Guyle	Helter
Gid (Davis)	Guymon Hooker	Helurd
Gideon	Guyon	Heman
Gilester	Habakkuk	Hence
Gilliam	Habis	Henlen
Gillie	Habor	Henry Clay
Gillion	Hagger	Henry Ward Beecher
Ginlock	Hale Sabbath	Hensy
Girt	Halee	Heonum
Glass	Halitosis	Herbert Hoover
Glean	Hallard	Hercial
Glee	Hallowed	Hercules
Glinner	Ham	Herlie
Gloster	Hamlet	Herman
Glouchester	Hammie	Hermie
Glydon	Hamp Smith	Hernia
Go Through (Smalls)	Hancy	Herod
God Be There	Handbag Johnson	Hershey
God Jesus Jolly	Handsome	Hershey Bar
Goin	Handy	Herthel Deresser
Gold	Hankie	Hesilcial
Gold Golden	Hannaball	Hestus
Gold Refined Wilson	Hannibal	Hewery
Golden	Hansom	Hezekiah
Golden Crum	Hansport	Hezzy
Goldsborough Hinkle	Hap	Hiawatha
Goldwire Merry Weather	Haphazard	High Water
Goliath	Hard	High Pocket
Golitha	Hard Jack	Highie
Golphin	Hard Times	Hilsire
Gonzales	Haron	Hillrab
Goobey	Harvest	Himself
Good Day	Harvin Thealphins	Hinder Ray
Good Will	Haskel	Hizer
Gooden	Hassie	Hoar Frost
Gosh	Hasty	Hobby
Gourd	Havanna	Hobsy
Governor	Havil Collins	Hohound
Grandy	Hawthorne	Hoke
Grant Lee	Hazard	Hokilas
Grease	Haze	Holland
Greenberry	Hazy	Holsey
Greenie	H. B.	Homie
Grubbe	H. C.	Homimy
Guillume	Heams	Hondon
Gull	Hearmey	Honor
Gumbo	Heathen	Honest
Gunner	Hebrew	Honey

479

Index of Unusual Names

Hood	Ino Geography	James Howell
Hood Wood	Inundation	James Madison
Hookin Cow	Iodine Williams	James Monroe
Hoopy Do	Iodus	Jan
Hoover	Irdell	January
Hopsum	Ireland	Japham
Horace Greeley	Iriot	Japsie
Horace Mann	Irovie	Jasie
Horade	Irvan	Jasper
Horal	I. S. Brooks	Jauncey
Hortenius	Isaac	Javance
Hosea	Isaiah	Jaw Bones
Hosey	Isador	Jawn
Holiah	Isadore	Jaxon
Hosie	Isah	Jay
Hot	Isaiah	Jay Bird Walker
Hot Ash White	Ishadol	Jay Gould
Hot Shot	Isham	Jazie
Hoxie	Ishmael	J. C.
Hozie	Ishman	J. D.
Hubbie	Ishmanel	Jed
Hudie	Ishmay Jones	Jeff Davis
Huey P. Long	Ishman Allen	Jehovah
Hughie P.	Ishom Sykes	Jelly Bean
Huey P. Washington	Isiah	Jemejo
Hula	Ismor	Jenifer
Hulet (Hood)	Isom	Jent
Hulion	Israel	Jeptha
Hulons	Israel J. Twitty	Jepthro Hawkins
Huriet	Issah	Jeremiah
Huritt	Italy	Jeremiah Chronicles
Husberry	Ivan	Jeremiah Major
Huse	Ivanhoe	Jeremiah Prophet
Huxley	Ivey	Jerkus
Hyce	Ivoria	Jerusee
Hymans	Ivory	Jesse De Priest Boyd
Iccie	Ivy	Jesse James
Ice Cream	I. Y.	Jess Willard
Ignacio	Izear Freeman	Jestine
Ignatius	Izfy	Jesus (Patterson)
Ignatz	Izzy	Jesus Christ Jones
Ike	Jabbo	Jesus Hoover Christ
Iley	Jabe	Jetco
Iliad	Jaben	Jeter
Ill Central	Jabie	Jethra
Illinois	Jabus	Jethro
Immanuel	Jack Johnson	Jethrow
Indella	Jaffree	Jett
Independence	Jaise Williams	Jetter
Independent	Jajor	Jettie
Industry	Jakie	Jewel
Inman	James Lloyd Garrison	Jezirus Elisha

Index of Unusual Names

J. H.	Juette	King Solomon
Jigg Oliver	Jug	King Solomon Jr.
Jiles	Jule	Kingfish
Jimbo	Jules	Kip
Jip	Julius Caesar	Kipling Washington
Jitney	July	Kit
Joachim	July Rice	Kiziah
Joah	Jumbo	Knosco
Joan	Juneboy	Knowledge
Joash Beezer	Junior	Knowledge Killums
Job	Junior, Jr.	Knute
Jobe	Juniper	Kondo
Jock	Junius	Kongulay
Jodie	Jupiter	Kossuth
Jody	Juriah	Kossouth Purifay
Joe Lewis	Jurias	K. P.
Joelouis	Jury Russell	L. A.
Joemiah	Justice	La Marquis
Johah	Justine	Lacase
John Bunyon	J. W.	Lacum
John Calvin	Kacem Ligar	Ladd
John Henry	Kaiser	Laddie
John Milton	Kansas	Laertes
John Quincy	Kanassa	Laivious
John D. Rockefellow	Kanze	Lake Erie
John Wesley	Karenza	Laken
Joll	Kazee	Lalaris
Jolly	K. C.	Laly
Jon	Keal O'Neal	Lamb
Jonah	Keens	Lance
Jonas	Kekey	Lancie
Jordan	Keleseed Jones	Land of Moab
Jororid	Kelly Miller	Landres
Jorrett	Kelsie Cross	Landslet
Josepho (Patterson)	Kennel	Landy
Josh	Kenoly	Laney
Josh Obed	Kessol	Lanis
Joshua	Kethus	Lank
Josiah	Kexekiah	Lannie
Josuway	Key	Lansey
Jourdan Waters	Kiah	Lany
Journey	Kid	T. Lanzoil Williams
Joanal Valley	Kidnap	Large Smash
J. P.	Kinckle	Largin
Jube	Kind	Lark
Juber	King	Larney
Judas Iscariot	King Aguppa	Lasher
Jude (Moore)	King David	Laska Leiner
Judge	King De Loach	Lassus
Judge Euphrian	King Fisher	Last Joe
Judge Samuel Longworth	King George	Laval Williams
Juel	King Henry III	Lavender

Index of Unusual Names

Lawless	Lemon	Limuary
Lawrence Dunbar	Lemon Brown	Limus
Lawyer	Lemon Custer	Lin
Laxatine Jones	Lemon Freeze	Lincoln
Layfield	Lemoru	Lindbergh
Layhew	Lemuel	Lindberg, Jr.
Lazarus	Len	Linere
Laze	Lenaz	Lingo
Lazelle	Lendy	Linious
L. C.	Lenis	Link
L. D.	Lennie	Linn
L. E.	Lent Gandy	Linzie
Le Grand	Lentie	Lioy
Le Mon	Lenzie	Lisbon
Le Roy	Leodus	Lisper
Leaby	Leoidas	Listerine Davis
Leacho	Leolus	Litho Range
Leacy	Leonidas	Litt Golden
Leader	Leophas	Little Boy
League of Nations	Leophius	Little Bit
Leak	Leoveter Tillman	Little Brother
Leamon	Lepolian	Little Freeman
Leander	Lesby	Little Nigh
Leandrew	Leslus	Litus
Leaner	Less	Lizander Lockett
Leanious	Lessie	Llewellyn
Leanshanks Pescod	Lessilia	Lloyd Garrison
Leaely	Lets Stay Here	Lloyd George
Leather	Levander	Lock
Leavy	Levenal	Lockie
Leb	Levi	Lodee
Lebra	Levie	Lodge
Led	Levis	Lodias
Ledger	Leviticus	Loer
Ledoscer	Levorgia	Log Cabin
Lee Dora (Smith)	Levy	Logi
Lee-Mar	Lew	Loin
Leevester	Lexes	Lokey (Moses)
Leffy	Lexius	Lon
Lefty Growd	Lexiux	Loncelion
Leflatte	Libel	London
Leger	Licey	London Miller
Legrande	Lief	London Sistrunk
Legrant	Lieutenant	London Squall
Leif	Lige	Londsa
Lem	Lightning	Long Ear
Lemander	Lightnin' Twicet	Longstreet Boozer
Lemious	Lillian (Boys)	Lonie
Lemmer	Limm	Lonnie
Lemmie	Limmer	Lonsy
Lemmon	Limmie	Lonzee
Lemmy Nations	Limmie Lee	Lonzie

Index of Unusual Names

Look (Johnson)	Maceo	Maso
Looney	Machine	Massadonia
Lord	Macklin	Massathaw
Lorenza	Macon	Massey
Lorenzo	Magazine	Master
Lotus Bun	Magellan	Master Mack Marboey
Louse	Magor	Masterkey
Louise Jannes	Mahomet	Math
Love	Mahuo	Mathis
Love Fitts	Main Road	Matthias
Loveless	Maine	Mavis John
Loverte	Major	Maybe
L'Overture	Mal	M. C.
Lovie	Malachi	McAdoo
Lowerton	Malkie	McKinley
Loy	Mally	M. D. (Holmes)
L. P.	Malson	Meat Grease
Lube	Malure	Mebane
Lucifer	Man	Meconium
Lucious	Man Child	Media
Lucious Woods	Manaerice	Mee
Lucius Kish	Manassah	Megie
Lucky	Manchild	Mell
Lucky Blunder	Mancy	Melodius
Ludwald	Manero	Memphis
Luff	Maniss	Meninges
Lug	Manila	Menor
Lugean	Mankind	Mention Taylor
Lum	Manner	Mentlow McCadden
Lumie Bridges	Mannessett	Mentor
Luminary Williams	Mannie	Merceed
Lummie	Manos	Mercury
Lummox	Manny	Mercy
Lumpkin	Manse	Mermen
Lunch	Mantly	Mertin
Luner	Manuel	Mertus Midas Pennyman
Lunie	Manzie	Mesiah Golphin
Lunt	Maple	Methodist Conference
Lureery	Marcel	South
Luscious (Higgins)	March	Metric Emanuel
Lusk	Marco	Micajah
Luster	Marcellus	Mice
Lutheral Clay	Marcus	Mick
Lutheran	Mardesso	Mickeral
Lutrell	Marine Spencer	Mid
Luttell	Marquis Lafayette	Midas
Luuwah	Mars	Midian
Luzel	Marshall Foch	Middie
Lybrant	Martial	Mile
Macaree	Martin Van Buren	Miley
Mace	Martinez	Milleaget
Macelroy Crawley	Maryland	Milledge

Index of Unusual Names

Million Dollar	Moses Locates Moody	Neamon
Milo	Moss	Nebraska
Milredge	Moss Green	Necoda
Mina	Mossy	Needa
Miner	Mothballs Johnson	Neeley
Minger	Mount	Neg
Mingle	Moure	Nehemiah
Mingo	Mouse Waltz	Neilus
Minor	Mozart	Nemiah Storey
Mint Bell	M. T.	Nemik
Minus	Mub Bub	Nemroy
Mirles	Mubub	Nero
Misber	Much Man	Nether Smith
Miscellaneous Duncan	Mud	Netters
Misery	Muddle	Nevada
Mish Cox	Mum	Nevard
Mission	Mumtez	Never More
Mississippi	Munjun	New Hampshire Maxey
Mississippi Flood	Munch	Nias
Mississippi Mud	Munsing Underwear	Nicholas Longworth
Mister	Murch	Nick Christmas
M. L.	Murdle	Nicodemus
Mobile	Mut	Nicodemus Button
Mock Smith	Mutt	Nickle
Mode	Mylas	Nimit
Modest	Naaman	Nimmie
Monday	Namon	Nimrod
Modic	Nancy Crosby	Nimus
Modiste (Kendrick)	Nando	Nish
Moggie	Nantee	Nitrus
Mond	Naper Stewart	No More Cross
Money	Napoleon	No Parking
Mongier	Naragansett Bay Jones	No. Seven
Monk	Narvel	Noah
Monkeyde Covington	Narvell	Noah Webster
Monnie	Narvis	Noak
Montana	Nary	Noas
Monte	Nary A. Red	Noawell
Montean	Nat	Noble
Montee Hoarse	Nathaniel Hawthorne	Noble King
Montoe	National	Noby D.
Montraville Isadore	Naulbert	Nodix Lee
Montrie	Nausea	Noe
Monzella	Navey	Noel
Moose	Navie	Nohanner
Moot	Navy	Nolie
Mordecai	Naxum	Nollie
Morean	Nay	Nong
Moron Washington	Nazarene	Nonzo
Morrisette	Nazaris	Noon
Mose	Nazaro	Noray
Moses	Nazro Barefoot	Normal

Index of Unusual Names

Index of Unusual Names

Index of Unusual Names

Index of Unusual Names

Romeo	St. James	Segaster Lee Smith
Romie	St. John the Baptist	Self Rising Taylor
Rommel	St. Julian	Selius Tillery
Romolo	Saint Paul	Selix
Rompom	Saint Phillip	Sellers
Romulus	Saleh	Selorn
Romus	Saliva Bungay	Selron
Ronery	Salonie	Selven
Roosevelt	Salvis	Selvin
Rose (Vine)	Saltas	Semi-Colon Divinity
Rosegarden	Salvda	Duke
Roseberg	Salvation	Semmial
Rosenwald (Remus)	Samp	Semmie
Roso	Sample	Semper
Rosomber	Sampson	Seneliaur
Rossi	Sampton	Senior
Rossie	Sancho	Sennie Richards
Rotan	Sanclarey	September
Roumania	Sanco	Sergia Sawyer
Rousseau	Sanctified	Serions
Rovine	Sandy	Session
Rowdy	Sank	Sessard
Rowsoll	Santa Fee	Setrick
Royal	Sanville	Seviela
Royal Fowlkes	Sapho	Shabo
Rozelle	Sargent	Shack
Rube	Sassaway	Shad
Rubie	Satan	Shaddie
Ruby	Saul	Shade
Rubystein Jones	Sausage	Shade Black
Ruddie	Savannah	Shadrack
Rudell	Saviour Jackson	Shady
Rudelle	Sawyer	Shallie
Rudy Vallee	S. B.	Shambo
Ruel Laverta	Scatmore	Shang
Rufus	Schene	Shark
Rugce	Scipio	Shave
Rulus	Scooner	Shead
Rumsey Meadow	Scottie Squalls	Shed
Rural	Scottish Rite	Shederick
Rush	Scumpy	Shedric
Rusha	Seaboard	Shedrick
Russie	Seaborn	Sheely
Rutherford B. Hays	Seafus	Shell
Sabre Hayes	Seal Gaston	Shellie
Sack Daddy	Seasess Banks	Shelman
Saint	Seattle	Shelva
Saint Augustine	Seba	Sherman
St. Clair	Sebastian	Sherry
St. Elmo	Sebion	Shib
St. Elmo Shivers	Sebron	Shillie
St. Elmore	Sefus Syphus Suffax	Shine

Index of Unusual Names

Shirley	Snowbird	Stock Holder
Shoofoot	Snowdrift	Stone
Shoot Lyons	Snowflake	Stonewall
Short	Social	Stonewall Jackson
Shorty	Socrates	Stoney
Shropshire	Soe	Strawberry Commode
Shubrick	Soliator	Jones
Shuea	Solice	Strawberry Hill
Shug	Solicitor Ransom	Strolizer
Shylock	Sollie	Suck
Si	Solomon	Sudery Emanuel
Si Baby	Solon	Suel
Sicily	Somer	Sug
Sile	Son	Sugar
Silent	Son Boo	Suite
Silver	Sonnia	Sumlar
Silvern	Sonnie	Sunday
Sim	Sonny	Sunday Night Supper
Simmie	Sonny Boy	Jones
Simey	Sonny Williams	Sunie
Simon Peter	Sonrose Williams	Super Six
Simp Williams	Southern Stonewall	Superior Circulator
Simsie	Jackson	Surveyor
Simuel	Sox	Suspencer
Singer	Spad	Swan
Sink	Spanish	Swatrel
Sip	Sparcus	Sweet William
Sipfield Edgfield	Sparkle Flint Rock	Sweetening
Sir Walter	Sparkplug	Sylvanus
Sir Walter Raleigh	Sparkies	T & P
Sirretter Ray	Special	Taff
Sirrouko	Spengeon	Taft
Six Bits	Spinish	Tal
Skeeter	Spnix	Taliferro
Skid	Spirall	Tallie
Slaughter	Spoonbill	Talty
Slaughter Bugg	Sprig	Tamlin
Slay	Spud	Tampa
Slim	Spurgeon	Tampie
Smalley	Spurgin	Tandy
Smart	Square	Tansel
Smilie	Squire	Tap
Smithie	Squirley Moore	Tapey
Smokey Stover	Squirrel Bowers	Tardy
Snake	Starbird	Tarnish
Snook	Starling	Tass Turner
Snooy	Starr	Tater
Snow	State	Tater Time
Snow Byrd	Stephany	Tar Baby
Snow Flake	Stephen Douglas	Taxee
Snow Melton	Stetson	T. B.
Snowball	Stew	T. C. I.

Index of Unusual Names

Teacher	Thermans	Toy
Teackle	Thermos	Toy Kidd
Teal	Theron	Trandus Norris
Tearatic	Theus	Trenton (Joel)
T'Early	Thirkel	Tris Van
Teat	Thomas Edison	Tritus
Tecumseh	Thomas Jefferson	Trolius
Tecumseh Fluellen	Thone	Trot
Teddy	Thursday	Trott and Go Back
Tee	Thymon	Trouble
Teem	Thyroid	Troupe
Teepee	Tias	Trout Walker
Telesphor	T. I. C.	Troy
Tell	Tick	Truboy Ola
Tellos	Tie	Truehart Wages
Telly	Tig	Truly
Tem Prude	Tin Pan	Truly Fue
Temnit	Tinner	Truly Friday
Temper	Tiny	Truly White
Tench	Tip	Trustee
Tennessee	Tipsy	Tuck Newman
Tennyson	Tite	Tullis
Terminal Tower	Tituba	Tump
Teroy	Titus	Tuna Barnes
Terris	T. J.	Tunis
Tew	Tobe	Tunstil
Texas	Tobias	Turb
T. G.	Tobie	Turnip
Thad Fries	Toby	Tut
Thales	Todie	Twain
Thales Malachi	Toil	Twenty Year
Thattis	Toilet Preparations	Twig
Theady	Tola	Twiggs
Thearthur	Toledo	Twiller
Theatus	Toledo Ohio	Twitty
Thelma	Toles	Two Bites
Thelman	Tollie	T. V. A.
Thelreg	Tom Collins	Tyree
Theodies	Toma	Tyrie
Theodius	Tomb	Tyrus
Theodore Lightning	Tomed	U. B. Phillips
Theodore Roosevelt	Too Late	Ula C.
Theodus	Toofay	Ules Long
Theola	Took	Ulesee Glen
Theophelus	Toosie	Uleses
Theophilus	Tot	Uley
Theophilus Elsaw	Total	Uleas
Theopolis	Toussant	Ulicius
Theoplus	Touissant Christian	Ulipes
Theodrick	Toussaint	Ullias
Theotis	Toussaint L'Overture	Ulma
Theotus	Towny	Ultima

Index of Unusual Names

491

Index of Unusual Names

Wm McKinley	Yankee	Zellus
William Taft	Yanty	Zelman
Wilmet Heard	Yewston	Zelmo
Wimpy	Yoke	Zelona
Winder	Yook	Zema
Wine	York	Zen
Wingee	You	Zena
Winston Salem	Young	Zendell
Wise	Young Old	Zener Taft
Wistee	Youngest	Zeno
Witha	Y. Z.	Zenophon
Wodsea Whitlow	Z.	Zenos
Wolf	Zaccharias	Zenri
Wonderful Zwingler	Zach	Zenus Gibson
Woodie	Zachariah	Zeophus
Wooding	Zachary	Zeph
Woodlee	Zachary Taylor (Jr.)	Zeppes
Woodraw	Zack	Zerel
Woodrow Wilson	Zak	Zero
Woody	Zan	Zeta
Woolie	Zannie	Zick
Wortabee	Zaro	Zid
Wortes	Zavilan	Zilal
Worthit	Zeak	Zim
Worthy	Zealous	Zimmie
W. P. A.	Zeb	Zinka
Wrazie	Zebe	Zion
Wrigley Moon	Zebedee	Zolda
Waylene	Zebron	Zoll
Xenephon	Zebulon	Zollie
Xray	Zedrick	Zollner
Xmas	Zeffy	Zone
X. Y.	Zeffrey	Zonnie
X. Y. Z.	Zek	Zooa Daniels
Yancy	Zeke	Zoon
Yank	Zell	Zore
		Zulean

Black Females

Abaline	Adda	Adlena
Abanda Stone	Addassa	Adlenia
Abia	Addel	Adora Boniface
Abie	Addie	Adrana
Abigail	Addielee	Adrea
Abobbie	Addis	Adrena
Abolena Sweat	Addyne	Adrenia
Abrilla	Adelphia	Adride
Accie Mae	Adesta	Adries
Acquilla	Adgelee	Adside
Acy	Adina	Aeril
Adakar	Adivell	Affie

Index of Unusual Names

Affree	Aletha	Alloivisia
Agah	Alethea	Almaire
Agala	Alethia	Almareta
Agatee	Alexandria Celestine	Almary
Agatha	Alexene	Almedea
Agatta	Alexina	Almeda
Agernora	Alexine	Alme da Garters
Aggy	Alexzina	Almena
Aguilla	Alexzine	Almeria
Ailese	Alfa	Almeta
Ainthy	Alfair	Almetta
Airlene	Alfeir	Almexill
Airlessa	Alferitia	Alnesta
Airzena	Alflorena	Alodoil
Aisula	Alfonia	Alona
Alabama	Alfonsa	Aloni
Alabama Louisiana	Alforetta	Alonia
Alam Corrina	Alfra	Alonza
Alamanza	Alfrana	Alpha
Alanza	Alfreda	Alpha Omega Campbell
Alaska	Alfrebell	Alpheaus
Alazena	Alfreddie	Alpheus
Albaline	Alfredia	Alphi
Albene	Alfredna	Alphia
Alberdeen	Alfreeda	Alphoni
Albertha	Alfreza	Alphonse
Albertine	Algee	Alphonza
Albertina	Algerita	Alrena
Albirda	Algertha	Alsada
Alca	Algia Pochier	Alsenia Carissa
Alcaen Odella	Algie	Alsteen
Alcee LaBranche	Algusta	Alta
Alcelia	Alice Roosevelt Hoggs	Altaire
Alcenia	Alicestine	Altamae
Alcestia	Alimae	Altamase
Alcester Parker	Alinae	Altamese
Al Chester	Alinez	Alterine
Alcia	Alinza	Altha
Alcibia	Alis Yvonne	Althea
Aldee	Alivan	Altheda
Aldernese	Aljourney	Althenia
Aldia	Alladine	Althoranzo
Aldira	Alleah	Arthurene
Aldonia Duncan	Alleanna Add	Altmae
Aldora	Allee	Altona
Alease	Allegia	Altonia
Aleaser	Allegra	Altoria
Aleathia	Allene	Altrue Lamar
Alena	Allie Besta	Alva
Alenna	Allonease	Alvaris
Alennia	Alloria	Alvelia
Alerine	Allouise	Alvera Vance

Index of Unusual Names

Alverda	Amreta	Arcee
Alvereet	Amzie	Arcelia
Alverna Florine	Anastasia Perewinkle	Archiola
Alveria	Jones	Arcola
Alversa	Anavestee	Ardailyer
Alversia	Andrena	Ardearie Gore
Alverta	Anethia	Ardeila
Alvesta	Angel	Ardelia
Alvetia	Angel Ann	Ardell
Alvida	Angel Mary	Ardella
Alvira	Angelface	Ardena
Alvolia	Angelie	Ardenia
Alwilda	Angeline	Ardessie
Alwilder	Angella	Ardie
Alwillie	Angeronia	Ardis
Alzada	Angina Keys	Ardure
Alzade	Anguila	Areather
Alzadie	Anis	Aredell
Alzarah	Anna Vesta	Arelece
Alzata	Annell	Arelia
Alzeda	Annie Laurie	Arena
Alzena	Annizella	Arence
Alzenia	Anoltha	Aressa
Alzonia	Anona	Aresta
Alzora	Antemesa	Areta
Alzuma	Antenority	Aretha
Amanas (Cushion)	Anthellothea	Arethea
Amanda	Antisluett	Aretta
Amandee	Antoinette Alva	Arflenda
Amarinth	Antola	Argellan
Amatine	Antonie	Argentina
Amazing Grace	Anzella	Arginta
Amberlean	Anzola	Aria
Ambia Aretha	Anzora	Arice
Ambria	Aphronia	Arie
Ambronettie	Appleblossom	Arietta
Ambrosia	Appyehonia	Arilia
Ambush	April (Deas)	Arimena
Amelia	Aptene	Arimentha Augusta
Amendo	Aquilina	Aringa
Amenthie Weber	Aquilla	Arinze (Bell)
Ameretta	Ara	Arizona
America	Arabia Scribner	Arkadelphia
Amertine	Arah	Arkansas Holmes
Amie Lee	Aralee	Arkless Eugenia
Aminda (Green)	Araletha	Arky
Amjogolh	Araminta	Arlandis Eastern
Ammie	Aramintha	Arlee
Ammonia	Aray	Arlelia
Amona	Arbelia	Arlena
Amorette	Arber	Arletha
Amoyda	Arbesto	Arlethia

Index of Unusual Names

Arlevia	Artemisia	Athenia
Arlie	Artence	Atheria
Arlinza	Artent	Atlanta
Arlinzie	Artesia	Atlanta Bryant
Arlogia	Artheamise	Athlene
Armanda	Arthecia	Attealia Charity
Armantha	Arthima	Attie
Armeatha	Artholia	Aubra
Armecia	Arthur Mae	Audella
Armendia	Arthuree	Audra
Armenia	Arthurine	Audramae
Armenta	Artice	Audrey
Armentie	Artie	Audrivalee
Armeta	Artificial Flowers	Audrybelle
Armetia	Artilla	Augella
Armentine	Artimichian	Augery
Armidia	Artorio	Augusta Wind
Armina	Arurlda Thompson	Augusta Wynn
Arminta	Arvadia Martin	Augustan
Armintha	Arvelle	Auguster
Armissie	Arveolla	Auline
Armistice Green	Arvester	Auntine
Armita	Arvetta	Aura
Armogene	Arvilda	Aurelia
Armster	Arvilla	Auretha
Arnasser	Arzata	Aurilla
Arneida	Arzelia	Aurlevia
Arnesa	Arzella	Aurodor
Arnetha	Arzola	Aurora
Arnether Nolia	Asalene	Aurora Indiana
Arnethia Christina	Asaline	Aurtha
Arnetta	Aseline Brown	Authalia
Arnette	Asia	Autharila
Arneza Goods	Asia Minor (Stone)	Authula
Arnice	Asilene	Austine
Arnita	Aslense	Australia
Arona Prudence	Aslina	Autree
Aronia	Asma	Auval Antionette
Arouslee Allen	Assie	Auvelia
Arpie	Aster	Auzie
Arquilla	Astimes	Avada
Arra	Astoria	Avadean
Arrabella	Astrea Sunshine	Avalon
Arria	Astria	Avannia
Arriana	Astria Ark	Ave Maria
Arrie	Atchie	Averitta
Arris	Atelia	Avice
Arsania	Ater	Avie
Arsenia	Athalia	Avis
Arsie Mitchell	Athelia	Awella
Arsula	Athelma	Awilda Everage
Arta	Athelstine	Axamia
Artelia	Athena	Axlina

Index of Unusual Names

Aza Belle
Azalea Edmoniá
Azalee
Azalia
Azalie
Azalien
Azalina
Azaline
Azalle
Azarene
Azarine
Azelea
Azelee
Azelia
Azeline
Azelle
Azerine
Azie
Azora
Azore
Azzalee
Azzie
Azzie Zivillus
Azzielee
Babe
Babie
Baby
Baby Doll
Baby Fox
Baby Lace
Baby Lou
Baby Ruth
Baby Ray
Baby Venue
Baina Harper
Baissie
Ballencia
Balumnioo
Bama
Bamma
Banna
Banner
Bannie Mae
Bantie
Bannana
Barcolia
Bardelie
Bargia
Barnetta
Barto
Bassar
Bazelia

Bazille
Beadie
Beady
Beaurina
Beaury
Beautiful Swindler
Beauty
Beauty Love
Beauty Marcelle
Beauty Pearl
Beblaha
Beck Esta
Beda
Bedelia
Bee
Bee Attress
Beechie
Bela
Belessa
Belina
Belinda
Bella Belle
Bella Scippio
Beloved
Belva
Belzara
Belzora
Benella
Ben Ella
Benerlyn
Benia
Benida
Benina
Benita
Bennie
Benoca
Benzena
Benjina
Beoria
Beornored
Bera
Berdie
Berdin
Beresenia
Berla
Berlene
Berma
Bernadette
Berta
Betha
Bethalena
Berthelle

Berthena
Berndella
Bernethia
Bernicetine Berdie Lee
Bermitha
Bero
Berrens
Berthola
Bertie
Bertina
Bertine
Besotra
Bethine
Bethula
Bertrude Burton
Beveretta
Betranna
Beuna
Beuna Mantooth
Beveline
Bevelyn Venue
Bicentennial
Biddie
Bina
Binah
Biney
Bionca
Bina Rozelle
Biozola
Birchie
Bird Cook
Birda
Birden Bunice (Chester)
Birdester
Birdia
Birdie
Birdie Bell Boypin
Birdine
Birnetha
Birtie
Blairyne
Blanche White
Blandina
Blantee La Vurn
Bleaker
Blendina
Bleka
Blessed B. Truly Blue
Blessed Virgin Murphy
Blivian
Blondella
Blondelle

Index of Unusual Names

Index of Unusual Names

Casteline
Castella
Castilla
Castoria
Castra
Catalina
Cathedral Spires
Catty
Candace
Causey
Caylona
Ceana Ophelia
Cebonia
Ceceleous
C. D. (Pack)
Cedell
Cedric
Cefernia
Celian
Celestia
Celestial Devine
Celestine
Celina
Cender Lee
Cenia
Central
Centry
Ceola
Ceretha
Cerilla
Cerise
Cerita
Chaddie
Chaine
Chainey
Chaisey
Chancellor Rose
Chaney
Chanie
Charel
Charity
Charity Bell
Charity Bunn
Charity Ward
Charlena
Charlene
Charles Etta
Charlesetta
Charlsie
Charleston
Charlesine
Charlestina

Charlie
Charlina
Charline
Charlise
Charlsie
Charmaine
Charsie
Chassie
Chatice
Chatnee
Chattie
Chehoney
Chemise
Cheri
Cheristeener
   (from Kerosene)
Cherokee
Cherribelle
Cherrie
Cherry
Cherry Tee
Cherrylane
Cherubina
Chessie
Chester
Chestina
Chico
Chinesa Baptiste
Chipso Green
Chlora
Chloria
Chlorie Godboldt
Chlorine
Chistee
Chloe
Chloroform
Chloteal
Choatee
Chorce
Choyce
Chrisey
Christalee
Christernelia
Christiana
Christie
Christille
Christinia
Christmas
Christmas Day
Christopher
Christy
Chrystal Brown
Cicero

Cidda Lou
Cile
Cilla
Cinda
Cindie
Cinderella
Cindy
Cintilla
Cis Nero Ciresco
Cisroe
Cissie
Cissley
Citronella
Citronola (corruption
   of Citrinella)
City
City Bell
City Lee
Cjntha Alexander
Clarazelle
Clardia Mae
Clareen
Clarnea
Clarenda
Claressa
Claretes James
Claretha
Claretta
Claricia
Clacinda
Clarine
Clarissa
Clarisse
Clary
Classie
Classie Childs
Classy
Glassy Gal Oats
Claster
Clatile
Claudell
Claudesta Ross
Claudie
Claudine
Clayee
Clayton
Clearness
Clearrander Bowen
Clearyse
Cleata
Cleathel Leafes
Clelia Regina
Clema

Index of Unusual Names

Clematis
Clemency Love
Clementina
Clementine
Clemmie
Clemenza
Clencie
Clenderline
Clendolia
Clennice
Clensie
Clentyne
Cleo Nero
Cleo Portio
Cleoard
Cleobelle
Cleodell
Cleodo
Cleola
  (Twin to Theola)
Cleomie
Cleony
Cleopatra
Cleopatra Blue
Cleopatria
Cleophia
Cleoporia Manilla
    Turner
Cleora
Cleotha
Cleottus
Cleva Maylor
Cleven
Clevia
Clidie
Clima
Climmie
Clinia
Clintola
Clio
Clodifa
Cloie
Clolelia
Cloreand
Cloreatha
Cloree
Clorene
Clorie
Clorine
Cloteal
Clotee
Clotha Kittles
Clotilde
Clotelle

Clotiel
Clotine
Clouise
Clover
Cloverett
Cloy
Cloybelle
Cloye
Cluck
Cluverious
Clydena
Clydester
Clymithe
Clyta
Clytee
Clytie
Coatsie
Coaxum
Cobretha
Coddell
Coebra Myrthal
Cogy
Cola
Cold Turkey
Coleen
Colena
Colia
Colie
Colie Demus
Colin Lampsey
Collatta Martinia
Colletta Vowry
  (Law Mis' us foun'
   hit in er book)
Collie
Collins
Colody
Colonius Spearman
Colorado
Columbia
Columbiana
Comfort
Comforter Duncan
Comfortsee
Comillas
Commeace
Commer (Combs)
Commoca
Con Mary
Concuella
Connie
Conscience Durant

Constant
Constantia
Constantine
Consuella
Consuelo
Contella
Cool Cosa
Cooperzanna Simpson
Coozie
Coranette
Cordia Mare
Cordie
Coreania
Coretta
Corilla
Corinda
Corines
Coritha
Cormae
Cormitta
Corne Belle
Cornelia Tonsil
Cornese
Corrie
Cosetta
Cosette
Cosmos
Cossie
Costella
Cotie
Council Mims
Couchie
Countess
Coy
Cozetta
Cozia
Cozie
Cozy
Cqueta
Cravalis
Creacy
Creamery
Creaniola
Creasie
Creasy
Crecilla
Credella
Creedie
Crenie
Creola
Cresa
Cresie

Index of Unusual Names

Cressie
Cresye
Cridele
Crisstella
Crocha
Cuba
Cuetta
Cullie
Cumialla
Cunise
Curdlee
Curlee Cline
Curley
Curlie
Curly
Cutie Eagle
Cutrena
Cuvata
Cydonia Japonica
Cylla
Cynthiabelle
Dahlia
Daisia
Daisie
Daisy (Washington)
Daisy Dell
Daisy Field
Dallas
Dallie Simmons
Dally
Dalomba
Dalsese
Dalzie
Dancer
Danice
Dannia
Danula
Darcas
Dardanella Gilstrap
Darksie
Darline
Darling
Darnella
Darsia
Darthula
Dashie
Dassie
Dasyl
Daszelle
Datie
Davidica
Davie

Davine
Davis Mae
Dawn
Day Dee
Dazelle Graster
Dazerine
Dazine
Dazzle Daniels
Dealla
De Anna
Deanna
Dear
Dearie Peoples
Dea Vera
Deavera
De Bell
Debirdie
Deborah
December
Decie
Declema
Dee
Deedie
Delacy
Delamare Calulius
Delcee Latham
Delcenia
Delcie
Delena Love
Delerious
Delerna
Deleria
Delias
Delight
Delilah
Delilah Royalty
E. Delita
Della Francis Bible
Dellagratia
Dellaphina
Dellaphine
Delliana
Dellie
Delois
De Lois
Delolah
Delorah
Deloria
Deloina
Delphena
Delphene
Delphi

Delphia
Delphin
Delphine
Delphinia
Delphis
Delphone
Delsey Semera
Delsie
Delsie Gee
Delta
Delvia White
Delvin
Demetris
Demetrius
Demolesta
Demorah
Dena
Denita
Denkie Jones
Dennette Arthur
Dennie
Denola
Depucious
Dequilla
Dera
Derathes
Dereola
Deresette
Dernice Nichol
Derotha
Desaline
Desdemona
Desire
Desirie
Desmar
Desmonia Deanna
Desrette
Dessa
Dessie
Detie
Detro
Deva
Develous
Devada Phelesta
Devella
Devoalia
Devota Persons
Dewatha
Dewey Frater
Dewey Meadows
Dexter Poindexter
Dezebee Studemire

500

Index of Unusual Names

Dezira
Diana
Dicey
Dichloramentine
Dicia
Dicie
Dickie
Dicy
Digesta
Dilcey
Dilcie
Dilla
Dillie
Dilsie
Dimeda
Dimmileane
Dimple
Dimples Rinse
Dina
Dinah
Dinna
Diola
Dion
Dionysia Amelia
Diptheria
Divine
Dixie
Doak
Dochie
Docia
Docie
Docile
Doctor Marion
Dode
Doffie
Dogmas Clarissa
Dolemia
Dolintha
Doll
Doll Baby
Dollbaby Henry
Dollena
Dollie
Dollina
Dollis
Dollista
Dollye Deloria
Dolphin
Dona
Donamerhle
Donella
Donie

Donnah
Donnie
Donzelle
Doosey
Dootsey (Subadger)
Dora Droe Dennis
D'ora
Dorazelle
Dorcas
Doree
Doreen
Doretha
Doria
Dorinda
Dorisca
Doristine
Dorlice Phillipotts
Dorphenie
Dorus
Dorwatha
Doshia
Doshie
Doskie
Dossie
Dot
Dotcary
Dotsie Spruell
Douche
Dove
Dove Tee
Doveeye
Dovey
Dovie
Dovie Bible
Doshia
Dovella
Doxie
Dozelle
Dozlia
Drewella
Drissa
Drucilla
Drunetta
Dubro
Duella
Dulcenia
Dumpie
Dumpsie Brown
Dura
Duris
Dusk
Dusky (Justice)

Dussie
Dutrelle
Dwellie
Dwendolyn
Dymple
Dymoush
Eadie Weaver
Eammarell
Eariest
Earlee
Earlena
Earlese
Earlie Mai
Earlie May (Mrs.
             Cutter)
Earline Bel
Early
Early True (Lee)
Earsel
Earsie
Eartha
Eartherlee
Eartheline
Eartherre Idarette
Earthline
Earthly
Earthy
Easlyn
Easter
Easter Bell
Easter Bells
Easter Dummy
Easter Glory Simpson
Easter Hunt
Easter Legg
Easter Lillie
Easter Lily
Eastern Star
Eatabee
Earvial
Eather
Ebbie
Eberline
Ebony
Ecra
Edalia
Edda
Eddie (Lee, Mae)
Edmonia
Ednelia
Edria
Edurna

501

Index of Unusual Names

Edvenia	Elluna	Emiel
Edwardine	Elma Murray	Emistine
Edwina	Elmere	Emmogene Miller
Edwina Electa Lowe	Elmetta	Emmaretta
Edwinner	Elmette	Emmie
Effie	Elmina	Emmie Ucullus
Effie Mae Bugg	Elmira	Emmogene
Effitee	Elmo	Empress
Egypst	Elmora	Ena
Egypt (Stone)	Elmyra	Endor
Eileithyia	Elnada	Enameline
Eilesse (Eaves)	Elnola	Endie
El Nora	Elnoria	Endora
ElRee	Elon (Lavonia)	Energine
Elawes	Elonia Cockrell	Enelean
Elbell	Elora Ardalia	Enevia
Elbertha	Elphanie	Enid
Eldeese	Elphreda	Enielda
Eldia Louise	Elreta	Enna
Eldora	Elroce	Ennis
Eldra	Elsena	Enola
Electa	Elvada	Enolia
Electa Allegra	Elvannah Bufyou	Enzy
Electra	Elvee Ulee	Epna
Elecyra Arnetta	Elvena Gloria	Eppie
Elereen	Elvenleen	Eppirese
Elesta	Elverta	Epsie
Elesta Etta	Elveta	Epsy Ann
Elester	Elveta Lytease	Equator
Elevator	Elvie	Era
Elexenia	Elvina	Erana
Elezar	Elvira	Ercelle
Elfleeta	Elvise	Ercie Mae
Elfrida	Elysis	Ergot
Elgartha	Elza	Ergotine
Elgetha	Elzaner	Erie Canal
Elgie	Elzatie	Eris
Elgirtha	Elzena	Erla
Elgria	Elzenobia	Erlena
Eliease	Elzera	Erlica
Elissa Jane	Elzeria	Erline
Elitea	Elzinda	Erly Mae
Elizah	Elzonia	Erma
Elizetta	Elzora	Ermene
Elijenine	Em Tecumseh	Ermenese
Elkanah Celestine	Emalee	Ermenia
Ellabelle	Emdella	Ermine
Ellaneese	Emeance	Erminie
Ellanese ·	Emelda	Ermyntrude
Ellease	Emelia	Erna
Ellestine	Emerald	Ernese
Ellie	Emerlyn	Ernestia

Index of Unusual Names

Erra	Etholia	Evashti
Ersaline	Ethylene	Evekena
Ersalyn	Etienetta	Eveler Bandman
Erseline	Etnah	Evelina (Thrasher)
Erselle	Etolia	Evena
Ersie	Etoy	Ever Leana
Ertha	Etrest	Ever Mae
Erycena	Ettie	Everga
Erylin	Ettyce	Evergreen
Erza	Eucalor	Everlee
Esabelle	Eudora	Everlena
Esatee	Eues	Everline
Esdelia	Eufaula	Evetta
Eselean	Eugenera	Evi Lena
Eslanda	Eugertha	Evna
Esnold	Eukalia	Evon Jackson
Esperance	Eula Bell	Evona
Essa	Eulah	Evora
Essaline	Eulalah	Ewa
Essel	Eulalia	Excelene
Essemers	Eulalie	Excema (or Exie)
Essie	Eulamoy	Excetta
Essielee	Euleas	Exeline
Esserlena	Eulene	Exema
Essolene	Eulie	Exermas Mathes
Esta	Eulila	Exie
Esteem Mareem	Euline	Extella
Estella Chotella Hill	Euphemia	Eyla Mae Arnold
Estellar	Euphrasia	Eyner
Estellena	Eura	Ezeka
Esterine	Eural	Ezell
Esterlene	Eurcelyn	Ezelma
Estine	Eurdie	Ezema
Estoria	Eureka	Ezetta
Estue Essie	Eureka Feolia	Facilla
Etah	Eurice	Fair
Eteria	Eurine	Fairy
Etha	Europenia	Fairy Bell Moses
Ethelbert Napoleon	Eusebe	Fairy Belle Collie B.
Ethelda	Eustase	Fairybell
Etheldra	Euther	Faith
Ethelean	Eutie	Fallopian
Ethelene	Eutocia	Falonia
Ethelind	Euzena	Fan Chon
Etheline	Evadean	Fancie
Ethella	Evadne	Fanilla
Ethelnell	Evalee	Fara
Ethelreeda	Evalena	Farina Willie Wheeler
Ethelwyn	Evalina	Farlie
Ethelyne	Evanda	Farntella
Ether	Evander	Farrie
Ethiopia	Evangeline	Fataque

Index of Unusual Names

Fate Cutts	Florella	Frankie
Fatima	Florene	Frankie Frisch
Fatrice	Florentine	Frankie June Munday
Fatring	Florenza	Frastina
Faucette	Floretta	Frazzie
Fausteen	Floria	Freda
Faustina	Florida	Fredda
Favoretta	Florida Lemon	Freddie
Favorite	Florida Orange	Freddie May Shivvers
Fay	Floride	Freddique
Feannette	Floridie	Freddye Madene
Fedalma	Florie	Frederica
Fedeliza	Florine	Frederice
Felicia	Floris	Fredericka
Felicie	Floriska	Fredie
Felixina	Florita	Fredima
Felman	Florrie	Fredna
Felony	Florzell	Fredonia
Female	Floss B.	Fredena Clementine
Femba	Flossie	Fredrica
Fenella	Flounda Fletcher	Fredrika
Fenezie	Flowers (Green)	Free Love
Feola	Floy	Free Press
Fern	Flowers	Frequette Fortune
Ferndina	Floyce	Frezette
Ferneva	Flozelle	Friendly
Fernine	Fluellen	Frissie
Ferraline Carter	Fluter	Frona
Ferryn	Flutsie	Froney
Fertilizer	Fly Kate	Fronia
Fesla	Fobola	Fronie
Finish	Focie	Fronnia
Finney	Foney Graves	Fronnie
Fizar	Fonie Lee	Frosty
Flabbie Hall	Fonsa	Frozee
Flamboylia	Fontana	Frozene
Flavelia	Fonzie-Mae Jenkins	Frozine
Flavella	Foots	Fruitsy Kertsy
Flavor	Forresta	Fruseanna
Flawilla	Fosia	Frizzie
Flaxie	Fostena	Future
Fleecie	Fosteria	Gabrielle
Fleta	Fostine	Gainsetta
Fletta	Fourthine	Galatea
Flithia	Fradonia	Galilee
Flo	Fragelia	Galiton White
Flocelia Cora	Fraidy	Gallie
Floecelia	Fraitus	Galma L.
Flogelle	Francena	Galzena
Flonteen	Franchelle	Ganzella
Floree	Francina	Garah
Florette	Francine	Garcia

Index of Unusual Names

Garcie	Gheretein	Gora Lean
Gardinia	Giffy	Gordia
Garna Mae	Gift of God	Goretha
Garthelia	Gilla	Gosie
Garthula	Gillie	Gotter Clinkscales
Gassie	Ginger	Governia
Gatha	Giora	Gozelle
Gather	Girlee (You're)	Gozy
Gaudy	Girlena Terrell	Gracy
Gawdy Lou	Girlie	Grafta
Gay Ada	Girllene	Granuloma
Gaynelle	Girtha	Gratha
Gazelle	Girthlee	Grazelle
Gearline	Girtie	Grazia
Gecana	Givenlaine	Greenleaf Meadows
Gelester	Gizzy	Grendetta
Gemargie	Gladie	Gretchen
Gena	Gladiola	Gretel
Genia	Glandora	Griselda
Genelallena	Glassy	Grizelle
General	Glavinia	Grizzelle
Geneve Eloise	Glenarna Cloteah	Guessella
Genil (Maples)	Glenda	Guinevere
Genner	Glendafay	Guleane
Genoa	Glennia	Gunoa
Genola	Glenola	Gurseal
Gensy	Glodine	Gurtha White
George Anna	Gloria Angela	Gussie
George Washington	Gloridine	Gustara
Georgella	Glorie	Gustava
Georgene	Glorious McGhee	Gustavia
Georgetta	Glory	Gustella
Georgie	Glossy	Gustine
Georgie Washington	Glynoil	Gustora
Georgine	Gold	Gutha
Geova	Gold Dollard (Johnson)	Guyoria
Geralyn	Gold Duster	Guyrene
Geranium	Golda	Gwendel
Gerella	Goldbeam	Gwince
Geretta	Golden	Gynell
Gerita	Golden Brown	Gypsophilia
Gerlene	Golden Rose	Habie
Gerlina	Goldie	Haddie
Gerline	Goldie Blondine	Hadessa
Germania	Goldie Tomaza	Hagar
Gerotha	Goldusta	Hager
Gertha	Golear	Hagra
Gertie	Golie	Haidee
Gertis	Gonadia	Haidee Hurrah Huff
Gerwausee	Gonzelle	Hailstine
Geshma	Gonzola	Halla
Geston Do	Good Day	Hallique

Index of Unusual Names

Hallorah	Hibernia	Idelia
Hammie	Hilda	Idell
Handsome	Hilda Vernetta	Idella
Hancy	Hilwe	Idelle
Hanna	Hinnie	Idelphine
Hannah	Hisetta	Idena
Happiness	Hissie	Idonia
Hardenia	Homezell	Idozier
Harrietha	Honey	Iduma
Harryette	Honey Child	Idylee
Harrylee	Honeybee	Idyles
Hartie	Honor	Ietta
Hartis	Hoodoo	Ietta Moon
Harvey Mae	Hope	Igetta
Hasner Terrell	Hora	Igetta Pullen
Hassie	Hornetha	Ikella
Hassoloba	Hosannah	Ila
Hattiebell	Hula	Ila Almetya
Hattoe	Hulda	Ilene
Havanah	Huldah	Ilia Mae
Havenia	Huretta Samuel	Illinois
Haysal	Hurice	Illistine
Hazeline	Huron	Illusta
Hazeltine	Hurtha	Ilma Anglique
Heaven	Hussie	Ilsye
Helan Monday	Hutie	Ima
Helen Taft	Hyacinth	Ima Rose Bush
Helena Nozelle	Hynetis	Ima Valentine
Heleria	Hytorria	Immaculate Conception
Heliotrope	Ianatha	Imogene
Hellena	Iantha Ugrthea	Imogene Gucken
Helmar	Ianthia	Imy
Helveitia	Ibbie Lee	Ina
Helvuis	Ice Cream	India
Hennie	Ice Cream Babbit	Indiana
Henriene	Icelea	Indiana Carolina
Henrienne	Icephine	Morgan
Hepsie	Icephine Butler	Indiana River
Herbine	Icie	Indie
Hercial	Icie Byrd	Indya
Herline	Icelean	Ineather
Hermania	Icephine	Ineffie
Hermaphalia	Icky	Inell
Hermenia	Icy	Inella Callier
Hermione	Icy Banks	Inest
Hernie	Icy Belle	Inetha
Hertha	Icy Blizzard	Inola Prizelle
Herticile	Icybell	Insolene
Hessie	Idalia	Inze
Heterogeneous	Idalette	Iodine
Hettie	Idama	Ioma
Hezekiah	Idele	Ione

Index of Unusual Names

Ionia	Ivory	Jenesa
Ionzell Sparks	Ivory Dew	Jenevera
Iota Morton	Ivory Keyes	Jency Lenon
Iowa	Ivory White	Jenilene
Iphagenia Olinda	Ivy	Jenlee
Ique	Iwalda	Jenna
Ira Kalantha	Iwilda Williams	Jense
Iralee	Iwilla	Jensie
Irazetta	Iwilla (Rainge)	Jeranium
Irealous	Izel	Jerlene
Irener	Izelia	Jermette
Iretha	Izella	Jerolene
Irewilla	Izera	Jerolian
Iris	Izetta	Jerona
Iristine	Izema	Jerusha
Irlene	Izma	Jerussia
Isadora	Izola	Jessica
Isadore	Izone	Jesseline
Isedora	Izora	Jestina
Isephense	Izora Magnolia	Jestine
Isetta	Izoria	Jesticer
Isis	Izzie	Jetta
Isio Bell	Jacequelin	Jettie
Islet	Jacola	Jetty
Isofine	Jadeline	Jewel
Isola	James Ellen	Jewel Pearl Dismikes
Isolene	Jamescina	Jeweline
Isolene Christmas	Jamie Mae	Jewette
Isoline	Jamimia	Jimella Jones
Isophalie	Jammie	Jimmie
Isophine	Janelle	Jimmizine
Isora	Janetha	Jinever Slaughter
Israella	Janetta	Jo Leatha
Issie	Janeva	Joan Crawford
Itaska Campbell	Janine Jones	Jobie
Itenia Boston	Japania	Jocelia
Itha	Japonica	Joe
Ithilla Fields	Jara Lee	Joehanna Rolen
Itlean	Jarodis	Joella Turbin
Iulca	Java	Joese
Iva	Javoo	Joetta
Iva Dime	Jayma	John Ellen
Iva Incision	Jeddie	Johnalee
Ivana	Jeffie	Johncie Sartor
Ivanetta	Jeletta	Johnelle
Ivanhoe	Jelma	Johnese
Ivanona	Jemima	Johnetta
Ivella	Jemina	Johnita
Ivery	Jemmy	Johngeline
Ivie	Jentie	Johnnice
Ivinola	Jenelle	Johnnie
Ivorie	Jenerette	Johnny
		Johnsie

Index of Unusual Names

Index of Unusual Names

Lavinia
Lavona
Lavonia
Lavuna
Lawsonia
Lawuna
Laxine
Layee Bobbie
Layette
Lazelle
Lazinko Epps Enigless
Le Grand
Lea
Leacie
Leahre
Lealette
Leana
Leanell
Leanetta
Leanna Griffin
Leany
Learline
Leaster
Leasure
Leatha
Leaver
Leavesta
Leavie
Leavima
Lebertha
Leborgia
Lecie
Leda
Ledger
Ledora
Ledpsia
Lee
Lee Vonia
Leeanna
Leeda
Leedie
Leedy Mae Bixon
Lehency
Leitha
Leittia
Lejunita
Lelaea
Lellie
Lemmie
Lemon
Lemona Lee
Lemone

Lemoyne Elnora
Lemuel
Lendie Gibson
Lenebell Delores
Lenera
Lenie
Lennie
Lenola
Lenolia
Lenonia
Lenora
Lenzy
Leobra
Leoda
Leola
Leolar
Leoma
Leomia
Leondas
Leonelle
Leonnie
Leonteen
Leontine
Leonzie
Leony
Leonzie
Leoppie
Leota
Lephis
Lera
Lerlie
Lerline
Lerla
Lerona
Lessie
Lestine
Letarheal
Letetia
Letha
Lethaneal
Lethia
Letitia
Letitia Demenii
Lettia
Lettie
Lettuce Fields
Leu Bosia
Leuscina
Levada
Levana
Levander Kinds
Levata

Levenia
Levessie
Levesta
Levice
Leverage
Leverta
Levina
Levinia
Leviticus
Levonia
Levora
Lewana
Lewine
Lewis
Lexana
Lexie
Lexine
Lexra
Li Mar
Libel
Liberta
Licey
Lida
Liddie Belle
Lilac Green
Lilliog
Lily White
Lima
Limousine
Lina
Linda
Lindy
Linnie
Linzie
Lisha
Lissie
Listerine
Lit
Litt
Littie
Littie Lo Willie
Little (Yancey)
Little Sister
Littlebit
Livilee
Liza
Liza Cucumber
Lizelle
Lizzel Vasta
Lizzell
Lizzerine
Lizziemine

Index of Unusual Names

Lobelia
Lobertha
Loda (B. Foy)
Loda Coal
Lodea Mar Pettiford
Lodee Antitain
Lodelle
Lodie
Lodieze
Lo Esther
Loester
Loetta
Logania
Loi Ethel
Loida
Loleta
Lolette
Lolita
Lolota Augustine Dreux
Lolittia
Lollie
Lolly Pop
Lolo
Lona
Loneday
Lonely
Longenious
Lonia
Loida
Lonie
Lonnette
Lonnie
Lonteshia
Lonzella
Lonzetta
Looney (Head)
Lorayne
Loree
Lorelle
Lorenza
Loresia
Loretha
Lorie May
Lorillard
Lorine
Lornella
Lossie
Lotharie
Lottee (Moaning)
Lotus
Lottya
Loualma

Louana
Louberta
Louccandia Lockett
Loudicia
Loudlgia Wilhelmina
Louetta
Louevenia Freeman
Louia
Louisiana
Louisiana Oats
Lounett
Louquency
Lourena
Lourie
Loustar
Loutilla
Loutishia
Louvenia
Louvicia
Love
Love Bird
Love Divine
Loveless
Love-li
Lovella
Lovely
Lovena
Lovenia
Loventrice
Lovey
Lovicia
Lovie
Lovey Lou Lane
Lovine
Lovitt
Lowly Joan
Loxie (Cates)
Loyal
Lozea Mae
Lualgia Clementine
Luanna
Luberta
Lubertha
Luby
Lucendia
Lucendya
Lucetta
Luchia
Lucienda
Lucinda
Lucine
Luckenga

Luckie
Lucky
Lucresia
Lucretia
Luda Alexander
Ludea
Ludeen
Ludella
Ludelle
Luders
Ludessa
Ludia
Ludie
Ludina
Ludine
Lue Birdia
Lue Ginger
Lueberta
Leugenia Moss
Lueneal
Lueraine
Lueretta
Luethel
Luetta
Lueverne
Luezzia
Lugene
Lugenia
Lugesta
Lugurtha
Lugusta
Luina
Luiza
Lujane
Lukie
Lulene Cantrell
Lulila
Lullia
Lullovee
Lumeta
Lumicie
Luminate
Luminary
Lumitia
Lummie
Luna
Lunell
Lunese
Lunette
Lunie
Luoda
Lura

Index of Unusual Names

Luranda	Macelroy Crawley	Maizie Zonetta
Lurania	Machie	Majenta
Lurena (Jones)	Macie	Majesta
Lurene	Macille	Majester
Lurina	Mack Lee	Major McGriff
Lurine	Mackamo	Maleatha
Lurla	Madam Queen	Malena
Lurlene	Madelle	Malenda
Lurline	Mademoiselle	Maletha
Lusina	Madena	Malinda
Lussie	Madera	Malisa
Lusta	Maderas	Malissa
Luster	Madesta	Malissie
Lutetia	Madey	Mallalieu
Lutherine	Madie	Mallie
Lutie	Madies	Malonla
Lutie Panola	Madine	Malsie
Lutis	Madonna	Malta
Lutisia	Madora	Malvenia
Lutitia	Mae West	Malverse
Lutril Amos	Maecile	Malvolia
Luvada	Maedell	Malysia
Luvata	Maejim Willingham	Mammie Lee
Luvelle Lucile	Maelyne	Mamnise
Luverna	Maezethia	Mammy
Luvendia Austin	Magelina	Mammy Asia
Luvenia	Magazine	Manassas Quinn
Luverna	Magdalena	Manatee
Luverne	Magdalene	Manda
Luvernia	Magdaline	Mande
Luvina	Magdeline	Mandelene
Luvinia	Magella	Mandena
Luverna	Magilene	Mandester
Luvisa	Magnoila	Mandleen
Luwenia	Magnolia	Mandy
Luwilla	Magnolia Fields	Manervia
Lux Teaberry	Magnolia Hill	Manetta
Luxora	Magnolia Zenobia Pope	Manilla
Luzenia	Magnotia	Manima
Lybertia	Mahala	Mannie
Lycille	Mahale	Manola
Lydie	Mahaley	Manytailfeathers
Lydya Lucetta	Mahalie	Manza
Lygia	Mahelia	Manzellie
Lygretta	Mahilia	Maonie
Lyncha	Mahita Bell Jane	Maple Lee
Lynetta	Johnson	Mapluma
Lyonell Clarence	Mahogany	Marcella
Lysbeth	Maida	Marcelle Martin
Lyzola	Maide	Marcelline
Mabelia	Maire Ximinia	Marcilite
Macedonia	Maisie	Mardess

Index of Unusual Names

Marechal-Neil	Matteen	Melinee
Mareda	Mattline	Melissa
Mareen (Green)	Mattis Modell	Mellanese
Margarine	Maubell Sexten	Mellie Durrett
Margella	Mauchie	Mellow
Margo	Maudelle	Melvayne
Margorilla	Maudest	Melvena
Margree	Maudestine	Melvene
Margretta	Maudine	Melvenia
Maria	Maudleine	Melvina
Mariah	Mauline	Melvira
Maire Antoinette	Maulsie	Melzetta
Mariella	Mavelle	Melzie Essielonia
Marigold	Mavis	Melzore
Marinba	Maxie	Memory
Marinda	Maxine	Mencie
Marinda Nevada	May Rose Pickens	Mendora
Mariola	Maycellette	Menergh
Marionella	Maydell	Menora
Marionette	Maydelle	Menses
Marire	Maydia	Mentha (Mae)
Marjoe	Mayette de Brossard	Mentie
Marline	Mayleen	Mentrell
Marossie	Mayola	Menzola
Marovia	Mayola DeGraffenried	Merceda
Marquita	Mayoso	Mercer Dese
Marria	Mayronia	Mercedes
Marstella	Mayzelle	Mercedes Acthea
Martelia	Mazarine	Mercedes Corra
Martha Washington	Mazella	Mercides
Marthena	Mazella Altha	Mercy
Marthenia	Mazie	Merdie
Martilla	Mazilie	Merida
Martini	Mazine	Merietta
Marvelle	Mazoe	Merissa
Marvelline	Mazola	Merlee
Marveltine	Me	Merline
Maryland	Mealy	Merodia
Maryline	Mearle Aristine	Merry Christmas
Marylonia	Mearleen	Merryce Altymese
Marzetta	Meconium	Mertha
Marzie	Meddie	Mertice
Massaleen	Medesta Alfosa	Mertie
Masselee	Medieth Elouise	Mesppotamia Tucker
Masseline	Medora	Meta
Massie	Mel Rosa	Metabell
Masue Esther	Melcina	Metella
Mathilda	Meleda	Meterine
Matia	Meledia	Methylene
Matilda	Melena	Mettie
Matitia	Melia	Meurion
Matoka	Melinda	Miargo

Index of Unusual Names

Mickie	Modeline	Murlean
Mida Gore	Modelle	Murline
Midget	Modena	Murmer
Midgie	Modeska Lyons	Murtice
Mignon	Modest	Murvain Moals
Mignora	Modesty	Musa
Milah	Modiest	Musette
Milbia	Mohaley	Musia
Miliada	Moirselles	Musie Manna
Milissa Sypes	Mola	Mussyle
Mincie	Moline	Mutelive
Minda	Molise	Muvina
Mineola	Mongoloa	Myneola
Minneola	Monia	Myoline
Minnesota Lee	Monica	Myria Mullens
Minnetta	Monily	Myrna Loy
Minnieola	Monnie	Myrtaline
Minola	Monta	Myrtee
Minor	Montesse Robinson	Myrtella
Minta	Montez	Myterious
Mintia	Montilla	Myrtie
Mintora	Monzella	Myrtis
Minunette	Morell	Mytrolene
Minyore	Morella	Nachel Harper
Miranda	Morena	Nadine
Mirian	Morphine	Nancean
Miril	Mortina	Naner
Mirina Brownreed	Morzillor	Nanetta
Mirl Martha	Mosella	Nannette Norine
Mirreaen	Moselle	Nannie
Miscellaneous	Mosetta	Nanon
Misher Cox	Moslette	Naola
Miss Daughter	Mossie Rainwater	Naomie
Missie	Motta	Narcie
Mississippi	Moundry	Narcissa
E. Missoura Brandyburg	Moxie Mae	Narcissa Flora
Missouri	Moyese	Narcissus
Missouri Riva	Mouesto	Narra (Woods)
Missouri Soup	Mozel (Orena)	Narvie
Missouri Woods	Mozella	Natalee
Missy	Mozelle	Natalie
Mistress	Mozetta	Natalya
Mittie	Mozie	Natha Lee
Mizelle	Mozilia	Nathel
Mizpah	Mug Jones	Nathia
Mizrach Shadrach	Mulvenia	Natine
Abendago	Murella	Nausaeous
Mizura	Murgie	Nazarie
Mobelia	Murice	Nazlee
Mobile	Murilla	Nazrinie
Moddie	Murine	Nealie
Modelia	Murlee	Neallie

Index of Unusual Names

Index of Unusual Names

Ometa
Omie
Omizell
Ommie
Ona
Onada
Oneida
Oneita
Oneiter Macknickle
Oneta
Onetha
Onetis
Onia
Onibel
Onida
Onie
Onilda
Onneda
Onous
O. N. T. Clark
Ontee
Ooman
Oouida
Opal
Opal Jewyle
Opera
Opera Lovely
Ophbelia
Ophlisa
Opia
Opra
O'pretty Hubbard
Ora
Oradene
Oral
Oralee
Oralee Derricoatee
Oralie
Orangeade
Orange Jello
Orange Lean
Orangene
Orangia
Orangie
Oratrice
Orcellia
Orea
Orean
Oreather
Orece Holman
Orelia

Orelius
Orella
Orellie
Oremia
Orena
Oreta
Oretha
Oria
Oriah
Orico
Orie
Orine
Orietta
Orise
Orita
Orlande
Orleans West
Orlena
Ormee
Ormenta
Ornamental
Ornee
Ornette Augusta
Oro
Orpha
Orrie
Orselola
Ortharia
Ortie Lee
Orttie
Orville
Ory
Osa
Oscarine
Oscella
Osceola
Oscie Ola
Oseler
Oseola
Oshell
Osia
Osie
Osie Ola
Osmadel
Ossa
Ossalee
Ossie
Otelia
Ote
Otelia Viviette
Otelia Zenobia
Otella

Otha
Othamae Gillylen
Othela
Othelia
Other Osculate
Other Tennessee
Othneil
Otie Reese
Otilie
Otillia
Ottice
Ottie
Ottalee Allonia
Ounilda
Ouida
Our Nora Crawford
Oval
Ovaltine
Ovein
Ovene
Overdis
Overflow
Oveta
Ovetta
Ovide
Owena
Ozana
Ozane
Ozela
Ozell
Ozell Brassel
Ozella
Ozelle
Ozemaid
Ozena Lee
Ozena
Ozene
Ozetta
Ozias
Ozie
Ozola
Ozora
Paceline Rosimae
     Mazore
Palastine
Palestine
Palhi
Pallee Goings
Pallie
Pally
Palmolive Jones
Palmyra
Paloma Jones

Index of Unusual Names

516

Index of Unusual Names

Index of Unusual Names

Render Rosser	Rhymie	Roma
Rene	Rica	Romaine
Reneer	Richard Arthur Jackson	Romelia
Remer	Jr.	Rometa
Remesba	Richardine	Romie Darling
Renetta	Richetta	Romlee
Renna	Richidine	Romena
Renova	Rietha Rigna	Rona
Reola	Rilla	Ronetta
Reseda	Rillar	Roralle
Reselle	Rillia	Rorie
Ressie	Rina Walker	Rosabud
Restena	Rissie	Rosabird
Restyne	Rita	Rosada
Reta	Rita Avista	Rosalle Clark
Retha	Rithie	Rosebud
Retha Flowers	Ritta	Rosebud Cafe
Retinelle Odelin	Riva	Rosebud Parrot
Retta La June	Rivanna	Rosea Hubbard
Rettia	Rivilne	Rosella
Reubelle	Rixie	Roselle
Reunice	Roanza	Rosena
Reva	Roba Pedrasa	Rosenia
Revelations	Robbie Edward	Rosetta
Revelia	Robbiesteen	Rosetti
Reversa	Robina	Rosia
Revia	Robenia	Rosilla
Rivian	Robertha	Rosina
Rezalia	Robertine	Rosy
Rezalla	Roberta Lee	Rothenia
Rhea	Robetta	Rothia
Rheba	Robie Lee	Rouesta
Rheola	Robenette	Rovenia
Rhene	Robnett	Rovina
Rheola Vashit	Robnette Patti	Rowena Littlepage
Rheolia	Rochelle	Roxella
Rhetta	Rocity	Roxie
Rhetta Cabrere	Rocksy	Rozelia
Rhina	Roda	Rozell
Rhiner	Rodelia	Rozella
Rhoda	Rodella	Rozelle
Rhoda Mops	Rodessa	Rozena
Rhoke Lipscomb	Roezina	Rozetta
Rhodia	Rogenia Anola	Rozzie
Rhodie	Rogenius	Rubena
Rhodima	Rohalia	Ruberta Calmes
Rhodina	Rohelia	Rubenia
Rholma	Rohninia	Rubina
Rholna	Rolanda	Rubinette
Rhonia	Rolena	Rubirda
Rhunette	Rolla	Rudella
Rhusses	Rollee	Rufa

Index of Unusual Names

Index of Unusual Names

Singing	Stayzola	Synestine
Sinie	Stella St. Cecilia	Synette Johnson
Sirelia	Stellarive	Synolve
Sirlonia	Stephanie	Syphronia
Sis	Steveanna	Syresdo
Sisley	Suarade	Syretha
Sisseretta Tibbedoe	Sudella	Syphillis
Sissie	Sudie	Syvilla
Sister	Suella	Tabbie
Sister Canada	Sugar	Taber
Sivolia	Sugar Pie	Tabitha
Sizzie	Sugartea Johnson	Tack
Smella Brownridge	Sula	Talitha
Smiley	Sulouise	Tallie
Smithie	Summer Butter	Talulah
Snobia	Summit County Bell	Taluta Mae Duckett
Snola	Sumptie Leonard	Tama
Snowdie Moore	Sunbeam Susniches	Tamar
Snowie Belle	Sunie	Tamer
Snowdrift	Sunny	Tammel
Snowdrop	Sunray	Tamzie
Snow Drop	Sunshine	Tango
Snowflake	Superior Calculator	Tannie
Snowrilla	Supreme	Tansy
Sociamelia	Supremia	Tanzie
Soda	Surderia	Tanzy
Solitude	Surener	Tara
Sollie	Surgest	Tarba
Soloda Young	Surice	Taretha
Solomie	Surilla	Tarquera
Solonia	Susannah	Tarsher
Solottie	Susibelle	Tatie
Sonnette Hughes	Susiella	Taz
Sonoma	Sussie	Te Bertha
Sonora Queen Ester	Susue	Teacake
Sophenia	Suvenna	Tearo
Sophia	Suzene	Teasie
Sophialea	Swannie	Tecora
Sophie	Sweet	Teddie
Sophronia	Sweet Blossom	Tedia
Sorrow Frusteri	Sweet Honey	Tedie Obelia
Sovina	Sweet Pea	Teena
Spicey	Sweet Potato Emmeline	Teenie
Spicy Fudge	Sweet Piccolo	Telia
Sree	Sweet Thing	Telitha
St. Anastasis	Sweet Violet	Tella
St. Cecelia Asnea	Sweetie	Teller Story
Staffie	Sweetie Goode	Telsee
Stafine	Syhel	Temp
Stanley (Nuckalls)	Sylvania	Tempey
Starchy	Sylxia	Tempia
State	Symora	Tempie
Stately	Synesta	Tempy

Index of Unusual Names

Tena	Theosodosia Elmira	Tomie Dee
Tencie	Theossa	Tomma Cobbs
Teneola	Thersa L. Cuffee	Tommey
Tenia	(Archer)	Tommie
Tenna	Thersia	Tommielil Odessa
Tennessee	Theresita	Tommisteen
Tennie	Thessolonia Roton	Tommy
Tenola	Thessia	Tomorra
Tenolia Ryan	Thessolonia Roton	Tompie
Tensie	Thetis Phrisell	Too Sweet
Teola	Thisby	Tootsie
Tera	Thomasena	Tootsie Burford
Te-ready-be	Thomasina	Top Knot
Teretha	Thomasine	Topaz
Terrecita	Thomisena	Topie
Teriessetta	Thongual	Topsie
Terine	Thoolene	Topsy
Tero	Thoralee	Torris
Teska	Thressiadel	Tossie
Tessie	Thursa	Tots
Tettie	Thyra	Tottie
Tex	Tilda	Toy Kidd
Texana	Tildy	Trandaler
Texas	Tilena	Trannie Mae
Texie	Tilla	Traversia
Textie	Timezena	Treasie
Thaddenia	Timma	Treasure
Thalia	Timpie Brooks	Tredda
Thamar McGhee	Tina	Trelaly
Thay Myrtle	Tinea	Trelawney Lonzetta
Thea Arnetta	Tinie	Tremetria
Theatis	Tinnie	Tremilla
Theatrice	Tinsa	Trendenner
Theda Bara	Tinsey	Treophia
Thedith Nita	Tiny	Treopia
Thela	Tiny House	Tressa
Thelga	Tiny Small	Tressie
Thelassie	Tisha Brooks	Trilla Walker
Thella	Tisher	Trinket
Thenis	Tissie	Trithemia
Thenie	Tissue	Troas
Theodocia	Tiverna	Trojia
Theodora	Tizzer	Trudelle
Theodosia	Toadva	Trudie
Theodrous	Tobie	Trudy
Theola	Tobitha	True Love
Theola Aleathia	Toddles	True Love (Smothers)
Theola Orealis	Tomasena	Truelove
Theolia	Tomasina	Truly
Theolina	Tomasine	Truly White
Theopocis	Tomasino	Truzella
Theora	Tomasitta	Truzelle
		Try-em-and-See

Index of Unusual Names

Tryphenlous Elizabeth	Valaska	Veatrice
Tryphene	Valda	Vee
Tryphrenise	Valedia	Veda
Tula	Valeira	Vedie
Tumeloin	Valencia	Vedva
Tumps	Valenda	Veldora
Tuna Barnes	Valentine	Velencia
Tunie Burns	Valera	Vella
Turalee	Valeria	Velleen
Tureenis	Valerie	Velsoria
Tusie	Valetta Allen	Velva Jean
Tweedie	Valina	Velvet
Tweety	Valisha	Velvo
Twila	Vallena	Velzora
Twilda	Vallie	Venay
Twinella	Valine	Vendetta
Tynie	Valonys	Vendura
Tyra	Valzora	Venella
Tyrie	Vanda	Veneller
Uab	Vandelia	Venera
Udoxie	Vandella	Veneria
Ulac	Vandola	Venetta
Ulebelle	Vandor	Venoris
Ullias	Vandora	Venus
Ulo Bobo	Vanela Adams	Veola
Uloise	Vanella	Veorah
Ulsee Germany	Vanetta	Verbia
Ulystine	Vanilla	Verda Mae
Una	Vannie	Verdee
Undine	Vantella	Verdell
Uniska	Vanzie	Verdelle
Unite	Variah	Verdery
Ura	Varina Road	Verdie
Urada	Varresse	Verdine
Uralee	Vasco	Verdra
Ursal Graspard	Vaseline	Verenous
Ursaline	Vaseline Malaria	Vergia
Ursula	Vaseline Rosa	Verla
Urusha Henrietta	Vashti	Verlalia
Utah	Vashti Jacinta	Verlee
Utensil	Vassar	Verlenia
Uterina	Vassie	Verlie
Uvula	Vastie	Verline
Uxenia Beryl	Vastine	Verian Christian
Uzee Tecomia	Vaudelle	Verily
Vacilla Poe	Vaytaslau	Verm
Vada	Vazelle	Verma
Vadies	Ve-Ella	Vermaline
Vagina	Ve Esta	Vermell
Vainey	Ve Esta Izella	Vernal Bishop
Val Lola	Vea	Vernandia
Valader	Veagelee	Verneka

Index of Unusual Names

Vernesse	Villa Eleta	Vonder
Verneda	Villa Lilla	Vonie
Verneeda	Viletta	Vonzella Cobb
Vernell	Villie	Vossie
Vernella	Villora	Votie
Vernelle	Vina	Vouncie
Vernessa	Vincenta	Vulina Villere
Vernetta	Vine	Vunies
Vernetta Magaline	Veneda	Vynetta
Verniat	Vinella	Vyrle Paris
Vernice	Viney	Wacile
Vernola	Viney Fields	Wahlena
Verona	Vinia	Walenia
Veronica	Vinicia	Waltena
Versa	Vinie	Wanda Lee
Versie	Vinnie	Wander
Vertella	Vinola	Wandy Lee
Vertelle	Vinus	Wanza
Vertie (Ven)	Viny	Wardelle
Vertille	Violetta	Wardene
Vertlee	Violet Ray	Warm
Vertrelle	Viole Barele Little	Warrena
Vestage	Vibeteen Victoria	Wattie
Vester	Virdas	Wavalee
Vesteria	Virdee	Wealthy
Vestora	Virdelia	Weeder
Veta	Virgie Lee	Weenie
Vhaness Eulalia	Virgil	Weeta
Vi Siba	Virgin	Weetha
Viana	Virgin Gentile	Welcome
Vianna	Virgin Mary	Welcome Good
Vibe	Virgin Moses	Wellena
Vic	Virginia Dace	Wenonah
Vice	Virginial	Werda
Vicie	Virgis	Wessie
Vick	Virlee	Westina
Victerine Quille	Virlie	Wheirda Mae
Victoria Delgrotia	Virtile	Wheirmelda
Victorice	Virtle Tene	Whelma
Victorine	Virtula	White Olive Branch
Victory	Vistula Hughes	Whitlene
Victrola	Vitamine	Whurria
Victrola Valentine	Vitaminye Murphy	Wida B. Hansome
Vida	Vitree	Wilberetta
Videl	Vitula	Wildetta Allien
Videlle	Viva Tryphina	Wildie
Videllia	Vivanene	Wiletta
Vidie	Vivilora	Wilhelma
Vienna	Viviolora	Wilhelmina
Viessa	Vizella	Wilhemenia
Vileria	Volena	Willa (Egberta)
Villa	Vonciel	Willa Wybee

Index of Unusual Names

Willadean Evans	Xavia	Zelpha
Willafred	Xenia	Zelta
Willene	Ximina	Zema
Willetta	Yanikae	Zemoria
Willia Silone	Yancienna Louise Perry	Zena
William	Yandell	Zenaby
Willianna	Yannzil	Zenis
Willie Jennings Bryant	Yetine	Zenobia
Williette	Yolande	Zenola
Willis	Yolenda	Zenolia
Willive	You Doll Perkins	Zeola
Willo Dean	Yours	Zeonbia
Willodess	Youree	Zepher Brown
Willodine	Ysabell	Zephenora
Willola	Frochlictistein	Zepherine
Willow Mae	Yvone	Zephia
Willya Sareta	Yvette Vereda	Zephria
Wilmenia	Zada	Zephys
Wilona	Zaddie	Zephyr Oretha
Wilphria	Zadie	Zepna
Wilsie	Zady	Zeporah
Wilzetta	Zadye	Zera
Winnie	Zalphan	Zerelda
Winnifay	Zana	Zerilda
Winona	Zanie	Zerlena
Winsel	Zannie	Zerline
Winsie	Zdara	Zernona
Winstona	Zeater	Zestell Neals
Wittonia	Zebedia	Zeta
Wodia	Zebede Knight	Zetha
Womangal	Zedda	Zettie
Wonderful	Zeffera	Zezebel
Woodia	Zeffie	Zidia
Woodie Fields	Zelda	Zidie
Woody	Zeldabelle	Zil
Worcester	Zeldar	Zilla
Wordie	Zeldia Perry	Zillah
Worthie	Zelean	Zillary
Wortie	Zelene	Zillie
Wormalee	Zelfia	ZilPha
Wottie	Zelia	Zilphie
Wrennie	Zelicia Cobb	Zilplyon
Wretha	Zeline	Zle Eggleston
Wylean (Montegromery)	Zelinor Wade	Zion
Wylena	Zell	Zipporah
Wylene	Zella	Zodiabelle
Wyllia	Zellean	Zodie
Wylona	Zellena	Zola
Wymon	Zelleni	Zoline
Wyneona	Zelma	Zollie
Wynetka	Zelna	Zona
Wynonia	Zelona	Zora

Index of Unusual Names

Zorato	Zula	Zurlene Zucker
Zore	Zulene Zucker	Zxlema Berryissa
Zorie Battie	Zuline	Zylpha
Zuella Savoy	Zuora	

White Males

Aaron	Alpa	Ariel
Abe	Alpheus	Aril
Abe Winkle	Alphonse	Aris
Abijah	Alphonso	Arkansas
Abraham	Alpine	Arkie
Abram	Alter	Arlie
Absolom	Alto	Arlo
Ace	Altona	Armand
Acey	Alvah	Armie
Achilles	Alvan	Arnel
Acie Lacey	Alver	Arnie
Acquilla	Alvie	Arno
Acree	Alvin	Arrie
Acy	Alvis	Arromanus
Ad	Alvy	Arsemus
Adna	Am	Artemus
Adolphus	Amalves	Artie
Adoniram	Amagus	Artis
Adron	Amedie	Aruna
Adrown Athins	Americus	Arvid
Agee	Amon	Arvie
Agens	Ancel	Arvil
Alabama	Ancelan	Arvine
Alaska	Ancil	Arzo
Albin	Ander	Asa
Albra	Andral	Asbill
Albro	Andre	Ashal
Alcander	Andrew Jackson	Ashamed
Alcide	Angelo	Ashira
Aldo	Anselm	Astroin
Aldophus	Antone	Athel
Alex	Antonia	Ather
Alexis	Antonio	Athol
Aljo	Anvil	Atlas
Allie	Aquilla	Atticus
Allone	Aran	Athel
Alma Puckett	Archelaus	Aube
Almon	Archelles	Aubin
Almond	Archillis	Audie Pennington
Almos	Ardis	August
Almus	Arengus	Aundee
Almyra	Argo	Aus
Alney	Argie	Ausmon
Alonza	Argyle	Aut
Aloysius	Arial	Autey

Index of Unusual Names

Index of Unusual Names

Index of Unusual Names

Du Val	Elm	Esker
Duff K. Cox	Elmo	Esso
Duffel	Elmou	Estee
Duffie	Elmus	Estus
Duffy	Elonza	Ethaney B. Egger
Dugger	Elphra	Ethelred
Duke	Elrie Brown	Etol
Duluth	Elroy	Etowah
Dumah	Elvie	Etral
Dunk Hemby	Elvis	Eudelle
Durie	Elvon	Euel
Dutch	Elza	Eulan
Dyce	Elzey Pope	Eule
Ealy	Elzie	Euley
Earlie	Elzy	Eulie
Early	Em	Eulis
Earon	Emanuel	Eulon
Earvan	Emel	Euly
Eason	Emelious	Eunon
Eaves	Emil	Eural
Eben	Emile	Eureka
Echo	Emilius	Euriah
Echols	Emit	Eutha
Ededin	Emlo	Evander
Edfert	Emmanuel	Everion
Edon	Emmette	Evon
Edries	Emperor	Ewel
Edwon	Emrie	Ewell
Eel	English	Exa
Efton	Enid	Exam
Egie	Ennis	Exey
Einar	Enoch	Exie
Either	Enos	Ezekiel
El Caney	Enrique	Ezra
Elam	Enzo	Fabian
Elbee	Ephraim	Fabious
Elder Dodson	Ephy	Fain Pink
Eldno	Era	Fairest
Elexis	Erasmus	Famon
Elgar	Erastus	Fance
Elgey	Erato	Fate
Eli	Erb	Fater
Elias	Erbie	Fendol
Elijah	Erby	Ferdi
Elisha	Erdice	Ferdie
Elistus	Eris	Fernando
Ell	Erlie	Fernie
Ellerlee	Ervell	Ferreol
Ellie	Ervil	Fes
Ellmaevous	Esca	Festus Wheeler
Ellonine	Escar	Ficken
Elly	Esco	Fidella

Index of Unusual Names

Filetus	Gensie	Hans
Finas Wooten	George Washington	Happy
Finfred	Gerd	Hapsey Hoover
Finis	Gerry	Harle
Flagus Ausborn	Gettis	Harlee
Flake	Gervaise	Haroland
Flanery Satter	Gevin	Harlos
Flare	Gid	Harva
Fleet	Gideon	Harvel
Fletcher Dickle	Gideons	Hastel
Flinn	Gilcin	Haven
Flint	Gillam	Havie
Florian	Gillian	Havis
Floy	Gillie	Haymon
Foi	Girthie	Haze
Fonds Wilbanks	Given	Hazzy
Fonza	Givens Hornsby	Healon
Fortune	Givezester	Heard
Fount	Glathan	Hebe
Fountain	Glendy	Hector
Foy	Glinn	Heinie
France	Goah	Heman
Francis Zavier	Gola	Hence
Frankie	Gonde	Henry Clay
Franklin Roosevelt	Goza	Henry Grady
Frantz	Gratis	Herbert Spencer
French	Greek	Hercules
Frenchie	Griff	Herlong
Frontis	Grover Cleveland	Hermus
Gabe	Guedon	Hero
Gailor Curtis	Guido	Heubel
Gallie	Guion	Hezekiah
Ganus	Gulian	Hezron
Gar	Gully	Hezzie
Gardelle	Gurley	Hi
Garden	Gurlie	Hiawatha
Garland	Guss	Hick McClanahan
Garien	Gussy	Hickory
Garnol	Gust	Hie
Garrie Lee	Gusta	High-Pockets
Gartine	Gustaf	Hilah
Gasaway	Gustan	Hilary
Gassie	Gustave	Hillrie
Gathra	Gustavus Adolphus	Hill
Gavil	Guy	Hilmar
Gay V. Conner	Gynne	Himsell
Gayle	Hadwin	Hinchie
Gaylor	Hadgarwan Tripp	Hobbie
Gedney	Halcon	Hodby
Gelo	Hallum	Hogrefe
General	Haman	Hoke
Genio	Hance	Holdutch

Index of Unusual Names

Holland	Jabus	Julese
Hollice	Jac	Julus
Honey-Waites	Jace	Jumell
Horan Powell	Jack Dempsey	June
Hosea	Jacques	Junie
Hosia	James Pershing	Junior
Hosmer	Jamis	Junius
Hoss	Jan	Justice
Hoy	Jap	Justino
Hoyt	Jarmie	Justus
Hub	Jason	Kaga
Huck	Jay	Kaleb
Huel	Jay Gould	Karin
Hugo	Jay Tee	Karvin
Hulet	Jefferson Davis	Kaybon
Hulette Noah	Jehu	Kedar Miller
Hulow	Jeller	Keeble
Huss	Jentry	Kell
Hydie	Jep	Keren
Hyle	Jepsy	Kersine
Hymie	Jeptha	Ketto
Iber	Jere	Kish
Idalo	Jeremiah	Kile
Iddo	Jess Willard	Killis
Idis	Jet	Kimber
Ignacie	Jeter	Kincer
Ignatius	Jethro	Kinch Exum Jr.
Ike	Jett	King
Iloff	Jettie	King David Sullivan
Iloah	Joab	Kip
Inus	Jobie	Kirt
Inzer	Jock	Kiser
Iram	Jodie	Kitt
Irbing	Joffre Pershing	Kleber
Ire	John Alden	Koith
Ireaneus	John Jacob Astor	Kolie
Ireland	John Milton	Kope
Isaac	John Randolph	Koran
Isadore	John Wesley	Kosey
Isaiah	Jonah	Krank
Isham	Jonce	Kreel Hopper
Isiah	Jose	Kusher
Isidore	Josh	La Clede
Israel	Joshiah	La Monte
Ivan	Joshua	La Verne
Ivie	Josiah	Laban
Ivy	Jonett	Label
Jabe	Jubal	Lablon
Jabes	Jude	Labon
Jabeus	Judge	Laddie
Jabez	Jule	Ladislav
		Lafayette

Index of Unusual Names

Lafe	Lessier	Luman
Lake	Lethur	Lummie
Lally	Levi	Lundy
Lamb	Levis	Lunus
Lance	Levo	Lurid
Lancelot	Levy	Lussie
Lando	Lexie	Lyda
Lanie	Libon	Lynt
Lanoyd	Lieutelle	Lysses
Lath	Lige	Macagal
Lathaddious T. Copelan	Lightning	Mace
Latona	Liku	Macel
Lattie	Liliburn Wilbanks	Madvell
Laurie	Lilius	Magness
Lavarius	Lindberg	Magnus
Lavelle	Linder	Major
Lavertice	Lindy	Malachi
Lavoisuer	Linnie	Malee
Law	Linus	Malen
Lawtis	Lion	Mallie
Laxie	Lish	Matter
Layel	Loather	Manah
Lazard	Loice	Manilla
Lazarus	Lom	Manin
Le Corte	Lomie	Manly
Le Garde	Lon	Mannie
Le Roy	Lon Garus	Manzie
Le Vere	Lonas	Marce
Leaketh	London	Marcel
Leander	Loney	Marcell
Leaser	Lonie	Marcelle
Lebe	Lonnie	Marcellus
Lecie	Lony	Marcus
Lecil	Looney	Mario
Leck	Lorie	Marius
Ledyard Vaughan	Lorin	Marne
Leibun	Lorne	Marte
Leize	Loron	Martin Luther
Lelio	Lot	Marvilee
Lem	Lottie	Marzine
Lemon	Loucious	Mathias
Len	Love	Mauldin
Lenia	Lovick	Maunsel
Leniel	Low	Mavice
Leno	Loyal	Maxino
Lent	Loyce	McKinley
Leoline	Lubie	Meador
Leonidas	Lucious	Medie
Lencio	Luck	Mefrin
Leriol	Luckey	Mel
Leron	Luckie	Mell
Lessey	Lum	Melvan

Index of Unusual Names

Melvin	Murgar	Odus
Melzar	Myra	Oertel
Menanda	Myron	Offa
Menarda	Nando	Ogie
Menza	Napoleon	Ohio
Meral	Napoleon Bonaparte	Olaf
Merel	Narvin	Olee
Meron	Nath	Olice
Mert	Navel	Olin
Mertie Brasher	Nay Lee	Ollest
Mertis	Nebraska	Ollie
Met	Neddo	Ollie Ambrose
Mettie	Nemo	Oma
Meubern	Neo	Omar
Mexie	Neptune	Omega
Micajah	Netrell	Omer
Milas	Nette	Omri
Milam	Newbell	Onan
Mildin	Nezzie	Oness
Milledge	Nias	Onie
Millwee	Nicolaos	Ools
Milo	Nim	Ople
Milosh	Nimrod	Oral
Mindorse	Ninevah	Oran
Miner	Nivars	Orange Scofield
Mingle	Noah	Orby
Minick	Noah Webster	Ord
Mink-eye	Nobie	Oren
Minor	Noble	Orel
Minous	Noel	Oreste
Minus	Nollie	Orgie
Minviah	None	Orie
Mirileau	Nonie	Oriel
Moe	Normal	Orien
Moise	Norval	Orion
Monica	Norvelle	Oris
Monte	Nuell	Orlan
Montezz	Numa	Orlando
Montie	Oarly	Orlo
Montreal	Obadiah	Oroon
Mood	Obed	Orpha
Moragne	Obeddoe	Orral
Mord	Obediah	Orrie
Mordecai	Obie	Orris
Mordie	Obry	Ortie
Mortie	Oce	Ortiz
Mosco	Ocie	Orus
Moscoe	Ocram	Orval
Mose	Octavius Gaddy	Orvell
Moses	Odelle	Orvis
Motry	Oder	Osbie
Mundy	Odie	

Index of Unusual Names

Osce	Philemon	Raub
Osceola	Phillipa	Readus
Osey	Philomena	Reagon
Osteen	Phineas	Reb
Ostell	Pichegru	Rector
Osye	Pick	Red
Otha	Piercy	Reedy
Othal	Pierre	Refo
Othel	Pincus	Regga
Othello	Pink	Reggie
Other	Pinkie	Reguile
Othmiel	Plato	Reh
Otho	Pleas	Rem
Othor	Pleasant	Remer
Ottia	Pliny	Remi
Ottmar	Plum	Remus
Otus	Poke	Rene
Ovid	Poley	Reno
Ovis	Polie	Respess
Oyer	Pompeo	Restees
Oza	Porcher	Reufine
Ozern	Postelle	Revis
Ozie	Potice	Rhomell
Ozmus	Powhatan	Rile Rooks
Ozy	Pride	Rimmer
Ozzie	Prieth	Rinaldo
Pardue	Prime	Roamie
Paris	Primus	Robert E. Lee
Parlie	Prince	Robin Weaver
Parmalee	Promeathus	Roby
Partee	Ptolemy	Rocie
Pascal	Purlee	Roco
Paschal	Pyron	Roddy
Pasco	Quay	Roelof
Pasquale	Quillin	Rollie
Patrus	Quin	Rolling Stone
Pearl	Quince	Rollo
Peak	Quint	Rolly
Pearre	Quintus	Romaine
Ped	Rabon	Roman
Pedro	Rainy	Romeo
Pee Wee	Ralsa	Romie
Penland	Ralston	Romuel
Pennie	Ramelle	Romulus
Pera	Ramie	Romus
Perk	Rance	Ronice
Perley	Ransom	Rooney
Perrigene Evelyn	Raphael	Roosevelt
Pershing	Ras	Rosendo
Petrons	Rashnel	Roupen
Pharris	Rasho	Royal
Philander	Rastus	Royd

Rozzel
Rozzie
Rube
Ruel
Rufus
Rush Smith
Russian
Russie
Sabin
Sailor
St. Elmo
St. John
St. Pierre
St. Piere
Salathiel Hollingsworth
Salvador
Salvatore
Samp
Sampson
Sandy
Sank
Saul
Saverino
Savoy
Schabil
Schooler
Scottie
Scutter
Seab
Seabron
Seavy
Sebe
Sebron
Secar
Seck
Seelye
Self
Seisel
Selix
Senate
Seraphim
Serbetus
Sereno
Shade
Sharon
Shed
Sherlock Holmes
Shier
Shines
Shiprah
Shire
Shirl

Shivers
Shoal
Shorty
Shula Lawrence
Sig
Sim
Simeon
Simmie Witt
Singer
Sion
Slee
Smiley
Socrates
Soggie
Sol
Sol Moog
Solomon
Solon
Son
Sonny
Sonny Boy
Soonny
Speed
Spires
Spivey
Spurgeon
Spurgeon Bonaparte
Square Vinton
Squire
Starlie
Starling
Steely
Stonewall
Stonewall Jackson
Stork
Sug
Summey
Sy
Taft
Taft, W. H.
Tampa
Tandy
Tanzie
Tarver
Tasso
Tate
Tavelyon
Te-Wyatt
Teague
Teddis
Teeps
Tenny

Tera
Terrace
Texas
Tharion
Tharon D. Edgewarth
Thea
Thears
Theoler
Theophilus
Theopolis
Therman
Thermon
Theron
Therron
Thetus
Theus
Thomas Jefferson
Thomas Nelson Page
Thomasian Cady
Tiffen
Tip
Tippie
Tivey
Tobe
Tobey
Tobias
Tobin
Toby
Toccoah
Toe-ax
Toledo
Tolly
Toofie
Toxey
Toy
Tracie
Trammel
Treber
Trez
Trice
Trinidad
Troad
Trois
Trosper
Troup
Trox
Troy
Troye
Truette
Truman
Truss
Truxton

Index of Unusual Names

Tuccoah	Veit Avil	Waddie
Tuckey	Velatta	Wade
Tull	Velatti	Waitus
Tullis	Veldon	Waitzel
Tully Thornbrough	Veljean	Waldemar
Tuney	Venancio	Wales
Turley Pincard	Venda	Wallend
Blackstone	Venice	Walter Scott
Tyne	Veo	Wash
Tyras	Verdie	Washington Irving
Tyre	Verdis	Wave
Tyree	Verelle	Weeber
Tyrus	Verl	Weems
Ual	Verlie	Welch
Ubie	Verna Pruitt	Welcome
Udelle	Verne	Weltz
Ulain	Verner	Welzie
Ular Gilbert	Verne	Wendell Holmes
Ulie	Vernie	Wetlie
Ulis	Versie Luke	Whetstone
Ulmo	Ves(t)	Whirley
Ulrick	Vesta	Wice
Ulysses	Vestal	Wig
Uphire	Vestel	Willied
Ural	Vester	Wiltz
Urath	Vestis	Windom
Urban	Vetall	Wingo
Uriah	Vetol	Wishard
Urie	Vezzie	Wistar
Urquhart	Victor Emmanuel	Woodie
Urvire	Victor Hugo	Woodrow Wilson
Usher	Villie Pique Shivers	Woody
Vadis	Vim	Word
Val	Vines	Worth
Valda	Vineyard	Worthin
Valdee	Virdel	Wray
Valden	Virgie	Wroe
Valentine	Virgil	Wyvurn
Valgean	Virgis	Yale
Valorous	Voen	Yankee
Valve	Void Null	Youles
Vanderbilt	Vol	Yuille
Vanard	Volney	Zachariah
Vanezzer	Vonceil	Zachrias
Varie	Vondas	Zack
Varley	Vonell	Zary
Varon	Vonnie	Zash
Vasco	Vonno	Zavel
Vasil	Voy	Zearl
Vascoe	Voyd	Zeb
Vassen	Vulard	Zebbie
Veatch	Vydell	Zebedee Nabors

Index of Unusual Names

Zebulon	Zemmie	Zid
Zeddie	Zenas	Zinn
Zedekiah	Zenno	Ziv
Zedic	Zeno	Zoar
Zedie Satter	Zenoph	Zoe
Zelsa	Zenus	Zollie
Zell	Zeo	Zolly
Zelle	Zeph	Zolomon
Zellick	Zeron	Zotas
Zem	Zerrel	Zuscha
Zema	Zethus	Zygfried

White Females

Abertine	Albertina	Almeda
Abiah	Albur	Almena
Abiatha	Alda	Almeta
Abigail	Aldah	Almira
Abigal	Aldine	Alneta
Abera	Aleaner	Aloris
Abrena	Aleitha	Alpha
Absye	Alema	Alpharetta
Adda	Alemie	Alpheus
Addill	Alesa	Alphia
Addilou	Aleta	Alta
Adeen	Aletha	Altha
Adene	Alethea	Althea
Adeon	Alethia	Altie
Aderade	Alexandra	Alto
Adgie	Alexia	Alst
Adiabelle	Alfaretta	Alva
Adiva	Alfie	Alvena
Adolphine	Alfrances	Alvah
Adrenna	Alfreda	Alvenia
Adrian	Alfredina	Alvertine
Adriana	Algeria	Alvina
Adris	Algia	Alyn
Aenard	Alida	Alyne
Aeria	Alieze	Alzerine
Agatha	Alisa	Alzie
Agnold	Alisia	Alzona
Ahava	Alita	Ama
Ahma	Alledes	Amanda
Ahrenna	Allee	Amandtine
Aili	Allefair	Amarinthia
Aina	Allena	Amazon
Aimee	Alletha	Amber
Aire	Allue	Ambra
Ala	Allyn	Amcely
Alacoque	Almalene	Amelia
Alazanah	Almaretta	America
Alba	Almarine	Americus

Index of Unusual Names

Amil	Arlita	Austelle
Amilee	Armanda	Australia
Amina	Armenia	Authena
Ammie	Armie	Ava
Amoree	Army	Avaha
Amret	Arnette	Avalee
Anastalia	Arnie	Avaline
Antasia	Aroezena	Avalon
Ancie	Aronell	Avella
Andra	Arrie	Avice
Andre	Arris	Avie
Andrea	Arsenah	Avil
Andreinna	Atta	Avis
Andrina	Artamesia	Avise
Andromedia	Artelia	Avo
Aner	Artemesia	Avonel
Angela	Arthemise	Avonia
Angele	Artie	Avra
Angelle	Artis	Azalea
Angelo	Aruelle	Azalee
Angelus	Arvonia	Azaline
Angie	Ary	Azie
Anjadell	Arystine	Azilee
Annas	Arzanna	Azzie
Annill	Arzula	Babe
Annulette	Asalee	Babette
Anos	Aselee	Baby
Anthesia	Asia	Balzora
Anulee	Asie	Bama
Aquilla	Astrid	Bamma
Ara	Atha	Barb
Arabella	Athalia	Barney
Arca	Athalie	Barrier
Archia	Athelene	Bartee
Ardecia	Athelin	Bartie
Ardelia	Athens	Bartow
Ardella	Athma	Basha
Ardene	Atossa	Baydie
Ardesia	Atta Ruth	Bazetis
Ardia	Attant	Bea
Ardis	Attie	Beachy
Areminta	Aubie	Bealie
Aretta	Aubra	Beauty
Argie	Audice	Bee
Argine	Audie	Bela
Arianna	Audley	Belma
Arie	Audrene	Belva
Arietta	Audrin	Bena
Arilla	Auline	Benita
Arizola	Aulsie	Bennie
Arizona	Aunala	Benola
Arkansas	Auriebell	Bennola

Index of Unusual Names

Bera	Blunnie	Candace
Berdie	Bob	Candia
Berdye	Bobbie	Cannie
Berma	Bobby	Capitola
Bernadette	Bobbye	Cappita
Bernadine	Bonetta	Cappie
Bernedene	Bonita	Carese
Bernie	Bonnie	Carfy
Bershe	Bonny	Caria
Berta	Bonnylee	Carlee
Bertia	Brazalee	Carlene
Bertie	Brenelle	Carlos
Bertis	Brezelia	Carlota
Berto	Bricie	Carmel
Besma	Briddie	Carmela
Bethel	Bright	Carmelita
Bethenie	Brina	Carmelite
Betheny	Brittie	Carnele
Betra	Bromah	Carnie
Beuria	Bronnie	Caro
Bevie	Brownie	Caro-Beth
Bexie	Brunie	Carola
Bicie	Bryettie	Carole
Biddie	Brejetty	Carolee
Biffle	Buena	Carulee
Bigamy	Buna	Carrie
Billie	Bune	Cassandra
Billy	Bunnie	Cascilla
Billie Burke	Burdette	Cassie
Billy Burke	Burma	Cassy
Bina	Burmah	Cat
Binah	Butroyce	Cattie
Birca	Butys	Cecetia
Birda	Byra	Cecil
Birdie	Byrdie	Cele
Birdiejell	Cabelle	Celena
Birma	Cadence	Celesta
Birmah	Cajetine	Celestia
Birtie	Calara Swansy	Celine
Bitsy	Caldonia	Celuma
Blannie	Caledonia	Ceola
Bleaca	Calene	Champia
Bleba	Caley	Channa
Blenie	Calista	Charity
Bliss	Callie Cloud	Charlene
Bloma	Calola	Charles
Blondelle	Camielle	Charlette
Blondie	Camilla	Charlie
Blondina	Camille	Charline
Bloom	Cammie	Charm
Blooma	Cammille	Chatnee
Blumie	Canada	Chebie

Index of Unusual Names

Index of Unusual Names

Index of Unusual Names

Elodie	Erla	Eupha
Elowea	Erladean	Euphania
Elphia	Ermile	Euphemia
Elphie	Ermine	Euphemie
Elspeth	Erminie	Eura
Elta	Erna	Eurena
Elthalia	Erroldine	Eusie
Eltine	Ersula	Eutropia
Elton	Erta	Evalena
Elva	Erva	Eve
Elvane	Eryth	Evell
Elvera	Escue	Evelle
Elvira	Esseline	Evene
Elviretta	Essie	Ever
Elvis	Estamae	Evetta
Elvise	Estie	Evie
Elvita	Estma	Exa
Elvy	Estoria	Exer
Elwa	Etha	Exie
Elzetta	Etheldra	Exielee
Elzona	Ethelvest	Exum
Emajean	Ethelwyn	Ezzie
Emarie	Ethelyne	Faby
Emerald	Ethelynn	Fairest
Emergine	Ethie	Fairy
Emile	Etholene	Faith
Emilia	Etoy	Falbia
Emmagene	Etruila	Falkia Diligence
Emmaline	Etruria	Fallie
Emogene	Ettie	Fanellen
Emola	Ettrall	Fanie
Emozene	Etty	Fannalee
Ena	Eucese	Fanneylu
Enal	Eudeana	Fanola
England	Eudena	Farra
Enid	Eudelle	Fate
Enise	Eudora	Fathie
Ennes	Euell	Faustine
Ennie	Eufaula	Faytie
Ennis	Eulah	Felcia
Enola	Eulala	Felicia
Eolian	Eulalia	Felma
Eolion	Eulalie	Felta
Epatha	Eulanie	Fena
Eppie	Eulatie	Fenny
Epsie	Eulaween	Feral
Era	Eulila	Fern
Erah	Eulis Delk	Ferna-Faye
Erdeal	Eulo	Fernande
Erika	Eumice	Fielda
Eris	Euna	Filie
Eritta	Eunie	Fillette

Index of Unusual Names

Finnetta	Freidi	Glenda
Finnie	Freva	Glendora
Flavia	Froella	Glenoris
Flavil	Fronia	Glycine
Fleda	Fronnie	Glynda
Flemma	Fuchsia	Golda
Fleta	Gabie	Golden
Fletta	Gabrella	Goldia
Fleurette	Gabriella	Goldie
Flewellyn	Gail	Gomeria
Floe	Gaithel	Gowdylook
Flonie	Ganell	Grace Flowers
Flordie	Garcia	Gratia
Floread	Garlande	Gretha
Floreid	Gatsye	Grosie
Floreine	Gay	Grussie
Florene	Gayril	Guessela
Floria	Gazette	Gussie
Florian	Gelatina	Guynelle
Florice	Geline	Gwendoyn
Florida	Genell	Gwennie
Floride	Genesta	Gyphene
Floriede	Genevia	Gypsy
Florie	Gennelle	Habbo Hanna
Florien	Gennevine	Hails
Florine	Genoa	Hallie
Florita	George	Halycon France
Florrie	Georgebell	Hanna
Flossie	Georgenia	Hannah
Floy	Georgie	Hannie
Fluiter	Gera	Hanora
Flute	Geral Dean	Hanoria
Fonda	Gerda	Hapsey
Fonella	Germaine	Harmel
Fontella	Gerome	Haroldine
Fontelle	Gerry	Harrydele
Foresteen	Gertha	Harryette
Fortuna	Gertie	Haseltine
Fostine	Gesina	Hassel
Francelia	Giagur	Hasseltine
Francesca	Gilley	Hassie
Frank	Gillie	Hassierne
Frankelene	Gincy	Hastine
Frankie	Ginia	Hazie
Frazier	Gippie	Hedda
Freda	Giralda	Hennie
Fredanna	Glad Tydings	Henri
Freddie	Gladiola	Hepsie
Frederica	Glarene	Hermie
Fredericka	Glata	Hermine
Freddie	Glatha	Hermoine
Freeda	Glencie	Hessie

Index of Unusual Names

Hethie	Indiana	Jeddie
Hettilu	Inee	Jeffie
Hilah	Ineith	Jeilee
Hildrathe	Iness	Jellie
Hildur	Ineta	Jemima
Hildyer	Inetha	Jena
Hilma	Inis	Jenelle
Hilmer	Iola	Jenetta
Hinda	Iona	Jenia
Hira	Iowa	Jenny Wren
Hixie	Iradelle	Jenora
Hollie	Irby	Jere
Honor	Irdelle	Jerene
Hope	Iree	Jerrie
Hulda	Iris	Jerusha
Hutchie	Irley	Jessamine
Hyacinth	Iruena	Jestine
Hypatia	Isadora	Jetta
Iantha	Isala	Jettie
Icey	Isalee	Jewel
Icie	Isla	Jewelene
Icy	Isma	Jhonnie
Icy Ree	Isolene	Jimetta
Icye	Isoline	Jimmie
Idalane	Isophine	Jimmy
Idalene	Istalena	Jodie
Idelia	Italca	Joe
Idella	Ities	Joe Nita
Idelle	Iuka	Joelena
Idena	Iuna	Joella
Iderstine	Iva	Joellen
Idonia	Ivalene	Johness
Idora	Iveene	Johniet
Ignell	Iva	Johnnie
Ika	Ivory	Johnsie
Ila	Ivylyn	Johntie
Ilene	Izella	Jolie
Ileva	Izetta	Jordie
Illa	Izola	Josela
Illeen	Izora	Joseph
Ilma	Jacque	Josia
Ilse	Jacqueline	Jossie
Ima	Jadie	Joueta
Imelda	Jala	Joy
Imena	Jamelle	Juana
Imer	James	Juelda
Imogene	Jamesetta	Jule
Imond	Jamesina	Julie
Ina	Janella	Junnie
Inabeth	Janelle	Juno
Inda	Januaria	Justine
India	Jaxie	Kansas

Index of Unusual Names

Kasimir	Laretto	Lennie
Kassie	Laroma	Lenova
Kathomas	Latishia	Leoline
Katibel	Latrina	Leoma
Katrine	Laudice	Leonida
Katurah	Laudie	Leonie
Keitha	Launa	Leontine
Kella	Lauree	Leoris
Kellah	Laurine	Leose
Kennette	Laurita	Leota
Kerlie	Lavada	Lephe
Kezzie	Lavada Frenchie	Lera
Kibble	Lavella	Lerah
Kimmie	Laverne	Lerline
Kinnie	Laverta	Lerna
Kirke	Lavetra	Lessie
Kissie	Lavina	Lestina
Kizzie	Lavine	Lestle
Klonda	Lavinia	Leta
Kosa	Lavolia	Letha
La Delle	Lavonia	Leth
La Fils	Lavonne	Lethe
La Lelle	Lawlos	Lethea
La Neldo	Lazelle	Lethia
La Nette	Lazile	Letitia
La Perle	Le Claire	Letta
La Rue	Le Noir	Leva
La Vada	Lea	Levada
La Verda	Leanna	Levancie
La Vere	Leano	Levenia
La Verne	Learline	Leventa
La Vida	Leatha	Levie
Laddieree	Leavy	Levina
Ladine	Lecie	Levis
Lady	Lector	Lexey
Lady Bird	Leda	Lexie
Laila	Lee	Lexine
Lala	Leeda	Liberia
Lalage	Leelia	Liberty
Lalla	Leetha	Lida
Lallah	Leilou	Lidda
Lallaiegh	Leiron	Liddie
Lallie	Leita	Liddy
Lalouise	Leither	Lidwena
Lamie	Lell	Lieuennie
Lamora	Lellie	Lili
Lanie	Lema	Lilla
Lannie	Lemma	Lillyetta
Lanora	Lemmer	Lilyon
Lantie	Lemora	Lima
Larceny	Lenamae	Lina
Laree	Lenna	Linda
		Liney

Index of Unusual Names

Linna	Loten	Lurania
Linnea	Lotsha	Lurelene
Linnetta	Louana	Lurid
Linnie	Loudie	Lurina
Linola	Louessie	Lurlene
Linzkey	Loueseba	Lurline
Liona	Louie	Luster
Lisa	Louisianna	Luta
Lise	Loulie	Lutheney
Lissa	Louranie	Luthie
Lissette	Louree	Lutie
Lissie	Lourene	Lutrelle
Littoria	Loutrell	Lurie
Livy	Louvenia	Luvenia
Liza	Love	Luverina
Lizette	Lovenia	Luvil
Lizula	Loventrice	Lyal
Lloyd	Lovey	Lycille
Loa DeLoach	Lovie	Lyde
Loamay	Lowa	Lyle
Lochie	Lowel	Lylette
Loisy	Loy	Lyn
Lockie	Loyce	Lyndall
Lodema	Loyola	Lynelle
Lodessa	Lozetta	Lynette
Lodie	Lu Mar	Lynie
Loduska	Luana	Lyra
Loduskia	Luanne	Lyrabeth
Loel	Lucenda	Mabla
Loie	Lucerne	Mabry
Loleta	Lucinda	Macedonia
Lolie	Lucretia	Macie
Lolita	Lucyhearn	Madell
Lolla	Luda	Madetine
Lollie	Ludie	Madie
Loma	Ludy	Madina
Lon	Luedna	Madolon
Lona	Lueisa	Madonna
Londine	Luerane	Maeten
Lone	Luiala	Mafra
Lonie	Lulleane	Magaline
Lonnie	Lullie	Magda
Loreda	Lulline	Magdalena
Loree	Lullyanne	Magnolia
Lorelle	Luma	Mahala
Loria	Luna	Mahalah
Lorie	Lunda	Mahalia
Lorine	Lundine	Maida
Lorinne	Lunetta	Maidelle
Lorita	Lunette	Maidie
Lorna Doone	Luouida	Mailland
Lossie	Lura	

Index of Unusual Names

Maitress	Marionette	Meara
Malah	Mariwilburn	Meaze
Malene	Marjean	Meck
Maleta	Marjee	Meda
Malinda	Marjevia	Medie
Malissa	Marlee	Medora
Malisse	Marlene	Meena
Mallie	Marnette	Mehlena
Malura	Marshlea	Meida
Malvina	Martel	Melanie
Mamai	Martha Washington	Melideen
Mame	Marthajean	Melinda
Mamie	Marthilda	Melissa
Mammie	Martine	Melisse
Mana	Marue	Mellie
Manda	Maruilla	Mellouise
Mandie	Marvel	Mellvina
Mandy	Mary Magdalene	Melna
Manerva	Maryan	Melodia
Manilla	Maryland	Melvina
Manine	Marylois	Melrose
Mannie	Marzie	Melvira
Manolia	Mascarene	Meme
Mansleat	Masquelette	Memory
Mantie	Matelenis	Mena
Mantine	Mathilda	Mennie
Maoma	Mathilde	Mercedes
Maple	Matilda	Merceree
Mar Leeta	Matilie	Mercini
Maradele	Matine	Merdelle
Marcel	Maudel	Merele
Marcella	Maudeen	Merial
Marcelline	Maudine	Meriba
Marcellus	Mauline	Merintha
Marcelynn	Mauree	Merita
Marcia	Maureen	Merle
Marcie	Maurine	Merlee
Mardelle	Mauritius	Merlie
Mardice	Mava	Merline
Mardite	Mavine	Merry Tydings
Marene	Mavis	Mersa
Margel	Mavolyn	Mersine
Margene	Maxine	Mertie
Margolese	Maydelle	Meta
Margorene	Maynie	Metha
Maria	Mayrene	Metrol
Mariada	Maysel	Metta
Mariella	Maytrel	Mettie
Marigayle	Mazel	Meula
Marillia	Mazelle	Mexie
Marina	Mazie	Midge
Marinelle	Mealie	Mignon

Index of Unusual Names

Mignonne	Mosetta	Needa
Milbra	Mossie	Neela
Mile	Mozell	Needia
Mimi	Mozelle	Negie
Mina	Mozeta	Nelda
Minalee	Mozie	Nelder
Minardi	Mural	Neldor
Minda	Murcillia	Nelia
Mindel	Murlene	Nellavease
Mineola	Musette	Nello
Minerva	Mynelle	Nelure
Minett	Myrdie	Nelwyn
Minna	Myrle	Nemy
Minnesota	Myrteline	Nena
Minnett	Myrth	Neola
Minnie	Myrtice	Nep
Minta	Myrtie	Neppie
Mintie	Myrtis	Neta
Mirial	Myrtrie	Netta
Miskel	Naab	Neva
Missouri	Nacy	Nevada
Mitchie	Nada	Nevelyn
Mittie	Nadia	Neville
Modelle	Nadian	Neue
Modena	Nadie	Newrie
Modene	Nadine	Ninette
Modest	Nalure	Nishie
Modesta	Nan	Nissa
Modie	Nana	Nitus
Moina	Nanaline	Nixie
Moleta	Nanelu	Nob
Mona	Nanie	Nobie
Monette	Nannie	Nodie
Monia	Nara Pearl	Noelle
Monica	Narcie	Noena
Monie	Narcis	Nola
Monita	Narcissa	Nolia
Monnie	Narvelle	Nomina
Mono	Nassie	Nona
Montez	Natala	Nonie
Montie	Natalee	Nonnie
Montina	Natalie	Noreen
Montine	Natalene	Noreene
Montyne	Nathalee	Norella
Mony	Nathalene	Norene
Monzora	Nathalie	Norice
Moree	Natilee	Norie
Morene	Naudine	Norine
Morma	Nealie	Nova
Morrah	Nealia	Novaline
Mortina	Neata	Novel
Moselle	Nealtha	Novella

Index of Unusual Names

Novis	Omega	Otheal
Nozelle	Omelia	Othel
Nubye	Omera	Othella
Nucia	Omie	Othello
Nula	Ona	Othera
Nuzzie	Ona Gazelle	Othma
Nyleen	O'Neal	Ottie
Nylodine	Oneida	Ottilia
Nyree	Onell	Othillie
Obelia	Onella	Ouida
Obera	Ones	Ouita
Oberia	Onesta	Ouraleen
Obie	Oneta	Ova
Occlo	Onida	Oval
Ocele	Onie	Oveda
Ocey	Onnie	Ovie
Ocie	Onza	Oxena
Oda	Onzelle	Oxie
Oddie	Ophal	Ozalea
Odelia	Ophie	Ozane
Odelle	Opie	Ozell
Odena	Opieree	Ozella
O'Desa	Ora	Ozelle
Odessa	Ordalia	Ozola
Odesso	Oregon	Ozzie
Odette	Orelle	Pallie
Odia	Orena	Paloma
Odie	Orene	Pamela
Odie Dee	Oretha	Panie
Odom	Oretta	Paralee
Odressa	Oria	Parma
Ody	Orie	Parmelia
Oella	Orlean	Parmella
Offie	Orlena	Parmie
Ofie	Orlie	Parrie
Ogarietta	Orma	Patia
Ogle	Ormie	Patience
Ola	Orneita	Patria
Olear	Ornie	Patro
Oleater	Orpha	Patti Gee
Olena	Orphia	Pattie
Olene	Orra	Paulee
Oleta	Orrie	Paulette
Oletia	Orzell	Pearlie
Olline	Osa	Pemie
Olsie	Osceola	Penelope
Olta	Oscie	Penny
Oluet	Osie	Pensacola
Oma	Ossie	Perci Mae
Omah	Oteli	Perla
Omar Dell	Otella	Perlila
Omeda	Otha	Permelia

Index of Unusual Names

Pernie	Randy	Rhoba
Persia	Ranie	Rhoda
Perthenia	Rannie	Rhodie
Petrea	Rassie	Rhodom
Petrony	Ratie	Rhonda
Phala Marie	Raven	Rhondabelle
Pharos	Rayanna	Rhonwynn
Phena	Re	Rhuea
Phil	Rea	Richardine
Philena	Readie	Richie
Philippa	Reana	Rieveland
Phillippa	Reatha	Rilda
Phillis	Rebe	Rilla
Philomena	Rebie	Rina
Phinetta	Rebion	Rinda
Phronie	Reda	Rinsie
Phryne	Reddie	Rintha
Phylis	Redolia	Rinthy
Piccola	Ree	Rippi Jean
Piety	Reena	Rissie
Pink	Regine	Rita
Pinkey	Reine	Riva
Pinkie	Rela	Robbie
Placida	Rella	Robbye
Pluma	Rellus	Robelle
Ponder	Relta	Robena
Popless	Rema	Robertelle
Portia	Remie	Robie
Pretto	Remmie	Roda
Primrose	Remona	Rodella
Princess	Rena	Roena
Priscilla	Renah	Roma
Prude	Renee	Romayne
Prudy	Renna	Romie
Prue	Renna Europa	Ronie
Q'Milla New	Rennie	Rose Marie
Quay	Rennis	Rosebud
Queen	Rentha	Roselle
Queenie	Ressie	Rosena
Quejetta Snodgrass	Restored	Rosette
Quila	Ret Needler	Rossie
Quilla	Reta	Rothe
Quillar	Retha	Roudine
Quinnie	Retta	Roxilu
Racie	Reva	Roy Elizabeth
Rada	Reverie	Rozell
Radie	Reville	Rozella
Rae	Rhea	Rozelle
Rama	Rheata	Rozzie
Ramelle	Rheta	Ruchia
Ramie	Rhetta	Rudine
Ramona	Rheufina	Ruedell

Index of Unusual Names

Ruffie	Settie	Sydnette
Rufie	Shadie	Sydney
Runette	Shelba	Sylvania
Rusha	Shellie	Tabitha
Russie	Shoshana	Taliah
Rutha	Sible	Taliela
Sabina	Sicily Sallis	Tallu
Sabra	Sidney	Talula
Sabry	Sidonie	Talulah
Sadonia	Sighnie	Tallulah
Saffrona	Sigma	Taltha
Sala	Signie	Tamar
Salantha	Siguce	Tandy
Salatha	Silva	Tankie
Salemma	Silverbud	Tannie
Salena	Silvernia	Tassia
Salome	Simmie	Tavia
Samantha	Simmye	Tecora
Samella	Sina	Teedie
Sammie	Sinnie	Teekie
Sammye	Skiddy	Tekla
Samuella	Snowie	Telatha
Sannie	Sola	Telesia
Santa	Solie	Thelitha
Santippe	Sonia	Tella
Saphronia	Sophia	Telma
Sarabel	Sophie	Tempe
Saracinesca	Sophronia	Temperence
Saraelen	Sophronie	Tempie
Sarah Burnhardt	Stacia	Tempy
Saree	Stevie	Tena
Savannah	Storia	Tennessee
Seabie	Subrina	Tennie
Sebelle	Sucie	Tennie Ike
Sedonie	Sudie	Tenolia
Segusta	S(h)ug	Tensie
Seibelle	Suke	Tera
Selecta	Sukey	Terah
Selena	Sula	Terasa
Selene	Sunie	Terrah
Selenia	Sunny	Tessie
Seleta	Sunshine	Tethys
Selina	Sureen	Tetia
Seney	Surella	Tex
Senie	Svea	Texas
Sennie	Swan	Texie
Senora	Swanee	Tezzie
Seppie	Swanell	Thais
Seraphim	Swannie	Thalia
Serena	Sybino	Thankful
Serepta	Syddie	Thea
Serita	Sydna	Theadocia

Index of Unusual Names

Theah	Tulon	Vannette
Thedro	Tura	Vannie
Theodosia	Turley	Vardaman
Theola	Tweetie	Varee
Theonia	Twila	Varette
Theopia	Tybell	Varie
Thermal	Typhene	Varina
Theta	U-Bell	Varner
Thomascine	Udelle	Varnetta
Thomasine	Udine	Varnie
Thressa	Udo	Vashti
Thursa	Ula	Vasie
Thyra	Ulie	Vastine
Tildie	Uline	Vaudie
Tildy	Ulla	Vaudine
Tillye	Ullaimee	Vaulda
Timozena	Ulva	Vaurice
Tina	Una	Veda
Tincy	Uni	Vee
Tineta	Urella	Vela
Tiney	Urlyne	Velara
Tinie	Ursel	Velda
Tinnie	Ursula	Velera
Tincy	Ursuline	Vella
Tinsie	Vada	Velma
Tint	Vadah	Velora
Tish	Vadgir	Velta
Tivis	Vadia	Velves
Toby	Vadiel	Velvie
Tommie	Vadis	Vena
Topie	Valaria	Venda
Tot	Valda	Venera
Totsie	Valeree	Venetia
Toy	Valeria	Venetta
Tracey	Valerie	Venia
Tracie	Valia	Venice
Trannie	Valla	Venie
Trasilla	Valley	Venita
Trennie	Vallie	Venne
Tressie	Vallusia	Vennie
Trix	Valoris	Ventral
Trizelle	Valrie	Ventrice
Trudie	Valsie	Veoma
Truedell	Vama	Verabel
Trugen	Vana	Verbye
Trula	Vander	Verd
Tula	Vandola	Verdelle
Tulamaye	Vandora	Verdia
Tulla	Vanella	Verdie
Tullie	Vanescel	Verdria
Tullulah	Vanita	Verea
Tululah	Vanner	Vergie

Index of Unusual Names

Verla	Vixie	Willene
Verlee	Volita	Willeda
Verlia	Volumnia	Willianna
Verlin	Vonceil	Williebill
Vermal	Voncile	Willilou
Vermel	Voncille	Willine
Verna	Voncine	Willodene
Vernell	Vondell	Willogene
Verner	Vonnie	Willons
Vernice	Vontese	Willula
Vernie	Vonzie	Willyne
Verona	Voris	Wilmanell
Veronica	Voula	Wilmoth
Versey	Voy	Wimbreth
Versie	Vurnia	Winney
Vertlee	Vyande	Winnie
Vervie	Vylen	Winona
Veryl	Wadine	Winta
Vessie	Waldeen	Wirta
Vesta	Walena	Woodie
Veta	Wallie	Woody
Vetella	Walterine	Wordna
Vevi	Walterrene	Wortie
Vi Vienne	Wanda	Wrenella
Vianah	Wander	Wrennie
Vicie	Wannie	Wuzzie
Victory	Warrenette	Wylena
Vida	Watha	Wylene
Vidue	Waverlyn	Wylodine
Vienna	Wavie	Wyndall
Vilandie	Weda	Wynell
Vilanta	Weeda	Wynette
Vilda	Weenonah Poindexter	Wynona
Vina	Weida	Wyolene
Vineta	Welcome	Ximena
Vinetta	Welda	Xymena
Vinia	Weleska	Yale
Vinie	Welthy	Yetive
Vinnie	Wepne	Yetta
Vinvie	Wessar	Yola
Vir	Wessie	Yolanda
Virdell	Wetta	Yona
Virdie	Whit	Yvette
Virein	Wilda	Yvonne
Virgia	Wildie	Zabie
Virgie	Wildella	Zada
Virginia Dare	Wilhemina	Zadah
Virginius	Wilkins	Zadelle
Virtie	Willa	Zadie
Visa	Willadene	Zahade
Vista	Willard	Zaidee
Vivienne	Willardine	Zailease

Black Names in America

Index of Unusual Names

Zanola	Zenie	Zira
Zannis	Zennie	Zita
Zara	Zenoba	Zoa
Zeara	Zenobia	Zoe
Zela	Zeola	Zahde
Zelda	Zeph	Zola
Zelena	Zerline	Zollie
Zelia	Zeta	Zona
Zelinda	Zetha	Zora
Zelirne	Zethar	Zorada
Zella	Zetta	Zoretta
Zellah	Zettie	Zorra
Zellamae	Zilca	Zovira
Zellee	Zilla	Zuandry
Zellia	Zillah	Zudie
Zellie	Ziller	Zula
Zelma	Zilliah	Zulieme
Zeloma	Zilpah	Zulma
Zemma	Zilphie	Zuna
Zena	Zimmie	Zurie
Zenia	Zipporah	Zylpha
		Zylphia

553

BIBLIOGRAPHY AND PRINCIPAL SOURCES

BOOKS

Abraham, Roy Clive. Dictionary of the Hausa Language. 2nd ed. London:
    University of London Press, 1962.

Allen, William Francis. Slave Songs of the United States. New York:
    A. Simpson & Co., 1867

Armstrong, Orland Kay. Old Massa's People: The Old Slaves Tell Their Story.
    Indianapolis: The Bobbs-Merrill Company, 1931.

Bardsley, Charles Wareing Endell. Curiosities of Puritan Nomenclature.
    London: Chatto and Windus, 1880.

Barnhart, Clarence L. New Century Cyclopedia of Names. New York: Appleton-
    Century-Crofts, 1954.

Beckwith, Martha Warren. Black Roadways: A Study of Jamaican Folk Life.
    Chapel Hill: The University of North Carolina Press, 1929.

Bently, William Holman. Dictionary and Grammar of the Kongo Language: as
    spoken at San Salvador, the ancient capital of the old Kongo empire, West
    Africa. Compiled and prepared for the Baptist mission on the Kongo river,
    West Africa. London: Baptist Missionary Society, 1887.

Billingsley, Andrew. Black Families in White America. New York: Prentice-
    Hall, Inc., 1968.

Block, Martin Friedrich. Gypsies, Their Life and Their Customs. Translated
    by Barbara Kuczynski and Duncan Taylor. New York: D. Appleton-Century
    Co., 1939.

Boris, J. J. Who's Who in Negro America. 2nd ed. New York, 1928-29.

Bowditch, Nathaniel Ingersoll. Suffolk Surnames. Boston: Ticknor & Fields,
    1858.

Bowman, William Dodgson. The Story of Surnames. London: B. Routledge and
    Sons, Ltd., 1931.

555

Campbell, John Charles. The Southern Highlander and His Homeland. New York: Russell Sage Foundation, 1921.

Carmer, Carl Lamson. Stars Fell on Alabama. New York: Farrar & Rinehart, Inc., 1934.

Catterall, Helen Honor Tunnicliff, ed. Judicial Cases Concerning American Slavery and the Negro. 5 vols. Washington, D. C.: Carnegie Institution of Washington, 1926-1937.

Clodd, Edward. Magic in Names and in Other Things. London: Chapman and Hall, Ltd., 1920.

Cobb, Joseph Beckham. Mississippi Scenes: or, Sketches of Southern and Western Life and Adventure, Humorous, Satirical, and Description, including The Legend of Black Creek. Philadelphia: A. Hart, 1851.

Cohn, David L. God Shakes Creation. New York, 1935.

Commins, John R., ed. Documentary History of American Industrial Society. 11 vols. Cleveland: The A. H. Clark Co., 1910-11.

The Documentary History of the State of New York. Arranged under direction of Christopher Morgan, Secretary of State. 4 vols. Albany, New York: Weed, Parsons & Co., 1849-51.

Donnan, Elizabeth, ed. Documents Illustrative of the History of the Slave Trade to America. Washington, D. C.: Carnegie Institution of Washington, 1930-1935.

Dougall, James W. C. Characteristics of African Thought. London: Oxford University Press for the International Institute of African Languages and Cultures, 1932.

Dow, George Francis. Slave Ships and Slaving. Introduction by Captain Ernest H. Pentecost, R.N.R. Salem, Mass.: Marine Research Society, 1927.

Ewen, Cecil Henry L'Estrange. A History of Surnames of the British Isles: A Concise Account of Their Origin, Evolution, Etymology, and Legal Status. London: Paul, Trench, Trubner, Ltd., 1931.

Farley, Reynolds. Growth of the Black Population: A Study of Demographic Trends. Chicago: Markham Pub. Co., 1970.

Flanders, Ralph Betts. Plantation Slavery in Georgia. Chapel Hill: The University of North Carolina Press, 1933.

Franklin, J. Hope. From Slavery to Freedom. 3rd ed. New York: Alfred A. Kogeb, 1967.

Frazier, E. Franklin. The Negro in the U. S. New York, 1949.

Genovese, Eugene D. The Political Economy of Slavery: Studies in the Economy and Society of the Slave South. New York: Vantage Books, 1967.

Goldie, Hugh. Dictionary of the Efik Language. Edinburgh: United Presbyterian College Buildings (1886?).

Herskovits, Melville Jean. The New World Negro: Selected Papers in Afro-American Studies. Bloomington, Indiana: Indiana University Press, 1966.

Herskovits, Melville Jean and Francis S. Rebel Destiny: Among the Bush Negroes of Dutch Guiana. New York and London: McGraw-Hill Book Company, Inc., Whittlesey House, 1934.

Innes, Gordon. A Mende-English Dictionary. London: Cambridge University Press, 1969.

Jones, George Noble. Florida Plantation Records. Ed. Ulrich B. Phillips. St. Louis, Mo.: Historical Society, 1927.

Jordan, Winthrop D. White Over Black: American Attitudes toward the Negro, 1550-1812. Chapel Hill: For the Institute of Early American History and Culture at Williamsburg, Va., University of North Carolina Press, 1968.

Lambert & Pei. Our Names. New York: Lothrop, 1969.

Macrae, David. The Americans at Home: Pen and Ink Sketches of American Men, Manners, and Institutions. Glasgow: T. Smith & Son, Ltd., 1908.

Malcolm X. The Autobiography of Malcolm X. New York: Grove Press, 1964.

Mallard, Robert Q. Plantation Life Before Emancipation. Richmond, Va.: Whittet & Shepperson, 1892.

Melzian, Hans Joachim. A Concise Dictionary of the Bini Language of Southern Nigeria. London: K. Paul, Trench, Trubner & Co., Ltd., 1937.

Mencken, H. L. The American Language. 4th ed. New York, 1936.

Migeod, Frederick William Hugh. The Languages of West Africa. London: K. Paul, Trench, Trubner and Co., 1911-13.

Phillips, Ulrich Bonnell. Life and Labor in the Old South. Boston: Little, Brown & Co., 1929.

Puckett, Newbell N. "Names of American Negro Slaves." Studies in the Science of Society. Ed. G. P. Murdock. New Haven: Yale University Press, 1937, pp. 471-94.

Schon, James Frederick. Dictionary of the Haussa Language. London: Church Missionary House, 1876.

Smith, Elsdon C. _Treasury of Name Lore_. New York: Harper and Row, 1967.

Stapleton, Walter Henry. _Comparative Handbook of Congo Languages_. Stanley Falls, Congo, Yakusa, 1903.

Steingass, Francis Joseph. _The Students Arabic-English Dictionary_. London: W. H. Allen & Company, 1884.

Turner, Lorenzo Dow. _Africanisms in the Gullah Dialect_. Chicago: University of Chicago Press, 1949.

Waddell, Laurence Austine. _The Buddhism of Tibet: or Lamaism, with its mystic cults, symbolism and mythology and in its relation to Indian Buddhism_.

Weekley, Ernest. _The Romance of Names_. London: J. Murray, 1917.

Weld, Theodore Dwight. _American Slavery As It Is_. New York: American Anti-Slavery Society, 1839.

Whitehead, John, Comp. _Grammar and Dictionary of the Bobangi Language: as spoken over a part of the upper Congo, West Central Africa_. London: Baptist Missionary Society, 1899.

Willams, Cynric. _A Tour Through the Island of Jamaica in 1823_. London: Hunt & Clarke, 1826.

Woodson, Carter Godwin. _Free Negro Heads of Families in the United States in 1830: together with a brief treatment of the free Negro_. Washington, D. C.: The Association for the Study of Negro Life and History, Inc., 1925.

ARTICLES

"Americana," _American Mercury_, X (1927), 303-304.

Brunini, John G. "By Any Other Name," _Catholic World_, 145 (1937), 336-339.

Carraway, Gertrude S. "Many Oddities in Tar Heel Names," _Greensboro (N. C.) Daily News_, Jan. 9, 1938.

Chappell, Naomi C. "Negro Names," _American Speech_, IV (1929), 272-275.

Clayton, Frank, pseud. "A Sketch in Black and White," _Atlantic Monthly_, 97 (May-June, 1906), pp. 600-610, 783-792.

Comba, Josiah. "Languages of the Southern Highlanders," _Publication of the Modern Language Association of America_, XLVI (1931), 1302-1322.

Frazier, E. Franklin. "The Negro Slave Family," Journal of Negro History, 15 (April, 1930), 198-259.

Gaither, Frances. "Fanciful Are Negro Names," New York Times Magazine, Feb. 10, 1929, p. 19.

Grace, Alonzo G. The Education of the Negro in the North With Particular Reference to Cleveland. (Ph.D. Thesis, Graduate School, Western Reserve University, Cleveland, 1932), 109-110. (Unusual names of students enrolled at Case-Woodland and Mayflower elementary schools between 1923 and 1929.)

Harrison, J. B. "Studies in the South," Atlantic Monthly (1882), 49: pp. 76, 740; 50: pp. 99, 750; 51: pp. 87+.

Holmes, Urban T. "A Study In Negro Onomastics," American Speech, V (1930), 463-467.

House Executive Documents No. 42. 38th Congress, 1st Session, Vol. IX (1863-1864), 1-79.

Hudson, Arthur P. "Some Curious Negro Names," Southern Folklore Quarterly, II (1938), 179-193.

Migeod, Frederick W. H. "Personal Names amongst some West African Tribes," Journal of African Society, 17 (Oct. 1917), pp. 38-45.

"Negro Names" (Editorial). Opportunity, 5 (Feb. 1927), pp. 35-37.

Pitman, F. W. "Slavery on British West India Plantation in the Eighteenth Century," Journal of Negro History, 11 (Oct. 1926), pp. 584-668.

Sizer, Miriam M. "Christian Names in the Blue Ridge of Virginia," American Speech, VIII (1933), 32-37.

Still, James A. "Christian Names in the Cumberlands," American Speech, V (1930), 306-307.

Trux, J. J. "Negro Minstrelsy, Ancient and Modern," Putnams Magazine, 5 (1855), pp. 73+. Reprinted in Maga Social Papers. New York: G. Putnams & Sons, 1867.

Woodson, Carter G. "Extracts from the records of the African companies," Journal of Negro History, 13 (July, 1928), 286-394.

STUDENT DIRECTORIES

Black Colleges

Agricultural and Technical College of N. C. ('30-'31 and '35-'36). Greensboro, N. C.
Alcorn Agricultural and Mechanical College ('32-'33), Alcorn, Miss.
Allen University ('35-'36), Columbia, S. C.
Arkansas State College ('30-'35), Pine Bluff, Ark.
Armstrong High School ('36), Richmond, Va.
Benedict College ('35-'36), Columbia, S. C.
Chaflin College ('34-'35), Orangesburg, S. C.
Clark University ('35-'36), Atlanta, Ga.
Colored Agricultural and Normal University ('32-'36), Langston, Okla.
Dillard University ('35-'36), New Orleans, La.
Dunbar Junior College ('31-'36), Little Rock, Ark.
Fisk University ('34-'35), Nashville, Tenn.
Florida Agricultural and Mechanical College ('32-'36), Tallahassee, Fla.
Florida Normal and Industrial Institute ('35-'36), St. Augustine, Fla.
Hampton Institute ('35-'36), Hampton, Va.
Howard University ('35-'36), Washington, D. C.
Knoxville College ('35-'36), Knoxville, Tenn.
Lincoln University ('20-'30), Jefferson City, Mo.
Morgan College ('36), Baltimore, Md.
Morris College ('35-'36), Sumpter, S. C.
Prairie View State Normal and Industrial College ('35-'36), Prairie View, Texas
Southern University and Agricultural and Mechanical College ('35-'36), Baton Rouge, La.
State Agricultural and Mechanical College ('35-'36), Orangeburg, S. C.
State Teacher's and Agricultural College ('33-'36), Forsyth, Ga.
Tennessee Agricultural and Industrial State College ('35-'36), Nashville, Tenn.
Tougaloo College ('35-'36), Tougaloo, Miss.
Tuskegee Normal and Industrial Institute ('35-'36), Tuskegee, Ala.
Virginia State College for Negroes ('35-'36), Ettrick, Va.
Virginia Union University ('35-'36), Richmond, Va.
Voorhees Institute ('35-'36), Denmark, S. C.
West Virginia State College ('36-'37), Institute, West Virginia
Wilberforce University ('35-'36), Wilberforce, Ohio

White Colleges

College of the Ozarks ('36-'37), Clarksville, Ark.
Florida State College for Women ('38), Tallahassee, Fla.
Louisiana State University ('35-'36), Baton Rouge, La.
Mississippi State College ('35-'36), State College, Miss.
Mississippi State College for Women ('34-'35), Columbus, Miss.
Mississippi Woman's College ('35-'36), Hattiesburg, Miss.
Oklahoma City University ('36-'37), Oklahoma City, Okla.
Texas Christian University ('37-'38), Fort Worth, Texas

Tulane University ('36-'37), New Orleans, La.
University of Alabama ('32-'33), Tuscaloosa, Ala.
University of Arkansas ('37-'38), Fayetteville, Ark.
University of Georgia ('35-'36), Athens, Ga.
University of Mississippi ('35-'36), Oxford, Miss.
University of North Carolina ('37-'38), Chapel Hill, N. C.
University of South Carolina ('36-'37), Columbia, S. C.
University of Tennessee ('37-'38), Knoxville, Tenn.
University of Tulsa ('38-'39), Tulsa, Okla.
University of Virginia ('37-'38), Charlottesville, Va.
Vanderbilt University ('37-'38), Nashville, Tenn.
Virginia Military Institute ('36-'37), Lexington, Va.
Woman's College of Alabama ('35-'36), Montgomery, Ala.
Woman's College of the University of North Carolina ('36-'37), Greensboro,
N. C.

CITY DIRECTORIES AND CENSUS REPORTS

Asheville, North Carolina. City Directory (1924).
Augusta, Georgia. City Directory (1877).
Augusta, Georgia. City Directory (1899).
Augusta, Georgia. City Directory (1919).
Augusta, Georgia. City Directory (1937).
Columbus, Mississippi. City Directory (1925).
Heads of Families At the First Census of the United States Taken in the Year
1790 (Md., Va., S. C. and N. C.) (Wash., 1908).
Lowndes County (Mississippi) School Census (1935). (Children).
Lowndes County (Mississippi) School Census (1935). (Parents).
Montgomery, Alabama. City Directory (1899).
Montgomery, Alabama. City Directory (1920).
Montgomery, Alabama. City Directory (1933).
Pine Bluff, Arkansas. City Directory (1936).
Richmond County (Georgia) School Census (1938). (City Schools).
Richmond County (Georgia) School Census (1938). (Rural Schools).
Senate Document 150. 28th Congress, 2nd Session (1844). Serial Number 458.